In Search of Global Patterns

edited by

James N. Rosenau

THE FREE PRESS
A Division of Macmillan Publishing Co., Inc.
NEW YORK

Collier Macmillan Publishers
LONDON

The Free Press
A Division of Macmillan Publishing Co., Inc.
866 Third Avenue, New York, N.Y. 10022

Collier Macmillan Canada, Ltd.

Library of Congress Catalog Card Number: 75-20950

Printed in the United States of America

printing number

1 2 3 4 5 6 7 8 9 10

Library of Congress Cataloging in Publication Data
Main entry under title:

In search of global patterns.

    Includes bibliographies and index.
    1. International relations--Research--Addresses,
essays, lectures. I. Rosenau, James N.
JX1291.I33   327'.07'2   75-20950
ISBN 0-02-927050-2

In memory of Norah

Contents

An Acknowledgment

An expression of my appreciation for the assistance of the several persons and institutions who made possible the compilation of this volume can be found in Chapter 1, as can an account of the circumstances that led to the essays of which it is comprised. Here I want to acknowledge the contribution of Norah Rosenau. I have thanked her many times in many prefaces, but this time my feelings must take the form of a memorial. She was killed in a senseless traffic accident July 5, 1974, on the Pacific Coast Highway in Malibu, California. Her death ended a rich and satisfying and ever-growing marriage of nineteen years, one that was founded on a deep commitment to open communication, an uncompromising readiness to confront problems directly, and an unceasing effort to enlarge and experience the full measure of our sensitivities.

Our marriage was also a colleagueship. Norah was a social psychologist profoundly interested in the dynamics of human affairs. We always shared our ideas and writings with each other, often developing new understandings through endless discussion. While she was never especially interested in the political dimension of human affairs, she read every word I ever wrote and her suggestions and criticisms always resulted in a more incisive, succinct, and integrated manuscript. She had a rigorous mind and a keen intellect that enabled her to see both the broad perspectives and the essential details through which cogent ideas are expressed and meaning conveyed.

But there is more to colleagueship than the exchange of ideas. It also thrives on a willingness to be direct, to indicate reservations and doubts when ideas are ambiguous, unsound, or otherwise inappropriate. Norah never compromised in this regard. She would not be deterred by my stubborn commitment to a particular wording or my insistence that a specific formulation was clear and well founded. Often it would have been easier to overlook the weaknesses of a paragraph or page, but she never took the easy way and always made me face the implications (or lack of them) of what I was trying to say. Marriages and colleagueships do not go readily together, but in our case Norah's courage and integrity allowed each to thrive on the other.

These same qualities that helped me professionally were even more central at a personal level. There is no question in my mind that I would be a very different person, and a much less humane, healthy, and effective person, had it not been for Norah and her relentless commitment to making our marriage grow. Norah believed in me, and she believed in us, and she believed that we could grow together, so she never stopped trying to make our relationship a better, more creative, and happier one.

And she was no less tough on herself. She had trouble believing in herself as much as she did in others. But she did believe that people can and should face up to their problems and try to surmount them. So she was working as hard at making herself a better person as she did at trying to help others. She never stopped learning and thinking and feeling and living. She never did anything half-heartedly or partly or somewhat. She did everything wholly, fully, and thoroughly, whether it was little household details or large intellectual tasks. In her own professional work self-doubt began to give way to a growing confidence that she could meaningfully probe the dynamics of child development, a concern and a confidence that culminated in three papers on the political education of children that are filled with insight and pervaded with clarity.

There is also an immediate sense in which the dedication of this book to Norah's memory is compelling. She was involved in all three of the conferences that yielded the papers compiled together here. All the senior authors of all the papers knew her, many as close and long-standing friends, and were aware of and valued her varied contributions to the proceedings that gave rise to this book.

Norah would have objected to my writing this memorial. She had no need—none—to call attention to herself and, indeed, she tended to play down praise and recognition Yet, in this one instance, I dare to act counter to what she would have wanted because this book is about a search for comprehension and my search is meaningless without an acknowledgment of her companionship and support. The search will go on, but henceforth it will be different, enlarged by what she gave me and diminished by her absence.

Pacific Palisades   J.N.R.
March 17, 1975

1. The Restless Quest

James N. Rosenau

Twentieth-century efforts to comprehend the political universe have not been nearly so extensive, conspicuous, or successful as those intended to unravel the secrets of the physical universe, but they have been no less intense. The same curiosity, the same fascination with unexplained events and patterns that moves physical scientists to probe the mysteries of the atom also sustains social scientists concerned with the vagaries of international relations (IR). The latter have not had the confidence of society enjoyed by the former and the financial support provided for their efforts has thus been minuscule by comparison. Indeed, probably few persons outside the halls of academe are even aware of the existence of a small community of investigators dedicated to the scientific study of world politics.

Notwithstanding the lack of societal and monetary support, the search for global patterns has been marked by the same restless quest for understanding found in all the sciences. The purpose of this book is to portray that quest—its origins and motivational dynamics, its accomplishments and failures—and to highlight the problems that must be solved if patterns are to be uncovered and knowledge cumulated.

THE SCIENTIST AS PUZZLE SOLVER

To stress that scientific inquiries into world politics spring from curiosity about recurring patterns is not to imply that this is the only source from which such studies emanate. As will be seen, a vast array of other motives, ranging from a desire to improve the human condition to a concern for personal advancement, may also be operative and, indeed, may well be more central than the satisfaction of curiosity. But the importance of curiosity— of an inquisitive mind puzzled by the dynamics of unfolding patterns and shifting trends—cannot be underestimated. Without an inquisitiveness of this sort, inquiry takes a much different form. In the absence of puzzlement over the nature and sources of underlying patterns, investigations of world politics tend to focus on specific problems, immediate causes, and short-range solutions. Indeed, most students of the subject are not provoked by the challenge of discovering and explaining underlying patterns and prefer, usually with good reason, to focus instead on particular situations and possible policies that might be applied to them.

The community of science-oriented international relations analysts is thus but a small segment of those who investigate the subject, and what sets them apart is the depth of their curiosity about recurring phenomena in global politics. As Newton was puzzled by the larger forces that made the apple fall, so are those in this small community stirred by the larger forces that shape international systems and condition the behavior of nations. For them, world politics is a vast and complex puzzle, the pieces of which are presumed to fit together despite their apparent disarray. And finding how, when, and why a piece fits into place provides a sense of triumph and exhilaration no less intense or satisfying than Newton must have experienced as he put together the pieces of the gravitational world.

This is not to say, or in any way to imply, that the curiosity of science-oriented analysts is purer, wiser, or otherwise better than the curiosity that sustains other investigators. The analogy to Newton is evoked not as a subtle indication of superiority but rather to give special emphasis to the role of curiosity. The routes to a more thorough comprehension of world politics are many, and it would be insufferably arrogant, as well as profoundly erroneous, to assert that one is superior to another. Nor is the denial of superiority merely an editor's lip service to the ideal of pluralism, a disclaimer intended to disguise and hide what is in fact a sense of superiority. For the search for understanding, as the ensuing chapters authored by more than forty analysts so clearly reveal, is marked by humility and doubt, not arrogance and certainty.

The stress on curiosity and puzzle solving is necessary in order to appreciate why IR scientists proceed as they do.[1] Whatever the other reasons for the inquiries they undertake, their curiosity about patterned international phenomena that recur across time and place infuses structure and continuity into their efforts. It explains why they are not content to look only at the immediate circumstances and policy implications of a single situation. It explains why they eschew historical narrative for quantitative analysis. It explains why they are preoccupied with methodology. It explains why they sometimes redo and often extend each other's studies. Without a persistent puzzlement over the nature and sources of underlying patterns, there would be no reason not to settle for comprehension of a single situation, the events that led up to it, and the implications it holds for the future. Impelled by curiosity, however, they need to determine what the particular situation is an instance of, and this necessitates examining a number of situations—i.e., quantifying data and tracing the patterns they form. Then, having teased patterns from a welter of events, their curiosity impels them further to question whether the uncovered patterns are reflections of empirical reality or artifacts of the procedures used to identify them—i.e., to a preoccupation with methodology and an inclination to replicate and elaborate each other's findings.

THE PLACE OF VALUES IN PUZZLE SOLVING

Emphasizing the role of curiosity poses the danger that scientifically oriented IR analysts may seem unconcerned about values and policy questions and convinced that through the scientific method they can engage in value-free inquiries. Concerned

[1] The notion of science as a puzzle-solving enterprise is compellingly elaborated in Kuhn (1970).

that the human condition is deteriorating ever more rapidly, some might say that pursuit of curiosity is a luxury that cannot be afforded in today's world, that those professionally involved in the building of knowledge about world politics should direct their talents toward the solution of pressing problems.

Such a reaction is ill founded. As many of the ensuing essays plainly reveal, a restless search for recurring patterns and an unyielding commitment to the realization of basic values need not be mutually exclusive. Few scientists in any field exercise idle curiosity. Rather the underlying patterns that fascinate them are usually central to the system on which they focus (else why be fascinated?), and the systems on which they focus their analytic talents are usually important to some aspect of the human condition (else why focus on them?). Thus it is clear that the values of IR analysts underlie their selection of the problems on which their curiosity is then unleashed. It is not mere coincidence, for example, that several of the autobiographical essays in Part One of this book eloquently describe how a concern for the problem of war underlay the decision to become professionally involved in the study of world politics. Nor is it coincidental that all—not just a few, but all—the scientific projects noted in the pages that follow focus on major alternatives for the human condition—cooperation or conflict, poverty or progress, dignity or suppression, peace or war.

Scientifically oriented analysts, in short, are no less concerned about values and policies than any other students of world politics. Rightly or wrongly, they are persuaded that the realization of values and the solution of problems is also served through the building of knowledge about underlying patterns, that immediate solutions of current dilemmas are at best temporary if they are not derived from a comprehension of the basic variables that shape human behavior. For them the pursuit of curiosity is not a luxury, but a necessity—a fundamental requirement of their commitment to the cumulation of a body of knowledge in which the recurring features of human experience are differentiated from the transitory phenomena explainable only in terms of specific times and places. As they see it, such a body of knowledge cannot be fashioned if curiosity is limited to specific situations, since to do so is to incur the risk of overlooking variables that may be relevant to the phenomena under investigation. So they set out in search of global patterns, allowing their curiosity to propel them in whatever directions their findings, hunches, and/or preconceptions may suggest. And they do so secure in the conviction that the methods of science—which include the checks of colleagues who may be dubious about the validity and reliability of their results—will constrain their excesses and bring them back into line if their curiosity leads them astray.

Since values underlie the choice of problems selected for investigation, it can hardly be said that scientifically oriented analysts engage in value-free inquiries. Nor do they see themselves as proceeding in such a fashion. Their goal is to uncover patterns that any observer following their methods for gathering and processing data will also uncover. To seek to render knowledge independent of those who generate it, however, is not to claim that it is free of values. Rather, the values are made explicit so that others can determine the extent to which they shape the results. Other observers may employ different values as the basis for identifying and organizing relevant data, and if they do and if different findings are thereby uncovered, then plainly alternative knowledge bases will cumulate.

Scientific inquiries into world politics, in short, are value-explicit rather than value-free. The notion of a value-free enterprise becomes crucial only after data have been identified on the basis of explicitly elaborated values. For obviously the rigorous application of scientific methods to trace recurring patterns entails procedures that must be free of the biases and whims of the investigators if reliable knowledge is to be cumulated.

To note that scientists neither are free of values nor claim to be, however, is not to ease the demands made upon them to be relevant. The dire urgency of the world's problems is such that many critics are unwilling to accept the notion that the unfettered expression of curiosity, subjected only to the constraints of scientific methodology, can serve in the long run to alleviate the human condition. Impatient with, even distressed by, the search for global patterns, they demand short-run applications and thus, regrettably, often succeed in diverting scientific investigations into propounding premature and unfounded policy formulations. It is hoped that the essays in this book will give critics pause. They may not be persuaded to champion scientific inquiry, but they may come to appreciate that *their* values can be served by the presence of a small but active community of analysts searching for global patterns.

A MULTIPLICITY OF SEARCHES

To refer to those who investigate world politics as a community is perhaps misleading. They share a curiosity about recurring patterns and a commitment to some of the basic tenets of scientific method, but their efforts are otherwise marked by diversity, even division. Stated differently, the premises and procedures they employ set them distinctly apart from analysts who focus on single situations and seek policy solutions, but when they are compared to each other the community of apparently like-minded analysts emerges as a variety of subcommunities engaged in a multiplicity of searches for a multiplicity of patterns.

Perhaps the most diverse array of subcommunities stems from the wide variety of international actors whose patterned attributes and behavior evoke curiosity. Some analysts focus on individuals, particularly foreign policy officials, in an effort to uncover the cognitive, attitudinal, motivational, and affective sources of their behavior. Others are intrigued by subnational collectivities—such as elite groups, voluntary associations, institutionalized organizations, sociocultural entities, and mass publics—and the sources and consequences of their activities directed abroad or toward foreign policy officials. Still others concentrate on national political systems in a search for the dynamics of the foreign policies whereby governments adapt to their international environments. A fourth subcommunity centers its attention on the attributes, structure, stability, and development of various kinds of international systems, from the two-nation dyadic system to the *n*-nation regional system to the global system consisting of all international actors. Still another subcommunity is fascinated by the dynamics of governmental and nongovernmental international organizations, their influence, structure, and functioning. And within and across all these levels of analysis, many other subcommunities of analysts can be found who are joined by a common interest in a particular type of functional area (e.g., economic, military), relationship (e.g., alliances, cultural), situation (e.g., crisis, détente), attribute (e.g., hierarchy, ideology), activity (e.g., propaganda, diplomacy), substantive problem (e.g., population growth, resource allocation), or methodology (e.g., simulation, content analysis).[2]

To be sure, there is considerable overlap among these foci; some analysts move back and forth easily and frequently among several subcommunities. But each focus has also attracted analysts whose curiosity is bounded by it and who are thus likely to proceed from different premises about the flow of causation in world politics. Those who focus on national foreign policies on the one hand and those concerned with international systems on the other—to cite one of the most obvious and controversial subcommunity differences—tend to view the sources and outcomes of international conflicts as stemming from the interplay of different variables, with the former stressing the perceptions, strategies, and impacts of governments and the latter emphasizing the coherence, structure, and stability of interaction patterns.

Methodologically, too, the IR scientific community is marked by subdivisions. Depending partly but not entirely on the substantive phenomena in which they are interested, analysts vary considerably in the techniques they use for identifying, gathering, processing, and analyzing data. Some code and quantify historical events and thereby compile large empirical data sets.[3] Others content analyze materials found in historical archives, legislative records, newspaper columns, or any central place where the words of actors are recorded and preserved. Still others eschew historical materials and instead generate data through simulations—man and machine—of real-world phenomena.

Each of these methodologies—as well as the many others that could be listed—tends to attract analysts who become specialists in their applica-

tions and thereby interact as a subcommunity within the IR scientific fraternity. Again, of course, the overlap among these methodological schools is substantial, with more than a few analysts acquiring skills that enable them to move freely among various methodologies. In each case, however, a core of specialists can be identified whose knowledge of and involvement in their methodology is so advanced as to set them apart, with few outsiders able (or willing?) to follow the logic and complexity of their procedures.[4]

Springing in part from methodological considerations, but also from basic philosophical convictions, another crucial division within the scientific community involves the distinction between those who search for patterns inductively in empirical data and those who seek to uncover them deductively through the development of theoretical and mathematical models. The former contend that it is fruitless to fashion theory unless the empirical world has been thoroughly—or at least adequately—mapped, whereas the latter argue that mapping cannot be adequately—or at least justifiably—undertaken unless observers have a clear and explicit conception (i.e., theory) of what they wish to map. Thus the deductionists tend to be drawn to analytical models and mathematical formulations and to the philosophies of social science that support such a choice, while the inductionists incline toward data-making techniques and philosophical works that legitimate their doing so. As a number of the ensuing essays reveal, these two very different assessments of the surest route to reliable and cumulative knowledge can markedly divide practitioners who otherwise share an intense curiosity about the dynamics of global patterns.[5] All concerned may pay lip service to the ideal of combining inductive and deductive procedures, and some in fact do proceed in this synthesizing way, but the issue is so central to how the search for patterns is to be conducted that most analysts tend to become specialists in one or

[2]For a systematic effort to uncover empirically the various subcommunities of IR analysts, see Russett (1970).

[3]For a succinct account of the events data movement, see Burgess and Lawton (1972).

[4]It has been estimated, for example, that only about "a dozen" persons in the IR scientific community can comprehend the advanced factor analytic techniques developed by the Dimensionality of Nations (DON) project; see Hilton (1971, p. 7).

[5]For an especially vigorous dispute on this issue, see Young (1969) and Russett (1969).

the other approach rather than developing skills at both.

Generational differences also tend to fragment the scientific IR community. Chronologically, the generations are not separated by more than five or ten years—or as long as it takes for the creation of new plateaus of knowledge from which curious pattern hunters can again depart—but they are far apart in terms of the ways in which they conduct their searches. At least, the first generation of IR scientists seems to be differentiated from their successors in their readiness to theorize on the one hand and to accept some of the tedium of scientific procedure on the other. These differences can be traced to the way in which scientific investigations of international phenomena were launched in the United States.

Starting in the late 1950s, as the effects of the behavioral revolution in the social sciences began to be felt in a field that had long derived its orientations from the historical and legal traditions of inquiry, a few analysts became enamored of the possibility that new and perhaps more reliable ways of uncovering the recurring patterns of world politics could be developed. This possibility became a reality in the 1960s, as funds became available from government agencies and private foundations to initiate major research projects founded on extensive (and expensive) data-gathering and data-processing activities.

The founders of these projects can properly be regarded as the first generation of IR scientists, since it was they who first provided the field with analytic and (in a few instances) theoretical frameworks supported by empirical data generated and analyzed through the methods of science. DON, SIP, WEIS, QIP, COW, CREON, COPDAB—to mention but a few of the acronyms for the early projects[6]—quickly became part of the lexicon of the IR scientific community as they infused a steady stream of research reports, methodological formulations, and theoretical propositions into the field. This flow of material from the early projects,

[6]The acronyms cited stand, respectively, for the following projects: the Dimensionality of Nations, Simulated International Processes, World Event/Interaction Survey, Quantitative International Politics, Correlates of War, Comparative Research on the Events of Nations, Conflict and Peace Data Bank.

not to mention the flow of graduate students trained in connection with them, in turn provoked a second generation of scientists to refine, test, and extend the frameworks, theories, methods, and findings fashioned by their predecessors.

Considerable consequences follow from the difference between propounding a theory and perfecting it, between creating a methodology and clarifying it, between generating findings and modifying them. The first-generation IR scientists tend to locate their searches in a broad theoretical context, while their successors are more content to seek patterns within narrowly defined theoretical frameworks. Stated in terms of the labels Kuhn (1970) uses to distinguish scientists who seek to build an ever widening knowledge base through the creation of new and competing research paradigms and scientists who aspire to strengthen the corpus of knowledge by locating and fitting the missing pieces of the puzzles posed by existing paradigms, the first-generation analysts tend to be practitioners of a "revolutionary" science while their successors are inclined to adhere to the practices of a "normal" science.

Some of the reasons for this generational distinction seem clear. One is that those in the first generation were compelled to pay attention to the larger theoretical context of their searches in order to justify and win support for the broad scope of their large-scale projects. Another, more important reason is that most of the first-generation scientists—and their projects—helped initiate the break with the traditional, nonscientific modes of investigating international phenomena, a task that required not only the perfection of new research techniques but also the allocation of considerable time to developing and arguing the philosophical case for scientific inquiry. As a consequence, many first-generation practitioners emerged with the orientations of the revolutionary scientist even as their work served to establish a normal science. The inclination to create new data bases, to experiment with new methodologies, and to construct new models became habitual for them—inclinations that run counter to the normal scientist's predisposition toward building a knowledge base in small increments through replications and extensions of previous work. As will be seen in subsequent chapters, in short, many first-generation IR scientists tend to be temperamentally too set in their ways to practice normal science or even fully to appreciate its products.

THE NATURE OF CUMULATIVE KNOWLEDGE

Given the multiplicity of searches and the differences among the various subcommunities that undertake them, the question arises as to whether a body of cumulative knowledge has emerged in the years since scientific methods were introduced into the study of international phenomena. To evolve a shared curiosity about global patterns is not to ensure greater clarity about the identity, nature, and direction of the patterns. To rely increasingly on quantification, mathematics, and computers is not to guarantee greater comprehension. To generate a vast outpouring of models, hypotheses, data, and findings is not necessarily to fashion a corresponding cumulation of reliable and enduring knowledge. To have attracted considerable attention, even prominence, as an emergent community within the IR field is not necessarily to achieve theoretical or empirical breakthroughs. Indeed, to grow as a self-conscious community, with open lines of communication and a tolerance for diversity, is not even to assure the initiation of a cumulative knowledge-building process. The existence of the community and the prominence it has gained may merely reflect the emergence of a vogue in which quantitative analysis serves as a substitute for, rather than an instrument of, the creative theorizing and rigorous hypothesis testing through which steady accretions are made to the understanding of global patterns.

What, in short, has the scientific IR community accomplished in its short lifetime? It is a measure of both the youth and the diversity of the community that the answer to this question is in itself a subject of lively dispute. Various practitioners and subcommunities simply do not agree on the extent and nature of the accomplishments. Some are so impressed with the rapid development of methodological sophistication and the outpouring of theory and data that they proudly view the years since the inception of the scientific community as a period in which great progress has been achieved. Others insist that progress must be

measured by the breadth and validity of the substantive knowledge base that has been fashioned and claim that on these grounds the community has little to show for its years of effort. Still others find a middle position on the question, pointing to some substantive areas where achievements have been recorded and to other areas where the record is essentially one of failure.

Central to assessment of intellectual progress in any field or discipline, and especially one that has only begun to cohere, is the philosophical problem of what is meant by knowledge and its cumulation. As will be seen throughout this book, the different interpretations of what the IR scientific community has accomplished spring from widely disparate conceptions of what it means to cumulate knowledge.

At one extreme are those who take a narrow view of cumulated knowledge, viewing it as consisting exclusively of those substantive findings and theories that have been sufficiently verified to the point where they become part of the foundations on which other analysts build their searches. The keys to this narrow conception are confidence and consensus—confidence on the part of the observer that the uncovered pattern does indeed exist and operate as indicated by the theory and data, and consensus among many observers that it is therefore scientifically valid, in subsequent inquiries, to treat the uncovered pattern as having been established. Stated differently, confidence in findings descriptive of the explanatory power of an independent variable or the operation of a dependent variable, or at least in findings that describe one or more conditions under which the interaction between the variables unfolds in a particular way, must exist if other analysts are to use the variables and investigate how they may interact under other conditions. Only in this way, it is argued, do findings pile upon findings in a sufficiently coherent and cumulative way to satiate curiosity and expand the base of reliable knowledge.

At the other extreme is a broad conception of cumulation in which the growth of knowledge is seen to consist of much more than the evolution of confidence in reliable, replicable, and interdependent findings. While agreeing that the aggregation of such findings in small, incremental steps is an important dimension of scientific progress, those who subscribe to the broad conception contend that this is not the only dimension of knowledge building and must be seen as but one part of a larger enterprise. They assert that the reconceptualization of core notions, the development of diverse methodologies, the discovery and pursuit of anomalies, and the emergence of competing theories and paradigms are as central, if not more, to the growth of a science of IR as the painstaking process of empirically delineating the interaction of independent and dependent variables. To the argument that the ultimate measure of the growth of a science is the substantive knowledge that it cumulates—that revised and sharply delineated concepts, diverse methodologies, and competing theories are of little value unless they result in an ever growing corpus of findings in which an ever widening community of scholars has confidence— those who take a broad approach to cumulation respond that the expansion of knowledge does not occur in neat and logical sequences, that scientific progress is discontinuous, even dialectical.

While these two perspectives on the nature of knowledge need not be so incompatible as some of their adherents may believe, they tend to correspond to, and possibly even underlie, different assessments of the progress that has been made by the scientific IR community since the late 1950s. Those who espouse the broad perspective point to the proliferation of theories and the evolution of methodological sophistication as indicating that the accomplishments have been considerable, and they thus tend to be sanguine about the future of the field. Those who cling to the narrow perspective emphasize the dearth of established findings and the scarcity of widespread consensuses on the nature of international phenomena, thereby tending to see little progress and to judge the period as essentially one of failure.

THE CHAPTERS THAT FOLLOW

All the foregoing themes—the search for patterns, the sense and structure of community, the shared aspirations and the common philosophical assumptions, the variability of substantive concerns, the conceptions of cumulative knowledge and progress, the generational distinctions, and the related but not identical tensions between normal and revolutionary scientists—recur often in the chapters that follow, along with a host of empirical findings and provocative theories relevant to one or another pattern of world politics. And perhaps most pervasive of all is the thread that ties all these diverse themes together, a restless curiosity about the dynamics of international life.

Three separate conferences served as the immediate stimuli to the preparation of the ensuing papers. One, held in Ojai, California, in June 1973, was convened under the auspices of the National Science Foundation[7] and brought together fifteen scholars who had received major research grants since the 1950s. The purpose of the deliberations was to assess what the IR scientific community had accomplished as a consequence of large-scale funding for a decade or more. Each of the participants was asked to prepare an autobiographical account and assessment of his or her project, with due attention being given to how it contributed to the growth of a cumulative science. In many instances these papers were substantially revised (and, in some cases, rewritten) as a consequence of the deliberations; eleven of them are reproduced in Part One.[8]

Somewhat contrary to expectations, at this conference the aforementioned differences over the nature of cumulative knowledge and the degree of progress in the field surfaced in a vigorous way. It had been anticipated, perhaps naively, that those in attendance had outlooks and experiences sufficiently similar to allow for concerted effort to delineate the successes and failures of a decade of sustained scientific work. Instead there emerged basic disagreements about what had been done in the past and what ought to be done in the future. These disagreements were detailed in an eighty-two page report on the deliberations (Rosenau, 1974a) that, in turn, served as the stimulus for a follow-up conference convened in Santa Monica,

[7]Through a grant (GS-37340) to the Ohio State Research Foundation. I am grateful to G. R. Boynton of the University of Iowa, then program director for political science at the National Science Foundation, for his help in planning the conference.

[8]The papers by Rosecrance and Singer were not cast in an autobiographical context and are thus more appropriately placed in Part Two.

California, in March 1974, under the auspices of the Institute for Transnational Studies of the University of Southern California,[9] and attended by fourteen younger scholars.

The rationale of the second round of deliberations arose from the interpretation that one reason the first conference fell short of expectations was that it had been attended exclusively by first-generation scientists who were still too close to the experience of founding a scientific community to be able to sustain a coordinated effort to assess the cumulation that had occurred and to which they had contributed so much. It was felt that perhaps a group of second-generation IR scientists would be better able to focus on the problem and make such an assessment. To ensure generational linearity, those at the first conference were asked to nominate the conferees for the second round, particularly persons who either had experience in their projects or otherwise had firsthand familiarity with the research methodologies they had helped to launch. Those invited to the second conference were given the report on the earlier deliberations and were asked to use it as a point of departure for a paper on the problem of cumulation. Eleven of these papers, also considerably revised as a result of participation in the deliberations, are reproduced in Part Two along with two papers from the earlier conference that focus exclusively on the cumulation problem (see note 8).

Once into Part Two, readers will soon appreciate that there are limits to the degree to which generational differences account for varying conceptions of knowledge and its development. Although not nearly so autobiographical and wide-ranging as the chapters of Part One, those in Part Two also reflect basic differences over the surest route to effective cumulation. The second conference was not so contentious as its predecessor, but the papers it stimulated reveal that basic philosophical issues, such as the dispute over whether the knowledge-building process is best served through a deductive or an inductive approach, do

not necessarily wane as new analysts enter the IR field and extend the work of prior generations.

The third conference arose from a very different set of circumstances. It consisted of a long-planned "retreat" on the part of the Inter-university Comparative Foreign Policy (ICFP) project, an informal organization of scholars who managed to sustain fruitful collaboration across seven years and some ten universities, but who had begun to wonder how and where their collective efforts should be directed in the future.[10] Concerned that they may have advanced the comparative study of foreign policy beyond the point where continued large-scale collaboration was possible and desirable, the group secured the support of the School of International Relations of the University of Southern California to convene for three days of deliberations.[11] In order to concentrate attention on the question of whether there were still important tasks the ICFP could perform, the fifteen participants agreed to prepare papers on some aspect of the problem of "where the comparative study of foreign policy should go from here." Fifteen papers, considerably revised and now bearing twenty-three authors' names, are reproduced in Part Three.

Despite the different and more extensive origins of the third conference, the papers it generated are pervaded with the same restless search for global patterns that mark those presented in Parts One and Two. Many of the ICFP papers are, to be sure, less philosophical and more empirical and methodological in their orientation than the others. They also differ in that their scope is confined to those global patterns that can be traced to the attributes and behaviors of nation-states. Since these papers spring from a deep-seated curiosity about the regularities of national behavior in the international arena, however, their contribution to an understanding of the scientific quest for meaning in world affairs is no less than that provided by the more autobiographical and philosophical papers

[9]The resources used to sponsor the follow-up conference were made available to the institute by the university's School of International Relations and its director, Ross N. Berkes, whose continued support is gratefully acknowledged. Kay Neves and Gary Gartin of the institute's staff also made valuable contributions to the success of the conference.

[10]For a history of the ICFP's collaboration, see Rosenau et al. (1973). For some of the substantive results of the collaboration, see Rosenau (1974b).

[11]It is a pleasure again to acknowledge the assistance of the school's director, Ross N. Berkes. Without his support the ICFP could not have come together for prolonged deliberations. Charles A. Powell of the University of Southern California gave unstintingly of his time in planning and implementing the deliberations.

that precede them. Indeed, the empirical and methodological concerns of the ICFP papers serve as an important complement to the materials of Parts One and Two. They clearly indicate how the curiosity of IR scientists that arises out of personal and epistemological considerations can be translated into a disciplined probing of specific phenomena and data.

Taken together, in short, the papers of the three conferences depict the broad range of levels at which the search for global patterns is conducted by scientifically oriented analysts. They do not delineate many of the patterns themselves, but collectively they demonstrate that the search for them is a serious and multifaceted undertaking and, accordingly, one that is likely to expand our comprehension of international life.

REFERENCES

Burgess, Philip M., and Raymond Lawton. 1972. *Indicators of International Behavior: An Assessment of Events Data Research.* Beverly Hills: Sage.

Hilton, G. T. 1971. *A Review of the Dimensionality of Nations Project.* London: Richardson Institute for Conflict and Peace Research.

Kuhn, Thomas S. 1970. *The Structure of Scientific Revolutions.* 2nd ed. Chicago: Univ. of Chicago Press.

Rosenau, James N. 1974a. "Success and Failure in Scientific International Relations Research: A Report on a Workshop." Mimeo. Los Angeles: Univ. of Southern California.

———. 1974b. *Comparing Foreign Policies: Theories, Findings, and Methods.* Beverly Hills: Sage.

———, Philip M. Burgess, and Charles F. Hermann. 1973. "The Adaptation of Foreign Policy Research: A Case Study of an Anti-Case Study Project." *International Studies Quarterly* 17 (Mar.): 119-44.

Russett, Bruce M. 1969. "The Young Science of International Politics." *World Politics* 22 (Oct.): 87-94.

———. 1970. "Methodological and Theoretical Schools in International Relations." In *A Design for International Relations Research,* ed. Norman D. Palmer, pp. 87-105. Philadelphia: American Academy of Political and Social Science.

Young, Oran R. 1969. "Professor Russett: Industrious Tailor to a Naked Emperor." *World Politics* 21 (Apr.): 486-511.

Part One

The Search

Autobiographical Perspectives

2. The Roots of Faith

R. J. Rummel

For several reasons I have difficulty navigating a brief paper through the questions posed for our Conference on the Successes and Failures of Scientific International Relations Research. First, I question the assumptions underlying our efforts, for I am reluctant to debate scientific techniques, approaches, data, theories, and the like, when the game's very rules and values are at issue.

Second, as a movement the quantitative scientific approach to international relations (IR) is only about 15 years old. This is hardly enough time to crystallize trends, methodologies, theories, and results, and to overcome the extreme variance among people in their competence, approaches, scientific sensitivity, and norms. With people of different traditions, training, skills, and perspectives working side by side, is it appropriate or fair to assess success and failure in this first working-out-the differences stage? At least a few more decades are needed to lessen significantly the impact of this generational and transitional variance on our self-assessments.

Third, there simply has not been sufficient time to assimilate as a group our separate research, except in broad, often misleading, outline. Each of us probably feels the others have no clear idea or understanding of our research and ideas, in spite of all our reports and publications. With so little mutual understanding, how can an adequate scientific evaluation take place? It can't. And because of the lack of any real mutual understanding of our research, our discussions will be elevated to philosophy, norms, standards, and general substance. Yet on this level, the conference is stacked pro science; the movement's *bêtes noires*—the Morgenthaus, Hoffmans, Kahns, and Bulls—are not involved.

Enough. My quandary is indicated and this paper's direction sufficiently prefaced. For rather than confront our successes and failures as a scientific movement, let me simply write a personal history of my involvement. I trust this will be of singular interest in spite of its length, while giving a helpful and heretofore unknown picture of the Dimensionality of Nations (DON) project.

At the outset, I should say that my critical tone about the scientific IR movement does not mirror a feeling that DON has not succeeded scientifically. Quite the contrary. I believe that DON has been rigorously scientific and successful in its concern for a programmatic development of systematic knowledge, accumulation of consistent results, replication, interaction between theory and data, theory confirmation, sensitivity to error and reliability, methodological competence, and theoretical integration, comparing results, policy relevance, scientific communication, and critical (à la Popper) interaction and exchange. Of special interest, therefore, is my questioning the fundamentals defining this success, since behavioral psychology would have it that the self rationalizes and supports its successes.

However, in this as in so many things, behavioral psychology is wrong. Man is not a stimulus-response automaton, but is an intentional being behaviorally integrated around a future superordinate goal (whether it be a college degree, a million dollars, heaven, or a communist utopia). A person's ideas and behavior can be given intelligible perspective only in relation to this superordinate goal.

My lifelong superordinate goal has been to eliminate war and social violence; only by understanding this goal's genesis and enveloping cognitive structure can DON's research and my current reorientation be grasped. For to me, science or quantitative research are not the aims, but tools to be pragmatically applied to doing something about war and, if found wanting, improved or discarded.

War has been the focus of my intellectual life since my undergraduate days, and my emotive issue since a tour of army duty in Japan during the Korean War. But I need to go back further, since my feeling about war developed out of a youthful aversion to conflict. As difficult as it is, with the slippery deceit of our memories of youth, to untangle the first strands of life's ambitions, motivations, and interests, we nevertheless have feelings and impressions, sometimes so vivid, so intense, and so much part of our current concerns as to be clearly a major root. For me, this is especially so with conflict.

My memory of youth is mainly of disagreements, arguments and fights between my parents, of my own unhappiness as a result. By the time I was twelve, they had separated (eventually to get divorced); and after living in one rooming house after another with a father who was seldom around and gave me little support, I struck out on my own at fifteen. Soon thereafter I dropped out of school (in the ninth grade).

This youth, with its deep and pervasive family conflict and later with the numerous conflicts associated with trying to support myself, to develop an identity, and to move within cultures in which I found myself holding contradictory values (such as working in a factory among men whose beliefs, norms, and habits I could not share, or rooming with people whose values I could not adopt), left both an appreciation and dislike of conflict. It left raw nerves that would later energize a drive to understand and control such conflict; and it left a sensitivity to the role that values and meaning play. Moreover, this background tempered me in ways that would prove valuable in later years as a college student and an academic.

A subsequent traumatic tour of army duty in Japan was to intensify my involvement with conflict and to lead me eventually to focus on war. To give some background, after three years of bouncing from job to job (as farm worker, lumber hauler, drill press operator, assembly line worker, fisherman, bait seller, salesman, book shop clerk, department store clerk, amusement park worker, bowling pin setter, package deliveryman), I found most were unacceptable drudgery. That I was basically lazy and hated to be given orders, of course, made me a less than suitable employee.

By seventeen, I was in a box without exit. I couldn't stomach most jobs which suited my lack of skills. Yet, I had to support myself. In retrospect, I am almost certain that crime would have been the natural consequence of this age had not chance worked otherwise. A few months before my eighteenth birthday, the Korean War broke out, and military recruitment ads began to sing the virtues of enlistment—learn a trade, see the world. They offered escape from my frustrations—a chance to travel, perhaps to learn a trade (operating heavy equipment was a vague hope). The army was honored with my enlistment for three years in March 1951.

This was my most significant decision, for it was in the army that I came in contact with college graduates (before enlisting I had hardly known college existed since most of my relatives, friends, and acquaintances had not even completed high school), and by comparing myself with them began to think of college as a possible future option. Moreover, I was given the opportunity to take and pass the military's graduate level examinations that certified (within the army) the equivalent of a high school education. I was later to use these exam results to enter college with the support of the Korean GI Bill.

My first station was in Fort Benning, Georgia, a place I soon grew to hate with a passion exceeded only by my repugnance for army life (for a boy hostile to hierarchical situations, headstrong and lazy, some self-assessment should have deterred me from enlisting). The summer heat of Georgia, the southern racial biases (as they then seemed), and the rigors and difficulties of barracks life motivated me to volunteer for transfer to Korea.

This was the second significant decision. For rather than being sent directly to Korea, I was routed through a camp in Japan just at the time a vacancy occurred in the 64th Cartographic Battalion stationed in Tokyo. By mistake (chance, again) I was pulled out of the Korean pipeline and sent to fill that vacancy and remained there for the next two and a half years. Because of its map-making assignments, the battalion had an exceptional number of highly educated personnel and a technically oriented atmosphere. It was in this environment that I first conceived of going to college.

Equally important, my experiences in Japan would later provide the fundamental motivation for my interest in war. The reason for this goes back to my youth during World War II, which began for the U.S. when I was nine. I was tremendously impressed by the anti-Japanese propaganda before and after Pearl Harbor. I still can remember the emotions associated with bubblegum cards graphically illustrating the Japanese bombing of Shanghai, with grotesque bodies, puddles of blood, and pieces of wreckage everywhere. I remember surreptitiously scanning, when no clerk was looking, pocket-size books with lurid covers on the Rape of Nanking. And I remember the pride and involvement with which I read comic books and

studied magazine pictures of the battles of Guadalcanal, Iwo Jima, and so on. After all this, my mental picture of Japan and its people was not exactly a complimentary one. That basic attitude which had developed during the war was hardly touched by a later teenage belief in tolerance and internationalism. It was a psychological shock, then, to be immersed suddenly in the Japanese culture. For the immediate traumatic confrontation between my prejudices and stereotypes and the reality of Japanese life generated emotions that turned themselves upon the institution of war.

That the Japanese could feel pain, love and cry, and find pleasure in poetry and the beauties of nature was an emotional surprise. As I write I realize how naive this may appear. Of course, by the age of eighteen I knew that people differed little except in their culture. By then war appeared an irrational, ridiculous, and inexplicable occurrence. I had seen the movie *All Quiet on the Western Front* twice and had been intellectually moved by its message. But all these are the rational veneer. Japan gave me a personal emotional experience and a lesson about man's fundamental unity, and the brutal, distorted images created by war.

Already deeply set against conflict, I now began to turn strongly antiwar. How is it that people who were fundamentally alike could kill, maim, and hate each other on such a massive, unbelievable scale? How could World War II have occurred? Wasn't also the Korean War, then raging, itself mass stupidity? These kinds of question reflected a pervasive hostility to war and its vehicles, the military and the state, and affected much of my behavior, from questioning U.S. defense efforts and taking a decided pro-North Korean position in information briefings we received, to refusing to salute the American flag when my superior officers were looking the other way. This antiwar attitude remains with me to this day. Its behavioral and intellectual manifestations, however, have undergone twists and turns as my intellectual framework for understanding war has been deepened and extended since my army days (and decades later would paradoxically result in my opposing the antiwar movement against the Vietnam War).

During my tour in Japan and for years after, my feelings about conflict and war could find outlet only in personal rebellion or political activity, or so I thought. I had no realization of any relevant academic field or professional activity. Nor did it occur to me that I could focus my emotions and values by doing scholarly or scientific peace research.

When I entered Ohio State University in 1954—as green a freshman about academic opportunities as I have met since—my majors were physics and mathematics. Why I chose these will be pointed out later. The outcome, however, was that it was soon clear that I was not interested in physics, for I preferred to read books about the Far East (and Japan in particular), political histories, philosophy, and such.

Meanwhile, I had heard that the University of Hawaii offered a program for majors in Far East studies. After checking on this, I transferred to Hawaii in 1956 via a five-month stay as a yardman on the Alaskan railroad. During my first year in Hawaii I was persuaded to major in political science, since it was a better career line than Far East studies (in which I could still concentrate as a political science major). In my junior year, through my courses in international relations, I began to see that war was not only a topic of academic concern, but that *there was a field fundamentally dealing with it*. War, its nature and resolution, thereafter became the hub around which all my studies were focused and remains so to this day. My interest in the Far East has not been lost and, indeed, can be seen in part of DON's research. But this interest has been secondary to what is surely a single-minded passion.

It is at this point that the scientific, philosophical, and mathematical strands of my intellectual development became integrated around the focus on war. Therefore, let me back up and untangle these threads as well. When I was about thirteen or fourteen, I came upon some pulp magazines (*Amazing Stories* and *Astounding Stories*, I think) while rummaging through a secondhand bookshop. I was immediately captured by these early and corny science fiction tales (Captain Future stories were my favorite), and from then on, up to my early college years, I read voraciously almost everything in this genre published in English.

Science fiction helped to provide me with my basic precollege education. From it I developed an appreciation for a variety of sciences, a belief in the value of diversity, a faith in science, a basic set of scientific-rationalistic norms, and a future's orientation. Authors like Arthur C. Clarke, Ray Bradbury, A. E. Van Vogt, and Isaac Asimov were my mentors. (Asimov's *Foundation* and *Robot* series still provide me great pleasure; of course, anyone in the know must realize that the DON Project has been designed to provide the same mathematical forecasts Hari Seldon provided his followers in *Foundation*.) Science fiction was also the entrée for me to more socially conscious literature, such as that of Aldous Huxley, E. Bellamy, H. G. Wells, Philip Wylie, and George Orwell.

It is not hard to understand, then, why I wished to major in physics when I decided to go to college, especially in those aspects of physics which would prepare me to do scientific research on rockets and space flight. But I realized once the decision had been made to go to college (and thus to take the armed services graduate level examination, which would be my entry card) and to major in physics that I must come to terms with my weakest areas: English grammar and mathematics. Grammar was clearly needed to pass the examination, and as far as mathematics is concerned, science fiction had taught me its value—the predominant reliance of science on it.

While in Japan, I began, on my own, to study both grammar and mathematics. I soon became acquainted with spelling, parts of speech, and composition; I made a special effort to improve my vocabulary. And a concurrent study of Japanese proved especially useful in learning my own language. If my knowledge of grammar was limited, my knowledge of arithmetic was nil.

I had to begin with adding and subtracting fractions, taking square roots and manipulating decimals. I approached this with the anxiety of one's first solo drive on the road, for it seemed I had little mathematical ability and after all, had flunked plane geometry in school. But doing problems and outlining the methods gradually increased my confidence. While in Japan I worked gradually through geometry, algebra, trigonometry, and the beginnings of calculus, so that I felt sufficiently prepared to enter college and to major in physics and mathematics (I had added it because it appeared necessary for a good physicist to have this level of mathematical ability). My first two college math courses (college algebra and analytic geometry) turned out to be a surprise; I had already covered the essentials.

When Far East studies beckoned, I dropped physics and mathematics but not the scientific attitude. From science fiction I had developed a perspective, an orientation, a set of norms, if not a career. This orientation took on new meaning when I began to study IR and to delve into the literature on war. In the late 1950s, the scientific approach to IR was a growing, already coherent movement. The emphasis on forces, generalizations, justifications, laws, and theories was very much in the air. Quincy Wright, Richard Snyder, Karl Deutsch, and Morton Kaplan were only among the better known of those pushing for the scientific approach. I was foreordained to adopt this view with the example of Quincy Wright's *A Study of War* (1942) and, later, Lewis Fry Richardson's mathematical and statistical applications to war (1960a, 1960b), to believe strongly in creating a science of peace. As a junior at the University of Hawaii, this became my religion.

After a year's study of international relations, I began to feel that mathematics could play the same role in this field as in physics (a position I no longer hold). Scholars, I saw, were continually writing in terms of relationships and associations, dependency and independency, change and probability, and constants and variables. Yet, the language for expressing these concepts precisely and clearly—mathematics—was not being widely employed. For this reason I returned to its study in my senior year; when I received an M.A. in political science three years later, I had also completed the B.A. requirements for a mathematics major.

In this manner, my repugnance for conflict developed as a youth, my strong antiwar feelings formed during my army tour in Japan, my love of science born out of science fiction, and my belief in mathematics as the most appropriate language and tool became fused before my graduate years. Two other separate strands came together around this time to make my intellectual personality a consistent and integrated whole.

The first of these was a philosophical interest and orientation that I had before I was captured by science fiction. Where this orientation came from in a boy whose parents, relatives, and friends did not deal with abstractions beyond their daily needs, work, and play is a mystery. School might have been a source, but I doubt it, since I remember being entirely repulsed by school, except for art classes. At any rate, my earliest memories of an intellectual involvement began with questions about God's existence, the nature of reality and truth. Before the age of twelve I had become an atheist, a value relativist, and a skeptic about truth and reality. Perhaps the experiences that provoked this kind of questioning and these conclusions may have been alternating between the Methodist church with my mother one Sunday and the Catholic church with my father the next, along with frequent moves from one neighborhood subculture to another.

My beliefs, my questioning of those around me, and my youthful eagerness to show others to be wrong (my skepticism did not extend to my own beliefs) had the predictable results. I became the smart alec, the show-off who was too big for his britches. My parents were only confused by my beliefs and each responded only by blaming the other for my ungodliness. I was an outcast from my peer group; those whom I could talk to were usually several years older. This reaction only fueled my questioning and I continued to seek support in my readings.

The how or why of my interest in reading, which extends back to my earliest school years, is also lost to memory, if indeed there is anything specific to recall. Neither of my parents read at all; I do not recall having seen books or magazines around the house. There was, however, a significant transition in what I read. The shift from animal stories and the usual children's books borrowed from the library took place during the wartime paper drives (1942-1943) to collect used newspapers and magazines for reprocessing. During these drives, people stacked old magazines and newspapers in front of their homes for pickup and provided me a golden opportunity for rummaging. From these piles I picked up an assortment of treasures, in particular, *Reader's Digest* and *Life* magazines. Their variety interested me and eventually I had a complete collection going back several volumes. In the years that followed I went through these from cover to cover.

I still recall the joy with which I approached my *Reader's Digests*, organized by month and year, and the anticipation with which I began to read an issue. From the ages of ten through thirteen, these magazines opened unknown worlds to me. Natural history, disasters, politics, biography, social history, science, and so on, were popularized in a digestible and fascinating fashion. This variety, and the comprehensible excursions into religion, morality, and philosophy extended my conceptual framework, improved the substance and logic of my positions (I do not remember changing any of my answers), and most importantly, opened up the philosophic thought of other men. Plato, Aristotle, Socrates, and Kant exemplify the names that became meaningful to me (certainly, I must have previously come across these philosophers in school; however, what I had learned about them had no significant impact on me).

When I had exhausted this magazine collection and began my science fiction craze soon thereafter, I found a higher level of philosophical discussion. Stories enjoyable for their adventure and gimmickry alone would often discuss, or implicitly consider, the nature of life, mind, intelligence, reality, time, space, perception, truth, and so on. I still feel that reading the better science fiction authors sharpens one's philosophic perspective (a conditioning helpful but not sufficient for understanding the truly great philosophers) in the same way that reading literary masterpieces, like those of Tolstoy, Dostoyevsky, and Shakespeare, deepens one's social philosophy.

By no means, however, did my informal philosophic education prepare me for coping at this early age with the philosophers themselves. I remember getting special library permission to borrow Kant's *Critique of Pure Reason,* and finding it absolutely opaque. Kant's analytic and synthetic, his discussion of cause and effect, and his treatment of space and time were gibberish to me. This frustrating inability to comprehend Kant left its mark. It was three or four years before I tried to read the basic works of other philosophers. (Aristotle I found dull, Plato fascinating. Socrates became my hero; I identified with his suffering,

and his manner of questioning was similar in style—or so I thought—to that with which I had alienated my peers. As an atheist I ignored the Christian philosophers and did not try to read St. Augustine or St. Thomas Aquinas until recently. For obvious reasons, I was much attracted to David Hume, Francis Bacon, and John Stuart Mill, and I felt for years that the greatest living philosopher was Bertrand Russell. I did not try to read Kant again until a few years ago and have now devoured most of his works. His influence will be seen in my current writing.

My interest and reading in philosophy have continued since my teens. But this aspect of my mentality did not become connected with my attitudes toward war, science, and mathematics until I took my first formal course in philosophy—in logic—while a college junior. Almost immediately, the value of logic for any work on war seemed apparent. It appeared fundamental to all thought and at the time I began to think of mathematics as a subfield of logic. Only lately have I reluctantly given up this point of view (largely because of the lack of success of Russell and Frege in reducing mathematics to logic, of the failure of Hilbert's program, and of Godel's incompleteness theorems). The next courses in philosophy all dealt with the philosophy of science, and the pure intellectual excitement they engendered far surpassed that of other courses throughout my college years.

In this philosophic perspective I found a thorough (although one-sided, which I did not realize at the time), fundamental and favorable discussion of science (my religion). I was easily captured by the Vienna Circle. Logical positivism became my philosophy; its major interpretation of meaning, the testability thesis, became my doctrine. I was even more convinced after taking a course from Herbert Feigl, a Carnegie visiting professor at Hawaii and one of the original members of the Vienna Circle. His lectures and collection of readings (with Brodbeck, 1953) poured my philosophic position into concrete for the next several years. Only recently have I begun to see logical positivism as sterile, inconsistent with its own metaphysical presuppositions, and a block to the development of knowledge.

At the time, however, this philosophic perspective fitted well my pro-scientific-mathematical approach to international relations and war. I could easily believe that war was a problem because we knew little about it. The reason we knew little was that those who studied it did so intuitively or speculatively. And what was clearly needed was a scientific study of war based on mathematics. Science fiction had infused me with a scientific spirit. Logical positivism gave me a metascientific vocabulary with which to fight the metaphysicians of international relations. Precision, hypothesis, theory, laws, deduction, data, prediction, and explanation were my orienting concepts; and testability was my thesis. Little did I realize then that man's most basic data, his own experiences (such as those I present here), are not testable.

The final strand that enters here is art. In my preteens I became adept at drawing. It was an activity I enjoyed and my route to approval and status. In retrospect I now think that I was unconsciously balancing through art the strong negative reactions my beliefs and attitudes aroused. Until I dropped out of school art was my favorite subject.

After leaving school, and subsequently having little stomach for laboring or clerk-type jobs (or environments), I began to attend evening classes at the Cooper School of Art in Cleveland. By comparison with other students, I could see that I had artistic ability, but for reasons I no longer recall (if there were actually any specific ones) I lost the motivation to apply myself consistently to the fundamentals of color, anatomy, perspective, and design. I left the school after about six months. Shortly after, the Korean War began and I joined the army.

Although lacking the motivation to do the work necessary to be an artist, I still enjoy art and take pleasure in painting or drawing. One of Japan's great attractions for me was the aesthetic nature of Japanese culture. The landscapes of Hiroshige, the bamboo prints of Eisen, the snow pictures of Hokusai, the flower arrangement, the architecture, the alcove for the pleasing vase or flower arrangement, and bonsai all contributed to an aesthetic feeling of oneness with the Japanese. No doubt this aesthetic attraction significantly influenced my dismay that we had made war on each other.

While I was preparing for college and involved in my first college years, the aesthetic part of my nature found little outlet—that is, until I moved into areas of advanced mathematics. Analytic geometry, spatial representations of calculus, and mathematical functions themselves provided me with great aesthetic joy. In drawing a hyperbolic function, representing a three-dimensional plot, or integrating a function, I found the same joy and the same aesthetic pleasure, the sense of the beautiful, the well formed, and well balanced as I had in a landscape or figure drawing. Years later, I would find these same joys in linear algebra and associated matrix algebra. And, in class I still may exclaim, after having derived the canonical regression model or Guttman's image analysis model, "Isn't that beautiful."[1]

Art gave me a spatial orientation, a desire to see things visually, that has been a central aspect of my approach to international relations and war. If there is a relationship between war and nationalism, how do we reflect this visually? If we theorize in terms of a social space, how is this spatially represented? If there is a technique to use, what is its geometric interpretation?

The cognitive appreciation of mathematics, visual orientation toward and aesthetic pleasure in it, linked strongly to my study of international relations and war. It was thus that as a college senior my mathematical and scientific focus on war through the narrow lens of logical positivism was an intellectually, emotionally, and morally integrated concern. The story since then is one of loosening this system, of broadening its elements and perspective, and of the metamorphosis of new perspectives—but always around the core concern with war.

One change came soon. Strongly antiwar in my undergraduate years, I tried to organize demonstrations (such as disrupting ROTC), but in terms of mobilizing followers I was ten years too early. I then felt that armaments were absurd and my

---

[1] My book *Applied Factor Analysis* (1970) is primarily a presentation of a technique in its many ramifications, but I find pleasure in viewing the book's diagrams, plots, figures, and equations as an artistic accomplishment.

major premise was unilateral disarmament for the U.S. or as a compromise turning our armaments over to the UN. Better red than dead was my belief; and anyway, I was then an ardent socialist. But as a first-year graduate student, I did a term paper on unilateral disarmament and the criteria for evaluating it among other disarmament alternatives. My criteria led me to a conclusion that I could not at first accept: no matter how I looked at it, I found that unilateral disarmament or turning our arms over to the UN was impractical and idealistic. These alternatives would be absolutely unacceptable to Americans; and even were the President so inclined, he could not so act without impeachment.

This experience of having *my* analysis contradict what *I* had been advocating dampened my subsequent activism. The result was to turn me to an insistence on analysis before advocacy and to initiate an erosion of my blanket antiwar and antimilitary views that eventually led me to support the Johnson and Nixon Vietnam policies (and separate me again from most of my peers). This does not mean a decrease in intellectual or emotional concern with the problem of war, but rather a broadening and disciplining of the cognitive framework within which I can understand and deal with the problem.

A second event of my early graduate years, not of immediate significance for changing my views, but which later was to have a profound impact on my view of science and its value, concerned applied statistics. As part of my mathematical study I had gone routinely through mathematical statistics and probability. As is usual at the textbook level, the analytic material was all neat, clean, and precise. When, however, I tried to apply the all-so-simple product-moment correlation to data for my M.A. thesis, all was fuzzy, messy, and frustrating. The thesis was that war resulted from a breakdown in the normative structure of international society and that technological change was the cause of the breakdown in this structure. (Sorokin, 1937, came to the same conclusion, but on a much firmer basis than I was capable of developing. I still hold to this thesis essentially, and it will be found in various forms throughout my current writing.) Thus, A (technological change) $\rightarrow$ B (breakdown in norms) and B $\rightarrow$ C (war), and therefore A $\rightarrow$ C,

where $\rightarrow$ means logical implication. As a good logical positivist I had to test this thesis, of course.

I wrongly felt at the time that A $\rightarrow$ B implies statistical correlation between data A and B. (Actually, it means only that whenever A, then B, *but not necessarily the other way around.* The proper implication to test correlationally is A $\rightarrow$ B and B $\rightarrow$ A. That is, that A must be necessary *and sufficient* for B.) Therefore, I wanted to use the product-moment correlation coefficient I had learned about in mathematical statistics to do this testing. My measure of technological change was the number of inventions over 25-year intervals, from 1648 (the beginning of the modern European nation-state system with the Treaty of Westphalia) to 1900; my dependent variables were the numbers of wars, battles, and killed among European nations at similar intervals. Trying various lag relationships, I spent several weeks calculating some 125 product-moments at a desk calculator. I then discovered that the assumption of normality had not been checked, and had to find such a test; then came the discovery that many of my distributions were nonnormal; then the search for an alternative correlation coefficient that did not assume normality; then the search for a test of significance, and so on. By the time I was through, I had learned something about the difference between mathematics and quantitative research and had uncovered my ignorance about scientific *research*. Incidentally, the thesis found that war occurs 25 years after intense technological change (as indicated by inventions). This experience directed me into social statistics and applied methodology, into a realm that began to show the strong qualifications of mathematics applied to international relations and the overzealous mistakes of such attempts as those of Nicholas Rashevsky.

After I received my M.A., I accepted a fellowship in the program of international relations at Northwestern University and subsequently became a Ph.D. candidate there. When I arrived at Northwestern, Harold Guetzkow's Internation Simulation project was the major research effort in international relations. The idea of simulation was not new to me and laboratory experimentation was a favored ikon of my religion. However, the notion of having high school or college students simulate nation-states in interaction, and controlling or intervening experimentally in the simulation to test or generate knowledge and international relations, seemed fundamentally mistaken. It was like trying to study the nature and problems of automobile driving by having people who had never driven and knew little about highways simulate traffic problems in a situation structured by experimenters whose only acquaintance with driving was through books. Moreover, I could not see how such simulations could advance knowledge about a system whose empirical states, variables, and parameters were still unknown.

Nonetheless, this was the major effort at Northwestern and I felt I should be acquainted with it. During my first year there, as part of a term paper for a course on factor analysis, I collaborated with two other students in an analysis of simulation data. To understand and generate these data required going into the simulation procedures and outcomes in detail. This effort only confirmed my bias and to this day I feel that one correlation coefficient between the actually observed behavior of nations, say trade and aid, is of more scientific use than all the simulations that have been run at Northwestern. To be clear, I am not referring to simulations used for teaching or for policy exploration purposes (e.g., simulations among decision makers to explore alternatives or the implications of particular scenarios), or to computer simulations (modeling). It was, and is, the use of people to simulate nations in a contrived environment—man-simulation—as a route to scientific knowledge of international relations that I find naive. Today my views on man-simulation have generalized to small group research itself (including the game studies *ad nauseum*), at which I would level the same criticisms well presented by Sorokin in his *Fads and Foibles of Sociology and Related Sciences.*

The complement of these negative views on simulation was the belief that the route to understanding international relations must be paved with observational or statistical data on the behavior of nations. Since war was my main focus, I also believed that data on international conflict were necessary (though not sufficient) for such understanding.

My logical positivistic credo thus gave data a clear role as the arbiter between metaphysical and scientifically meaningful statements, as the final judge of truth and falsity, as the test of our theories. Years before attending Northwestern, I felt the need for a general theory of war. Theory was required to order our data, to provide explanation and a basis for prediction. Data paved the road to understanding, but theory dictated its direction and contours. My conception of an adequate theory was dictated by my positivistic views. It was narrowly defined as a logico-mathematical system, comprising axioms, theorems, rules of correspondence, primitive terms, theoretical concepts (the problems these create for the logical positivistic criterion of meaning were not to be seen until years later), and so on. American political science graduate students are now weaned on this sterile (for the social science) view of theory through their reading of Hempel (1965) and Rudner (1966). Not until several years after leaving Northwestern did I see the retarding influence that this Procrustean conception of theory had on my research and outlook, and on behavioralism generally.

But during my graduate years I firmly believed that the missing element in dealing with war was *Theory,* as defined above. The thoughts of such scholars as Morgenthau, Deutsch, Thompson, Kennan, Aron, Carr, Liska, and Snyder I dismissed as untestable metaphysical speculations. (This is written with a sigh, for the arrogant assurance that, as a senior and graduate student, without any of the personal experience with international relations problems of a Kennan or the deep scholarly acquaintance of a Morgenthau or Carr, I could shrug off their views was an attitude that for years walled me off from the very understanding I was seeking.) Quincy Wright's work, as exemplified in his chapter "Measuring International Relations" in *A Study of War*, was a step in the right direction, I felt. But the only true *Theorist* was Lewis Fry Richardson.[2] I dissected his arms race models piece by piece as a graduate student at Hawaii. His

---

[2] I had discovered Richardson through an obscure footnote that mentioned his mathematical approach to war. Excitedly I tried to locate his works or references to him without much success. Finally, one of my professors heard about the *Journal of Conflict Resolution*'s full issue on Richardson (see Rapoport, 1957). This opened the door to all his research. For many years one of my treasures was the posthumous, two-volume collection of his works (1960a, 1960b)—a birthday gift from my wife.

mathematical theory was of the kind I was after, but his actual theory seemed to me to have problems involving the number of parameters and their measurement, and to be too restricted in application (as I later wrote in a term paper criticizing his efforts). What I wanted was a *Theory* that would deal with war causation and predict the occurrence of wars.

My M.A. thesis was an effort in this direction, but I considered my technology → norms → war linkage a hypothesis. It needed formulation in a set of interrelated mathematical equations in order to be a *Theory*.

I carried this two-sided research conception—formulate mathematical *Theory* and test it with behavioral data—to Northwestern, and except for my hike into the simulation wilderness, this conception framed my efforts there. Until the DON project opportunity, I tried various routes to developing a set of *Theoretically* interrelated equations. For example, I studied game theory and used its mathematical system to model Organski's power transition speculations (I thought). But game theory seemed of little use for structuring *Theory* of a predictive kind (I still think so, Riker's valiant efforts notwithstanding). Calculus (as used by Richardson) seemed inappropriate at the level of measurement possible for the concepts to be imbedded in the *Theory*. (Calculus simply is inapplicable to variables measured on an ordinal scale. One can transform these variables to appropriate scales by using multidimensional scaling, smallest space analysis, or factor analysis. The scale could then be the operationalization of the concepts, but I did not realize this at the time.) So I concentrated on manipulating algebraic functions.

I still have a file titled "Conflict Theory: Ideas" containing my notes and attempts of those years (1961-63). Consistent throughout these notes is the attempt to define international conflict, at the dyadic level, as dependent on value and technological differences, power parity, and geographic distance. These elements still, ten years later, form my core conception of war, even to my emphasis on the dyad. The reason I did not deal then at the system or national levels, which were more popular (J. David Singer's classic "Level-of-Analysis" paper does not even include the dyadic level), is probably the joint influence of Wright and Ri-

chardson, who both defined their equations in terms of nation dyads (Wright's less familiar differential functions are in *A Study of War*). And it made good pragmatic sense to be able to deal with war in terms not only of those who engaged in it, but also those toward whom it was directed.

Toward the end of my first year at Northwestern, Guetzkow and Jack Sawyer decided to submit a proposal to the National Science Foundation (NSF) primarily to delineate "real-world" dimensions for Guetzkow's simulations and, secondarily, to replicate Raymond Cattell's (1949, 1952) factor analyses of nations. I was then taking a course in factor analysis (as part of my attempt to master applied social statistics) from Sawyer, a visiting professor in the Psychology Department, and Guetzkow knew of my interests and mathematical background. Thus they asked me to join them as an assistant on the project, even though I was assured of a fellowship the next year.

While my initial inclination was to decline, my final agreement to join them proved to be one of my more fateful decisions (I write now in the eleventh year of the project). I shied away from this proposal for three reasons. First, I was not interested—and am still not—in data *collection* and *analysis* per se. Although I saw the value of replication and felt that such a factor analysis would make a contribution, it would consume time and energy. Second, theory about war was my interest, and data analyses appeared useful only for testing such theory. No theory existed in the proposed project. Finally, I was emotionally wary of such collaboration. A loner since my early teens, I have been self-generating, dependent on my own wit, and with beliefs usually strongly at variance with my peers. What few classroom group projects I had been involved in had been frustrating. I could not eagerly anticipate such a team effort.

In spite of these reasons, two opposing considerations were decisive. My attempts to develop a *Theory* of war faced the difficulty of operationalizing the basic concepts (in spite of my positivistic belief that *Theory* involves theoretical concepts in part, I treated all my concepts as empirical) such as values, technology, power, and conflict. Power was the easiest to deal with since I could use Organski's (1958) measure (national income) or Wright's (1955) index (energy production times population). I was not happy with the measure of technology (inventions) I had used in my M.A. thesis and was really stymied as to how to measure values or conflict. Around this time I wrote in my notes that value difference

> is the difficult index to get at. Might be done via a factor analysis of all possible indices ... of values. Probably political values most important. Therefore might include dichotomous measures like: monarchy or not; dictatorship or not; women's suffrage or not; no election, one party without effective primary, one party with effective primary, multiparty; censorship, etc. On the other hand, the proposition that overlapping group membership is an indication of similar values might be explored, viz. number of international organizations of which both a member; multilateral treaties.

Besides, however I chose to operationalize the concepts, I was still confronted with a lack of data. Of course there were the Wright, Sorokin, and Richardson collections of useful data on values. (I do not know how at the time I could have used Sorokin's war data and ignored his rich tabulations on values or technology.) It was evident, therefore, that I needed relevant concepts which were more empirically grounded and from which data could be generated in order to develop a testable *Theory*. I saw the proposed factor analysis of nations as the means to this end.

On this basis, I joined the Guetzkow-Sawyer effort and wrote the proposal's first draft. Much revised by both Sawyer and Guetzkow, this DON proposal with a two-year budget was subsequently submitted to and approved by NSF; Guetzkow was the principal investigator, Sawyer was a consultant, and I was an assistant.

From the very beginning, the project involved a bewildering variety of questions: what variables to select with what criteria; what sources to use; how best to measure the variables; what units to use; what computer programs; what correlation coefficient, factor model; and so on. Over the months between NSF approval and the project's starting date, I tried to survey the applied research literature and, especially, actual projects doing similar research. What seemed a relatively simple task when laid out in a proposal became a can of worms when the data and methodological issues began to surface—and no books or articles or other projects (such as Cattell's, 1949, which we were trying to replicate) provided much help.

In all my years in school, the closest I came to education as interactive learning was in the frequent Guetzkow-Sawyer conferences we had during DON's first year. I prepared the agenda (on such issues as how our variables can index prevailing international relations conceptions, or how to measure censorship), outlined the solutions, and provided the justification. They accepted or criticized these and often provided new considerations for me to check into. In this manner, we covered a broader range of topics than I had ever considered in my previous courses or my own research.

There is no need here to detail the questions and my answers, nor the results of these conferences. My conclusions on methodology are in the "Operationalization" section of *Applied Factor Analysis*; this book also contains the total findings of my research on factor analysis itself. The research procedures, criteria for selecting variables, considerations on error and so on, as well as the empirical results of this phase of DON, are in my *Dimensions of Nations*.

Many of the early problems in doing the DON analysis defied packaging or even easy communication. Therefore, I felt it wise to do a pilot analysis involving a small number of variables before entailing the expense of analyzing the 200-plus variables we foresaw. The conflict variables (nine domestic conflict variables such as riots, demonstrations and assassinations; thirteen foreign conflict variables, including wars, threats, and protests) interested me most so I selected them for a first run through our complete design. Since I needed a Ph.D. dissertation at this time (my second year at Northwestern), I decided to use the results for that purpose also, but secondarily.

The pilot analysis was successful. It showed me what to avoid in running computer programs and helped me to plan the 200-plus variable (eventually 236 variable) runs. It showed that our analyses of these kinds of variable could be interpreted and thus substantively meaningful. It showed that systematic error could be dealt with. And in the preparation of these conflict data for analysis, it showed the necessity for considering the effects of outliers and distributions on the need for transformations. It also gave me a dissertation.

I was not happy with the dissertation. It had no theory, and little philosophy or substance. But in a field which lacked such previous analysis of domestic or foreign conflict, it seemed a contribution. For that reason I trimmed the dissertation and submitted it to a journal for publication (Rummel, 1963). In retrospect, it is ironic that a pilot study, which had a primary purpose other than to factor-analyze conflict, and which lies on the periphery of my interest, should forever set my professional image as an "atheoretic factor analyzer of conflict data."

I received my Ph.D. in 1963 and in September of that year I began teaching at Indiana University. Guetzkow, Sawyer, and I agreed to try to transfer DON to Indiana with me as principal investigator and with Guetzkow and Sawyer acting as consultants. With some trepidation NSF agreed to this arrangement.

The Indiana Government Department (since then renamed Political Science) was a friendly, facilitative beginning for my career. Walter Laves, then chairman of the department, was most considerate of my needs. I was given sufficient space for DON and soon had research assistants (one of whom was Ray Tanter) to help in the effort.

The move, however, caused considerable difficulties for our analysis. By the time the project was shifted to Indiana, all the data had been collected on 236 variables and initial data screening and transformations had been completed (mainly by Richard Chadwick). Also I had made sure that Indiana had the same computer system (an IBM 750) so that our laboriously prepared computer programs could be run there.

What I had not realized was that even though computers may be mechanically the same, each computer center writes its own system to process programs. Thus, I soon found out that our programs would not run at Indiana and that revising them would take considerable effort. Fortunately, the director of Indiana's computing center was sympathetic and also interested in getting our programs into his library. He gave me much personal help and made a programmer available, so that by the spring of 1964 all our programs were working. From this time on I made sure that programming costs were a major part of DON's budget; a fortunate decision, for time and again over the next ten years I found that the major analysis headache was in revising our programs to make them compatible with a new system.

Out of necessity I had taught myself some programming (calculating over a hundred product moments for my M.A. thesis on a desk calculator had motivated me to learn FORTRAN), but it was not something that I wished to go into deeply or keep up with. The reason for this was clear. Mathematics is, once learned, unchanging: $y = a + bx$, therefore $a = y - bx$ always and forever, A substantive specialty or philosophy, although not so invariant as mathematics, provides basic principles, ideas that change slowly; the ideas of Plato or Aristotle are still pertinent and much discussed today.

But computer languages and systems do not share this invariance. The manner in which language and system lock together to enable one to program a specific computer is an ever evolving unity, changing often from month to month. Keeping up with the rapidly changing technology therefore requires a high expenditure of time. If one has a substantive focus, as I did on war, and computers are only tools (although perhaps a great route to status among methodologists and the behaviorally inclined), then spending more time on computers than that needed to process programs written by others or to communicate with a programmer appeared to me then, and still does, wasteful. (Understandably, I have found curious the practice of taking a significant portion of class time in political science to teach programming.)

At Indiana the major analysis planned at Northwestern was completed and subsequently published, years later, in *The Dimensions of Nations*. Also at this time I was still trying to improve my understanding of factor analysis. This was DON's primary method, and I wanted to be sure of what the results meant, if anything. I had gone through all the basic factor analysis works, but there were many contradictions (for example, with respect to the proper number of factors or best factor rotation scheme to use), and almost all discussions were in the context of psychological tests and samples. By contrast, DON was dealing with a population of nations and with such data as GNP per capita, riots, and censorship.

The best way to handle these uncertainties, I felt, was to move down to the mathematical foundations of factor analysis and then deal with the applications. For this reason I spent much of my time at Indiana studying linear and matrix algebra.

This, in conjunction with my previous mathematical training, had four significant effects on my future path. First, it enabled me to see through the fog of myths and misunderstandings that had grown around factor analysis (e.g., that linear relationships are assumed, that results are arbitrary, or that it is only a data reduction technique). Second, I saw for the first time the mathematical unity of the whole range of bivariate and multivariate methods, such as the product-moment coefficient, multiple regression, factor analysis, and discriminant analysis. Later, I would see smallest space analysis and canonical analysis also as part of this mathematical whole; they are all variants of the same mathematical system. Since then I have avoided arguments as to which of these is a better technique and have only shaken my head at the causal analysis of smallest space analysis fads. Saying that one technique is better, or overused, or *the* approach in the abstract is like saying that the quadratic equation is better, or overused, or *the* equation compared to the cubic. The question is which of these mathematical variants are appropriate for the substantive problem at issue and the theory or hypothesis of concern relative to one's assumptions and long run scientific goals. Third, I saw that factor analysis was not simply a technique of data manipulation, but a fundamental mathematical approach that was widely used in the physical sciences and engineering (based on the characteristic equation and similarity transformation) for a variety of purposes. I saw that factor analysis proper was only a simple scaling of the eigenvector solution to the characteristic equation and that the eigenvector-eigenvalue equation was of general scientific use.

Finally, and most importantly to my later intellectual development, it became clear that the basic mathematical approach implied a profound philosophical and paradigmatic shift from the traditional Cartesian view; the same shift involved in the move from a mechanical nature implied by classical physics to a probabilistic indeterminate nature implicit in quantum theory. My philosophical interests were much aroused by this and I remember still the fascination with which I read Ahmavaara and Markkanen's discussions of this point.

Aside from my mathematical study at this time, an important question had to be faced: whether to continue the DON project, which was due to end in the summer of 1964, even though the analyses completed went far beyond what had been originally proposed to NSF. In the early days of DON I had suggested to Guetzkow and Sawyer that instead of doing an analysis of national characteristics as Cattell had done, we could do a dyadic analysis of international behavior (which seemed to me more relevant for international relations). Both were wary of this idea, for there was no precedent in the psychological literature for this kind of design (it seemed that psychologists could not move outside the monadic mold that dominated virtually all academic research), and anyway they basically wanted to follow Cattell's path.

I did not forget the idea and when the replication at Indiana was completed, I again thought seriously of moving to the dyadic level and focusing on international behavior. Specifically, I wanted to analyze data on dyadic war within the context of dyadic conflict and all within the context of dyadic international behavior, such as trade, aid, and treaties. This goal reflected the first significant mental shift in my positivistic-mathematical-scientific focus on war.

I had participated in DON in order to generate data and empirical concepts for a *Theory* of war. Paved with data-based tests, *Theory* was the road to eliminating war. However, perhaps due to a wide reading and synthesis of the basic international relations literature in preparation for my Ph.D. exams, or to my lack of success in developing or finding such a *Theory*, I began to feel that war could not be dealt with alone. It must be considered as part of a behavioral matrix (what I would later call a field). A *Theory* about war must be a *Theory* about international relations, or so it began to seem. I began to see Richardson's approach (and of course, my previous position) as fundamentally wrong. Considering war in isolation from the system of behavior of which it is a part was like studying heart disease without considering its relationship to other diseases or comparing the diseased constitution to healthy ones. Years later this shift in view would ripen into a field conception: that war must be understood in the situation, in context, as a part of a whole that constitutes the sociocultural and psychological system. But at the time it simply broadened my focus: war was now to become part of a *Theoretical* concentration on international relations, although still (as now) the normative core of my efforts.

This shift had another significant aspect. My positivistic epistemology had centered on *Theory*. "Understanding" was psychological state arrived at through familiarity with a well-tested law or theory. Often science makes advances that are hard to understand or against the common sense of the time (as with the Copernican system), but through reiteration and use the strange becomes familiar and understandable. Therefore, understanding had no reality, no aspect of truth to it, and no useful epistemological status. Perhaps the intensive two-year long emotional and intellectual investment in data, technique, procedures, variables, selection criteria, factor interpretation, and so forth, that the DON project entailed gradually eroded this naive view. In any case, I began to try to understand international relations and war within this matrix and apart from *Theory*. The work of the project appeared in this new light as contributing to understanding, and I began to think of a dyadic level analysis as providing a new insight. Clearly my reluctant association with DON for the purposes of data and concepts—empirical grist for the *Theoretical* mill—had now accommodated to an interest in analysis itself. Possibly I belabor here what may appear a subtle distinction. However, this was the first movement away from a rigid perspective and toward eventually abandoning the whole positivistic philosophy.

Although cognitively I grew to appreciate more the value of DON and see its continuation as desirable, I found little pleasure in directing it. Introverted, extremely shy, with little social experience, I was psychologically the last person to manage people. Yet, I found myself of necessity with a secretary and research assistants to direct. Throughout the years I was to find this situation uncomfortable and in the beginning even felt apologetic about making a request of my secretary. I longed for the quiet and solitude of the simple scholar-scientist, but clearly this was not yet to be. Only recently have my cognitive framework and personal longings merged to the point where I could significantly alter the project as it has operated since 1962.

In the spring of 1964 I submitted a proposal to NSF for a Phase II, requesting double the amount previously granted. Phase II constituted the dyadic analysis of international relations behavior and complemented the completed analysis of nation characteristics. NSF subsequently approved this proposal for two years. This meant that I now had complete control over DON's research direction (remember the previous two years were largely devoted to a design that had been jointly agreed upon with Guetzkow and Sawyer) and that NSF had implicitly approved of my handling of the research.

Before the dyadic phase began, I accepted a position at Yale University, and transferred DON there in 1964. At Yale I completed the proposed dyadic analysis by a simple straightforward application of the methodology developed previously. Most important to me, however, was the development of social field theory, which until recently I considered the *Theoretical* breakthrough I had sought.

An aspect of my mentality is that I try to organize things into a common framework, to move to a level of abstraction where I can connect diverse ideas. In 1964 at Yale, I felt under a definite intellectual strain in trying to reconcile what appeared to be two different studies: the national level analysis completed at Indiana and the dyadic level then under analysis. The strain was mathematical: on one hand I had a matrix whose rows were defined by nations; on the other, a matrix whose rows were defined by dyads. Consequently, these matrices implied two different vector spaces which seemed mathematically unconnectable. I wanted a transformation that would enable me to move from one space to another. That is, *I was after a mathematical linkage between national attributes and international behavior*. Suddenly one morning, as I drew both vector spaces on a blackboard, the solution appeared: the distance vector between nations in the space of their attributes would connect this space to that of their behavior. Dyadic behavior mathematically could be the resultant of the dyadic distance vectors. This really simple insight caused me to shiver with delight. For I saw immediately the implications of these distance vectors *as a representation of sociopolitical, economic, and cultural distances*. Wright, of course, had made various distances a central aspect of his operational theory of international relations (not in his field theory, but in his dyadic level distance based theory in *A Study of War*), and I was familiar with some of the sociological uses of this concept. Moreover, in my previous attempts to formulate a *Theory* of war, value and technological distances had been core variables.

Since I felt that the factor equations upon which the distances would be based had significant philosophical implications, that the dimensions were probability densities covering the range of dyadic behavior and nation attributes, and that the whole thing could be developed axiomatically, this appeared to be my general theory. This discovery gave me my one and only "Eureka!"

I gave this *Theory* the name social field theory because of Quincy Wright's field theory conception in *A Study of International Relations*. He had plotted the change in the location of nations in their capability and value spaces, and had thought of the coordinate axes as factors based on his analysis of international relations. This was *intuitively* close to the nature of my nation attribute space, so I used the field theory label.

This has created some misunderstanding about the nature and origin of social field theory. Some have felt or written that it is a mathematical treatment of Wright, a simple extension of his field theory, or that I have been simply testing his field theory. I highly respect Wright's work and have tried where possible to build on it, but in this case social field theory in its structure bears little mathematical or substantive resemblance to Wright's theory. He simply proposed plotting nations in their capability and value spaces and asserted that their relative movement in these spaces measured the movement of the system away from or toward a stable balance of power and international integration.

Wright's field theory follows by 15 years his theorizing about distances and his differential equation predicting the rate of change in the probability of war from rates of change in dyadic distances. These two conceptions, one of nations changing in a space representing a field and the other of rates of change in distances affecting behavior, were kept separate by Wright. In my *Theory*, these two conceptions were brought together (with a different mathematical interpretation of the effects of distances) in one substantive mathematical interpretation.

Once the distance vector linkage was conceived, the rest followed. In subsequent months I established the axioms and described the structure of field theory. It was eventually published (Rummel, 1965), but understandably has drawn little attention. Its mathematics—linear algebra—is little known among social scientists, and in form (but not in fundamental idea) it constituted a fundamental departure from what is usually considered theory among political scientists (although among logical positivists it would be *Theory*). Clearly, as I realized at the time, further development and dissemination of the theory is needed if it is ever to attract critical attention.

What impact field theory has had is on DON itself. Up to the discovery of the distance vector linkage, DON was concerned with the dyadic analysis of international behavior. As anyone involved soon sees, analysis as a goal (even focused on an understanding of war and the development of relevant empirical concepts) does not define many of the links in the research design chain connecting data and results. Throughout 1964 I experimented with various methodological choices to determine their effects, such as the particular transformation or correlation coefficient used, or factor model applied (such as image analysis versus component analysis). With the development of field theory in 1965 all this experimentation was phased out. DON priorities were reordered and all new design choices were made within the constraints of the *Theory*. The concern was now to provide the results defining the nation attribute and dyadic spaces and distance vectors and to use these results to test the central theoretical axiom: that dyadic behavior is a resolution of distances between nations in the space of their attributes. It was this testability of the whole conception that convinced me that I had a *Theory,* rather than just a framework, a method (as Lewin, 1951, thought of his field theory), or a statistical research design (as many would allege over the following years). Remember, I was a good positivist.

From this time until 1970, my efforts moved along three distinct but related tracks: operationalization, interim testing, and theoretical elaboration. First, considerable effort was needed to operationalize the nation attribute and dyadic behavior spaces such that field theory could be tested. Masses of data had to be collected, sub-spaces (like UN voting) had to be defined and analyzed, and hundreds of variables had to be factor analyzed to delineate the coordinate axes of attribute and behavior spaces. In the spring of 1966 I submitted another two-year proposal to NSF to continue this effort. Although I did describe field theory in the proposal, my sensitivity to the interests and prejudices of the proposal's possible evaluators led me to stress the quantitative results as a mapping of the international dyadic and attributive domains. I asked for continued support to do a factor analysis of 1963 and 1965 attribute data and 1965 dyadic behavior. (The 1963 behavior space analysis already had been completed.) This proposal was approved and the project was transferred to the University of Hawaii in 1966, where I had just accepted an appointment.

I realized at the time I made this proposal that the funds (about $70,000) were not sufficient in the long run. The reason was that I had to deal with a number of different years to do an adequate testing of field theory. I had asked the maximum of NSF I thought my reputation and their interest in my results could demand, but I foresaw the need for a series of NSF grants over more than a decade. Other foundations had no interest in quantitative international relations analyses per se. In 1966 I was, therefore, eager to increase DON's support, but saw no alternative to NSF.

In this context Ray Tanter played a central role. He had been an assistant on DON during its year at Indiana. By coordinating Indiana's computing center's rewriting of our programs developed at Northwestern and running our 236-variable factor analyses, he was most responsible for completing DON's analysis there. Through him I learned that the Defense Department's Advanced Research Project's Agency (ARPA), Behavioral Science Division, funded quantitatively oriented, applied projects, and that this might be the source of the large funding that I needed.

I did not share many of my colleagues' prejudices against the Department of Defense or defense related research. For one thing, I was not anti-Vietnam War. I saw our original involvement in the late 1950s as a mistake, and Kennedy's investment of U.S. prestige through increasing our

military commitment as *the* fatal blunder; but I saw Johnson's policies as the best way to resolve the war while maintaining a stable nuclear environment.

Second, my normative focus on war and doing something about it had begun to mean bringing war under political control. It meant helping policy makers evaluate alternatives so that they do not stumble into war, especially nuclear war. It meant providing the forecasts that would enable policy makers to foresee the war-provoking consequences of their actions. I saw defense policy makers as sharing the desire to understand and avoid war, and I strongly believed, as I still do, that involving social scientists in the Defense Department's analyses and decisions is a method of diluting a strictly military perspective.

In 1967, I wrote to ARPA briefly sketching what I needed funds for (again with the emphasis on the analysis results—the operationalization—and not the theory testing) and asking whether I could get support. The response was negative, arguing that the Vietnam War left little research funds available for such efforts. Soon after this exchange Tanter joined ARPA as an assistant director of the Behavioral Science Division. And, of course, I reopened the whole issue of a five-year DON program. A program involving training as well as research appeared most supportable at the time; and I subsequently wrote a draft proposal for discussion. A training program lacks rigorous definitions and for that reason I ran into difficulty in ARPA. Accordingly, Tanter advised me to submit a research proposal like those to NSF, which I did in 1968. It outlined the parallel analysis of dyadic behavior and nation attributes for 1950, 1955, 1960, 1963 and 1965, a reanalysis for the Asian region, a computer simulation model based on field theory, and the analyses results. This proposal outlined all that was necessary to test field theory without elaborating on the *Theory* as its basic focus.

Our discussions and this proposal stimulated Tanter to develop a Quantitative International Relations Program in ARPA that would support DON as well as the research projects of Bruce Russett, Charles McClelland, and Harold Guetzkow. Tanter fought this program through the Department of Defense and administered it during his stay at ARPA. It has continued under his successors, Davis Bobrow and George Lawrence, in spite of difficulties with Congress over DOD social science support and the pressures on the defense dollar from the Vietnam War. ARPA provided the consistent support necessary to quantitatively operationalize field theory in the shortest possible time.

Operationalization was the first track. The second was interim testing. To define the behavioral and attribute spaces quantitatively and sufficiently enough to do the necessary testing required the completion of the five years of research proposed to ARPA. But some interim testing could be done, I thought, to explore the theory and get a feel for the testing methodology (canonical analysis). A first such "test"—really inadequate to testing the theory as such but done before the 1955 behavior space was analyzed— previously published as "A Field Theory of Foreign Conflict," had been helpful in elaborating field theory itself. Accordingly, when the 1955 and 1963 behavioral and attribute spaces were empirically defined, field theory tests were run. Moreover, tests were made for all dyads involving the U.S. as actor in 1955; separate tests (see Rhee, 1971) were made similarly for China on 1955 and 1963 data.

The experience gained from these tests had much influence on the interpretation of field theory. Most importantly, they showed that attribute distances have differential effects in the international field depending on the actor. However, the effects of distances are patterned (as predicted by the *Theory*) as object nations vary for the same actor. Equally important to me, they showed that distances to explain a considerable part (over 50 percent!) of the variation in international dyadic behavior, including conflict. These results were always tentative, however, until the five years of data collection and analyses could be completed, and the full-scale longitudinal tests of the *Theory* could be run.

The third track was theoretical elaboration. One aspect of this involved working out the mathematical and substantive implications of the theory (for example, the basic model that would represent the distance vector linkage). Model I—which implied that the differential effects of attribute distances were similar, regardless of actor

nation—was abandoned in 1969 for a Model II interpretation representing distance effects as dependent on the acting nation. Another consideration involved the way time fit into field theory. After some study, I felt that calendar time only functioned to order the data; that time, as part of the field, was social and psychological in nature and effects; that it was a coordinate axis of attribute and behavior spaces; and that there may be more than one social time dimension. A third important consideration was the mathematical relationship between the dyadic level of field theory and the nation-centered analyses current in the literature. Most quantitative analyses are still concerned with the interrelationships between a nation's total behavior, such as its trade, aid, treaties and conflicts, or between its total behavior and attributes. I found a simple mathematical relationship between the dyadic and nation-centered results for Model I of field theory, but not for Model II.

Besides working out the theoretical implications I also tried to fit field theory into the literature. I had not read Lewin's work prior to developing field theory, but soon did. I could not agree with much of Lewin's work as it seemed to be pseudomathematical hopes rather than sound method or *Theory*. However, I found much similarity in perspective (such as the need to deal with the whole) and assumptions (such as simultaneity of causation). At this time (1966) I also studied Arthur Bentley, whose notions of social space and belief in a social geometry attracted me, and Parsons, who felt at one time that his pattern variables defined the coordinate axes of social space. Neither was very useful.

In the international relations literature there were many ideas I felt were subsumable or related to field theory. Here Rosenau's linkage theory seemed a special case of field theory; Wright's distances and field theory were, of course, aspects of my field theory; Organski's power transition theory, and theories of integration such as those developed by Deutsch and Russett, were interpretable within the *Theory*. I sketched these relationships in a paper, a test of field theory, Model II, on the U.S. (Rummel, 1972b).

I was especially happy to see that general systems theory (as developed and interpreted by Bertalanffy) and mathematical communications theory had much in common with field theory. The former's whole-part assumption, emphases on interdependence and the system state, concern with parameters, and mathematical orientation (leaving aside Bertalanffy's belief in differential equations) are shared in field theory. For communications theory and field theory, the mathematical structures have much in common (for example, the measure of entropy is directly related to the eigenvalues of the principle axes defining the probability densities in the field), enabling many aspects of field theory to be defined in or translated to communication theory terms. Thus, I soon began to see that field theory was not a unique development at ninety degrees to the field, but a development that promised precise operational and testable synthesis of many disparate ideas and theories.

Of particular interest had been Johan Galtung's application of status theory to international relations. I was fascinated by the theory because of the explanatory strength status it had in sociology, because it easily lent itself to mathematization, and because it seemed a fruitful direction in predicting dyadic behavior. Accordingly, I was interested in determining the relationship between field theory based on distances and status theory based on rank and status disequilibrium. I spent about a year going through the status literature and determined that status theory could be integrated within field theory and form a fundamental part of it. On this basis I reworked the axioms of field theory (some were clearly not independent, so this change was long overdue) and added new ones to incorporate status concepts and propositions.

The revised theory, which I called status-field theory, was subsequently published. As a revision this development was clearly an improvement. It gave more meaning and substance to the stipulated relationship between dyadic behavior and distances and it predicted particular relationships between conflict and cooperation on the one hand, and economic development and power distances on the other. This added precision and fruitfulness without changing the mode of operationalization or testing the theory.

This work on status-field theory was the last gasp of *Theory* as my positivistic bias had defined it. Because of my immersion in the status and

international relations literature, the accumulated effects of teaching substantively oriented courses, and the on-the-job methodological and scientific lessons I was learning, a change in my integrated mentality took place. From about 1959 to 1970, a logical positivistic philosophy, faith in science, a mathematical and aesthetic orientation, and a concern with war were unified in my research and analyses, and in the development of field theory. Some minor changes in this mental system had taken place, like the growing acceptance of analysis and understanding aside from *Theory* and the refocusing on war within the contexts of conflict and international relations. However, only the lighting had changed, the picture remained the same through these years.

What altered this picture fundamentally was the coming conclusion of the ARPA five-year research program. I saw that by the summer of 1972 we would have collected the planned five years of data, completed the analyses of dyadic behavior and attribute spaces, and completed the necessary tests of field theory. Clearly, it was time for the evaluation and synthesis of all this research and for posing the crucial question: *after ten years of effort and expenditure, what do we now know about war that is new and will help control or eliminate it*? Before any new research was planned this evaluation appeared absolutely necessary. On the strength of this evaluation, then, additional or different lines of theoretical or empirical effort might be indicated. This evaluation would be a comprehensive philosophical, theoretical, empirical, and policy-oriented treatment of war. Field theory would be the foundation, with DON's many results as the evidence and the end. This would be the first general treatment to come out of the DON project, a treatment now possible because of the projected completion of the first range of field theory tests.

Over 50 research reports, some three dozen articles, and two books had emerged from DON since 1962. All had been technical reports, either directed to like researchers or written for a lay audience. Some hoped to communicate the methodology; others, the technical results. Many of the results and approaches of DON were of general interest in their own right and, it seemed, should not be buried in a more comprehensive volume. Moreover, the field theory was formulated in 1965 and subsequent research was directed to its full scale testing in 1972. I was reluctant to write up the substantive-philosophical context until the foundation was tested. And third, it was good grantsmanship to maintain a steady flow of publications to support my frequent proposals (the ARPA funding was on an annual basis). In 1970, the need to consolidate all these (which I am now doing) was clear.

Fortunately, I had appointed assistant directors of DON, Warren Phillips, 1969-1971 and Sang-woo Rhee, 1971-1973 who assumed DON's daily research administration. This enabled me to concentrate on background and general reading in preparation for the evaluation. To free most of my time I decided to write no more until I could begin the book, to reduce my administrative commitments, to refuse more such positions, and to reduce travel to a minimum.

And then I began to read. This was a reeducation and updating in history, philosophy, social science, and international relations, for other than DON's research interests and material related to my substantive teaching, I had not read widely since my graduate years. This reading period has turned out to be my happiest academic years, and has refreshed and reshaped my perspective. I read without pressure and without restriction as to approach, philosophy, or relevancy to field theory of war. One guide was my feeling about those areas (such as international relations theory) where I needed refreshing, was weak (as in history), or lacked any background (such as religion); a second guide was my desire to deal with the best works, those that time and the critical acclaim of the scholarly community had singled out from the multitude that enjoy an ephemeral life each year. Thus, I reduced my professional reading of journals and the latest research articles and books to a minimum. Keeping up with these materials was increasingly expensive in time, as most merited either a footnote or a kind oblivion. The value of relying on a scholarly and time-honed consensus as to the important works has increasingly become evident.

In this way I relaxed my concerted and focused efforts on DON. I ignored the time-consuming problem of its research design (such as systematically estimating missing data, or controlling for data error), the seductive mathematical questions of field theory (such as the relationship between dyads of persons and dyads of groups involving those persons as members), and its important theoretical relationships (such as to game theory). Freed from the hard taskmaster—the DON design—which I had obeyed for 10 years and which (except for some courses I taught) had completely co-opted my intellectual energy, I enjoyed spending hours reading Toynbee, Fies, Finer, A. J. P. Taylor, Pareto, Weber, Marx, Durkheim, Sorokin, Plato, Aristotle, Thucydides, Confucius, Lao-tse, St. Augustine, Spinoza, Descartes, and the like. I am inclined to call this the liberal education of R. J. Rummel. I now saw the strength, beauty, and importance of much of this literature. I no longer simply (sneeringly?) dismissed such concerns as metaphysics or irrelevant free will, purpose, morality, intuition, causation, or man and nature.

Disengaged from DON and from my research and administrative commitments, relaxed and totally immersed in the great works, the system that was my mentality was rapidly transformed. It had been ready to change, the cracks that had appeared have been noted above; all that was needed was intellectual removal from DON and a broad immersion in man's knowledge and speculations about himself.

My current writing will manifest this change and I need not detail it here. In broad outline, my focus on war in the context of conflict and international relations was broadened even further to include man, society, and culture. Logical positivism I began to perceive as quite starkly narrow, sterile, and naively mistaken. I now only wonder at how I could have been so wrong for so long. In place of this former philosophy I now see a necessary partnership of intuition, reason, and sensation; of metaphysics, science, and experience. If anything, my views now are a mixture of Kant, Popper, and Cassirer; of Cattell, Sorokin, Sartre, and Alfred Adler; and of Aron, Rousseau, and E. H. Carr. In contrast to a former value relativity based on an emotional interpretation of the "is-ought" dichotomy, I now see many strong qualifications and alternative positions. The role of ethics and values has become a paramount concern.

Instead of a view that the mathematical logical approach is supreme, the argument for more intuitive and less precise verbal approaches now makes sense. Increasingly I see the contributions to understanding of poetically rich prose, less exact than logic or mathematics, ambiguous to be sure, and without the *therefore*s, *thus*es, and *because*s of reason, but vibrant with meaning and understanding.

Regarding international relations, a somewhat militant opposition to the traditional approaches of observers like Bull, Morgenthau, Fox, Thompson, Aron, and Hoffman (all of which I had read in my graduate years) has been replaced by an admiring appreciation of their scholarship. They were uncovering layers of understanding untouched by the quantifiers and positivists. Moreover, I have begun to see their works as a philosophical-normative-theoretical-policy unit that no quantitative effort had been approached. A case in point is Aron's *Peace and War*. On first reading it in 1968 I could not finish it. I found it speculative, unsystematic, without operational concepts or variables, and rife with untested generalizations; Young's (1969) hostile, positivistically oriented review of the book reflected my attitude. Three years later I found it a brilliant analysis of international relations.

Regarding *Theory*, which for 10 years had a capital *T* for me, I started to question the value of the geometric analogue: axiom, primitive terms, deductions, theorems. Theory, without capitalization, as a loosely related system of ideas began to have value in itself. I saw the positivistic—Hempelian—definition as possibly stultifying; it seemed to sacrifice meaning and usefulness for seductive precision and deductability. Why deny the label and role of theory to the works of Morgenthau, Durkheim, Sorokin, or Marx just because the formal analytic structure is lacking? And with this change of *Theory* to theory, I began to loosen up on my thinking about field theory. Now I began to consider the role of man's nature and culture even though they cannot be neatly fitted into a formal theory. I began to consider the fundamental principles underlying international relations and the roots of war even though they are not operationalizable or testable. Ignoring the requirements for a deductive *Theory*, I now had a diverse literature to enrich my understanding and the field conception.

Whether in fact or value I have only deluded myself in another direction is for others to judge. The results of these twists and turns lie in my current work, which probably will not be published for at least another five years. For the purposes of these proceedings, however, I might suggest where DON's efforts now fit into this reorientation. Am I discarding all DON has done? Am I saying that the effort was misconceived? That field theory is to be abandoned? The answer is no.

The work of DON and field theory in the larger philosophical-normative context are even more important than before. I saw the elimination or control of war as requiring mathematics, *Theory*, and systematic observation. Now, I see this triad as but part of a perspective we have on what we blindly call reality. This perspective includes our intentions, our metaphysical suppositions, our values, as well as our theories, logic (such as mathematics), and experience (observations). This perspective is thus a manifold of intuition, reason, and experience. I see the project as bringing together reason and certain kinds of experience, and field theory as providing the structure for understanding the perspective through which war has meaning for us. But I see also a metaphysics—an ontology—and man's nonscientific experience—his autobiographies, memories, speculations, perceptions—as infusing this perspective.

Finally, where I had previously seen values as functioning to select our research problems and to decide how research results would be utilized, I now see them as interwoven throughout our research enterprise—as giving light to our perspective on war. (Of course $1 + 1 = 2$ always and forever regardless of ideology. However, the choice of this number system, the content or meaning of the numbers, and the implication to be drawn are part of our values.) And for this reason, praxis has become as important a part of my research as *Theory* once was.

The upshot of all this is my willingness now to state views that formerly I would have considered unscientific (not based on *Theory* and data). For example, one of the more important results of DON is my conclusion that war is inevitable within the behavioral-positivistic perspective and insofar as people are persuaded (as are most Americans) of it. I think the only way to break this iron law of history that is war is through the realization (1) that man, not physical nature, is the center of reality, (2) that man's behavior is not subject to the same cause-effect processes we ascribe to physical reality, but rather is teleologically guided by his future goals, and (3) that man is mainly self-determined and morally responsible for his actions. To wit: the future lies in his hands and not in some causative features of his environment such as distances, power, geography, poverty, deprivation, and underdevelopment. It has taken me many years to see finally that my own history and that of DON exemplify this self-determining power.

REFERENCES

Ahmavaara, Y., and T. Markkanen. 1958. *The Unified Factor Model*. Helsinki: Finnish Foundation for Alcohol Studies.

Aron, R. 1967. *Peace and War*. New York: Praeger.

Bertalanffy, L. von. 1968. *General Systems Theory: Foundations, Development, Applications*. New York: Braziller.

Cattell, R. B. 1949. "The Dimensions of Culture Patterns by Factorization of National Characters." *Journal of Abnormal and Social Psychology* 44: 443-69.

———. 1952. *Factor Analysis: An Introduction and Manual for the Psychologist and Social Scientist*. New York: Harper & Row.

Feigl, H., and M. Brodbeck, eds. 1953. *Readings in the Philosophy of Science*. New York: Appleton-Century-Crofts.

Galtung, J. 1964. "A Structural Theory of Agression." *Journal of Conflict Resolution* 11: 15-38.

———. 1966. "Rank and Social Integration: A Multidimensional Approach." In *Sociological Theories in Progress*, ed. Z. A. Berger. Boston: Houghton Mifflin.

Guetzkow, H., C. F. Alger, R. A. Brody, R. C. Noel, and R. C. Snyder. 1963. *Simulation in International Relations: Developments for Research and Teaching*. Englewood Cliffs, N.J.: Prentice-Hall.

Hempel, C. G. 1965. *Aspects of Scientific Explanation*. New York: Free Press.

Lewin, K. 1951. *Field Theory in Social Science*. New York: Harper & Row.

Organski, A. F. K. 1958. *World Politics*. New York: Knopf.

Rapoport, A. 1957. "Lewis F. Richardson's Mathematical Theory of War." *Journal of Conflict Resolution* 1 (Sep): 249-99.

Rhee, Sang-woo. 1971. "Communist China's Foreign Behavior: An Application of Field Theory Model II." Ph.D. dissertation, Univ. of Hawaii.

Richardson, L. F. 1960a. *Arms and Insecurity: A Mathematical Study of the Causes and Origins of War*, ed. N. Rashevsky and E. Trucco. Pittsburgh: Boxwood.

———. 1960b. *Statistics of Deadly Quarrels*, ed. Q. Wright and C. C. Lienau. Pittsburgh: Boxwood.

Riker, W. H. 1962. *The Theory of Political Coalitions*. New Haven: Yale Univ. Press.

Rudner, R. 1966. *Philosophy of Social Science*. Englewood Cliffs, N.J.: Prentice-Hall.

Rummel, R. J. 1963. "Dimensions of Conflict Behavior within and between Nations." In *General Systems Yearbook*, Vol. 8, pp. 1-50. Bedford, Mass.: Society for General Systems Research.

———. 1965. "A Field Theory of Social Action with Application to Conflict within Nations." In *General Systems Yearbook*, Vol. 10, pp. 183-211. Bedford, Mass.: Society for General Systems Research.

———. 1966. "A Social Field Theory of Foreign Conflict Behavior." *Papers, Peace Research Society (International)* 4: 131-50.

———. 1970. *Applied Factor Analysis*. Evanston: Northwestern Univ. Press.

———. 1972a. *The Dimensions of Nations*. Beverly Hills: Sage.

———. 1972b. "U.S. Foreign Relations: Conflict, Cooperation, and Attribute Distances." In *Peace, War, and Numbers*, ed. B. M. Russett, pp. 71-114. Beverly Hills: Sage.

———. Forthcoming. "A Status-Field Theory of International Relations." In *Field Theory Evolving*, ed. R. J. Rummel. Beverly Hills: Sage.

Singer, J. D. 1961. "The Level-of-Analysis Problem in International Relations," In *The International System*, ed. K. Knorr and S. Verba, pp. 77-92. Princeton: Princeton Univ. Press.

Sorokin, P. A. 1937. *Social and Cultural Dynamics*. New York: American Book.

———. 1956. *Fads and Foibles in Modern Sociology and Related Sciences*. Chicago: Regnery.

Wright, Q. 1942. *A Study of War*. Chicago: Univ. of Chicago Press.

———. 1955. *The Study of International Relations*. New York: Appleton-Century-Crofts.

Young, O. R. 1969. "Aron and the Whale." In *Contending Approaches to International Politics*, ed. K. Knorr and J. N. Rosenau, pp. 129-43. Princeton: Princeton Univ. Press.

3. Apologia pro Vita Sua

Bruce M. Russett

Rudy Rummel's conference paper[1] was the first to arrive at my office. In some ways I had dreaded its arrival. In his DON project Rummel has pursued the development of cumulated data and analysis, rigorously centered on a particular theoretical approach, more single-mindedly and perhaps more successfully than any of the other projects with which members of this conference are associated. I fully expected that the receipt of his paper (or perhaps that of Dave Singer, or of some other member of the club) would arouse some guilt feelings about my own failure to be so single-minded in the development of a corner of our science. While I think there is much in my work that has been cumulative, I also have been a gadfly, changing my theoretical and substantive foci repeatedly within the general field of international conflict studies. And yet when I read Rudy's paper, it became clear that he and I are closer intellectually than I had thought, or probably than we had been earlier. Without retreating from his scientific commitments, here was Rudy defending eclecticism! My guilt subsided.

SOME CUMULATION FROM THE WORLD DATA ANALYSIS PROGRAM

But before giving too much away, or before being misunderstood, let me first detail some of the ways in which my projects over the past decade have, I think, been cumulative in the scientific sense of which we presumably approve. Most obvious of all is, I suppose, the work that went into, and that stemmed from, the two editions of *World Handbook of Political and Social Indicators*

[1] See Chapter 2.

(Russett et al., 1964; Taylor and Hudson, 1972). Much of this is detailed in the foreword and introduction to the second edition, and in Taylor (1968). In a survey I did only four years after the appearance of the first edition, I found that the data had been used in preparation of nearly 150 papers, articles, and books. By now that figure should be multiplied several times, perhaps by five or more. Thirty-five or more of these works were produced by co-authors of either the first or the second edition, with the rest done by other scholars who worked from the printed page or from the computer tape on deposit at the Inter-university Consortium for Political Research in Ann Arbor, Michigan.

Some of these authors used the data in merely anecdotal or incidental form, but many have used them in increasingly rigorous, cumulative ways, building in part on the primitive examples of data analysis that Hayward Alker and I gave in part B of the first edition. By refining methods and combining *World Handbook* data with bits and pieces of other quantitative materials, scholars have produced some important and convincing findings about political development and stability. In this context I think most vividly of the exemplary book by Hibbs (1973) and forthcoming work by Edward Tufte. Other important work, refining, revising, and confirming earlier propositions, has been done on the political effect of intranational and international inequalities, communications, and military activities. The data, hypotheses, methods, and initial findings of our work in and from the *Handbooks*, all have been integral parts of this cumulative process. Furthermore, these materials, especially as made available through the Consortium, have played a major role in the education of many hundreds of graduate students who have not yet entered into the above publication count. I suspect that a continuation of this data-gathering and dissemination process, with increasing attention being paid to diachronic analysis, in a theoretically informed manner, would be one of the most fruitful ways of insuring cumulation in important realms of comparative and international political research.

I recently finished preparing the manuscript for a book compiled from my articles on international politics written over the past 14 years (Russett, 1974a). In doing so I was surprised by the durability of several threads of continuity, and the sense that some cumulation was occurring. One such thread was in deterrence theory, manifested in three articles written over the course of a decade (reprinted as chaps. 13-15 in Russett, 1974a). The first article was a theoretical formalization and empirical test of some hypotheses about the importance to effective third-party deterrence of various aspects of the dyadic relationship between the defender and the state it was trying to defend. This was further developed, at a rather leisurely pace, in the subsequent two articles, and has been the subject of further testing, refinement, and formalization by a number of other writers (most notably George and Smoke, 1974, and Doran, 1973).

Another thread, beginning with *Community and Contention* (Russett, 1963) and continuing off and on through a number of articles, is my work on international integration. This began, inspired by Karl Deutsch, as an effort to operationalize a variety of propositions he and I had worked out. Even though further refinement and testing has continued over the years, by Donald Puchala, Hayward Alker, David Handley, Steven Brams, and others, the results have not been so successful. The reason, I think, is a failure of theoretical convergence. While we all agreed on the apparent importance of certain variables, especially those representing communication and transaction flows, we did not agree as to precisely what hypotheses ought to be tested with what indicators. As a result we have frequently talked past each other, employing similar data to reach opposite conclusions (see Russett, 1974a, chap. 18). We simply waited too long to articulate careful theory.

The other major focus in my work during the 1960s was on international systems, and especially "regional" or other subsystems. This combined aspects both of the work on integration and the work Hayward Alker and I did on the UN (Alker, 1964; Alker and Russett, 1965; Russett, 1967). Of the other major quantitative IR projects, it draws most heavily on Rummel's DON project, and probably has been of greater relevance to his work than to the others. Interaction between the two projects has, I think, produced some significant cumulation. And quite a number of other scholars have taken one aspect or another of this work and made some modest contribution to cumulation. I say modest, however, because in my opinion (and, I suspect, Hayward's), much of this other work has been mechanical, devoid of important theoretical interests, and almost cavalier about modifying the design in replications. Instead of modifying the design systematically, one element at a time, in the typical report several modifications are made at once, and it is therefore impossible to tell which is responsible for any difference between the results of the initial effort and that of the supposed replication. On the whole, however, the differences produced have not been great, which argues for the existence of a fairly robust structure in the underlying data, insensitive to moderate methodological variations. But the replications typically have not taken the form advocated by Boynton,[2] such as the systematic introduction of third-variable controls. Here we see the baleful effects of the absence of a broad and accepted theoretical paradigm. I think we also see the limited nature of the results to be expected from demanding cumulation too quickly in the absence of such a paradigm. I will have more to say on this below.

The work outlined in the last paragraph was concerned overwhelmingly with macro analysis; that is, with the effects on national behavior of international system, subsystem, dyadic, or national system variables, to the substantial exclusion of attention to the effect of intranational system variations. This work, and that of other quantitative IR researchers at the macro level, led me to be much impressed with the stability of the

[2]See Chapter 13.

international system (largely with the post-World War II stability, but also, and importantly, continuities with the prewar system as well). The empirical convergence of a great deal of work built up this finding, whose implications I dealt with at some length in the essay, "Macroscopic View of International Politics," that I did in 1968 for the Rosenau, Davis, and East volume (reprinted as chap. 2 in Russett, 1974a). The theory to explain these findings is a good deal less impressive than are the empirical data, however, so we again see a major limit on the value of the cumulativeness that has so far emerged.

One other piece of evidence for the thesis that important cumulation has nevertheless occurred in our work—and here I am thinking of interproject cumulation—is the set of articles that went into *Peace, War, and Numbers* (Russett, 1972a). The Rummel, Wallace, and Wilkenfeld articles—the first two concerned with a variety of systemic and dyadic hypotheses, the third more with attributes and behaviors of single nation-states—are rather impressive in the way they test and modify a variety of important hypotheses from the previous work of other quantitative researchers; we really do know more than we did before those articles were written. Others that also display a cumulative building of knowledge, though more intra- than interproject, are the Singer and Choucri articles. The cross-fertilization of data, hypotheses, and findings throughout the book is very noticeable. Considering the young state of our science, am I claiming too much to point to this collection as real evidence that we are building in the cumulative way that scientists ought to do?

RESEARCH ON MILITARY EXPENDITURES

In returning to *my* project autobiography, however, I would like now to point up a noticeable shift in my own research focus, a shift which began almost immediately after I completed my essay on the macroscopic view. While I certainly have not abandoned my "macro" interests, I have become increasingly concerned with the effect of subnational influences on United States national security policy. The reasons for the shift are

reasonably clear to me: a substantive concern with the topic in light of particular actions in and by this country in recent years, a sense of some of the limits of the macroscopic view, and a conviction that the quantitative IR community was, in general, neglecting these subnational variables in its systematic research. The result was (in addition to some speculative pieces, informed by this perspective but for which I certainly do not claim the label of science) a set of quantitative studies, by me and by my students, of such variables and their interaction with U.S. military policy. Thus I think one of the best examples of cumulation in our work involves our examination of the determinants (*other than* the interactive, "arms race" ones) of national levels of military expenditure.

In his intensive and extensive review of the arms race literature drawing on the Richardson tradition, Peter Busch (in Russett, 1970a) noted some of the severe deficiencies in work to that point. Among them were data of poor quality, data of very limited quantity for any particular set of interactions (and hence a severe limitation in the degrees of freedom available for statistical analysis), and perhaps most important, serious theoretical deficiencies. The latter were manifested both in frequent rather mechanical and politically uninformed borrowings from physical and economic models, and in a relative neglect of intranational influences on arms acquisition, especially on the ways other nations' arms expenditures would be perceived. Furthermore, he noted that even in the best empirical studies of the arms race, no more than about half the *variance* in arms expenditures was explained, and the *levels* around which the variance occurred were explained hardly at all. Nor do they say who *initiated* the interaction. These conclusions led us to a variety of efforts to explore the effect of other possible determinants of arms spending, focusing primarily on the United States but frequently using other nations' experience as a basis for comparison.

[1] Attempted international explanations of military spending have focused largely on conflict interactions, to the neglect of intra-alliance bargaining and burden sharing. General, rather atheoretical cross-national studies of military expenditure levels have shown a consistent relationship between

nations' size and the share of their resources devoted to military efforts (Russett, 1964, and Russett et al., 1964, part B.1). Some work, however, has been done on alliance burden sharing from the perspective of collective goods theory, notably by Olson and Zeckhauser (in Russett, 1968) and by Pryor, Ypersele de Strihou, and Burgess and Robinson (references are in Russett, 1970a). They have shown that in certain kinds of alliances the theory predicts disproportionate military spending by the various states in the alliance, whereby the larger states spend even more than would be predicted from the relatively larger size of their economies, and this prediction is confirmed by empirical evidence. Russett (1970a, chap. 4) further develops the theory to specify what kinds of alliances it can be expected to apply to (deterrence, not defense or wartime alliances) and the kinds of states which would, despite the alliance, spend greater-than-predicted amounts on military goods (states which lacked confidence in the big power's deterrent resolve or ability, or where military spending provided important particular benefits not provided by the alliance; e.g., internal security, research and development, control of colonies, or where they are coerced to greater efforts by the big power in control of the defense policies of the alliance members). Empirical results using data gathered at Yale (Taylor and Hudson, 1972) showed that disproportionate large-power expenditure occurred in those alliances meeting the conditions for application of the theory (NATO, recent Warsaw Pact experience and, with modifications, SEATO and the Rio Pact) and failed to occur in those alliances not meeting the specifications of the theory (CENTO and the Arab League). Recent work by a former member of the Data Program (Starr, 1974) has confirmed and strengthened our findings for the Warsaw Pact (see also Beer, 1973).

[2] Several scholars (including Huntington, Gray and Gregory, and Cobb, references in Russett, 1970a) had examined the role of the legislature, specifically the differential rewards to various legislative constituencies in stimulating or maintaining high levels of military expenditure. The results of these studies were indeterminate, due largely to methodological difficulties I discussed in Russett (1970b). However, further analysis (Russett, 1970a, chaps. 2 and 3) showed clearly that legislators from districts with high proportionate military employment (but *not* military contracting) were more likely to favor high levels of military spending than were other legislators. Moreover, and more interesting, such legislators were more likely to approve of a variety of hawkish foreign policy acts than were legislators from districts of low military employment. This finding has been challenged (Cobb, 1973) but has been reconfirmed by further studies at Yale (Moyer, 1973 and forthcoming) and elsewhere (Clotfelter, 1970).

An additional very important finding has emerged from this work of Moyer: legislators' positions on issues of military spending and foreign policy are much better explained by their general ideological perspectives than by the military dependence of their districts. While the latter variables typically explain about 5 percent of congressional voting on foreign policy issues, the former typically explain about half the variance. In recent years at least (since 1967), various indexes of conservatism on domestic issues (e.g., civil rights, civil liberties, welfare) are very powerful in explaining foreign policy voting. This finding of a relative unidimensionality, and hence polarization, in the political system does not apply to earlier post-World War II years, but there is some indication that a similar pattern existed in the 1930s. This has led us to studies of change over time in military spending in districts of members of selected legislative committees (Arnold, 1973), further supporting the initial finding about the effect of military employment and strengthening the causal inferences, and to a major study of changes in ideology and consensus in American politics over a 25-year period (Rosenberg, forthcoming). The result has been cumulation in theory, methodology, and findings.

[3] Study of the domestic sources of support and opposition to arms expenditure also requires examination of the relative economic gains and losses from military spending accruing to various segments of the economic system. In Russett (1970a, chaps. 5 and 6), I found that in the United States the proportion of the GNP devoted to military spending varied in important degree inversely with expenditures for fixed capital formation and

for governmental expenditure on social investment in health and education. Similar but less sharp or consistent tradeoff patterns were found in the other Western countries examined (Britain, Canada, and France), and I suggested some tentative theoretical explanations of these differences. Again, these results have been challenged on methodological grounds (Hollenhorst and Ault, 1971) but have been further confirmed by our work at Yale (Russett, 1971; Lee, 1973; Hartman, 1973).

[4] These results, and related findings from very different data bases by Choucri and North (1975), have encouraged us in further explorations of various influences, other than conflict-laden arms race interactions, on military spending. One of these is my study, using public opinion data over a 30-year period, of attitudes among the American populace toward military spending (Russett, 1972b). This shows a recent sharp change in the level of support for military spending, especially a reversal of attitudes among the attentive public, and tests various hypotheses in an effort to account for the change. Another is our study (Hanson and Russett, 1973) of the response in the stock market to various escalatory and deescalatory events in the Korean and Vietnam wars. Here we tested various hypotheses, derived in large part from neo-Marxian theory, about attitudes in the business community. In general, we failed to confirm these hypotheses, and in the later years of the Vietnam War we even found evidence against some of them. These results led us to a major study employing interviews, questionnaires, content analysis, and event data, of key American elite groups, notably major corporation executives and senior military officers (Russett, 1974b, 1975; Russett and Hanson, 1975).

A BROAD DEFINITION OF CUMULATION

If I can claim so much, why (aside from the possibility that the claims may be inflated) then did I start out by saying I sometimes felt guilty? The reason, of course, is that I have not worked, over the 15 years since receiving my Ph.D., within a single paradigm. The result has been a variety of pieces of cumulative research. But these pieces are,

in Harold Guetzkow's famous term, "islands of theory" rather than continents. With the resources so generously available to me, I could perhaps have built and tested a general theory of substantial breadth, touching fewer bases than I did indeed touch, but making a focused contribution—a narrower but deeper impact on the field. For example, I have a great deal of respect for the model of scholarly behavior that Rudy's DON project has set before us. Yet I also have very substantial sympathies with his latest statement, and I have tried to follow its implications for some time. We simply do not have an all-inclusive paradigm for international relations research or, with one or two exceptions, for any major segments of the field.

I do not yet feel able to build one. Perhaps some of my colleagues do, and I am merely speaking from my own inadequacies as a theorist, but I strongly suspect that the problem is more general. For this reason I am not really apologetic about any eclectic, gadfly aspects of my behavior. I feel we must, and surely can, attend carefully to cumulative theory-building and testing within various islands, and, particularly, always be alert to ways of bridging the islands. We could, and should, demand more rigorous cumulation within some of these islands, for example, integration research. But to demand or even expect a broader synthesis is premature.

Worse still would be a demand that quantitative IR research focus almost exclusively on the one or two or three islands, where the narrow cumulating model works most effectively, to produce a host of studies, each making marginal improvements (e.g., as is done in experimental gaming, or in some other areas of experimental psychology). This would seem to me to be the worst possible course for the IR community. The phenomena outside any of the scientific islands that currently are at all well developed are too many and too varied; there are too many questions, vital to the survival of the race, on which we need evidence and insight. The experience of other sciences, especially the behavioral sciences, that have concentrated their resources on a few limited islands surely should be an object lesson to us.

In fact, the problem is even more severe for quantitative IR studies than for most other social sciences. Compare our situation with that of psychology, for example. In most major universities the entire political science department is smaller than that of psychology; only a minority of those political scientists deal with IR, and only a fraction of them have any significant training in quantitative research. Scientific methods have had far fewer years to produce anything in their field, and the research resources available to most political scientists are, by comparison to those in psychology, woefully small. Political scientists' teaching loads are typically much heavier. (Most of us teach graduate or undergraduate survey courses in IR; of how many psychologists can the equivalent be said?) We are responsible for vast areas of theory and substance. Under these circumstances the total intellectual resources available for scientific work in IR are small indeed.

Obviously we need cumulative research, much more than we have gotten so far. Much more attention should be paid to connecting one piece of research to another. I would never argue otherwise. But I remain skeptical that a narrow and exclusive application of the cumulating model would produce marginal returns comparable to those to be expected from maintaining, along with it, a more broad-based attack on IR theory and substance.

In any case, it seems important, even when looking at a particular set of variables or a particular problem, that the discipline remain committed to an eclectic, multimethod approach, and also one prepared to work at more than one level of analysis. As an example of the basic problem, take Dave Singer's excellent Correlates of War project—a fine example of careful and imaginative cumulating research. It operates within certain confines, notably a commitment to a data base where the nation is the unit of analysis for data-gathering purposes, and within a limited (but by no means short) historical period. A great deal of "theory" purporting to explain the propensity of nations for war exists, but it is frequently imprecise, rarely rigorously deductive, and in the past has equally rarely been subjected to rigorous empirical testing. Under the circumstances one is forced to consider a great many variables, in a great variety of possible interactions, with what is

by comparison a very small number of wars or nations. The result is a problem of degrees of freedom, where it becomes difficult to negate convincingly, let alone support, complex and therefore interesting hypotheses.[3] No matter how painstaking, clever, and incremental the data manipulations, there are serious limits to the confidence we are able to place in the project's findings. The results clearly are more valid than most of what passed as knowledge previously (based on intuitive generalization from far fewer cases), and Singer and his colleagues are trying to surmount their problems through computer simulation and other approaches. Yet it is quite apparent that other people, with different theoretical levels of analysis, and methodological skills (including the use of carefully designed case studies, see Russett, 1974a, chap. 1) will have to build on the project's results before its greatest value will emerge.

All this is to argue for a broader definition of cumulation. We of the IR research community should encourage it, in ourselves and in the students we train to join the enterprise. I think this would make good sense at any state of the discipline, but doubly so now when it has not yet fully evolved from a revolutionary science into a science that makes orderly progress with one or a few accepted paradigms. Similarly, critics and funding agencies of IR research should not treat it as a fully established science. Critics should not expect that all research be within a narrow focus, nor should funding agencies provide support for only those projects that operate within a well-worn paradigm; they should not expect an initial proposal to detail all the hypotheses and methodology that the researcher intends to use. International relations is too important to leave exclusively to the Rummels, Russetts, Singers, et al. when they have their cumulating hats on.

---

[3] A similar example of a need to test complex hypotheses is seen in Wilkenfeld's article (in Russett, 1972b), which reexamines the Rummel and Tanter reports of no relationship between domestic and foreign conflict. Few sophisticated analysts would have expected to find simple bivariate relationships; when Wilkenfeld applies multivariate models with time lags, some positive findings do appear. But again the necessarily limited sample size and the level of analysis chosen impose some serious restrictions.

REFERENCES

Alker, Hayward R., Jr. 1964. "Dimensions of Conflict in the General Assembly." *American Political Science Review* 58 (Sep.): 642-57.

——— and Bruce M. Russett. 1965. *World Politics in the General Assembly.* New Haven: Yale Univ. Press.

Arnold, Douglas. 1973. "Defense Impact on Constituencies of Members of the House and Senate Armed Services Committee." Mimeo. New Haven: Yale Univ.

Beer, Francis. 1972. *The Political Economy of Alliances.* Beverly Hills: Sage.

Choucri, Nazli, and Robert C. North. 1975. *Nations in Conflict: National Growth and International Violence.* San Francisco: Freeman.

Clotfelter, James. 1970. "Senate Voting and Constituency Stake in Defense Spending." *Journal of Politics* 32 (Nov.): 979-83.

Cobb, Stephen. 1973. "The United States Senate and the Impact of Defense Spending Concentrations." In *Testing the Theory of the Military-Industrial Complex,* ed. Steven Rosen, pp. 197-224. Lexington, Mass.: Heath.

Doran, Charles. 1973. "A Theory of Bounded Deterrence." *Journal of Conflict Resolution* 17 (Jun): 243-69.

George, Alexander L., and Richard Smoke. 1974. *Deterrence in American Foreign Policy: Theory and Practice.* New York: Columbia Univ. Press.

Hartman, Stephen W. 1973. "The Impact of Defense Expenditures on the Domestic American Economy, 1946-1972." *Public Administration Review* 33 (Jul-Aug): 370-90.

Hanson, Betty C., and Bruce M. Russett. 1973. "Testing Some Economic Interpretations of American Intervention: Korea, Indochina, and the Stock Market." In *Testing the Theory of the Military-Industrial Complex,* ed. Steven Rosen, pp. 225-46. Lexington, Mass.: Heath.

Hibbs, Douglas. 1973. *Mass Political Violence: A Cross-national Causal Analysis.* New York: Wiley.

Hollenhorst, Jerry, and Gary Ault. 1971. "An Alternative Answer to 'Who Pays for Defense?' " *American Political Science Review* 65 (Sep): 760-63.

Lee, Jong Ryool. 1973. "Changing National Priorities of the United States." In *Military Force and American Society,* ed. B. M. Russett and A. Stepan, pp. 61-105. New York: Harper & Row.

Moyer, Wayne. 1973. "House Voting on Defense: An Ideological Explanation." In *Military Force and American Society,* ed. B. M. Russett and A. Stepan, pp. 106-42.

———. Forthcoming. "Congress and Defense Policy, 1937-1972." Ph.D. dissertation, Yale Univ.

Olson, Mancur, and Richard Zeckhauser. 1968. "An Economic Theory of Alliances." In *Economic Theories of International Politics,* ed. B. M. Russett, pp. 25-50. Chicago: Markham.

Rosenberg, Douglas. Forthcoming. "Collective Belief and Collective Behavior: An Enquiry into the Levels-of-Analysis Problem in International Relations Theory and American Cold War Policy." Ph.D. dissertation, Yale Univ.

Russett, Bruce M. 1963. *Community and Contention: Britain and America in the Twentieth Century.* Cambridge: MIT Press.

———. 1964. "Measures of Military Effort." *American Behavioral Scientist* 7 (Feb): 26-29.

——— et al. 1964. *World Handbook of Political and Social Indicators.* New Haven: Yale Univ. Press.

———. 1967. *International Regions and the International System.* Chicago: Rand McNally.

———, ed. 1968. *Economic Theories of International Politics.* Chicago: Markham.

———. 1970a. *What Price Vigilance?* New Haven: Yale Univ. Press.

———. 1970b. "Communication on Defense Spending and Foreign Policy Behavior." *Journal of Conflict Resolution* 14 (Jun): 287-90.

———. 1971. "Some Decisions in the Regression Analysis of Time-Series Expenditure Data." In *Mathematical Applications in Political Science,* ed. James Herndon and Joseph L. Bernd, vol. 5. Charlottesville: Univ. Press of Virginia.

———. 1972a. "The Revolt of the Masses: Public Opinion toward Military Expenditures. In *Peace, War, and Numbers,* ed. B. M. Russett, pp. 299-319. Beverly Hills: Sage.

———, ed. 1972b. *Peace, War, and Numbers.* Beverly Hills: Sage.

———. 1974a. *Power and Community in World Politics.* San Francisco: Freeman.

———. 1974b. "Political Perspectives of U.S. Military and Business Elites." *Armed Forces and Society* 1 (Fall): 79-108.

———. 1975. "The Americans' Retreat from World Power." *Political Science Quarterly* 90 (Spring): 1-21.

——— and Elizabeth Hanson. 1975. *Interest and Ideology: The Foreign Policy Beliefs of American Businessmen.* San Francisco: Freeman.

Starr, Harvey. 1974. "A Collective Goods Analysis of the Warsaw Pact after Czechoslovakia." *International Organization* 28 (Summer): 521-32.

Taylor, Charles L., ed. 1968. *Aggregate Data Analysis.* The Hague: Mouton.

——— and Michael C. Hudson. 1972. *World Handbook of Political and Social Indicators.* 2d ed. New Haven: Yale Univ. Press.

4. Individual Achievements Rarely Sum to Collective Progress

Hayward R. Alker, Jr.

Among the small perplexities recently generated by a modest degree of prominence as a quantitative international relations researcher have been the following:

1. A course-related letter from a midwestern undergraduate asking me what was the most important book shaping my professional life;
2. A recent convention encounter with an earnest graduate student who introduced himself by noting that he had "replicated" nearly everything I had ever done (meaning most of my factor-analytic UN roll-call studies);
3. A request from James Rosenau that I autobiographically review my evolving commitments to international relations research, including my recent thoughts on the nature of scientific cumulation, reflections that may also be of value to undergraduates considering entering the field; and
4. A plea from an old acquaintance that I make accessible the main themes connecting my scholarly work, which began with a Ph.D. dissertation (1963) factor analyzing selected UN roll calls, and most recently included papers on such apparently diverse topics as: "Research Paradigms and Mathematical Politics" (1971b), "On Political Capabilities in a Schedule Sense: Measuring Power, Integration and Development" (1973), "Are There Voluntaristic Structural Models of Public Goods Generation?" (1974a), and

SPECIAL NOTE: I have benefitted from the assistance of my brother, Henry Alker, and the editor of this volume, James N. Rosenau, in the redrafting of the present paper. As this is a personal statement, I have only noted research support at appropriate points in the text below. The reasons for my choice of title should become apparent to the reader. My doubts about writing an autobiography at thirty-seven, even one focused on developmentally significant work in the international relations area, should, however, be publicly recorded at the outset.

"Analyzing Collective Security Regime Alternatives" (Alker and Greenberg, forthcoming).

SOPHOMORIC BEGINNINGS

Upon reflection, I answered the first question by citing Herbert Marcuse's *Eros and Civilization* (1955). It was a symbolic answer. Controversies involving members of the Frankfurt school (the early Fromm, Adorno, Horkheimer, Marcuse, Habermas) would have been more accurate. One book rarely shapes an entire career, but Marcuse was the exemplary teacher of my first political science course, while I was an MIT sophomore. His treatment of the history of modern political theory was judicious, informed, Socratic, and unobtrusive. In the last class, our second week on Hegel, he lectured much more than usual, suggesting some amazing ideas which I later discovered had appeared in his books, *Eros and Civilization* and *Reason and Revolution* (1941).

Individual successes rarely yield collective progress. At that time, while taking Marcuse's course, I was first in my MIT class, but the world was creaking through harrowing Hungarian and Suez crises. The threat of nuclear war felt very real—many of us spent days watching televised meetings of the United Nations Security Council. Major war was avoided; UN results were good regarding Suez, otherwise bad concerning Hungary.

More important personally, my family world also fell apart disastrously in a way that had an alienating effect, without leaving me entirely free of responsibility. Marcuse's discussions of the dialectical destructiveness of logic, reason, and the reality principle—his "left Hegelian" combination of Marx and Freud into a social theory of repression—became extensions of personal knowledge as I tried to understand and deal with my situation.

Gradually, I have come to see how an impressive theorist of repressive tolerance could at the same time be a great teacher of liberating ideals and a defender of scholarly autonomy.[1] And the relevance of modified versions of these ideas to world affairs has become clearer, for what I hope are not primarily personal reasons. My personal response to crisis has thus had an academic dimension joined with a commitment to cope methodologically and substantively with the deeper causes of destructive conflicts on a wider scale.[2] Teachers and teaching are as important for me as the joy and anguish of research. Normative issues, including policy and research directives, have always struck me as more important than the purely empirical ones on which they sometimes depend. To avoid defensive or destructive reactions to conflict, I have always tried to be logically and methodologically self-critical. And when such criticisms apply to others, I have set myself the harder, constructive, synthetic task of improving upon previous inadequacies. All these early tendencies crystallized through the continuing experience of my graduate education.

YALE TUTORIALS

Having discovered the social sciences while at MIT—they combined what I might be good at with what I felt important—I chose political science as a profession because it was the most normative field among them. It avoided the dehumanizing instrumentalism of economic rationality conceived of as profit maximization. It dealt with important ques-

[1] This reflection is out of autobiographical context, but relevant to someone who has been thought of by many as a stimulator of student revolts in the late 1960s and by others as a betrayer of fundamentalist Marxism. An important reference is his "Repressive Tolerance" in Wolff, Moore, and Marcuse (1969).

[2] This does not mean I have not been occupied with family considerations. My response to episode 2 above was first a fatherly one: "Have you met my three daughters?" I then asked the student if he had read "Statistics and Politics" (my last UN roll-call study) or any of the more recent papers noted in 4 above. He had not. I made arrangements to get some of these papers to him.

tions of justice and equity, coercion and consensus, freedom and responsibility. In particular world politics, the international relations of war and peace, treated these questions impersonally, scientifically, epochally, and globally.

All of my teachers and many fellow students at Yale helped continue my education. At least four of my professors maintained close relations over a long enough period, well past the year of my Ph.D., 1963, for me now to think of them as tutors: Robert Abelson, Robert Dahl, Karl Deutsch, and Harold Lasswell. When I hear these men discussed, I am often appalled at how inaccurately they are described and how superficially their scholarly contributions are evaluated. Let me briefly review those of their impacts on my education that have most affected my international relations research.

Robert Dahl

In my first graduate class at Yale, I argued vigorously with Robert Dahl about the essential truthfulness of C. Wright Mills's *The Power Elite* (1956). (In the cafeteria the night before I had been *surprised* by overhearing someone remark that Dahl didn't like the book!) The book contained too many resonances with my personal history and too many obvious but painful truths for me to disown it.

Moreover, Mills's *The Causes of World War III* (1960) had nearly convinced me to go to Columbia. An interview with him had impressed me personally—what a sensitive, gentle, lonely, abused man he was, a radical Quaker. But his avowed research methodology, of gathering as much evidence as possible to support his case, had bothered me.

Dahl taught me: a causal analytical approach to power relations (in which Oppenheim's *Dimensions of Freedom,* 1961; Harsanyi, 1965, on opportunity costs; and Bachrach and Baratz, 1962, on nondecisions readily found a place); a process-oriented understanding of the limits and virtues of polyarchical democracy; a positivist philosophy of social science that edged toward Hanson's rather Kuhnian *Patterns of Discovery* (1965); and the great value of passionate, informed resistance to oppression.

Because I shall discuss both positivism and pluralism later, let me here elaborate on two of these points, the last one first. When I was rather unclear why and whether the United States should be fighting in Vietnam, Dahl, more than any other Yale political scientist, was speaking to public rallies against American escalation. I recall arguments about neocolonialism, Cold War hysteria, and civil war interventionism. Add lots of liberal hubris, technological overkill plus realpolitik, and the indictment strikes me, some years later, as basically correct. On many of these points Dahl and Mills agreed. American self-righteousness has rarely yielded world peace.

My papers[3] "Causal Inference and Political Analysis" (1966b) and "Political Capabilities in a Schedule Sense: Measuring Power, Integration and Development" (1973) owe much to Dahl's analytical approach to power, even though we may still disagree on certain points. Thus he helped me see the logic, set out in the first paper, behind my earlier intuitive identification of coping responses with the use of causally effective policy instruments. Because causal power relations are theory-based statistical formulas linking one actor's means and ends to another's, power theories may be falsified and need not be merely tautological or ideological.

The Weber-Lasswell-Dahl-Harsanyi treatment of exercised power as basically a coercive, opportunity-cost-sensitive, counterfactually relevant causal relation (Dahl, 1968) deeply informs the model described at the beginning of the second paper. An explication of this approach and the careful definition of my related models would take many more pages than I have here, but the following few sentences may help the puzzled reader. It is possible, but difficult, causally to measure how exercised power hurts some, even when it might help others; potential power is even harder to study. Assessing power as an ability requires

[3] A chronological listing of my works cited in the text is given in the bibliography. My occasional textual citation of titles is not narcissism, but reassertion of meanings their readers seem frequently to have missed. Citations to the work of others may sometimes be confusing because selected, currently available relevant works often have later reference dates than the ideas and materials I refer to in the text. A full bibliography would be voluminous, and still would do injustice to the persons and positions being referred to.

knowledge of potential limits to action as well as foreclosed possibilities of action; both kinds of knowledge refer "counterfactually" to unrealized events and to hypothetical causal relations. Analyzing foregone opportunities thus points beyond directly observable causal relations to underlying, partly observable systems-change/systems-maintenance practices which allow or cancel certain action opportunities. At the end of that paper, by embedding power relations in a changing but explicit decisional context, I present a testable version of power-elite-type arguments that elite-serving agenda-formation processes prematurely foreclose certain issues (resulting in "nondecisions"). The same respecifications might be applied to Singer's work on inter-nation influence, and adapted to the Collective Security system, as a way of studying the slippery connection between national power and global peace.

Robert Abelson

Abelson, more than Dahl and Deutsch, reinterested me as a social scientist in mathematics, statistics, and computers. I was recommended to him as a potential programmer for the nonadditivity part of his simulation study (Pool, Abelson, and Popkin, 1965) of the 1960 presidential election. Having graduated from MIT in mathematics, I shared the prejudices of my peers that social science mathematics was trivial, and that computers offered only dull "hackwork." And I was ambivalent about the dehumanizing aspects of mathematical reasoning, preferring verbal subject matter. Not being able to convince Abelson of these points, I did volunteer to help the election study by learning FORTRAN and programming his statistical interaction analysis: "Do Predispositional Factors Summate?" (in Pool, Abelson and Popkin, 1965). By and large they did, with the important exception of party identification. Thus region, class, sex, age, have additive effects on many political attitudes, except that party allegiances nonlinearly enhance or contract such tendencies. Together with the Blalock-Lazarsfeld treatments of covariance analysis, (see Alker 1964b for details) this gave me some of the ideas used later in "The Long Road to International Relations Theory: Problems of Statistical Nonadditivity" Alker (1966a). Statistically speaking, aggregate political outcomes rarely summate individual predispositions, even at elections.

Abelson's courses on multivariate statistics and mathematical models for psychologists had a number of important lessons for me. One was the fundamental difference between psychological orientations toward measurement and (by comparison) econometric ones. Not only do psychologists take as extremely problematical what economists take as axiomatic, viz. rationality, they are also strongly *dispositionally* oriented. Technically, attitudes or preferences are unmeasured variables, while economic propensities to consume are unmeasured coefficients. Both kinds of measurement have identification problems. A great variety of techniques exist in psychology for inferring dispositions. (Anyone thinking of doing a factor analysis should first have read Coombs et al., *Introduction to Mathematical Psychology*, 1970, Torgerson's *Theory and Methods of Scaling*, 1958, and the Romney, Shepard, and Nerlove volumes, 1972, so that a more intelligent choice among measurement models is possible.) Abelson suggested factor analysis for my thesis because large multidimensional scaling analyses were then not feasible, and alignment predispositions might be expected to behave like attitudes. These points later contributed to my multidisciplinary review of causally oriented statistical practices (Alker, 1970b).

Both Deutsch and Abelson reviewed Richardson's arms-race models in their classes. Abelson's own derivation of these in attitudinal terms (1960) engrossed me. But it was his gradually evolving work with Rosenberg on psycho-logics which has been the most revealing regarding scientific cumulation. This literature pointed toward logics-in-use that had the ring of verisimilitude about them, while at the same time being normatively flawed by comparison with the stricter axioms of orthodox symbolic logic. For example, "The U.S. distrusts the U.S.S.R.; the U.S.S.R. and India are friendly; *therefore* the U.S. distrusts India" is *good* psychologic but bad sentential logic. Abelson's substantive focus on the rationalizing hot-cognition of Cold War ideologues in particular, and closed minds in general, points toward important kinds of defective, destructive reasoning. Thus mathematics could be used critically, to show the failures of human reasoning.

Abelson's 15-year effort to criticize and improve upon his earlier mathematical work is extremely suggestive for those (Rosenau, 1974) who have attempted to assess scientific progress primarily in terms of such crude measures of cumulation as the extent to which one's data are used by others. Abelson's work has gone through three or four fundamental and, many would say, progressive transformations. These have variously involved empirical inadequacies being taken into serious consideration, formal/conceptual respecifications, and substantive refocusing that requires different kinds of data. Now, for example, his work can be described in theoretical/methodological ways fundamentally different from the 1958 paper: it is conceptual-dependency, memory-rich, cold-cognition, artificial intelligence, and true-believer oriented. (See Abelson, 1973, for the technical meanings of most of these terms.) The unity and development of this research program can best be understood historically and philosophically, by knowing the people involved, their sociopolitical contexts, the ideas, the problems, and the literature they are responding to. When one still finds economically oriented political scientists ignoring altogether relevant literatures on rationalization (e.g., Abelson and Carroll, 1965), or others still getting excited *in print solely* about the earliest psycho-logic paper (Abelson and Rosenberg 1958), one must react with one more variant of the central theme of this paper. As noted in two papers (Alker, 1971b, 1974a) subdisciplinary specialists frequently communicate like opposed politicians or propagandistic diplomats. Work in interdisciplinary fields like international relations has little of the sustained, global, cumulative quality characteristic of a mature, paradigmatic natural science. As outlined in more detail in the concluding section of this paper, this means that individual scholarly achievements, or the developments of a small cluster of cumulating scholars, are rarely integrated into globally shared knowledge systems.

Karl Deutsch

Karl Deutsch has the same broad-gauge grounding in history and political thought on major normative issues that I admired in Marcuse, but with fewer traces of the synthesis of Marxian and Freudian theory characteristic of the Frankfurt school. In a way, I now see his work as the antithesis of earlier Marxian arguments. Thus his work on nationalism belies the nearly exclusive attention given to class cleavages in some Marxian writings. His demonstration of the existence of pluralistic security communities among capitalist states contradicts Marxian arguments about the inevitability of international class conflicts, even when it shows similar assessments of imperial exploitation and irrational international conflicts. As formally reviewed (Alker, 1970a) the integration theories of Deutsch, Ernst Haas, and their students nonetheless evidence strong parallels with Marxian sociology. All these writers emphasize the importance of structural/transactional bases, shared political-economic values or ideologies and the innovative role of political-economic elites. As a theory of international system change and system maintenance attempting to supplant the inhumanity of power-balancing realpolitik, however, integration theory offers a consensual, pluralistic alternative, both as science and practice, to revolutionary socialism. Voluntaristic, pluralistic integration of the sort discussed in Haas (1958) and Deutsch et al. (1957) has often even been opposed politically by communist or socialist parties, for reasons that to me have only recently been understandable.

My early work for Deutsch was on a much less exalted level. I was hired as a research assistant to sort out an inaccurate FORTRAN program for computing relative acceptance (RA) coefficients for trade flow data on European and global integration. It turned out that the original Savage and Deutsch article (1960) contained a crucial statistical misprint. When working later with Puchala, I published my recomputed RA's, and added to the article what I had learned from social psychology about the need to test for construct validity using multimethod measures.

As Deutsch has argued, sustained, increasingly salient, freely chosen, mutually rewarding transactions can help integrate peoples into cooperative, noncoercive problem-solving arrangements. To test these ideas, both breakdowns and successes in integration are worth looking at. In my "Integration Logics" (Alker, 1970a), I suggested such

tests using Klingberg's international hostilities measures (reported in the appendixes of Wright, 1968), that predicted World War II alignments rather well. Using similar trade indices, Russett has shown weakening U.S.-U.K. ties. Puchala (1971) and Merritt (1966) have shown important positive transactional trends associated with American confederation and the ending of centuries of French-German emnity, historic achievements no one seems even to notice anymore.

No methodological area in quantitative international relations research has been more poorly served, however, by the attendant sequence of papers and arguments. Jokes about mail flow analyses that don't read the letters are legion. Inconsequential technical debates about which version of the RA to use have been endless.

None of the critiques I have yet seen has seriously confronted RA studies of community formation with radical arguments about exploitive trade relations. An eye-opening book for me in this regard was *Unequal Exchange* (1972) by Aghiri Emmanuel, a Greek structural Marxist teaching in Paris. (This book is much discussed in Third World countries.) If trade flow studies are to be reoriented to ask when and why one finds community and/or exploitation, questions Deutsch and Marxist writers have always been interested in, additional subnational distributional data on trade-generated value gains and losses must be included in the analysis. Differential *effects* on subsequent beneficial exchange generating *capabilities* must also be investigated (Baumgartner and Burns, 1974).

Here too the basic phenomena are nonadditive. Voluntaristic exchanges by economic elites may be mutually beneficial for them in Pareto efficiency terms (what liberal economists call maximizing global welfare), but other groups excluded from profit sharing, or at different levels of technological development, may be simultaneously relatively deprived or exploited. Having only recently discovered the radical critique of liberal trade theory, I now think it doubtful that collective economic welfare is uniformly enhanced through individualistic economic success. Theories about the necessary conditions (e.g., the assumption of equity and fairness) for this to be true strengthen this expectation. Even though pointed in the right direction, RA's measure the wrong nonadditivity effect.

In my first course with Deutsch, I was confronted with another problem that has had a growing significance for me: Prisoner's Dilemma (PD). We all read and liked Rapoport's *Fights, Games and Debates* (1960). It introduced me to alternate research paradigms for studying conflict relations; Deutsch pointed me toward empirical research with normative significance. Later thought, reading, and teaching have convinced me that PD problems generalize to the most interesting economic research for political theorists interested in the ideas of Hobbes, Locke, Rousseau, or Marx on the basis for a consensual public order: the public goods literature as recently propounded and developed in Samuelson (1969) and Frohlich, Oppenheimer, and Young (1971). With Deutsch's help I came to see the collective irrationalities generated by PD-like arms race situations as an essential model of how the collective interest in mutually satisfactory conflict resolutions fails because of uncoordinated, individualistic, maximizing behavior. Even though there are many other ways systems can fail, this suggested a very American way in which two individual "rights" could make a collective "wrong."

Several of these arguments are spelled out in Alker (1974a). In the present context a few additional reflections may be in order. First of all, the empirical literature on PD has been discontinuously self-correcting, as it has attempted to integrate insights from the rational, the deterministic, and the conversational orientations reviewed in Rapoport's book. Still other points of view are needed. The Kuhnian thesis that science progresses dialectically across revolutionary thresholds does not fit the data-based generalization-making philosophy sometimes espoused by Deutsch, Russett, Singer, and Rosenau, but Kuhn's relevance seems especially clear to me in the PD case. As argued in "Voluntaristic Structural Models" (Alker, 1974a), with references to Simon, Shubik, Emshoff, Burns, et al., the introduction of a *cognitively oriented* learning approach to gaming behavior explains plausibly the residuals generated by earlier, causally mechanistic or rational treatments. The resistance to such a methodological reorientation is surely paradigm-linked.

The dynamics of coalition formation for superadditive collective benefits (a process footnoted at the end of my "Long Road to Theory" (Alker, 1966a), in which payoffs to coalition members exceed those individually obtainable) is at the heart of sequential plays of PD, as well as of an important new area of research in rational modeling literature (see Cotter, 1973). The liberal political economy approach has also spilled over into the alliance formation area. Because alliances, or prisoners' tacit contracts, generate a public good— a good such as security whose consumption by one actor does not prevent its simultaneous consumption by another—much possible intellectual integration between social psychologists, political scientists, economists, and game theorists is possible in the PD context even though, again, rarely achieved.

From a contextual, structural, or Marxian perspective, the most serious problem with such collective action dilemmas is their underspecification. The options of collectivizing the means of benefits production, including the transformation of individualistic utilities, need to be discussed. Just as liberal economics assumes certain political-economic structures to be constant, game theory formalisms and theorems based on them hold constant or minimize underlying social structures. Respecifying PD relations is called for if the dilemma is to be resolved. Are not PD's three-actor games, asymmetric control relations where a manipulative third actor, the district attorney, holds most of the cards? His payoffs, and those of the society he presumably represents, are crucial to the real resolution problem. Are prisoners like slaves, without lawyers and the right to private communications, or like dependent trading states, without helpful market alternatives, or are they the just recipients of the district attorney's machinations? Without coercive central institutions, new modes of joint benefit production, and/or shared ideological alternatives to distrustful "possessive individualism," prisoners rarely maximize their collective interests in public goods production, even when the goods are security communities.

As a Deutsch student, the stasis of contemporary work on regional integration theory, noted in Alker (1971b), strikes me as a puzzling phenomenon, especially when Frohlich et al. (1971), Russett and Sullivan (1971), and Ruggie (1972) have also noted exciting overlaps of integration and collective goods theory. My explanatory hypothesis would be that the most exciting opportunities for cooperation, for transforming the Hobbesian state of nature, have shifted with détente back from the regional to the global, or nearly global, levels. Regional integration as policy has significantly but unevenly progressed in Europe; it has faltered elsewhere. A weaker, but jointly positive form of superpower interdependence might be in the offing at the superpower level; preintegration institution building is called for among members of the "free world."

As argued in Alker (1970a), the scientific aspect of integration theory was still heavily pretheoretical: it lacked contextually explicit, falsifiable, dynamic causal statements. Nonetheless, as reviewed in Alker (1974b), public goods generation problems are central to current discussions about globalizing détente, and managing interdependence. Ecological balance, monetary abundance, nuclear security, and communal integration involve similar considerations. But public good generators may turn into "regulated," expensive arms races or *1984*-type self-perpetuating personal insecurity systems. Free world integration may perpetuate the dependency of the technologically less developed. Collective goods, or bads, increasingly preoccupy international relations policy makers, who are less and less able individually to provide such goods or prevent such bads.

Cybernetics was another Deutschean world. (The student will find almost all relevant references discussed below in Buckley, 1968.) Rosenblueth and Weiner, McCulloch and Pitts untied a philosophical Gordian knot by defining and exhibiting a class of *teleological mechanisms*. Purposes could be causes; voluntaristic "structural models" (an econometric "causality" notion) could exist. Dahl's distrust of functional arguments since Aristotle (and including Marx) need not be definitive. Almond's structural-functionalism (Almond and Coleman, 1960) need not omit Parsons' fifth and most important pattern variable—self versus collectivity orientation. But it was Sommerhoff's work on "directive behavior" (see Alker, 1968a, and the Sommerhoff excerpt in Buckley, 1968) that showed me how cybernetic images of quasi-teleological behavior could be rigorously extended to the systems level. Deutsch's creative treatment

of these ideas suggested that low-coercion, information-coordinated, capability-enhanced systemic wholes could, in theory, be more than the sum of their parts. They could also be less.

The Nerves of Government was the basis of a particularly exciting Deutschean advanced graduate course. Besides reviewing much of current theorizing, the rich emphasis on systems pathologies resonated with my radical proclivities. The possibility of creative, nonalienating, symbolic, self-conscious, combinatorial mathematics excited me. Both Chomsky (on generative linguistics) and Simon (on artificial intelligence) have been excited by similar visions, even if the latter emphasizes managed choice and conservative responses. (See Simon, 1969, and Chomsky, 1972, for nontechnical accounts.) Reflexive reason, unfettered by structural constraints and able to build consensual understanding, is at the heart of the goal of "communicative competence," espoused by Habermas. Although the profaning of such creative potentialities regularly occurs, the scientific similarities of Marxian and Western cybernetics—both focused on coordination, autonomy, planning, and control—need not evaporate in the final analysis *if* the political interests informing them significantly and positively converge.

Harold Lasswell

More than any other of my teachers, Harold Lasswell taught me the way to critical self-awareness through interminable, comprehensive political analysis. His brilliant book *World Politics and Personal Insecurity* (reprinted 1965) linked together what I had tried to keep apart. As a "partially inhibited rage type," I have learned about myself and others from his writing on rationalizing private passions in terms of public interests. His work on political propaganda analysis (cited in Lasswell, 1965) motivates the methodologies of quantitative content analysis and political linguistics. It presaged Abelson's true-believer research. His contextual, transactionalist approach to power precedes and predicts Mills, Dahl, and Deutsch.

It was in his class that I rediscovered *Eros and Civilization* when asked to restate its major arguments within the Lasswellian framework. The argument fits very well: Marcuse's goal is less repressive solidarity communities—"affection institutions" in Lasswellese. Families also belong in the same category.

It is not really surprising that Lasswell, who turned Marx on his head using Freudian arguments (Lasswell, 1965), would come close, at important points, to certain viewpoints of the Frankfurt school. Lasswell's demythologized use of developmental constructs, be they communism, world commonwealths close to Haas-Deutsch models of pluralistic, low-violence security systems, or the more terrifying garrison states so like *1984,* helps us orient ourselves between past and future. His brilliant delineation of the "democratic personality" dialectically responds to Adorno's "authoritarian personality." His distinction between contemplative and manipulative orientations encompasses what Habermas and many other Europeans call positivistic and hermeneutic knowledge interests. His "Must Knowledge Serve Power?" in Lasswell (1963) vividly links political interests to knowledge development, a point that troubles behaviorists in discussions of scientific cumulation. He argues that scholarly conversions in knowledge interests to those searching for global human dignity must be nearly simultaneous with each other for such conversions to be effective.

Strangely, Lasswell's unmathematical writings have had a marked effect on my more mathematical work. His fascinations with symbol manipulation helped me see my changing UN roll-call factor loadings and contextual regression coefficients as political variables in a higher order political context, a central reason for the emphasis on multilevel causal models in Alker (1974a). His conception of political analysis prefigures my most hard-earned scholarly achievements.

UNITED NATIONS STUDIES

Most of my papers have been fairly general, usually methodological, and often philosophical. They have evolved in the context of spoken or silent dialogues with my tutors, dialogues which have been carried on in my own teaching as well. An equally important source of methodological insights has been my own substantive research on the United Nations, its successes and failures in

conflict resolution. With the help of several collaborators—principally Bruce Russett at the postthesis stage, Cheryl Christensen and Bill Greenberg more recently—these studies have spanned more than a dozen years, and produced more than a dozen books or papers. Reviewing their development here may make my thoughts on cumulation more specific and concrete.

If I continue to stress philosophical or methodological issues in this research, it is because I feel they are at the heart of any debate over how to improve scientific knowledge, Rosenau's preferences for the priority of substantive findings notwithstanding (Rosenau, 1974). As Kuhn has shown, new research paradigms involve Polanyi-like "new ways of seeing," new ways of interpreting laboratory experience, new standards of validation. Such has been my experience, although few have come along the same roads with me.

A Pluralistic Approach: Conflict Factors Regressed to National Attributes

My first "way of seeing" the UN political process was heavily influenced by Dahl-Lipset-Haas-type pluralism. And it was grounded in my personal commitments. World cleavages might not be so cumulatively destructive if they did not reinforce each other. U Thant had called to public attention the evolving complexity of the United Nations, a multidimensionality of alignments that those preoccupied with the Cold War should pay more attention to. UN disagreements obviously reflected environmental forces. Because of the divisiveness of these pressures, little *global* integration could be expected, even though some interesting temporary convergences might be visible, associated with U Thant's depolarization tendencies. Haas's discussions of multifunctional bargaining by the superpowers with the Third World at the UN in the late 1950s was a hopeful sign. Perhaps a meaningful pluralism, responsive to the disadvantaged, was more visible globally than in the politically conservative United States of the 1950s. Before arguing the scientific appropriateness of radical theories, plausible pluralistic ones would have to be tested.

Methodologically, Duncan MacRae's *Dimensions of Congressional Voting* (1958) was my exemplar, although I wanted somehow to multi-dimensionalize his Guttman scales and bivariate cross-tabulations. And I was tantalized by Harsanyi's introduction, at a summer workshop, to rational bargaining theories, and Duncan Black's (1958) elegant, ordinalist way out of the voter's paradox—individual preference orders don't consistently add up to a collective one—using single-peaked preference curves.

Pluralist bargaining models would require good data on preinfluential preferences. As cited by Torgerson (1958), Abelson had published multidimensional scaling articles with elegant, ideologically interesting perference peaks cum acceptability contours; but generating these required prebargaining, comparative rankings of many alternatives. From diplomats such data just weren't available. Nor were the alternatives they were to compare very clear.

Just exactly how preference peaks, agreement clusters, cumulative scales, and orthogonal factors were related also bothered me, a technical puzzle (in Kuhn's or Lakatos's terms) that I was not fully to resolve until seven years after my thesis was completed (Alker in Lipset, 1970). That one Guttman scale would produce several factors was statistically expected: the roll calls on one end of a scale would be highly intercorrelated, producing a factor; the same was true for the other end, and intermediate groups of votes as well. Guttman scaling implied nations cumulatively preferred all resolutions with at least a threshold's amount of something, e.g., pro- or anti-Communist zeal. Single-peaked preferences were not cumulative in this sense: resolutions would only be voted for with the right amount (e.g., neutralist amounts) of such zeal. Factor analysis assumed each roll call tapped more or less clearly one or more orthogonal, general alignment predispositions, e.g., the Cold War or anticolonial self-determination. Cluster analysis on percent agreements did not assume an underlying Euclidean space at all. Which data theoretic assumptions were appropriate for my data? Self-critically I wasn't sure.

Then there was the issue of explaining the determinative significance of Yale Data Program-type environmental variables. The obvious way of assessing relative impacts on alignment predispositions was multiple regression analysis, which I used

in my thesis. But it seemed wrong to say simply that aid bought votes, when the opposite argument was equally plausible. Just as I was not very sure that independent alignment predispositions additively caused actual votes (the basic assumption of the factor model, even when oblique factor analysis is possible), so I worried about the causal significance of the regression coefficients of environmental "determinants." Moreover, some people at the Yale Computer Center used stepwise regression procedures: I didn't know for sure which approach was better nor how to decide.[4]

The main findings of my thesis, as reported in Alker (1964a) and later in *World Politics in the General Assembly* were somewhat surprising. Four or five multiple alignments regularly existed—especially if one used the rotated factors. The corresponding data theoretic assumptions—that the rotated factor loadings would be simply structured, close to zero or one—struck me as substantively more real in the UN context than the assumption that variance explaining efficiency, giving unrotated principal components, alone was a powerful enough assumption to find what really underlay roll-call votes. (In subsequent discussions about our book, Russett did not seem to worry so much about data theory; he preferred parsimoniously to use my issue-vague North-South and East-West components.)

The finding that self-determination, Palestine, and postcolonial intervention alignments were almost orthogonal to Cold War alignments seemed both to offer promise of multi-issue bargaining and to chasten Dulles-type Cold War monomania.[5] But, perhaps contrary to Haas's "realistic" assumptions about the absence of global integration, there regularly also appeared a UN supranationalism dimension, reflected in some small powers and

[4]As a self-critical methodologist interested in what "really" was going on, I was obviously predisposed to find Simon-Blalock causal modeling and its relatives extremely exciting: it could answer such questions, and did in a footnote to Alker (1970b). But such techniques were not yet visible in the political science literature, even though they had existed in biometry and econometrics for decades.

[5]This does not mean they had any policy effect. Bloomfield (1968) notes State Department reactions as confused and resistant. Their practice of quantifying roll calls in percent agreement with the U.S., percent agreement with the U.S.S.R., apparently did not change.

nonaligned states' resolutions (occasionally with the U.S.) seeking to strengthen the UN's developmental and security-enlarging roles. Soviet-U.S. early cooperation on Palestine was visible and obliquely correlated with supranationalism. Some quasi-legislative power-sharing was also found, a Dahl-type "minorities rule," in which most states, *as sponsors,* won more than they lost. Russett found quasi-representative processes as well which linked predispositional socioeconomic characteristics to the assembly voting of the more pluralistically structured states.

More surprising, however, was the constancy, even the decline according to some indicators, of voting complexity from 1947 through 1962, despite U Thant's remarks. Variances accounted for by the most frequent "important" votes (an operationally defined category) showed such a trend. Certainly Cold War-colored perceptions had led many to miss the multidimensional complexity of 1952 and 1957. But maybe factor cum regression analyses were not adequate models of the complexity U Thant had been talking about. Against a fairly stable pattern of conflicts and alignments, some interesting but technically unexplained movement could be found in particular subjects. Chinese membership, for example, began to load on, or tap, self-determination predis-dispositions as well as Cold War ones. China and Cuba moved a lot in factor score space. Scandinavia gradually disassociated from the colonial powers. Aid and trade vote regressions increased at the height of the Cold War; caucusing group voting solidarities improved. Alger's (1965) stress on the UN as a delegate-learning experience, combined with his emphasis on nonresolutional processes, suggested that gradual consensus building might be going against or around relatively stable conflict predispositions.

Here was a methodologically problematical situation, preliminarily resolved by the emphasis on metapolitics mentioned above, and articulated in my replication study (Alker, 1966c). Given that regression cum factor analysis revealed slowly and meaningfully *changing coefficients,* they could *not* be considered causal law generators. As Lasswell had argued in analogous class discussions of content analysis, resolution wording and diplomatic sloganeering became symbolically meaningful.

Although I had "realistically" discounted verbal arguments in looking beneath them for basic voting conflict dimensions, it then became compellingly clear that my changing coefficients *measured the effects of* a multilevel, symbolic, diplomatic, structure-linked but still argument-oriented political process. Diplomatic interviews, discussions with Tom Hovet, and several good case studies reinforced the heuristic premise that resolutions are often diplomatically drafted and cosponsored in a way designed to mobilize the greatest degree of predispositional support for preferred policies/interpretations on salient issues. Such, after all, was part of the prevote persuasion/bargaining process. Charter citing, noncritical wordings, and democratic and nonaligned sponsorship all helped secure support for UN task-enhancing activities, for example. Membership for Communist China could be argued for as a Third World self-determinism issue over against equally political claims of Cold War alliance primacy. A larger, unstudied realm of political process became susceptible to scientific analysis.

Statistical Self-criticisms[6]

Having helped, with Rudolph Rummel and others, to introduce factor cum regression analysis into quantitative international relations research, I soon began to criticize, in print, my own previous publications. Several reasons for doing so were technical and methodological. Others were substantive. It is worth noting, but certainly not characteristic of "mature" science, that the most important criticisms toward which I directed my attention were usually not from my peers in quantitatively oriented international relations studies. Most of them were either self-generated—as I read outside the political science/IR literature and wondered why others analyzed their data differently—or engendered by insightful scholars,

[6]Except for methodological work on interdependence controversies for the Department of State, most of the UN research discussed in the rest of this paper has been funded by the National Science Foundation. One paper (Alker and Brunner, 1969), and associated causal modeling work were funded by the Joint War Games Agency through Harold Guetzkow's Simulated International Processes project. No correspondances between my views and those of these agencies should be inferred.

like Stanley Hoffmann, usually critical of the behavioral movement. A psychological and professional need to be critical of myself, and by implication others, was balanced by the tougher demand of providing constructive alternatives.

In Alker (1966a) I followed up some of Hoffmann's contextualist critiques, testing them using Lazarsfeld-Blalock covariance analysis. As elaborated in "Regionalism versus Universalism in Comparing Nations" (Alker 1964b), this procedure points toward substantively deeper, multiplicative (nonadditive) specifications of regression relationships. Generalizing this idea to regional factor analyses helped me to *test* the linear additivity assumptions of the factor model. The reader may recall that the roll-call-relevant specification of this additive model is:

aid-vote interdependence could be formally articulated. And it was possible, constructively, to specify the alternative, more complex causal theories in systems of nonlinear, nonadditive equations, and to test for their validity. The cumulative dialectic of hypothesis formulation, test and reformulation was very appealing. Positivist philosophy at last fit statistical method when I found the causal modeling literature.[7]

A clinching idea, of relevance for my UN studies, was the Sewell Wright demonstration (repeated in Alker, 1970b) that factor analysis too had a causal interpretation. For my results to be causally valid, Equation (1) must correspond to oneway causal arrows from factors (and their regressed determinants) to otherwise unlinked votes. If, and only if, this model was true, then factor-

$$(1) \qquad V_{ji} \quad = \quad a_{j1} \quad \times \quad F_{1i} \quad + \quad a_{j2}F_{2i} \quad + \ldots + \quad a_{jK}F_{ki} + U_{ji}$$

$$\underbrace{\phantom{V_{ji}}}_{\substack{\text{vote on} \\ \text{roll call } j \\ \text{by nation } i}} = \underbrace{\phantom{a_{j1}}}_{\substack{\text{loading of} \\ j \text{ on factor } 1}} \times \underbrace{\phantom{F_{1i}}}_{\substack{\text{score of nation} \\ i \text{ on factor } 1}} \qquad + \ldots + \qquad \underbrace{\phantom{a_{jK}F_{ki}}}_{\substack{\text{ungeneralizable} \\ \text{part of } i\text{'s vote} \\ \text{on roll call } j}}$$

Doing factor analyses for contextually similar regions allows us to check if the loadings, like a_{j1} and a_{j2}, are constant for different parts of the globe. If they are not, then the linear additivity of factor analyses is suspect. Rotated factor loadings survived the test of their substantive significance better than unrotated ones; but even for the relatively homogenous content area being analyzed, the findings were not wholly satisfactory.

Surely the most fundamental critque of my statistical work came to me from reading the Simon-Blalock causal-modeling literature and its many relatives. Political influence as causal forcing fitted my earlier understanding perfectly. Separate regression equations themselves might not add up. Regressing from one dependent variable on one page and from another on the next, when the dependent or independent variables were themselves interrelated, usually produced causally spurious results. Systems of causal relations, possibly involving some kind of negative or positive feedback, required *simultaneous* estimations and testing. Now my discussions with Russett about

loading coefficients were not spurious. But the problem was that they might well be so.

Soon I began having two corresponding visions. First of all, everything seemed to be structured by some underlying causal models. Many verbal arguments, even human interactions, seemed to conceal underlying causal mechanisms, such as matrix-formulated structural equations could specify.[8]

Figure 1 was a product of that period, 1964-1968, even though it was not published until much later in an overview paper about computer simulation. It allowed me to express most of my

[7]This argument is suggested more fully in Alker (1966b). The most interesting extensions of it recently to come to mind are the links of type I and type II errors to sophisticated falsificationism (noted by Lakatos) and the fit between Campbell's evolutionary epistemology and his quasi-experimentalism. An even more dialectical, critical view of statistics now seems desirable.

[8]Alker (1966b) presented the relevant econometric formulation; Alker (1970b) pulled together alternative causal representations; Boudon, Jöreskog, and Goldberger went even further in this direction, as noted in Alker (1974a).

Figure 1. Some possible causal connections among votes (V's), vote factors (F's), unknown influences (U's), Subjectively interpreted situational characteristics (S's), resolution wordings (W's), and environmental determinants (X's) in the United Nations General Assembly for a hypothetical country i

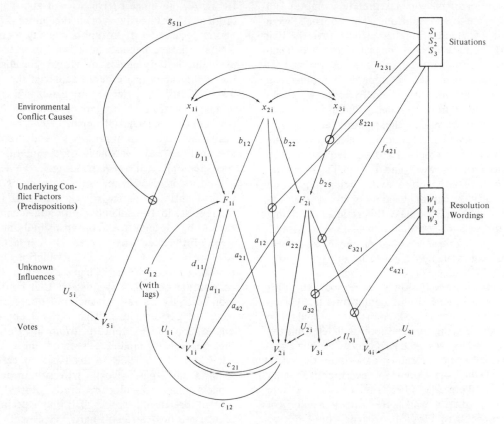

NOTE: Simple arrows represent direct causal relations. Intersections represent multiplicative relations. Exogenously correlated variables are represented by double-headed arrows. Time lags in causal chains are not precisely specified. Each type of coefficient is given a different letter. Thus factor loadings are a's with depndent variables first in their subscripts; b's link factors to their environmental determinants; c's refer to vote trading effects; d's indicate modifications in basic predispositions due to vote commitments; e's suggest multiplicative effects of resolution wordings on factors affecting particular votes; f's measure how situations similarly enhance or diminish factors affecting particular votes; etc. This figure is adapted from Alker (1968b).

misgivings about factor analysis in terms of a potentially testable, alternative model. Thus Haas-type vote trading, if it occurred very frequently, seriously violated the factor analysis' assumption that roll-call interrelations were spurious, due only to the effects of underlying, independent factors. (Note the c_{21}, c_{12} coefficients between V_{1i} and V_{2i} in the figure.) Alger-type learning required

d-type links from voting experiences to subsequently modified factor predispositions. The symbolic politics of resolution writing to maximize votes required e-type predisposition mobilizations. At the very least environmental variables should be assumed to be exogenously correlated (drawn using double-headed arrows). Nonlinear situational events obviously, metapolitically shaped the effects of environmental polarizers (as in the arrows with g and h coefficients).

The corresponding, negative vision was that my previously published correlation matrices (including factor loadings, which correlate variables and factors) were often spurious. The journals were also full of them. Simplistic field reviews like Jones and Singer (1972) make too much of such findings. Computer programs for generating correlation measures were coming into widespread use. (Even unstandardized coefficients were obviously spurious in many cases.) The more lectures and papers I gave making these points, and suggesting constructive causal-modeling alternatives, the more I felt ill at ease with the growing series of replications of my work and Rummel's. I still do, hence my dissatisfaction with being replicated without any apparent awareness as to the vulnerability of simplistic data theoretic or modeling assumptions. Such a practice may be educational, *if put in the context of more recent, better work;* but sold as gospel, it is degenerate, not progressive science.

Whereas Rummel slowly retreated from his prior technical and causal commitments by generalizing his underlying data-analytic models into acausal, simplifying, linear theories, I felt that the important point was to try to choose among alternate, causally interpretable, data-theoretic possibilities, of the sort Coombs, Dawes, and Tversky (1970) and Torgerson (1958) reviewed. *New* data and *better* data theories were usually needed for this purpose. Complex phenomena could not always be linearly, additively analyzed.

A visit to Japan and discussions with Michitoshi Takabatake at Yale helped me resolve an outstanding statistical puzzle concerning single-peaked preference interpretations of my data. As spelled out with citations in Alker (1970b) Hayashi's quantification scaling techniques, which paralleled Guttman-Lingoes's nonmetric Multivariate Analysis of Contingencies, could generate post-influence single-peaked preference spaces (relevant references appear in my 1970a review paper). *Guttman* had long known how to distinguish cumulative from peaked scales. Hundreds of copies of Alker (1970b) were distributed within a month of its presentation at the 1967 political science meetings. Although its commitments to causal

data analysis have diffused fairly widely throughout political science, no one has ever taken its constructive critique seriously regarding subsequent UN roll-call studies. Within the quantitative IR world, the more I have learned about the limitations of my early work, the more attracted others became to it. In replicating my work, they seemed to have become even less interested in the problematical dynamics of global pluralism, and the technical improvements achieved through my own self-criticism. Here again Rosenau's emphasis in his invitation to prepare a note for the NSF conference in 1973 (Rosenau, 1974, p. 18) on "using my data or hypotheses" and "replicating my analyses" as an aspect of cumulation seems very incomplete, if not misleading.

Methodologically and substantively, I wanted to find better evidence of supranational progress (or regress) in UN collective problem-solving, task-expanding, integrative, consensus-building activities. Influenced by personal contacts with Abelson's and Guetzkow's simulation work, I therefore proposed to Chadwick Alger that we collaborate on a UN simulation that could focus more directly on resolutional and nonresolutional parts of UN activities. This move from conflict explication and exploration to an integrative conflict resolution modeling seemed more directly relevant in 1967-1968 to my basic concerns than redoing my thesis work with nonlinear causal models and actor-roll-call, jointly plotted, single-peaked preference spaces. Although preinfluence predispositions were still hard to assess, the newer procedures could be used to provide data and mechanism estimates for a more richly specified simulation of parliamentary diplomacy. Figure 1 surely pointed in that direction. As outlined in my review paper (Alker, 1968b) certain insights from my early work and Alger's would be useful for doing so, even if they were not the insights others had gained from those studies.

Computer Simulations of Collective Security Practices

Two accidents deflected me from fulfilling this original intent: Alger's research on international organization task expansion was moving away from the UN in a scientifically profitable, comparative direction; and Ernst Haas published a theoretically appealing, functionally specific, multi-institutional, but methodologically weak, empirical study on collective security and the future international system, reproduced in Haas (1969). Clearly a process-oriented, more adequate treatment of UN peace making should also involve the Security Council, regional security organizations and, perhaps, the Secretary General. Haas revealed how, during the Suez crisis, Dag Hammarskjöld "adapted" the UN Charter to allow a General Assembly-backed, superpower-supported, bypass of a veto-locked Security Council. This neofunctionalist analysis, plus some hopeful statistical generalizations about UN performance on different issue classes, deepened my understanding of the UN's peace-making accomplishments in the Suez crisis. Its ideas of quasi-teleological system adaptation resonated with those of my "Directive Behavior" UN example (Alker, 1968a). His Apter-derived model of a future low-violence, pluralistic, international reconciliation system fitted my own research hopes and concerns. Given the extremely elementary statistical analysis in his study, plus the problematical fit of his very Lasswellian future construct with his data, I decided to try and improve upon his work, incorporating my own substantive and methodological understanding where possible.

The lessons of this period of research, 1968-1972, have been rather fully reported in "From Causal Modelling to Artificial Intelligence: The Evolution of a UN Peace-making Simulation" (Alker and Christensen, 1972), and in the second illustrative case of my "Structural Models" (Alker, 1974a). The lessons include:

1. An important methodological shift to Simon-March-Guetzkow type simulations—very complex, multilevel causal models—as *representationally* more adequate than ordinary causal (structural) models as ways of specifying and testing theories of institutional development and decay;

2. A more intensive focus on one functional area, collective security practices, appeared the best way to learn more deeply where the UN is going;

3. Also generated were some methodologically innovative ways of studying how charter norms affect UN practice and in turn are modified by them;

4. A very stimulating set of hypotheses, requiring *new verbal data,* has been developed about the *precedent logics* that are used like psycho-logics to interpret historical successes and failures;

5. Haas's substantive findings of modest UN successes have been more deeply supported by future simulations suggesting evolutionary adaptation of UN peace-keeping capabilities within a fairly narrow range of issues;

6. The need to pluralize evaluative success judgments and associated memory structures has been recognized;

7. Surprising similarities and differences between a norm, or regime-type evolutionary focus and legal, institutional studies, have been defined and explored, e.g., the role of legal categories in agenda processes;

8. The non-UN role of coercive or conciliatory practices—unilateral, bilateral and regional causes of, and responses to, conflict—clearly dwarf UN accomplishments and deserve explicit attention.

My awareness of the kind of revolutionary excitement and conflict associated with criticisms against technically and substantively dominant paradigms was heightened. And new research directions soon emerged.

Artificial Intelligence Concerning Quasi-regime Alternatives

Stimulated by continuing work with Greenberg, Christensen and Bennett, (Bennett and Alker, 1973) reflecting about its possible relevance to contemporary normative/conceptual empirical debates about evolving global interdependence and still concerned about the extent to which global pluralism exists and serves larger collective interests, I now see a new research agenda before me. Its topics derive more or less continuously from the points listed above.

The first emphasis is a reconceptualization of an earlier work, "The UN Charter" (Alker and Greenberg, 1971), in quasi-regime terms (Alker and Greenberg, forthcoming). Modifying earlier operational systems norms to include a prior agenda phase, in which states try to put or keep (avoid) issues within the arena most (least) favorable to them, gives a model of rule systems informally but effectively governing the behavior and expectations of two or more transnational/transgovernmental actors. Such quasi-regimes should be distinguished from the globally consensual, legitimate, institutionalized regimes of which international lawyers often speak, as well as nonregimes based on coercive terror or total indifference.

As noted in "Methodological Implications of Interdependence Controversies" (Alker, 1974b), less than global quasi-regimes for insecurity management appear to be the order of the day in many issue areas—among regional alliance members, within particular monetary areas, and between superpowers trying to avoid nuclear war. But underneath the conservative consensus of the superpowers one can see a global system of antagonistic, repressive great-power pluralism.

From a quasi-regime perspective, my collective security studies have led me beyond the narrow realm of virtually consensual UN security practices to the search for the effective, largely informal, structures of peace possibly operative in the past and the future.

Often these structures are force-linked and bilateral. "Minorities rule" inside the Security Council because of the veto; outside the formal collective security system they practice local hegemony. Many minority groups cannot even get their disputes recognized because they lack statehood. Regional resolution efforts that are successful often rely more on hegemony than consensus building and conciliation. In each case the degree of collective regime-like legitimacy through pluralistic accomodation is problematic. Relevant considerations extend well beyond conventional international security relations to include transnational/transgovernmental economic and political issues as well. Only in this latter realm are there appreciable signs of pluralistic bargaining practices.

In my earlier work on "operational charters" (Alker and Greenberg, 1971) I followed the "Political Capabilities" (Alker, 1973) philosophy that causally valid systems theories of political institutions were necessary for assessing the effectiveness of normatively significant alternative "charters." Counterfactual arguments depend on causal models. Haas (1969) argued that the UN did surprisingly well on Cold War issues. A cost analysis of Cold War inhibitions on UN effectiveness would have to be made in terms of unrealized but causally *feasible* alternatives. Similarly, UN future potentials were contingently mappable in terms of plausible, alternative, operational system norms. This emphasis on counterfactual analysis was reflected in the subtitle of the Alker and Greenberg paper (1971) on the UN Charter: "Alternate Pasts and Alternate Futures," now being revised and republished as "Analyzing Collective Security Regime Alternatives" (forthcoming).

One of the problematic features of most behavioral studies for me has been their fascination with what is, rather than with (counterfactual) alternatives to actuality. A reformist logical discovery suggests that facts ought to be perceived as deviations from what is not, but ought to be, and possibly could be. The possible-but-ought-not-to-be also deserves consideration. Nothing could be more sharply true in my mind than the corresponding lacunae of operational collective security practices. A major collective judgment the UN offered on Bangladesh was a General Assembly resolution calling for a genocidal status *quo ante*. Biafra and Vietnam, as much of the Cold War before these conflicts, are left in the most euphemistic terms to regional or extra-UN conciliation practices. The Sino-Soviet conflict never makes the United Nations, even after the United States and the Soviet Union ambivalently assented to changed Chinese representation. In fact, the nonregime of force, or the threat of its use, is more often the final arbiter of peace. The UN system, even when informally, operationally described in quasi-regime terms, fits an ecological niche: handling those cases state representatives are not able legally to deny the existence of, nor able or willing unilaterally or bilaterally to resolve by coercive or noncoercive means. Haas's surprising evidence of UN Cold War successes reflects the existence of these deeper processes, which occasionally place certain more manageable disputes in the UN context.

Hence the research priority of radically redefining Haas, Butterworth, and Nye (1972) conflict data to include power considerations—capabilities, costs, and intents or interests where possible. The realities of deterrence somehow influence UN effectiveness in a way our earlier studies do not reflect: another failure of the *ceteris paribus* ("other things being equal") thinking associated with ordinary statistical modelling. And the need appears to make non-UN insecurity management practices modelable options within a deeper agenda-conscious simulation of operational collective security practices. The nondecisional politics of the agenda process needs to be added to the metapolitics of issue or resolution shaping and coalition building. Important state-system legal categories—"domestic jurisdiction," "second-class veto power," "nonthreats" to the peace, non-membership in the state system—should be internal to the analysis.

Thus a related research direction arises from the need for more acute, politically sensitive, epistemological self-consciousness, a central feature of Marxian epistemology (e.g., Habermas, 1970) and artificial intelligence modeling. Routine data-coding decisions reflect politically relevant alternatives, as Galtung's arguments about the reality of structural violence suggest (e.g., Galtung, 1971, and his later articles in the *Journal of Peace Research*). These alternatives are often, occasionally after the fact, matters of political consciousness as well. Somehow the way the global insecurity management system *interprets* potentially relevant conflicts should be part of an adequate processual simulation.

Artificial intelligence is as well a design-oriented, normative modeling tradition whose specificational primitives are qualitative, list-processing languages with recursive functions. These allow self-simulation, self-reflection about program alternatives treated as data, and systemic self-transformation. As socially constructed, reality and its normatively evaluated alternatives become equally problematical. Individual facts can be reinterpreted as minor reflections of unrealized, but emergent wholes.

CONCLUDING POSTSCRIPT: SOME OBJECTIVE THESES

Many of the lessons of the above discussion are individualistically reported. Yet most of them concerning scientific cumulation can be objectified, I believe, as theses about contemporary interna-

tional relations research. In a less autobiographical style, this postscript contains the main points of my original response to Rosenau's conference invitation (in Rosenau, 1974). Scholarly background information, as well as relevant evidence, is contained in Alker (1971b, 1974a, 1974b).

As in many of the preceding textual comments, the language of the present theses is undeniably Kuhnian. *The Structure of Scientific Revolutions* (Kuhn, 1970) was for me an eye-opening account of the social, dialectical nature of natural scientific progress. Reading it in 1970 brought to mind earlier discussions by Merton (1968), Barber and Hirsch (1962), and Bernal (1939) that I had found particularly helpful. The manifold literature of subsequent discussion, most impressively Lakatos's (1970) long, critical, Popperian reconstruction of Kuhn's argument, has influenced me as well (see citations and discussion in Alker, 1971b). Kuhn's reformulations of his earlier work, and his continuing difficulty in communicating with rationalist philosophers are also worthy of special attention.

> *Thesis 1.* Very little international relations research has produced cumulative scientific knowledge in the strong sense that:
> (a) it is transnationally accepted as empirically, causally or objectively true; and
> (b) it is theoretical, lawful, and/or generalized knowledge; and
> (c) among those sharing a scientific orientation, such knowledge is consensually accepted and taught in codified form as the basis for further intensive investigation.

Specifically, where are the textbooks that have been widely used in different countries with different dominant ideologies? Aren't the current texts one might be tempted to cite here limited in their cultural/ideological appeal? IR theory is frequently taught from such nationalistic or culturally limited perspectives that most textbooks or theses of one country would not be acceptable in another, even if translated and provided with local historical examples.

Literatures that survive across temporal, national, and cultural boundaries usually do so as distinctly political realist, liberal or Marxist political theories, in the classic sense. Little genuine discussion of the *relative empirical validity* of these theoretical traditions exist except in terms laden with ideological predispositions, or burdened by crude falsificationist standards. As such, these literatures are genuinely valuable, but when writers one, two, many decades ago have as much to tell us theoretically as contemporary texts, cumulation past them is indeed problematic. For example, is the EEC a manifestation of integration, power balancing or neoimperialism? Current international relations scholarship all too often reads like high-class diplomatic propaganda.

But if we still allow the likelihood of some kind of weak, parochial cumulation, this doesn't exhaust the problems inherent in scientific progress.

> *Thesis 2.* The causes for the lack of such scientific cumulation include:
> (a) the complexity of international phenomena, in particular their interdisciplinary, historical, and largely nonexperimental nature;
> (b) the divergences of political orientations among IR scholars, in particular nationalistic and ideological differences;
> (c) the scarcity of sufficiently intelligent, well-trained, scientifically committed, adequately supported IR scholars;
> (d) the prevalence within much of the contemporary American oriented IR world of crude positivistic philosophies of social science.

In addition to the political, ideological, and philosophical parochialisms especially endemic in the world politics field, Thesis 2 highlights a lack of talent equal to the difficulty of the subject matter. It is true that global studies allow meaningful planetary *ceteris paribus* assumptions analogous to astronomical studies of our solar system; but the interdisciplinary nature of the subject matter, and the difficulties of reproducing such phenomena in the laboratory make anything like causal analysis very difficult (but not impossible if some rather complex, rarely mastered and applied quasi-experimental techniques are carefully used). The historicity of our self-conscious subject matter also makes the unqualified (probabilistic) determinism of natural scientific explanations suspect. One might seek instead either some kind of systematic, precausal, interpretive (hermeneutic) understanding of "constructed" international phenomena in between popular or diplomatic cognitions and environmental constraints. Artificial intelligence as design theory comes close to this

position, but may be too technocratic an orientation. Of course, morally we can be thankful that nuclear weapons have been used only twice, but the consequences include the nonscientific nature of most nonempirical deterence theory.

The manifest interdisciplinary nature of our phenomena introduces several complications. First of all, each substantive discipline invades the IR field, subsuming its phenomena with superficial success under its professional orientations. When a theory doesn't work *in practice,* resultant anomalies are often attributed to variables outside the disciplinary nexus. Thus the strong tendency for leading economic powers to be the strongest advocates of, and beneficiaries of, free trade contradicts (in a scientific cum policy sense) the theory of comparative advantage, but these anomalies can be attributed to benighted politicians (rather than a superficially depoliticized economic theory which ignores equity or surplus value questions).

An opposite tendency is to try to incorporate every phenomenon within the rubric of a single profession. If everything is reduced to multidimensional power balancing, the semiautonomy of political economic considerations of a liberal or Marxian sort is never recognized. Putting economic costs on every aspect of security policy is similarly problematic, as are the difficulties of rejecting some kinds of Marxian functionalism.

Both tendencies mean that synthetic cross-disciplinary cumulation is harder to do, given the biases of professional training.[9] Given the relative rarity of global research agencies, the international locus of IR phenomena further contributes to the difficulty of funding cumulative cross-cultural studies. Work funded by nationally organized policy agencies often holds constant many perspectives shared by national elites, when it is just those "blinders" that inhibit the vigorous criticism required to ensure scientific progress. The ignorance of many American scholars regarding dependency theories results in part from their unawareness of the way America's power influences both their scientific interests and validation standards. For example, how many small powers sponsor much *statistical* research on all 140-plus countries?

---

[9]My brother refers to an excellent paper on this subject by D. T. Campbell: "Ethnocentrism of Disciplines and the Fish-Scale Model of Omniscience." I do not know the exact citation, but I applaud the metaphor.

All the above cleavages limit the breadth and depth of the scholarly communities which must be the bearers of a cumulative scientific tradition.

Thesis 3. Cumulative social science knowledge is usually the product of a closely related scholarly community sharing most features of a research paradigm:

(a) metascientific orientations (including conceptions of social forces, query-solving inference modes, and certain sociopolitical values such as objectivity and scholarly autonomy);

(b) exemplars and positive heuristics (including also preoperational models);

(c) preferred symbolic generalizations (both in their original, interpreted and revised forms, and as part of significant mathematical theories); and

(d) a positively valued, sizeable follow-up literature.

Since this thesis is elaborated upon at much greater length in Alker (1971b), only a few illustrative arguments are necessary here.

First, I argue in that paper that the Richardson reaction process (arms race) literature has had the character of a multiadic, relatively nonparochial research paradigm achieving genuine but uneven scientific progress. Other scientific achievements tend to be more parochial and limited. Integration theory, for example, could be seen as no longer advancing in even parochial terms for some of the reasons already given in the text above. The events data movement seems more progressive now, but rather atheoretical and not clearly generalizeable cross-culturally. The Alker-Christensen-Greenberg work reviewed above fits more within the organization process paradigm originated by members of the Carnegie Tech School than any analogously developed IR subspeciality. INS/IPS simulations (discussed elsewhere in this volume) represented genuine paradigmatic progress within American IR for a time, but the scale and bases implied by Theses 2 and 3 are no longer present. If nothing else, judgments of this level of generality are worth trying to elaborate and sustain in a more thorough fashion.

Thesis 4. Scientific progress in weak and strong terms involves:

(a) the voluntaristic consolidation of a moderately large (25-50?) research community around exemplary achievements;

(b) the incremental pursuit of anomalies and puzzles generated by the paradigmatic generalization of such exemplars; and

(c) the revolutionary supersession of old research paradigms by new ones differing fundamentally in several of their central components.

Again, the basic ideas fit the fundamental respecifications of Richardson's (1960) "reaction process models" as governed either by a kind of economic rationality or a more complex psycho-logic than that of Abelson's earlier papers. But how many nonbehavioral scholars will appreciate Choucri and North's radical revisions of the Richardson tradition? The Haas-Nye work on collective security never integrated enough scholars cross-nationally for conditions (a) and (b) above to be fully met. Russian or French or British scholars do not cumulate from their work. My above findings of the need for revolutionary reworkings of pluralistic collective security theory must be seen as still within the realm of unreceived knowledge.

REFERENCES

Abelson, Robert. 1963. "A Derivation of Richardson's Equations." *Journal of Conflict Resolution* 7 (Mar): 13-15.

———. 1973. "The Structure of Belief Systems." In *Computer Models of Thought and Language,* ed. Roger Shank and Kenneth Colby, pp. 287-339. San Francisco: Freeman.

——— and J. Douglas Carroll. 1965. "Computer Simulation of Individual Belief Systems." *American Behavioral Scientist* 8 (May): 24-30.

——— and M. J. Rosenberg. 1958. "Symbolic Psycho-Logic." *Behavioral Science* 3 (Jan): 1-13.

Adorno, T. W., Else Frenkel-Brunswik, Daniel J. Levinson, and R. Nevitt Sanford. 1969. *The Authoritarian Personality.* New York: Norton.

Alger, Chadwick. 1965. "Personal Contact in Intergovernmental Organizations." In *International Behavior,* ed. Herbert Kelman, pp. 521-47. New York: Holt, Rinehart & Winston.

Alker, Hayward R., Jr. 1962. "An IBM 7090 Program for Transaction Flow Analysis." *Behavioral Science* 7 (Oct): 498-99.

———. 1963. "Dimensions of Voting in the General Assembly." Ph.D. dissertation, Yale Univ.

———. 1964a. "Dimensions of Conflict in the General Assembly." *American Political Science Review* 58 (Sep): 642-67.

———. 1964b. "Regionalism versus Universalism in Comparing Nations." In *World Handbook of Political and*

Social Indicators, ed. Bruce M. Russett et al., pp. 322-40. New Haven: Yale Univ. Press.

———. 1966a. "The Long Road to International Relations Theory: Problems of Statistical Nonadditivity." *World Politics* 23 (Jul): 623-65.

———. 1966b. "Causal Inference and Political Analysis." In *Mathematical Applications in Political Science,* ed. Joseph Bernd, Vol. 2, pp. 7-43. Dallas: SMU Press.

———. 1966c. "Supranationalism in the United Nations." *Papers, Peace Research Society (International)* 3: 197-212.

———. 1968a. "Directive Behavior: A Desirable Orientation for Mathematical Social Science." In *Mathematics in the Social Sciences in Australia,* UNESCO Seminar. Sydney: Univ. of Sydney.

———. 1968b. "Computer Simulations: Bad Mathematics but Good Social Science?" In *Mathematics in the Social Sciences in Australia,* UNESCO Seminar. Sydney: Univ. of Sydney. [Revised and reprinted as "Computer Simulations: Inelegant Mathematics and Worse Social Science." *International Journal of Mathematical Education in Science and Technology* 5 (1974): 139-55.]

———. 1970a. "Integration Logics: A Review, Extension, and Critique." *International Organization* 24 (Autumn): 869-916.

———. 1970b. "Statistics and Politics: The Need for Causal Data Analysis." In *Politics and the Social Sciences,* ed. Seymour M. Lipset, pp. 244-313. New York: Oxford Univ. Press.

———. 1971a. "Assessing the Impact of the UN Collective Security System: An Operational, Multicultural Approach." *Proceedings, American Society of International Law* 65: 33-39.

———. 1971b. "Research Paradigms and Mathematical Politics." In *Proceedings of the IPSA Roundtable,* ed. Rudolph Wildenmann et al. Mannheim (forthcoming).

———. 1973. "On Political Capabilities in a Schedule Sense: Measuring Power, Integration and Development." In *Mathematical Approaches to Politics,* ed. Hayward R. Alker, Jr., Karl W. Deutsch, and Antoine Stoetzel, pp. 307-74. New York: Elsevier.

———. 1974a. "Are There Structural Models of Voluntaristic Social Action?" *Quality and Quantity* 8: 199-246. [A version given in Montreal was entitled "Are There Voluntaristic Structural Models of Public Goods Generation?"]

———. 1974b. "Methodological Implications of Interdependence Controversies." In *Analyzing Global Interdependence,* ed. Hayward R. Alker, Jr., Lincoln P. Bloomfield, and Nazli Choucri. Cambridge: MIT Center for International Studies.

——— and Bruce M. Russett. 1965. *World Politics in the General Assembly.* New Haven: Yale Univ. Press.

——— and Donald Puchala. 1968. "Trends in Economic Partnership: The North Atlantic Area 1928-1963." In *Quantitative International Politics,* ed. J. David Singer, pp. 287-316. New York: Free Press.

——— and Ronald D. Brunner. 1969. "Simulating International Conflict: A Comparison of Three Approaches." *International Studies Quarterly* 13 (Mar): 70-110.

——— and William J. Greenberg. 1971. "The UN Charter: Alternate Pasts and Alternate Futures." In *The United Nations,* ed. Edwin H. Fedder, pp. 113-42. St. Louis: Univ. of Missouri, Center for International Studies.

——— and William J. Greenberg. Forthcoming. "Analyzing Collective Security Regime Alternatives." In a book being edited by Mathew Bonham.

——— and Cheryl Christensen. 1972. "From Causal Modeling to Artificial Intelligence: The Evolution of a UN Peace-Making Simulation." In *Experimentation and Simulation in Political Science,* ed. J. A. LaPonce and Paul Smoker, pp. 177-224. Toronto: Univ. of Toronto Press.

Almond, Gabriel A. and James S. Coleman, eds. 1960. *The Politics of the Developing Areas.* Princeton: Princeton Univ. Press.

Bachrach, Peter, and Morton S. Baratz. 1962. "Two Faces of Power." *American Political Science Review* 56 (Dec): 947-52.

Barber, Bernard, and Walter Hirsh. 1962. *The Sociology of Science.* New York: Free Press.

Baumgartner, Thomas, and Tom Burns. 1974. "Unequal Exchange." Mimeo. Durham: Univ. of New Hampshire.

Bennett, James, and Hayward R. Alker, Jr. 1973. "Restructuring Processes in the Global Stratification System: An Outline of a Simulation Model." Paper presented at the Annual Meeting of the International Studies Association, New York.

Bernal, J. D. 1939. *The Social Function of Science.* New York: Macmillan.

Black, Duncan. 1958. *The Theory of Committees and Elections.* Cambridge: At the Univ. Press.

Blalock, Hubert M., Jr. 1967. *Causal Inferences in Nonexperimental Research.* Chapel Hill: Univ. of North Carolina Press.

Bloomfield, Lincoln P. 1968. "The Political Scientist and Foreign Policy." In *Political Science and Public Policy,* ed. Austin Ranney, pp. 179-96. Chicago: Markham.

Buckley, Walter, ed. 1968. *Modern Systems Research for the Behavioral Scientist.* Chicago: Aldine.

Burns, Thomas, and Walter Buckley. 1974. "The Prisoner's Dilemma Game as a System of Social Domination." *Journal of Peace Research* 11: 221-28.

Campbell, Donald T. Undated. "Evolutionary Epistemology." Mimeo. Evanston: Northwestern Univ.

Chomsky, Noam. 1972. *Language and Mind.* Enlarged ed. New York: Harcourt Brace Jovanovich.

––– and George A. Miller. 1963. "Finitary Models of Language Users." In *Handbook of Mathematical Psychology,* ed. R. D. Luce et al., vol. 2. New York: Wiley.

Choucri, Nazli, and Robert C. North. 1975. *Nations in Conflict.* San Francisco: Freeman.

Coombs, Clyde, Robyn Dawes, and Amos Tversky. 1970. *Mathematical Psychology.* Englewood Cliffs, N.J.: Prentice-Hall.

Cotter, Cornelius P., ed. 1973. *Political Science Annual,* vol. 4. Indianapolis: Bobbs-Merrill.

Dahl, Robert. 1956. *A Preface to Democratic Theory.* Chicago: Univ. of Chicago Press.

–––. 1961. *Who Governs? Democracy and Power in an American City.* New Haven: Yale Univ. Press.

–––. 1965. "Cause and Effect in the Study of Politics." In *Cause and Effect,* ed. Daniel Lerner, pp. 75-98. New York: Free Press.

–––. 1967. *Pluralist Democracy in the United States: Conflict and Consent.* Chicago: Rand McNally.

–––. 1968. "The Power Approach to Political Analysis." In *International Encyclopedia of the Social Sciences,* ed. David L. Sills, vol. 12, pp. 405-14. New York: Macmillan and Free Press.

Deutsch, Karl W. 1963. *The Nerves of Government.* New York: Free Press.

––– et al. 1957. *Political Community and the North Atlantic Area.* Princeton: Princeton Univ. Press.

Emmanuel, Aghiri. 1972. *Unequal Exchange.* New York: Monthly Review Press.

Frohlich, Norman, Joseph A. Oppenheimer, and Oran R. Young. 1971. *Political Leadership and Collective Goods.* Princeton: Princeton Univ. Press.

Galtung, Johan. 1971. "A Structural Theory of Imperialism." *Journal of Peace Research* 8: 95-115.

Goldberger, Arthur S., and Otis D. Duncan, eds. 1973. *Structural Equation Models in the Social Sciences.* New York: Seminar Press.

Haas, Ernst. 1958. *The Uniting of Europe.* Stanford: Stanford Univ. Press.

–––. 1964. *Beyond the Nation-State.* Stanford: Stanford Univ. Press.

–––. 1969. *Tangle of Hopes.* Englewood Cliffs, N.J.: Prentice-Hall.

–––, Robert Butterworth, and Joseph Nye (1972). *Conflict Management by International Organizations.* Morristown, N.J.: General Learning Press.

Habermas, Jürgen. 1970. *Toward a Rational Society.* Boston: Beacon.

–––. 1971. *Knowledge and Human Interests.* Boston: Beacon. Hanson, Norwood R. 1965. *Patterns of Discovery.* Cambridge: At the Univ. Press.

Harsanyi, John C. 1965. "Measurement of Social Power, Opportunity Costs, and the Theory of Two-Person Bargaining Games." In *Human Behavior and International Politics,* ed. J. David Singer. Chicago: Rand McNally.

Jones, Susan D., and J. David Singer. 1972. *Beyond Conjecture in International Politics.* Itasca, Ill.: Peacock.

Jöreskog, Karl. 1970. "A General Method for Analysis of Covariance Structures." *Biometrika* 57 (Aug): 239-51.

Kuhn, Thomas. 1970. *The Structure of Scientific Revolutions.* 2d ed. Chicago: Univ. of Chicago Press.

Lakatos, Imre. 1970. "Falsification and the Methodology of Scientific Research Programmes." In *Criticism and the Growth of Knowledge,* ed. Imre Lakatos and Alan Musgrave, pp. 91-195. Cambridge: At the Univ. Press.

Lasswell, Harold. 1963. *The Future of Political Science.* New York: Atherton.

–––. 1965. *World Politics and Personal Insecurity.* New York: Free Press.

Lipset, Seymour Martin. 1959. *Political Man: The Social Bases of Politics.* Garden City, N.Y.: Doubleday.

–––, ed. 1970. *Politics and the Social Sciences.* New York: Oxford Univ. Press.

MacRae, Duncan. 1958. *Dimensions of Congressional Voting.* Berkeley and Los Angeles: Univ. of California Press.

Marcuse, Herbert. 1941. *Reason and Revolution.* New York: Oxford Univ. Press.

–––. 1955. *Eros and Civilization.* Boston: Beacon.

Merritt, Richard. 1966. *Symbols of American Community, 1735-1775.* New Haven: Yale Univ. Press.

Merton, Robert K. 1968. *Social Theory and Social Structure.* Rev. ed. New York: Free Press.

Mills, C. Wright. 1956. *The Power Elite.* New York: Oxford Univ. Press.

–––. 1960. *The Causes of World War III.* New York: Ballantine.

Oppenheim, Felix. 1961. *Dimensions of Freedom.* New York: St. Martin's.

Pool, Ithiel, Robert Abelson, and Samuel Popkin. 1965. *Candidates, Issues, and Strategies.* Cambridge: MIT Press.

Puchala, Donald. 1971. "International Transactions and Regional Integration." In *Regional Integration,* ed. Leon Lindberg and Stuart Scheingold, pp. 128-59. Cambridge: Harvard Univ. Press.

Rapoport, Anatol. 1960. *Fights, Games and Debates.* Ann Arbor: Univ. of Michigan Press.

––– and Albert M. Chammah. 1965. *Prisoner's Dilemma.* Ann Arbor: Univ. of Michigan Press.

Richardson, Lewis F. 1960. *Arms and Insecurity.* Pittsburgh: Boxwood.

Romney, A. Kimball, Roger Shepard, and Sara Nerlove, eds. 1972. *Multidimensional Scaling.* 2 vols. New York: Seminar Press.

Rosenau, James N. 1974. "Success and Failure in Scientific International Relations Research." Mimeo. Los Angeles: Univ. of Southern California.

Ruggie, John. 1972. "Collective Goods and Future International Collaboration." *American Political Science Review* 66 (Sep): 874-93.

Russett, Bruce M. 1963. *Community and Contention: Britain and America in the Twentieth Century.* Cambridge: MIT Press.

——— and John D. Sullivan. 1971. "Collective Goods and International Organization." *International Organization* 25 (Autumn): 845-65.

Samuelson, Paul. 1969. "Pure Theory of Public Expenditure and Taxation." In *Public Economics,* ed. Julius Margolis and H. Guitton, pp. 98-123. London: Macmillan.

Savage, I. Richard, and Karl W. Deutsch. 1960. "A Statistical Model of the Gross Analysis of Transaction Flows." *Econometrica* 28 (Jul): 551-72.

Simon, Herbert. 1969. *The Sciences of the Artificial.* Cambridge: MIT Press.

——— in collaboration with Harold Guetzkow. 1957. *Models of Man.* New York: Wiley.

Singer, J. David. 1963. "Inter-Nation Influence: A Formal Model." *American Political Science Review* 57 (Jun): 420-30.

Torgerson, Warren. 1958. *Theory and Methods of Scaling.* New York: Wiley.

Wolff, Robert P., Barrington Moore, Jr., and Herbert Marcuse. 1969. *A Critique of Pure Tolerance.* Boston: Beacon.

Wright, Quincy. 1968. *A Study of War.* Chicago: Univ. of Chicago Press.

5. The Researcher in the United Nations: Evolution of a Research Strategy

Chadwick F. Alger

My main purpose in the ensuing pages is to indicate how a research strategy evolved as I became progressively more involved in trying to understand the dynamics of international organizations. The account is presented in some detail because, in retrospect, it illustrates the large extent to which our research strategies are shaped by our subject matter even as they also shape our findings. Research strategies cannot be fully explicated in advance. They evolve as one gets deeper and deeper into the phenomena one is trying to comprehend. They also evolve because individuals, institutions, and societies under investigation have an impact on the researcher. This would seem to be especially so if one's research site puts him in personal contact with people from virtually all countries who are involved with a global agenda of issues.

With the advantage of hindsight it is now apparent that my research was guided by five assumptions. All of these can be discerned in the following account, but it is perhaps useful to explicate them at the outset. First, the documentary residue provided by officials and journalists offer only a very partial view of the activities and impact of institutions such as the United Nations. While it is important that this residue be carefully studied, scholars may make serious errors in interpretation of these documents if they do not independently acquire information through firsthand efforts. In retrospect, most of my work at the United Nations, in New York and Geneva, can be viewed as experiments in the development of methods for supplementing official documents and journalistic accounts with "scholarly documents" that are reasonably systematic.

Second, the political and social processes of international institutions such as the United Nations are not fundamentally different from those in other political and social institutions. They involve processes such as communication, socialization, decision making, voting, etc., that can be found in local, national, and international organizations, both governmental and nongovernmental.[1] This is more widely accepted than when I began my work, but much teaching and research still makes artificial distinctions that inhibit social scientists from analytic movement across these "laboratories."

Third, it follows from the above that international organizations can be studied with the same kind of research techniques, including field investigation, that are used in local and national organizations.

Fourth, no single research technique is adequate for handling a significant research question. Each is only able to provide one perspective, one approximation, of what is going on. I sensed this before my work at the UN but experiences in this "laboratory" deepened my understanding of the value of multimethod research. Documents, voting records, interviews, informants, observed behavior, all can be seen as pieces of a mosaic. Each piece was placed there for a purpose by the actor and must be understood in terms of its special purpose. Each piece of the mosaic has effects that the actor may not understand and sometimes may not even perceive. But a number of pieces must be viewed in order to comprehend fully the context of a single piece.[2] This simple truth is most obviously, and repetitively, violated by many who do UN voting studies—those who exhibit a naive unconcern with the context of the voting data they manipulate.

Fifth, an ever deepening belief in the importance of observation, both systematic and more anthropological—as a research tool—and as a way of sensitizing users of data acquired through other techniques.

My "experiments" in field research at the UN, ILO, and WHO have stimulated a number of my own graduate students and students at other institutions to engage in field research in both international organizations and national capitals. Thus, demonstration of what is possible seems to have had some impact on others. For the reasons described above I believe this work has made an important, although quantitatively very modest, contribution. Most important, I think, are the insights this work has contributed on the potential of international organizations as agents of change in the international system—through socialization, changes in communications patterns, and the generation of new agendas for national governments.

On the other hand, it seems that my work has had no effect whatsoever outside a small sector of scholars in North America and Western Europe who have replicated some aspects of my work, asked for my data, and cited my articles. It has not had any effect on the realm of activities we study.[3]

INITIAL IMPRESSIONS OF THE UN

The seeds from which my research strategy grew were planted in September 1958, on the day I first walked into the delegate's lounge of United Nations headquarters and wandered through the corridors of the conference building during the General Assembly. Textbooks, scholarly articles, newspapers, and television reporting of Security Council and General Assembly meetings had not prepared me for this experience.

I had pictured the lounge as a quiet and somewhat austere room, resembling the lounges of English clubs as they are portrayed in films. But the scene I observed was more like a lounge in a busy airport. As Assembly committees broke for lunch I was enveloped in a sea of humanity. The scene that I observed simply did not jibe with my image of diplomatic behavior. People stood three deep, and sometimes more, at the L-shaped bar, trying to outwit each other in acquiring a drink. Since there is no table service those who were lucky enough to acquire a place to sit carried their own drinks to their seats. Ambassadors were observed carrying trays of drinks to their guests. For those eating a quick lunch a line formed at the snack counter. The rack provided for briefcases was overflowing, and briefcases spilled out onto the floor. Some delegates patiently picked their way through the crowd, searching for each other;

---

[1] This argument is made more fully in Alger (1963a).
[2] This discussion is extended in Alger (1970a).

[3] For a more general assessment of the minimum extent to which systematic research into international organizations has been undertaken, see Alger (1970b).

others asked one of the hostesses to page another delegate. But hostesses paging delegates over a public address system were barely audible over the noise created by a multitude of conversations.

What were these people doing? What might the consequence of their activity be for the goals of the organization described in the familiar words of the UN charter? It took many years to find partial answers to these questions. To a large degree they are still unanswered. Put in the simplest terms, these people were doing the same kinds of things that men everywhere do when they gather in conventions, assemblies, and congresses. They were looking for their luncheon companions. They were searching out members of their own delegation to find out the latest news from home. They were talking with members of committees other than their own to find out what was going on. They hoped to see again an attractive blonde whom they had met in the lounge yesterday. They were trying to get support from other delegates for a proposal. They were looking for old friends who had been in the Assembly in earlier years but whom they had not seen as yet. And some were so wearied by the endless debate of the morning that they felt unable to face the afternoon speaking schedules without first being fortified by a couple of martinis.

If one has keen interest in and fascination for behavior of men in assemblies, parliaments, legislatures, and conventions, the first encounter with the corridors and lounges of the United Nations is an exhilarating experience. The languages, costumes, faces, and the decor are reminders that these men represent virtually all the nations of the world. The fact that they are all gathered together, proclaiming their support of the charter and pledging their nations to the peaceful resolution of all international problems, gives renewed hope where pessimism had abounded. Observing representatives of unfriendly nations in friendly conversation encourages this hope. But the UN simultaneously provides experiences that check false optimism. A few hours spent listening to Assembly debates or talking with a delegate involved in one of the conflicts on a UN agenda is all that is required. The continuous intrusions of the world outside, and their reminders that the UN is not separate from, but an integral part of, this world, tend to drive one alternately to despair and hope—despair that some of the big conflicts can ever be resolved, hope engendered by continued amazement that the UN exists and can, in some ways, thrive despite an inhospitable international environment.

Close observation of the United Nations makes it seem much more difficult to assess its affects on world affairs than when appraising it from afar. The task seems hard enough in the documents room of a university library. To which of many organs should attention be given? If, as an example, the General Assembly is chosen, which of the seven committees should be chosen? Which of the over one hundred agenda items should be covered? Which of over one hundred nations should receive attention? But the researcher who desires to supplement the documentary view of the United Nations must contend with these choices and more. Shall he focus on public debate, private negotiations, regional groups, delegations, secretariat, relations of secretariat and delegations with home governments, the press, or nongovernmental organizations?

But observation of the UN draws attention to an even wider range of events, moods, and impressions:

> The sense of vacuum and aimlessness that one felt at the UN in the days immediately following the death of Dag Hammerskjöld—a striking measure of the importance of his leadership.
>
> The bewildered look on the face of an Arab diplomat when he finds that he has unwittingly been engaged in conversation with an Israeli diplomat in the delegate's lounge.
>
> A touching scene in which a Saudi Arabian representative leads a UN colleague of some years, the Albanian ambassador, from the rostrum of the General Assembly after he has been gaveled down as out of order by the Assembly president from Ghana and is unwilling to remove himself.
>
> Ambassador Zorin (U.S.S.R.) and Ambassador Lodge (U.S.), not long after scathing exchanges in the political committee of the Assembly, serenely enjoying Brahms's Fourth Symphony played by the Boston Symphony in the General Assembly hall on UN Day.
>
> An African delegate in tribal robe washing his feet in the wash basin of the men's room in the delegate's lounge.

A black U.S. delegate standing up in the midst of the U.S. delegation in the assembly hall to applaud the passage of a historic anticolonial resolution which the United States delegation had opposed.

A normally verbose and buoyant French delegate disdainfully reading a statement as a clear signal to foreign colleagues of many years that he is opposed to his government's policy.

Adjournment of a debate of the Second Committee of the General Assembly on economic development at the request of the U.S. delegation because (privately known but not publicly stated) the State Department and the Treasury Department have not yet reached agreement on the position the U.S. delegation should take in the debate.

An Irish diplomat personally delivering his afternoon speech to the United Press so it will be sure to make the morning papers at home.

The contempt expressed, even by delegates from friendly countries, when the U.S. Permanent Representative becomes involved in the work of a committee for the first time by making a speech that once again goes over ground covered many times in the preceding weeks—obviously for the television audience of the six o'clock news.

The private thoughts of a weary secretarial official who has publicly, and patiently, again explained the details of UN budgetary procedures to delegates uninformed on the issues for which they are responsible.

The contents of a humorous poem written by a delegate, and privately circulated to selected colleagues from other delegations, ridiculing a colleague campaigning for a committee post.

The friendship of delegates to a UN committee from India, Israel, and New Zealand—all graduates of Cambridge University.

The camaraderie and jovial mood of some night committee meetings.

An Anglican clergyman presenting taped appeals to the UN from leaders in Southwest Africa—tapes smuggled across borders in a hollowed-out volume of *Treasure Island*.

A multitude of snapshots of UN life were viewed, primarily between 1958 and 1964, when some two months were spent at the UN each year—normally during the sessions of the General Assembly. In addition to attendance at virtually every kind of public meeting, assemblies, councils, committees, etc., an effort was made to experience as wide a selection of UN life as possible (in snack bars, restaurants, receptions, private homes, bars, corridors) and to establish contact with as wide a range of participants as possible—career diplomats, delegates from many walks of life (foreign ministers, parliamentarians, businessmen, clergymen, housewives), bartenders, secretariat, nongovernmental organization representatives, and journalists. A research strategy was developed incrementally from these experiences.

FACTORS UNDERLYING RESEARCH STRATEGY

In retrospect, four factors underlying this evolving strategy may seem more apparent now than they did at the time. First, impressions acquired from initial exposure to the UN milieu raised questions that persisted and intensified through time. These impressions, providing a dramatic contrast with the image of the UN obtained from the literature, reshaped my initial research agenda. I had gone to the UN to discern how firsthand inquiry could supplement documentary records of the conflict management activities of the UN—specific conflicts such as the Middle East and Kashmir. But my attention was immediately consumed by an effort to understand what was going on in the intensely active and heterogeneous UN community in which I found myself. Clearly the consequences of this activity for the global system of intergovernmental relations was not captured in the decisions of public bodies. What difference does it make when several thousand people from all over the globe gather together on a few acres of land to prepare for and debate a common agenda, struggle to win others to their point of view, strive to obtain some consensus, and interact intensely in a variety of settings? What happens to the people? What happens to the agenda of governments? What happens to norms for intergovernmental relations?[4]

Second, initial UN experiences reinforced previously held assumptions about the similarities of human behavior across a variety of political entities and arenas. It had seemed to me that distinc-

[4] These initial impressions and questions were presented in Alger (1961a).

tions made between diplomacy, national politics, and local politics were overdrawn, and that differences in customary labels (e.g., the use of the term *public diplomacy* in the UN and legislative behavior in the U.S. Congress) inhibited perception of the common attributes of political behavior in different arenas. Certainly there is much that is different, and this is important. But men from a variety of territorial units who come together to grapple with common problems must, because of shared biological, sociological, technological, and normative factors, engage in strikingly similar kinds of activities. To overlook these similarities limits understanding by inhibiting the application of knowledge across arenas of human activity. It also causes neglect of some of those things that are found everywhere that men gather to reach collective decisions—things that make it possible for an institution like the UN to exist—public exchange of views under agreed procedures, drafting of alternative proposals to be debated and amended, procedures for designating representatives of larger groups, appointment of secretariats to carry out decisions, sharing food and drink as both relief from and an extension of more formal debate and negotiation, and utilization of a variety of means widely used in human face-to-face contact to create trustful relationships.

Third, there had yet been virtually no firsthand, systematic study of the United Nations. In 1958 systematic fieldwork on national and local politics was rapidly growing, but it was generally believed that field research techniques could not be applied to the behavior of diplomats. This meant that there was virtually no past experience on which to build. Indeed, I was warned by scholars, and others with firsthand knowledge of the UN, that it would be impossible for a researcher to do systematic interviewing, and impossible for him to really find out what was going on because of the great sensitivity of most of the issues with which delegates were occupied. This meant that my research not only sought to answer substantive questions but at the same time represented experiments in discerning relevant and feasible methods for carrying out research in international organizations and demonstrating their utility.

Fourth, I frankly admit that I enjoyed firsthand exploration of the UN community, and investigated the less obvious paths, as well as the thoroughfares, because of a compulsive inquisitiveness about all aspects of this community, and because of continual doubts that those things on which journalists and scholars had traditionally focused their attention were necessarily most important. This enjoyment of face-to-face contact with members of the UN community was partly the result of a personal need to see the individuals and institutions whose behavior I am studying. This gives me greater confidence that I really understand what is going on. Others acquire the same feeling from printed documents and statistics, such as voting data. Of course, we all justify our choice of methods on other grounds, and these grounds are often scientifically valid, but choice of research methods also seems to correlate with the personal characteristics and needs of researchers. My enjoyment of firsthand exploration of the UN community was also partly a result of the stimulation I received from interacting with people from all parts of the globe who were concerned with virtually all of the problems confronting mankind as a whole. This satisfied my own need to think about and to develop a personal posture toward mankind as a whole, both in an analytic and a normative sense.

INTERVIEWS OF ASSEMBLY DELEGATES AND MEMBERS OF PERMANENT MISSIONS

The research strategy that evolved was shaped significantly by my broadening awareness of the characteristics and processes of the UN community, through personal experiences in this community and calculations about what kind of research method might work in investigating questions generated by this experience. The first question that was systematically investigated was the impact of experience in the UN on the participants. Data for this project were collected by interviewing new General Assembly delegates before and after their first experience in the Assembly in September and December 1969. There is no doubt that my own experiences in the General Assembly of 1968 partly influenced the choice of this topic. It seemed to me that new delegates would be as surprised as I was at the contrast between expectations and the actual UN. Change in delegate attitudes toward the UN, toward some UN issues, and toward specific countries were measured by asking questions about those issues before and after delegates had served in the Assembly. Experience with this project underlined the value of checking out impressions gained through conversations with informants (selected on the basis of chance encounters, introductions from other informants, etc.) with information gathered through more systematic methods. Conversations with many UN participants in 1958 had convinced me that UN delegates were indeed having significant learning experiences at the UN. But my informant sample did not alert me to the fact that many UN delegates just don't *have* explicit attitudes about many aspects of the UN, many UN issues, or many nations in the UN. Their knowledge and experience is not adequate enough for these attitudes to be developed.[5]

The second systematic inquiry investigated the difference between diplomatic activity at the United Nations and that in national capitals. In early 1960 one person from each permanent mission was randomly selected and asked questions about diplomatic practice at the United Nations. Most of the questions asked those responding to make comparisons between their experiences in New York and those in national capitals. Although the questions asked developed out of my exploratory work at the UN (Alger, 1965), this study was designed and executed by Best (1960). While this study tended to confirm differences between UN and national capital diplomacy that were suggested by informants, the value of systematic inquiry was once again underlined. For example, it had been hypothesized that delegates from Eastern European countries would find the UN less different than those from other countries because they seemed to be less integrated into the full range of UN activity at the time of the research. But Latin Americans were the only regional group that provided responses significantly different from the world as a whole.

Along with these efforts to deepen understanding of the effect of the UN on individuals and on diplomatic procedures and norms, a continual effort was being made in discussions with numerous UN participants to become acquainted with a broad range of UN issues. Initially, an effort was made to sit in on all of the seven main committees

of the Assembly as well as the plenary. Sampling all committees was deemed important because press and scholars in the U.S. have given primary attention to the two political committees. This provided insight into diverse viewpoints on priorities for the UN and also drew attention to some of the UN subcultures, composed of experts in international law, human rights, disarmament, economic and social development, UN budgetary procedures, etc. This breadth of experience gradually made it possible to have fruitful exchange with a wide variety of UN participants. Although my primary interest in the early phases of my UN research were in socialization and communication, most participants quite naturally wished to discuss agenda issues. Only through discussing issues could information be obtained on the social processes of the UN. Few informants were both interested in discussing and able to discuss abstract generalizations about those processes.

RESEARCH ON THE POLITICAL PROCESS

An effort was also being made to understand the political process in UN public bodies, particularly the General Assembly. One quickly becomes aware that much so-called public diplomacy is not public. I was able to experience scattered pieces of more private activity in the company of delegates in the lounge and corridors, and at receptions and parties. But I had to depend on informant accounts of group meetings and a variety of kinds of negotiating sessions at the UN, at national missions and elsewhere. Unfortunately, a research strategy that facilitated the development of a broad overview knowledge of UN issues seemed to be less and less useful in obtaining a deep knowledge of the political process. It became increasingly apparent that this would require me to focus on a single General Assembly committee for a period of time. This would permit me to concentrate on issues being debated by this committee and to become as informed about these issues, and their related documentation, as the delegates. It would also enable me to cultivate informants from one committee so I could develop a deeper understanding of those aspects of the political process carried on outside the public meetings. While I had gathered snippets of information on these behind-

[5] This study was published as Alger (1963b).

the-scene activities, I felt like I was floating on the surface, dependent on a few informants for reporting on a very complicated process in which different participants had very different perspectives. Also, I felt the need personally to follow through some issues from beginning to end, to record events and participant perspectives as the political process developed. On a number of occasions I had found participant accounts of what had happened unreliable. For example, there is a tendency for participants to rationalize outcomes so that they believe, or at least assert, that they are the expected product of a deliberate strategy. But these same participants, if interviewed several times as the political process unfolds, may give quite contradictory interpretations at different stages.

All of these reasons contributed to a decision to follow the political process of one General Assembly committee intensively for an entire session (approximately three months). (A research fellowship gave me the opportunity to spend a year in New York.) The Fifth Committee of the General Assembly was chosen (Administrative and Budgetary Committee). This committee was considering exceedingly important, and highly controversial, issues related to the financing of the Middle East and Congo peacekeeping operations, and was the only committee to meet at a special session of the General Assembly that convened in May and June 1963. Because members of the committee in permanent missions were active between the two sessions, although not in public meetings, it was possible for me to follow committee activities intensively for nine months. In retrospect, the fall session of the committee provided an opportunity for laying the groundwork (through learning the issues, contacting informants, and experimentation with research techniques) for an intensive study of the special session of the same committee. But this was a completely unanticipated opportunity that did not emerge until the General Assembly passed a resolution calling for the special session in December. This unexpected opportunity increased the value of the research product manyfold.

Development of an Observation Technique

It was obvious that an in-depth study of the UN political process would require the use of a variety of information and data collection techniques. The records of public meetings and documentation were important for understanding the public sessions. Informants would be needed for obtaining information on activities outside the public arena, and some systematic interviewing would be needed as a check on informants. All of these techniques had already been used. For some time it had seemed to me that some kind of systematic observation technique would be useful in UN research. The opportunity that the researcher has for observation of much UN activity should make systematic observation particularly relevant. While relatively ad hoc observation of a variety of kinds of UN behaviors had contributed much to my understanding of the UN, I found it difficult to develop a systematic technique useful in studying important research questions, although my notebooks already contained much information acquired through observation (in addition to information obtained from conversations). I found that recording observations not only made me much more attentive to what was going on around me, but these observations often provided a basis for asking questions of informants. The delegate's lounge provides a remarkable opportunity for getting snapshots of the interaction patterns of the UN community, but the number of participants is so large that one can only recognize a few of them, and the number present at one time is often so great that it is impossible to see what is going on except for the persons in your immediate vicinity. My favorite daydream was the possibility of blowing a whistle at randomly selected times and asking all present to file out of the lounge past me, and to tell me why they were there and what they were doing when the whistle blew.

The observational method eventually used in my study of the political process in the Fifth Committee in 1962 and 1963 emerged between midnight and two in the morning in September 1960, at a session of the Security Council on the Congo peacekeeping operation. As I was making notes on the debate, I found myself making notes also on the delegate interaction that was taking place simultaneously with the debate. These notes simply recorded who talked to whom, and who took the initiative. They were particularly interesting as they revealed the considerable interaction that took place during the consecutive translation of speeches. (Most delegates do not listen to these translations because simultaneous translation is also provided.) This tended to confirm the often expressed belief that consecutive translation provides time for private consultation that would not otherwise be available. In order to gain insight on the potential for observation techniques in UN meetings, I made copies of a report on these observations available to some of the participants, with a request for comments (Alger, 1961b). In general, delegates tended to think that this kind of simple observation would not be very useful. For example, a highly effective, and widely respected, U.S. delegate wrote to me:

> How many of the conversations concerned pretty girls in the gallery and last week's parties I don't know. At any rate you can't assume that all conversations, even in a crucial period such as that one, were related to the business at hand; a considerable amount of other United Nations business gets done at such times, as does a considerable amount of personal conversation.

Academic colleagues who were knowledgeable of the UN, and of international relations in general, were also skeptical about the usefulness of simple observation, particularly because it was impossible to learn the content of those private conversations. Nevertheless, I decided to use simple observation in my study of the Fifth Committee. The most important reason was a rather compulsive curiosity to learn more about the significance of these private conversations. It seemed to me that knowledge of patterns would give additional leads to processes behind the public debate. This would require systematic data collection and analysis, because casual observation, without systematic records and analysis, did not reveal the patterns. Persistence was also dictated by my determination to develop some way to capitalize on the observational opportunities that the UN provides as a part of a multiple method strategy. While my interaction notes in the Security Council were made in early morning hours without deliberate plan, this activity was preceded by much thought about how systematic observation might be applied and intense inquisitiveness about the importance of those aspects of public debate that could be seen but not heard.

It took exceptional curiosity about the interactions observed for me to have the patience required to record interactions in 70 meetings of the Fifth Committee in the fall of 1962. Despite this high motivation, I thought of quitting many times. The first 18 meetings were utilized for developing the ability to recognize over 100 participants, and the last 52 meetings for recording 2,662 interaction situations (most with two participants, but some with more). Very early in this effort it became quite clear that interactions were related to highly significant parliamentary activity, and not just random movements of bored delegates. Observed patterns provided the basis for asking questions of informants that would not have occurred otherwise. Also, it gradually became evident that, regardless of what the interactors were talking about, they tended to be a select group, i.e., those most intimately involved in the behind-the-scenes parliamentary activity, working toward some kind of consensus or decision following the public debate. For the most part, those who were highly active in interaction seemed to be highly informed on what was going on behind the scenes. High interactors seemed to be much more useful in this regard than those most active in public debate.

The results of a "fishing expedition," in which I searched for systematic relationships between interaction patterns and the reputation of delegates for being capable and informed, noncommittee roles of delegates, regional groups, investment of money and men in the UN by nations, national characteristics, and participation in public speaking (Alger, 1968), were sufficiently interesting to warrant replication of interaction data collecting in the special session the following May and June.[6] The analysis of the special session revealed the value of interaction analysis in studying the UN political process. Of particular importance in this case is the fact that the interaction network was virtually a mirror image of the negotiation system behind the scenes—more useful as a guide to this network than participation in public debate. Thus, interaction observation came to be a very useful element in the array of techniques used in the study of the UN political process (Alger, 1971a).

Relations with Informants

My daily routine for intense study of the political process in the Fifth Committee was as follows:

[6]The two sessions are compared in Alger (1969).

1. Picking up relevant UN documents and reading them before the committee's activities began.

2. Arriving at committee sessions before starting time (10:30 A.M.) in order to talk with delegates who passed my seat, in the front row of the press gallery.

3. Taking notes on interactions and debate throughout meetings (in the special session a research assistant made a record of interactions), taking advantage of any opportunity to talk to delegates that passed.

4. Joining the stream of delegates moving to the lounge and the bar after morning and afternoon meetings.

5. Sitting in the lounge when the committee was not in session, taking any opportunity to observe members of the Fifth Committee or to talk to them about committee activity behind the scenes.

6. Occasionally lunching with participants. Although it would have been possible to have lunches with delegates every day, either at my initiative or theirs, UN lunches often take as much as two hours. Since this required spending too much time with one person, I tended to float around the lounge during the lunch hour and have a sandwich or impromptu lunch with someone about 2:00 P.M., one hour before the committee normally resumed meeting.

7. Utilizing all available free time to record information obtained from conversations.

8. Arriving home around 7:30 or 8:00 P.M. and, after dinner, spending an hour or two typing up notes on the day's conversations with delegates. Reading these notes, looking at interaction patterns, and reading documents picked up during the day, provided an agenda of questions for discussions with delegates the following day.

After both the fall session and the special session, informants were interviewed for additional information on issues, the political process, and the activities of individual participants. In addition, informants, including a member of the secretariat, read a descriptive account of the negotiations in the special session and gave corrections and reactions on this draft to me.

In contacts with delegates I gave priority to informants, whom I had selected because of their knowledge of, and involvement in, behind-the-scenes activity. Most of these delegates are exceedingly busy. Why would they take time out of their busy day to tell a researcher what was going on? I never asked this question, although I have some hunches. It seems that the most fruitful relationships develop between researcher and participant when both have something to gain from the relationship. The researcher is likely to be most successful in achieving his goals if he is sensitive to what he is giving the participant in exchange, although it may often be the case that the participant has not even made the exact nature of the exchange explicit to himself. What can the researcher give the participant?—enjoyment from talking to someone intensely interested in his activity who has a different perspective than other participants, an opportunity to try out new ideas on someone who is not a participant, an opportunity to acquire knowledge about academic work on the UN, and an identification of the participant with academic life in the past and/or an aspiration for becoming so associated in the future. Attention from an academic researcher implies that the participant is engaged in something considered worthwhile by outsiders. And finally, the participant may desire to convey to others his knowledge of what the UN is really like or to ensure that the views of his nation or region of the world are adequately reported.

As a regular attendant at the Fifth Committee, spending virtually full time at this activity, I was surprised to find that I was much more informed on the activities of the committee and some of the issues being debated than many of the delegates, particularly some from smaller delegations that were simultaneously following other committees and perhaps had responsibilities for other matters at their mission. This knowledge was something I could exchange with delegates. Many times, as committee members passed me on entering the room I would be asked simple factual questions. "When are we expected to vote on this issue?" "Has a resolution been introduced yet?" "Are we going to have a meeting tonight?"

Maintaining relations simultaneously with some twenty-five informants from one committee, who are involved in intense interactions, and who all observe each other in conversations with the researcher, make the researcher self-conscious about how his activities are being perceived by participants. It is important for him consciously to endeavor to act so as to engender no suspicion that he is working for the delegation of his own country. Perhaps this is most difficult for the researcher from a superpower. As contacts develop it is important not to create the impression that you are working for one bloc or regional group. But, as you are observed in contact with many nations from many regional groups, will this not inhibit anybody from telling you anything? No, and one reason that it does not is that there is much that the researcher needs to know that is already known by many delegates from many nations and groups. For example, information on negotiations between groups is known by many but can only be obtained by the researcher from the participants themselves.

It is clearly more difficult to obtain information about negotiations and debates *within* groups and *within* delegations, as well as opinions and attitudes about the performance and abilities of other delegates. But it is possible over a period of time for the researcher to develop a sufficiently close relationship with individual delegates so that they will provide information and opinions on these kinds of issues. One never fully understands why trust develops between two delegates, or between a delegate and a researcher, but I had a strategy that I hoped was helpful. I expressed genuine interest in the opinions, attitudes, and perspectives of all, and tried to keep my own views to myself as much as possible. Although I learned many things that I knew were known only to a few (e.g., the name of the author of a specific resolution that was actually sponsored by others), I kept these things to myself. I resisted a frequent temptation to parade my knowledge before a delegate in order to impress him. This was done primarily to give informants the impression that I could keep confidences, since I was sometimes told things with the request that I keep them to myself. It seemed that one way to demonstrate to an informant that I could keep a confidence was not to tell him things I learned on the same basis from other people. This restraint on passing on information was also imposed by my wish to intrude on the process I was trying to study as little

as possible. Actually this was a more stringent restraint than keeping confidences requested by delegates.

NEED FOR A COMPARATIVE PERSPECTIVE

While United Nations headquarters involves representatives of virtually all nation-states in a broad range of issues, it is only one of many headquarters of international governmental organizations, and only one of many headquarters of organizations in the UN system. As time passed, I became increasingly uneasy that the conclusions of my work were based on activity at only one of these headquarters. Therefore, after eight years of research focused on the United Nations in New York, I spent fourteen months in Geneva, in 1966-1967. Geneva is a secondary United Nations headquarters, where UN activities such as the United Nations Conference on Trade and Development and the UN High Commissioner for Refugees are located. It is also the headquarters of several specialized agencies in the UN system: General Agreement on Tariffs and Trade, International Labor Organization, World Health Organization, and World Meteorological Organization. The value of a comparative perspective was overwhelmingly confirmed by my work in Geneva, and I learned many things from this comparative effort that were unanticipated.

While a basic element of my strategy in Geneva was to learn as much as possible about the substantive issues and differing organizational forms of the Geneva institutions, I planned to do this while replicating certain aspects of my research on the political process in New York. I was interested in finding out if patterns of cooperation and conflict varied across different organizations and issues. Could it be said that participation in the United Nations was creating patterns of affiliation and cooperation that cut across political alliances, thereby tending to restrain violence in the international system?

An important unanticipated consequence of this effort was insight on the degree to which methods are influenced by the cases which they examine. For example, I attempted to replicate observation of General Assembly committees in New York by observing assemblies of the Geneva agencies at the Palais de Naciones. The layout of the committee rooms in the Palais made this impossible. In New York observers sit on a higher level than the delegates, with an excellent view of all activity in the room. If one wished to construct a laboratory for observing UN activity, he would not do it much differently. But in Geneva the observer sits close to the committee, on the same level, and cannot get an adequate overview for systematic observation. Thus, comparable data just could not be obtained.[7]

It was possible to observe the smaller governing councils of the Geneva agencies who assemble in meeting rooms in their own headquarters. Yet even here there were difficulties. For example, the council of the World Health Organization adjourns during each session for a coffee break, deliberately intended to provide an opportunity for informal discussion. This diminishes the tendency of delegates to move about during the meeting, and interaction is clustered during the coffee break, when it is impossible for an observer to obtain a systematic record.

If overlapping patterns of alignment are to be measured, data on voting patterns are very useful. This, of course, requires roll-call votes. But the Geneva agencies very rarely have roll-call votes. When they do, it is often in the context of the intrusion of an item on the New York agenda into a Geneva agency—such as the Middle East conflict, disarmament, Vietnam, etc. Thus, the extensive roll-call vote analysis applied to General Assembly votes is useless. Alternative methods must be sought to study alignment patterns.

Following an ongoing political process through contacts with informants was also exceedingly more difficult because the "central switchboard" was missing in the Palais—i.e., the delegate's lounge. There was a lounge in the Palais, but it was small and did not serve the same function, partly because it was not as central to the delegates' traffic pattern as the New York lounge, and also because newspapers, telephones, and paging services were not provided. Food and bar service was on a much smaller scale. Because of the arrange-

ment of central corridors and lounges in New York, you can hardly fail to see any delegate present—unless he has a careful plan for avoidance. In Geneva you must make much greater effort. This requires a much more explicit strategy for developing and maintaining contact with informants.

While the different Geneva milieu disrupted my advance comparative research strategy, nevertheless, I obtained important comparative insights. My Geneva experience demonstrated the impact of architecture and the availability of personal services (such as telephones and refreshments) on political processes. The very small number of roll-call votes, and their slight relevance to actual issues being handled in Geneva not only demonstrated the limited usefulness of highly developed methods for analyzing roll-call votes but also suggested a reexamination of General Assembly roll-call vote analysis. While more numerous, they are a rather skewed sample of UN issues (Alger, 1973, p. 223).

The Geneva experience also intensified my anxiety about the nation-state unit of analysis that did and does dominate international relations research. Earlier I was concerned that researchers establishing data banks on nation-states erred by blithely collecting and manipulating data on units as different as Malta and the United States. The Geneva experience challenged the nation-state unit of analysis in yet another sense. For example, in Geneva people from several national government departments are observed sitting behind the sign "United States." These representatives reflect a diversity of professions, governmental and private interests, and values—in regard to human rights, medicine, labor, meteorology, etc. Members of Congress and a variety of private citizens also participate. It is a tremendous intellectual leap to treat all of these participants, with their diversity of regional and functional clientele—within the United States and outside—as a single actor. Yet all of this activity is coded in data banks as "United States," without any explicit justification. This is not to say that this coding custom might not be useful in answering certain research questions. But it is not appropriate for all research questions, and it obscures the ability to perceive important dimensions of international relations.

_____

[7]Nevertheless, the Geneva experience stimulated a systematic comparative study of documentary records of debates (Alger, 1971b; 1973).

SOCIALIZATION OF THE RESEARCHER

Perhaps the most important benefit from the Geneva experience was disengagement from intense involvement in the network of international relations researchers in the United States, thus giving me an opportunity to evaluate this experience and relate it to alternative networks in Europe. This enabled me to sense more clearly than ever before the degree to which the substantive interests and methods of U.S. scholars are shaped by the society in which we live, and the slight degree of awareness we have of the impact of the interests and norms of specific sectors of United States society on our work.

Observation of the economic and social activities of the United Nations in Geneva was helpful in this regard. At the time I went to Geneva, United States scholars were giving but slight attention to these activities. While some economic and social programs are headquartered in New York and extensively debated in the General Assembly and other bodies, the United States press, public, and scholars give them slight attention. In Geneva they are at the center of the stage. Here the emerging confrontation between the rich and the poor nations seemed much more pronounced. The degree to which the United States (along with other big powers) was blocking effective response of the UN system to these issues was more clearly perceived.

In this context, which now included the headquarters of UNCTAD, the degree to which the United States scholars were obsessed with conflict resolution was more readily perceived. Even when economic and social issues were considered, it was in terms of their likely contribution to conflict reduction. Yet the different agenda and milieu of Geneva caused me to wonder why conflict was the dependent variable of so many United States international relations scholars. Why was social and economic justice not considered as an end in itself? A quite plausible answer is that American society, particularly the institutions that support most research, give priority to international order. It is not surprising that the research of United States scholars, as with scholars in other countries, is affected by their social context. Yet, the lack of awareness that most United States international

relations scholars had (and still have) of the influence of certain sectors and institutions of their society on their research paradigms is surprising in the light of our self-consciousness about research methods.

Viewing United States scholarship from outside the country also helped to stimulate my slowly emerging perception of international relations within social science, and the degree to which these relationships have an impact on the achievements and potential value of our work. It had never occurred to me before that international systems of social scientists tend to mirror the nation-state system. Thus, the "big powers" in social science are the same as the "big powers" in the nation-state system. Social scientists in these countries have the most resources, dominate international associations, export their methods and research paradigms, attract a brain drain of talent, and have a great influence in determining which problems are studied through the control of a high percentage of research grants. This dominance by scholars from a few countries creates the same suspicions of the powerful that are found within the nation-state system, and is a deterrent to the development of knowledge about international relations that will be perceived as useful outside the countries that produce it. Yet, the sector of United States social science with which I identify aspires to produce knowledge that is universally valid and useful.

In retrospect, it is ironic that one of the first concerns in my research on the United Nations was the socialization of participants *in* the United Nations. I was not as aware as I might have been of the impact of the research "laboratory" on the researcher. Certainly I understood that my evolving research strategy was a product of the learning that was taking place as I attempted to apply new methods in social contexts that I had not experienced before. But I was not aware of the degree to which research involvements were having an impact on my basic orientation toward methods, toward the United States research community, and toward the basic issues of international relations.

It is also ironic that I early saw the value of observation as a research method in the United Nations "laboratory." As my research evolved I even became quite aware of my own involvement in the political process and attempted to minimize my impact while maximizing data collection opportunity. I even observed myself by including my own interactions with committee members in my observational data. Yet, only in retrospect do I realize the full impact on me of the global perspectives of the participants and the global array of issues I encountered in New York and Geneva.

OUR COLLECTIVE FUTURE

The foregoing research experiences, along with reflection on the state of our field, leads me to several overall conclusions. These are stated in the form of problems that we collectively face as we look to the future in the light of our collective efforts over the past decade. Four problems strike me as especially important:

First, and fundamental, has been our inability to break away from the nation-state as a unit of analysis. We are in the same position as a man standing in a field of daisies who is wearing pink-colored glasses—while looking for pink daisies. Of course, he sees them everywhere. By analogy, Barbados is a nation-state and the USSR is a nation-state and our nation-state glasses enable us to file away their attributes in data banks as though they were the same thing. On the other hand, we have depended on schools of business administration to collect data on multinational corporations, and data on the international activities of banks are not to be found in our data banks at all (although the assets of First National and Bank America exceed the GNP of all but 17 nation-states). This is because our nation-state glasses filter them out. Likewise, the activities in cities, the nodes of most international transactions, escape our attention. It is not only that our nation-state glasses prevent us from seeing the world as it really is, our tenacious preference for the nation-state unit of analysis also incapacitates our students and the public from thinking about alternative futures. How can they? We even destroy their capacity for seeing the present.[8]

[8] The concerns presented here have led to an effort to develop data on the international relations of cities, using Columbus, Ohio, as a "laboratory." Procedures developed in this project are now being replicated in several other cities. See Alger (1974; 1975).

Our nation-state "hangup" becomes more pronounced the more we depend on data for our research because this is the way virtually all data is aggregated—for nation-state units. This is partly our fault, but largely the result of the customs of national government statisticians. It is fair to say that nation-states, at least our perceptions of them, are largely the creations of statisticians. How can we develop data banks that are not self-fulfilling prophecies?

A *second* problem has been created by our lack of sensitivity to the impact of the geographic scope of our scholarly organizations, and the society in which we live, on our research. We have habitually, and without question, organized ourselves in the image of the things we study—into *national* organizations. We have not been mindful of the way in which the affluence of our nation, as well as its size, has affected our research agenda. Nor have we been conscious of the way in which our social class has affected our agenda. Yet we have pretensions that we are creating a universal science. Why have *we* been so concerned with "power" while our Latin American colleagues have been so concerned with "dependency?" Why are *we* so concerned with the management of conflict and the prevention of violence while our African colleagues are more interested in social justice? Why do *we* tend to see social justice as a means for preventing violence rather than as a condition to be pursued for its own sake? When we consider the special environment in which we work (affluent citizens in a big power) in comparison to most of our colleagues around the world, how can we think it possible for us alone to generate knowledge about international relations that has universal value? Because of the interdependency of major problems, and our penchant for focusing on ones that are important to *us*, is it not necessary for a research community to reflect the diverse priorities of the global system it is attempting to understand? For those of us who wish our findings to be applied, must we not have a community reflecting diverse interests for our work to be considered legitimate by practitioners representing different interests? Certainly the knowledge we generate will have little impact on the world if our findings are applied in only one country. Yet there is little likelihood that the findings of affluent white citizens from North America will be considered valid by the vast majority of the world who do not share these characteristics.

If we accept the necessity of creating a community of scholars that incorporates representatives whose interests in the international system are more diverse, how could we do it? How would it be possible for us to establish such a community in the face of the tremendous advantage in resources and facilities available for our interests in contrast with those available to our colleagues in Africa, Asia, and Latin America? (Have you seen any research lately on dominance and dependency in international social science?) Can patterns of dominance and dependency in our own transnational "community" be changed without first changing the international system which our own "community" reflects?[9]

Third, it is most unfortunate that our methodological training almost completely ignores observation. While training in observation would feature instruction in the development of quantitative indicators of social interaction, this is not really the basic issue. Training in observation would begin with the development of the researcher's sensitivity to his social context—his identities and social contacts, constraints on research priorities imposed by sources of financial support and the theoretical and value biases of these constraints. This training would also include the generation of an awareness of international knowledge systems, discussed in the last paragraph, in which all social scientists are involved. Observation training would train the young researcher to exercise restraint in drawing conclusions from data analysis until some form of observation (whether personal or through reading) had provided understanding of the context of the data. Sensitivity to context could be obtained by providing observational training in local institutions. But wherever possible any student planning major research on specific institutions should not consider his research complete without a period of personal observation.

Fourth, we have been negligent in sharing the fruits of our labors with our local communities, while relatively overly concerned with sharing our research with national governments. (Is this par-

tially a result of our tendency to look at international relations as primarily relations between national governments?) Are we concerned about the increasing dominance of the executive in our national government, particularly as it results from the increasing importance of foreign affairs? Are we concerned about the minimal interest and widespread ignorance of the public in international affairs. Are we concerned about the decline in international relations teaching at all levels? Has our own behavior helped to create these problems? Do we relate too much to Washington and distant communities of scholars and not enough to our own communities? Do we have a responsibility to help generate strong and highly informed international interest groups in our own communities?[10] If we agree that we have too narrowly defined the potential users of our research, how can we build the necessary global community of scholars and relate to our own communities at the same time without completely neglecting our responsibilities toward national governments? What, moreover, are those responsibilities?

The four main questions above, and those that flow from them, are difficult, but they underline the fact that we need to make more explicit the interdependencies between the character of our research community and our research findings. We also must make more explicit our choices of the groups and communities we serve. While we have been remarkably systematic and explicit in our study of people out there, we have been distressingly opportunistic and ad hoc in decisions about what we study and what we do with our research products, and woefully unconcerned about *why* we make the kind of decisions we do.

In conclusion, the title of this chapter could have been identical to one of my articles: "Participation in the United Nations as a Learning Experience." In terms of what those who enter its "classrooms" learn about the whole world, I believe the United Nations is the greatest university in the world—whether the participant be diplomat, doctor, lawyer, journalist, or scholar. Reflection on my own research experience there

---

[9]For further discussion see Alger and Lyons (1974).

[10]See Alger (1974; 1975) for one method by which international relations scholars can help to extend local awareness, comprehension, and involvement in international issues.

suggests that we should take exceptional care in choosing the "laboratories" in which we work and learn. Some "laboratories" offer experiences that liberate, so we can help students, colleagues, and a diversity of communities to face evolving future worlds more effectively. Other "laboratories" may imprison creative potential and inhibit capacity to develop analytic postures that can encompass future worlds. What we study, where we do it, and whom we serve largely determines what we become.

REFERENCES

Alger, Chadwick F. 1961a. "Non-resolution Consequences of the United Nations and Their Effect on International Conflict." *Journal of Conflict Resolution* 5 (Jun): 128-45.

———. 1961b. "Private Conversation in Public Diplomacy: A Microscopic Analysis of One Hundred and Twenty-four Minutes in the United Nations Security Council " Mimeo. Evanston: Northwestern Univ., Program of Graduate Training and Research in International Relations.

———. 1963a. "Comparison of Intranational and International Politics." *American Political Science Review* 57 (Jun): 407-19.

———. 1963b. "UN Participation as a Learning Experience." *Public Opinion Quarterly* 27 (Fall): 411-26.

———. 1965. "Personal Contact in Intergovernmental Organizations." In *International Behavior,* ed. Herbert Kelman, pp. 523-47. New York: Holt, Rinehart & Winston.

———. 1968. "Interaction in a Committee of the United Nations General Assembly." In *Quantitative International Politics,* ed. J. David Singer, pp. 51-84. New York: Free Press.

———. 1969. "Interaction and Negotiation in a Committee of the United Nations General Assembly." In *International Politics and Foreign Policy* (rev. ed.), ed. James N. Rosenau, pp. 483-97. New York: Free Press.

———. 1970a. "Methodological Innovation in Research on International Organizations." In *Political Science Annual, 1969-1970,* ed. James A. Robinson, 2: 209-40. Indianapolis: Bobbs-Merrill.

———. 1970b. "Research on Research: A Decade of Quantitative and Field Research on International Organizations." *International Organization* 24 (Summer): 414-50.

———. 1971a. "Negotiation, Regional Groups, Interaction, and Public Debate in the Development of Consensus in the United Nations General Assembly." In *The Analysis of International Politics,* ed. James N. Rosenau, Vincent Davis, and Maurice A. East, pp. 278-98. New York: Free Press.

———. 1971b. "Decisions to Undertake New Activities in Assemblies and Councils of the U.N. System." In *The United Nations,* ed. Edwin H. Fedder, pp. 165-88. St. Louis: Univ. of Missouri, Center for International Studies.

———. 1973. "Decision-Making in Public Bodies of International Organizations (ILO, WHO, WMO, UN): A Preliminary Research Report." In *Political Decision-Making Processes,* ed. Dusan Sidjanski, pp. 205-29. Amsterdam: Elsevier.

———. 1974. "The International Relations of Cities: Creating Images of Alternative Presents." Mimeo. Columbus: Ohio State Univ. Mershon Center.

———. 1975. "Your City in the World: The World in Your City: Discovering the International Activities and Foreign Policies of People, Groups and Organizations in Your Community." Mimeo. Columbus: Ohio State Univ., Mershon Center.

——— and Gene M. Lyons. 1974. "Social Science as a Transnational System." *International Social Science Journal* 26, 1.

Best, Gary. 1960. "Diplomacy in the United Nations." Ph.D. dissertation, Northwestern Univ.

6. The Stanford Studies in International Conflict and Integration

Robert C. North

My determination to study the origins of international conflict and war was an outcome of island-hopping experiences in the Pacific. Prior to Pearl Harbor I had been enrolled in graduate history courses, with a class in anthropology on the side, but nothing I had learned in them provided any rationale for the tasks I was called upon to perform in a string of engagements with Japanese forces. The whole enterprise impressed me as a supremely tragic and irrational way of resolving human differences. During frightful pauses, when there was nothing else worth thinking about, I wondered if there were not some more disciplined and insightful way, other than immersing oneself in the chronicles of earlier diplomacy and wars, to probe the sources of international conflict and violence. Perhaps there were better approaches to an understanding of the human condition than those I had tried.

During the week immediately following the explosion of the nuclear bombs over Hiroshima and Nagasaki, while transports combat-loaded for a landing on Kyushu were still anchored just off shore from our staging area on Mindanao, a column from a popular news magazine came to my attention. In it the author identified problems in international relations as among the most critical issues of the postwar world and identified several new programs that were already being organized in American universities for the training of future specialists. That night I wrote letters of inquiry to each of those institutions. Nine months later I was enrolled as a graduate student at Stanford University, attending classes in one of those programs.

From the way world affairs looked to me during the summer of 1946 I decided that relations between the Soviet Union and China would be a critical factor in world affairs during the years ahead. I therefore focused upon this issue and spent the next ten years studying it. In retrospect, I do not regret the time and energy expended, but by the mid-1950s I was growing more and more dissatisfied with my investigations. I had survived the Joseph McCarthy era relatively intact, and there was growing evidence that some of my intuitions about the Sino-Soviet relationship might soon be validated. But I had no satisfactory explanation for my personal rejection of some of the assumptions that had been shaping many public, governmental and even scholarly assessments of the Soviet Union, the People's Republic of China, the Cold War, and the general drift of international politics. To explain the course of events in terms of a communist determination to rule the world, or in terms of capitalist imperialism seemed entirely too simplistic. But prevailing balance of power theories also impressed me as inadequate. One evening, in the course of a long and candid discussion with a friend and colleague, I developed a sense of intolerable frustration. Although he knew a great deal about both China and the Soviet Union, and although, as citizens, our political inclinations were similar, I discovered that we proceeded from quite different assumptions and had almost wholly different views of the processes that were operating. It seemed to me that there must be some better way to proceed, some theory, some methodology, that would advance from explicit assumptions, observe some recognized canons of investigation, and yield findings that could be accepted or rejected according to some rational criteria and that would tend to be cumulative.

A few weeks later I read, quite by chance, an article in *Harpers Magazine* about a "new philosophy" that had emerged from physics, had invaded biology, and was beginning to influence some of the social sciences. The emphasis was on nesting systems and subsystems and upon a complicated interactivity of variables throughout—both "horizontally," between systems, and "vertically," within a single system. By a shift of perspective, any subsystem can be viewed as a system with subsystems of its own. The idea was presented that any substantial change in one part of a system, *whatever its causes,* was likely to bring about changes in other parts of the system and in the system as a whole. And any substantial change in a system, *whatever its causes,* could be expected to effect changes in any other system with which the first system was interacting. The emphasis was thus upon networks of interactions and upon complex patterns of *multi*causality.

Living systems (also, some nonliving systems) have certain characteristics in common. They encompass informational or signal subsystems that include the capability of making choices or decisions, and energy processing subsystems, that is, they can absorb energy from the environment, transform it in various ways, and apply it, through some effect or arrangement, in order to act, to perform work. They display allometry, which involves the tendency for a more efficient system (or subsystem)—a system able to metabolize or otherwise transform energy more effectively than others—to acquire a proportionately greater share of energy-rich resources than a less efficient system. And living systems are also characterized by equifinality, which means that different systems can reach approximately the same state by different paths of activity or development.

These ideas struck me like the proverbial thunderbolt. If they applied to human beings and their work—including nations and the international system—then it could be misleading to focus upon the Soviet Union and the People's Republic of China, per se. Rather, one needed to look at processes, interactions, relationships, interdependencies, flows—the behaviors of numerous variables relating numerous actors under a considerable range of different conditions. But what variables? What interactions? What relationships?

The article had mentioned the writings of three men, none of whom I had heard of previously: Erwin Schrödinger (a physicist), Ludwig von Bertalanffy (a biologist), and Kenneth Boulding (an economist). None of the writings referred to were in the main library at that time, but I eventually found them in the biology library—on the librarian's desk. He was surprised and delighted to learn that I was from political science, and I went back several times to discuss them with him.

Shortly thereafter Easton Rothwell, who was then chairman of the Hoover Institution where I was working at the time, encouraged me to obtain a seed grant from the Ford Foundation. With modest funds in hand, I was then all but immobilized by the dimensions of the undertaking. It was not a task that a lone political scientist could embark upon with equanimity. For a time Rothwell and I fostered a small faculty discussion group with representatives from different disciplines. But with a few exceptions, they tended to be so caught up in their own responsibilities and perspectives that they were not inclined to take the enterprise seriously. So we decided to mount a larger research project that would allow us to probe some historical situations in depth. About this time Rothwell left Stanford to become president of Mills College. After several months of investigation and discussion, I came to the conclusion that an examination of two or three international crises would be a good way to start. With a considerably larger Ford Foundation grant in hand, we initiated a study of the 1914 crisis.

At the start, I intended to complete the World War I study in a few months, and then move on to another crisis. That was in the autumn of 1958. By the early 1960s the research staff and I were still plowing our way through the six weeks between the assassination of Francis Ferdinand in late June 1914 and the outbreak of war in early August. It was a vastly larger undertaking than we had anticipated. Having decided upon content analysis as a methodology, we discovered that the translation of pertinent documents from the various languages into English was a formidable task to begin with, and the subsequent preparation of materials for content analysis was a task of Herculean proportions. The latter work was especially trying for student coders. The requirements of keen insight, precision, and seemingly endless drudgery were an invitation to nervous breakdowns. As the price was recognized as being too high, we began experimenting with machine content analysis, and Ole Holsti made a successful adaptation of the General Inquirer program which Philip Stone and others had developed at MIT.

During these years, the graduate students who worked on the project were the sustaining asset. Numbers of them rose above the drudgery to make contributions of the greatest importance. To watch them move on into productive careers of their own has been one of the most satisfying rewards of the enterprise.

By 1964 it was possible to assess in a general way what the yields and limitations of the crisis studies were going to be. The limitations were largely unavoidable—at least for the time being. Some of them stemmed from the methodology which, despite automation, was still enormously expensive in terms of time and effort as well as money. Thousands of hours still had to be spent in the collection and hand preparation of documents before any analysis could be undertaken. We experimented with simplified "high-speed" programs of analysis that required less manual work, and had some success—but with considerable losses of information, precision and nuance. Perhaps, when the technology of optical scanning is further developed, some of this massive preliminary drudge work can be eliminated, but in the meantime, the efficient application of content analysis is limited to relatively small amounts of documentation. The other limitation emerged from the nature of the crisis phenomenon itself.

Crudely put, a crisis is like the tip of an iceberg. It is a critical part—but still only a small part—of a much larger reality "down below." A crisis does not merely erupt. It is the outcome of powerful antecedent processes. From our studies of crisis, moreover, it was my conclusion that the intense, escalatory processes that characterize the phenomenon are so unstable that successful "crisis management" is likely to be chancy, at best. With respect to the Cuban missile crisis of 1962, for example, it is conceivable that if either Khrushchev or Kennedy had been someone else (or possibly, if either one had happened to be in a somewhat different state of mind), the outcome might have been quite different. It also disturbed me that our investigations so far had been confined almost wholly to the informational, signal, decision-making aspect of the systems under study. Where did the energy acquisition, energy transformation, energy application aspects of the system fit in? What about allometry? Was there not something in the concept of allometry that might clarify the relative growth and exercise of power among nations and differences in their ability to acquire, control, and exploit territory and a wide range of critical resources?

My concerns did not imply that crises should not be studied. Certainly, there are "better" and "worse" ways to make decisions in crises, and it is highly desirable that statesmen and their advisers know as much as possible about their dynamics. In a nuclear age, however, it is probably of equal importance to learn as much as possible about what "drives" nations to behave the way they do and about how crises might be avoided.

During the academic year 1964-1965 I was teaching on the Stanford University campus in Florence, and the slower pace of life in the villa was conducive to contemplation. Moreover, I found in the library there several volumes of the Cambridge history series—ancient, medieval, and modern—as well as Toynbee's *A Study of History* and a number of other standard works. I decided to go through these volumes, reading rapidly, and keeping a list of the "causes" of various wars as they were identified by distinguished historians. Suddenly, history began to make sense. The undertaking was so fruitful that I subsequently continued the search through a number of anthropology books and appropriate ethnologies.

In the course of this reading, I found many references to the "nature of man," to his greed, ambitions, love of power, reactions to uncertainty, fear, and threat, and so forth. Yet overall, my list of "causes" turned out to be considerably shorter than I had expected. What caught my particular attention, however, were scattered references to population growth, the effect of new technologies, and the unrelenting search for resources. Again and again it was noted that ample resources often contributed to increased populations. But increased populations, in turn, generated demands for more resources. And a technological advance often enabled a people to reach out for more resources. Some technologies made it possible to uncover domestic resources that had previously been unattainable, or to put old resources to new uses. But often a relatively advanced technology—technology in the sense of applied knowledge and skills—gave a people the capabilities, organizational cohesion, and political as well as military power to conquer their neighbors, or threaten them into submission, enslave them, drive them off, or exploit them in any number of ways, and thus gain access to new resources. Or, as frequently, they invaded sparsely settled, low capability regions that were rich in needed resources.

Occasionally (only occasionally) I came upon the suggestion that advances in technology also tended to generate new demands for resources—both greater amounts and wider ranges of resources required to fashion tools (and later, factories), to provide energy (slaves, draft animals, eventually wood, coal, oil), and materials for processing (minerals, fibers, foodstuffs, and so forth). Hence, population increases combined with advances in technology created increased demands which often led to a kind of lateral pressure, a reaching out for land, cheap labor, a variety of resources, and also markets. It was further evident that certain combinations of population growth and technological and economic growth tended to correlate with the development and exercise of political and military power. States and empires generating high lateral pressure tended to dominate, if not conquer, peoples with substantially lower capabilities—and to compete and often fight cataclysmic wars with high capability, high lateral pressure rivals.

This was explosive history, but the historians, while making frequent, though widely scattered references to all these phenomena, seemed never to have related them systematically, never to have perceived the theoretical potentials inherent in them. Nevertheless, to the extent that these propositions "tested out" when used in other modes of analysis, a certain cumulativeness would be achieved. At moments, during the first weeks in Florence, I had felt twinges of guilt from living serenely in this finest of all cities while other members of the project continued to code endless amounts of material for content analysis. Now I suddenly concluded that all this time in the villa library had been amply well spent.

On returning to Stanford, I assumed that in the course of a few months we could develop at least a "proto-theory," gather together a body of population statistics, indicators of technology, military and naval budgets, colonial populations and territories, casualty statistics, and other data and complete an analysis of the 1870-1914 period in the course of a year or two—a vast improvement over the drudgery and expense of content analysis. This turned out to be the worst sort of fantasy. Space does not allow a discussion of the many difficulties, but I was wrong on all counts (although the methodology does become cheaper and more efficient as refinements are accomplished): the theoretical propositions remained fuzzy and would not link together; we did not know how to translate them into equation form; far more data were required than I had ever imagined; there were gaps in the records, and alternate sources were sometimes grossly inconsistent. The casualty data were hopeless, and men-under-arms were not much better. There were problems of currency conversion. I had not the slightest notion of the appropriate methodology, and when I consulted with colleagues in economics, statistics, and elsewhere, most of them answered with grave caveats or a shaking of heads. Gradually, I got an inkling that there were some very serious difficulties associated with time series analysis.

As she was completing her doctorate at Stanford, Nazli Choucri came to work on the project. For the first year or two she spent most of her time expanding and refining the data (I suspect we shall be refining and expanding the data the rest of our lives), but then she took a summer of intense training in statistical methods at the University of Michigan, and soon she was doing path analyses of major power attributes and behavior during the 1870-1914 period. Some months later we had stacks of print-outs and a draft manuscript weighing about ten pounds and utterly unintelligible to anyone but us. We thought we had made spectacular progress.

Then Hayward Alker came out to the Stanford Center for Advanced Study in the Behavioral Sciences, which is located in the hills back of the campus. When he saw what we had done he was ecstatic and appalled at the same time—ecstatic over the basic conception of what we were doing, but appalled by the way we were doing it. This was a turning point: whatever we did thereafter, we knew that Hayward was watching with an intensely critical but sympathetic eye.

Just as the "proto-theory," the data, and the methodology seemed to be straightened out, we confronted serious problems of funding. We had survived more than a decade on the generosity of the Ford Foundation, but Ole Holsti was now winding up the content analysis studies at the University of British Columbia, and his book, *Crisis, Escalation, War* (1972), which reported on the 1914 research, was well under way. If the Ford Foundation felt that they had invested enough in the enterprise it was understandable. Fortunately, Tom Milburn, as director of Project Michelson at the Naval Ordnance Test Station, China Lake, California, had been giving us supplementary support, and when that gave out the Office of Naval Research and ARPA picked up the tab. We owe considerable debts to Raymond Tanter and others for helping to see us through this difficult period. Then, during the campus protests of the early 1970s, we began to receive student criticism, sometimes quite bitter, for accepting Defense Department funds. The main charge was that whereas we might be investigating the antecedents of war with benign intent, there was nothing to stop our sponsors from adapting our findings for their own purposes. I was personally dubious about this argument. It was difficult to identify anything in that ten pound 1870-1914 opus that could advance the United States cause in the Vietnam War—unless it were dropped from an airplane. But the protesters had a point, and it also became evident soon enough that Defense funding in the social sciences, even in small amounts, offended some of our colleagues, embarrassed the university, and did indeed involve some moral ambiguities. Fortunately, at the last possible moment, we received a grant from the National Science Foundation.

When Nazli moved to MIT, she began working with the TROLL system, which brought a whole array of rigorous statistical controls to bear upon time series analysis. This was a godsend and, like Hayward's generous involvement, a major turning point. By this time, Nazli was using econometric techniques, rather than path analysis, and she had

developed a promising system of simultaneous equations which was an enormous advance over our earlier arrangement of equations. Although we were still dissatisfied with several aspects of what we had done, the work began to look almost respectable. It was none too soon. Fourteen years had now elapsed since the inception of the project, and one of the more unnerving aspects of the enterprise had been the occasional flicker of doubt in the eyes of a respected colleague or friend. Fortunately, there were many people who never wavered in their support. Also, Ole Holsti's book was now in press, and we had a shorter, greatly revised, and much more readable manuscript underway on the 1870-1914 period. There were still some weaknesses in our longer-range study (we had handled trade improperly, for one thing), and if we had known at the beginning some of what we knew toward the end, we would have done a number of things quite differently. But we felt confident that we had established an important bench mark in this type of research.

One of the more promising advances Nazli had achieved was the capacity for simulation and forecasting. Using the causal analysis of the time series data as a base, and the system of simultaneous equations, she was now able to simulate the processes of the 1870-1914 period and do "retrospective forecasting." That is, she could enter data from the early part of the period, allow the simulated output to track the "real world" behavior of an independent variable, and measure the error. This procedure served as a rigorous test of the hypotheses that were being exercised.

It would be satisfying to report that—having advanced from some explicit assumptions and having observed some recognized canons of procedure—we could now report upon a fully tested and fully validated theory. This is not yet possible. By switching to this type of research from more conventional approaches, we seem to have traded one set of difficult problems for another. Yet, despite this consideration, I think we do have findings in *Nations in Conflict: Domestic Growth and International Violence* (Choucri and North, 1975) that can be accepted or rejected or qualified according to some fairly rational criteria. And while making full allowance for our own errors of judgment, I suspect that many of the difficulties are deeply inherent in the reality we are investigating.

Although our findings tend to support the general thrust of the "proto-theory," we found that our initial assumption of equifinality was being well demonstrated. In other words, as reported in *Nations in Conflict: Domestic Growth and International Violence,* each of the major powers during the 1870-1914 period followed its own particular path toward large-scale violence, and this led to a considerable amount of inconsistency among the findings. This means that the theory as a whole is still inadequate and that a large amount of further research and testing will have to be done with other countries and other time periods before a full-blown theory can be presented.

As the work now stands, we cannot be certain exactly where the adjustments and corrections need to be made, since there are numerous possible sources of error that may account for our current inability to explain the inconsistencies. These include errors in the data sources we relied upon; faulty verbal hypotheses; faulty translation of the hypotheses into equations (we *know* that trade was improperly entered into the equations); and faulty choice or construction of indicators. This latter consideration—the correct choice and construction of indicators—represents a major enterprise in itself. It is a problem that will require vastly more thought and experience. We need to develop an underlying "theory of indicators." A further difficulty is the fact that one is dependent, in the choice and construction of indicators, upon the data that have been collected and made available by governments and other agencies.

The quality of data presented difficulties at every step. Many of the most serious errors and inconsistencies reside in the sources we depended on, but others were of our own making. Some data gatherers and processors are better than others (the work requires a certain disposition, as well as skill and intellect), but I am gradually coming to the conclusion that no single data handler can be relied upon, and even back-up systems are fallible. (This consideration gives me chills when I contemplate the implications of intelligence, police, credit bureau, and other data banks gathering information on the citizenry.) There is no substitute for refining and re-refining the data.

A fundamental methodological difficulty emerges from what James Caporaso has referred to as a three-way tug of war among empirical fit, parsimony, and falsification: a shift of emphasis in any one of these three directions tends to involve trade-offs with the other two. No doubt our handling of the problem can be improved upon, but I am not at all sure that the problem itself can be satisfactorily solved. In recent decades the "hard" scientist has learned that "reality" is extremely elusive, that even efforts to identify it can bring about alterations in it. For the social scientist the reach for reality can be like grasping at vapors.

Given these realities, we can only report: (1) what we have done; (2) how we have done it; (3) what the tentative findings are: (4) what the failures are; (5) some possible explanations for the failures; and (6) how we think they can be corrected.

In the meantime, we are cautiously optimistic about the potentials for this type of quantitative research. Since the inception of the project in 1958, we have used three broad types of data: attribute data, cognitive data, and action data. The *attribute data* fall into two main categories of variable: (a) fundamental "master variables" such as population, technology, territory, and energy and other resources; and (b) allocation data (investments in agriculture, industry, services, military expenditures, expenditures for health, education, welfare, and the like). The *cognitive data* include perceptions, attitudes, decisions, the affects or emotions that affect attitudes and decisions, statements of goals and interests, policies, and the like. And the *action data* include (a) imports and exports, troop movements, currency flows between nations, and so on and also (b) metricized or scaled action data, such as those data produced by Charles McClelland, by the Lincoln Moses-Richard Brody scale, by Edward Azar, and others.

In the long run I expect the development of tools that will make it feasible to use all three types of data simultaneously and interactively in computerized modelling, simulation, and forecasting. But this eventuality will depend upon a great many improvements in tools (satisfactory optical scanning, for example) and in methodology. In the meantime, we stumbled upon a simple-minded insight which enhances the possibilities for relatively easy but controlled consideration of values and decisions in the quantitative analysis.

During our attribute analysis the objection has frequently been raised that we deal only in "dry," "inhuman," or "dead" statistics that have nothing to do with real people, or with what they value or with how they feel. In one sense, this is correct. But it gradually dawned on us that every single datum we employed in the attribute analysis was the result, the "trace," so to speak, of a very human decision that someone had made in the past. Every increase in a country's population is the outcome of a decision made, consciously or unconsciously, by some man and some woman, to have a child. Every transfer or transformation of a resource is the outcome of a human decision. Every allocation is the result of a decision to commit time, energy, resources, knowledge, and skills to one undertaking rather than another. And so it goes.

Much of the confusion about values and decisions, we now believe, emerges from the failure to distinguish between professed values—the values that are enunciated in speeches, proclamations, protests, treaties of friendship, statements of national intentions, values, goals, and the like—and the values that are actually invoked and which thereby produce whatever data are collected and preserved. In these terms, a nation's budgetary allocations, its expenditures, the conditions of its trade, its acquisitions of territory, its movements of troops, its establishment of military bases overseas, and so forth—these are quantifiable (and often chillingly accurate) indicators of the *operational* values of that society (though not necessarily the operational values of any individual citizen, except insofar as he or she has become involved in a particular outcome by paying taxes, for example, even though disapproving of their expenditure on a war in Vietnam or an invasion of Czechoslovakia).

Viewed this way, attribute data allow the investigator to infer the operational values of a society, *retrospectively,* with considerable confidence. They are inherent in his data. But what about future-oriented simulations and forecasts? How can the experimenter foresee what values a society is likely to invoke in the future? Clearly, there is no possibility of a "crystal ball" type of forecast. The values that are operationalized may change substantially. Couples may "decide" to have fewer children. Statesmen, under pressure or through their own volition, may decide to allocate less to the military establishment and much more to health or education or welfare. Environmental considerations may begin to override the disposition toward growth, and so forth. But these uncertainties do not necessarily eradicate the potentials of the tools we have in mind.

If retrospective analysis reveals the trends and outcomes of the last twenty-five or fifty years—and by strong inference the values that were more or less consistently invoked by various societies over that period of time—the investigator can then make "base-line" projections over the next twenty-five years on the assumption that the trends (and the margins of error in his own retrospective "forecasts") will hold for that period of time. Then, employing sensitivity analysis, he can introduce, in a controlled way, whatever different values he thinks might be invoked—fewer children, less money for armaments, more money for education, less growth, more attention to the environment—and observe the consequences. In this way it should be possible to generate not one, but dozens, perhaps hundreds, perhaps thousands of alternate futures. As the methodology improves, the investigator might be able to specify some of the costs and benefits associated with each major alternative, together with some indication of who is likely to share in the benefits and who seems likely to bear the costs.

Like the findings from the work that we have accomplished so far, the results of this type of research will be somewhat different from what I envisaged during the mid-1950s. In those days I had a somewhat simplistic notion that it should be possible to "prove something." Now it seems to me unfortunate that, beginning somewhere around junior high school, we are encouraged to believe that the purpose of social science research is to "prove" some thesis. Except in a rather narrow, legal sense, I doubt that any such thing is possible, and what is more, life might be much less livable if it were. What this kind of research does is to offer alternate explanations and suggest probabilities. It clarifies relationships and processes, rather than final states. It provides new world views and new feelings for life. It greatly expands one's awareness of possible alternatives. For me, it has wholly transformed my perspectives: I shall never again be able to view people or nations or the international system or the world at large the way I viewed them before we began—nor do I contemplate the future in anything like the same way. I now see all human affairs and their relation to the natural environment as intensely interactive. Along with Jay Forrester and others, I see large and complex social systems as exceedingly difficult to analyze, control, or even understand. I perceive every "improvement" as involving some more or less commensurate "cost." What we refer to as "progress" is likely to involve some trade-off between advancement on one dimension and retrogression on another. It often amounts to sawing out sections of the floor to enlarge the roof. I am dubious about "solutions." I am also suspicious of dogmas and ideological imperatives. Yet, year by year, I become more egalitarian in my dispositions. I am increasingly persuaded that more nearly equal access to resources and benefactions for all the people of the world may be a prerequisite for the long-term survival of humankind. For me, my new and continually unfolding perspectives of the world have made the research undertaking eminently worthwhile.

Notwithstanding all the uncertainties, I consider rigorous research into human affairs—the search for a better understanding of large and complex social systems—to be a major priority. There are certain dynamic patterns that I think will be found in many situations and on different levels of analysis. For example, we had fully expected the classical Richardsonian type of arms-race spiral to be common to many different situations. In fact, what the attribute analysis revealed was an ubiquitous but even more complicated set of processes. Domestic growth (population, technology, and so forth) contributed to competition between countries in arms expenditures, and on other dimensions. Thus, the Richardsonian action-reaction process was explained partly in terms of country A's response to country B (and vice versa), but also in terms of both countries' domestic growth. Moreover, just as domestic growth contributed to competition between A and B, so

also did the competition contribute to the domestic growth of A and B.

The arms race was a competition for superiority —for the number-one position in the hierarchy of military power. But we would expect to find a similar pattern described in a variety of situations where two or more countries are competing for a scarce resource. In part, at least, the demand of each country for the resource is likely to be generated by domestic growth. Moreover, to the extent that two or more countries, in seeking to satisfy their respective demands, are caught up in an action-reaction spiral, the competition is likely to encourage further growth, a further enhancement of demands, and an impetus for more competition. If the availability of the desired resource begins to diminish, the process is likely to be exacerbated—up to some threshold point where at least one of the rivals is no longer willing or able to participate in the competition.

The identification of such process patterns on a number of levels and in a variety of different situations will contribute to cumulativeness in the field of international politics. And a clearer understanding of such processes may prove useful in future policy making.

There are high risks in this type of research. No doubt some of us will go down many blind alleys and suffer several failures before truly positive results are reported. But I am persuaded, by now, that this is the way most substantial advances are achieved.

REFERENCES

Azar, Edward. 1970. "Analysis of International Events." *Peace Research Reviews* 4, 1 (Nov):1-113.

———. 1972. "The Potential of Events Research in International Relations: Investigating the 'Normal Relations Range.'" Studies of Conflict and Peace, Report No. 8. Mimeo. Chapel Hill: Univ. of North Carolina, Dept. of Political Science.

Choucri, Nazli, and Robert C. North. 1972. "Dynamics of International Conflict: Population, Resources, Technology, and Some Implications for Policy." *World Politics* 24 (suppl.): 80-122.

——— and Robert C. North. 1975. *Nations in Conflict: Domestic Growth and International Violence.* San Francisco: Freeman.

Forrester, Jay W. 1971. "Counterintuitive Behavior of Social Systems." *ZPZ National Reporter* (Jun): 1-5.

Holsti, Ole R. 1972. *Crisis, Escalation, War.* Montreal: McGill-Queen's Univ. Press.

McClelland, Charles A. 1964. "Action Structures and Communication in Two International Crises: Quemoy and Berlin." *Background* 7 (Feb): 201-15.

Moses, Lincoln E., Richard A. Brody, Ole R. Holsti, Joseph B. Kadane, and Jeffrey S. Milstein. 1967. "Scaling Data on Inter-Nation Action." *Science* 156, 3778 (26 May).

North, Robert C., and Nazli Choucri. 1972. "Population and the International System: Some Implications for United States Policy and Planning." In *Governance and Population,* vol. 4, ed. A. E. Keir Nash. Washington: GPO.

7. From Correlation Analysis to Computer Forecasting: Evolution of a Research Program

Nazli Choucri

One of the most important challenges in the study of international relations today is the development of reliable means of forecasting international outcomes. Forecasting is a problem of reasoning, of reducing uncertainty, and of bounded and disciplined speculation. It involves bringing theory, data, and methodology to bear upon our understanding of a specific substantive issue and translating this understanding into scientific terms for systematic testing, validation and replication (Choucri, 1974a, p. 63). Exploring the unknown, identifying possibilities associated with different outcomes, and isolating likelihoods of occurrences constitute the essence of forecasting.

The purpose of our work is to identify the determinants of conflict among nations and isolate the policies that could reduce the probabilities of international violence. Specifically, we have been developing empirical models to assist in (a) understanding the relationship among the multiple and interactive causes, (b) exploring the implications of alternative policies, and (c) undertaking contingent forecasts of alternative futures. This paper presents a critical review of our work to date, delineates its cumulative aspects, presents some specific findings, and describes our research program of forecasting in the field of international relations.

THEORETICAL DEVELOPMENTS: EMERGING PERSPECTIVES ON INTERNATIONAL CONFLICT

International conflict has been accounted for in a variety of ways—in terms of territoriality, aggressive tendencies, the protection of trade routes, the "mad" leader, imperialist drive, and so forth—but few systematic efforts have been made to provide some order among the contributing causes of conflict. Our approach has been to decompose the problem of war and, through quantitative analysis, identify various determinants and isolate the weights attributable to each (Choucri and North, 1972, p. 80). The basic procedure employed is to isolate those aspects of international behavior that are most amenable to systematic inquiry, develop indicators of their underlying characteristics, and employ these as the initial basis for developing and testing empirical models of international conflict. In any investigation of this kind, however, a certain parsimony is required which, if unchecked, can border on oversimplification. The problems encountered were extensive, and, at each stage, our solutions have reflected both the achievements and limitations of the field of international relations at that point.

In operational terms, our research procedure was to (1) begin with simple correlation analyses of military and economic variables; (2) isolate their relative weights in contributing to conflict and warfare; (3) develop models of these interrelationships; (4) test these models against empirical data from different historical situations and cases; (5) observe the results and abstract functional relationships; (6) reformulate the model, taking into account misspecifications, changes in the phenomena under investigation, and so forth; and (7) respecify the model for purposes of forecasting and policy analysis.

We began with an analysis of national profiles and found that international behavior appears to be related to national attributes and capabilities. It gradually became clear that the underlying determinants of conflict behavior may lie less in observable factors which are readily defined as political, than in aspects of national orientation and characteristics which have conventionally remained outside the bounds of politics: Much of what we call politics may be shaped and constrained by factors which often lie beyond the political sientist's disciplinary concerns.

On the basis of empirical analysis we have gradually developed the view that the dynamics of *population growth,* those of *resource* constraints, flows and utilization, and those related to *technological* developments and transfers together shape political behavior and determine the parameters of permissible outcomes (Choucri, 1972).

Careful and often painstaking analysis of different situations, different nations, different times and different places yielded important clues regarding the relation of these three aggregate variables to conflict behavior. Analyses of the origins of World War I, the interwar period, Germany and Japan, the Scandinavian countries over a century, and the Middle East today, among others, provided the basis for this population-resource-technology

perspective. The causal network appears to be as follows:

Population acquires political implications when the combination of growing population and developing technology places increasing demands upon resources, resulting in internally generated pressures. The greater the pressures, the higher is the likelihood that national activities will be extended outside of territorial boundaries. If two or more countries with high capability and high pressure tendencies extend their interests and their psycho-political border it is highly probable that the two opposing spheres of interest will intersect. The more intense the intersection, the greater the chance that competition will assume military dimensions. When this happens, competition may be transformed into an arms race or a cold war, and perhaps even into a conflict. At the more general level of abstraction, provocation can be considered the final stimulus for large-scale conflict or violence. But an event will be considered as provocation only in a situation that has already been dominated by expansion, competition, armament tensions, and increasing levels of conflict behavior.

We have found that: (1) the dynamics underlying the development of conflict situations are highly volatile; (2) they change over time; and (3) longer-range causes differ from shorter-range, more immediate considerations. Rarely is the outbreak of war a random phenomenon; it is the consequence of developments which originate in aggregate demographic, ecological, technological, and economic factors. *This is not determinism.* It is an explicit attempt to formalize the constraints on national behavior and on political outcomes. The purpose is to reduce our uncertainties concerning future trends and events within some range of probability. The philosophical tone is one of probabilism.

Such a perspective is necessarily interdisciplinary, drawing upon current work in demography, in the economics and politics of resource allocations, flows and distributions, and in problems and processes of technological development. It has expanded our theoretical interests into directions which were not foreseen during the early years of our research. We also became concerned with the ways by which long-term considerations provided the parameters for short-term behavior and with the operational linkages between long-term dynamics and short-term imperatives. The connections are still loose, and neither our own empirical analyses nor those of other scholars have provided sufficient indication as to the nature of the operational linkages. This problem emerges as one of the greatest shortcomings of quantitative approaches to international relations, and one which we are profoundly aware of. So, too, the problem of "intersection" among time perspectives remains largely unresolved.

The major theoretical developments resulting from earlier empirical analyses was a movement from profile analysis to *process* analysis and an awareness that the determinants of international conflict must be viewed as a dynamic process, and not simply as a series of correlational factors. An important step in the direction of process analysis has been to depict the general behavioral dispositions of nations with different population-resource-technology profiles, and, on that basis to identify war-prone and peace-prone tendencies (Choucri with the collaboration of North, 1972).

Developing the theoretical bases for modelling the dynamic processes that generate these (and other) *alternative* international behaviors amounted to a major challenge. Estimating the coefficients of a process model was only one side of the coin, the other is understanding the intricacies by which the model output is generated. It is extremely difficult to specify (conceptually and theoretically) the consequences of several second and higher order nonlinear feedback relations. This type of conceptual requirement is often posed by our attempts to understand the determinants of international behavior.

We attempted to further identify theoretically and empirically those factors that might be manipulable by national leaders for changing national behavior, and the associated costs of manipulation. Isolating the identifying manipulables and the policy instruments that might be employed to change the behavior of a system has now become a central concern of our work. Thus, providing the theoretical linkages between the underlying determinants of international violence, and the day-to-day concerns of the policy maker amounts to a challenge, one we have only begun to confront.

In sum, the theoretical basis of our investigations has been highly cumulative: We began by seeking to isolate the key variables that, on the basis of pilot investigations, appeared to be important in conflict situations and moved to: (a) developing profiles of attributes and behavior, (b) mapping different profiles unto different observable patterns of international behavior, (c) focusing on the interrelationship among population, resources, and technology as three critical macrosocietal determinants of international behavior, (d) adopting this three-dimensional perspective of international behavior as the basis for developing process models of international conflict, (e) seeking to link empirically long-term causes to short-term decision, and finally (f) adopting a policy focus and seeking to identify the interventions and instruments that might be employed to modify the behavior of a system or to reorient a war-prone system to alternative directions.

The present emphasis is on policies, instruments, and manipulables. It is on developing the theoretical basis for thinking about, modeling, and simulating future behaviors. And it is on delineating the theoretical and methodological bases for forecasting in the field of international relations. Our current investigations focus on the ties that bind nations in their attempts to meet their individual needs. Our substantive concerns are now extended to determining the parameters of *interdependence* among nations, the mutual sensitivities and vulnerabilities, and shared utilities (Choucri with Ferraro, 1974). We now seek to identify empirically the ties that bind nations in their attempts to meet their individual demands and to forecast future patterns of links and ties that may lead to conflict or violence. Analyzing patterns of global interdependence thus represents the most recent stage in the development of an evolving theoretical framework in the analysis of international conflict.

METHODOLOGICAL DEVELOPMENTS:
PROBLEMS OF A CUMULATIVE
RESEARCH STRATEGY

The first attempts in analyzing quantitative data were primarily of a correlational nature in that indicators of conflict were correlated with indicators of national attributes and characteristics, with the expectation that some preliminary inferences could be drawn from observable associations. Through trial and error more precise theoretical guidelines were developed and we acquired a more sophisticated perspective on international behavior and conflict that went beyond the statement in our initial request for support from the National Science Foundation.

From an interest in associations and correlations, we moved to dependence analysis (regression and path analysis) and gradually the questions we raised necessitated multi-equation causal modeling and eventually computer based simulation.[1] The errors we made at each stage can be described only as monumental, and in retrospect we remain impressed by the collective ignorance of such methodology in the field as a whole.

It is only in retrospect that we appreciate the time and effort spent on seemingly technical matters. Because there appeared no precedence in the field for such work, at each stage we remedied our own errors. Consultations with colleagues in other fields were invaluable. But the danger of acquiring some moderate sophistication in one methodology lies in attributing to it greater capabilities than is warranted by the algorithms involved. For this reason we began to look at *alternative* options available for the analysis of international processes. And we redefined our generic methodological problem as one of *identifying the best type of algorithms for analyzing different aspects of conflict behavior.*[2]

A combination of skepticism and eclecticism gradually governed our approaches to questions of methodology. We became concerned as much with ways of analyzing past data as with methods of drawing inferences concerning alternative futures. These developments led to an initial assessment of the philosophical underpinnings of the orthodox behavioral approach in the study of international relations. The assumptions underlying statistical analysis also became the subject of greater scrutiny than they had been during earlier years. And a

systematic search for alternative research paradigm resulted.

A concern with the costs and benefits of alternative methodologies for examining long-range system behavior led to an experimentation with system dynamics. System dynamics refers to a philosophical approach to complex systems as well as a set of algorithms for depicting nonlinear feedback relationships. Despite the current controversies concerning the uses of system dynamics as a methodology, we have found that its requirements pose serious challenges to our conceptualization of the processes leading to war. The first effect in this direction was revealing—though halting and tentative (Choucri, Laird, and Meadows, 1972). Since then we have attempted to combine the data requirements of statistical and econometric methodologies with the conceptual demands imposed upon the investigator by an approach, such as system dynamics, which requires as complete a specification of system behavior as possible.

In spite of the many uncertainties and the problems we encountered, we strongly feel that our methodological development has been highly cumulative. Alternative views concerning the nature of casuality and its operational indicators and alternative methodological approaches have become part of the methodological repertoire in most international relations courses. This is an extremely worthwhile development. The view of international "realities" has been broadened and many pertinent questions regarding the assumptions of the orthodox behavioral position have been raised.

In earlier years we were concerned primarily with linearities in variables and with the intricacies of bivariate analysis. The current challenges include modelling endogenous system change, taking into account system breaks and nonlinearities, specifying decision algorithms and learning processes, and so forth. We now lend greater emphasis to negative findings, to patterns of residuals, and to statistical anomalies or artifacts than we have tended to do in the past. Our present assessment is that our investment in time and energy over the past several years has yielded a high return at the methods level, one that perhaps exceeds the return at the theory level since gaps remain between the theoretical framework and the methodology. How-

---

[1] For these stages in the development of our work, see North and Choucri (1968), Choucri and North (1969), and Choucri (1973).

[2] An initial illustration is provided in Choucri (1974a).

ever, major developments in the analysis of international conflict have resulted.

THE DEVELOPMENT OF DATA SERIES:
PROBLEMS OF COLLECTION
AND DOCUMENTATION

Undoubtedly the most painful aspect of our work involved the development of time series data on the attributes, capabilities, and behavior of 12 powers from 1870 to the present. These data were collected at annual intervals from a series of sources, a system that provided a check against any inherent bias in the reliance on single source. In this respect we believe that we have contributed substantially to the availability of longitudinal data for the analysis of international relations. Portions of these series are now available to the academic community; others are still being refined. We have been hesitant to allow either colleagues or students to employ these data extensively until we have some estimate of measurement error for each individual variable.[3] This task is now completed.

In view of our interests in the underlying determinants of international behavior we have begun to collect information on resource flows—both mineral and energy—so as to identify the major networks of interdependencies among nations along a dimension which appears crucial to national security and international behavior. The current controversies concerning energy issues have reinforced our belief that much international behavior can be clarified by a careful analysis of transactions along the resource dimension. This perspective amounts to a variant on contemporary analyses of trade and aid flows and provides some useful additions to existing data banks. (See Choucri with Ferraro, 1974.)

The preoccupation with data collection has been accompanied by a tendency to "allow the data to speak for themselves," a situation that could be potentially misleading if theory is grounded entirely in observable data. Measurement error can often result in erroneous inferences. Data must be placed in their proper perspective; they must be used to seek out alternative explanations of observable phenomena. The present focus is

upon (a) articulation of the premises underlying the use of alternative data series, (b) the development of extensive documentation for each datum collected, and (c) the specification of the theoretical link amg underlying concept, empirical variable, and operational measure.

Documentation is itself a threefold issue: first, it must specify attributes and assumptions underlying individual data series; second, it must delineate the expected linkages among data, operational indicators, and underlying theory; and third, it must document the uses of empirical data in alternative strategies of analyses of computer modeling. Developing adequate documentation for underlying theory, operational model equations, computer language, and empirical data is acquiring an increasingly important role in our approach to quantitative analyses of international behavior.

SOME EMPIRICAL FINDINGS:
ILLUSTRATING A CUMULATIVE
RESEARCH STRATEGY

By way of illustrating the developments in theory, methodology, and quantitative analysis, we present some empirical findings from recent investigations. This is a highly selective review with only the most brief references and explanations given. However, sufficient information data bases, methodology, and sources are provided; the interested reader may refer to the original study.

National Growth and International Violence

The following findings are drawn from a recent study on the determinants of international violence.

[1] There are complex causal links among indicators of national growth and indicators of external expansion and violent behavior.

[2] Population growth and technological developments contribute to military capability: the relation is positive, causal, and direct.

[3] The higher the budgetary allocation to the military, the greater appear to be the expansionist tendencies of nations and the more violent the intersections among their spheres of influence. Such intersections, in turn, contribute to increasing military expenditures.

---

[3]This work represents one of the many collaborative efforts with Robert C. North, Stanford University.

[4] National growth, increasing military expenditures, and greater intersections among spheres of influence contribute to move violent international behavior.

[5] Military competition results more from domestic growth and expansion than from external factors. However, allocations to the military influence patterns of international alignments and, through feedback effects, military competition; thus, arms races are accentuated.

[6] Once competition sets in, action leads to reaction, and violent behavior results in more violence. A classical Richardson process describes the dynamics of interactions among nations which results from the expansion of national interests outside territorial boundaries.

[7] A conflict system is more sensitive to upward swings in military expenditures than to downward swings. Policies designed to decrease military expenditures have less impact on the direction of a conflict spiral, and are generally less effective, than are policies designed to increase military allocations. Such upward swings move the system toward greater competition, expansion, allocations to the military, and violence.

[8] A conflict system is characterized by strong inertial effects. Once the conflict spiral is set in motion, the underlying process determines overall system behavior, rendering almost all interventionist policies largely ineffective.

The theoretical base for these investigations, presented initially in verbal terms, is specified further in the form of a probabilistic model linking national attributes to international behavior. The empirical data are composed of annual observations for six countries over a 45-year period. The methodology employed is econometric analysis for estimating the coefficients of a system of simultaneous equations. The analysis was undertaken in TROLL/1, an interactive computer system developed by the National Bureau of Economic Research, which was designed to estimate, simulate, and forecast econometric models. Simulating the model has allowed for experimentation with alternative values of key coefficients in order to examine the implications of alternative policies upon the behavior of the system modelled (Choucri and North, 1975).

Determinants of National Expansion

The following findings are drawn from a simulation and forecasting model of lateral pressure, a term employed to refer to national propensities for external expansion. The forecasts to the year 2000 are based on a good fit between simulated and empirical data for 1930-1970 and on a set of assumptions generally accepted by social scientists, namely, that an ideal U.S. economy is one that is characterized by being balanced, with no petroleum shortages, and with a military budget that is no more than half the total government budget.

[1] An increase in technology generates an increase in the society's excess productivity, thereby increasing lateral pressure or propensities for external expansion.

[2] A decrease in technology generates a partial depression and, by extension, causes less lateral pressure.

[3] Any marked decreases in petroleum reserves create economic shortages that generate a decrease in Gross National Product and, by extension, a decline in lateral pressure.

[4] An increase in military expenditures leads to a slowing down of the GNP, to depression, to overproduction, and to technological stagnation.

[5] Although an increase in military expenditures generates lateral pressure, the effects are mediated somewhat by the negative impacts upon GNP; the net expansionist propensities are thereby lower than would be the case were GNP to continue to increase.

[6] An increase in the fraction of the total government budget allocated to civilian use allows GNP to grow faster, thereby generating underproduction and less propensity for expansion. The greater the civilian budgetary allocations, the lower lateral pressure appears to be.

[7] A decrease in population growth leads to a lower increase in GNP, which, in turn, causes less lateral pressure than would be the case were population to continue to grow.

The theoretical bases of these investigations are specified in a system dynamics process model of the structure of lateral pressure. The data are composed of annual observations for the United States, 1930-1970. These observations enabled the estimation of coefficients for the model, on the basis of which forecasts to the year 2000 were undertaken. The above results refer to the forecasts beyond 1970 (Choucri and Bousfield, 1975). The model was built in DYNAMO, a system dynamics language designed to model functional relationships in a feedback nonlinear system.

International Implications of Population Dynamics

The following findings are based on a cross-national study of population dynamics and international conflict.

[1] The role that population variables play in a conflict situation varies extensively: in some cases population factors provide the parameters of a situation and define the context within which a conflict unfolds; in others, population provides a multiplier effect upon a conflict by exacerbating the preexisting form or model; in still other instances, population may act as a variable, when in itself might change in the course of a conflict, or alternatively, cause a change in the nature of the conflict.

[2] In 38 of 45 cases of conflict in developing areas (1945-1971) population factors have been sole determinants in four cases. They were of (a) central importance in 11 conflicts; (b) major irritants in 10 situations; (c) minor irritants in 7 cases; (d) of background significance in 6 cases; and (e) they had no appreciable influence on the development or conduct of the conflict in 7 of the 45 cases examined.

[3] Population appears most frequently as a *parameter* of a conflict situation, then as a *multiplier* effect, and last in order of frequency, as a *variable* in a warring situation.

[4] Population *size* is most frequently a parameter; population *change* emerges most often as a multiplier upon an already existing conflict; population *distribution* is also a multiplier; and population *composition* emerges most often as a parameter of a conflict situation.

[5] There is no evidence that population density per se leads to conflict and violence.

[6] But there is a statistically significant positive correlation between the rate of population change and its criticality in a conflict situation in developing areas. The higher rate of growth, the more salient a factor population increase appears to be in the development of conflict and violence.

These findings are drawn from a study of population dynamics and international violence. Forty-five cases of conflict in developing areas were examined, drawing upon the files in CASCON (Computer Aided System for the Analysis of Local Conflict) and employing comparative case study analysis (Choucri, 1974b).

Energy Politics and Global Interdependence

The following findings are drawn from an analysis of the links, policies, priorities, and constraints that bind nations in their attempt to meet their respective energy needs (Choucri with Ferraro, 1974).

[1] There have been dramatic changes in the structure of the world petroleum system over the past 20 years. These changes are reflected in patterns of production, consumption, imports, and exports.

[2] These changes include (a) a transformation from the West as the focal point of petroleum production and exports to focal points in other areas of the world, and (b) changes in the rank order of exporting countries, again with a receding importance of the West.

[3] These changes have led to an increased reliance of consumer countries upon imports, an increased trend toward diversification in the sources of imports, and to clear asymetries with respect to mutual dependencies between imports and exports. In some cases the asymetries favor the importer, in others they favor the exporter.

[4] There have been important structural changes in the world petroleum system, particularly in the roles of multinational corporations and that of the Organization of Petroleum Exporting Countries.

[5] Although oil-producing countries rely heavily on consumer countries for trade in capital-intensive commodities, these commodities can be obtained from the consumers interchangeably, thereby providing the producers with a certain economic and political maneuverability.

[6] The balance of payments problem, from the perspective of the consumer countries is, in

fact, a problem of absorptive capabilities and surplus revenue from the perspective of the producers. This dual issue illustrates most dramatically the economic interdependencies in the world today.

[7] There are emerging networks of interdependence among the oil-producing countries, based on differentials in attributes and capabilities and upon complementarity in such differentials. This interdependence is having, and will continue to have, a strong influence upon global interactions and upon the future shape of the world petroleum system.

[8] Continued increases in petroleum prices will increase the consumer countries' investments in alternative sources of energy. A global energy system based on alternatives to petroleum will be characterized by different networks of links, ties, policies, priorities, and different configurations of inequalities in the international system.

[9] The major requisites for alternative global energy systems are defined by (a) alternative patterns of control over energy resources; (b) the distribution of energy resources; (c) the attendant price structure; and (d) the development of regulatory mechanisms for moderating global energy transactions.

[10] The nature of these system requisites would be very different depending on the type of international regime developed to regulate transactions and flows of energy. At least four different regime alternatives are identifiable: a free market regime, a joint regime, a multilateral regime, and an international regime. Each will invariably be characterized by different patterns of control, distribution, price, and regulation.

These findings are based on a cross-national analysis of the energy profiles, production, consumptions, and imports of the major consumers and producers of petroleum over the past 25 years and on a systematic assessment made regarding the implications of a world energy system based on an alternative to petroleum. The analysis included coal, nuclear energy (fission and fusion), solar energy, geothermal energy, tar sands and shale oil, and other exotica. Four dimensions of interdependence were considered in each of these cases: (a) economic issues and their political implications, (b) impact on terms of national security

and military strategy, (c) implications for global or regional community building, and (d) impacts upon the environment.

These are some brief illustrations of empirical findings based on recent work. There have been many drawbacks and many false starts and stops. But each stage drew upon the previous one and the progression from associations and correlations to causal modeling, simulation, and forecasting clearly represents a cumulative research effort. At the present time, the emerging focus on alternative forecasting methodologies, and on bringing them to bear upon our attempts to reduce uncertainties about the future, represents new directions of research. We now seek to develop reliable means of identifying the probabilities associated with alternative futures and policy interventions that might increase (or decrease) these probabilities.

FORECASTING IN INTERNATIONAL RELATIONS: A RESEARCH PROGRAM

Forecasting refers to the development of contingent and probabilistic statements regarding alternative future outcomes.[4] A successful forecast must account for (a) the direction of the activity modeled, (b) the direction of sharp breaks or reversals and the extent of change, (c) the period over which change is likely to persist, (d) the points in the system most amenable to manipulation and (e) the costs of policy interventions. The critical distinction between prediction and forecasting is one of contingencies and probabilities. A prediction usually dispenses with probabilistic interpretations; it is generally made in terms of a specific point or event. Forecasting, by contrast, focuses upon probabilities, contingent outcomes, and the specification of alternatives.

Forecasting in international relations is particularly challenging in view of the large number of variables in question, the magnitudes of the unknowns, and the propensities for random factors or exogenous shocks. All the methodological complexities associated with forecasting as such are compounded by the uncertainties of tomorrow's international realities.

[4]The following observations are based upon, and expand, the arguments in Choucri (1974a).

Forecasting forces us to think of *alternatives.* "Goods" and "bads" assume the same theoretical importance in a forecasting design: the distinction is imposed upon future realities by the motivations, preferences, and expectations of the forecaster. The major components of our research program in international relations forecasting include: (a) specifying the structure of the system to be forecasted; (b) identifying the role of theory; (c) comparing and experimenting with alternative forecasting methodologies; (d) delineating the different purposes and the different time horizons for alternative forecasts; (e) specifying the policy implications of forecasting and illustrating its relevance for the development of appropriate policy interventions; (f) systematically altering the values of key coefficients or variables to test the consequences of different policies; and (g) designing alternative futures and specifying the interventions needed *now* to realize alternative future designs.

Together, these seven issues have provided the foundation of an evolving approach to international relations forecasting.

So far we have completed two major empirically based forecasting studies in international relations. The first was designed to replicate the behavior of nations in conflict and to identify the policies that would have an impact upon the expansion of national behavior outside territorial boundaries as well as those that might reduce armament competition (Choucri and North, 1975). The strength of this study lies in a sound theoretical base, an empirically validated model of international conflict, a good simulation of system behavior, and some initial probes into the effect of alternative policies. However, the major effort has been in model building and simulation. The forecasting aspects of this study remain preliminary and tentative. In addition, its purpose was to examine the impact of alternative policies upon past behavior, raising the counterfactual "what if" query; systematic forecasts into the future, beyond known data, were not undertaken.

The second study was designed specifically to examine the impact of alternative policies on future behavior. Its purpose was to identify the extent to which national growth and economic development in the United States increase the country's propensities for external expansion and conflict behavior. The model was validated against empirical data for 1930-1970 and alternative forecasts were undertaken to the year 2000. (The choice of a terminal date is arbitrary; our purpose was to examine the impact of alternative policies over a short, as well as long, range.) It represents a clear extension and elaboration of the first study, and an attempt to incorporate the earlier experience into a cumulative research perspective. Thus, while the earlier model of *Nations in Conflict* (Choucri and North, 1975) is designed as a system of simultaneous equations, with some feedback relations, the specifications in *The Determinants of Lateral Pressure* (Choucri and Bousfield, 1975) represent a system of nonlinear, dynamic, feedback loops specified as a complex process in which change is endogenous, determined by variables in the model and not by exogenous factors. Such a specification is a more complete representation of the processes modeled and poses a greater theoretical and methodogological challenge than the earlier formulation. But it is a model of the internal determinants of external behavior and their implications for conflict; it does not take into account the interactions among nations. The modeling of these is clearly the next step.

These studies, and related efforts, have led to the adoption of ten theoretical and methodological requisites for forecasting in international relations:

1. a dynamic process-oriented approach to the substantive issues at hand;

2. an awareness of the implications of the choice of methodology for modeling and understanding the behavior of the system at hand;

3. a realization that the images of the future and the policy interventions selected are conditioned by prevailing assessments of the past and the present (a built-in regression toward the present need is to be consciously avoided in specifying the structure of the model);

4. systematic evaluations of what present trends are likely to produce if no interventions were undertaken, and specifications of the ranges of expected outcomes and (ideally) the probabilities associated with each;

5. a comparison of alternative research paradigms to evaluate their comparative relevance for modeling different aspects of international behavior (different methodologies are appropriate for different problems);

6. simulating the behavior of a system over the historical (known) past to articulate expectations regarding alternative futures, and systematically alternating the key coefficients and variables in a model to observe their impact on system behavior; and

7. specifying the alternative causal mechanisms underlying future outcomes articulating or identifying the different "paths" that could lead to the same (or alternative) futures;

8. adopting a multiperspective view of the issues modeled to test for the consequences of alternative political orientations:

9. articulating the values underlying different specifications of the system modeled; and finally,

10. systematically "importing" the future into the present by evaluating the implications for the present if certain futures were realized.

Together, these 10 directives have yielded the basic "rules" of an evolving research program in international relations forecasting. Research support from the National Science Foundation is enabling the systematic comparison of alternative forecasting methodologies for evaluating the consequences of resource constraints for the United States in international politics. As can be seen, considerable trial and error marked the development of a research strategy that had begun with correlation analyses of the determinants of violent conflict and is now centering around forecasting in international relations. The present investigations represent the latest stage in a cumulative research strategy.

REFERENCES

Choucri, Nazli. 1972. "Population, Resources, Technology: Political Implications of the Environmental Crisis." *International Organization* 26 (Spring): 175-212.

———. 1973. "Applications of Econometric Analysis to Forecasting in International Relations." *Papers, Peace Science Society (International)* 21: 15-39.

———. 1974a. "Forecasting in International Relations: Problems and Prospects." *International Interactions* 1: 63-86.

———. 1974b. *Population Dynamics and International Violence: Propositions, Insights and Evidence.* Lexington, Mass: Heath.

——— and Marie Bousfield. 1975. *The Determinants of Lateral Pressure: A Forecasting Model of the United States, 1930-2000.* Cambridge: MIT Center for International Studies.

——— with Vincent Ferraro. 1974. *Energy Interdependence.* Vol. 2 of *Analyzing Global Interdependence,* ed. Hayward R. Alker, Jr., Lincoln P. Bloomfield, and Nazli Choucri. Cambridge: MIT Center for International Studies.

———, Michael Laird, and Dennis L. Meadows. 1972. *Resource Scarcity and Foreign Policy: A Simulation Model of International Conflict.* Cambridge: MIT Center for International Studies.

——— and Robert C. North. 1969. "The Determinants of International Violence." *Papers, Peace Research Society (International)* 12: 33-63.

——— and Robert C. North. 1972. "Dynamics of International Conflict: Some Policy Implications of Population, Resources, and Technology." *World Politics* 24 (suppl.): 80-122.

——— and Robert C. North. 1975. *Nations in Conflict: National Growth and International Violence.* San Francisco: Freeman.

——— with the collaboration of Robert C. North. 1972. "In Search of Peace Systems: Scandinavia and the Netherlands, 1870-1970." In *Peace, War, and Numbers,* ed. Bruce M. Russett, pp. 239-74. Beverly Hills: Sage.

North, Robert C., and Nazli Choucri. 1968. "Background Conditions to the Outbreak of the First World War." *Papers, Peace Research Society (International)* 9: 1-13.

8. Sizing Up a Study in Simulated International Processes

Harold Guetzkow

EVALUATION PERSPECTIVE

We who are interested in a science of international relations are concerned with identifying patterns of global behavior. As we postulate explanations of these behavior patterns, we begin to formulate a theory, a statement of *which* activities recur in the international sphere and *why*. The question posed here is how do simulations size up in this investigation of international affairs?

SPECIAL NOTE: The writing of this essay was made possible by the author's occupancy of the Gordon Scott Fulcher Chair of Decision-Making at Northwestern University. My gratitude is unbounded for opportunities to pursue international relations research with risk as to "payoff." My seminal stay during 1956-1967 at the Center for Advanced Study in the Behavioral Sciences in Stanford was financed by the Ford Foundation. Exploratory runs of the Inter-Nation Simulation were underwritten in 1957-1959 by funds from the Carnegie Corporation of New York. During 1959-1963 the research was supported by the Behavioral Sciences Division of the U.S. Air Force Office of Scientific Research (Contract No. AF49 (638)-742 and Grant No. AF-AFOSR 62-63). During this period special tasks were undertaken for Project Michelson of the Department of the Navy (N1 23 (60530) 25875A). From 1964 into 1972 the work was financed by a contract from the Advanced Research Projects Agency (SD260) of the U.S. Department of Defense, with funds during 1971-1973 from the Carnegie Corporation of New York permitting the project to be brought to an orderly termination.

I am grateful to my colleagues, Richard C. Snyder and Chadwick F. Alger, for their sustained encouragement of my efforts in this endeavor, both while we were working together at Northwestern and later when we were separated. They have helped me constructively with this essay in 1973, even though they disagree (and at times disagree strongly) with my speculations. My new partner in the development of our all-computer work in the simulation of international affairs, William Ladd Hollist, reworked the paper on my behalf during the fall of 1974, following many suggestions made by the editor of this volume. I am grateful for the fine work of Glenna O. Calderone (formerly of Northwestern) and Susan E. McCarthy (newly of Northwestern) in handling many of the details involved in the preparation of this piece. Northwestern University, holder of the copyright, granted permission for publication of this essay to The Free Press. ©1975 by Northwestern University. All rights reserved.

Two rather disconcerting treatments of "islands of theory"[1] in international politics can be noted. First, seldom do scholars in international relations engage in further validating another scholar's work. Perhaps in our wish to be noted as "originators" of theory, we underplay the vital contribution we might make in further validating and subsequently reworking an "island of theory" postulated by another. This lack of cumulative enterprise unfortunately results in inadequately tested, though perhaps plausible, theories of various subsets of materials. Second, the various "islands" are seldom synthesized. We are not, it seems, sufficiently concerned with integrating the parts into a network of patterned relationships.

Though I question my own objectivity in evaluating the pluses and minuses of the Simulated International Processes (SIP) project, validation and integration have eventuated. Man-computer simulation techniques provide a vehicle for furthering theory validation and theory integration. It is a useful device for validating various islands of theory in international relations and for bridging gaps in formulating a theory network, encompassing global patterns.

In rendering judgments in this essay, I hope to develop with the reader some basis for making his own evaluation of the usefulness of the project for the furtherance of knowledge concerning inter-

[1] The original thinking concerning an "islands of theory" approach to the construction of more general theories of international relations is sketched in Guetzknow (1950).

national relations. Most of the ensuing presentation is organized in terms of questions posed by the editor in his invitation[2] to the conference which occasioned the preparation of this essay. But I do not regard my comments as answers to Rosenau's queries; we know too little about which research strategies produce desired outcomes to offer clear-cut responses at this stage. Before we can do justice to a project evaluation, we need "research on social science research."

During the gestation period of the SIP project, 1957-1959, effort was devoted to exploring the possible usefulness of a simulation methodology for the study of international relations. It then seemed that some amalgamation of existing all-manual games and all-computer simulations might provide a viable tool for theory construction and examination.[3] From 1959 to 1969, activity in SIP centered on man-computer simulations the efforts of which are described by Guetzkow (1970) in a bit more detail elsewhere. Toward the end of the project (1969-1972) ventures were begun in an all-computer format. A new effort is now underway which focuses upon cumulating all-computer simulations for decision-making in international affairs (Guetzkow, 1974).

Throughout its existence, the SIP project connected with the interests of many, most of whom were off the Northwestern campus.[4] In developing simulation as a tool for work in international affairs, our focus was upon research, both in terms of the problem of validity and in terms of potential for retrospective analysis as well as for the exploration of alternative futures. Serious effort was devoted to interesting the policy community in simulation, but such activity met with little success during the life of the project. On the other hand, with leadership from Alger (1963), there was a proliferation in the use of all-manual and man-computer simulations by teachers in colleges and universities, then in high schools, and more recently even in elementary schools. It is curious to note that the moderately great attempt to involve the project in policy developments yielded few apparent dividends; on the other hand, the relatively modest effort given to providing simulations for teaching induced widespread utilizations.

As contrasted with other international relations projects of considerable size undertaken in the 1960s, this project did not in the main develop new "pre-theories," nor did it "make data." Rather, emphasis was placed on (1) exploring explicitly stated pre-theories postulated largely by others, (2) constructing simulation vehicles capable of handling substantively complex sets of concepts and quantitative material in an integrated network, and (3) providing a means for meshing theory with extant empirical findings, the validity problem. Experience was gained in the use of man-computer simulation in the mounting of international relations theory, empirically grounded, so that this aspect of the "science of the artificial"[5] might one day become capable of handling the complexity needed for creative utilization of knowledge, both in policy work and in teaching.

RESPONSE TO QUERIES

As stated above, Rosenau has suggested a series of questions to be utilized in the development of a critical evaluation of a social science project in international relations. However, our SIP project had some peculiar characteristics which perhaps lessen its direct relevance to Rosenau's suggested queries. We in the project were content to work in the development of theory in simulation formats, using the pre-theories of others. Its hypotheses were largely borrowed, sometimes quite systematically.[6] Likewise, there was but a minimal allocation of resources to produce data for checking the validity of the simulations. It was possible in most

[2]Letter from James N. Rosenau, dated January 12, 1973.

[3]We reasoned that such a hybrid might highlight the advantages while reducing the disadvantages of both all-manual games and all-computer simulations. For a further explanation of this decision see Guetzkow (1963, 1970).

[4]Russett (1970), on the basis of an empirical analysis of citations in the international relations literature, found that persons using simulation constituted something of a "school" unto themselves.

[5]This phrase comes from the work of Simon (1969) and refers to the science of "man-made" objects and phenomena.

[6]For example, Leavitt (1971) built upon Liska's (1962) writings in his work on alliances.

situations to benefit from the data collection work of others.[7]

Given these characteristics, there is concern whether responses to Rosenau's questions are appropriate as ingredients for an autobiography of the SIP project (Guetzkow, 1970). However, rather than starting anew (as is so often done), let us attempt to utilize the queries posed by Rosenau, even though they seem framed for projects concerned centrally with the deriving, measuring, and testing of hypotheses. When it seems useful, we will modify the questions to accommodate the posture of our work in SIP.

Who (or how many) have requested use of your [data] products? For what purposes? What kinds of things have they done with the [data] products?

Perhaps three to five hundred people have used outcomes of the project for research, for policy, and for teaching.

There was a moderate number of requests for outputs from researchers, seeking access in the main to unpublished materials. Scholars made critiques of the simulations; of the Political Military Exercise, an all-manual game (Fischer, 1972); of the man-computer simulation (Coplin, 1966; Modelski, 1970); and of all-computer simulations (Gorden, 1968). Simulation's theoretical contributions are appreciated only by a narrow circle of scholars in international affairs. Although many grieve over a contemporary lack of widespread interest in theory, few recognize the potential contribution of simulation in overcoming this deficiency. Few understand that simulation is not game-playing, or even the theory of games; few understand that simulation is but a useful vehicle for mounting and exploring complex theories.

Sometimes scholars have carried forward research on their own, exercising their interest in man-computer simulations as vehicles for theory exploration. Burgess and Robinson (1969), operating within this research strategy, found in their examination of the economic theory of public goods that voluntary associations which sup-

[7]Empirical materials were borrowed from numerous data banks during the course of the project; resources of the Inter-university Consortium for Political and Social Research were valuable.

plement collective benefits with private benefits are more cohesive and effective than those that produce only collective benefits.

There have been those who have radically revised the Inter-Nation Simulation (INS) because of their scholarly convictions. Coplin (1966), emphasizing issues in international politics, developed his World Politics Simulation (WPS). This was subsequently revolutionized (Coplin et al., 1971) into an interactive, all-computer simulation in "A Programmed International Computer Environment" (PRINCE). In quite another stream the INS was revised by Smoker (1968, 1973) into a more encompassing man-computer International Processes Simulation (IPS), and later by Bremer (1970) as an all-computer simulation processor (SIPER). These revisions evolved as documentation of the Inter-Nation Simulation became available.

The military has had much greater interest in simulations than other branches of the federal government concerned with international affairs. There was ample opportunity to present various forms of simulation by such people as Abt and Gorden (TEMPER, 1969), Bloomfield (Rand/MIT Political Military Exercise), and ourselves to policy makers within both the U.S. Departments of Defense and State.

Bloomfield succeeded in government more than other researchers, even serving as director for a number of the exercises undertaken by the Pentagon's Joint War Games Agency (Bloomfield and Gearin, 1973). Working through the National Gaming Council and such periodic gatherings as the Inter-Agency Group on Strategic Studies, it was possible to explain political-military simulation in full detail to those who might have need for such. Twice initiative was taken by the government of the United States in asking us for special materials which might be applicable to a particular problem an agency was facing, once with respect to Brody's work on nuclear futures (1963, 1969) and the other time with respect to the operation of intelligence indicators within simulations of international affairs.

Despite the many briefings given, and the continuous communication maintained with personnel in the Joint War Games Agency (JWGA) and (its successor organization) the Studies, Analysis, and

Gaming Agency (SAGA) in the Office of the Joint Chiefs of Staff, the project seemed to have little impact, not even on such rudimentary aspects of methodology as the need for replication in the use of simulation, so that war games would not be "over-read." Was it that the dissatisfaction felt during the mid-1960s by members of the Joint Chiefs of Staff with respect to an all-computer simulation effort in their military political gaming lowered the esteem of those concerned with all-manual and man-computer gaming for policy work, thereby inhibiting the development of more adequate models and designs for policy work in the subsequent five to eight years after their termination of all-computer work in the field of military political exercises? Despite much top level encouragement, members of the Senior Seminar of the Foreign Service Institute of the U.S. Department of State twice rejected, four years apart, first the potential of man-computer and then later interactive, all-computer simulation.

Most of the requests for use of the project's material came from those concerned with teaching, including a long-term, impressive utilization in the U.S. Industrial College of the Armed Forces through the initiative of Colonel William Thane Minor, USAF. Minor, George L. Draper, and Charles D. Elder mounted three generations of man-computer simulations in a very systematic way. Although our project per se was not directed toward the utilization of simulation for educational purposes, there were pressures upon us to supply information and materials so that educators throughout the world might utilize developments in the simulation of international processes. For example, twice, midstream and near the termination of the project, we were coopted into conferences by the U.S. Industrial College of the Armed Forces to acquaint American military educators with potentials, as well as with the knowledge available at that point, for utilization in the war colleges and the military academies.

There seemed to be no possibility of imposing standards upon the utilization of our simulation in educational endeavors, even if such were to be desired. The project by and large found itself without resources to do more than attempt to shift the burdens for communication with regard to its work to others, such as in publishing in 1966 an

"INS Kit" through Science Research Associates, Inc.

In the use of materials in the simulation of international affairs, scholars have often asked questions about the validity of our materials. Policy makers have been skeptical with respect to the Inter-Nation Simulation's veridicality, especially in terms of its predictions. Educators have plunged forthwith ahead, seldom asking whether or not the theories embodied in the constructions corresponded to the referent systems which they were attempting to bring into their classrooms.

Have any of the (hypotheses derived from) [simulations developed in] your project been (tested) [checked] by others? With what results?

It was toward the end of the preliminary stage in working with man-computer simulations that we realized that a man-computer simulation was importantly *unlike* an experiment in social psychology. We finally recognized that human participants, enmeshed with computed programs constituting "nations," served but as surrogates for decision-makers of the nation-states and were not necessarily representative of interpersonal phenomena as captured in the laboratory by the social psychologist. The outputs of political military exercises and of man-machine simulations are not observed data as created and captured by laboratory and field social scientists. Neither are the outputs events data, as developed through analysis of historical documents and/or journalistic reports. Instead, simulation outputs are analogous to the output of symbols obtained in the printout of computers. Simulations are analytic constructions, and the outputs of the humans and machines are the "consequences" thereof.[8] Simulations express variable relationships as analytic constructs, and the results of simulations are outputs derived therefrom. In testing the validity of a simulation, the researcher compares simulation outputs with "real-world" phenomena. The investigator observes whether the outputs of the model's processes, as involved humans and machines, correspond with the outcomes of the associated "real-world" processes.

---

[8]Not all agree that simulations are analytic heuristics, especially when they involve humans rather than symbols alone. This is evidenced in the severe criticisms of Powell (1969).

Simulation is fundamentally different from the enterprise of empirically testing relationships among variables, as done with rigor in data-grounded projects. However, if the reader recognizes the utility of simulation for advancing theories in social science, he perhaps will be willing to evaluate SIP on a somewhat modified criterion.

One may reformulate Rosenau's question by asking the extent to which the simulations of SIP were transferred to other sites. All-manual forms of crisis-like games have richly proliferated with many variations. It is my guess that some 30 to 50 variants have blossomed. Although the Inter-Nation Simulation (INS) may have existed in fifteen to 25 variations in the past decade and a half, no one has duplicated its successor model, Smoker's IPS (1970), perhaps because of the latter's enormity. (It involves almost a hundred persons meshed with on-line computer facilities.)

There has been considerable proclivity to utilize the basic framework of the INS, even though the hypotheses explored by a given investigator differ quite widely from those examined by another. Coplin, whose World Politics Simulation (WPS) and PRINCE simulation have been more differentiated from those central to the SIP project than many, found himself using features of the INS, even though his issues orientation resulted in constructions in which emphasis was given to foreign policy rather than to international relations processes. As far as this researcher knows, there are now five somewhat all-encompassing international simulations in existence, only two of which are being pursued with sustained effort, namely the Political Military Exercise (PME) and the Simulated International Processor (SIPER).

If we invert Rosenau's query "Have any of the hypotheses derived from your project been tested by others?" to "Have any hypotheses tested by others been used by your project?" the reply then is "Indeed so." In some 30 validity studies undertaken with respect to one form or another of the simulations of international affairs, the correspondences between empirical findings (usually obtained by others) and our simulation outputs have been examined in some detail (Guetzkow, 1968). This work provides a loose integration of the results of many partial, more fragmented investigations. In the overall tallies, the Inter-Nation

Simulation model reproduces in the main the empirical relationships in some two-thirds to three-quarters of the cases. These outcomes seem to be of the same magnitude, roughly, as the (64 percent) hits scored by Jensen's foreign policy experts (1966) in making about three and a half thousand predictions. Solid studies continue to appear confirming the even greater validity of the International Processes Simulation (IPS), as in Soroos's work (1975) which includes the successful use of reference materials from McClelland's shop (Fitzsimmons, Hoggard, McClelland, Martin, and Young, 1969).

Sometimes the strength of the relationships exhibited in the simulation were found to be weaker than the corresponding relationships in the referent materials, as is true for Soroos. Sadly, no pattern in the failures of the simulation to replicate the empirical studies could be found. For example, there were as many successes in the processes surrogated by interacting humans as in those in which the decision-making was handled by the computer programs. Furthermore, the simulations seemed to handle the mirroring of the reference material whether such were examined at the level of the global system, the nation-state, or at the internal organizational and individual levels.

These validation studies are deemed most important by the author. From my point of view, it is lamentable that private and governmental funding policies deprived Coplin and O'Leary of an opportunity to check out the validity of their simulations as they moved from INS to WPS to PRINCE, but then recently encouraged them rather to disseminate PRINCE (still unvalidated) in educational circles. It is deplorable that bureaucratic problems within the military discouraged both the Joint War Games Agency and the U.S. Industrial College of the Armed Forces from even seeking ample resources for mounting validity studies for their particular formulations of their simulations, to assure a firmer empirical grounding of their policy and educational tools. "Eyeball" checks are hardly tolerable, given the international significance of the outputs.

The importance of work in validating simulations becomes most apparent as one gains a better feel for the simulation enterprise. Simulations are concatenations of hypotheses, demanding that the investigator order interrelations among variables. Simulations specify conditionalities and simultaneously lead and lag interactions among variables. When data-based research is exhausted— and during the past decade and a half, as Jones and Singer abstracts testify (1972), there were relatively few empirical studies available—conjecture often takes over. Simulation provides a means for overcoming some of the problems deriving from data inadequacies. This is illustrated in Smoker's significant transition from the INS to IPS in which he built speculatively but carefully upon the shortcomings of the former, given his global orientation. He simultaneously also built upon the empirical work of McClelland and Hoggard (1969) and Rummel (1966).

As a methodology, simulation encourages one to sift the extant verbal literature, attempting to gain clarification from the material in hand. Raser and Crow (1964), in their study of the capacity for delayed response in nuclear exchanges for Project Michelson, first surveyed the literature to identify pertinent variables and expected relationships. They then went about filling the gaps in the resultant model through intuition. Simulation does permit one to be less data-bound, even though it requires more explication than other forms of theory. Seen in this perspective, simulations are a heuristic for the composition and integration of verbal hypotheses not yet empirically disproved. It is interesting to note that Crow and Raser found instabilities in their simulations when flexible response was permitted in nuclear confrontation, contrary to military doctrine of the time.

Has the feedback provided by the users of your [data or concepts] (developments) had an effect on your thinking and the evolution of the project? If so, how?

The generous feedback provided by users, collaborators, and critics of our simulations had tremendous overall impact on the evolution of the project. The many validity studies involved in the research constituted targets for colleagues in international relations, inasmuch as the material provided quite explicit standards by which the model development could be appraised. It was ever sobering to relearn from the verbally skilled policy makers how the validity studies indicated noncor-

respondences in a quarter to a third of the cases. We eventually found that our continued efforts in validation yielded diminishing returns. This occurred even though we attempted to use tighter designs and more appropriate reference data. Despite the urging of our friends to do "just one more" validity study, it seemed wise to place our resources elsewhere as the project continued.

We may illustrate our incorporation into the model of feedback from others by tracing the evolution of the project. In our initial attempt to make INS an encompassing construction, Sullivan (1963) searched verbal models implicit in a series of some 10 textbooks in international relations. Important parts of the Inter-Nation Simulation were composed therefrom. The project clearly used the notions of others to feed into its initial formulations. When Smoker later rethought the construction of this earlier simulation, he insisted that INS needed an enlargement, including nongovernmental organizations as actors. He based his argument on empirical findings from his doctoral dissertation at Lancaster. This effort eventuated in an evolution of the INS into IPS, in which validity was found to be of improved magnitude (Smoker, 1970). Smoker's contentions were reinforced by receiving almost simultaneously from Modelski (1970) a similar critique of the shortcomings of the Inter-Nation Simulation, even though his documentation was not as complete then as is now available in his recent textbook (Modelski, 1972). Feedback persists, once people become taken with the problems. This is illustrated in Sullivan and Noel's recent piece on INS' premises (1972) written ten years after Smoker's IPS had replaced the INS. It still seemed useful to these authors and their editors to reexamine the assumptions involved in their earlier work with the principal investigator.

The use of a hybrid form of simulation involving both persons and machines created opportunity for feedback from social scientists concerned with laboratory experimentation. Those who conceive the man-computer simulation as an experiment in social psychology felt that our methodology was gross, when measured against the refined standards and elegance of the laboratories available to "small group" psychologists. Inasmuch as the project conducted work in the psychology of the surrogate decision-makers themselves, as in the

Driver (1965) and Hermann (1965) studies, it is easy to understand why there was an identification of the man-computer simulation with but one of the phenomena involved in its construction, i.e., the human beings who served as "subjects" in the simulation runs.

Policy makers felt fundamentally disturbed by the use of high school and college participants. Later involvement of adults active in the foreign policy community within the Chicago area, and even participants drawn from the upper ranks of embassies in the United States for simulation runs at Arlie House outside Washington, did little to assuage their misgivings. As we listened to the feedback provided by the policy community, we wondered whether we would ever be able to involve participants of adequate background and stature to meet their demands for our work in SIP.

Two feedbacks contravened the vigorous development of the project. There were many pressures for doing work within the utilization of Inter-Nation Simulation (INS) for teaching, perhaps deriving from the excitement which simulations often deliver in the classroom. It is surprising how many high school and college undergraduates have been exposed to a simulation experience in the United States. Many educators throughout the world were quite willing to reshape the contents of their simulations in light of INS findings, working interactively in quite creative ways. However, we often wondered whether utilizing simulations as educational games, without demanding validity, would discredit the ability of simulations to evolve into serious research instruments, let alone policy tools. Unfortunately, the ventures into simulations by educators and their students were often taken as games for play rather than serious learning exercises.

Were policy makers in our federal government more tied to their offices in the long run, their negative feedbacks with respect to their prognosis on the usefulness of simulations would be quite handicapping to further work. However, they go and new ones come, as they transfer from post to post. Should the negative effects of their exposures to "games" in learning situations not spread too widely, it may be that as the total climate toward the usefulness of social science in policy making grows more positive, newcomers will arrive

with a willingness to be involved in the construction of simulations for their policy work. Let us hope that scholar-researchers do not lose perspective when they are plagued by mis-utilizations. Rather than being pressed into practicality by the exigencies of immediate teaching and policy situations, it may be that the academic members of those groups concerned with international relations are the ones who must keep sights clear, working constructively with each other, so that fragile ideas are not crushed by discouragement before they have had time for fruition.

It is interesting to note how feedback guided the evolution of the project, sustaining the investigators' early judgments of worthwhileness while transforming its contents fundamentally. The project's various advisory groups of most knowledgeable persons tutored as well. They proved further to be valuable as links in communication among the communities concerned with simulations in international affairs.

The substance of our simulations, although continuing to emphasize an all-encompassing scope, moved from a restricted, somewhat "billiard ball"-type model to include enriched, global patterns. The leveling off of the strength of the validity findings with continued replication opened us to alternative modes of procedure. We came to wonder whether one perhaps should build simulations which represent empirical findings, rather than attempting to locate data-based materials against which an a priori construction might be checked. We guessed that perhaps there would be payoff in a turnaround, looking at simulation construction inductively and grounding modular development in empirical work. The notion of inverting the direction of the empirical approach of our simulation was crystallized by Singer, when he and Jones began preparing their abstracts of data-based research (1972). We reasoned that one might go "beyond conjecture" by moving from the use of the global deductive schema to inductively developed modular materials assembled into global simulations, as was later sketched by Guetzkow (1974).

Throughout the life of the project, there was an overall increase among social scientists in the use of simulation, much of which was gravitating to all-computer formats, a trend which was monitored.[9] Some of my younger associates were quite responsive to these new opportunities. For example, the use of on-line computer facilities in both the IPS and some versions of the WPS broke barriers artificially erected by the difficulties encountered by overly ambitious efforts in TEMPER. Our feedback was impressive enough in quality and quantity so as to induce a decision by Bremer to move from man-computer to all-computer simulation as the project neared its end. Bremer (1970) presented the investigator with SIPER, a well-documented, all-computer version of the Inter-Nation Simulation (for which he won the Reid Award for the "best doctoral dissertation completed and accepted during 1970 and 1971 in the field of international relations, law, and politics"). At the end of the project, Leavitt (1971) had produced an all-computer, partial model of alliance behavior as outlined by Liska (1962). Not only was computer time becoming cheaper, but some of the difficulties in all-computer simulation, which Gorden (1968) so insightfully enumerated on the basis of his work with TEMPER, were being handled as experience was gained.

If you could do it over again, equipped with your present understanding, what would you do differently?

It is intriguing to muse about what one would do differently, were he able to "do it over again." Fundamental decisions about the project were taken during 1956-1957, while the investigator was a Fellow at the Center for Advanced Studies in the Behavioral Sciences. Recall the state of international relations then: Morgenthau (1954) had recently issued the second edition of his text—and realism rode high in the Cold War climate. Wright's important assessment of the field (1955) had just been published. Snyder's early work on decision-making in foreign affairs (1958) was creating excitement. The first of the Rosenau readers (1961) had not yet been published. The International Studies Association (ISA) was then a regional group on the west coast of the United

States. There was no COPRED (Consortium on Peace Research Education and Development) or Peace Science Society (International). Were I to start anew today, given the experiences of the last decade and a half, things would be done quite differently. Some parts of the project would remain unchanged; others would be modified. Let us loosely explore the different possibilities, taking full advantage of hindsight.

In our proposal to the Advanced Research Project Agency in the spring of 1964 we aimed to "begin work in the integration of studies in the simulation of international behaviors, so that coherent theory may be developed and tested for utilization by military and political policy-makers." Through the course of the contract (1964-1972) we were but partially effective in meeting this objective. This has led me to ask some rather critical questions concerning project organization.

How does one organize a project to motivate colleagues simultaneously for cumulativeness and creativity? Did the project operate too freely in permitting scholars to pursue their personal proclivities? Or did our contracting-out procedures circumscribe the researchers too severely? Perhaps the attempt to make our efforts cumulative was somewhat needless, inasmuch as the generally less capable scholars often could not deliver and the generally more capable scholars were often partially cumulative anyway. Were the project to be redone, an attempt might be made to buy more effort for longer periods of time from the interested and the more capable analysts.

Had the investigator not failed thrice in securing the long-term services of an assistant director, perhaps his energies would not have been so diverted into administrative matters. It is easy to dream that one needs an assistant director who can handle things. I found that when I recruited a person of quality, each time I also had a person motivated to move in his own research directions autonomously. Yet it was imperative to seek people of such quality. Simulations, regardless of their format, attract the gadgeteer—be he the laboratory tinkerer or the computer bum. Perhaps it would have been better to employ simultaneously two assistant directors of quality, chancing that perhaps one would have the long-term patience with academic detail necessary to permit the direc-

---

[9]Two volumes, edited by the principal investigator (Guetzkow, 1962, 1972), served as vehicles for continuous contact with researchers in the social sciences but outside the field of international relations.

tor more substantive opportunities to develop the project per se in a tighter, more cumulative fashion.

In retrospect, especially in light of the null findings of experimentation in the classroom (Cherryholmes, 1966; Wentworth and Lewis, 1973), it seems clear that the project would have been better off had it not attempted to work with the educational side of the use of simulation. The project's deep involvement with military educators proved somewhat futile from the point of view of gained insights for model construction. Civilian educators throughout the world placed heavy demands upon the project, despite the effort to disperse our material through commercial channels. Just as PRINCE is now being shoved ahead of its substantive foundation by demands from the Education Commission within the International Studies Association and COPRED, such was the case in the lifespan of INS. Furthermore, people within the military who were utilizing the outputs of the project in their educational work were not able to convey the utility of simulations to policy makers and researchers within the Department of Defense.

Many variations of INS included one or more international organizations, such as a United Nations or a World Bank. IPS featured actors other than the nation-state. Yet, by the time the patterns of the international system were analyzed as a whole, in addition to the nation-states themselves, there seemed to be little impetus for work on international organizations per se. Was this due to the way in which the Morgenthau viewpoint permeated international relations thought, often unconsciously? Was it the result of a declining American interest in the United Nations and its associated groups as well as a subtle shaping of our interest by our users? Were one to do it again, it seems that this serious default would need to be remedied. Although not directly connected with our project, only Hoole (1971) developed a simulation of an international organization—an all-computer model of budgetary processes in the World Health Organization. Though a number of our collaborators examined alliance behaviors, it is curious that none felt impelled to contrast alliance formation with regional and/or global organizations. In my judgment these omissions are important shortcomings of the project.

Similarly, legal aspects of international systems have been neglected. Although the moot court, a kind of all-manual simulation, has been around a goodly number of years, no one took seriously the need for simulating legal aspects of the international system. To date, not even Coplin has moved into this area, despite his frequent verbal explications of the importance of international law.

In developing opportunities for use of simulation by policy-related offices, it would have been advantageous to have direct comparisons of the ability of simulations to handle concrete materials in international relations and to make predictions therefrom, with the ability of policy makers to make verbally based predictions. A plan aborted midstream to this investigator's great regret, Jensen's work (1966) being but an initial start. As it is important to know how well formulations within a simulation are data-grounded, so it might have been constructive to know how the evolving simulations were poorer or better than the implicit theories of those working day-by-day in the international affairs community. Yet, in retrospect, one realizes that few of the practitioners would have been persuaded that the project's simulations were to be taken seriously, especially if the comparison had disadvantaged their judgments.

In retrospect, it would have been wiser to have sought direct involvement of operating personnel within the United States government, so that the simulations might have evolved in the very offices of the relevant decision-makers. Then there might have been some chance of acceptance of the findings, with rich feedback to the simulation from ongoing field activity. An attempt was made to secure such relationships in the latter part of the project. Yet neither within the Office of International Security Affairs of the Department of Defense nor within the Office of the Under Secretary in the Department of State did such collaboration prove feasible, despite my intensive effort to secure such an arrangement for joint activity.

Should there have been more consolidation as one went along? Yes, such would have been advisable even though Smoker did consolidate both empirical work and the results of earlier INS runs in his IPS. However, to date, pleas for coherence have drawn little response from other scholars.

Through the device of contracting out it was possible to partially link the work in simulation with many other ongoing activities in international relations. Yet in the end, it proved impossible for this investigator to work closely with contractors on other campuses, with but three or four exceptions.

Most textbooks on simulation, regardless of their field, urge that one should not attempt simulations until verbal and mathematical theory within the area of the simulation has been well formulated, so that the model can be adequately constructed. From that point of view, the initial decision to go ahead with man-computer simulations was ill advised. Yet a decade and a half later we still await formulation and consensus among international relations scholars of such a definitive, all-encompassing verbal theory, as the disparate papers in this volume demonstrate. Most contemporary work is either empirical and somewhat fragmented or highly abstract and ambiguously presented in ordinary verbal language. At least in PRINCE and SIPER we have broad, relatively well-articulated constructions of theory, even if they are a bit lopsided in emphasizing foreign policy when compared with some of the contemporary literature of international relations.

An opportunity was lost in not having monitored more systematically the literature of ordinary language. Sullivan's (1963) frustrations in handling the contents of the ten texts as input into the initial formulations may have been unduly discouraging. Pfaltzgraff, in his comparisons of simulations and verbal theory in international relations (1972), found that the former placed significantly more emphasis on the domestic components of foreign policy, while the later gave more prominence to system-wide behavior. Tighter vigilance of verbal theories may have led to a quicker realization of this difference.

To gain further perspective on "what went wrong," it may be useful to highlight a few features of the initial decisions which "went right," even on the "Monday after." In general, it seems we were able to keep an overall perspective in the research, operating with the slack appropriate to the stage of the enterprise. In our work on validity most of the analyses were done with a degree of precision befitting the coarseness of the data and the simulations. Our simulations gained from a close study of the incongruities between empirically tested relationships among variables and the predicted outputs of simulation runs.

Some promising work was incorporated into the overall model. This was largely the result of our decision to attempt to require researchers to (1) validate their own work, and (2) to program their research into the project's general framework. For example, the intriguing prospects which Elder (1966) and Pendley (1966) held out, when they did fruitful micro-analyses of political and economic features of INS, did materialize in changes of the model (IPS) when Smoker (1968) re-engineered the INS. The suggestion (Zinnes, 1966) that we modify the assumptions in the INS regarding communication processes was also carried out. Zinnes's studies of these assumptions in the context of events on the eve of World War I indicated that we were in error in permitting face-to-face communication among foreign offices, thereby neglecting the buffering associated with mediation via embassies. Again Smoker allocated time and resources to making this revision (1968).

Despite the harshness with which more rigorously trained behavioral scientists seemingly urged precision for its own sake, Guetzkow's refusal (1966) to dump resources into such an all-consuming task still seems to have been wise. There will be another round by some team or other; perhaps that will be the time to try for a significant gain in validity. Let us not now rashly assume that extant characterizations of the reference system are flawless enough to warrant an all-out struggle for higher validity at this time.

Given the state of the field, and the finite funds available in the project, it seems wise that Chadwick's (1972) suggestions from his midstream exploration using more sophisticated statistical methodologies were not followed up within the man-computer context. It was recognized early that simulations are but one tool by which complex formulations may be mounted. Inasmuch as regression work, causal inference technology, and econometric modeling were just in the initial stage of exploration in international relations (Smoker, 1965a, 1965b, 1967), the decision to proceed with man-computer simulation in "splendid isolation" may have been wise. This headstrongness permitted the field to become acquainted with simulation qua simulation, without requiring expertise in the statistical and mathematical devices that are integral parts of present-day simulation, especially the all-computer variety. The leverage and elegance one can gain by including simulation as a part of the sophisticated technologies used in research on international relations is now being demonstrated in the more recent work of Alker and Christensen (1972) and Choucri and North (1975). Such reach in the 1960s might have spread our already over-extended capabilities too thinly; besides there were only three or four of our collaborators at that time who had sufficient competence to handle meaningfully the intricacies of such an enterprise. The author regrets that such stubbornness had not been taken with our forays into the utilization of simulation in education.

The basic paradigm used from the beginning of the project was that simulation might be employed as a way of exploring pasts, presents, and futures, grounding the work as much as possible in empirical materials—but without being "data-bound." There was much excitement in Evanston for the few days during which Smoker (1969) developed an antithesis to the project's paradigm: Smoker argued, in effect, mold the world after the simulation, rather than the simulation after the world! We all had been intrigued by findings from his IPS that young high school students had "run the world" with less conflict than mature adults knowledgeable about foreign affairs. Should we now change direction, attempting to build realities to correspond to our simulation? Perhaps it was the sketchiness of our elaboration of this "brave new world" which inhibited a turnabout. Given our limited resources, were we to tackle recreating the reference system? We did not even have funds sufficient to make our own "real" data, let alone to remake the reference system from which to make such data! The project persisted in its original paradigm, despite Smoker's (1968) tempting proposal that we respond to its antithesis.

Stated immodestly (or modestly), how is the IR field better off by virtue of the funds and time invested in your project?

In the development of social science it seems imperative that importantly different options be kept open for significant periods of time. Simula-

tion as a vehicle for theory construction has been in existence for less than a quarter century; its alternative in ordinary lanaguage theory has been practiced since the days of Herodotus, over ten thousand times longer. Little wonder it is difficult to gain perspective at this time on the outcomes of this project in international relations, inasmuch as its resources have been but a minute fraction of those devoted by legions over many centuries in verbal theory.

Let me be reckless: the international relations field is "better off" because of the development of the Inter-Nation Simulation (INS), and the International Processes Simulation (IPS), and the Simulated International Processor (SIPER) in the Simulated International Processes (SIP) project. The field now has more adequate understanding of the various formats of this new vehicle for mounting theories in a data-related way. Simulations permit one to tackle immense problems of great complexity, involving large numbers of variables in both foreign affairs and international relations. The modules within the simulations tie relationships among variables into bundles, giving opportunity for the display of interacting processes. Furthermore, the project developed simulations which are data-related, not mere conjectured gadgets. The reconstructions are not without validity. The simulations also permit one to work on alternative formulations without being data-bound. Nevertheless, we realize that simulation is but one of the array of tools with which we gain "better" coherence as we accumulate knowledge in the field of international affairs. It is encouraging to realize that over half of the contributors to this volume are now using simulation in their work—not as a focus, but as a complementary tool in developing their substantive interests, as Guetzkow argued some years ago (1969).

The international relations field is "better off" because SIP catalyzed development of simulations. By occupying a middling position, attempting to capitalize upon the advantages of both the all-manual simulation and the all-computer simulation, it bridged differences between the two extremes, providing a screen for their mutual growth. There has been fascinating competition among simulators, giving users considerable choice. For example, the political military exercise now encompasses the noncrisis situation, no longer focusing only upon crisis. On the other hand, in the all-computer arena there has been demonstration that this format need not be thought of as suitable only as a research tool, but that it may also be used interactively in the classroom. The international relations field is "better off" because its all-manual and all-computer simulations have reacted to the shortcomings of man-computer simulations by improving contrasting formats.

The international affairs field is "better off" because the SIP project helped create a readiness to shift from all-manual and man-computer simulations to all-computer simulations. Would we yet be content in all-manual simulation if it had not been for the nudging of the man-computer simulation? Would our courage to go ahead into all-computer simulation now be less had we not had a period within man-computer simulation? Could we have skipped the man-computer phase, going directly from limitations of the manual exercise to the all-computer simulation, given the state of the field at the end of the 1950s? Or was an intermediate form necessary to spur young and old to gain the methodological competence required to work in an all-computer format? A decade and a half later one guesses that had the development of the project not been with magnitude and speed, it would have not helped in creating today's widespread readiness to work with global and modularized simulations. As some of us see things, the development in simulation has more than matched the important changes that have occurred on the empirical side in the study of international affairs.

SUMMARY AND COMMENT

Northwestern's project in international processes (1957-1972) fashioned simulations in international relations, enabling scholars, practitioners, and educators to develop and use their complex theories with greater coherence and validity. The central achievement of the project was the building of the Inter-Nation Simulation (INS) and the International Processes Simulation (IPS), first- and second-generation man-computer constructions, respectively. The project's evolution from a concern with man-computer simulations to all-

computer models is embodied in the Simulated International Processor (SIPER), a third-generation, all-computer version of the INS. The validity of these simulations varied; correspondences between their outputs and data from the references of the "real world" centered on target between two-thirds and three-quarters of the time. The diffusion of the simulations in the decade and a half of the project's existence differ for three classes of users, being greatest among educators, employed somewhat by scholars for research, with little interest shown by policy makers. The feedback obtained from users of the project's products was great, as was the constructiveness of most of the project's critics. The shortcomings of the work were many, some relating to its organizational failures and others to its inability to communicate persuasively with its users, actual and potential. In addition to its production of simulations, the project may have served—especially because of the scope of its operation through subcontractors—to help develop readiness within the field of international relations to move from all-manual to all-computer simulations, thereby keeping pace in its theoretical capacities with its newly acquired capabilities in data-making and data-archiving.

Speculation vs. Research: Yet Another Plea for the Funding of "Research on Research" in the Social Sciences

Although I have from time to time urged more funding of "research on research," as have some of my colleagues, I seldom have felt as uncomfortable in discussing questions like those Rosenau has posed for a project autobiography. Perhaps now it is time for someone to mount a long-term, rigorous and systematic examination of research in international affairs, so that we all may do better with the resources we have. It will be fascinating to know whether or not small projects, centering in a single scholar or two, are better than larger projects involving teams. It is important to know whether or not a net of close communication is useful among investigators, so that their works may dovetail more adequately, or does such a social structure among scholars tend to diminish innovation? Just as we no longer want to rely upon surmises and guesses in the substance of our knowledge in international relations, so we no longer want to rely upon philosophical conjectures and hunches as to the adequacy of our research procedures.

How Can We Get Things to Add Up?

Others often challenge, "What, you're still working in simulation?" Yes, I'm still working in simulation; and it is my hope that I can spend the rest of my life in this venture, at once concerned with the problems of war and peace, the problems of development—both overdevelopment and underdevelopment—and the problems of justice and freedom. There is much to be done in attempting to develop more coherence and more validity in the work. Although Smoker's inversion of the project's basic paradigm is most exciting, in my judgment we still have a long and expensive way to go before I would have enough boldness to want to model the world after our simulations. Simulations have made the international relations field "better off" for sure—but not that much better.

REFERENCES

Abt, Clark C., and Morton Gorden. 1969. "Report on Project TEMPER." In *Theory and Research on the Causes of War,* ed. Dean G. Pruitt and Richard C. Snyder, pp. 245-62. Englewood Cliffs, N.J.: Prentice-Hall.

Alger, Chadwick F. 1963. "Use of the Inter-nation Simulation in Undergraduate Teaching." In *Simulation in International Relations,* by Harold Guetzkow et al., pp. 150-89. Englewood Cliffs, N.J.: Prentice-Hall.

Alker, Hayward R., Jr., and Cheryl Christensen. 1972. "From Causal Modeling to Artificial Intelligence: The Evolution of a UN Peace-Making Simulation." In *Experimentation and Simulation in Political Science,* ed. J. A. Laponse and Paul Smoker, pp. 177-224. Toronto: Univ. of Toronto Press.

Bloomfield, Lincoln P., and Cornelius J. Gearin. 1973. "Games Foreign Policy Experts Play: The Political Exercise Comes of Age." *Orbis* 16 (Winter): 1008-31.

Bremer, Stuart A. 1970. "National and International Systems: A Computer Simulation." Ph.D. dissertation, Michigan State Univ.

Brody, Richard A. 1963. "Some Systemic Effects of the Spread of Nuclear Weapons Technology: A Study through Simulation of a Multi-nuclear Future." *Journal of Conflict Resolution* 7, 4 (Dec): 663-753.

――― and Alexandra H. Benham. 1969. "Nuclear Weapons and Alliance Cohesion." In *Theory and Research on the Causes of War,* ed. Dean G. Pruitt and Richard C. Snyder, pp. 165-75. Englewood Cliffs, N.J.: Prentice-Hall.

Burgess, Philip M., and James A. Robinson. 1969. "Alliances and the Theory of Collective Action: A Simulation of Coalition Processes." *Midwest Journal of Political Science* 13, 2: 194-218.

Chadwick, Richard W. 1972. "Theory Development through Simulation: A Comparison and Analysis of Associations among Variables in an International System and an Inter-Nation Simulation." *International Studies Quarterly* 16, 1: 83-127.

Cherryholmes, Cleo. 1966. "Some Current Research on Effectiveness of Educational Simulation Implications for Alternative Strategies." *American Behavioral Science* 10, 2: 4-7.

Choucri, Nazli, and Robert C. North. 1975. *Nations in Conflict: National Growth and International Violence,* Chap. 17, pp. 255-76. San Francisco: Freeman.

Coplin, William D. 1966. "Inter-Nation Simulation and Contemporary Theories of International Relations." *American Political Science Review* 60, 3 (Sep): 562-78.

―――, John Handelman, Stephen Mills, and Michael K. O'Leary. 1971. "A description of the PRINCE Model." Mimeo. Syracuse: Syracuse Univ.

Driver, Michael J. 1965. "A Structural Analysis of Aggression, Stress, and Personality in an Inter-Nation Simulation." Mimeo. Lafayette, Ind.: Purdue Univ.

Elder, Charles D., and Robert E. Pendley. 1966. "An Analysis of Consumption Standards and Validation Satisfaction in the Inter-Nation Simulation in Terms of Contemporary Economic Data Theory." Mimeo. Evanston, Ill.: Northwestern Univ.

Fischer, Lucas R. 1971. "The Rand/MIT Political-Military Exercise and International Relations Theory." In *Simulationen Internationaler Prozesse,* ed. Lucian Kern and Horst-Dieter Ronsch, pp. 219-38. Germany: Opladen.

Fitzsimmons, Barbara, Gary D. Hoggard, Charles A. McClelland, Wayne Martin, and Robert Young. 1969. "World Event/Interaction Survey Handbook and Codebook." World Event/Interaction Study, Technical Report No. 1. Mimeo. Los Angeles: Univ. of Southern California.

Gorden, Morton, 1968. "Burdens for the Designer of a Computer Simulation of International Relations: The Case of TEMPER." In *Computers and the Policy-Making Community,* ed. Davis B. Bobrow and Judah

L. Schwartz, pp. 222-45. Englewood Cliffs, N.J.: Prentice-Hall.

Guetzkow, Harold. 1950. "Long-Range Research in International Relations," *American Perspective* 4, 4 (Fall): 421-40. [Reprinted in *International Politics and Foreign Policy*, ed. James N. Rosenau (New York: Free Press, 1961), pp. 53-59.]

———. 1962. *Simulation in Social Science: Readings.* Englewood Cliffs, N.J.: Prentice-Hall.

———. 1963. "A Use of Simulation in the Study of Inter-Nation Relations." In *Simulation in International Relations,* by Harold Guetzkow, et al., pp. 24-38. Englewood Cliffs, N.J.: Prentice-Hall.

———. 1966. "Simulation in International Relations." In *Proceedings of the IBM Scientific Computer Symposium on Simulation Models and Gaming,* pp. 249-78. Yorktown Heights, N.Y.: Thomas J. Watson Research Center.

———. 1968. "Some Correspondences between Simulations and 'Realities' in International Relations." In *New Approaches to International Relations,* ed. Morton A. Kaplan, pp. 202-69. New York: St. Martin's.

———. 1969. "Simulations in the Consolidation and Utilization of Knowledge about International Relations." In *Theory and Research on the Causes of War,* ed. Dean G. Pruitt and Richard C. Snyder, pp. 284-300. Englewood Cliffs, N.J.: Prentice-Hall.

———. 1970. "A Decade of Life with the Inter-Nation Simulation." In *The Process of Model-Building in the Behavioral Sciences,* ed. Ralph M. Stogdill, pp. 31-53. Columbus: Ohio State Univ. Press.

———, Philip Kotler, and Randall L. Schultz, eds. 1972. *Simulation in Social and Administrative Science: Overviews and Case-Examples.* Englewood Cliffs, N.J.: Prentice-Hall.

———. 1974. "Collaboration in Computer Simulation for Decision-Making in International Affairs." *International Studies Notes* 1 (Spring): 8-9.

Hermann, Margaret G. 1965. "Stress, Self-esteem, and Defensiveness in an Inter-Nation Simulation." Ph.D. dissertation, Northwestern Univ.

Hoole, Francis W. 1971. "The Simulation of Alternative Budgetary Futures for the World Health Organization." In *The United Nations,* ed. Edwin Fedder. St. Louis: Univ. of Missouri, Center for International Studies.

Jensen, Lloyd. 1966. "American Foreign Policy Elites and the Prediction of International Events." *Papers, Peace Research Society (International)* 5: 199-209.

Jones, Susan D., and J. David Singer. 1972. *Beyond Conjecture in International Politics: Abstracts of Data-based Research.* Itasca, Ill.: Peacock.

Leavitt, Michael. 1971. "A Computer Simulation of International Alliance Behavior." Ph.D. dissertation, Northwestern Univ.

Liska, George. 1962. *Nations in Alliance: The Limits of Interdependence.* Baltimore: Johns Hopkins.

McClelland, Charles A., and Gary D. Hoggard. 1969. "Conflict Patterns in the Interactions among Nations." In *International Politics and Foreign Policy,* ed. James N. Rosenau, pp. 711-24. New York: Free Press.

Modelski, George. 1970. "Simulations, Realities and the International Relations Theory." *Simulation and Games* 1, 2: 111-34.

———. 1972. *Principles of World Politics.* New York: Free Press.

Morgenthau, Hans J. 1954. *Politics among Nations.* 2d ed. New York: Knopf.

Pendley, Robert E., and Charles D. Elder. 1966. "An Analysis of Office Holding in the Inter-Nation Simulation in Terms of Contemporary Political Theory and Data on the Stability of Regimes and Governments." Mimeo. Evanston, Ill.: Northwestern Univ.

Pfaltzgraff, Robert L. 1972. "Simulation and International Relations Theory: A Comparison of Simulation Models and International Relations Literature." Mimeo. Medford, Mass: Tufts Univ.

Powell, Charles A. 1969. "Simulation: The Anatomy of a Fad." *Acta Politica* 4, 3: 299-329.

Raser, John R., and Wayne J. Crow. 1964. "WINSAFE No. II: An Inter-Nation Simulation Study of Deterrence Postures Embodying Capacity to Delay Response." China Lake, Calif.: U.S. Naval Ordnance Test Station, Project Michelson.

Rosenau, James N., ed. 1961. *International Politics and Foreign Policy.* New York: Free Press.

Rummel, Rudolph J. 1966. "Some Dimensions in the Foreign Behavior of Nations." *Journal of Peace Research* 3: 201-23.

Russett, Bruce M. 1970. "Methodological and Theoretical Schools in International Relations." In *A Design for International Relations Research,* ed. Norman D. Palmer, pp. 87-105. Philadelphia: American Academy of Political and Social Science.

Simon, Herbert A. 1969. *The Sciences of the Artificial.* Cambridge: MIT Press.

Smoker, Paul. 1965a. "Trade, Defense and the Richardson Theory of Arms Races: A Seven-Nation Study." *Journal of Peace Research* 2: 161-76.

———. 1965b. "The Arms Race: A Wave Model." *Papers, Peace Research Society (International)* 4: 151-92.

———. 1967. "The Arms Race as an Open and Closed System." *Papers, Peace Research Society (International)* 7: 41-62.

———. 1968. "International Processes Simulation: A Man-Computer Model." Mimeo. Evanston, Ill.: Northwestern Univ.

———. 1969. "Social Research for Social Anticipation." *American Behavioral Scientist* 12, 6: 7-13.

———. 1970. "International Relations Simulations." *Peace Research Reviews* 3, 6: 1-84.

———. 1973. "An International Processes Simulation: Development, Usage, and Partial Validation. Part I: 'International Processes Simulation: A Man-Computer Model.' Part II: 'Analysis of Conflict Behaviors in an International Processes Simulation and International System, 1955-1960.'" Ann Arbor, Mich.: University Microfilms.

Snyder, Richard C. 1958. "A Decision-Making Approach to the Study of Political Phenomena." In *Approaches to the Study of Politics,* ed. R. Young, pp. 3-38. Evanston, Ill.: Northwestern Univ. Press.

Soroos, Marvin S. 1975. "Patterns of Cross-national Activities in the International Processes Simulation and a Real-World Reference System." In *International Interactions,* ed. Edward E. Azar. New York: Gordon & Breach.

Sullivan, Dennis. 1963. "Toward an Inventory of Major Propositions Contained in Contemporary Textbooks in International Relations." Ph.D. dissertation, Northwestern Univ.

——— and Robert Noel. 1972. "Inter-Nation Simulation: A Review of Its Premises." In *Simulation and Gaming in Social Science,* ed. Michael Inbar and Clarice S. Stoll, pp. 111-24. New York: Free Press.

Wentworth, Donald R., and Darrell R. Lewis. 1973. "A Review of Research of Instructional Games and Simulations in Social Science Education." *Social Education* 37, 5 (May): 432-40.

Wright, Quincy. 1955. *The Study of International Relations.* New York: Appleton-Century-Crofts.

Zinnes, Dina A. 1966. "A Comparison of Hostile Behavior of Decision Makers in Simulate and Historical Data." *World Politics* 18, 3: 474-502.

9. An Inside Appraisal of the World Event Interaction Survey

Charles A. McClelland

A request to render an accounting of one's own past research efforts produces a disquieting effect. An initial reaction is that evaluations ought to be done by others; it appears to ask too much to be impelled to recall half-forgotten motivations and to judge consequences, worthy and otherwise, arising from the work undertaken according to those motivations. Turning to the use of the past tense is, in itself, mildly disconcerting. This stimulates ideas that seem faintly illicit: what would one expect to hear from a dear departed if he had a chance to participate actively in the celebration of his own wake? A venture into this question contains the possibility of a protest. What if the loved one should suddenly come upright to bawl out the lyrics of a popular song, "we've only just begun . . ."? There is, of course, a more likely scenario. The gathering might be entertained by a glowing self-tribute to heroic struggles undertaken against great odds—entertained, but with full knowledge that the accounting is a fabrication, a pack of lies. As those who study politics come to realize, the seasoned prevaricator exploits one great resource, the absolute and solemn declaration that he speaks only the truth.

Hence, reader beware: what follows is the brief but truthful, unbiased, and unvarnished narrative of the origins, purposes, developments, and accomplishments of the World Event Interaction Survey (WEIS). The story begins in the fall of 1954 with the discovery of the relevance of general systems "theory," which was propounded in a prospectus circulated by Ludwig von Bertalanffy (and later incorporated into a 1956 article) on behalf of the founding of a systems research society. General systems theory, it was perceived, has a bearing on the understanding of international relations. The contact with the systems concept put together programmatically in one's mind a lot of floating, erstwhile disconnected pieces of the phenomena of international relations. The subject matter of international affairs should be thought of altogether as the material of a dynamic, open, exchanging, adaptive, and complex system. Existing ordering ideas and organizing explanations about the relations among nations might be associated, compared, and integrated within the broad conceptual domain of "systems." Thus, an essay on that topic was published (McClelland, 1955) in pursuit of such conceptual reconciliation and unification. Broad homomorphisms were detected in the variety of conceptualizations which, just then, passed as the theory of international relations. That time was the beginning of the period of the inward rush to the study of international relations of conceptualizations from the "behavioral" fields—sociology, psychology, anthropology, and biology.

The unanticipated appearance in 1957 of Morton Kaplan's formulation of a systems application to international politics pushed the idea to the foreground. There was much puzzlement over what Kaplan was saying. His book was seen very quickly as a landmark event but just what it encompassed and designated for long remained unclear. What is an international system? The Western state system was an old and established term. Was that the real topic, only garbed now in new and hard-to-understand terminology or was it something else? If the concept of systems was a pregnant idea for international relations, the students of the field wanted information on what the promise was. The borrowed abstractions, even after their refashioning by Kaplan, did not seem to come to grips with this requirement. In the same period, Karl Deutsch (1952, 1953, 1954) was writing very interesting things about the relevance of systems, cybernetics, communication, and control to the study of politics. Some important innovation seemed to be lurking in the background but it would not come forward into full sight. The systems approach was a naked body searching for clothing. The empirical referents of the idea needed anchoring.

The advantages of hindsight and rationalization now allow us a more coherent view of the ferment of a decade and a half ago. Neat, summarizing sentences can be presented. The impulse, for which the systems conceptualization became an instrument, was to find some way to push back confining definitions that equated international politics with international relations, that identified political action with the exercise of power, that made power out to be a quasi-mystical substance one either had or lacked, and that, in any case, was weighed on some kind of balancing scale in the assessment of foreign policies.

In trying to think back carefully and to recall the intellectual milieu prevailing fifteen or twenty years ago, I find reasons to say that some liberating definitions have been achieved, indeed, and that "systems thinking" contributed importantly to the change.

John Burton's characterization of the old and the new thought goes too far, in my opinion, when he puts a "billiard ball-power" formulation in opposition to a "cobweb" of interactions approach (Burton et al., 1974). It is not a case of one displacing the other, but rather of the new shifting the perspective and modifying the old. Similarly, the idea that inter-state relations have lost meaning and legitimacy and that an orientation toward a world society is required now is a misconception. Instead, current prevailing definitions make room for multiple concepts of international, transnational, and supranational phenomena. The play of power and influence has come to be understood as a highly variable process of interaction including about as much psychology as military hardware. The increasing dependencies and vulnerabilities of nations call for more collaborative efforts, but they also sharpen the awareness of the need for national self-defense. As Michel Jobert, the former minister of foreign affairs of France, reminded his colleagues during the energy crisis of 1974, when affairs are going well, international collaboration also goes well, but when affairs go badly each country looks to ways to assure its own safety.

It is a systems concept that the substance of international relations is a flow of interaction. It is a systems concept that relations are established and disestablished by the sequential occurrences of events, that events are the basic units of observation, and that changes of state in relations are the central topics of theory and research for world politics. A systems concept is being used when it is said, as it often is today, that there are circular flows of policy and action moving both within and between nations in complex patterns. Some international activities are highly organized and patterned while others are more chaotic and are contingent on policy choices that are too individual or too arbitrary to be foreseen or countered. Finally, the notion has become very familiar that the relations of most nations, most of the time, find an ordinary level of operation in a kind of steady state of exchange and interaction. From time to time, there are breaks or interruptions of this steady state. Such disturbances most often have localized properties, but they frequently can spread along the networks of interaction to affect many governments and countries. Crises, confrontations, and violent conflicts are among the visible manifestations of these sudden and usually short-lived disturbances.

Regular behavior defines a system. Although it is still little understood, the matter of distinguishing between system and non-system behavior need not be based on insight and intuitive judgments. Very definite analytic procedures for identifying system states exist, whether they are a steady state condition, under disturbance, or in transition between the two. Empirical research along appropriate lines is necessary to discover the rules of change of regular behavior before the determination of the actuality of a system can be made. Since the late 1950s, most of my inquiries have been directed to the search for actual system manifestations in international behavior. The disturbances—the crises and confrontations—have remained the most challenging topics.

By 1958, my research attentions were being drawn to applications of the systems approach to the data of Cold War crises such as the Berlin Blockade and the Suez conflict of 1956. These episodes appeared to be disturbances in the flow of steady state relations of nations. The problem was to show what the system approach meant in concrete, historical terms. This might be done by demonstrating that there were regular and reappearing forms of behavior in the crises. If it were shown how the crises came and went in a sequence of stages following identified rules of change, a practical use of the systems conceptualization would be illustrated. A way had to be found to

index data so that the appearance of a phase or stage could be discerned clearly. This requirement was the beginning of the categorization of specific international events by "elemental" type. The concept was that the volume of the event flow and the combinations of event types might, together, provide the method of indexing. The evidence of the efforts to clarify and develop the ordering idea of event accounting can be found in several journal articles (McClelland, 1961, 1962, 1964). Several studies of the sequential development of stages of particular crises according to changes in the event flows were made in this period, but were never published. The means of handling data gathering and data aggregation remained uncertain, and the conceptualization itself lacked stability.

By 1964 a system for coding international events had been hit upon—it was the forerunner of the 63 WEIS codes—and the Berlin crisis study was underway as a test of a first quantitative application. The results were subsequently reported as a chapter in a collection of essays on quantitative international politics (McClelland, 1968). In the concluding paragraphs of that chapter a theoretical worry was expressed about the missing parts of systemic analyses of international crises. The onset and abatement of a particular crisis ought not to be treated in isolation from the particular setting in which it occurred. This was characterized as the problem of the context. The logic in the problem was this: if crises were manifestations of severe disturbances of the steady state conditions of the relations of nations that constituted the system, then knowledge of the character of the steady state—its interaction patterns, its behavioral boundaries, its variations and fluctuations—would appear to be essential to the understanding of crisis phenomena. Crises arise in the context of pre-existing situational settings and they lapse eventually into subsequent situational settings. Analyses of crises ought not to be isolated from these before and after conditions. The new question was, how might one go about providing an index—a set of measures—for the flow of international action and interaction when crises are not occurring? The origin of WEIS is to be found in the motivation to try to answer this question.

A step ahead was taken in 1965 in the China Lake research project on "The Chinese Performance in Crisis and Noncrisis." This study of the Taiwan confrontations (McClelland, 1967) was launched on the initiative of a small group of graduate students who wrote the proposal, did the group research, and struggled with the drafts of the report on the work. My role was that of advisor, conflict manager, and rewrite man. The Taiwan investigation was a case study. The non-crisis analyses covered only a sector of system interaction and not the whole. The real need was to arrive at an accounting of the ongoing event flows for crises and noncrises covering developments in the interstate relations of all countries. Coverage of a single conflict arena was not enough; a world survey was needed.

Whether or not a small group operating in a university environment could cope with the data-gathering problems of a world survey of reported international events was a serious and intimidating question. In addition to gathering the reporting in a data file, the needs were to learn the techniques of converting the material to computer-usable forms, to organize and reduce the material so it could be analyzed, and to produce research results at the end of the data management process. In 1966, the WEIS category scheme was refined and stabilized during a period of collaborative inquiry with Wayne R. Martin and Robert A. Young, a period that I now recall as the most creative within my experience. Concurrently, a pilot effort was launched to see if it was really feasible to make a day-to-day survey of reported governmental activities across national boundaries using a major newspaper source. The proposal for the funding of WEIS followed when we decided the work could be done.

The World Event Interaction Survey was supported by the Advanced Research Projects Agency, Behavioral Sciences between 1967 and 1973. In addition to the identification of the steady state conditions of international interactions that were conceived as baseline contexts of international crises, the survey had other motivations. We wanted to revive the group research activity of the China Lake experiment. There was the challenge to learn the current quantitative methodologies and computer procedures that were then being thrust into the foreground of attention in the field. It was important to provide financial support for some graduate students in work related to the advancement of their skills and knowledge on the way to a degree in the discipline. The critics of the systems approach who were coming into full hue and cry about the empty character of the notion, the failure to produce results, etc. should have answers, not by counter-argument but through the appearance of research results. We would work to make clothes for the naked systems body.

In the spirit of self-tribute, I would make the declaration that the WEIS effort, between 1966 and 1973, worked: we created computerized chronologies, tested the coding, devised an inventory of computer-based analytical tools for studying the phenomena, and, finally, set up and made initial tests with an analytical "package" for making short-range projections of what should happen in the future, given the record of past event flows. We did what we promised to do. Feasibility was demonstrated and applications were carried out in several ways.

The end of funding for WEIS in August 1973 has stimulated further the question of what was accomplished. My reaction has been toward protesting against that usage of the past tense. As I see it, the circumstances are those of beginnings rather than endings. As noted above, the immediate goals of a world survey of international events were reached during the five years of development, but these lay in the direction of techniques of data acquisition, data management, and practical aspects of monitoring and projecting. What about gains of a more fundamental kind? Will the work, as it continues, eventually make contributions to theory in the study of international relations? Does the approach show signs of producing cumulative results? Self-involvement prompts one to give positive answers to all these questions. The skeptics who suspect that the system perspective has little to offer to theory, and the critics who doubt that the indexing of the flow of international behavior is useful, will provide all the negative reactions that are needed.

In the matter of providing empirical covering for the skeleton of international systems, I see the achievement to date through event analysis to be a miniscule part of what yet can be attained. The guiding concept of steady state behavior flows in the relations of nations interrupted by short-lived disturbances maintains its value when confronted by event data. Many analyses confirm that both the total reported event flow and the event flows between the 25,000 pairs of national actors stay within steady, predictable ranges of performance under most month-by-month observations. The difficulties lie in establishing a firm taxonomy by which one not only could name the types of steady state and normal range behavior configurations, but also could specify the common change sequences of one pattern type succeeding another. One research result is sure: there is no simple and determinate pattern or sequence in the reported stream of public international events. Despite some published claims to the contrary, event analysis has not developed to the point of accurate projections covering those occasions when a break out into crisis or severe conflict can be foreseen to interrupt the day-to-day flow of regular international interactions. The testing for regularity in action-response patterns—in other words, the identifying of actual system in the conceived system—is still close to the beginning. Thus, the expected contribution to basic theory with regard to the identification of what is stochastically regular in the system remains to be demonstrated.

One serious handicap is the short run of the time series of world surveys of events. Experience in other fields where the accumulation of data of dynamic phenomena is a central concern suggests that a 20- to 30-year time series is an adequate baseline against which current developments can be compared. WEIS has had only a seven-year data base—a time span obviously too short to allow numerous reappearances of patterned interaction phenomena. Opinions vary on the best ways to extend the series; the problem is that data acquisition activities tend to dominate event research unless they are carefully curbed. I have had a strong preference to build files in "real time" and to acquire experience in analyses by attempting projections to short-range futures, rather than by investing the effort to go back to earlier years.

A second handicap that restricts the prospect of making fundamental contributions is the prevailing lack of variety in the recoding systems for events. The insight into the complexity represented by the notion of international systems would appear to

require the development of rather large numbers of perspectives on international events. The latter ought to be observed from a number of viewing angles. The WEIS event category scheme constitutes a window that opens on the current historical manifestation of action and response going on between and among national governments, but it is only one window. Other perspectives should develop so that additional dimensions can be added to systems and event studies.

It is gratifying, if not flattering, to see relatively large numbers of international relations students adopting the WEIS categories and extending, reshaping, and refining them for a variety of studies. No complaint can be issued on that account. The argument that international event data investigations represent an example of research cumulation hinges mainly on the evidence that many students have been borrowing and building in a mutually reinforcing effort. Burgess and Lawton (1972) have mobilized the pertinent details in their inventory of the events data movement. Nevertheless, I remain concerned about the narrowness of the existing perspectives on international event research. What some of the other windows opening on the study and indexing of international behavior may be is not difficult to specify. Elsewhere, I have tried to attract attention to other perspectives and other data analysis problems that "compound the dependent variable," but there is little current indication that we are widening the scope of event research as we should.

Two points must be emphasized in the correction of such liabilities: (1) it is necessary to realize that the filling out of the systems approach to international relations is still close to its beginnings, despite the years that have passed since the idea was first broached and, (2) much more empirically oriented research and much more "data confrontation" lie ahead.

The last contention flies in the face of the prevailing belief that the critical task in advancing international studies is the improvement of theory. By calling for more research, I place myself in the group of industrious tailors to a naked emperor (Young, 1969). In the context of the critical literature of the field in recent years, this position suggests a devotion to mindless data grubbing and to inductionist analyses that are almost certain to be infertile in results that "contribute to theory." The advocates of deductive theorizing and the enthusiasts who cleave to the prescriptions of the philosophy of science have so gotten the upper hand in the evaluations of research in international studies that they have everyone intimidated. Russett (1969) has reacted to this "virtual rejection of inductive procedures" by saying he finds the argument unprofitable and silly. I would add that I believe the prevailing attitudes about theory are damaging to innovation and to the widening of knowledge in the field. An appropriate counter attitude is in the advice, "let theory take care of itself." It cannot be commanded into being. It does not arise from campaigns to produce it because it is needed. It does not take any one particular form and, certainly, its generation does not depend on pledges to conduct inquiries by deduction or by induction. Insight and the recognition of relationships are, in my view, the vital operations in the origination of theory. Observation, induction, and deduction are intellectual activities that intermingle in research, but with no particular ordering in their usage. Theory floats free from research in the sense that it may, on some occasions, come before research is initiated, on others, it may follow it by way of generalization or conclusion, and, on still others, it may make no appearance whatsoever. My reaction to the question "Where have all the theories gone?" (Phillips, 1974) has two parts: there were precious few to slip away in the first place and they cannot be induced to come forward, by the pressures of endless theorizing about theorizing. The attempt to force theory development has become, in my judgment, a third major handicap to event research and analysis as well as to other kinds of international inquiry.

The "heroic decade" between the mid-1950s and the mid-1960s was marked by the struggle to calibrate and integrate the inflowing conceptualizations from the behavioral fields for international relations. It was followed by the "theory and method" decade, a period given over to self-inspection and the burnishing of the tools of the trade. The hope is that now academic international relations will resume its task: simply, to provide the accounting for and the interpretation of what is transpiring and developing on the globe in the human enterprise. The prospect is not that of a return to current affairs descriptions of interstate relations as these were developed in the 1930s. The unfolding event flows within and between nations are still the prime raw materials of international relations analysis; it is to be presumed that two decades of making ready through concept articulation and tool sharpening will result in a much improved processing of these materials.

We are aided now by the insight that we are dealing with manifested behavior in large, complex, adaptive systems of relations arising among component parts that become increasingly interdependent and interactive. There is, too, a general awareness that we are among the beneficiaries of the revolution in technology related to data acquisition and data management. Whole earth perspectives become practical if we can expand our mental grasp to the dimension of this technological advance, already consolidated and coming just now into full operation. These are the considerations that I am convinced give reason for expecting transforming, beneficial changes in international studies. The recent past of the field should be seen as beginnings, not culminations. Research enterprises such as WEIS merely kicked the ball onto the field. The game begins now.

REFERENCES

Bertalanffy, Ludwig von. 1956. "General System Theory." In *General Systems Yearbook,* vol. 1, pp. 1-10. Bedford, Mass.: Society for General Systems Research.

Burgess, Philip M., and Raymond W. Lawton. 1972. *Indicators of International Behavior: An Assessment of Events Data Research.* Beverly Hills: Sage.

Burton, J. W., A. J. R. Groom, C. R. Mitchell, and A.V.S. DeReuck. 1974. *The Study of World Society: A London Perspective.* Pittsburgh: International Studies Association.

Deutsch, Karl W. 1952. "On Communication Models in Social Science." *Public Opinion Quarterly* 16 (Fall): 356-80.

———. 1953. *Nationalism and Social Communication: An Inquiry into the Foundations of Nationality.* New York: Wiley.

———. 1954. *Political Community at the International Level.* New York: Doubleday.

Kaplan, Morton A. 1957. *System and Process in International Politics.* New York: Wiley.

McClelland, Charles A. 1955. "Applications of General System Theory in International Relations." *Main Currents in Modern Thought* 12 (Nov): 27-34.

———. 1961. "The Acute International Crisis." *World Politics* 14 (Oct): 182-204.

———. 1962. "Decisional Opportunity and Political Controversy: The Quemoy Case." *Journal of Conflict Resolution* 6: 201-13.

———. 1964. "Action Structures and Communication in Two International Crises: Quemoy and Berlin." *Background* 7 (Feb): 201-15.

———. 1967. "The Communist Chinese Performance in Crisis and Noncrisis: Quantitative Studies of the Taiwan Straits Confrontation, 1950-1964." China Lake, Calif.: U.S. Naval Ordnance Test Station.

———. 1968. "Access to Berlin: The Quantity and Variety of Events, 1948-1963." In *Quantitative International Politics,* ed. J. David Singer, pp. 159-86. New York: Free Press.

Phillips, Warren R. 1974. "Where Have All the Theories Gone?" *World Politics* 26 (Jan): 155-89.

Russett, Bruce M. 1969. "The Young Science of International Politics." *World Politics* 22 (Oct): 87-94.

Young, Oran R. 1969. "Professor Russett: Industrious Tailor to a Naked Emperor." *World Politics* 21 (Apr): 486-511.

10. War, Presidents, and Public Opinion

John E. Mueller

In the 1960s a large body of public opinion data was deposited at and made accessible by the Roper Public Opinion Research Center at Williams College. The data consisted of original survey materials accumulated over several decades by major organizations such as the American Institute of Public Opinion (Gallup Poll), the National Opinion Research Center, and various state and regional polls.

For the most part these materials had been usable previously, if at all, only with enormous effort, by working through the research libraries (if that's what they could be called) of the individual polling agencies. Beyond that one had to rely on published poll results which, because of a journalistic necessity for timeliness, were often incomplete, directed to the wrong question, or self-contradictory.

My National Science Foundation (NSF) project was initially directed at exploiting these newly available data (as well as other relevant materials and research) for use in my topic of interest: public opinion in wartime. Essentially, the poll data were to be used as historical materials reflecting the public's state of mind in times past. I was, therefore, at the mercy of the whims and vagaries of the polling process; if Gallup in February 1951 chose not to ask a certain question that I had come to regard as vital, no amount of mourning on my part could undo that fact. Because of this, the kinds of questions and notions (sometimes known as hypotheses) to be explored were limited, and serendipity probably was unusually important in my research.

At the outset I found little previous research that was very helpful and, when my interests changed somewhat, this became even more the case. I was first led into the area through an interest in public opinion data from World War II; the interest was encouraged by many hours of exploration through the Cantril and Strunk compendium (1951). Research on attitudes toward World War II was fairly extensive, although most of it reflected a psychological or social-psychological perspective and a methodology (for example: What do my sophomores think about war?) that was not entirely helpful for my purposes. Furthermore, almost all of it had been done during the war and tended to be more timely than timeless.

As my own research evolved, however, I was led to concentrate on attitudes toward the wars in Korea and Vietnam more than on World War II. This occurred for two reasons. First, it became clear that the poll data from the later wars were more reliable as the agencies had gained experience and improved their methods (the 1948 election prediction disaster was no small incentive). Thus, the later data could stand more kicking around. Second, I became convinced that a *comparative* perspective is almost the only valid way to deal with public opinion data. The comparison of sub-groups, of the same questions asked at different times, and of questions with different wording all led to the possibility of a rather grand compari-son—that of public attitudes toward two similar wars—which was especially appealing.

The amount of existing research on which to build was very small in this area. Partly because of the unavailability of the poll data, the research studies on attitudes toward Korea consisted mostly of one analysis of student opinion, one study of opinion on the United Nations, including its handling of the war, one study of the Truman-MacArthur controversy, and miscellaneous mater-ials in election studies. And it was, of course, impossible to find previous research on Vietnam because the war was going on at the time I was doing *my* research.

In addition, broader studies of public opinion and foreign policy were consulted that were help-ful from time to time in suggesting lines and con-cepts of inquiry. However, these were usually less data-oriented than I would have preferred and many of the suggested notions could not be tested with the existing data.

The cumulative nature of this research, there-fore, is found more in its relation to what was happening concurrently than to what had been published previously. In that sense, the cumulation seems to have been considerable; it was dramatized several times almost by a race to publish. The most striking example of this occurred when the book I had written was in galleys (Mueller, 1973). Andre Modigliani sent me a paper, subsequently pub-lished in 1972, that overlapped heavily with one of the chapters in my book. Working completely independently and with almost opposite initial perspectives, we nonetheless had come to very similar conclusions. We have since been trying to reconcile our differences—an attempt made all the more interesting by our broad base of agreement. This may not be a very efficient way to operate. It would have been better, I suppose, had we known about each other *before* putting our pontifications on paper, but it does suggest, I think, that the data we used maintained a certain integrity under con-siderable manipulation, something that does not seem to be universal in the data-based interna-tional relations research I have seen.

This confidence in the data is further bolstered by much of the other research in the area. Some of it has been pretty terrible, but most of it hangs together rather well. There has been some replica-tion of findings and a considerable filling-in of chinks.

Another research project accomplished under the NSF grant is an exploration of presidential popularity. Since the early stages of the project I have been interested in doing trend analysis of public opinion poll data. It has often proved diffi-cult to satisfy this interest because the polling agencies have a frustrating habit of becoming bored with questions that are no longer topical.

In the case of the presidential popularity ques-tion, however, they have proved more constant; there is a long line of data results for this question, from 1945 to the present. I used regression tech-niques to assess the behavior of this line and, in determining how to establish a set of independent variables, I found existing literature on the presi-dency to be most helpful. There is a considerable amount of learned speculation on how people should, or do, relate to their president (for example, do they rally to his support at the time of crisis?). It was possible to build some of this into the regression analysis.

I have published the results of my explorations (Mueller, 1970, 1971, 1973, 1974) and have given the data to several other researchers who are work-ing toward refinements and/or refutations. I have begun to extend the analysis to subgroups of the population and it may also prove possible to extend my findings to later administrations. (How Watergate can be handled, I'm not sure, perhaps with a dummy variable.)

In approaching data analysis, I am most comfortable using a kind of inductive approach. I spend a considerable amount of time becoming familiar with the data until I feel confident that I have a feel for how they behave and for what they can—and cannot—be made to say. This involves many hours of sorting through—staring at—data arrayed in its rawest state. I also use cross-tabulations since this is a data analysis technique that loses no information. I only use measures of association after I have first satisfied myself that they truly reflect what is going on in the data. My tolerance for successive homogenizations of the data through the sequential application of data reduction techniques (correlation to factor analysis to regression analysis, for example) is extremely limited.

My purpose for using this approach is to ferret out regularities that may be generalizable to some degree. To be worthy of further exploration a finding must appear in a variety of circumstances across a broad set of polls; it is possible to prove anything with a single example. My results, then, are a series of data-based generalizations, some linked, some not. It seems to me that this approach strains the data least and lends itself most readily to replication and cumulation.

If I am reasonably comfortable with what I and others have done in the field of public opinion research, it stems in large part from the conviction that the poll data really do measure something, that they do have a basic integrity. What is measured is not always what the polling agencies *think* they are measuring, and frequently the polls are being used to supply answers to questions they are incapable of answering (for example, "How many people favor the bombing of Cambodia?") But in the examination of hundreds of surveys, conducted under all sorts of circumstances, I keep seeing the same results and the same interrelationships come up over and over again: subgroups will relate in an expected way to the war; alterations in the wording of a question will change response patterns in a rather precisely predictable way; support for a war at its end can be expected to fit a time series equation based on data gathered in the beginning and middle phases of the war.

As indicated, there are considerable limitations to the data; most of them, like most historical materials, were not originally created with a view toward later analysis. And the public opinion poll itself is only reflective of a rather primitive stimulus-response situation where poorly thought-out answers are casually fitted to questions that are often overly ingenuous. As with other data, it is entirely possible to push these too far, to try to wring from them, through the unthinking application of overly elaborate research strategies, statements about the real world they are incapable of supplying. But used with care and caution, public opinion data can supply a base for coherent, cumulative research.

REFERENCES

Cantril, Hadley, and Mildred Strunk. 1951. *Public Opinion 1935-1946.* Princeton: Princeton Univ. Press.

Modigliani, Andre. 1972. "Hawks and Doves, Isolationism and Distrust: An Analysis of Public Opinion of Military Policy." *American Political Science Review* 56 (Sep): 260-78.

Mueller, John E. 1970. "Presidential Popularity from Truman to Johnson." *American Political Science Review* 64 (Mar): 18-34.

———. 1971. "Trends in Popular Support for the Wars in Korea and Vietnam." *American Political Science Review* 65 (Jun): 358-75.

———. 1973. *War, Presidents and Public Opinion.* New York: Wiley.

———. 1974. "Public Opinion and the President." In *The Presidency Reappraised,* ed. Rexford G. Tugwell and Thomas E. Cronin, pp. 133-147. New York: Praeger.

11. Bridging the Gap between Theory and Practice

Alexander L. George

In 1966, while with the Rand Corporation, I started a project on "Theory and Practice in International Relations." My objective was to demonstrate, by means of a carefully selected series of studies, how empirical research on international relations could assist in reducing the gap between scientifically oriented theory and the needs of the policy maker for prescriptive theory.

The problems investigated were chosen with several criteria in mind, including the relevance of each topic to the needs of foreign policy making and indications that academic researchers were already interested in some aspect of the problems.[1] It was my hope that initial exploratory research on each of these problems would be successful and interesting enough to interest other investigators to participate in a fuller study.

This research project was continued and expanded somewhat when I moved to Stanford in 1968. It was supported by the Committee on International Studies at Stanford and, during 1971-1973, by a National Science Foundation (NSF) grant for completing a study of deterrence theory and practice.

In developing policy-relevant theory I distinguish between "substantive" theory and "process" theory.[2] Both are needed, and they can complement each other in efforts to improve the effectiveness of foreign policy.

SUBSTANTIVE THEORY: STUDIES OF COERCIVE DIPLOMACY AND DETERRENCE

Substantive theory deals with problems that arise repeatedly in the conduct of international relations—for example, deterrence, coercive diplomacy, crisis management, war termination, alliance management, foreign aid, etc. If policy makers have access to well-developed substantive theories on each of these familiar types of undertaking in international relations, they are likely to diagnose situations more adequately and to choose more effective policy options.

Given the objective of my research program—i.e., to reduce the gap between theory and practice—it has been necessary to clarify the policy maker's need for substantive theory. It is possible, by studying real-world policy making, to understand better the kinds of theories policy makers need and the ways in which they use them in diagnosing situations and prescribing for them. This in turn gives us a better understanding of the kinds of theories to strive to develop via systematic empirical research. I have characterized my understanding of the nature, requirements, and use of policy-relevant theory in a number of publications (George, 1968; George, Hall, and Simons, 1971; George and Smoke, 1974; Smoke and George, 1973; George, 1974c), and will only briefly recapitulate a few points here.

Policy makers need substantive theories for each type of undertaking that they may resort to from time to time in the conduct of foreign policy.[3] General theories—such as on "bargaining"—can also be of some utility in policy making. But more differentiated theories of task-

---

[1] The problems selected for study were: (1) deterrence; (2) coercive diplomacy; (3) detente theory and practice; (4) operational code belief systems; and (5) policy-oriented forecasting. Subsequently I added, as noted below, a study of management strategies for coping with dysfunctional effects of "bureaucratic politics" on policy making. Substantial work has been done on all of these topics, with the exception of detente theory and practice.

[2] For another elaboration of this distinction, see Chapter 20.

[3] I use the concept of "undertaking" along the same lines as was discussed by Rosenau (1968).

specific bargaining or interaction activities—such as deterrence, coercive diplomacy, or détente—will be more useful for policy-making purposes.

The substantive theory of each type of undertaking most relevant for policy making is one (a) that attempts to identify the *conditions* under which that type of undertaking is applicable and likely to prove to be a viable policy; and, in addition, (b) that attempts to provide a differentiated explanatory model that accounts for the *variance in the outcomes* for that kind of undertaking in terms of multiple independent and intervening variables, including those over which the policy maker has some control or leverage.

This approach to developing policy-relevant theory is informed by an awareness of the important *diagnostic* function that substantive theory can have in policy making. The policy maker needs empirically based theories that help him with the critically important task of diagnosing emergent situations. Much available theory gives policy makers little or no help in diagnosing situations. The diagnostic function of theory is often ignored or minimized in academic research aimed at producing theory.

The approach outlined here also emphasizes the need to develop substantive theory in the form of *conditional generalizations* which account for, and help predict, the variance in the dependent variable. Theory of this kind is helpful to the policy maker who must find, if possible, a reasoned, empirical basis for making the contingent predictions that are inherent in policy analysis.

In order to develop this kind of substantive theory for two types of foreign policy undertakings—deterrence and coercive diplomacy—I have employed a comparative case study approach (George, Hall, and Simons, 1971; George and Smoke, 1974).

I have described this research strategy in some detail in several publications (George, 1968; George, Hall, and Simons, 1971; George and Smoke, 1974; Smoke and George, 1973). Briefly recapitulated here, in both the deterrence study and that of coercive diplomacy I have employed the *method of structured, focused comparison.* This is a qualitative methodology for theory development that assures cumulation of empirical findings from case histories by following several

procedures. A set of standardized general questions are developed to reflect adequately the theoretical focus and to generate the data required for the focused analytical comparison. The same set of standardized general questions (with minor adaptations and with elaborations) are asked of each case in order to bring out the similarities and differences among them. The historical cases are carefully selected to comprise instances of the type of undertaking in question (for example, deterrence, coercive diplomacy, détente, etc.) and to provide as much variance in outcomes as possible.[4]

As the preceding remarks imply, and as I would like to emphasize now, political scientists have finally learned how to do case histories in ways that can avoid the disappointing experience of so many years with this type of study. Since Rosenau (1968) wrote his sober critique of the nonscientific, noncumulative character of foreign policy case histories, a number of political scientists working in different problem areas have independently achieved a similar breakthrough in devising a research strategy for systematic comparative study of case histories in ways that contribute to theory development.[5]

I would like to respond at this point to the request by Rosenau and Boynton for specific indications of the extent to which the research activities reported by conference participants have been linked to the work of other researchers. My deterrence study was influenced by the important thrust, as well as what I regarded as the limitations, of Russett's earlier efforts at empirical analysis of deterrence outcomes (1963, 1967). In turn, my own deterrence study has provided useful inputs to Gerald Shure's project at UCLA, which is examining deterrence problems via simulation and computer techniques.

Similarly, my coercive diplomacy study was informed by some of Schelling's observations regarding "compellance" (1966) and, in turn, some of the results of my study have been utilized and

[4]The sample may also include cases in which that type of undertaking was not adopted as policy, in order to provide variance in choice of policy as well as variance in outcomes achieved by that type of undertaking.

[5]In addition to my own use of the method of structured, focused comparison, see also Verba (1967), Russett (1970), Eckstein (forthcoming), Young (1968), Holsti (1972), Paige (1972), Smoke (1971), and Bloomfield (1974).

tested in Ray Tanter's project, Computer-Aided Conflict Information System (CACIS) at the University of Michigan. Also, some of the concepts and findings of my coercive diplomacy study have been incorporated into Glenn H. Snyder's effort to develop a more general bargaining theory (Snyder, 1972).

While the empirically derived theories of coercive diplomacy and of deterrence reported in my studies are presented at the verbal level, I have attempted to state them in a form that lends itself to replication and additional study by means of other research approaches, and to eventual restatement in mathematical form.

PROCESS THEORY

Process theory, on the other hand, deals with the question of how to structure and manage the policy-making process to increase the likelihood of producing effective decisions and of implementing them successfully. The availability of good substantive theory cannot by itself assure effective policies and outcomes—information must still be acquired and processed to produce a valid, incisive diagnosis of the situation as it emerges and evolves; and relevant policy options must be identified and properly analyzed so that substantive theory can be employed to sharpen the judgment that enters into the choice of a course of action and to heighten receptivity of the choice to feedback.

A closer look at process theories identifies two variants, one which focuses on improving the *structural design* of policy-making systems, and another which places emphasis on the day-to-day *management* of policy-making and policy-implementing systems rather than on structural design.

Despite numerous efforts in the past to restructure the machinery and procedures of foreign policy making (e.g., Clark and Legere, 1969; Destler, 1972), resulting improvements in policy performance have been marginal and uneven. While structural reorganization can aid in the quest for more effective policy, there is no single structural formula by means of which the chief executive and his staff can convert the functional expertise and diversity of viewpoints within and outside

the executive branch into consistently effective policies. This sober observation coincides with the evaluation of a broader range of experience in many different kinds of complex organizations (e.g., Bennis and Slater, 1968; Altschuler, 1968; Hilsman, 1964). As a result, organizational theorists have increasingly emphasized that efforts to improve policy making must go beyond the traditional tinkering with organizational structure and reformulation of standard operating procedures to the development of strategies for managing the policy-making system. The latter requires timely identification and correction of the kinds of malfunctions to which all complex organizations are prone (Wilensky, 1967; Downs, 1967; Maier, 1963; Vroom and Yetton, 1971).

My own work on process variables has gone in three directions.

[1] My dissatisfaction with certain aspects of research on bureaucratic politics led me to examine *alternative management strategies for coping with the dysfunctional aspects of bureaucratic politics* (George, 1972). This article identifies a number of questions and hypotheses for additional investigation both in field research and in the laboratory.

[2] I have also been engaged in mapping out a research program on the *types of stress encountered in political decision making and methods of coping with it.* (George, 1974a, 1974b). To study the effects of stress on foreign policy making requires a conceptual framework that takes into account three interrelated subsystems: the *individual-executive;* the *small group* context of face-to-face relationships the executive enters into with a relatively small number of advisers; and the *organizational* context of hierarchically organized processes involving the various departments and agencies concerned with foreign policy matters in the Executive Branch. Each of these three subsystems is capable of generating a special set of adaptive and maladaptive ways of coping with the impact of stress on decision making. The three subsystems often interact with each other in producing foreign policy outputs. The dynamic processes associated with each subsystem can affect the efforts to cope with the impact of stress on decision making within the other two subsystems favorably or adversely. My work on mul-

tiple advocacy, and on coping with stress in political decision making, has been linked for several years with parallel work by Irving Janis (1972). More recently, Ole Holsti and I have been collaborating in this area (Holsti and George, forthcoming).

[3] For several years, together with a number of collaborators, I have been exploring the utility of the operational code belief system approach to the study of political decision makers. Several years ago I outlined a standardized approach for operational code studies (George, 1969). Some eight or nine studies based on it have been completed or are underway. Several have already been published (Holsti, 1970; McLellan, 1971). Other studies focus on Dean Rusk, Senator Arthur Vandenburg, Senator William Fulbright, Ramsay MacDonald, Kurt Schumacher and Willy Brandt, Mao Tse-tung and Liu Shao-chi, and Getulio Vargas.[6]

Another study by one of my students, David Lampton, identifies changes in the U.S. image of the Chinese Communist leaders over a period of time and attempts to assess the influence of that image on American policy in three U.S.-Communist China foreign policy crises (Lampton, 1973). A comparative analysis of these operational codes is underway and Holsti is planning a follow-up series of studies of operational code beliefs of American foreign policy makers since World War II.

THE STATUS AND PROSPECTS OF INTERNATIONAL RELATIONS THEORY

My remarks on this topic will necessarily be brief and will draw upon some of the points made in my recent talk to the International Studies Association (1974c) and in the paper on policy-oriented forecasting (1973).

The familiar questions regarding the scientific or nonscientific character of research on international relations and whether such research is cumulative need to be reexamined in the light of the greater awareness that has emerged recently that the contending approaches to study of international relations are in good part not really compe-

titive; rather each serves a different purpose and does a somewhat different job.[7] Not only this, but we have begun to see ways in which these alternative approaches can complement and interact with each other in more complex research frameworks and in longer-range development strategies for improving both our knowledge of international affairs and our ability to use it more effectively.

The questions of the scientific character of international relations research and whether it cumulates adequately or rapidly enough need to be considered within a broader framework. The prior questions have to do with the purposes of the international relations theories we are attempting to develop and the uses which are to be made of them.

What Herbert Simon (1969) calls "design theory"[8] provides a focus and a comprehensive framework within which other approaches to accumulation of scientific knowledge and various kinds of theories can find a place. The theory of design is best understood as a comprehensive analytical framework. It explicates in a useful way the general types of problems, requirements, and procedures for translating knowledge into action in ways that are sensitive to values.

"Design exercises" are specific efforts to identify a preferred state of affairs and to judge whether such an objective is feasible, how it may be brought about, by what means, and at what cost. Design exercises, therefore, are a special form of prediction or, as I would prefer to call it, *analytical forecasting* for policy purposes. An analytical forecast is the output that a design exercise is supposed to produce. A full-blown analytical forecast attempts to specify the *necessary and sufficient conditions* for a given outcome, and also to indicate the *transitional strategies* and *scenarios* by means of which to bring about that desired outcome.

Obviously, most analytical forecasts can only approximate this; many of them will fall well short of this objective. Instead of disparaging design exercises that fall short of providing a full-blown

---

[6] For a more complete discussion of these studies, see Chapter 12.

[7] For a balanced statement along these lines see Bobrow (1972, pp. 11 ff.), Russett (1970), and Singer (1972).

[8] This is roughly the same as Bobrow's (1972) "engineering analytical framework" and what others have had in mind in using the terms "developmental models" and "policy science."

analytical forecast to which high confidence can be attached, both the forecaster and the policy maker would do better to regard them as exercises which help to clarify the uncertainties imbedded in the policy problem at hand. In identifying the various relevant uncertainties, the analytical forecast will provide useful inputs for the policy planner whose task it is to devise flexible plans and decision strategies for dealing in a more rational way with those uncertainties.

Design exercises of this kind can have considerable heuristic value for the further development of international relations theory. They can also be beneficial in stimulating multidisciplinary work. Thus, it should be noted, design exercises and analytical forecasts typically require an *intellectual synthesis* which can be achieved only by combining different analytic frameworks and different bodies of specialized knowledge, and by blending general international relations theory with specific historical models.

It is in this important sense, within the framework of design, that we shall find that many of our seemingly competing approaches to study of international affairs will complement each other and interact to produce analytical forecasts.[9] Thus, for example, we can readily see that different types of predictive models can perform complementary roles in design experiments. True, design theory does emphasize the necessity for predictive models that identify causal processes and, in particular, those causal variables over which the policy maker and other actors can exert some leverage in order to influence outcomes.

But design theory also recognizes—or should recognize—the contribution that can be made by statistically significant correlations that generate probabilistic forecasts without identifying the intervening causal processes. The latter type of

predictive model of course does not tell us how to avoid or to reduce the probability of an undesired outcome or how to increase the likelihood of a preferred outcome. But the probabilistic forecast is not thereby without policy relevance; it can be useful for designing a system for monitoring the environment, for providing "warning" of untoward developments or "indicators" of favorable opportunities, thereby alerting policy makers to the possible need for action of some kind.

9When a policy (or design) problem is broad and complex, analytical forecasting requires several different kinds of expertise. It also requires special procedures by means of which analytical interactions among the various specialized experts can take place within the framework of a holistic approach to problem solving. Analytical interaction among diverse experts is particularly necessary since there is usually no single theory that is adequate to serve as a forecasting model for the policy problem in question. Indeed, the analytical interaction of relevant experts may be regarded as an effort to create an ad hoc theory for the purpose at hand.

REFERENCES

Altschuler, A. A., ed. 1968. *The Politics of the Federal Bureaucracy.* New York: Dodd, Mead.

Bennis, W. G., and P. E. Slater. 1968. *The Temporary Society.* New York: Harper & Row.

Bloomfield, L. 1974. *Theories of State: Analyzing the Policy Process.* Beverly Hills: Sage.

Bobrow, D. 1972. *International Relations: New Approaches.* New York: Free Press.

Clark, K. C., and L. J. Legere, eds. 1969. *The President and the Management of National Security.* New York: Praeger.

Destler, I. M. 1972. *Presidents, Bureaucrats, and Foreign Policy.* Princeton: Princeton Univ. Press.

Downs, A. 1967. *Inside Bureaucracy.* Boston: Little, Brown.

Eckstein, H. Forthcoming. "Case Study and Theory in Macropolitics." In *A Handbook of Political Science,* ed. F. Greenstein and N. Polsby.

George, A. L. 1968. "Bridging the 'Gap' between Scholarly Research and Policy-Makers: The Problem of Theory and Action." Paper prepared for the Conference on Research on American Foreign Policy, Univ. of Denver, Graduate School of International Studies and the Social Science Foundation.

———. 1969. "The 'Operational Code': A Neglected Approach to the Study of Political Leaders and Decision-Making." *International Studies Quarterly* (Jun): 190-222.

———. 1972. "The Case for Multiple Advocacy in Making Foreign Policy." *American Political Science Review* 66 (Sep): 751-85.

———. 1973. "Policy-Oriented Forecasting." Mimeo. Stanford: Stanford Univ.

———. 1974a. "Policy-Oriented Forecasting." *International Studies Notes* 1 (Spring): 1-5.

———. 1974b. "Adaptation to Stress in Political Decision-Making: The Individual, Small Group, and Organizational Context." In *Coping and Adaptation,* ed. G. V.

Coelho, D. A. Hamburg, and J. Adams. New York: Basic Books.

———. 1974c. "Report on Minimizing 'Irrationalities.'" Paper prepared for the Commission on the Organization of the Government for the Conduct of Foreign Policy, Washington.

———, D. K. Hall, and W. E. Simons. 1971. *The Limits of Coercive Diplomacy.* Boston: Little, Brown.

——— and R. Smoke. 1974. *Deterrence in American Foreign Policy: Theory and Practice.* New York: Columbia Univ. Press.

Hilsman, R. 1964. *To Move a Nation.* New York: Doubleday.

Holsti, O. R. 1970. "The 'Operational Code' Approach to the Study of Political Leaders: John Foster Dulles' Philosophical and Instrumental Beliefs." *Canadian Journal of Political Science* 3 (Mar): 123-57.

———. 1972. *Crisis, Escalation, War.* Montreal: McGill-Queen's Univ. Press.

——— and A. L. George. Forthcoming. "The Effects of Stress on the Performance of Foreign Policy-Makers." In *Political Science Annual,* vol. 6, ed. C. P. Cotter.

Janis, I. L. 1972. *Victims of Groupthink: A Psychological Study of Foreign Policy Decisions and Fiascos.* Boston: Houghton Mifflin.

Lampton, D. 1973. "The U.S. Image of Peking in Three International Crises." *Western Political Quarterly* 26 (Mar): 28-50.

Maier, N.R.F. 1963. *Problem-Solving Discussions and Conferences.* Belmont, Calif.: Brooks/Cole.

McLellan, D. 1971. "The 'Operational Code' Approach to the Study of Political Leaders: Dean Acheson's Philosophical and Instrumental Beliefs." *Canadian Journal of Political Science* 4 (Mar): 52-75.

Paige, G. 1972. "Comparative Case Analysis of Crisis Decisions: Korea and Cuba." In *International Crises,* ed. C. F. Hermann, pp. 41-55. New York: Free Press.

Rosenau, J. N. 1968. "Moral Fervor, Systematic Analysis, and Scientific Consciousness in Foreign Policy Research." In *Political Science and Public Policy,* ed. A. Ranney, pp. 197-238. Chicago: Markham.

Russett, B. M. 1963. "Calculus of Deterrence." *Journal of Conflict Resolution* 7 (Mar): 97-109.

———. 1967. "Pearl Harbor: Deterrence Theory and Decision Theory." *Journal of Peace Research* 2 (Jun).

———. 1970. "International Behavior Research: Case Studies and Cumulation." In *Approaches to the Study of Political Science,* ed. M. Haas and H. S. Kariel. San Francisco: Chandler.

Schelling, T. 1966. *Arms and Influence.* New Haven: Yale Univ. Press.

Simon, H. 1969. *The Sciences of the Artificial.* Cambridge: MIT Press.

Singer, J. D. 1972. *The Scientific Study of Politics: An Approach to Foreign Policy Analysis.* Morristown, N.J.: General Learning Press.

Smoke, R. 1971. "Controlling Escalation." Ph.D. dissertation, Massachusetts Institute of Technology.

——— and A. L. George. 1973. "Theory for Policy in International Affairs." *Policy Science* 4 (Dec): 387-413.

Snyder, G. H. 1972. "Crisis Bargaining." In *International Crises,* ed. C. F. Hermann, pp. 217-56. New York: Free Press.

Verba, S. 1967. "Some Dilemmas in Comparative Research." *World Politics* 20 (Oct): 111-27.

Vroom, V. H., and P. W. Yetton. 1971. "Normative and Descriptive Models of Participation in Decision Marking." Paper prepared for Joint U.S.-Soviet Seminar on Organizational Design, Kiev, U.S.S.R.

Wilensky, H. L. 1967. *Organizational Intelligence.* New York: Basic Books.

Young, O. R. 1968. *The Politics of Force.* Princeton: Princeton Univ. Press.

12. Foreign Policy Decision Makers Viewed Psychologically: "Cognitive Process" Approaches

Ole R. Holsti

It is often difficult to recall exactly when and why one made many of the choices that ultimately led to a given line of investigation rather than to any of the alternatives. Luck, unanticipated consequences, and other unplanned factors have no doubt played an important role in many cases. I do, however, have a clear recollection of the circumstances that first awakened a persisting interest in the limitations of rational choice models for foreign policy analysis and, as a result, in the belief systems of decision makers.

As a second-year graduate student at Stanford I was awarded a teaching assistantship for a course in American public policy. Toward the end of the quarter two weeks were set aside for issues of foreign and defense policy, among them the doctrine of "massive retaliation" which had been developed and given official sanction some six years earlier by Secretary of State John Foster Dulles. I had known of the doctrine and the controversy it had set off, and I had some familiarity with critiques written by Henry Kissinger and others. But it was in the process of preparing for discussion sections that I became aware of how significantly the concept of massive retaliation was based not only on considerations of geopolitics,

weapons characteristics, and the like, but even more importantly, on a set of assumptions and beliefs about the nature of international politics, the role of rational calculation in decision making, and the nature of the adversary and his beliefs, motivations, and decision processes.

This teaching experience was the immediate stimulus that led my interests in a particular direction, but there were also more general factors that sustained them. A number of books and articles published in the preceding half decade seemed to offer interesting new ways of thinking about foreign policy and international politics. The Snyder, Bruck, and Sapin monograph (1962), although not yet available in book form, was widely read and discussed by graduate students. Of special relevance was its core premise that foreign policy choices could usefully be analyzed from the decision maker's perspective and his "definition of the situation." Kenneth Boulding's *The Image,* (1956) followed by an article (Boulding, 1959) that stressed the importance of images in international politics, was another important influence. A new interdisciplinary publication, *The Journal of Conflict Resolution,* provided an outlet for a number of articles by social scientists who questioned the assumption, widespread in conventional academic theories as well as in foreign offices and defense ministries, that foreign and defense policies could best be understood and formulated exclusively on the basis of rational choice models (Bauer, 1961; Osgood, 1959a; Wheeler, 1960). These authors suggested that important foreign policy decisions were sometimes made on the basis of "psycho-logic" rather than logic, and that failure to recog-

SPECIAL NOTE: An earlier and somewhat different draft of this chapter was prepared for the International Conference on Cognitive Models of Foreign Policy Decision-Making, London, March 17-24, 1973; it will be published as a chapter in *The Structure of Decision,* edited by Robert Axelrod. Axelrod and Matthew Bonham offered useful comments on earlier drafts. This chapter was written while I held fellowships from the Center for Advanced Study in the Behavioral Sciences and the Ford Foundation. Acknowledgement of my gratitude to the above does not imply their endorsement.

nize the fragility of rationality in choice situations, especially those decisions made under intense stress, might ultimately prove catastrophic for the nation, if not for mankind.

My interest in the limitations of rational choice models eventually led to a dissertation on John Foster Dulles that analyzed his belief system and images of the Soviet Union, and the manner in which these served as filters through which new information about the U.S.S.R. was processed and interpreted.

As a graduate student I had known of the existence of a pathbreaking project at Stanford—unofficially known as the "conflict project"—directed by Robert C. North. Its focus was on conflict dynamics, with a special attention devoted to the role of perceptions and misperceptions in creating, sustaining, or exacerbating conflict among nations (Koch et al., 1960; North et al., 1960; Zinnes et al., 1961). Among the project's many and varied activities was an intensive study of the processes by which the assassination of Archduke Franz Ferdinand on June 28, 1914 led to the outbreak of a general European war some six weeks later.

I had not been among the graduate students who had been associated with the 1914 study since its inception, but I joined this project upon completion of my dissertation. I was thus afforded a magnificent opportunity to extend my own education well beyond the bounds of my Ph.D. program, to pursue my interest in belief systems and perceptions in decision making within the context of a data-based project, and to share in the reformulation of important parts of the 1914 project (for example, all of the documentary materials were recoded to reflect intensity of perceptions as well as frequency, and several new categories were being added). Most importantly, it gave me the chance to work closely with Bob North, a gentle and wise scholar who always encouraged his colleagues to pursue new ideas.

Although the goals of the 1914 project were substantive and theoretical, a good deal of time was also devoted to methodological problems: identifying relevant documentary materials for coding, developing categories appropriate to our central interests in the perceptions of top-ranking decision makers, and working on techniques of content analysis that would permit replicable quantitative analysis. A number of alternative methods were developed and used in various studies (for summaries of these, see North et al., 1963; for applications see, among others, Zaninovich, 1964; Zinnes, 1962, 1968; Holsti, 1972). With the invaluable help and generous collaboration of Philip J. Stone—a Harvard social psychologist who had recently developed the "General Inquirer"—we also devised a method of thematic computer content analysis (Holsti, 1964), which was subsequently used in studies of the Cuban missile crisis and its aftermath (Holsti, Brody, and North, 1964; Clarke, 1964), alliance cohesion in NATO and the Warsaw Pact (Hopmann, 1967; Holsti, Hopmann, and Sullivan, 1973), Sino-Soviet relations (Holsti, 1966), the dynamics of the Soviet-American conflict during 1961-1963 (Morton, 1972), and conflict in the Middle East (Siverson, 1972).

These efforts did not, however, altogether resolve one of the persisting barriers to this type of research. Except for some very mechanical forms (for example, word counting), content analysis is usually tedious and laborious work. It is far more difficult to develop vast data banks comparable to those that exist for UN voting, event interaction data, and the like. As a result, the studies of the 1914 and other crises have inspired a modest amount of subsequent research compared, for example, to the McClelland WEIS project, the intellectual progenitor of the many "events data" studies.[1] Nevertheless, these studies have demonstrated the possibility of rigorous analysis yielding replicable data on perceptions and beliefs. They have also provided some empirical support for the general proposition that there are some circumstances in which decisions and conflict processes cannot fully be understood without reference to cognitive processes. This point is developed more fully later in this chapter.

My interests continue to center on cognitive processes in decision making, especially in the context of American foreign policy since World War II. Alexander George's (1969) reconceptualization of the "operational code" offers an approach to the role of belief systems in decision making that has, during the past half decade, inspired an im-

[1] See Chapter 9.

pressive number of case studies, as well as several efforts aimed at conceptual and methodological refinements (these are also described in more detail later in this chapter). The operational code approach will guide the research being undertaken by George and me on recent American foreign policy decisions.

The pages that follow attempt to survey some studies on cognitive processes and foreign policy, to assess some objections and barriers, and to provide a somewhat broader context against which to evaluate the progress and prospects for research of this type. Some emphasis will be given to the theme that engaged much of our attention at the Ojai conference—the problems and prospects of developing a cumulative literature.

COGNITIVE PROCESS APPROACHES TO FOREIGN POLICY

In the long run, if not in the short run as well, the course of international history seems likely to be shaped mainly by the convergence of forces in which the talents, aspirations, and perspectives of particular individuals are of relatively minor importance.

—Rosenau (1972)

Beliefs of foreign policy decision-makers are central to the study of decision outputs and probably account for more of the variance than any other single factor.

—Shapiro and Bonham (1973)

It is generally recognized that our behavior is in large part shaped by the manner in which we perceive, diagnose, and evaluate our physical and social environment. Our perceptions, in turn, are filtered through clusters of beliefs about what has been, what is, what will be, and what ought to be. Thus our beliefs provide us with a more or less coherent code by which we organize and make sense out of what would otherwise be a confusing array of signals picked up from the environment by our senses. Foreign policy decision makers are no different in this respect.[2] Yet, as the above

quotations indicate, students of international politics and foreign policy are far from agreeing about the central relevance or utility of research on the belief systems and cognitive processes of foreign policy leaders.[3] Analysts who take the affirmative side on this issue—in the sense that their research designs either focus upon, or at least leave room for the possible importance of, cognitive factors—appear to be in a distinct minority. Although there are some indications of a change in this respect,[4] to date there has been a relative neglect of systematic research focusing on the relationship among: belief systems; the manner in which such complex cognitive tasks as diagnosis of the situation, search for policy options, and evaluation are undertaken; choice behavior; and coping with feedback resulting from the selected policy.

This assessment can be documented in several ways. In many of the most prominent data-based research projects—for example, Dimensionality of Nations, WEIS, Correlates of War, Studies of International Conflict and Integration,[5] and Compara-

---

[2]Observations and examples throughout their paper tend to be drawn from studies of foreign policy decision making. Although circumstances under which cognitive process models are useful may occur with greater frequency in the foreign policy issue area, many of the observations on the utility, problems, and prospects of this perspective would apply with equal force to decision

making in other issue areas, or in other political contexts (cf. Converse, 1964; Cobb, 1973; Bennett, 1971; Putnam, 1973; Hammond, forthcoming).

[3]Belief systems and cognitive processes should be distinguished from ideology or mere policy preferences. Belief system refers to a more or less integrated set of beliefs about man's physical and social environment. In the case of political leaders, beliefs about history and the nature of politics may be especially important. Cognitive processes refer to various activities associated with problem solving (broadly conceived), including perception, appraisal, interpretation, search, information processing, strategies for coping with ambiguity, decision rules, verification, and the like. These cognitive activities are assumed to be in an interactive relationship with the individual's belief system, as well as with the environment.

[4]Signs of growing interest include the International Conference on Cognitive Models of Foreign Policy Decision-Making, as well as a number of projects in progress, some preliminary results of which are cited in the bibliography. Recent studies advocating greater attention to decision makers' beliefs, *and doing so on the basis of empirical evidence,* include: Art (1973), Steinbruner (1968, 1974), Stassen (1972), and Cottam (1973). Among broader assessments of alternative approaches to international politics, compare Alker (1973) and Boulding (1972).

[5]Although past studies of crises were concerned with cognitive and perceptual variables, more recent ones have been devoted to technology, population, and resources. "Our earlier analyses have focused on individual leaders' perceptions and cognitions. At this point we are not at all

tive Foreign Policy[6]—input-output models and those that stress attributes of the nation and the international system are clearly dominant. Empirically the research is heavily dependent on events data and aggregate data of various kinds. And few of these projects include analyses of decision making—the internal political process is usually black boxed—much less of belief systems and their effects on policy outcomes.

Limited systematic investigation of the linkages between beliefs and decision making characterizes not only the discipline as a whole, but also the research of those who have found a congenial intellectual home in the interstices between political science and psychology. A perusal of two reviews of the literature on foreign policy and international politics, undertaken from a social psychological perspective (Kelman, 1965; Etzioni, 1969; see also the extensive bibliography in Knutson, 1972, pp. 283-325), reveals that public attitudes, images and stereotypes; the effects of travel or personal contacts; and other forms of cross-national interaction have received considerable attention. Research on foreign policy leaders and their beliefs, perceptions, information processing strategies, and the like have been a secondary area of concern, even among those whose investigations are informed by theories, concepts, and data of a psychological nature. It may be useful to speculate on some general and specific reasons for this state of affairs, if only because doing so may point to genuine problems that stand in the way of developing rigorous theories and a cumulative body of empirical findings.[7]

There are a number of theoretical, methodological, and practical problems that have inhibited extensive application of cognitive process perspectives to foreign policy decision making. These include: disillusionment with some previous efforts of related kinds; skepticism about the relevance of psychological theories, insights, and evidence for analysis of political phenomena; the canon of parsimony; and difficulties of access to data, the laboriousness of coding, and related methodological problems.

Critical Reactions to Earlier Approaches

The continuing influence of critical reactions against previous efforts to deal with the individual and his psychological traits as primary units of analysis possibly contributes to the relative neglect of research on foreign policy officials, their cognitions and perceptions.

[1] The thesis that "war begins in the minds of men" acquired a substantial following after World War II, especially among behavioral scientists who sought to apply the insights of their own disciplines to the eradication or amelioration of international conflict. The optimistic vision of an almost infinitely malleable human nature and the tendency to ascribe conflict largely to misunderstanding, lack of communication, inadequate knowledge, or misperception were inviting targets for critical reaction (e.g., Waltz, 1959).

[2] Some approaches focused on the manner in which psychological aberrations or pathological needs of decision makers were projected into the international arena. The examples of Hitler and Stalin seemed to provide special relevance to this perspective. But, without denying that attention to nonlogical aspects of personality may provide some insight into the behavior of individual leaders, critics (e.g., Verba, 1961) questioned whether such explanations were either sufficient or necessary for understanding important international phenomena.

---

sure that such a focus represents the best possible choice. Our strategy now is to explore the capabilities of longer-range models to their fullest." Choucri and North (1972, p. 99).

[6]A consortium of scholars at various universities under the intellectual leadership of James N. Rosenau. Rosenau's extensive work on comparative foreign policy (1970, 1971) neglects neither internal political processes nor idiosyncratic variables, but most of those associated with the project have placed their emphasis elsewhere. A notable exception is the CREON project (Ohio State University) which is concerned with the effects of belief, attitudes, and decision styles on information processing and on foreign policy outputs. Data have been gathered for such variables as cognitive complexity, dogmatism, and belief in internal control of events (M. Hermann, 1972a, 1972b). For a summary of CREON research, see Rosenau, Burgess, and C. Hermann (1973) and Rosenau and C. Hermann (1973).

[7]Critiques of the premises, methodologies, or specific research results that have been employed in or emerged from various cognitive process studies include: Haas (1967), Hilton (1970), Jervis (1969), Mueller (1969a, 1969b), Goldmann (1971), and Brodin (1972).

[3] The "power school" which reached a position of dominance following World War II was also rooted in psychological theories of political man. It portrayed him as ambitious and egoistic or, in some versions, as touched with original sin. This is not the place to evaluate these visions of *Homo politicus*. Suffice it to say that global psychological properties such as those posited by the "first image pessimists," to use Kenneth Waltz's term, did not lend themselves very well to rigorous empirical research. As in the case of the "war in the minds of men" school, these explanations were subject to trenchant critiques (e.g., Waltz, 1959; Hoffmann, 1960) that cast doubt not only on the specific theories, but also on the more basic proposition that the decision maker and his psychological attributes should be at the core of our analyses.

[4] Decision-making approaches (e.g., Snyder, Bruck, and Sapin, 1954; Frankel, 1963) were in part a reaction to deficiencies of earlier theories. The most prominent of these, the framework developed by Snyder and his colleagues, placed the individual decision maker—with his values, attitudes, information, perceptions, and definition of the situation—at the center of a complex network of organizational and other influences. After an initially enthusiastic reception, this approach came under considerable criticism. There is no need to rehash here the now familiar arguments of the critics (e.g., McClosky, 1956; Rosenau, 1967; Hoffmann, 1960), but one point is perhaps worth noting. The major empirical application of the framework—the American decision to resist the invasion of South Korea (Snyder and Paige, 1958; Paige, 1968)—made fairly extensive use of the organizational and information variables of the scheme. It also explored at some length the internal and external setting of the decision. But relatively little attention was devoted to the belief systems and cognitive processes of those involved in making the decisions. Put somewhat differently, although the original decision-making framework drew upon both sociological and psychological theories and insights, in its application to the Korean decision the former seemed to outweigh the latter by a considerable margin.[8]

[8]The fact that there was relatively little disagreement within the policy-making group on the decision to resist aggression does not necessarily reduce the relevance of

The Relevance of Psychology

It is no secret that many political scientists consider the analyses of foreign policy and international politics undertaken by some psychologists to be well-intentioned, but often of dubious realism and relevance.[9] Questions have also been raised about the value of introducing the premises, theories, concepts, and to some extent the methodologies of other disciplines into the core of foreign policy analysis (e.g., Hoffmann, 1960, p. 172). These objections take several forms. One is that the relevant literature in psychology[10] has emerged from the artificial setting of the laboratory, using subjects who are, for reasons of age, experience, knowledge, and other important attributes, quite unlike foreign policy officials. Moreover, the laboratory subjects have been engaged in tasks that bear only a faint likeness to the complex cognitive tasks that occupy political leaders,

cognitive factors, nor need it imply that a "unitary rational actor" model would provide the most potent and parsimonious explanation. The analyst might, for example, wish to examine the decision makers' beliefs about the nature of international politics, the adversary (e.g., who, if anyone, was behind the North Korean invasion, and why), and the like. High consensus on both goals and the means of achieving them within a decision group representing diverse agencies within the government would, however, seem to diminish the relevance of a "bureaucratic politics" perspective, a point developed in more detail by Art (1973).

[9]Debate over the relevance of psychology to political subjects cuts across the so-called "traditionalist-behavioralist" controversy. For example, Morton A. Kaplan, an outspoken critic of traditional approaches, has also derided psychology as "the science that predicts that Russian leaders will behave the same way during the missile crisis that a female sophomore does on a date. If this is a caricature, it is only mildly so" (Kaplan, 1968, p. 694). Prominent efforts by psychologists to deal with problems of foreign policy and international politics include de Rivera (1968), Frank (1967), Janis (1972), Kelman (1965), Klineberg (1964), Milburn (1972), Osgood (1962), Stagner (1967), and White (1970). Psychologists are themselves in less than complete agreement about the relevance of their theories, concepts, and insights to analyses of international politics and foreign policy. See, for example, the exchange between White (1971) and Arnstein (1971).

[10]Similar doubts have been expressed about the relevance of models and concepts drawn from economics. See, for example, various assessments of the field by Morgenthau (e.g., 1968).

especially when they are faced with awesome crisis decisions.[11]

Some critics also question the wisdom of borrowing theories and concepts from another discipline when psychologists themselves have failed to achieve complete consensus on important questions about belief systems, attitude change, and related concerns. Even prominent formulations such as various cognitive consistency theories—approaches that share the premise that man seeks congruence between his behavior, beliefs, and attitudes—have been the source of vigorous debate among advocates of competing explanations (Abelson et al., 1968). Why, the argument goes, should students of foreign policy, rarely trained to deal critically with the results of experimental research, add to their own burdens by introducing the controversies of other disciplines into their work?[12] Doing so may render them no less vulnerable than the psychologist who assumes that the world of international politics is merely his research laboratory writ large.

It may indeed be true that many theories and findings from experimental settings are too fragile to withstand direct and unqualified transfer into other arenas. It seems unlikely that relationships correlated at 0.70 in the laboratory will have a -0.70 or even a 0.00 correlation in foreign offices; however, the issue of scope can only be settled empirically, not by an a priori definition of relevance.[13]

[11]It is interesting to note in this respect that a leading cognitive psychologist has recently suggested that "the best strategy for such research (on cognitions, emotions, and coping processes) is ideographic and naturalistic rather than nomothetic or normative and experimental." (See Lazarus, n.d., p. 42.)

[12]Needless to say, this argument has also been applied against personality studies employing concepts and insights of depth psychology. See, for example, Kaplan (1968, pp. 694-695).

[13]Jervis's forthcoming study of perception and international relations is highly suggestive in this respect. Drawing broadly on both experimental and historical evidence, he develops (but does not subject to definitive test) a number of hypotheses on the scope and limitations of psychological explanations. See also some of the studies cited in note 9, especially de Rivera (1968) and Janis (1972).

Parsimony

Perhaps the most widely articulated arguments against a cognitive processes approach to foreign policy decision-making center on theoretical parsimony and research economy. One can, it is asserted, account for more of the variance in international behavior by starting with—and perhaps limiting oneself to—other levels of analysis. The predominance of the Model I (unitary rational actor) approach to the study of foreign policy and international politics has been documented by Allison (1969, 1971). Advocates of Model I acknowledge that it is, like every model, an oversimplification of reality, but they assert that it nevertheless provides as good an explanation as we are likely to achieve at any reasonable cost. Even severe critics of the power school, Sovietologists, or deterrence theorists—three of the major groups that share a Model I approach to the subject—do not necessarily reject the premise that it is uneconomical to focus much research attention on the individual decision maker. Such analyses are often deemed superfluous for one or more of several reasons. One view is that role, institutional, and other constraints limit the area within which a leader's traits can affect policy. Another is that there is, in any case, little variance among leaders with respect to their decision-making behavior in any given circumstances; that is, whatever their individual differences they will tend to respond in similar ways. The following paragraphs illustrate, but by no means explore exhaustively, the thesis that explanations centering on the cognitions and perceptions of even the highest-ranking leaders are unlikely to extend our understanding in a significant way.

[1] Foreign policy decisions are made within complex bureaucratic organizations that place severe constraints on the individual decision maker (Verba, 1961). Organizational memory, prior policy commitments, parochial vested interests, standard operating procedures, normal bureaucratic inertia, and conflict resolution by bargaining, all of which are deeply entrenched within the bureaucratic organization, serve to restrict the impact on the policy output of the leader's beliefs of other cognitive traits and processes. It should perhaps be noted, however, that a focus on

bureaucratic bargaining need not exclude a concern for cognitive processes. That is, bargaining may develop as a result of divergent diagnoses and prescriptions which derive, in turn, from different beliefs about the nature of politics, the character of opponents, and the like—and *these differences may not be correlated perfectly with bureaucratic position.* The recent "bureaucratic politics" literature perhaps overemphasizes the notion that bargaining within government arises almost solely from parochial interests ("where you stand depends on where you sit"), to the exclusion of genuine intellectual differences that may well be rooted in broader concerns than the narrow interests and perspectives of one's bureau or agency.[14]

[2] Foreign policy is the external manifestation of domestic institutions, ideologies, and other attributes of the polity. The notion that political, economic, and other internal institutions determine the nature of foreign policy is an old one, extending back to Kant and earlier. Contemporary advocates of this position include, among others, hard line analysts who attribute all Soviet or Chinese foreign policy behavior to the imperatives of Marxism-Leninism and communist totalitarianism. Many revisionist American historians adhere to a comparable position: that the institutional requirements of capitalism are not only a necessary, but are also a sufficient explanation for the nature of American foreign policy. Theirs is usually a Model I (unitary rational actor) analysis *par excellence.* Individual decision makers and their attributes are of little concern, as they are allegedly merely the agents of the system who faithfully reflect the needs of the dominant ruling class. Names and faces may change, but interests and policies do not, because they are rooted in more or less permanent features of the polity.[15]

Those whose work is informed by what Waltz (1959) has called "second image" theories—that the causes of international conflict can be located in the malignant institutions of certain polities (it should be noted that their numbers are not limited to cold war superhawks or to revisionist historians)—clearly have little reason to introduce into their analysis such concepts as bounded rationality, cognitive dissonance, information processing capacity, coping with stress, and related concerns of cognitive process models. These are regarded not merely as unnecessary embellishments that complicate the investigator's task; they are diversions that cloud the analyst's insight into the fundamental sources of international behavior.

[3] Structural and other attributes of the international system shape and constrain policy choices to such an extent that this is the logical starting point for most analyses (Singer, 1961). Many who adhere to this position would concede that in order to explore the dynamics of the system it may, at times, be desirable and necessary to conduct supplementary analyses of political processes within the nation or even within its major institutions; few would extend the argument to the point of analyzing cognitive processes within the heads of even the highest-ranking leaders.[16]

---

[14]More detailed critiques of some aspects of the recent bureaucratic politics literature appear in George (1972), Rothstein (1972), Art (1973), and Ball (1974).

[15]"A society's goals, in the last analysis, reflect its objective needs—economic, strategic, and political—in the light of the requirements of its very specific structure of power. Since this power structure in America has existed over many decades in a capitalist form its demands are the common premises for the application of American power—one that theorists attribute to social consensus and sanction, but which in reality has always reflected the class structure and class needs. With time, such structural imperatives and limits appear to take on independent

characteristics, so that whether academics or businessmen administer it, *the state invariably responds in nearly identical ways to similar challenges.* Apart from the fact that no bureaucrat, however chosen, could rise to a position of responsibility without continous and proven conformity to norms of conduct and goals defined by the society's economic power structure which is, in the last analysis, the source of national goals, *there is little intrinsic significance in the nature of the bureaucratic selection process and administrative elite"* (Kolko and Kolko, 1972, p. 19, italics added). For a critique of these theories, see Holsti (1974). The criticism is not that national attributes are unrelated to external behavior, but rather that this premise has often been applied in a simplistic manner. Thus, one needs to distinguish between single-factor explanations (e.g., that foreign policy directly reflects Marxist ideology or capitalist power structure), and systematic multitrait analyses of the kind found in the work of Rummel, Wilkenfeld, Rosenau, Charles and Margaret Hermann, East, Kegley, McGowan, Ivo and Rosalind Feierabend, Salmore, and many others.

[16]A case for this position is summarized by Singer: "I urge here a clear and sharp distinction between behavior and the intrapsychic processes that precede and accompany behavior of the individual; let us simply equate behavior with action. By doing so, we are free to speak of the behavior or acts of any social entity, from the single person on up, and need never be guilty of anthropomor-

In summary, the argument is that by the time one has taken into account systemic, societal, governmental, and bureaucratic constraints on decision makers, much of the variance in foreign policy making has been accounted for; attributes of the individual decision maker are thus often regarded as a residual category which may be said to account for the unexplained variance. Although many contemporary students of foreign policy and international politics accept some variant of one or more of them, it is not wholly unfair to suggest that these arguments are often the initial premises that guide, rather than the considered conclusions that emerge from, systematic research. We are short of comparative studies that might reveal the circumstances under which alternative premises—for example, that "beliefs of foreign policy decision makers are central to the study of decision outputs and probably account for more of the variance than any other single factor" (Shapiro and Bonham, 1973, p. 161)—might be applicable. In many cases, and for many analytical purposes, it is clearly unnecessary to undertake detailed investigations of decision makers' belief systems in order to achieve and adequate explanation of policy outputs. However, research on international crises, as well as a number of other studies, suggest that doing so may prove rewarding in circumstances when one or more of the following conditions exists.[17]

1. Nonroutine situations that require more than merely the application of standard operating procedures and decision rules; for example, decisions to initiate or terminate major international undertakings, including wars, interventions, alliances, aid programs, and the like.

2. Decisions made at the pinnacle of the government hierarchy by leaders who are relatively autonomous—or who may at least define their roles in ways that enhance their latitude for choice.

3. Long-range policy planning, a task that inherently involves considerable uncertainty, and in which conceptions of what is, what is important, what is desirable, and what is related to what are likely to be at the core of the political process.

4. When the situation itself is highly ambiguous and is thus open to a variety of interpretations. (Ambiguity may result from a scarcity of information; from information of low quality or questionable authenticity; or from information that is contradictory or is consistent with two or more significantly different interpretations, coupled with the absence of reliable means of choosing between them.)

5. Circumstances of information overload in which decision makers are forced to use a variety of strategies (e.g., queuing, filtering, omission, reducing categories of discrimination, and the like) to cope with the problem (cf. Holsti, 1972, pp. 81-118, as well as the literature cited therein).

6. Unanticipated events in which initial reactions are likely to reflect cognitive "sets."

7. Circumstances in which complex cognitive tasks associated with decision making may be impaired or otherwise significantly affected by the various types of stresses that impinge on top-ranking executives (compare George, 1974; Holsti and George, 1975; and the literature cited therein).

These categories are not mutually exclusive or exhaustive, nor is it suggested that they are of relevance only for foreign policy decisions. It has been noted, however, that structural uncertainty often characterizes important foreign policy choice situations (Steinbruner, 1968, pp. 215-16; cf. Snyder, Bruck, and Sapin, 1962, p. 104). To the extent that this is more frequently the case in international than in domestic situations, we might expect the cognitive models would more often be applicable in issues of the former type.

---

phizing our social system. To use the metaphor of the S-R (stimulus-response) psychologists, we can treat all the psychological and physiological processes that occur within an individual as if they unfolded in a 'black box' which cannot be penetrated, and try to understand external behavior (or output) strictly in terms of its empirical association with external stimuli (or input)." (See Singer, 1971, pp. 19-20.)

[17]Empirical support for this list may be found in many studies, including, among others: Art (1973), Ball (1974), de Rivera (1968), C. Hermann (1969), M. Hermann (1972), Holsti (1967, 1972), Janis (1972), Jervis (1968, forthcoming), Krasner (1972), Lowenthal (1972), May (1973), Milburn (1972), Paige (1968), Snyder and Paige (1958), Stassen (1972), and Steinbruner (1968, 1974). More extensive discussions of the circumstances under which individual traits of leaders are likely to "make a difference" may be found in Greenstein (1969, pp. 42-62) and M. Hermann (1972a, pp. 3-11).

As Allison (1969, 1971) has persuasively demonstrated, any given level and units of analysis serve as beacons that guide and sensitize the investigator to some bodies of data and potential explanations; they may also be conceptual blinders, desensitizing him to evidence that might support competing explanations. At some point it is not altogether satisfactory to assert that the choice of levels and units of analysis is merely a matter of taste or theoretical preference. Nor is it always sufficient to assume that the higher (e.g., systemic) levels of explanation establish the limits within which choices are made, whereas lower ones serve to fill in the finer details; the different foci may lead to significantly different explanations. What is needed is rigorous comparative research that addresses itself to the issue, not in the spirit of evangelism on behalf of one theoretical position or the other, but rather in response to the questions: for what range of research and policy problems is any given perspective or combination of perspectives likely to prove necessary? Sufficient? What is the relative potency of various clusters of independent variables on not only the decision-making process (Rosenau, 1966), but also on the substance and quality of the policy output?

We have relatively few such studies, but of the examples that come to mind, a number seem to provide support for a cognitive process approach. Rosenau's (1968) research on the behavior of United States senators indicated that it was governed largely by role rather than personal or idiosyncratic attributes. An imaginative reanalysis of the data revealed, however, that preferences and belief-sets of the senators in fact provided a *more powerful* explanation for their behavior than did role (Stassen, 1972). Allison's study of the Cuban missile crisis did not extend the analysis to a consideration of a cognitive process model, but the potential value of doing so was suggested in the conclusion (1971, p. 277). It seems a reasonable hypothesis that such a study would have illuminated further several aspects of the decision-making process in Washington, for example, the early consensus that the Soviet missiles must be removed, the lineup of hawks and doves on the most appropriate and effective means of doing so, or the shifting of policy positions as new information became available and new interpretations were adduced.

Such a study might be especially useful because Allison's work—the most complete analysis of the missile crisis to date—did not reveal any significant correlation between bureaucratic role and decision making. That is, neither in the diagnoses of the situation created by the emplacement of Soviet missiles in Cuba, nor in their prescriptions of how best to cope with the problem did all members of the "Ex Com" act in ways that are readily predictable from the assumptions of the bureaucratic politics literature. For example, it is not clear that Robert McNamara's initial diagnosis of the Soviet emplacement of offensive missiles in Cuba ("a missile is a missile"), a judgment not widely shared by his colleagues, could be predicted from his bureaucratic role in the Kennedy administration; thus, whether or not a leader defines a situation as a "crisis" perhaps depends at least in part on basic beliefs about the political universe, and these will not always correspond to or be predictable from his role. Moreover, with the possible exception of members of the Joint Chiefs of Staff and UN Ambassador Adlai Stevenson, no consistant relationship between role and policy prescriptions was evident. This suggests at least some limitations to the core premise of the bureaucratic politics literature: "Where you stand depends on where you sit." A comparable analysis of Kremlin leaders would be no less intriguing but, needless to say, it would encounter serious data problems.

Steinbruner's study of the proposed multilateral force (MLF) for NATO tested four alternative conceptions of decision making: the rational, adaptive rational, bargaining, and cognitive process models. He concluded that "the handling of multiple objectives and the response to structural uncertainty required explanations at the level of the individual decision-maker, and it was the cognitive process model which provided the best fit with the phenomena observed" (Steinbruner, 1968, p. 538). As multiple objectives and uncertainty characterize many occasions for foreign policy decisions, the implications of the Steinbruner study would appear to extend well beyond the MLF case. Trotter (1971) examined the Cuban missile crisis from the perspective of nine different models, and concluded that a cognitive perspective provided the best explanation for American decision making during that episode. The latter study fails, however, to develop its models as fully as Steinbruner, Allison, or Stassen, nor is it as persuasive in demonstrating critical differences in the outcomes that could be derived from each. Finally, in a more anecdotal survey of some recent episodes in American foreign policy, Art (1973) concluded that the more important decisions are better explained by the mind-sets of top leaders than by a bureaucratic politics perspective.

Research Difficulties

Finally, not the least potent constraint has been the very real and persistent problems of doing systematic empirical research. At a time when the discipline itself was becoming more self-consciously scientific and was applying more stringent standards of theoretical rigor and methodological sophistication, these problems became increasingly visible. One obvious difficulty is access to data. Unlike the analyst who can index his variables with such measures as GNP per capita, arms budgets, trade figures, or votes in the UN General Assembly, those interested in the beliefs of decision makers have no yearbook to which they can turn for comparable evidence, much less quantitative data presented in standard units. One result is relatively limited agreement on the appropriate categories into which to code whatever data are available. A no less potent difficulty concerns transformation of available biographical, documentary, and other evidence into data that are both replicable and directly relevant to the theoretical question at hand. Moreover, such data are usually in a form that does not lend itself easily to sharing or depositing in archives. Hence, unlike figures on budgets, trade or voting, each data set developed for a cognitive process study is likely to be used only once. In the third section of this paper we shall return to some of these research problems.

Although these four arguments against expending considerable research resources on the cognitive attributes and processes of decision makers are not without some merit, the tentative conclusion is that their universal validity is open to serious question. Nevertheless, in the eyes of most foreign policy analysts they place a considerable burden of proof on those who assert that not only

are efforts toward developing cognitive process models of foreign policy decision making worth undertaking, but also that their use could survive a fairly rigorous cost-benefit analysis. The existing literature is insufficient to provide a definitive and compelling assessment, but there appears to be a reasonable case in support of the following proposition: For important classes of decisions (e.g., those cited above) a cognitive process perspective is necessary—*and not just as a way of filling in details*—although probably not sufficient. Put somewhat differently, the proposition is that for some decisions a cognitive process perspective is fundamental and should be at the starting point of the analysis, rather than a luxury to be indulged in order to reduce some of the variance unexplained by other, more powerful, approaches.

EXISTING FOREIGN POLICY RESEARCH: DIVERSITY IS THE RULE

Existing studies are characterized by diversity in conceptualization, sources of theory, research site, subject, and data-making (categories, coding rules, data analysis procedures) operations. They range from rather traditional single-case analyses of specific leaders to efforts aimed at developing computer simulations of cognitive processes (Abelson, 1971). The landscape of cognitive studies is also littered with possibly useful models that have failed to generate empirical follow-up studies (e.g., D'Amato, 1967), but there are some preliminary signs that this may be changing. For example, the "operational code" construct developed by George (1969) has inspired a continuing stream of research,[18] and a content analysis coding scheme, developed to extract materials for the construction of "cognitive maps" from documents, has been employed in a number of studies, including Axelrod (1972), Shapiro and Bonham (1973), Bonham and Shapiro (forthcoming), and several chapters in Axelrod (forthcoming). Nevertheless, research to date on belief systems and cognitive processes is

[18]Anderson (1973a, 1973b), Ashby (1969), Dye (n.d.), Gibbins (n.d.), Malone (1971), Gutierrez (1973), Heradstveit (1974), Holsti (1970), Johnson (1973), Kavanaugh (1970), Lawrence (forthcoming), McLellan (1971), Stassen (1973), Thordarson (1972), Tweraser (1973), Walker (1975), and White (1969).

suggestive and eclectic rather than focused and cumulative. For an enterprise that is of relatively recent interest within the discipline, and is still essentially in the "pre-takeoff" stage, diversity is probably desirable and, in any case, inevitable. To expect anything other than a broad range of approaches would be to imply nothing less than the existence of a paradigmatic theory of cognition and choice.

Underlying the variety, however, are two shared premises. First, there is a general suspicion that simple S-R (stimulus- response) or black box formulations are insufficient bases for understanding decision outputs, either of individuals or nation-states. That is, intervening processes are often the locus of powerful explanations of choice behavior. Second, it is assumed that the content and structure of belief systems, information processing styles, strategies for coping with stress, and the like are systematically related to the manner in which leaders perceive, diagnose, prescribe, and make choices, especially in situations of uncertainty. Both shared and idiosyncratic attributes and processes are of interest. For example, the premise that most, if not all, persons experience predecisional and postdecisional pressures for cognitive consistency, and for congruence between beliefs and behavior, informs many studies. But the propensity to favor one or another strategy for coping with discrepancies between elements of the belief system, attitudes, and behavior can vary widely across individuals, with potentially important implications for decision-making behavior.

Diversity in the existing foreign policy literature can be described briefly along several dimensions.

Theory. – There is a wide range of models which, in turn, are informed by different theoretical literatures, and even different disciplines. These include, but are not limited to, various cognitive consistency theories, personality theory, communication theory, decision theory, as well as many others.

Scope. – Much of the existing research is focused on a single leader, but some of it also deals with relatively large samples of elites (e.g., Burgess, 1967; Mennis, 1972; see also the studies described in Raser's review article, 1966). Moreover, some studies are concerned with a single concept, cognitive task, or stage in policy making, whereas others can be described as efforts at developing or exploring the entire decision-making process, encompassing various types of cognitive activities (Axelrod, 1972, 1973; Shapiro and Bonham, 1973; Holsti and George, 1975; Jervis, forthcoming).

Categories and concepts. – Not only do analytical concepts vary widely; even the language for describing them ranges from ordinary prose to the formal notation of set theory.

Data. – The studies draw upon vastly different empirical domains for data and illustrations. At one end of the spectrum are detailed analyses of a single decision maker, based on interviews and/or content analyses of primary documents, and supplementary secondary sources. Jervis (forthcoming) draws on the voluminous record of diplomatic history, as well as reports of experimental research, to illustrate the relevance of existing hypotheses, to generate new ones, and to demonstrate the limitations or inapplicability of other explanations. Still other studies combine data from real decision makers with those from surrogates, including man and machine simulations (Hermann and Hermann, 1967; Zinnes, 1966).

Analytic procedures. – There is no less variety in this respect, a point to be discussed further in the next section.

It should not be necessary to belabor the point further. A somewhat oversimplified summary of some existing studies appears in Table 1. Although it is illustrative rather than comprehensive, the table may serve some useful purpose in illustrating the relationship between conceptions of the decision maker, stages or tasks in the decision-making process, theories, and concepts. It also suggests a number of other points.

1. Decision-making, encompassing several states or tasks, is a shorthand label for a number of different cognitive activities, a fact that may be insufficiently recognized in much of the literature on foreign policy decisions.
2. As might be expected given the diverse theoretical roots of existing studies, the literature

Table 1. Some "Cognitive Process" Approaches to Decision Making

Decision Maker as[a]	Stage of Decision Making[b]	Theoretical Literature[a]	Illustrative Constructs and Concepts	Illustrative Studies of Political Leaders
Believer	Sources of belief system	Political socialization Personality & politics	First independent political success Mind Set	Barber (1972) Glad (1966) George and George (1956)
	Content of belief system	Political philosophy Ideology	Image Operational code World view Decisional premises	Operational code studies Brecher (1968) Cummins (1973) Stupak (1971)
	Structure of belief system	Cognitive psychology	Cognitive balance/ congruity Cognitive complexity Cognitive rigidity/ dogmatism Cognitive "maps"/ style	Axelrod (1972b) M. Hermann (1972a) Osgood (1959b) Shneidman (1961, 1963, 1969)
Perceiver	Identification of a problem	Psychology of perception Cognitive psychology	Definition of situation Perception/mispercep- tion Cognitive "set" Selective perception Focus on attention Stereotyping	Jervis (1968) Jervis (forthcoming, chaps. 5, 11, and 13) Zinnes (1966) Zinnes et al. (1972)
Information Processor	Obtain information	Cognitive consistency theories	Search capacity Selective exposure	Abelson (1971) Holsti (1967, 1972)
	Production of solutions	Theories of attitude change	Psycho-logic Tolerance of ambiguity	Jervis (forthcoming, chaps. 4 and 6)
	Evaluation of solutions	Information theory Communication theory	Strategies for coping with discrepant information (various) Information overload Information processing capacity Satisficing/maximizing Tolerance of inconsistency	
Decision Maker/ Strategist	Selection of a strategy	Game theory Decision theory Deterrence theory	Utility Risk taking Decision rules Manipulation of images Ends-means links Bounded rationality	Jervis (1970) Jervis (forthcoming, chap. 3) Stassen (1972) Burgess (1967)
Learner	Subsequent learning and revisions (post-decision)	Learning theory Cognitive dissonance theory	Feedback "Lessons of history"	Jervis (forthcoming, chap. 14 and unnumbered chap. on "learning from history") Lampton (1973) May (1973)

Left margin (spanning Believer through the table): Pre-decision: conceptual baggage that DM bring to decision-making tasks

Right margin: Axelrod (1972a, 1972b); Bonham and Shapiro (forthcoming a, forthcoming b); Shapiro and Bonham (1973); Steinbruner (1968, 1974)

[a]Columns one and three were suggested by, but differ somewhat from, the framework provided by Axelrod (1972a).
[b]Column two was drawn from Brim et al. (1962, p. 1).

abounds with a plethora of concepts which, taken together, are marked by considerable overlap and something less than complete consistency in usage.

3. There is a small but growing empirical litera- ture (note that most cited studies have appeared since 1965) that provides some basis for optimism about research of this genre.

Not depicted in Table 1, but of potential rele- vance at all stages of decision making, is another concern: The impact of cognitive processes on choice behavior may vary according to the nature of the situation, for example, the degree of uncer- tainty and the number of objectives (Steinbruner, 1968, 1974; Axelrod, 1973). The distinction be- tween circumstances of high and low stress is also likely to be of special interest.[19] The literature on decision making under stress is far too voluminous to review here.[20] Suffice it to say that research in both experimental and natural settings indicates that intense and protracted stress may have a con- siderable impact on those qualities of cognitive structures and abilities that are most needed to cope with the complex intellectual problems posed by many decision-making situations.[21]

SOME PROBLEMS OF EMPIRICAL RESEARCH[22]

Access to Data

Occasionally the investigator will have direct ac- cess to his subjects, although rarely until they

[19]For other ways to conceptualize situations, see C. Hermann (1969).

[20]Summaries may be found in Lazarus, Deese, and Osler (1952), Horvath (1959), Janis and Leventhal (1968), Lazarus, Averill, and Opton (1969), Broadbent (1971), Holsti (1972), Milburn (1972), Hermann and Brady (1972), and Holsti and George (1975).

[21]There is a dissenting note in the literature on bureau- cratic organizations. Some, including Wilensky (1967), Verba (1961), and Lowi (1969), suggest that the patho- logical impact of distorted information, bureaucratic politics, and decision making by bargaining among rep- resentatives of parochial vested interests is reduced in crisis, and that, in fact, decision making in such circum- stances more closely approximates a rational choice model.

[22]The comments in this section are addressed pri- marily to research on real rather than surrogate decision makers.

leave office. Examples include research on the Korean decision (Snyder and Paige, 1958; Paige, 1968), the MLF case (Steinbruner, 1968, 1974), McLellan's (1971) analysis of Dean Acheson's "operational code," and Gutierrez's (1973) study of Dean Rusk. These are, however, exceptions; as a rule documentary evidence of various sorts will serve as the primary source of data.

Whether the investigator relies on interviews, questionnaires, or documents, the situations for which he is most likely to incorporate cognitive process models into his analysis are precisely those in which access to relevant data is most difficult. Moreover, documentary materials that are avail- able in such situations may be contaminated in one way or another. The "color books" issued by various European governments immediately fol- lowing the outbreak of World War I are notorious examples but, unfortunately, far from unique, as the history of the war in Southeast Asia has amply demonstrated. "Credibility gap" may be a con- temporary phrase, but the phenomenon it de- scribes is far from a recent invention.

Research that is heavily dependent on docu- mentary evidence must almost always be con- ducted in circumstances of data scarcity, but this does not, of itself, distinguish it from other types of inquiry. Perhaps of greater importance is the fact that available materials may not represent an unbiased sample. Two types of biases may occur. First, the available evidence for any given case may be skewed; for example, formal documents may be overrepresented, whereas verbatim reports of de- bates within policy-making groups are underrepre- sented. Second, the cases for which sufficient evidence is available to permit systematic investiga- tion may not represent an unbiased sample of foreign policy decisions. The sample is likely to be skewed toward those that are:

1. At least n years old, n being determined by the rules that govern each archive.

2. From nations losing major wars, such as World War I and World War II, that result in the destruction of the existing regime. Often the most salient archival evidence becomes available following major wars, but even then it is usually the losers' documents that become available first; only later, if ever, do

we gain access to those of the winning nations.

3. At least in the short run, from "successful" decisions rather than from disasters that may reflect adversely on the competence of those responsible for them. In the longer run, we may gain access more readily to data from the "disasters."

4. From "modern" governments in which vast foreign offices maintain equally vast archives.

5. From democratic rather than authoritarian governments because the former seem more willing eventually to open their archives voluntarily. They are usually less likely to rewrite history retrospectively to meet the needs of the regime in power, an enterprise that requires tight control over even seemingly innocuous or trivial archival materials.

For many purposes, reports of group discussions represent the most desirable category of evidence, especially when the group is divided not only on preferences about possible outcomes, but also in beliefs about causation. Such data would also enable us to examine the often complex interaction between individual cognitive processes and the supports provided and constraints imposed by the decision-making group. Although we have resumés or retrospective reports about discussions in such groups as those that formulated policy on the decision to attack Pearl Harbor (Ike, 1967), the Bay of Pigs invasion, and the Cuban missile crisis, Axelrod's (1972) analysis of the British Eastern Committee is one of the very few for which actual verbatim records were kept and eventually made public. Other transcripts and records that might be analyzed are listed in Axelrod (forthcoming, app. II).

Inference from Documentary Data

Aside from access to the most relevant data, there are other difficulties in working with documentary evidence, especially public documents. One problem concerns the logic of inference. Barring the use of older materials that have worked their way through governmental declassification procedures, or fortuitous circumstances such as publication of the "Pentagon Papers," analysts will be forced to rely on documents that are in the first instance intended to convey information to the public, to legislatures, or to foreign governments. As likely as not, they are also intended to persuade, justify, threaten, cajole, manipulate, evoke sympathy and support, or otherwise influence the intended audience. Words may convey explicit or implicit clues about the author's "real" beliefs, attitudes, and opinions; they may also be intended to serve his practical goals of the moment. Consider, in this connection, former Attorney General John Mitchell's comment to observers at the beginning of the first Nixon administration: "Watch what we do, not what we say."

The issue being raised here centers on alternative models of communication—the "representational" and the "instrumental"—and the validity of inferences about the communicator that may be drawn from his messages.[23] The representational model assumes that verbal expressions are valid indicators of the communicator's beliefs, motivations, and the like, whereas the instrumental view begins with the premise that words are chosen to have an impact on the target of communication. According to the latter position the analyst must therefore take into account a good deal of the context of communication in order to make valid inferences from verbal behavior.

If we could always assume that the representational model is valid, research life would thereby be greatly simplified. It seems safer to treat it as a tentative hypothesis, the validity of which is better left to empirical confirmation than to untested premise. At minimum it would appear useful to take some elementary precautions to determine whether in fact the premises of the representational model are valid for the particular case in question. A comparison of private and public mes-

[23]These problems have been explored at some length in Pool (1959), George (1959a, 1959b), Jervis (1969), and Mueller (1969a, 1969b). A variant of the "representational-instrumental" debate occurs in a criticism of the "operational code" approach, which is charged with a failure to distinguish between official and operative ideologies (Singer, 1968, p. 145). The criticism may or may not be valid in the case of any given study, but the problem is not an inherent attribute of operational code research. That is, such investigations need not be tied to a single data source (i.e., official pronouncements or doctrinal "classics"), nor need they assume that operational code beliefs remain unchanged either for an individual or an elite group.

sages (Glad, 1966), interviews with the subject or his colleagues (Steinbruner, 1968, 1974; Zacher, 1970), or possibly, use of an expert panel, might offer some means of doing so. If only public messages are available, comparing results across audiences (Holsti, 1962, pp. 150-154, 183-187) could provide estimates of which are core beliefs, and which are sufficiently elastic to change according to the target of communication. Even private documents may need to be used with caution. Pressures for "instant history" and leaks of confidential papers may inhibit some decision makers.

Authorship

Establishing authorship may also pose difficulties for the student of cognitive processes. Government documents are often prepared by unidentified bureaucrats, or they are the product of committees, going through various drafts and passing through many hands before appearing over the signatures of their nominal authors. Widespread use of ghostwriters raises comparable questions about public addresses, statements to legislative committees, and even autobiographies and memoirs.[24]

One way of coping with the problem of authorship is to use only materials drawn from interviews and press conferences (M. Hermann, 1972). Given penetrating questions, spontaneous responses can be a rich source of evidence about beliefs, but there are also some drawbacks to this method. Interviews or press conferences are rarely granted during crises and other nonroutine circumstances in which cognitions of leaders are most likely to have a significant impact on policy choices. Indeed, there is no guarantee that they will be granted at all; note, for example, the wide disparity among recent American presidents in the frequency with which they engaged in direct contact with the press. It is possible that the structure and content of a belief system are relatively stable attributes and that measurements taken in one set of circumstances are therefore likely to be valid in

others. But for some purposes this assumption introduces a static quality to the analysis. Moreover, many of the most interesting research questions center on the interplay of situation and cognitive processes. There is, finally, considerable evidence that cognitive traits and abilities do not necessarily remain unchanged under varying levels of stress.

Exclusive reliance on interviews and press conferences also tends to rule out examination of initial reactions to a situation, when it may be relatively unstructured, and when there is the greatest latitude for cognitive "set" to have an impact on the definition of the situation and on the subsequent cognitive tasks associated with decision making. Consider, for example, first reactions to the news of President Kennedy's assassination in Dallas. Some liberals, predisposed to associate Dallas with extreme conservatism, jumped to the conclusion that John Birchers or other radical groups of the political right had been responsible. Lyndon Johnson, on the other hand, feared that the assassination was part of a larger communist plot to destroy the American government.

By this point it should be evident that there are no easy rules of thumb by which the investigator can overcome problems of access to and inference from documentary data. Those who undertake this type of research have recourse to one of two broad strategies. The first is to work with materials that have passed through the critical scrutiny of skilled archivists and historical detectives (e.g., the various collections of documents relating the outbreak and conduct of World War I and, increasingly, World War II). Alternatively, should they wish (for normative or other reasons) to undertake research on more contemporary situations, they will themselves have to approach available documentary evidence with the same skills and skepticism as the well-trained historian.

Data Analysis

When the research goal is to formulate hypotheses, rigor in techniques of data analysis is rarely the top priority. Anecdotal evidence, skillfully used, may suffice to inspire creative speculation, to develop and test the face validity of hypotheses in

---

[24]Propensity to use ghostwriters seems to vary with the individual and probably according to the situation. For example, John Foster Dulles is reputed to have written many of his own speeches, and Richard Nixon is reported to have handwritten all 10 drafts of his speech on the Cambodian invasion (Barber, 1972, p. 430).

a preliminary way, or to serve as examples. For hypothesis testing more explicit methods of coding and data analysis are usually required. Most studies of cognitions and perceptions are heavily dependent on documentary evidence—whether produced by diplomats in foreign offices or by surrogates in laboratory simulations—systematic analysis of which implies some form of content analysis.

Using a sample of recent studies as a base, Table 2 relates some techniques of content analysis (recording units and systems of enumeration in which the results are presented) to the types of inference that are drawn from the data. The re-

Table 2. Some Systems of Content Analysis and Types of Inference about Decision Makers

Recording Unit	System of Enumeration			
	Appearance	Frequency	Intensity	Contingency
Word/Symbol		*Cognitive complexity* (M. Hermann, 1972b), *Personality traits* (M. Hermann, 1972a), *Values* (Eckhardt and White, 1967; Cummins, 1973; Eckhardt, 1967).		Cognitive structure (Osgood, 1959b).
Theme/Sentence	*Philosophical and instrumental beliefs* ("Operational code" studies; Thordarson, 1972), *"World view"* (Brecher, 1968), *Perceptions of IR* (Stupak, 1971), *"Strategic image"* (Burgess, 1967).	*Perceptions of alternatives* (Hermann, 1969; 1972; Holsti, 1972), *Perceptions of threat, hostility, etc.* (Zinnes, 1966).	*Attitudes* (Stein, 1968), *National images* (Holsti, 1967), *Perceptions of threat, hostility, etc.* (Zinnes et al., 1972).	
Logical Idiosyncracy		*Cognitive "style"* (Shneidman, 1961, 1963, 1969).		
Causal Assertion	*"Cognitive map"* (Axelrod, 1972b; Bonham and Shapiro, forthcoming; Shapiro and Bonham, 1973), *"Script"* (Abelson, 1971, 1973).			
Sentence, Paragraph, Item	Not used in research of this type; too crude to be of very much value.			

cording unit refers to the specific segment of content that is characterized by placing it in a given category. These range from units as small as the word to such complex ones as causal assertions. Once the appropriate content units have been identified, there are various ways of counting them. Frequency measures count each appearance; it is assumed that repetition indicates salience or importance, and that each item should be given equal weight. When these premises appear inappropriate, the analyst may choose merely to record the content attribute as present or absent (appearance), or to adopt some type of weighting scheme (intensity). Contingency analysis assumes that inferences may be drawn from the proximity of two or more content attributes within a specified context (sentence, paragraph, 100 words, etc.).[25] Table 2 reveals that, even when the purposes of inquiry are similar, there has been little uniformity of methods, much less development of standard categories into which the content units are to be placed. An important gap is the paucity of studies that examine the same body of data using two or more methods with a view to assessing the strengths and costs of each. A few of the many alternatives include evaluative assertion analysis (Osgood, Saporta, and Nunnally, 1956), value analysis (White, 1951), contingency analysis (Osgood, 1959b), and various types of causal or structural analyses (Axelrod, 1972; Abelson, 1973; Shapiro and Bonham, 1973). A definitive assessment of research methods is beyond the scope of this paper, but a few observations may be in order.

There has been heavy reliance on qualitative content analysis in studies that focus on the *content* of belief systems. Qualitative content analysis is not, as is sometimes asserted (e.g., Berelson, 1952), a contradiction in terms, nor need it imply the absence of systematic methodology. Indeed, as George's (1959a, 1959b) explication of the methods used to analyze Axis propaganda during World War II makes clear, qualitative methods may involve very sophisticated rules of inference linked to an explicit model of the communication process. Nevertheless, the various "operational code" studies reveal some of both the benefits and costs

[25]For a further discussion on coding content data, see Holsti (1969, pp. 94-126).

of qualitative analysis. George's (1969) reformulation of the operational code construct developed by Leites (1951, 1953) has guided all of the studies. Using this framework analysts have been able to range widely across whatever materials were available for the given subject. It is doubtful that even a small fraction of the same material would have been coded using the more rigorous and time-consuming methods of quantitative analysis.

However, freedom from some of the more onerous chores of coding for quantitative analysis have also reduced the immediate imperatives for explicating the rules for inclusion in each category, and delineating the boundaries between them. As a result, although there appears to be wide agreement that the questions about history and politics encompassed in the operational code construct are central to any leader's belief system, not all of the case studies have addressed sufficient attention to the issue of category definitions. Thus, individual studies are not always easily compared and, as a result, they are less cumulative than they might otherwise be. A possibly useful development would be to combine the theoretical and substantive richness of the operational code with some other forms of content analysis, either quantitative or with a focus on causal linkages.[26] Continuing interest in operational code studies, including efforts directed at further explication of the construct itself,[27] gives rise to some optimism about

[26]For many types of research on belief systems the case for developing systematic and replicable sampling, coding, and data analysis schemes is quite compelling. Consider the following case. We wish to examine linkages between X's decision-making behavior and his belief system. But often we already know a great deal about his decision-making behavior, and there is the danger that the analysis of beliefs will be contaminated by that knowledge. For example, we know that Richard Nixon visited China and the U.S.S.R., placed controls on the American economy, and attempted to dismantle parts of the poverty program. There is no way of avoiding that knowledge. There may then be a very natural, even if not conscious, tendency to search for and interpret materials on Nixon's beliefs in light of that knowledge, especially if one is working on the hypothesis that there is in fact a close relationship between beliefs and decision-making behavior. Rigorous and explicit methodologies can provide a partial safeguard against this type of contamination.

[27]A further discussion of some aspects of this problem will be found in Anderson's (1973b) dissertation on Senator Arthur Vandenberg, as well as in a shorter paper based on that study (Anderson, 1973a). David Dye, a doctoral candidate in political science at Stanford, has

future developments on this aspect of research on cognitive processes and decision making.

Research on specific personality or cognitive traits (e.g., cognitive rigidity) that may be relevant to decision making tends to be at the other end of the qualitative-quantitative continuum. Inferences are often derived from various measures of word frequencies. These methods offer several clear advantages. They draw on a rich, although not especially cumulative,[28] literature on theory and method. Dividing the data into units poses no difficulty and quantification is relatively easy. Moreover, developments in computer content analysis programs, theoretically oriented dictionaries (Stone et al., 1966), and disambiguation routines (Stone et al., 1969) offer the promise of freedom from the sheer drudgery of counting. Offsetting these obvious attractions are some problems that are less than completely resolved. The most critical of these center on questions of inference; the validity of many constructs based on word-symbol frequencies remains to be firmly established.

Methods that yield data about the structure of belief systems generally involve onerous tasks of unitizing and coding, and relatively limited opportunities to use computers, at least without considerable precomputer syntax identification. Coding difficulties have no doubt been a deterrent to further use of Shneidman's method of drawing inference from logical fallacies; it does not appear to have been employed beyond the original studies of John F. Kennedy, Richard Nixon, and Nikita Khrushchev.

In speculating about the prospects for, and likely payoffs from, the various approaches to documentary analysis, very safe answers are that diversity will only slowly give way to much standardization of method, and that the choice of methods will, in any case, depend on the purpose. A somewhat more venturesome guess is that, despite the laborious coding involved,[29] the

methods listed under "causal assertions" in Table 2 appear promising for various purposes:

1. To explicate in detail the belief structure of a leader as it is operative in a given situation.
2. To compare a leader's belief system in different circumstances. For example, this might permit testing hypotheses such as those predicting that cognitive structures become simpler, or less logical and more "psychological," in circumstances of intense and protracted stress.
3. To compare the belief systems of two or more leaders in a given situation.

This method may also be adapted to a variety of other research problems centering on both the content and structure of belief systems and, where deemed useful for the problem at hand, causal linkages may also be analyzed in such quantitative terms as frequencies and intensities.

The Dependent Variable

The student of foreign policy is interested in beliefs and cognitive process because these are assumed to be among the independent or intervening variables that are systematically related to the substance and quality of decision outputs. But linkages to, or even conceptualizations of, the dependent variable are not always satisfactory.

This problem is by no means confined to studies of belief systems; it may be found in several areas of a discipline that has fared somewhat better in dealing with the inputs to the political process than in conceptualizing decision making or developing performance measures for the outputs. Many studies that focus on the content of belief systems seem somewhat vulnerable on this score. It is not uncommon to find a statement in the conclusion to the effect that "the preceding analysis of X's belief system establishes its utility for understanding X's political behavior." It is less common to find an explicit and compelling demonstration of why this is the case. Greater attention to a clearly articulated model of decision making, explicating the critical cognitive tasks that must be undertaken, would facilitate and encourage more systematic efforts at establishing the nature of the linkages between belief systems, the performance of these cognitive tasks,

---

done useful work toward developing typologies of belief systems. Dye's efforts draw upon a number of the previously cited operational code studies.

[28]See the critical reviews in Auld and Murray (1955) and Marsden (1965).

[29]The coding scheme developed by Wrightson (forthcoming) appears much more manageable for large bodies of data than that described in Abelson (1973).

and the substance and quality of the decision output. Among the merits of recent studies by Axelrod (1972a, 1972b), and Shapiro and Bonham (1973) is that their concerns with cognitive processes are embedded within explicit models of the decision-making process.

CONCLUSION

Aside from developing precise, communicable concepts and methods of inquiry that ultimately lead to a cumulative literature, there remains the longer-term task of integrating research on cognitive processes with other conceptualizations of foreign policy decision making. Exaggerated claims on behalf of these models are likely to be even less convincing than those made on behalf of competing frameworks. It will not suffice to assume that foreign policy decisions merely reflect the beliefs of any given leader, or even group of leaders. Hence research on belief systems must ultimately be embedded in a broader context, and the problems of linking and interrelating theories and concepts that are oriented to the individual decision maker—as are most of those in columns 3 and 4 of Table 1—to the behavior of groups and organizations need to be addressed directly. Put somewhat differently, a cognitive process model of foreign policy decision making will not represent a great step forward if it simply becomes another Model I analysis, assuming that foreign policy is the product of a unitary (subjectively) rational actor. Thus, even those who focus on crisis decisions that are made by a small and relatively autonomous group of top-ranking leaders are likely to profit by exploring possible linkages with models of group dynamics (Janis, 1972; George, 1974), bureaucratic organizations (Allison, 1971; George, 1972; Allison and Halperin, 1972; Halperin, 1974). Some of the more theoretically oriented approaches to comparative foreign policy also suggest a broader context within which the relative potency of leadership variables—including the cognitions of decision makers—can be assessed systematically (Rosenau, 1966, 1970; M. Hermann, 1972a, 1972b).

Integration across analytical levels is not an end in itself, however, nor is it likely to occur unless we can identify specific questions, the answers to which will require the analyst to focus directly on the linkages between processes in various decision-making contexts. For example:

1. How does the decision maker define his cognitive tasks and needs, and how are these satisfied, modified, or constrained by the small group or bureaucratic organization?
2. What tensions exist between the decision maker's cognitive style and role requirements, and how does he attempt to cope with them?
3. What are cognitive concomitants of organizational differences (Steinbruner, 1968, p. 500)?
4. What group processes are associated with a premature bolstering of shared beliefs? With systematic examination of decisional premises?

Similar questions may also be couched in normative or prescriptive terms. For example: Given an executive's cognitive style, what types of normative interventions at the group or organizational level will increase the probability that his cognitive needs are met? Will increase the likelihood that beliefs and decisional premises are subjected to critical analysis?

This list is by no means an exhaustive one. It merely illustrates a few of the questions relating to cognitive processes in decision making that can only be answered by considering also the broader context within which policies are made.

REFERENCES

Abelson, Robert P. 1971. "The Ideology Machine." Paper prepared for the Annual Meeting of the American Political Science Association, Chicago.

———. 1973. "The Structure of Belief Systems." In *Computer Simulation of Thought and Language,* ed. Kenneth Colby and Roger Schank. San Francisco: Freeman.

———, Elliot Aronson, William J. McGuire, Theodore M. Newcomb, Milton Rosenberg, and Percy H. Tannenbaum, eds. 1968. *Theories of Cognitive Consistency: A Source Book.* Chicago: Rand McNally.

Alker, Hayward R., Jr. 1973. "Research Paradigms and Mathematical Politics." Paper prepared for the IPSA Roundtable on Quantitative Methods and Political

Substance, Mannheim, Germany.

Allison, Graham T. 1969. "Conceptual Models and the Cuban Missile Crisis." *American Political Science Review* 63 (Sep): 689-718.

———. 1971. *Essence of Decision: Explaining the Cuban Missile Crisis.* Boston: Little, Brown.

——— and Morton H. Halperin. 1972. "Bureaucratic Politics: A Paradigm and Some Policy Implications." *World Politics* 24 (suppl.): 40-79.

Anderson, Joel E., Jr. 1973a. "The 'Operational Code' Approach: The George Construct and Senator Arthur H. Vandenberg's Operational Code Belief System." Paper prepared for the Annual Meeting of the American Political Science Association, New Orleans.

———. 1973b. "The 'Operational Code' Belief System of Senator Arthur H. Vandenberg: An Application of the George Construct." Ph.D. dissertation, Univ. of Michigan.

Arnstein, Fred. 1971. "Comment on 'Three Not-So-Obvious Contributions of Psychology to Peace' by Ralph K. White"; "Response to White's Rejoinder." *Journal of Social Issues* 27 (Nov): 207-9; 212-20.

Art, Robert J. 1973. "Bureaucratic Politics and American Foreign Policy: A Critique." *Policy Sciences* 4 (Dec): 467-90.

Ashby, Ned. 1969. "Schumacher and Brandt: The Divergent 'Operational Codes' of Two German Socialist Leaders." Mimeo. Stanford: Stanford Univ.

Auld, P., and E. J. Murray. 1955. "Content Analysis Studies of Psychotherapy." *Psychological Bulletin* 52 (Sep): 377-95.

Axelrod, Robert. 1972a. *Framework for a General Theory of Cognition and Choice.* Research Series No. 18. Berkeley: Univ. of California, Institute of International Studies.

———. 1972b. "Psycho-Algebra: A Mathematical Theory of Cognition and Choice with an Application to the British Eastern Committee in 1918." *Papers, Peace Research Society (International)* 18: 113-31.

———. 1973a. "An Experiment on How a Schema Is Used to Interpret Information." Mimeo. Berkeley: Univ. of California.

———. 1973b. "Schema Theory: An Information-Processing Model of Perception and Cognition." *American Political Science Review* 67 (Dec): 1248-66.

———. Forthcoming. *The Structure of Decision.*

Ball, Desmond J. 1974. "The Blind Men and the Elephant: A Critique of Bureaucratic Politics Theory." *Australian Outlook* 28 (Apr): 71-92.

Barber, James David. 1972. *The Presidential Character: Predicting Performances in the White House.* Englewood Cliffs, N.J.: Prentice-Hall.

Bauer, Raymond A. 1961. "Problems of Perception and the Relations between the United States and the Soviet Union." *Journal of Conflict Resolution* 5 (Sep): 223-29.

Bennett, Stephen Earl. 1971. "Modes of Resolution of a 'Belief Dilemma' in the Ideology of the John Birch Society." *Journal of Politics* 33 (Aug): 735-72.

Berelson, Bernard. 1952. *Content Analysis in Communications Research.* Glencoe, Ill.: Free Press.

Bonham, Matthew, and Michael Shapiro. Forthcoming a. "Explanation of the Unexpected: The Syrian Intervention in Jordan in 1970." In *The Structure of Decision.* ed. Robert Axelrod.

——— and Michael Shapiro. Forthcoming b. "Simulating Foreign Policy Decision-Making: An Application to the Middle East." In *Simulation Yearbook,* ed. Joseph Ben-Dak. New York: Gordon & Breach.

Boulding, Elise. 1972. "Peace Research: Dialectics and Development." *Journal of Conflict Resolution* 16 (Dec): 469-75.

Boulding, Kenneth E. 1956. *The Image.* Ann Arbor: Univ. of Michigan Press.

———. 1959. "National Images and International Systems." *Journal of Conflict Resolution* 3 (Jun): 120-31.

Brecher, Michael. 1968. *India and World Politics: Krishna Menon's View of the World.* New York: Praeger.

Brim, Orville, David C. Glass, David E. Lavin, and Norman Goodman. 1962. *Personality and Decision Processes.* Stanford: Stanford Univ. Press.

Broadbent, D. E. 1971. *Decision and Stress.* London: Academic Press.

Brodin, Katarina. 1972. "Belief Systems, Doctrines, and Foreign Policy." *Conflict and Cooperation* 8 (5): 97-112.

Burgess, Philip M. 1967. *Elite Images and Foreign Policy Outcomes.* Columbus: Ohio State Univ. Press.

Choucri, Nazli, and Robert C. North. 1972. "Dynamics of International Conflict: Some Policy Implications of Population, Resources, and Technology." *World Politics* 24 (suppl.): 80-122.

Clarke, David E. 1964. "Persisting Attitudes and International Tension: A Study in the Use of the Stanford General Inquirer." Ph.D. dissertation, Stanford Univ.

Cobb, Roger W. 1973. "The Belief-Systems Perspective: An Assessment of a Framework." *Journal of Politics* 25 (Feb): 121-53.

Converse, Philip E. 1964. "The Nature of Belief Systems in Mass Publics." In *Ideology and Discontent,* ed. David Apter, pp. 206-61. New York: Free Press.

Cottam, Richard, W. 1973. "Foreign Policy Motivations." *International Studies Newsletter* 1 (Winter): 52-60.

Cummins, Howard W. 1973. "Value Structure and Political Leadership." In *Sage Professional Papers in Inter-*

national Studies, ed. Vincent Davis and Maurice A. East. Beverly Hills: Sage.

D'Amato, Anthony A. 1967. "Psychological Constructs in Foreign Policy Prediction." *Journal of Conflict Resolution* 11 (Sep): 294-311.

de Rivera, Joseph. 1968. *The Psychological Dimension of Foreign Policy.* Columbus, Ohio: Merrill.

Dye, David R. Undated. "A Developmental Approach to the Political Style of Getulio Vargas." Mimeo. Stanford: Stanford Univ.

Eckhardt, William. 1967. "Can This Be the Conscience of a Conservative? The Value Analysis Approach to Political Choice." *Journal of Human Relations* 15: 443-56.

――― and Ralph K. White. 1967. "A Test of the Mirror-Image Hypothesis: Kennedy and Khrushchev." *Journal of Conflict Resolution* 11 (Sep): 325-32.

Etzioni, Amitai. 1969. "Social-Psychological Aspects of International Relations." In *The Handbook of Social Psychology* (2d ed.), ed. Gardner Lindzey and Elliot Aronson, vol. 5, pp. 538-601. Reading, Mass.: Addison-Wesley.

Frank, Jerome D. 1967. *Sanity and Survival: Psychological Aspects of War and Peace.* New York: Random House.

Frankel, Joseph. 1963. *The Making of Foreign Policy: An Analysis of Decision-Making.* London: Oxford Univ. Press.

George, Alexander L. 1959a. *Propaganda Analysis.* Evanston, Ill.: Row, Peterson.

―――. 1959b. "Quantitative and Qualitative Approaches to Content Analysis." In *Trends in Content Analysis,* ed. Ithiel de Sola Pool. Urbana: Univ. of Illinois Press.

―――. 1969. "The 'Operational Code': A Neglected Approach to the Study of Political Leaders and Decision-Making." *International Studies Quarterly* 13 (Jun): 190-222.

―――. 1972. "The Case for Multiple Advocacy in Making Foreign Policy." *American Political Science Review* 66 (Sep): 751-85, 791-95.

―――. 1974. "Adaptation to Stress in Political Decision-Making." In *Coping and Adaptation,* ed. G. V. Coelho, D. A. Hamburg, and J. Adams. New York: Basic Books.

――― and Juliette L. George. 1956. *Woodrow Wilson and Colonel House: A Personality Study.* New York: John Day.

Gibbins, Roger. Undated. "The Political Leadership of William Lyon MacKenzie King." Mimeo. Stanford: Stanford Univ.

Glad, Betty. 1966. *Charles Evans Hughes and the Illusion of Innocence: A Study in American Diplomacy.* Urbana: Univ. of Illinois Press.

Goldman, Kjell. 1971. *International Norms and War be-*

tween States: Three Studies in International Politics. Stockholm: Laromedelsforlagen.

Greenstrin, Fred I. 1969. *Personality and Politics: Problems of Evidence, Inference, and Conceptualization.* Chicago: Markham.

Gutierrez, G. G. 1973. "Dean Rusk and Southeast Asia: An Operation Code Analysis." Paper prepared for the Annual Meeting of the American Political Science Association, New Orleans.

Haas, Michael. 1967. "Bridge-Building in International Relations: A Neotraditional Plea." *International Studies Quarterly* 11 (Dec): 320-38.

Halperin, Morton. 1974. *Bureaucratic Politics and Foreign Policy.* Washington: Brookings Institution.

Hammond, Thomas. Forthcoming. "Complexity Reduction in Contemporary Politics." In *The Structure of Decision,* ed. Robert Axelrod.

Heradstveit, Daniel. 1974. *The Outline of a Cumulative Research Strategy for the Study of Conflict Resolution in the Middle East.* Oslo: Norsk Utenrikspolitisk Institutt.

Hermann, Charles F. 1969. *Crises in Foreign Policy.* Indianapolis: Bobbs-Merrill.

―――, ed. 1972. *International Crises: Insights from Behavioral Research.* New York: Free Press.

――― and Margaret G. Hermann. 1967. "An Attempt to Simulate the Outbreak of World War I." *American Political Science Review* 61 (Jun): 400-416.

――― and Linda P. Brady. 1972. "Alternative Models of International Crisis Behavior." In *International Crises,* ed. Charles F. Hermann, pp. 281-320. New York: Free Press.

Hermann, Margaret G. 1972a. "Effects of Leader Personality on National Foreign Policy Behavior: A Theoretical Discussion." Mimeo. Columbus: Ohio State Univ.

―――. 1972b. "How Leaders Process Information and the Effect on Foreign Policy." Paper presented at the Annual Meeting of the American Political Science Association, Washington.

Hilton, Gordon. 1970. "The 1914 Studies: A Reassessment of the Evidence and Some Further Thoughts." *Papers, Peace Research Society (International)* 13: 117-41.

Hoffmann, Stanley, ed. 1960. *Contemporary Theory in International Relations.* Englewood Cliffs, N.J.: Prentice-Hall.

Holsti, Ole R. 1962. "The Belief System and National Images: John Foster Dulles and the Soviet Union." Ph.D. dissertation, Stanford Univ.

―――. 1964. "An Adaptation of the 'General Inquirer' for the Systematic Analysis of Political Documents." *Behavioral Science* 9 (Oct): 382-88.

―――. 1966. "External Conflict and Internal Consensus:

The Sino-Soviet Case." In *The General Inquirer,* ed. Philip J. Stone et al., pp. 343-58. Cambridge: MIT Press.

———. 1967. "Cognitive Dynamics and Images of the Enemy." In *Enemies in Politics,* by David J. Finlay, Ole R. Holsti, and Richard R. Fagen, pp. 25-96. Chicago: Rand McNally.

———. 1969. *Content Analysis for the Social Sciences and Humanities.* Reading, Mass.: Addison-Wesley.

———. 1970. "The 'Operational Code' Approach to the Study of Political Leaders: John Foster Dulles' Philosophical and Instrumental Beliefs." *Canadian Journal of Political Science* 3 (Mar): 123-57.

———. 1972. *Crisis, Escalation, War.* Montreal and London: McGill-Queen's Univ. Press.

———. 1974. "The Study of International Politics Makes Strange Bedfellows: Theories of the Radical Right and Left." *American Political Science Review* 68 (Mar): 217-42.

———, Richard A. Brody, and Robert C. North. 1964. "Measuring Affect and Action in International Reaction Models: Empirical Materials from the 1962 Cuban Crisis." *Journal of Peace Research* 1: 170-90.

———, P. Terrence Hopmann, and John D. Sullivan. 1973. *Unity and Disintegration in International Alliances: Comparative Studies.* New York: Wiley-Interscience.

——— and Alexander L. George. 1975. "The Effects of Stress on the Performance of Foreign Policy-Makers." In *Political Science Annual,* ed. C. P. Cotter, pp. 255-319. Indianapolis: Bobbs-Merrill.

Hopmann, P. Terrence. 1967. "International Conflict and Cohesion in the Communist System." *International Studies Quarterly* 11 (Sep): 212-36.

Horvath, Fred E. 1959. "Psychological Stress: A Review of Definitions and Experimental Research." In *General Systems Yearbook,* ed. Ludwig von Bertalanffy and Anatol Rapoport, vol. 4, pp. 203-25. Bedford, Mass.: Society for General Systems Research.

Ike, Nobutaka. 1967. *Japan's Decision for War: Records of the 1941 Policy Conferences.* Stanford: Stanford Univ. Press.

Janis, Irving L. 1972. *Victims of Groupthink: A Psychological Study of Foreign Policy Decisions and Fiascoes.* Boston: Houghton Mifflin.

——— and Howard Leventhal. 1968. "Human Reaction to Stress." In *Handbook of Personality Theory and Research,* ed. Edgar F. Borgatta and William W. Lambert, pp. 1041-85. Chicago: Rand McNally.

Jervis, Robert. 1968. "Hypotheses on Misperception." *World Politics* 20 (Apr): 454-79.

———. 1969. "The Costs of the Quantitative Study of International Relations." In *Contending Approaches to International Politics,* ed. Klaus Knorr and James N.

Rosenau, pp. 177-217. Princeton: Princeton Univ. Press.

———. 1970. *The Logic of Images in International Relations.* Princeton: Princeton Univ. Press.

———. Forthcoming. *Perception and Misperception in International Politics.* Princeton: Princeton Univ. Press.

Johnson, Loch. 1973. "Operational Codes and the Prediction of Leadership Behavior: Senator Frank Church at Mid-Career." Paper prepared for the Annual Meeting of the American Political Science Association, New Orleans.

Kaplan, Morton A. 1968. "A Psychoanalyst Looks at Politics: A Retrospective Tribute to Robert Waelder." *World Politics* 20 (Jul): 694-704.

Kavanagh, Dennis. 1970. "The Operational Code of Ramsey MacDonald." Mimeo. Stanford: Stanford Univ.

Kelman, Herbert C., ed. 1965. *International Behavior: A Social-Psychological Analysis.* New York: Holt, Rinehart & Winston.

Klineberg, Otto. 1964. *The Human Dimension in International Relations.* New York: Holt, Rinehart & Winston.

Knutson, Jeanne N. 1972. *The Human Basis of the Polity: A Psychological Study of Political Men.* Chicago: Aldine-Atherton.

Koch, Howard E., Robert C. North, and Dina A. Zinnes. 1960. "Some Theoretical Notes on Geography and International Conflict." *Journal of Conflict Resolution* 4 (Mar): 4-14.

Kolko, Joyce, and Gabriel Kolko. 1972. *The Limits of Power: The World and United States Foreign Policy, 1945-1954.* New York: Harper & Row.

Krasner, Stephen D. 1972. "Are Bureaucracies Important?" *Foreign Policy* (7): 159-79.

Lampton, David M. 1973. "The U.S. Image of Peking in Three International Crises." *Western Political Quarterly* 26: 28-50.

Lawrence, Donald. Forthcoming. "The Operational Code of Lester Pearson." Ph.D. dissertation, Univ. of British Columbia.

Lazarus, Richard S. Undated. "The Self-regulation of Emotion." Mimeo. Berkeley: Univ. of California.

———, James Deese, and Sonia Osler. 1952. "The Effects of Psychological Stress upon Performance." *Psychological Bulletin* 49 (Jul): 293-317.

———, James R. Averill, and Edward M. Opton, Jr. 1969. "The Psychology of Coping: Issues of Research and Assessment." Paper prepared for the Conference on Coping and Adaptation," Stanford Univ. Dept. of Psychiatry.

Leites, Nathan. 1951. *The Operational Code of the Politburo.* New York: McGraw-Hill.

———. 1953. *A Study of Bolshevism.* Glencoe, Ill.: Free Press.

Lowenthal, Abraham F. 1972. *The Dominican Intervention.* Cambridge: Harvard Univ. Press.

Lowi, Theodore J. 1969. *The End of Liberalism: Ideology, Policy, and the Crisis of Public Authority.* New York: Norton.

Malone, Craig S. 1971. "The Operational Code of Lyndon Baines Johnson." Mimeo. Stanford: Stanford Univ.

Marsden, G. 1965. "Content Analysis Studies of Therapeutic Interviews: 1954 to 1964." *Psychological Bulletin* 63 (5): 298-321.

May, Ernest R. 1973. *"Lessons" of the Past: The Use and Misuse of History in American Foreign Policy.* New York: Oxford Univ. Press.

McClosky, Herbert. 1956. "Concerning Strategies for a Science of International Politics." *World Politics* 8: 281-95.

McLellan, David. 1971. "The 'Operational Code' Approach to the Study of Political Leaders: Dean Acheson's Philosophical and Instrumental Beliefs." *Canadian Journal of Political Science* 4 (Mar): 52-75.

Mennis, Bernard. 1972. *American Foreign Policy Officials: Who They Are and What They Believe Regarding International Politics.* Columbus: Ohio State Univ. Press.

Milburn, Thomas W. 1972. "The Management of Crisis." In *International Crises,* ed. Charles F. Hermann, pp. 259-77. New York: Free Press.

Morgenthau, Hans J. 1968. "Common Sense and Theories of International Relations." In *Theory and Reality in International Relations,* ed. John C. Farrell and Asa P. Smith, pp. 23-30. New York: Columbia Univ. Press.

Morton, Elaine L. 1972. "The Dynamics of Dyadic Conflict: The United States and the Soviet Union, 1961-1963." Ph.D. dissertation, Stanford Univ.

Mueller, John. 1969a. "Deterrence. Numbers and History." Mimeo. Los Angeles: Univ. of California, Security Studies Project.

———. 1969b. "The Uses of Content Analysis in International Relations." In *The Analysis of Communication Content,* ed. George Gerbner et al., pp. 187-98. New York: Wiley.

North, Robert C., Howard E. Koch, and Dina A. Zinnes. 1960. "The Integrative Functions of Conflict." *Journal of Conflict Resolution* 4 (Sep): 355-74.

———, Ole R. Holsti, Martin G. Zaninovich, and Dina A. Zinnes. 1963. *Content Analysis: A Handbook with Application for the Study of International Crisis.* Evanston: Northwestern Univ. Press.

Osgood, Charles E. 1959a. "Suggestions for Winning the Real War with Communism." *Journal of Conflict Resolution* 3 (Dec): 311-25.

———. 1959b. "The Representational Model and Relevant Research Methods." In *Trends in Content Analysis,* ed. Ithiel de Sola Pool. Urbana: Univ. of Illinois Press.

———. 1962. *Alternative to War or Surrender.* Urbana: Univ. of Illinois Press.

———, Sol Saporta, and Jum C. Nunnally. 1956. "Evaluative Assertive Assertion Analysis." *Litera* 3: 47-102.

Paige, Glenn D. 1968. *The Korean Decision.* New York: Free Press.

Pool, Ithiel de Sola, ed. 1959. *Trends in Content Analysis.* Urbana: Univ. of Illinois Press.

Putnam, Robert D. 1973. *The Beliefs of Politicians: Ideology, Conflict, and Democracy in Britain and Italy.* New Haven: Yale Univ. Press.

Raser, John. 1966. "Personal Characteristics of Political Decision-Makers: A Literature Review." *Papers, Peace Research Society (International)* 5: 161-81.

Rosenau, James N. 1966. "Pre-theories and Theories of Foreign Policy." In *Approaches to Comparative and International Politics,* ed. R. Barry Farrell, pp. 27-92. Evanston: Northwestern Univ. Press.

———. 1967. "The Premises and Promises of Decision-Making Analysis." In *Contemporary Political Analysis,* ed. James C. Charlesworth, pp. 189-211. New York: Free Press.

———. 1968. "Private Preferences and Political Responsibilities: The Relative Potency of Individual and Role Variables in the Behavior of U.S. Senators." In *Quantitative International Politics,* ed. J. David Singer, pp. 17-50. New York: Free Press.

———. 1970. *The Adaptation of National Societies: A Theory of Political System Behavior and Transformation.* New York: McCaleb-Seiler.

———. 1971. *The Scientific Study of Foreign Policy.* New York: Free Press.

———. 1972. Book review. *American Historical Review* 77 (Dec): 1415-16.

———, Philip M. Burgess, and Charles F. Hermann. 1973. "The Adaptation of Foreign Policy Research: A Case Study of an Anti-Case Study Project." *International Studies Quarterly* 17 (Mar): 119-44.

——— and Charles F. Hermann. 1973. "Final Report to the National Science Foundation on Grant GS-3117." Mimeo. Columbus: Ohio State Univ.

Rothstein, Robert L. 1972. *Planning, Prediction, and Policymaking in Foreign Affairs: Theory and Practice.* Boston: Little, Brown.

Shapiro, Michael J., and G. Matthew Bonham. 1973. "Cognitive Processes and Foreign Policy Decision-Making." *International Studies Quarterly* 17 (Jun): 147-74.

Shneidman, Edwin S. 1961. "A Psychological Analysis of Political Thinking: The Kennedy-Nixon 'Great Debates' and the Kennedy-Khrushchev 'Grim Debates.' " Mimeo. Cambridge: Harvard Univ.

———. 1963. "Plan II: The Logic of Politics." In *Television and Human Behavior,* ed. L. Arons and M. A. May, pp. 178-99. New York: Appleton-Century-Crofts.

———. 1969. "Logic Content Analysis: An Explication of Styles of Concludifying." In *The Analysis of Communication Content,* ed. George Gerbner et al., pp. 261-79. New York: Wiley.

Singer, J. David. 1961. "The Level-of-Analysis Problem in International Relations." *World Politics* 14 (Oct): 77-92.

———. 1968. "Man and World Politics: The Psycho-Cultural Interface." *Journal of Social Issues* 24 (Nov): 127-56.

———. 1971. *A General Systems Taxonomy for Political Science.* Morristown, N.J.: General Learning Press.

Siverson, Randolph M. 1972. "The Evaluation of Self, Allies, and Enemies in an International Crisis: Suez, 1956." *Journal of Conflict Resolution* 16 (Jun): 203-10.

Snyder, Richard C., H. W. Bruck, and Burton Sapin. 1962. *Foreign Policy Decision Making.* New York: Free Press.

——— and Glenn D. Paige. 1958. "The United States Decision to Resist Aggression in Korea: The Application of an Analytical Scheme." *Administrative Science Quarterly* 3 (Dec): 341-78.

Stagner, Ross. 1967. *Psychological Aspects of International Conflict.* Belmont, Calif.: Brooks/Cole.

Stassen, Glen H. 1972. "Individual Preference versus Role-Constraint in Policy-Making: Senatorial Response to Secretaries Acheson and Dulles." *World Politics* 25 (Oct): 96-119.

———. 1973. "Revising the 'Operational Code' Method." Paper prepared for the Annual Meeting of the American Political Science Association, New Orleans.

Stein, Janice Gross. 1968. "Krishna Menon's View of the World: A Content Analysis." In *India and World Politics,* Michael Brecher. New York: Praeger.

Steinbruner, John D. 1968. "The Mind and the Milieu of Policy-Makers: A Case History of the MLF." Ph.D. dissertation, Massachusetts Institute of Technology.

———. 1974. *The Cybernetic Theory of Decision.* Princeton: Princeton Univ. Press.

Stone, Philip J., Dexter C. Dunphy, Marshall S. Smith, and Daniel M. Ogilvie, eds. 1966. *The General Inquirer: A Computer Approach to Content Analysis in the Behavioral Sciences.* Cambridge: MIT Press.

——— et al. 1969. "Improved Quality of Content Analysis Categories: Computerized Disambiguation Rules for High Frequency English Words." In *The Analysis of Communication Content,* ed. George Gerbner et al., pp. 199-222. New York: Wiley.

Stupak, Ronald J. 1971. "Dean Rusk on International Relations: An Analysis of His Philosophical Perceptions." *Australian Outlook* 25 (3): 13-28.

Thordarson, Bruce. 1972. *Trudeau and Foreign Policy: A Study in Decision-Making.* Toronto: Oxford Univ. Press.

Trotter, R. G. 1971. "The Cuban Missile Crisis: An Analysis of Policy Formulation in Terms of Current Decision-Making Theory." Ph.D. dissertation, Univ. of Pennsylvania.

Tweraser, Kurt. 1973. "Senator Fulbright's Operational Code as Warrant for His Foreign Policy Advocacy, 1943-1967: Toward Increasing the Explanatory Power of Decisional Premises." Paper prepared for the Annual Meeting of the American Political Science Association, New Orleans.

Verba, Sidney. 1961. "Assumptions of Rationality and Non-rationality in Models of the International System." *World Politics* 14 (Oct): 93-117.

Walker, Stephen G. 1975. "Cognitive Maps and International Realities: Henry A. Kissinger's Operational Code." Paper prepared for the Annual Meeting of the American Political Science Association, San Francisco.

Waltz, Kenneth N. 1959. *Man, the State and War: A Theoretical Analysis.* New York: Columbia Univ. Press.

Wheeler, Harvey. 1960. "The Role of Myth System in American-Soviet Relations." *Journal of Conflict Resolution* 4 (Jun): 179-84.

White, Gordon. 1969. "A Comparison of the 'Operational Codes' of Mao Tse-tung and Liu Shao-chi." Mimeo. Stanford: Stanford Univ.

White, Ralph K. 1951. *Value Analysis: The Nature and Use of the Method.* Glen Gardner, N.J.: Libertarian Press.

———. 1970. *Nobody Wanted War: Misperception in Vietnam and Other Wars.* Garden City, N.Y.: Doubleday.

———. 1971. "Rejoinder"; "Counter Response." *Journal of Social Issues* 27 (Nov): 209-12; 220-27.

Wilensky, Harold L. 1967. *Organizational Intelligence: Knowledge and Policy in Government and Industry.* New York: Basic Books.

Wrightson, Margaret. Forthcoming. "The Documentary Coding Method." In *The Structure of Decision,* ed. Robert Axelrod.

Zacher, Mark W. 1970. *Dag Hammarskjöld's United Nations.* New York: Columbia Univ. Press.

Zaninovich, Martin G. 1964. "An Empirical Theory of State Response: The Sino-Soviet Case." Ph.D. dissertation, Stanford Univ.

Zinnes, Dina A. 1962. "Hostility in International Decision-Making." *Journal of Conflict Resolution* 6 (Sep): 236-43.

———. 1966. "A Comparison of Hostile Behavior of Decision-Makers in Simulate and Historical Data." *World Politics* 18 (Apr): 474-502.

———. 1968. "The Expression and Perception of Hostility in Prewar Crisis: 1914." In *Quantitative International Politics,* ed. J. David Singer, pp. 85-119. New York: Free Press.

———, Robert C. North, and Howard E. Koch. 1961. "Capability, Threat, and the Outbreak of War." In *International Politics and Foreign Policy,* ed. James N. Rosenau, pp. 469-82. New York: Free Press.

———, Joseph L. Zinnes, and Robert D. McClure. 1972. "Hostility in Diplomatic Communication: A Study of the 1914 Crisis." In *International Crises,* ed. Charles F. Hermann, pp. 139-62. New York: Free Press.

Part Two

Cumulative Processes
Philosophical Perspectives

13. Cumulativeness in International Relations

G. R. Boynton

The most straightforward way to discuss cumulativeness in international relations is to suggest what is known now that was not known before and what can be done now that could not be done before. However, it would be presumptous for someone not trained in the field to take on this task. This chapter will, therefore, address two more general questions. In the first section of the chapter it is suggested that cumulativeness in any discipline is, at least in part, a frame of mind of the practitioners of the field. This is not to suggest that the results of the research efforts of the field are unimportant in cumulation, but it will be argued that the perspective that one takes toward these research efforts is important in the conclusion one comes to about the extent of cumulativeness in the field. The second section challenges two rather standard operating procedures in our research. These procedures are hypothesis testing and aggregation of multiple cases in testing one's theory. Both have an important role in research, but it will be argued that our normal way of doing

these two things is as often misleading as it is clarifying, and that as ordinarily practiced they do not lead to the theoretical cumulation that we desire.

CUMULATIVENESS AS A FRAME OF MIND

In Chapter 34 of this volume—a paper originally prepared for a conference on Comparative Foreign Policy—Michael O'Leary recodes the World Event Interaction Survey (WEIS) data set of interactions among nations in order to determine the policy issue content of these interactions. He is able to show that there was substantial variation in the level of conflict and cooperation between pairs of nations from one issue area to another. The overall conflict and cooperation scores for the pairs of nations concealed this important source of variation.

How should one interpret this finding? A reading of that paper and private conversations with

O'Leary indicate that he believes this finding requires a major break with past research on conflict and cooperation. He concludes his paper in the following way.

> This short statement, of course, far from confirms anything about the argument as to exactly where the study of comparative foreign policy should be moving. But it hopefully at least fails to falsify the hypothesis of this paper, that there is a range of quantitative and qualitative richness to foreign policy behavior which has not yet even been measured systematically let alone analyzed. To move systematically and rigorously into the complex field of issue analysis is not easy. But in the long run the costs may not be as great as continuing in the present path of statistical impotence and theoretical vacuity.

Thus, I think, he would score this finding as one with noncumulative implications. Let me write a somewhat different conclusion.

> These findings make possible a major advance in our understanding of cooperation and conflict between nations. Previous research has demonstrated that it is possible to understand the basic mechanisms in cooperation and conflict, but the theory has not been as precise in its predictions as is desirable. Breaking down measures of cooperation and conflict by issue area will permit more precise measurement of the cooperation and conflict between nations, and this alone should improve our understanding. More important, it will make possible refinement of the theory through examination of the conditions under which patterns of conflict and cooperation in the interaction of nations diverge in different issue areas and conditions under which they converge.

Let me quickly add that this is a rhetorical conclusion. My knowledge of international relations is limited. I wanted to choose an example from this field, and this was a piece of research that I had thought about and which could serve as an example. The point is that two very different conclusions can be drawn from a single empirical finding. One can interpret the empirical finding as having cumulative or noncumulative implications. This is part of what I mean in saying that cumulativeness is a frame of mind.

The most obvious characteristic of cumulative thinking is that it is a temporal frame of reference which incorporates the past, present, and the future. From this perspective it is assumed that the present research could not have been done except for the work that preceded it. Just as this frame of mind joins past and present work, it also sees past and current research as leading to research in the future. The past and present point the way to future advances in understanding by suggesting leads which are unearthed in those research efforts. The cumulative frame of reference assumes that one will be able to elaborate and make one's understanding of the empirical phenomenon being studied more precise by following new leads which grow out of a given piece of research.

The cumulative frame of reference assumes that previous research is that without which the current research could not have been done. It is sometimes asserted that cumulativeness means that current research *builds* on previous research. But the more stark characterization, *that without which this work could not be done,* carries less connotative "baggage" and may therefore be a clearer way to present what is basic to the cumulative perspective.

Past research has three important aspects for cumulativeness. First, there is the importance of past research in the current recognition of a problem requiring new research. Returning to O'Leary—without the prior research that did not differentiate issue areas in constructing measures of conflict and cooperation, he would not have been able to argue as forcefully as he does for the need to segment cooperation and conflict along issue area lines. The problem does not exist so long as one talks about nations in concrete and discrete terms—something approaching diplomatic history. The problem also does not exist so long as one talks about the interaction between nations in general terms—as in general interpretations of, or theorizing about, events without the benefit of precise definitions or empirical data. It is only when one attempts to become precise in theoretical formulation and in empirical measurement that the "problem" becomes a problem. Thus, O'Leary's research required the previous research of those utilizing events data in their studies of conflict and cooperation in order to locate his research problem.

A second important aspect of past research is the procedure or the technology of research. Current research is based on procedures which have been developed in the past. While new research may refine those procedures, cumulativeness in the technology of research is an important aspect of cumulativeness. In research on the interaction of nations the development of events data is an important technological innovation. It permits precision in description and measurement that was not possible before its "invention." Again returning to O'Leary—his work clearly could not have been done without the prior development of events data. I do not mean that he only reanalyzed a data set which had been collected by others, although that is not a trivial part of the technological cumulativeness in an observational science but, more important, events data coding has extended our measurement capacities to areas where measurement was not possible before. Before this data collection procedure was developed O'Leary and his colleagues could have argued at great length, but they would not have been able to settle their differences by references to the empirical world except in an anecdotal manner. Anecdotes are, unfortunately, not a very satisfactory or conclusive way to answer empirical questions. Thus, in a second important way his research was dependent upon previous research.

The third aspect of past research which is important for cumulativeness is theoretical integration. Theory plays the useful function of intellectually coordinating the findings from one research effort with much other research on the same phenomena. It is, undoubtedly, at this point that political scientists feel most uneasy about the cumulativeness of the discipline. There are both more theories or theoretical perspectives than we can cope with and yet much of the research seems to be basically atheoretical. Much of what is called theory is so general that it does not prescribe any particular research; it is a framework for giving heuristic order to work that has already been done. It is also insufficiently precise to permit testing, that is, one cannot quite figure out what would count as evidence for or against it. I believe that there are signs that this is beginning to change, and an example is presented in the following section.

Cumulative thinking is a merging of past, present, and future. The problems set for research now grow out of research in the past. Much of the technology of present and future research grows out of past research. Increased understanding and precision in the future can be predicted by observing that it is possible to go beyond what has been done in the past. The steps that must be taken to move toward increased understanding in the future will be different at distinct historical junctures; theoretical reformulation may be required, there may be a need for better measurement techniques, there may be the necessity of establishing the generality of the theory, or other types of activities may be required. To the extent that one sees any of these diverse activities as growing out of past research and leading to increased understanding of the phenomenon under investigation in the future, one is engaged in cumulative thinking.

STRATEGIES FOR THEORY DEVELOPMENT IN RESEARCH

There are two rather standard procedures used by political scientists in their research which ought to be critically examined by asking—Do they really contribute to theoretical cumulativeness? First, most of the empirical/quantitative research in political science is described by researchers as a process of testing hypotheses. The ultimate aim is averred to be the development of theory, and hypothesis testing is assumed to be the way to arrive there. Political scientists have been busy testing hypotheses for more than 20 years, and one can still conclude that there has been little theoretical development in coordination with research findings. This should lead us to question the utility of hypothesis testing, in and of itself, as a road to theory. Second, the standard procedure in data collection and analysis is to collect a large number of pieces of information (variables) on a large number of cases and then perform one or another statistical analysis in order to see how the "independent" variables are "related" to the "dependent" variable(s). I will try to show, with an example and a brief discussion, that a few cases can be used to test certain interesting types of theories, and that, in general, theory development may proceed more efficiently by examining each case individually than by combining them in the analysis. The general question being raised here is—is there a strategy of theory development that is potentially more productive than our normal procedure?

An example may make what otherwise would be an unduly abstract discussion more concrete. Here I must depart from international relations and discuss research with which I am more familiar. The example, taken from a paper by Sprague (n.d.), is a small part of a much larger study of the growth and decline of social democratic parties. Despite the limited scope of this example, in the context of the broader problem it illustrates a relevant strategy for theory development.

Assume that one wants to understand the growth of social democratic parties, and also assume that the growth of the Democratic coalition between 1920 and 1948 is an example of the phenomenon to be investigated. A relatively simple way of conceptualizing the process is to think of it as a process of gains and losses. Growth in support for the Democratic party can be thought of as a process in which there are more gains than losses. Equation 1 states this accounting relationship.

$$\triangle M = -fM_t + g(L-M_t) \qquad (1)$$

where M is percentage Democratic vote
  f is the loss rate from the group who already support the Democrats
  g is the gain rate from those not in the group and potentially susceptible
  L is the upper limit on the proportion of the population who may become members

The equation simply says that change in Democratic support, $\triangle M$, is produced by loss from those who were Democratic supporters at one time, $-fM_t$, and gain from those who were not Democratic supporters, g. Because it seems implausible that all voters would become Democratic, some upper limit is set on the amount of gain possible, L in $g(L-M_t)$.

Equation 1 is only an accounting formula and is not substantively very interesting. However, it is possible to develop an understanding of the process based on this conceptualization. We know that voting is an habitual act. Most voters vote for the same party election after election. This can be

taken into account by defining habit in the following way.

$$h = (1-f) \qquad (2)$$

where h is habit
  f is the loss rate

Habit is a property of individuals. One would not expect this property to vary substantially from one context to another. Thus, if one estimates habit in several different contexts (counties in the analysis to follow) one would expect the parameter estimates to be approximately the same in each context. The recruitment of new supporters is not a property of the individual, but is a function of the context in which the individual finds himself and the influences working in that environment which are more favorable to one party than the other. New organizations were created during the period 1920-1948, particularly labor unions, which were favorable to the Democratic party. These organizations flourished in urban but not in rural areas. We can assume that communication and interaction are greater in urban areas. This also leads to an expectation of greater gain rates in urban areas. Rewriting equation 1 to incorporate habit and estimating the model with counties of varying levels of urbanization will permit one to test these ideas.

$$M_{t+1} = (h-g)M_t + gL \qquad (3)$$

After some "fancy footwork," presented in the original paper but not presented here, one can estimate the parameters of the model. These are presented in Table 1.

Note first that in 1920 the counties were very similar in their support for the Democratic party (see column Observed Value 1920). The model was developed on the assumption that whatever changes took place would be related to either habit or differential rates of gain due to the different degree of urbanness of the counties. It was assumed, however, that habit as a property of individuals would be constant across all contexts. The estimates for these four counties indicate that this assumption proved to be true for these counties (see column Habit or Retention Rate). The effect of the forces working in the direction of

Table 1. Parameter Estimates for Democratic Presidential Voting in Four New York Counties, 1920-1948

County	Observed Value in 1920	Gain Rate, g	Loss Rate, f	Habit or Retention Rate $(1-f)$, h	Upper Limit on Recruitment Pool, L	Long-run Limit, M^*	Observed Value in 1960
Jefferson	0.26	0.18	0.08	0.92	0.57	0.40	0.39
St. Lawrence	0.23	0.25	0.11	0.89	0.56	0.39	0.43
Oneida	0.30	0.29	0.09	0.91	0.69	0.53	0.52
Bronx	0.30	0.44	0.08	0.92	0.84	0.71	0.68

Source: John Sprague, "Three Applications of Contextual Theses: Cross Section, Across Time, and Across Parameters." Mimeo. Undated. Reprinted by permission of the author.

Democratic support or the context of the individual was assumed to vary from one county to another. This gain proved true (see column Gain Rate). The gain rate for the most urban county (Bronx) is the highest, and the gain rates for the two least urban counties (Jefferson and St. Lawrence) are the lowest. Notice also the long-run limit and the Democratic support in 1960 (see the last two columns in Table 1). The long-run limit is the predicted level of support when equilibrium is reached (this concept is developed in Sprague's paper). The election of 1960 was one in which the two presidential candidates were closely balanced, and is therefore a reasonable test of whether the long-run limit had been reached. The predicted values of the long-run limit and the actual support in 1960 are very close.

The point of presenting this example is to contrast it with more normal research procedures of testing hypotheses with statistical analysis of large numbers of variables and cases. What might the more familiar procedure look like? First, a measure of change in Democratic support would have to be developed for all counties (or a sample of counties) in a given state, nation, or combination of nations (since others were undergoing similar increases of growth of support for social democratic parties). Second, a series of measures of independent variables—urbanness, occupational structure, income distribution, etc., would be generated. Third, a regression analysis would be performed. This procedure would determine rather precisely what kind of counties changed, but it tells very little about the *process of change*. Both procedures utilize regression in making estimates, but the example presented above permits the effects of the important components of the process to be estimated. Because it is modelled as a process, it is also possible to estimate the limits on the process of growth, something which cannot be done in normal hypothesis testing.

Let us return to the two general points of this section. Our normal procedures of hypothesis testing are not likely to lead to cumulative theorizing. First, hypotheses such as "the greater the concentration of working class in a community, the greater the increase in support for Democrats" tell us where different rates of change take place, but they tell us very little about the process of change itself. Thus, we end up with historically conditioned descriptive information rather than an understanding of the process of change. Second, the normal hypotheses are not integrated—mostly they just stack up; without integration they have the unsatisfying quality of discrete pieces. "Getting it all together" is the product of a theoretical system and not just multivariate analysis. The model taken from Sprague's work, on the other hand, provides a theory of change, and with this beginning theoretical statement it is possible to investigate *how* the rate of change will differ from one context to another. A next step in the theoretical development might be to bring context explicitly into the model in order to elaborate the theory and to predict different rates of change more formally. The point is that there is a theory, and there is some initial empirical validation of the theory. The theory can be elaborated in a number of directions and can be further tested by bringing more empirical evidence to bear in the testing.

I also asserted that collapsing all of the cases in a single analysis was likely to be misleading. Each county is undergoing the same process of change in the above analysis, but we would have learned very little if a single set of parameter estimates for all the counties had been produced. Each of the counties is different, and it is these differences that allow inferences to be drawn about the assumptions that go into the model. The same is undoubtedly true for all dyads of nations. For example, all are, more or less, involved in the process of cooperation and conflict. We are more likely to develop and elaborate a theory of cooperation and conflict by looking at them individually than we are by lumping them together in an analysis. This does not mean that testing for generality is not important. Clearly, it is necessary to test the model presented above on more than four counties in New York State. But it is possible to test and elaborate that model more effectively by proceeding with careful analysis of individual cases than by looking for general descriptions.

CONCLUSION

What is the prospect for cumulativeness in international relations? I have argued that in certain important ways cumulativeness already exists in international relations. Current research problems frequently arise out of research that has been done in the past. An example was presented at the beginning of this chapter; it could be multiplied many times. The technology of international relations has changed and, in the process, improved. These techniques do not have to be reinvented or, when borrowed, rediscovered. Finally, I think there are signs that our theory will become more explicitly integrative and testable—the *sine qua non* of cumulativeness. International relations has made great progress during the past twenty years, and this progress should be reflected in our perspective on what has happened in research in this field.

REFERENCE

Sprague, John. Undated. "Three Applications of Contextual Theses: Cross Section, Across Time, and Across Parameters." Mimeo.

14. Noticing Pre-paradigmatic Progress

Richard K. Ashley

For the field of international relations, the concept of paradigm represents a vaguely envisioned utopian destination which, like Hilton's Shangri-La, is not marked on any map. Of the little that is known of this hidden destination, its most alluring feature is its orderliness—not the orderliness of a totalitarian regime, but the Rousseauesque orderliness that comes when consensually shared beliefs, values, and expectations motivate a society's members to serve common ends by common means. It is widely believed that in a paradigmatic society each member's labor constitutes a cumulative contribution to the society's

SPECIAL NOTE: Thanks are due to Hayward Alker, Nazli Choucri, and Harold Guetzkow for their valuable comments on an earlier draft.

product, for each member is certain of the form that the product has taken and is taking. The member is not nagged by doubts about the sturdiness of the prior contributions upon which he builds; after all, these have been subjected to reliable quality controls that screen out those contributions in which he should not be confident. He even knows the general form that his contribution must take if it is to "fit." The society frequently encounters puzzles. But these are invigorating rather than debilitating, for each member is sure that such puzzles constitute challenges that are surmountable within the framework previously constructed. Committed to the product and sure of society's rewards to those who contribute to it, he and his colleagues eschew pursuits that might detract from the product, devoting their energies exclusively to improving it. Ordered, cumulative development in a rewarding environment combining the excitement of discovery with the constant reassurance of a firm prior foundation—this is the promise of the paradigm vision.[1]

Scanty yet compelling, this common vision of paradigm exerts a subtle influence on our views of the pre-paradigmatic field of international relations and progress within it. Because the vision provides no roadmap by which we may find our paradigm(s), it often seems that we are left to rely on serendipity. Yet a mode of search characterized by chaos, uncertainty, and risk is a mode those most strongly attracted to the order and certainty of the vision are least disposed to accept. In seeking an alternative, we frequently advocate emulation of components of the vision; the vision of

paradigm becomes more than a possible future destination; it becomes a contemporary standard for our work. Even though we readily (albeit painfully) admit that our field is pre-paradigmatic, we persist in measuring our progress by reference to a vision of scientific enterprise more appropriate to—and in fact borrowed from—other fields.

Thus we tend to discuss cumulation in the building-block sense of the paradigm vision, and we are disappointed. We are disturbed by the scarcity of firm theoretical propositions on which to build. We are concerned by the absence of cooperation: the disregard that others seem to have for our contributions, the vaporous qualities of others' contributions. We demand the use of confidence enhancing quality controls, but we are frustrated by the fact that many of the ones we now have are themselves of questionable quality while others lend credence only to unrelated theoretical components of overly specific utility. We are confused and perplexed by the number of competing blueprints and the fact that each is incomplete. We often conclude that, by the standards set by our vision, our progress has been dismal. And in seeking solutions, we prescribe behavior more in conformity with our image of the paradigmatic scientist, better quality controls, more judicious use of them, and more clearly defined blueprints; we reaffirm our belief that our vision of paradigm embodies standards that must be met, not later, but now.

The present paper reflects suspicions (1) that the prevailing vision of scientific paradigm is at best a partial standard by which to measure pre-paradigmatic progress; (2) that the vision has been misequated with science itself, obscuring important facets of a scientific enterprise while overemphasizing others; and (3) that the resulting concentration on high confidence, proven, and strictly theoretical statements in our intra-field communications has limited opportunities for cumulation to the building-block form—a form which might well be the norm in some future international relations paradigm(s) but which today represents a prochronistic expectation. The present paper reflects the conviction that, for a pre-paradigmatic field, cumulation cannot be confined to theory, but must be understood as a social process wherein scientists' evolving beliefs about

---

[1] The vision of scientific paradigm depicted in this paragraph is most similar to the concept of prerevolutionary paradigm developed by Kuhn (1970). Although Kuhn's version is controversial (as are the others with which it contends), it remains a prominent, benchmark version familiar to most social scientists. This paradigm vision is here treated as a destination without a roadmap because, as Kuhn readily declares, the paradigm construct is suggestive of a dynamic process of social interaction and scientific development only after the threshold to normal science is crossed; i.e., after a successful, exemplary, and unprecedented research achievement—one that excites further inquiry along similar lines while drawing scientists away from other scientific modes—is performed. The paradigm construct is not particularly illuminating concerning the nature of a scientific enterprise in advance of a galvanizing exemplar.

international phenomena are influenced by their evolving levels of confidence in their own and others' techniques.

Offering an idealized description of this process, and not a program for the field, this paper tries to suggest two forms of cumulation which can occur at confidence levels much below those demanded in our paradigm image but which nevertheless are potentially significant in their effects on continuing research. It indicates one way in which the interaction of these two forms of cumulation might be taken as evidence of the presence or absence of research nuclei and progress within them. And, noting that such inferences are inhibited by our tendency to selectively report on our research as if we already shared a paradigm, it also suggests a modification of our reporting styles. One step toward pre-paradigmatic progress is an expansion of our collective consciousness about the forms it might take.

TWO CRUDE CONSTRUCTS

In addition to the building-block type of cumulation, participants in a pre-paradigmatic field might consider two other types: one of these might be called *expansive* cumulation, and the second might be labeled *selective* cumulation. Expansive cumulation can be defined as a process in which, among a group of scientists, research horizons are broadened and there is a shared sense that an expanding variety of formerly neglected notions "should not be overlooked." The major thrust of expansive cumulation processes is to produce an expanding, commonly perceived catalogue of models, concepts, variables, indices, relationships, data, and techniques that have been shown to be significant or useful under one or more sets of circumstances and which are widely acknowledged to be *potentially* significant or useful in others. Expansive cumulation provides a storehouse of research options. It does not discriminate among them.

Selective cumulation, by contrast, can be defined as a process of evolving shared *expectations* about models, relationships, variables, techniques etc. such that a group of scientists' selections among these increasingly will be informed by prior experiences, including empirical research. That is,

we can envision a group of scientists' shared expectations regarding the promise (e.g., explanatory, predictive, idea-generating, problem-solving promise) of alternative models, relationships, data sets, and techniques. Where expansive cumulation occurs as the variety of these alternatives is increased, selective cumulation may be said to occur when the scientists' shared expectations regarding the promise of these alternatives evolves away from a perfectly even distribution across alternatives: shared expectations for one model (or technique or type of data) increase relative to expectations for others as a result of shared experiences. Selective cumulation processes should not be equated with one possible (but far from inevitable) end product—a growing stockpile of confidently accepted and excluded theoretical propositions—for selective cumulation in expectations can occur for technical as well as theoretical components of a scientific enterprise, and it can occur well below (arbitrarily defined) levels of statistical significance. A key dimension is consensus: if the evolution of expectations is not uniform across a group of scientists, selection processes are disintegrative.

When selective cumulation occurs among a group of scientists sharing common research-relevant values, the process tends to guide inquiry; it increasingly performs (Lakatos-like) positive and negative heuristic functions (see Lakatos and Musgrave, 1970)—indicating, often in a nonarticulated (but also nonmystical) way, which research alternatives to pursue and which alternatives to postpone, ignore, and avoid. In a developing, self-sustaining process, selective cumulation (along with shared values) guides further expansive cumulation; in a degenerating process, expansive cumulation is decreasingly subordinated to selective cumulation.

NOTICING PROGRESS IN PRE-PARADIGMATIC IR

Looking at the field of international relations as a whole, it seems clear that our cumulation processes have been primarily expansive in nature. Concepts, techniques, data archives, and models have proliferated; and about most of these we generally agree, they should not be ignored, they are potentially useful. That this is the major thrust of field-wide cumulation is evidenced by the fact that a common theme in general IR theory courses is simply that several sets of phenomena deserve investigation and that a set of phenomena can be investigated from several angles. The student emerging from such a course ordinarily has a catalogue of ideas but little commitment to any of them. In fact, field-wide expansive cumulation demands only shared tolerance, only a generalized sense that others are doing work that might (above some very low confidence threshold) satisfy some of our values and from which we might have occasion to borrow. In part, the extent of field-wide expansive cumulation is attributable to a degree of commonality in our values (including our evaluation of tolerance). In larger part, it reflects the fact that the field is not truly divisible into paradigms.

This last statement deserves elaboration. To say that the field does not contain paradigms is simply to say that within the field there are no groups of scientists who satisfy the absolute definitional criteria for "schools," "invisible colleges," "research programmes," or "disciplinary matrices" as these concepts have been developed in the literature.[2] According to Hayward Alker's valuable synthesis (see Table 1), these criteria include a scholarly community within which the following are well developed and consensually shared: metascientific beliefs and values, originating exemplars and positive heuristics, symbolic generalizations, and a linearly cumulative literature reporting of exemplar application and reinforcement, of puzzle/anomaly identification, and of successful, generalization-based puzzle solutions.[3] The conclusion that there are no such paradigms in our field is possibly an unhappy one; but it is an accurate one.

This is not, however, a conclusion of despair. The presence or absence of paradigms (as strictly defined) is a hopelessly misapplied measure of scientifc progress in a pre-paradigmatic field. We need to look for ways to measure progress prior to the nearly absolute self-assurance-in-knowledge

---

[2]See, for example, Kuhn (1970); the contributions of Lakatos, Kuhn, Masterman, and Popper in the essential volume edited by Lakatos and Musgrave (1970), Merton (1968), Price (1963), Hanson (1950), Wolin (1968), and Polanyi (1958).

[3]See Alker (1973). The table from which these criteria are drawn is attached with Alker's permission.

that the paradigm construct implies. We need to recognize that there is no void (between thorough ignorance on the one hand and high confidence, high commitment science on the other) in which scientists' behaviors are dictated only by whim and in which no real scientific progress occurs. If new measures of pre-paradigmatic progress are found, one can try to examine the field, identify nuclei of progress, and make contributions.

It is toward this end that the selective cumulation and expansive cumulation constructs have been introduced. They are proposed as crude, partial, and approximate indicators of pre-paradigmatic development in the field. They are intended, in a sense, to liberate us from the artificially absolute, burdensome, and often misconstrued conceptual baggage that usually accompanies attempts to locate paradigms, proto-paradigms, and schools as centers of progress in the field.

Following this tack, one would ask whether, among a group of scientists in our field, there is evidence that selective cumulation—with respect to models, concepts, techniques, variables, data, substantive foci, etc.—has occurred as a result of their shared experience. The questions are not "What presumably workable puzzles have you identified and tried to solve? What common symbolic generalizations have you employed? To what extent is your literature composed of a linear development of generalizations from past findings? What do you as a group know with certainty that you did not know before?" Rather, they are "What shared heuristic (i.e., research-guiding) expectations are you developing as an outgrowth of your common experiences? To what extent is expansive cumulation guided by selective cumulation?" These latter questions demand less certainty but more thought. They go more directly to the heart of pre-paradigmatic progress. When a group of scientists sustains more or less uniform selective cumulation and the selective process guides expansive cumulation within the group, one can speak of a *developing research nucleus*. When selective cumulation ceases, is no longer uniform across the group, or decreasingly dominates expansive cumulation within the group, one can speak of a *degenerating research nucleus*.

Using these gross measures, it is possible to spot only a few of the more formidable research nuclei

Table 1.   Definitional Components of a Research Paradigm Complex

Components	Related Concepts or Examples
1. *Metascientific Beliefs and Values*	1a) Ontological commitments; metaphysical principles; negative
a) Metaphysical paradigms	heuristics; Wright's orienting concepts: field, equilibrium,
b) Research-related value commitments,	organization, plan, community.
including policy interests	b) Kuhn's good reasons for paradigm change, Lakatos' standards,
c) Paradigm schemas, problems, or	regarding progressive problem shifts; Popper, Kuhn,
question sets	Barber, Merton on scientific norms and institutions;
	Kepler's concern with calendar crisis.
	c) Lasswell's politics, Merton's sociology of knowledge paradigm,
	action schemas, Allison's modes of appropriate problem
	response.
2. *Originating Exemplars and Positive Heuristics*	2a) Laboratory experiments; quasi experiments, e.g., Galilean
a) Applications of analogies or preoperational	pendulum experiments and Einstein's explanation of
mechanistic models in a problematic	black body radiation anomalies.
context	b) Lavoisier's heating of mercury oxide to produce oxygen;
b) Technical exemplars including experi-	Fisher's experimental designs with associated variance
mental devices, associated techniques,	analysis; Lazarsfeld's quasi-causal marginals-partials
and related mathematical procedures	analysis of spurious correlations; the Skinner-box;
c) Positive heuristics of model development	Stanford-Binet IQ test.
d) Original evidence of exemplar success	c) Gradual relaxations of point mass assumptions by Newton
	and Galileo; growth in nonsubjective reinforcement
	mechanisms of learning theory.
	d) Usually this includes explanation of crisis-inducing anomaly
	cluster.
3. *Symbolic Generalizations*	3a) Merton's deviant behavior taxonomy; Weber-Parsons action
a) Ideal types on constructs	typologies; Ashby's homeostat.
b) Quasi-tautological symbolic laws	b) Newton's laws; Von Neumann's game theory; Keynes-Kalecki
c) Preliminary or revised, testible	models of macroeconomics.
specifications of exemplars	c) Point-mass, frictionless versions of original Galileo,
	Newton models of pendulum, planetary motion; the
	revolution of psychometric IQ measurement.
4. *A Cumulative Literature,* based on	4a) Kepler's tables at last gave more accurate planetary locations
exemplars, mediated through symbolic	than Ptolemaic ones.
generalizations	b) Discoveries of new planets, new elements, new behavioral
a) New evidence of descriptive and explana-	regularities like structural unemployment; new isotopes
tory success of originating exemplars	distinguished through physical separation means.
and applied positive heuristics	c) Revolution-hiding textbook reinterpretations and
b) New data discoveries, changing and	mathematiczations of earlier work; continuing scholarly
usually tougher standards; heuristic,	journals with only very recent footnotes.
corroborated auxiliary theories	d) Newtonian astronomy led to the discovery of irregularities
c) A linearized literature of successful	in the orbit of Venus, etc.
generalization-based puzzle solutions	
d) Renewed list of evocative puzzles and	
anomalies	
5. A scholarly community sharing the "research	5. Kuhn's scientific communities organized in terms of a
paradigm" (1-4 above). If a "normal"	disciplinary matrix (roughly 1-4 above); other paradigms
scientific community, many components of	and professional structures might also be present. A
of a reserach paradigm would be	notion similar to Price's invisible colleges. An obvious
globally adhered to.	example would be Pavlov-Skinnerian learning theorists.

Source: H.R. Alker, Jr., "Research Paradigms and Mathematical Politics." Revision (1973) of a paper presented at the
1971 IPSA Roundtable on "Quantitative Methods and Political Substance: Toward Better Research Strategies,"
Mannheim, Germany. Reprinted by permission of the author.

in the field. The "events data movement" as a generic phenomenon probably deserves to be called a developing research nucleus. It has been characterized by a very large measure of expansive cumulation over the years (e.g., McClelland, CREON, Azar, Moses-Brody, Rosecrance). And this might have suggested degeneration except that shared experiences (both successes and failures) are slowly giving rise to a widely shared adherence to a variety of selectively identified precepts that will increasingly guide future research.

Another developing nucleus (or molecule) is the work on arms races in the Richardson tradition. Reviewing the relevant literature, Alker (1973) went so far as to conclude that this work represents a multiadic research paradigm complex centering on the basic question: why do nations arm against each other as if they were in a mechanical reactive process? Alker named three (sub)paradigms in this complex: the psycho-logic, rational action, and social causation paradigms. Whether or not one agrees with the use of the term paradigm,[4]

it does seem clear that over the last fifteen years each of these has been characterized by a sustained selective cumulation process reflecting shared exemplars and experiences;[5] within each of these, expansive cumulation has generally been guided by selective processes.

The comparative foreign policy area is (at least if taken as a whole) an example of a static or degenerating research nucleus. Once fairly well united by shared commitments to common research interests, this group has never exhibited any uniform, sustained selective cumulation, and expansive cumulation has dominated the area. It may be the case, however, that some subgroup or spin-off nuclei are emerging.

Another static research nucleus is the INS/IPS simulation area. Unlike the comparative foreign policy area, this area did in fact exhibit a sustained selective cumulation process over a period of many years. Its heuristic products have been impressive. And though it crossed several theoretical "paths," this movement was guided by the evolution of shared expectations about the promise of the design and changes that could be made in it. The current, apparently static nature of the area is largely (but probably not wholly) due to a rapid evolution of expectations about funding prospects—

---

[4]My disagreement with Alker on this point is minor but deserves to be spelled out. It stems from my interpretation of his definitional criteria as fairly absolute (like Kuhn's description on which they are largely, though not exclusively, based) and from my belief that research in the Richardson tradition has not fully satisfied these criteria. In particular, it is highly questionable whether the bodies of literature associated with the three groupings have been cumulative in the linear sense (see note 5) and whether the "scholarly community" associated with each approach is in fact bounded and bonded to the degree that "paradigm" usually implies. Moreover, while each "community" does evidence a consensual sharing of metascientific beliefs, exemplars, positive heuristics, and symbolic generalizations, there are rarely specified well enough, and adherence to them generally is not strong enough or uniform enough, to form a background against which anomalies might be perceived and distinguished from puzzles, thereby generating genuine crises.

Alker, by contrast, does not see these criteria as nearly so restrictive, asking only that "at least some of the 4 or 5 definitional components be widely shared, perhaps in some reconstructed form." Thus he can view research in the Richardson tradition as an "uneven, abnormal, multiadic research paradigm complex," using it as a vehicle by which to pinpoint components of mathematical politics exhibiting paradigm-like qualities, to further our understanding of obstacles to sustained paradigmatic progress in mathematical politics, and, finally, to significantly revise and enrich the paradigm concept, and the research relevant expectations we associate with it, so that it may prove more immediately relevant to mathematical politics.

My only objection to this important and commend-

able work is terminological: I wish that an alternative to "paradigm" had been used, for I fear that many readers will neglect the significant refinements in the Kuhnian depiction that Alker's research paradigm represents, will assume that Kuhn's paradigm and Alker's research paradigm are identical, and will therefore mistakenly conclude that mathematical politics contains a variety of Kuhnian paradigms, with all that this connotes.

It is interesting to note that, as two lengthy conversations have revealed, my selective cumulation construct and Alker's research paradigm construct lead us to the same conclusions about areas of IR that are progressive and degenerative—an observation that leads me to conclude that selective cumulation might be understood as a product of Alker's conceptually richer research paradigms.

[5]As Harold Guetzkow reminded me in a personal communication, the Richardson exemplar was neglected for two decades—an indication that the long-term selective cumulation process has not exhibited the smooth progression that the adjective "sustained" might imply. This is true. It illustrates the dependence of selective cumulation processes on externalities: in this case, the Cold War and the persistent antagonism of Soviet-American arms policies, together with the availability of new, computer-aided techniques, served to catalyze interest in armament/tension processes and the Richardson exemplar.

a very real consideration when one considers the promise of a model, technique, or type of data.[6]

But much beyond these formidable, well-publicized sorts of research areas, it is difficult to apply these measures of progress. One obstacle is particularly prominent: *our intra-field communications generally neglect the information most crucial to the identification of research nuclei and to the evaluation of progress within them.* Both selective and expansive cumulation are processes, not static conditions; and selective cumulation, a process usually operating well below expectational levels of statistical significance, is crucial to pre-paradigmatic progress. Yet our current reporting norms dictate the use of variants on an artificially static hypothetico-deductive reconstructed logic which concentrates on "proof." This is a reporting style often associated with the paradigmatic scientist. Apparently we have confused it with science itself.

SURMOUNTING AN IMPEDIMENT TO NOTICING

Following Kaplan (1964), a *logic-in-use* is a scientist's cognitive style—his way of thinking about his work, raising questions, and looking for answers. Applying the selective cumulation construct, it can be said that within any developing nuclear group of scientists, their common logic-in-use will in part be a product of their shared values and their shared selective cumulation process. This logic-in-use is not necessarily explicit. A *reconstructed logic* is an attempt to explicitly formulate a logic-in-use. As Kaplan points out, the two cannot be taken to be identical or to correspond exactly. A reconstructed logic does not describe a logic-in-use but rather idealizes and refines it, usually in a highly selective way.

In the empirical/quantitative international relations literature, most reporters on research proj-

---

[6]Unfortunately, funding is largely an externality with respect to selective cumulation processes. To the extent that funding agencies neglect these processes and demand the production of substantive, high confidence, theoretical building-blocks, they introduce cross pressures which distort, even undermine, these processes. Surely funding agencies cannot be blamed for making such demands. After all, we have done more than acquiesce. We have repeatedly pronounced these the appropriate demands for our field.

ects seem to aspire to the hypothetico-deductive reconstruction. In this reconstruction, the scientist begins by offering a set of postulates governing the phenomena under study and deduces some observable consequences. Next, he introduces a technique, and using it he tests these consequences by confronting them with evidence, thereby confirming or disconfirming the initial postulates. Throughout, there is an emphasis on proof. When strictly adhered to, such a reconstruction is neat; it is easy to follow. It converges nicely with statistical techniques (quality controls) in which we have been trained and on which we profess reliance ("Why, I can just thumb to the tables to find out what he had to say!"). It offers a semblance of logic and a sense of elegant accomplishment (or, occasionally, of classy failure). Reports using this reconstruction are the ones that we are supposed to be the most anxious to receive, and they are therefore the ones that we feel constrained to send. The hypothetico-deductive reconstructed logic, in short, stands as a symbolic standard of "goodness" in research reporting.

To conform to the hypothetico-deductive norm, however, is to do considerably more than faithfully reconstruct a logic-in-use. It is to be selective to the point of offering the reader only a tightly framed snapshot, and perhaps a somewhat distorted one, of a complex, dynamic research process. The snapshot suggests to the reader that he is reviewing the record of a critical experiment in which substantive hypotheses generalized from a firm theoretical base are tested with tried and reliable techniques. In fact, this is only a pretense. The dominant characteristic of a pre-paradigmatic research enterprise is that shared expectations about, and commitments to, nearly every aspect of research—models, hypotheses, data, indices, techniques, concepts of validation, problems addressed, etc.—are to a greater or lesser degree in a state of flux. Among the scientists within any research nucleus, empirical investigation can simultaneously affect selective cumulation with respect to a variety of research dimensions; it can, for example, affect their expectations about the validity of an indicator as well as (or in lieu of) their expectations regarding the theoretical significance of the concept purportedly measured; and it can affect their sense that, say, ordinary least squares is an appropriate estimating approximation as well as their expectations regarding the presence or absence of a specific factor in a causal chain. But the hypothetico-deductive mode hides most of this, offering the reader an artificially static representation and pretensions to proof.

Consequently, the reader examining several snapshot reports emerging from what he takes to be a research nucleus may note movement (e.g., new techniques, new indices, recoded data, respecified models, new test hypotheses, problem shifts) but may be at a loss to infer the presence or absence of progress. Is this movement evidence of expansive cumulation unguided by prior research (and hence degeneration)? Is it guided by selective cumulation? Perhaps the reader has misidentified the boundaries of the nucleus? The individual trying to assess progress in the field by relying on reports conforming to the hypothetico-deductive norm is usually right if (to switch metaphors) he concludes that some of the most important parts of the research drama are played backstage or between scenes.

None of this is intended to suggest that the hypothetico-deductive reconstruction ought to be banished. Nor is this to advocate the lowering of our research standards. The hypothetico-deductive reconstruction offers an important, generally recognized means of ordering thought, maintaining contact with "reality," enhancing our own and others' confidence in our work, and advancing selective cumulation among our colleagues. This is only to suggest that we should broaden our criteria of goodness in research reporting to make room for reports that more adequately reflect our logics-in-use—that place hypothesis testing in a dynamic context of greater scientific richness. There is more to science than proof.

The reporting styles more appropriate to our field would be decidedly developmental in nature. They would begin with a frank exposition of the researcher's interests and his evolving expectations as to the promise of alternative models, concepts, indices, data types and data sets, techniques, and so on. In exposing these, the researcher ought to do more than footnote the relevant literature. And he ought to do more than list the substantive "findings" of other reports that he hopes to refine, support, add to, challenge, or refute. The re-

searcher ought to report on his own selective processes in light of his perceptions of the strengths or weaknesses of other research reports; e.g.:

> I am not sure that he has sufficiently accounted for higher order autoregressive processes, so I suspect that his t-statistic for X_3 is inflated, and I am not convinced that X_3 is a causal link.
>
> Their conclusion that no institutional learning occurred seems premature, for their data is much too aggregated to catch the subtleties of learning.
>
> I'll use A's transformation rather than B's—even though B's index seems to be a slightly better predictor—because B's obscures the policy-manipulable variables, and I want to be able to say something to policy-makers.

In addition, the researcher ought to report upon his own vital 'preliminary" inquiries, describing developmentally how they influenced his decisions-under-uncertainty and shaped his effort. And finally, after displaying an estimated model or tested hypothesis, the researcher should try to articulate the implications for his own selective processes across a range of research alternatives. Where next, and why?

Having done this, the reporter will have introduced the reader to his logic-in-use, and he will have prepared and invited the reader to evaluate his research, not only for what it says about the (often highly specific) theoretical propositions directly examined, but also for what it has to say about the future course of research in the area. The reader reviewing several such reports will at least possibly be able to note the boundaries of research nuclei in the field, to infer progress or degeneration within these boundaries, and (if he is interested) to make contributions.

REFERENCES

Alker, H. R., Jr. 1973. "Research Paradigms and Mathematical Politics." Revision of a paper presented at the 1971 IPSA Roundtable on "Quantitative Methods and Political Substance: Toward Better Research Strategies," Mannheim, Germany. [To be published in *Proceedings of the IPSA Roundtable,* ed. Rudolph Wildenmann et al.]

Hanson, N. 1950. *Patterns of Discovery.* Cambridge: At the Univ. Press.

Kaplan, A. 1964. *The Conduct of Inquiry.* San Francisco: Chandler.

Kuhn, T. 1970. *The Structure of Scientific Revolutions.* 2d ed. Chicago: Univ. of Chicago Press.

Lakatos, I., and A. Musgrave, eds. 1970. *Criticism and the Growth of Knowledge.* Cambridge: At the Univ. Press.

Merton, R. 1968. *Social Theory and Social Structure.* Rev. ed. New York: Free Press.

Polanyi, M. 1958. *Personal Knowledge.* Chicago: Univ. of Chicago Press.

Price, D. deS. 1963. *Little Science, Big Science.* New York: Columbia Univ. Press.

Wolin, S. 1968. "Paradigms and Political Theories." In *Political Experience,* ed. P. King and B. Parekh, pp. 125-52. Cambridge: At the Univ. Press.

15. A Contra-Kuhnian View of the Discipline's Growth

Richard Smith Beal

Revolutions are common political phenomena to any student of international politics. The history of international relations is replete with attempts by discontented parties to supplant the current political order with an alternative one. Revolutions, revolts, civil wars, insurrections, uprisings, guerrilla warfare, coups d'etat, rebellions, and mutinies are representative of the activities designed to replace, usually by violence, the status quo with a more fulfilling political order. But the view that basic "scientific" frameworks are replaced rather than modified, and fall rather than change when faced with contradictory evidence, has only recently gained widespread acceptance in the social sciences. Since Kuhn's *The Structure of Scientific Revolutions* (1962) there have been marked efforts to fit Kuhn's model, fashioned initially for the natural sciences, to the social sciences generally and to international relations specifically (Wolin, 1968; 1969; Easton, 1969; Lijphart, 1974).

Wolin and Lijphart, for example, accept Kuhn's general thesis about the growth of knowledge in the natural sciences as an ideal model of development for the social sciences as well. Wolin sets out to extend and apply the theory to political science while Lijphart serves as a carrier to international relations. Very little effort is made by either Wolin

or Lijphart to respond to the criticisms of Kuhn by his detractors (Lakatos and Musgrave, 1970; Blackowicz, 1971); Kuhn's normal science/paradigm revolution scheme is endorsed without serious modification by either scholar. Rather their intentions are to represent scientific change in the social sciences in terms of Kuhn's perspective, and not to amend his point of view.

While the more intricate facets of Kuhn's thought are still being explicated and the controversy over the exact meaning of some of his ideas continues unabated, the basic logic of the model is straight forward and easily grasped. Kuhn, following the lead of Sir Karl Popper, rejects the proposition that science progresses by accretion and adopts instead a relatively random change perspective. Science is, therefore, best characterized by two fundamental periods: normal science and scientific revolutions. These periods essentially reflect the status of a paradigm in any given discipline. During periods of normal science, a single paradigm (meaning theory in this context) guides research, organizes constructs and data, and serves as a kind of "religious credo" for members of the scientific community. Virtually all of the active members of a scientific community adhere to its precepts, methods, and guidelines. By contrast, scientific revolutions are periods when the paradigm ceases to serve these functions adequately. The prevailing paradigm repeatedly fails to explain the anomalies generated by empirical research, and a new paradigm surfaces to replace it. A crisis develops and members of the community abandon their commitment to the older paradigm in favor of the new one. Scientific revolutions are, by their very nature, noncumulative developments. They are radical breaks with past paradigms; they are possible only insofar as they destroy the very foundations upon which the previous paradigm was based. When the new paradigm directly confronts the older one, the scientist is forced to make an uncompromising choice: either he stands with the older paradigm and puts himself out of the mainstream of intellectual practice, or he repudiates some of his most cherished beliefs and "converts" to the new one.

All scientific activities conducted during periods of normal science are governed by some paradigm (i.e., the dominant theory). The correspondence between the paradigm and research is never perfect, nevertheless the authenticity of the paradigm is never really challenged. Anomalies between research and paradigm are simply puzzles to be solved. Kuhn is careful to point out that testing in normal science means puzzle solving. It is the ingenuity of the individual scientist which is tested, not the paradigm itself. Tests with negative results do not invalidate the theory, instead they call into question the experimenter's skills. Only during a crisis of confidence do tests challenge the credibility of a paradigm. These periods of scientific revolution, when "extraordinary science" occurs, are abnormalities, exceptions rather than the rule. Preoccupied with puzzles and satisfied with the general veracity of the paradigm, scientists only rarely devote themselves to the task of extraordinary science and paradigm displacement.

A scant treatment of Kuhn's model of scientific growth cannot possibly do justice to the subtleties of his thesis. But the central objective here is not to make a thorough evaluation of the merits of Kuhn's thinking. Rather, it is to ask whether the model accurately describes the general developmental pattern in international relations. Should students of the discipline expect increases in knowledge as a function of normal science and paradigm replacement?

Lijphart, for one, has already answered this question in the affirmative; theory development in international relations, especially what he calls "classical theory," conforms nicely to the Kuhnian perspective. The traditional paradigm, according to Lijphart, rests on a common image of international relations—namely that the critical factors of classical diplomacy were state sovereignty and international anarchy. And the prevailing theories of world government, balance of power and collective security follow logically from these two factors. The notions of sovereignty, balance, social contract, anarchy, security, and world government provided analysts with all the necessary puzzles and clues to their solution to occupy themselves with during the pre-1945 period. The scientific revolution emerged in the 1950s when a variety of new models, theories, approaches, conceptual frameworks, and methodological innovations arose to "challenge the hegemony of the traditional paradigm." Lijphart acknowledges that no single new approach claimed exclusive dominance or that any scientist was necessarily faced with the uncompromising choice between paradigms. Nevertheless, the "behavioral paradigm" constitutes a significant substantive as well as a methodological assault on the traditional paradigm. In a most telling way, Lijphart asserts that the rivalry between the two paradigms is thoroughgoing, dramatically incommensurable, and irreconcilable. They are based on different commitments, methods, relevant questions, and metaphors of world affairs. "Each school considers the other's results to be not just wrong, but absurd. In fact, the result is not necessarily wrong at all; it is the problem to which the other school addresses itself that is wrong. And the answer to a wrong question can only be irrelevant and absurd" (Lijphart, 1974, pp. 62-63).

Certainly harsh words have passed between the most ardent adherents of the rival schools of thought. The paradigm replacement scheme begins to break down as a model of development for international relations when the inquiry is made whether scientists had to reject categorically the traditional paradigm to accept the behavioral one. Kuhn is clear, even adamant, about the necessary incompatibility between rival paradigms. They operate on entirely different premises; in fact, the new paradigm owes its existence to a decisive attack on the premises of the older paradigm. This assault is so definitive that scientists cannot straddle the fence; to accept the new paradigm, the scientist must reject, and abandon, the old paradigm. And conversely, to remain loyal to the older paradigm meant the scientist had to reject entirely the new paradigm. But for all of its radical dimensions, the behavioral revolution in international relations sought to retain, not destroy, many of the metaphors, concepts, anticipated relationships, and categories of the traditional paradigm. This activity contradicts the Kuhnian view that knowledge is advanced by challenging and supplanting previous paradigms.

Scholars of the behavioral persuasion looked to the traditional theories for definitions, concepts, and testable hypotheses. Their major contribution was not in terms of new metaphors, images, or analytical relationships, but in rendering the search for explanation and description systematic and subjecting traditional propositions to empirical tests. This strategy conforms more to knowledge by accretion rather than by revolution. To the extent they did challenge the traditional paradigm it was to restrict its scope and amend its reliance on single variable explanations. For example, it became increasingly evident the realist position, and particularly Morgenthau's formulation of the power and influence model, did not explain all politics among nations. It was unsatisfactory to view foreign policy strictly in terms of power politics. Snyder, Bruck, and Sapin (1962) offered decision making as an alternative frame of reference to the realist position advanced by Spykman, Niebuhr, and Carr of the 1930s, and Morgenthau, Kennan, and Fox in the 1940s and 1950s. Decision making sought to rectify certain inadequacies in the power model, to suggest optional categories for research and to focus analytical attention on decision makers involved in action-reaction-interaction processes. It was not a theoretical alternative to the power model because it was not a theory.

Decision making, systems theory, communication theory, integration theory, deterrence, and so on have unquestionably redirected the traditional focus of international relations, but they have not forced students of the discipline to make uncompromising choices. It is common, even widespread, that members of the community accept sovereignty, balance, and anarchy as essential components of their prevailing image of international affairs and still adopt conflict theory and use analysis of variance. It was also possible to reject the major components of the behavioral movement and yet remain a vital force in the discipline, à la Hoffmann, Aron, Tucker, Osgood, Claude, Brzezinski, Morgenthau, Bull, and Jervis. Furthermore, it has become perfectly acceptable to adopt almost wholesale a systems terminology without ever employing the theory or its input-output methodology.

The claims to a scientific revolution in international relations are questionable given that (1) the traditional versus behavioral rivalry did not force members of the community to make uncompromising decisions about their allegiances, (2) the behavioralist approach brought procedures of systematic inquiry to the traditional perspective and not destruction to its very premises, (3) the behavioralist looked, despite what they may have asserted from time to time, to the traditional literature for testable hypotheses (Handleman and others, 1973), and (4) traditionalists, though their numbers may have decreased proportionately, are alive and well.

Under these conditions, Lijphart's application of the Kuhnian model appears misguided, inappropriate or at the very best, premature. Lijphart has confused the magnitude of the methodological revolution accompanying the behavioral movement for a paradigm onslaught against the traditional perspective. In a Kuhnian sense, a revolution without the force of a single, dominant theory is not a structural revolution. When there is no prevailing paradigm, there can be no paradigm displacement.

There are serious doubts about whether international relations has undergone a structural revolution, but this does not dismiss the prospect of such a paradigm transition in the future. After all international relations may be in a pre-paradigm period; perhaps with time the Kuhnian model will be verified. This is highly unlikely, however, Kuhn's thesis about structural revolutions depends on the widespread acceptance throughout a discipline of one dominating theory. A paradigm exists only in those instances where one theory monopolizes the field. No rivals are permitted. International relations, by its very complexity and transforming character, precludes this possibility. To accommodate its diversity and dynamic, a proliferation of theories is natural and not conducive to the emergence of one overriding paradigm. Consequently, our revolutions are likely to continue to be political and not paradigmatic.

REFERENCES

Blackowicz, James A. 1971. "Systems Theory and Evolutionary Models of the Development of Sciences." *Philosophy of Science* 38: 178-99.

Easton, David. 1969. "The New Revolution in Political Science.'. *American Political Science Review* 63: 1051-61.

Handelman, John R., John A. Vasquez, Michael K. O'Leary, and William D. Coplin. 1973. "Color It Morgenthau: A Data-based Assessment of Quantitative International Relations Research." Paper presented at the Annual Meeting of the International Studies Association, New York.

Kuhn, Thomas S. 1962. *The Structure of Scientific Revolutions.* Chicago: Univ. of Chicago Press.

Lakatos, Imre, and Alan Musgrave, eds. 1970. *Criticism and the Growth of Knowledge.* Cambridge: At the Univ. Press.

Lijphart, Arend. 1974. "The Structure of the Theoretical Revolution in International Relations." *International Studies Quarterly* 18: 41-74.

Snyder, Richard C., H. W. Bruck, and Burton Sapin. 1962. *Foreign Policy Decision-Making: An Approach to the Study of International Politics.* New York: Free Press.

Wolin, Sheldon T. 1968. "Paradigms and Political Theories." In *Politics and Experience,* ed. P. King and B. C. Parekh, pp. 125-52. Cambridge: At the Univ. Press.

———. 1969. "Political Theory as a Vocation." *American Political Science Review* 63: 1062-82.

16. The Problem of Cumulation

Dina A. Zinnes

In recent years a general feeling of disquiet has prevailed among researchers in the field of quantitative international politics (QIP). The disquiet centers around the questions asked implicitly by Young (1972), Phillips (1974), and others, and which were a motivating force behind Rosenau's (1974) call for the Ojai, California, conference on international relations research: Where have we been? Where are we going? The director for political science of the National Science Foundation, G. R. Boynton, suggests a reason for the disquiet: "One of the outstanding characteristics of research in political science during the last several decades has been it non-cumulativeness." Although, in his critique, Boynton (1974) cites examples from American politics, his statement offers a clue to QIP researchers. It highlights the growing concern that QIP research is fragmented, that it consists of correlation coefficients, amounts of variances explained, significances, factors, etc., that cannot be, or have not been, put together in a meaningful way and thus, that we know little about international political phenomena as a whole. QIP researchers have been using quantitative-statistical analyses for approximately 25 years. It is time to take stock, to see where we have been and where we are going—and to examine the extent to which Boynton's critique is valid for QIP research.

Clearly, before we can answer Boynton's charge we need to know what we mean by "cumulation."

SPECIAL NOTE: This chapter has been prepared under the auspices of the National Science Foundation, Grant GS-36806.

What criteria will be used to assess the cumulativeness or noncumulativeness of the field? In the letter referred to above, Boynton proposes: "At the simplest level I would take cumulativeness of research to be the following: a second research effort on a topic can rely on findings of a first research effort in such a way that it does not have to start from scratch." We note first that a key word in this statement is "findings," for it eliminates, as a criterion for cumulation, the increasing use of certain methodologies. Thus, while multivariate techniques have gained in acceptance, as is easily attested to by the number of published articles using multivariate statistics, this cannot be construed as evidence of cumulation. Cumulation refers to the *growth of knowledge,* not to the increasing acceptance of certain methodologies. Hence, the widespread use of multivariate techniques is not an indicator of cumulation, but a measure of the increasing degree of sophistication in the field.

But while Boynton's definition of cumulation represents a good first approximation, at another level it becomes somewhat ambiguous. The problem lies in the word "rely." Is cumulation achieved when one study pays homage to the literature by citing a half dozen articles in which similar problems have been tackled? Boynton himself would probably say no. Yet this second study has clearly relied on earlier studies. The problem is that we want "rely" to have a more rigorous interpretation. We want to say somehow that the findings of the first study were "crucial" to the research of the second, that the second could not have been accomplished without the first having taken place, or conversely, that the second study has incorporated the first and gone beyond it. But these statements are still inadequate; we have substituted for the ambiguous word "rely" the equally ambiguous word "crucial" and "incorporated." In looking at two studies, how do we access whether the first was crucial to the execution of the second?

Having puzzled over these definitions I have come to the conclusion that there is probably no satisfactory answer and that the solution perhaps lies in distinguishing between kinds of cumulation, or, more appropriately, levels of cumulation. Thus far I see at least two. For simplicity let me call them (1) additive cumulation and (2) integrative cumulation. By "*additive cumulation*" I mean that one study adds some information to the existing literature on the subject. Thus, the study that cites previous research in the literature by quoting relevant studies is cumulative in the additive sense. If I analyze the alliance formation process with a Poisson model and in that study refer to Liska's (1962) previous work on alliances, I have added some knowledge to the study of alliance phenomena. If I reanalyze Rummel's (1969) data as Wilkenfeld (1973) did, holding a new variable constant, or, if I incorporate the new variable into the analysis, as Hazelwood (1973) subsequently did, then the results have provided more information on the general issue of the relationship between domestic and foreign policy variables. Clearly then, all research is cumulative in the additive sense, and QIP is no exception.

"*Integrative cumulation*" is somewhat more difficult to define, for we are again using words like "crucial." But while a precise definition may not be possible, perhaps a general characterization will at least differentiate it from additive cumulation. Integrative cumulation means that a study ties together and *explains a set* of research findings. In this sense the earlier research is "crucial" since it suggests what processes and variables should be examined in the later one. Suppose I review the Rummel, Wilkenfeld, and Hazelwood results that indicate what types of variables are related under what conditions. Suppose further that I make certain assumptions about the foreign policy decision process that allow me to conclude logically how the variables of the three studies must be related under certain conditions. My study would be cumulative in the integrative sense. The earlier studies were "crucial" in that they suggested what kinds of phenomena needed to be looked at and explained; the subsequent study built upon, incorporated, and went beyond the earlier studies by providing an explanation in the form of assumptions about the decision-making process.

In light of the above characterization it is obvious that additive cumulation is a necessary ingredient of integrative cumulation. We discern what kinds of variables we need to account for and what kinds of processes require explanation from our observations of the occurrences and co-occurrences of certain events. In short, additive cumulation suggests the puzzles that require solution. However, it is also equally obvious that most of us would not be satisfied with additive cumulation, with tacking a new piece of information on to older bits and pieces of knowledge. Most of us want to see a total picture. Thus, while the very nature of research is necessarily always additive, its principal goal is to eventually become integrative. The question then is "To what extent has QIP been cumulative in the integrative sense?"

This is where I believe the dissatisfaction arises. Many of us who look across the field of QIP see scattered bits and pieces of intriguing, but difficult to comprehend, findings. We see that alliances and wars tend to co-occur in one time period but not in another (Singer and Small, 1968). We note that certain state characteristics do not appear to be related to certain kinds of foreign policy activities (Salmore and Hermann, 1969), yet measures of disruption within countries (which can be considered a type of characteristic when controlling for types of government) do seem to be associated with foreign conflict activity (Wilkenfeld, 1973). We find that a stimulus-response explanation works for one type of alliance but not for another (North, Brody, and Holsti, 1964). We discover, contrary to popular belief, that there is no observable covariation between the formation of international organizations and the subsequent outbreaks of war (i.e., international cooperation does not necessarily lead to a decrease in conflict activity), yet international conflict tends to lead to greater subsequent amounts of international cooperative activity (i.e., there is a frantic rush towards international cooperation following wars) (Singer and Wallace, 1970). In short, QIP has accumulated a large number of very explicit pieces of information and in the process has implicitly proposed a great variety of puzzles. The difficulty is that the challenge to solve these puzzles has not been met by QIP researchers. Rather than switching research strategy from additive to integrative, rather than attempting to seek answers to the numerous already existing puzzles, we continue to collect more and more data and to generate more and more analyses of covariation. Why?

There are at least two plausible answers to this question. First, there are some researchers who believe that they have not sufficiently isolated the parts of their puzzle. They argue that they need to collect and analyze more data before they can

fully comprehend the limits of their problem; they must determine the variables to be examined and what kinds of covariation exist among them. In short, these researchers argue that they need to observe more before they can begin the task of integration. They have a valid point. As we noted earlier, one must have some ideas about a problem before an attempt can be made to put the pieces together into a more general picture. We cannot begin explaining crisis decision making until we have observed the processes a number of times and noted key variables and covariations. However, this answer is not satisfactory. At what point does the researcher feel he has enough comprehension of a problem to begin constructing an explanation?

There is, however, a second and perhaps more fundamental reason for the lack of integrative cumulation in QIP. I have become increasingly convinced that QIP research has been captured by what might be called the additive mentality. The principal characteristic of the additive mentality is its belief that integrative cumulation will occur of its own accord through the simple process of adding more and more facts and relations to a body of knowledge. It is assumed that integrative cumulation is the consequence of a sufficient quantity of additive cumulation; the bits and pieces will in effect arrange themselves into meaningful packages, if only enough parts of the puzzle are supplied. This, of course, is a statement of the inductivist school of thought. The problem is, as many philosophers of science have noted and a careful scrutiny of the physical sciences shows, we cannot achieve explanation through induction. At some point someone must make the leap and *propose* an explanation. While the accumulated facts may be highly suggestive of the broad outlines of that explanation, it takes a human mind to make the final jump, to assemble the pieces into a meaningful explanation. Pieces do not assemble themselves.

If we seem to be headed in the wrong direction, it is reasonable to ask what the causes of this misdirection are so that we might alter it. How did we arrive at the conclusion that total explanations would emerge if we added more and more facts? I can isolate four factors which, in combination, seem to account for this additive mentality: (1) the heavy emphasis on data collection and the establishment of large data sets, (2) the extreme dependence on statistical techniques. (3) easy accessibility to advanced computer technology and (4) something of a misunderstanding of the total scientific enterprise. Let me be more specific on each of these points.

The arguments made for the establishment of data sets seemed plausible enough when they were first put forth some years ago. Namely, it was contended that the scientific study of international politics, unlike many other fields, would suffer because there was a greater difficulty in obtaining data on the international phenomena that we wished to study. Thus, it seemed useful, indeed necessary, to begin collecting data. It seemed eminently reasonable at the time to collect, collate, and store data and that this enterprise, while motivated by some general ideas as to broad classes of variables of interest, could largely be done independently of specific theoretical concerns or explicit hypotheses. If the data were stored in centrally located depositories, much as documents and primary sources of the traditional political scientist had previously been stored in libraries, the work of future researchers in QIP would be greatly simplified. But what few of us saw at the time was that this analogy between data banks and libraries was fallacious. We began to believe in our data sets as if they contained some kind of objective truth, forgetting that someone had to make decisions on what was to be measured, and how. Having invested large amounts of time and money into the data collection it was now necessary to demonstrate to ourselves, and to funding agencies, the usefulness of these collections by producing "findings." Since the data sets were not generated to test specific theories, the findings that were subsequently produced were, in effect, simply descriptions of the data sets.

Perhaps these problems would not have been so severe had it not been for the introduction of statistics into QIP studies. This tool made it extremely easy to produce findings, and we began to believe that they were explanations rather than descriptions of data sets. Most researchers would agree that a mean or a variance is a simple descriptive property of a data set, but a correlation coefficient or a factor analysis can be an equally descriptive characteristic of the data set. Unless the statistic is used to assess the degree of fit between a *theoretically derived hypothesis* and a set of observations, the statistic represents nothing more nor less than a description of certain regularities within the data. And significance tests only tell us how likely it is that we will observe similar patterns in other sets of data.

While means, variances, and even correlations can be done by hand or with the aid of a desk calculator, multiple regressions, factor analysis, analysis of variance, etc. require a considerable amount of time and patience to perform by hand. Thus, had it not been for the extraordinary advances in computer technology, many a researcher would have thought twice before beginning a statistical analysis. But with the advent of ever more sophisticated computer programs it was no longer necessary to consider the usefulness or meaning of a particular analysis. Since the computer did all the work with considerable ease, it seemed eminently reasonable to employ many types of analyses. Indeed, we could correlate everything with everything else, regress all variables on all possible combinations of remaining variables, and factor analyze, etc. The computer printout, with the addition of a few sentences indicating how the data were collected and a summary paragraph of interpretation, became a fast and easy publication in a world of publish or perish. We began to succumb more and more to the belief that explanations were found in amounts of variance explained or in levels of significance. Even our hypotheses, which at one time we formulated before examining data, now became products of statistical results—when bivariate correlations were significant we then formulated the relevant hypothesis.

Thus, it was our overemphasis on the empirical-observable world, combined with the power of statistics to elegantly describe those data and the advances in computer technology that made analyses simple to perform, that led to a seeming misinterpretation of the scientific enterprise. We were scientists as long as we clearly stated our measurement rules for collecting data on variables, indicated what analyses were performed, and did not attempt to generalize too much beyond the results obtained from the computer printout. While these are certainly key ingredients of the scientific approach, they make sense only when combined with an additional criterion: the purpose of examining data is to determine whether initial ideas about the structure of the world correspond to what we observe. In short, we must be systematic, objective, and explicit not only in culling evidence, but even *more* precise in stating the theory which led us to the examination of a particular set of data. All our research is but extensive and elegant description without this critical ingredient.

When the behavioral, or scientific, revolution reached the field of international politics some 20 years ago, those who took up its banner claimed that the new approach was superior to the old, more intuitive one because it was explicit. The behavioralists said that the traditionalists did not lay enough cards on the table: When an argument was made, the reasoning behind it was unclear; when evidence was brought to bear on a proposition, the methods used in collecting and assimilating it were vague; when conclusions were drawn, the logic supporting the data analysis was not explicit.

A conversation I had with Robert North, who is a convert, so to speak, from the traditional to the behavioral approach, will illustrate this point. I asked him why he had given up an established career as a specialist on the politics of mainland China in order to learn the methods of scientific research, in particular QIP, which required considerable retraining as well as study. North answered with a story. A conversation he had with a colleague some years ago about a basic aspect of China's political system turned into a debate that lasted far into the night; no mutual agreement was reached. North remembered that as the debate progressed he began to realize that he and his colleagues were making different assumptions and speaking from different data references about the same issue. This perplexed North. Something was wrong when two scholars, specialists in the same area of study and knowledgeable about the same facts, were unable to agree on a basic issue. North concluded—and his conversion was the result—that his inability to state an explicit basis for argument was what was wrong.

Similar thoughts and conclusions led me, and others, into QIP. However, we all seem to have overlooked the fact that the scientific approach requires explicitness at *all* stages of the research endeavor. We seem to have conluded that the scientific approach is principally a set of rules for marshalling evidence and have forgotten that the dictum of explicitness is equally, and perhaps more significantly, relevant to the initial statement of our argument.

Thus, we cannot hope to obtain integrative cumulation without the explicit construction of theories. To understand how theories can be used as integrative tools it is necessary to understand what is meant by "a theory." A theory contains at least three sorts of ingredients: First, a set of assumptions which proposes an interpretation of the kind of world in which we live; second, an agreement on the valid rules of inference that will be applied to the set of assumptions, i.e., the canons of logic; third, certain conclusions or deductions drawn from the set of assumptions, using the canons of logic. Taking these three parts together, a theory may be roughly defined as an "if-then" statement. If the world operates as postulated by the assumptions then, according to the rules of logic, certain consequences will be observed. The final ingredient, is the testing of the deductions to see whether they do in fact correspond to what is observed in the real world. If, following the tests, we find that the conclusions from the theory appear to fit our observations in the world, we contend that the theory is a reasonable explanation of the set of phenomena under study and we agree to accept this explanation for the time being. The theory is considered valid until (1) we obtain additional evidence that refutes our deduction, or (2) find a more parsimonious set of assumptions that lead to the same deduction. Theory construction, of course, is a continuous process; even if we never find evidence that conflicts with our deductions, we are always searching for more parsimonious theories or more general theories whose deductions are the assumptions of an earlier theory.

Although this exposition of theory construction is brief and superficial, it is perhaps sufficient to highlight the integrative features of theories. First, it is important to point out that we have gone beyond simple observations of patterns to explanations of why those patterns occur. Thus, a theory is integrative because it makes sense out of a catalogue of observations. Second, it is frequently the case that the same set of assumptions produces more than one deduction. In effect the theory groups together those hypotheses which are deductions from the same interpretation of the world. The theory is therefore an organizing device that demonstrates how hypotheses are linked. Third, explicit theory construction makes it possible for researchers working at a distance from one another to engage each other's help in the solution of problems. It makes unstructured team work possible. If the arguments that a researcher uses to conclude a particular hypothesis are explicitly stated, then other researchers can work within the context of that same problem, and they may be able to demonstrate additional consequences that follow from the theory. When evidence fails to support a particular hypothesis, other researchers can suggest what might be altered in the structure of the theory to account for the lack of confirmation. Thus, explicit formal theorizing, where each stage of the argument and design is explicit and there is universal agreement on the rules of inference (logic), makes a concerted disciplinary effort towards the solution of important problems possible.

But let me pause at this juncture, so that my argument is not misunderstood. In case some of the foregoing has been misinterpreted, let me clearly point out that I am *not* opposed to data collection, nor against the use of statistics and the wonderful resources of the computer. My point is not that we should do away with these facets of the research enterprise, but rather that we should put them into perspective. Data collection, statistics, and computer technology must be subservient to, rather than master of, a problem. My concern is that we have done too much "observing" and rather little thinking. We need to de-emphasize data collection and statistical analysis and spend more of our energies analytically examining substantive problems.

If the reader has followed my argument to this point he might reasonably query: So what do we do about it all? How do we begin the operation of theory construction? It is all well and good to argue for the explicit statement of assumptions and the formal and logical derivation of consequences, but how does one go about such a task? The answer, it seems to me, lies in learning the language of mathematics. In the same way that many of us discovered some years ago that the collection and processing of data required additional skills in research design, statistics, and com-

puter programming, we must now realize that the theoretical enterprise—thinking logically and deductively—is also a skill. And skills require training. We fought long and hard to include statistics as an acceptable part of a graduate program in political science, and while we must retain this component, we must now add to it carefully selected courses in applied mathematics. While statistics will continue to help us assess hypotheses, mathematics is a language that can help us be precise and explicit about the construction of our arguments.

REFERENCES

Hazlewood, Leo A. 1973. "Exernalizing Systemic Stress: Inter-national Conflict as Adaptive Behavior." In *Conflict Behavior and Linkage Politics,* ed. Jonathan Wilkenfeld, pp. 148-90. New York: McKay.

Liska, George. 1962. *Nations in Alliance.* Baltimore: Johns Hopkins.

North, Robert C., Richard A. Brody, and Ole R. Holsti, 1964. "Some Empirical Data on the Conflict Spiral." *Papers, Peace Research Society (International)* 5: 1-14.

Phillips, Warren R. 1974. "Where Have All the Theories Gone?" *World Politics* 26 (Jan): 155-88.

Rosenau, James N. 1974. "Success and Failure in Scientific International Relations Research." Mimeo. Los Angeles: Univ. of Southern California.

Rummel, Rudolph J. 1963. "Dimensions of Conflict Behavior within and between Nations." In *General Systems Yearbook,* vol. 8, pp. 1-50. Bedford, Mass.: Society for General Systems Research.

Salmore, Stephen A. and C. F. Hermann. 1969. "The Effect of Size, Development and Accountability on Foreign Policy." *Papers, Peace Research Society (International)* 14: 15-30.

Singer, J. David, and Melvin Small. 1968. "Alliance Aggregation and the Onset of War, 1815-1945." In *Quantitative International Politics,* ed. J. David Singer, pp. 247-86. New York: Free Press.

——— and Michael Wallace. 1970. "Inter-governmental Organization and the Preservation of Peace, 1816-1965: Some Bivariate Relationships." *International Organization* 24: 520-47.

Wilkenfeld, Jonathan. 1973. "Domestic and Foreign Conflict." In *Conflict Behavior and Linkage Politics,* ed. Jonathan Wilkenfeld, pp. 107-23. New York: McKay.

Young, Oran R. 1972. "The Perils of Odysseus: On Constructing Theories of International Relations." In *Theory and Policy in International Relations,* ed. Raymond Tanter and Richard H. Ullman, pp. 197-203. Princeton: Princeton Univ. Press.

17. Tribal Sins on the QIP Reservation

J. David Singer

When the Reverend J. Owen Dorsey wrote up his "Omaha Sociology" for the Smithsonian Institution in the late 1870s, he surprised some ethnologists by noting that there was something less than unanimity among his informants. Particularly when he was describing the Omahas' war practices, his accounts are sprinkled with comments to the effect that "Two Crows denies this" or that a given interpretation is "disputed by La Fleche and Two Crows." Whereas most ethnographic reports tended to suggest that all the informants agreed as to what the dominant practices were in a given tribe or culture, Dorsey was willing to report diverse recollections and interpretations, leaving the synthesis and reconcilation up to those who would later try to generalize from these field studies. He relies particularly on Two Crows' interpretations to challenge the majority views as to how decisions were made for going to war, how war was conducted, and how victory and defeat were marked.

In the quantitative international politics (QIP) tribe, there may be a parallel problem, with the danger that outsiders will not be aware of the cultural variations within. More specifically, there seems a real likelihood that outside observers will conclude from these proceedings that we are all in essential agreement not only on "how they do it" in our community, but on how successful we have been at it. Lest that dangerous illusion be conveyed, it is necessary for someone to take on the role of Two Crows, and to offer a deviant—and much less optimistic—picture of the QIP culture. Having taken that role at the conference, let me continue it into the report; future observers of our culture may find this trace, and thus know that some members were less sanguine about our tribal ways.

In the autumn of 1968 (Two Crows began), members of the QIP tribe could be forgiven their optimism. Things looked very promising. Not that the corridors of power were suddenly inhabited by other "believers," or that foreign policy reportage was regularly couched and interpreted in scientific terms. But on the academic side, both in the U.S. and in Europe, many of the informal indicators pointed toward real progress. Three peace research journals *(Journal of Conflict Resolution, Journal of Peace Research*, and the *Peace Research Society Papers)* had appeared and were, by the standards of our hardscrabble existence, flourishing, and bringing forth a respectable harvest of high quality work. Also, a symbolic first anthology of commissioned, data-based, papers (Singer, 1968) had just appeared, and others were soon to be completed (Russett, 1972).

Moreover, even though the sound of our drums had barely been heard on the reservations at Cambridge, Princeton, Chicago, or Berkeley, they *had* been heard elsewhere. That is, such political science departments as Stanford, Yale, Ohio State, Northwestern, Minnesota, Hawaii, British Columbia, and Michigan had introduced an appreciable element of the scientific method into their international politics curricula, especially at the graduate level. On top of these hints that we may have been on the verge of take-off was the strong interest (or curiosity) of American and other foreign policy elites in our progress and in ways that our research might improve the quality of the decision process. On the research, the teaching, and the policy fronts, it looked—in sum—as if the scientific approach might well be entering a self-amplifying feedback phase.

But within two years, this rosy picture was shattered. While it may be too strong to say that our not-so-invisible college was in a shambles, it seems no exaggeration to refer to a serious setback. My intention in this chapter is to touch upon a number of the elements that might possibly account for this snatching of defeat from the jaws of victory, not so much with the aim of placing the blame, but in the hope that, if we can turn things around once more, we will not be deflected a second time from the path of righteousness.

ECOLOGICAL ELEMENTS

In the absence of hard evidence to the contrary, it is usually safe to assume that any change in fortune, favorable or not, can be explained partially by ecological, extra-systemic elements, and partially by those that characterize the subject system itself. And since there is virtually no reproducible evidence available, and this chapter will be very impressionistic, I intend to follow that prudent strategy.

As to those factors over which we in the QIP fraternity had little control, many of them fall into what is best—or at least conveniently—labeled the Vietnam War syndrome. On my checklist, the most potent element was the extent to which those who "planned" and executed the U.S. role in that human disaster were associated with the quantitative approach. Reference is to the highly visible role of Rand and ex-Rand personnel, and similar "types" in and around the systems analysis group in the Department of Defense. Across all too wide a sector of the liberal and radical spectrum was the assumption that the brutality, incompetence, and dishonesty of that adventure could be traced to the introduction of quantitative methods and computerized analyses.

To be sure, I think this was, and remains, an exaggeration, and that things would not have been very different even if no one in the establishment had learned how to count or to read computer printout. The Americans in the Philippines, the British in India, and the French in North Africa and Indochina, had all, over the previous 70 years or so, committed the same kinds of sins with no help at all from the "whiz kids" or their functional equivalents. However, the critics do seem to have a point when they urge that the people around the Administration knew more about computer software and differential equations than about people or politics. From there, it was an effortless leap to infer that this was true of all macro-social quantifiers.

This reaction nourished, in turn, what might be called the "new Luddite" movement. As the social sciences in general, and the world politics field in particular, were progressing toward greater rigor and precision, a good many of our traditional colleagues began to suffer from varying degrees of threat perception. Some felt threatened because they lacked the capacity or motivation to tool up, and thus were eager to belittle the movement toward a more scientific approach. Others, nurtured on the dubious proposition that scientific and humanitarian values must inevitably be in conflict, perceived the QIP tendencies in highly charged, normative terms. Not surprisingly, these groups had no trouble recruiting from both the left and the right ends of the ideological spectrum. The left wing in the Western nations opposed the American role in Vietnam largely in the context of anti-imperialism, and were willing to believe that QIP types were either "value-free" technicians who were merely available for hire to the imperialists, or eager participants who were ideologically sympathetic to counter-revolutionary strategies. And the right, with approximately equal logic and rigor, interpreted the quantifiers as part of the "New Frontier crowd," willing to take on foreign policy adventures, but not to see them through. From the Bay of Pigs to Operation Rolling Thunder, the best and the brightest looked—to the critics of the right—as if they had to make up in technique and mystique what they lacked in political perspicacity and strategic courage.

Another element over which we had little control was the post-behavioral syndrome in political science and sociology. While QIP scholars may have contributed slightly to this tendency, the major culprits, in my view, were those students of American or comparative society who focused on what *they* called political behavior. By this, unhappily, they meant little more than what respondents told interviewers and what aggregates of voters did at the polls. It takes a pretty limited outlook to believe that survey and electoral research would either uncover the regularities of political behavior or lead to an understanding of political systems. But the bulk of the more quantitatively oriented scholars seemed to be working from that assumption. And, almost inevitably, those associated with the Caucus for a New Political Science and parallel groups in the related disciplines assumed that virtually all of their behaviorist/behavioralist colleagues did the same sort of thing. Given how little of our work they had read, this was an inevitable conclusion.

On top of the new left's skepticism as to the theoretical sophistication of the number crunchers, there was a perhaps more devastating criticism. A good many of these critics argued—and I think with some justification—that much of our research was basically conservative, if not reactionary. This conservative impetus was alleged to come from both the social system and from the methodology itself. The former allegedly derived from the "fact" that the western economic and political establishments had become very statistics- and data-oriented, and that quantitatively inclined scholars would thus be regarded more favorably than their pre- or anti-quantitative colleagues, with symbiosis and cooptation as the inexorable result.

A slightly less dubious line of argument was that the more scientifically oriented scholars tended to embrace the models of the structural-functional type, perhaps because they were so indoctrinated in graduate schools which, in turn, were dominated by the quantitative sociologists and political scientists of the academic establishment. Fat cats, it was suggested, prefer models that focus on system persistence, not system transformation. Another argument revolved, as I understand it, around the notions that (a) quantification was applicable only to the obvious and superficial variables and (b) therefore, none of the really important variables—those that might account for exploitation and oppression of the many by the few—would ever be scrutinized by us.

One other element worth noting under this rubric is the extent to which the frustrations of the anti war people led them to give up on virtually *all* matters of war and peace, and to divert their energies into such issues as domestic injustice and global exploitation. On the presumption that the American establishment might be more vulnerable or malleable on such issues as air and water pollution, consumer protection, city beautification, mass transport, and electoral reform, a good many of the former war resisters turned their efforts in these directions. It is safe to assume that this large group of concerned individuals contained a fair number of former and potential peace researchers, whose role in the QIP movement had

been considerable. And for those who shifted their emphases away from the dangers of global holocaust to those of human exploitation, the loss may have been even more serious. That is, while the peace researchers who turned in an intra-national direction tended to continue using fairly rigorous methods, those who turned to matters of imperialism, global conspiracy, and the like tended to either forget any criteria of evidence or to urge that scientific evidence is essentially ideological and a class-conscious delusion, and instead began to invest heavily in *their* brand of ideological jargon and dogma.

Finally, this catalog would be incomplete were it to ignore the simple matter of the counter-culture syndrome. Whereas a good fraction of the reformers turned their energies from foreign to domestic ills or to imperialism, I suspect that an even larger fraction turned them to nothing at all. Or, to be more precise, they turned to self-understanding, self-expression, mind-expanding activities, and other forms of narcissism. Included, again, were quite a few who had been—or might have become—serious students of international politics. So much, then, for a few of the exogenous constraints, as they say in econometrics.

INTERNAL ELEMENTS

If my catalogue of external events and the sins of others leaves us in the QIP fraternity feeling unencumbered and guilt-free, let me hasten to assure that this was not my intent. It was only my way of identifying the variables over which we appear to have *little* control, so as to better understand how much of the variance might be left over, to be accounted for by our own intellectual inadequacies. To put it another way, I take second place to no one in my despair over the intellectual obtuseness of our anti-scientific critics, but if ever a group of academic reformers contributed to its own failures, we were that group. I have neither the space nor the patience to specify all of our failings, but it behooves me to mention a few of those that may have been particularly critical in the abrupt reversal of our fortunes. While they might be arranged under the more formal headings of typology, taxonomy, and epistemology, let me deal with them in a more journalistic fashion, under the general rubric of intellectual style or tribal culture. Space limitations preclude any detailed buttressing of my allegations, or full exegeses on the consequences of these alleged sins, but to the extent that each of us recognizes his/her own transgressions along the ill-charted path to cumulative knowledge, such evidence and inference will hardly be necessary.

Turning first to matters of vocabulary, and the verbal symbols we use to convey information, I note how fashionable it has become in recent years to dismiss any preoccupation with terminological precision as unnecessarily rigid, and to aver that "it doesn't matter what you call it, as long as you define your terms." Not a bad piece of advice, if only we had the time to read and write papers twice the normal length and to include all those idiosyncratic definitions in parentheses, footnotes, or glossaries. Alternatively, each of us could prepare a machine-readable dictionary, and have it stored on disc so that when a reader begins to peruse one of our literary gems, he/she would merely go to the nearest terminal and punch in (for example), PRINT LASSWELL CLEAR-SPEAK. Out would come, a few microseconds later, that pre-recorded glossary, and we would know (for example) the difference between scope and domain, or between core and base values.

A conscious effort to maximize effective communication both within and without our esoteric circle is preferable, it seems to me. Thus, we might begin with some common practice vis-à-vis two of our most abused terms: "theory" and "data." The latter can be disposed of quickly, if we agree that the term applies to information that is in scientifically useful form, and does not apply to every scrap, snippit, fact, impression, or recollection that finds its way onto paper. For example, to expect to find data in a diplomatic historian's narrative or in a foreign minister's communiques is naive; what we find are lots of facts and assertions that can, via operational coding rules, be *made* into data.

As to "theory," I fear that we have an even more difficult issue, and every time I raise this one, I feel like Don Quixote. Nevertheless, why not differentiate between a theory on the one hand, and such useful but inferior constructs as

hunch, suspicion, scenario, model, or paradigm on the other hand? As I see it, we do research in order to build, test, and refine theories; seldom do we *start* with one, but occasionally, we might *end* with one. If every half-baked scheme that passes through one's head qualifies as a theory, there is little need for all that scientific activity whose objective is to produce a theory. I could go on.

Two other terms that seem to be overworked and abused in our circle are "nature" and "structure." The former I would completely banish, on the grounds that it conveys virtually no information. A political philosopher may speak of the "nature of Plato's thought," and we need not be surprised. With brevity not a virtue, and semantic precision often a vice, our author can just keep on cranking out the sentences and paragraphs, and eventually, by the brute force of sheer redundancy, we come to some understanding as to just what is subsumed under "the nature of." But for cumulative science, I suspect we might do better to specify the characteristic of the social unit or the dimension of the event (for example) to which we refer, and to avoid such mystifications as the nature (or essence) of the phenomenon at hand.

As to "structure," I may once again be face-to-face with the familiar windmill. If a social system, for example, can be described in terms of its most salient structural, cultural, and behavioral characteristics, why not differentiate among them? That is, social scientists normally think of culture as embracing peoples' ideas, or more precisely, perhaps, the dominant preferences, perceptions, and predictions manifested in a given population. Similarly, we certainly can tell the difference between ideas and behaviors. Finally, if we observe any social system, and focus on the bonds, links, relationships, and distances among the people or other units in the system, we normally think of the resulting configuration as the system's structure. Why, then, obliterate these critical distinctions by using "structure" to embrace any real or imagined regularity in the system, be it ideational, behavioral, *or* structural?

Closely related to our casual tendencies in terminology, but perhaps even more destructive to cumulative progress, is our approach to taxonomy and typology. Idiosyncrasy run rampant strikes me as an apt description. Not only is there little convergence or comparability between and among the schemes of different scholars; many of us even go so far as to modify our own, from study to study, with no explicit notice or justification. And if the corpus of a *single* researcher's work is not cumulative, how can we expect cumulativeness across the work of *several* people?

What are some of the transgressions that come to mind? Without citing name, rank, and serial number of the offender, let me mention a few. The most serious, I suspect, and the most easily avoidable, is the failure to set up typologies whose dimensions are explicitly operational and whose categories not only rest upon variation along these dimensions but are also (a) mutually exclusive of one another and (b) logically exhaustive of all possible combinations. This is essential not only for comparability and integration of concepts and findings, but also to avoid drastically erroneous inferences from one's empirical results. Oddly enough, we would never analyze only two of the columns or rows in a 3 x 3 contingency table, but we often fail to note that it *should* have been 3 x 4.

Another serious problem is the construction of taxonomies (i.e., several typologies brought together so that comparative description can lead to systematic explanation) that do not include, or sufficiently specify, the actors or social entities in the scheme. It may be liberating to speculate about behavior patterns, interaction sequences, and role configurations, but if these phenomena are experienced by disembodied figments, we are unlikely to move to empirical observation. And without such observation (and measurement) we never, in any cumulative sense, use or apply the taxonomy.

Somewhat related is the problem of drawing boundaries around our social "systems," and I mean this as much in the temporal as in the spatial sense. If we use the concept of system in our taxonomies to represent a time- and space-bound empirical referent, some care ought to be taken. One implication, of course, is that distinctions between and among social, economic, cultural, or political systems (to take the Parsons example, 1951) or between conflict and integrative systems (à la Boulding, 1962) is doomed to disaster. In both of these cases, the social entities are (pre-

sumably) identical across the allegedly different systems, with the only change being the observer's shift in preoccupation from one set or mix of activities to another. It should come as no surprise to find that taxonomies based on coterminous— but allegedly different—systems are often the ones that also have no referent world actors in them. One might say that when the actor is a wraith, it can easily move from one system to another without any action whatsoever. It is, as they say in old left circles, "no accident" that models based on these multi-systemic taxonomies are seldom associated with empirical discoveries; no one would know what to observe and measure.

Also related to the use of the system concept is the problem of taxonomies whose systems seem to appear and disappear with alarming frequency. Rather than refer to one system existing alongside others at the same moment in time, these sinners refer to one system replacing another *through* time. In such taxonomies, the researcher tends to terminate the life of a system the moment that some pattern within it—observed or hypothesized—undergoes some sharp change. Thus, there is a brand new European system in 1849 or 1872 or 1919, and a brand new international system after German unification, the collapse of the Ottomans, the appearance of military aircraft or atomic bombs, or the Smithsonian devaluation of 1971. How can we combine findings and integrate them in a cumulative fashion if they are each based on observations in a "different" system? Why not merely note that certain attributes of large social systems do indeed undergo change through time, and let these changes be used to mark the state of that same system across time?

Yet another obstacle to cumulativeness is our attitude toward our paradigms. We look, to this participant-observer, painfully like our friends the historians or perhaps even the couturiers. We are almost as trendy, and seem willing to scrap and return to our paradigms with the same alacrity as historical revisionists or fashion designers. It might be instructive, if painful, were we to content analyze our texts and journals to ascertain the frequency with which the imperialism, real-politik, cognition-perception, or bureaucratic politics paradigms have moved in and out of favor during the past several decades. Why must we rediscover and promptly forget the relevance of such factors as these over and over again? To put it crudely, we need a lot less paradigm replacement and a lot more paradigm improvement.

Let me shift now to the matter of epistemology and the kinds of criteria we use before taking a model or an alleged finding seriously. One of the most important points of contrast between the world politics work of earlier days and that which began to emerge in the late 1950s was the preoccupation with rules of evidence. Whereas our field, from Thucydides through Morgenthau, has tended to accept *plausibility* as sufficient, the behavioral science emphasis became one of *reproducibility*. We finally began to appreciate how frail the human intellect is when operating in an undisciplined manner; creativity, however essential, was recognized as insufficient. On top of the several sins outlined in the above paragraphs, the field was characterized by selective recall of history, momentarily appealing analogy, and the authoritative assertion.

With considerable effort, quite a few of us began to tool up and to learn something about the generation and analysis of data and the relationship between such data and the models we use in order to provide some coherence and integration. Admittedly, the payoff from that effort was still quite minimal in the late 1960s, a decade after the epistemological transition had begun to crystallize. But given the complexities of our subject matter and the extent to which taboo and dogma have inhibited our efforts to comprehend, there had been *some* modest progress. But much of it looked like finger exercises or intellectual gymnastics, and not enough like solid cumulative knowledge; as a consequence, both we and our critics began to wonder aloud as to when the prologue would end and the curtain would rise on the real thing (Marshall, 1966).

Unhappily, the momentum just was not there. In response to the exogenous factors mentioned earlier and the growing skepticism from within, many of us seemed unable to "keep the faith." Some of us over-responded to the vulgarized versions of Mannheim *et al.* (1954) and began to believe that *every* paradigm is so contaminated by epoch, place, and social role that no cumulativeness would be possible. Others accepted an extension of that proposition to the effect that since

research must be funded and supported, the researcher must arrive at conclusions that are acceptable to those who—in a given epoch and place—provide that support and expect the appropriate findings. Then there was the notion that anything that could be measured and scaled must be trivial. Yet others knuckled to the assertion that "history is bunk" and therefore can teach us little about the future.

But the point of view that embraced many such criticisms of scientific method and also reflected the changing worldview or counter-culture in the West was a version of romantic escapism. This escapism contaminated those who feared that science was constricting and antithetic to creativity, those who believed that science necessarily worked for political repression, and those who thought that the only way to make a better world was to join that counter culture, and retreat into the privatism of drugs, esoteric religion, and communal living. By a tragic irony, those who had been most individualistic, working on problems *they* believed were important, adhering to the canons of scientific method, and ignoring the dogma and shibboleth of industrial society, often joined the new conformity and succumbed to the tyranny of a culture shaped by jaded old men and puerile youngsters. In sum, there just had not been enough time for the norms of social science to take root, and our more fainthearted colleagues and would-be colleagues were soon right back where they used to be or where they would have been had the QIP community never appeared on the scene.

CONCLUSION

In wrapping up this brief, let me point out that a lot more is at stake than either an academic discipline or the credibility of a handful of its members. I, for one, am quite persuaded that the global system is headed for a series of catastrophes, of which nuclear war will be only the most horrible and dramatic, and that one way to head off these catastrophes is through the application of scientifically generated knowledge. To be sure, humanity may well get one or two (perhaps three) reprieves through good fortune and inertia alone, but unless some radical overhaul is begun soon, it seems to me that we will all go down in one disaster or another. It could be the swift and dramatic disaster of a major nuclear exchange, or it could be the slow and incremental dissolution of the fragile ecosystem, symbolic and material, on which human life depends.

If that overhaul is to begin in time and lead in constructive directions, it had better rest on something more substantial than one or another of today's political ideologies. Without going into detail, I am persuaded that none of these ideologies will suffice, largely because they have no built-in mechanisms for self-correction. That self-correction mechanism must, of course, lead to changes in the explanatory and predictive models that undergird the ideology, when the evidence calls for such change. But today's dominant ideologies contain their own peculiar epistemologies, and thus tend to use highly selective criteria as to what constitutes evidence. In addition, their explanatory models rest heavily on certain key assumptions, and those assumptions in turn lie beyond the pale of empirical questioning.

To put it another way, virtually all of today's contending paradigms for comprehending the global society depend for their acceptance on one form or another of mystification. That mystification today, as throughout history, depends upon at least three conditions. One of these is the ignorance of the elites and another is the epistemological naiveté of the public; the third is, of course, some degree of public faith in the competence (and decency) of the elites. My view here is that the elites know very little about governing—beyond, admittedly, how to achieve and maintain power—and trot out one "explanation" and "remedy" after another, trying to cope with disease, urban blight, famine, crime, pollution, or war. And since the general publics usually have even less knowledge, as well as no epistemology that might permit them to question the alleged evidence behind the elite articulations, who is there to gainsay the conventional wisdom of the time and place? Further, given the utterly prescientific way that we think about governing, it is little wonder that the publics prefer to believe, to forget, and generally to leave things to the putative experts.

As I see it, then, the scientific approach to understanding and modifying social systems does not *guarantee* success. Science is no more a panacea than fascism, socialism, capitalism, communism, syncretism, humanism, or even altruism. But scientifically generated knowledge may be the key. *Without* it, we will continue to stumble and muddle our way to catastrophe. *With* it, we have a chance of building a viable world community, despite stupidity, laziness, and avarice. But that knowledge will not come from us as long as we carry on as we have in the past. It may well be that social scientists are drawn from essentially the same bio-cultural pool as everyone else, and will therefore be as lazy, careless, trendy, and narcissistic as the rest. But if we *are* no different in either our basic intelligence or what we do with that intelligence, the picture is grim indeed.

Conversely, if we turn to our research in a sustained and serious way, we may yet produce the requisite knowledge, make it intelligible to the governed and the governors, and help equip the former to continually evaluate the latter. Eternal vigilance may be the price of survival as well as of liberty, but vigilance that is not tough-minded and competent as to the quality of evidence will be of little use. In sum, we have a great deal of important work to do, and the sooner we get on with it, the better our chances for survival. The rest of the tribe may say that we *are* getting on with it, but Two Crows says no.

REFERENCES

Boulding, Kenneth E. 1962. *Conflict and Defense: A General* Theory. New York: Harper.

Mannheim, Karl. 1954. *Ideology and Utopia.* New York: Harcourt, Brace.

Marshall, Charles Burton. 1966. "Waiting for the Curtain." *SAIS Review* 10, 4 (Summer): 22-26.

Parsons, Talcott. 1951. *The Social System.* New York: Free Press.

Russett, Bruce M. 1972. *Peace, War, and Numbers.* Beverly Hills: Sage.

Singer, J. David, ed. 1968. *Quantitative International Politics: Insights and Evidence.* New York: Free Press.

U.S., Bureau of Ethnology. 1884. *Third Annual Report of the Bureau of Ethnology to the Secretary of the Smithsonian Institution, 1881-82.* Washington: GPO.

18. The Failures of Quantitative Analysis: Possible Causes and Cures

Richard Rosecrance

There are many who consider American work in the quantitative study of international relations to be a failure. These views are held not only by protagonists of traditional methods but also by some who would like to be persuaded that the quantitative study of international politics has merit. To many it appears that most of the generalizations or propositions offered by one set of quantitative specialists have been questioned or refuted by another set. One study shows that there is a relationship between domestic and international conflict (Denton, 1966), another that there is no such relationship (Rummel, 1963; Tanter, 1966). One observes a relationship between economic development and internal conflict such that conflict declines with development (McNamara, 1968), another that internal conflict is actually exacerbated by rapid economic development (Lipset, 1960). One notes that there is a connection between the balance of power and movements toward a balance and war (Choucri and North, 1972; Singer, Bremer, and Stuckey, 1972), and another that balances of power help to produce peace (Singer, Bremer, and Stuckey, 1972).[1] Some studies indicate that it is the disparity between power and status which causes conflict (Wallace, 1971), others conclude the precise opposite (Ray, 1974; Rosecrance, Alexandroff, Healy, and Stein, 1974). It is uncertain whether the development of alliances is a force for peace, and conclusions on this issue differ for the nineteenth and twentieth centuries (Singer and Small, 1968). Some conceptual studies contend that multipolarity should display fewer conflicts than bipolarity (Deutsch and Singer, 1964), but empirical evidence suggests the reverse (M. Haas, 1970). In short, there is virtually no strand of theory, quantitatively buttressed, which is not subject to the check or contradiction of other quantitative analyses. It is easy, therefore, to understand how even those most favorably disposed to scientific and quantitative research in international relations might conclude that the effort has not yet been worth the candle.[2]

Far from producing a cumulation of verified propositions, in other words, the record of data-based international relations studies is well nigh self-canceling. Why is this? And what can be done about it? These are the two questions I want to address.

CAUSES

The causes of our present plight clearly have to do with the various research strategies which different investigators have used. Unless one believes that social statistics are essentially frivolous, it could not be the case that two investigators seeking to validate the same hypothesis on the basis of the same data sets and the same manipulative and computational procedure could reach different mathematical conclusions. If differences in their results emerge it must be because of differences in one or more of four areas: (1) data base; (2) chronological period and geographic context sur-

[1] Singer, Bremer, and Stuckey found that in the nineteenth century a further concentration of power was associated with war (supporting the balance of power argument). But the reverse was true for the twentieth century.

[2] Arthur Burns, one of the earliest protagonists of quantitative analysis, wrote recently, "Any war, despite all its unintended aspects, is a deliberately-continued conflict and is amenable to particular historical explanation only, not to general functional explanation" (1974, p. 103).

veyed; (3) mathematical or manipulative procedure; and (4) research paradigms. Each of these realms is worth a few comments.

Data Base

One of the greatest sources of disagreement among quantitative investigators is differing types of data. Bull actually believes that no type of quantitative data can be adequate for the study of international affairs. It is impossible to reduce his arguments to a single aphorism, but if one exists for his essay "International Theory: The Case for a Classical Approach," it is "What is significant can't be measured; and what can be measured is insignificant." He contends that the development of proxy variables (trading, communications, financial, transactions) as substitutes for the "real" political variables of diplomacy and military statecraft is totally unsatisfactory. Measures of trade are not measures of political closeness or similarity of interests, but merely measures of trade (Bull, 1969, p. 35). Political and historical relationships, Bull claims by implication, cannot be measured. Whether Bull's contention is right or not, it certainly is true that analyses utilizing trade, economic, and financial data have often reached different conclusions from those which seek to chart political variables. Deutsch et al. predicted that European integration efforts would flag at precisely the time when they were (temporarily) gaining momentum (Deutsch, Edinger, Macridis, and Merritt, 1967). Haas seemed to believe that his functionalist "spill-over" would force the path of integration at the time when the political impact of the Gaullist regime was in the precisely opposite direction (E. Haas, 1964). Russett found a secular decline in the solidarity of the Anglo-American relationship since 1890 when political trends would indicate an episodic deepening and intensification of that relationship at least until 1956 (Russett, 1963). Bull's contention, therefore, that proxy variables and political trends often point in different directions is partly substantiated.[3]

[3] This does not mean, however, that a *general* case has been effectively made to date against longer term transactions indicators as partial measures of political closeness and divergence. What has been effectively questioned has been the validity of short-term fluctuations in such data as indicators of changes in political attitude and policy.

Bull assumed, however, that there was no way of treating political occurrences mathematically and thus that such treatment could only be applied to economic and other already quantified indices. The enormous development of events data sources since 1966 (see Hoggard, 1973; Peterson, 1973; Leng, 1973; Phillips, 1973) casts doubt on this assumption. Providing that a valid record of important events can be compiled, events data captures the politically significant happenings among states; it is "real" not proxy data. Data on alliances and wars add an additional dimension. It therefore can no longer be claimed that what is significant cannot be measured.

But the development of events data and other real political indicators does not remedy disagreements among quantitative practitioners. Singer has used historical statistics for data about frequency and magnitude of conflicts. Rummel and McClelland have employed the *New York Times Index, Facts on File, Deadline Data on World Affairs,* and other sources to create events data. Azar has added a great number of sources to this list, some of which are regional in their coverage. Data from newspaper and contemporary event compilations suffer from the fact that much of what passes between states remains (for long periods at least) private. Public sources, then, fail to include much of the probably largely cooperative iceberg of events which lies beneath the surface. This suggests, at minimum, that conclusions based on open compilations need to be checked and replicated by analyses performed using sources based on all documents public and private.

A further problem resides in the unevenness of reporting of events. If regional or monographic accounts are added to public and general source compilations, the data will be skewed accordingly. Some crises in some regions will be treated in much greater detail than others. A problem in generalization of the behavior in question to other crises (concerning which the data may not be so rich) emerges. Where regional and monographic sources are employed, no general systemic conclusions can be reached. A necessary alternative is to look for data sources at a given level of generality. Merely adding events to a list does not improve the data base, *unless events are added at the same level of generality*. At minimum, one should insist that conclusions based on studies employing unevenly compiled data need to be replicated using data collected on the basis of uniform treatment and generality. Finally, conclusions reached on the basis of data on wars, alliances, and so on need to be checked by analyses using uniform events data compilations.

Time Period and Geographic Context

But even if all investigators used the same data constructed on precisely the same bases, disagreements would still exist. What is true of the nineteenth century may not be true of the twentieth. Data generated for European countries may not hold for Asian, African, or Latin American contexts. There is a major difference between cross-sectional and longitudinal data. Rummel has rendered great service in developing cross-sectional measures of the international system in 1954-1956 (Rummel, 1969a, 1969b). But there is the implicit question whether data in 1955 or even the data of the post-World War II period were characteristic of the entire period of the modern state system. If there was little relationship between domestic and international conflict measures for one period, would that be true at another (Rummel, 1963)? Cross-sectional studies, of course, have been supplemented by the longitudinal work of Singer's Correlates of War project (Singer, 1972). Longitudinal relationships have turned out to be particularly crucial in this case, for nineteenth- and twentieth-century findings have varied on a number of counts (Singer, 1972; Wallace, 1971; Singer, Bremer, and Stuckey, 1972). Relationships in one time period do not necessarily obtain in another. Further, Singer's longitudinal analyses have included only military forms of conflict and have largely neglected (with the exception of alliance measures) cooperation data.

With a few notable exceptions most investigators have assumed that the more recent the chronological period surveyed, the better. But this assumption rests on the possibly dubious ground that understanding of a fundamentally bipolar system will greatly help with understanding of a more multipolar system in the future. With this disjunction in mind, some investigators have con-

centrated their attention upon nineteenth-century precedents (Choucri and North, 1972; Singer, Bremer, and Stuckey, 1972; Rosecrance, Alexandroff, Healy, and Stein, 1974) where the operation of a more multipolar system can be most clearly observed. They have also centered attention upon the impact of a closing of the gap between two powers on the rest of the system. Here the relevance of the Anglo-German rivalry has important precedents for the U.S.-Soviet experience (see Choucri and North, 1972; Rosecrance, Alexandroff, Healy, and Stein, 1974; Doran, 1971).

There are several contentious issues on geographical context. A complete systemic survey of world politics is highly desirable from the standpoint of coverage, but there remain cogent arguments for treating continents separately at least until the general integration of a world system after 1945. In any nineteenth-century survey of the entire world, Latin American developments may greatly influence general systemic conclusions. The extrapolation of those conclusions to the major power European system would be quite unwarranted. There is also the related question even today, of whether it is desirable to separate the major powers (the central system) from other states. It is at least arguable that the major power subsystem is most highly interreactive. Systemic conclusions which are partly based on loose-knit relationships among developing states could turn out to be misleading for the central system. As Russett has shown, the real "regions" in international politics are not geographic, but functional (Russett, 1967). A focus on such functional subsystems may reveal much that a general systemic analysis would obscure.

Mathematical or Manipulative Procedure

But even if the same data sets are used to examine the same countries in the same time periods, there still remain reasons for disagreement. Since data sets may be analyzed in a number of different ways, and since different computational routines may influence the result obtained, a further degree of uniformity in procedure is necessary. As an example of this requirement, many have noted that there may be a difference between the behavior of a system as a whole and the behavior of individual members of the system. Not to recognize this difference is to commit the "ecological fallacy." But often studies which are aimed at description of purely systemic outcomes and effects may lead readers to make erroneous conclusions about member relationships (see Wallace, 1971; Ray, 1974). To produce manipulative identity, the same unit of analysis should be taken in each case, and where possible, both systemic and member relationships should be examined.

Mathematical procedure may produce substantial differences in the results achieved. As many have shown (see particularly Mueller, 1969) factor analytic procedures may be manipulated in such a wide variety of ways that many different outcomes are possible. Even where the number of factors chosen and the method of rotation are held constant, the "naming" of the factor (which determines the theoretical significance of the result) is distinctly a matter for judgment and intuition. Other investigators could affix different names. "Wealth or affluence" factors can become "industrialization or modernization" factors. Labels like "East-West" and "North-South" can obscure nearly as much as they reveal. The choice of other mathematical procedures, like least squares or smallest space analysis, is less ambiguous but also gives ground for differences. Unless the very same mathematical and manipulative procedures are employed and the same steps are followed in the same order, investigators will come to different conclusions. The very proliferation of mathematical techniques and packaged computer programs offers such a wide choice to the investigator that the likelihood of absolutely *isomorphic* replication is remote.

Even the formulation of hypotheses to be tested presents ground for error or at least ambiguity. In many studies there is no precise advance formulation of hypotheses, but rather a mere processing of data, in which there is an enormous temptation to manipulate the data and procedures until a significant and striking result is obtained. Since this is a mere curve-fitting enterprise, no hypotheses have been tested at all; and the significant hypotheses proferred will not be tested until a replicative study is performed. Few investigators, however, wish to replicate identically the studies of others.

The best way to proceed is to formulate specific testable hypotheses prior to the data-gathering stage. In order to get a very strong test, one should search for periods of history, country-contexts or other predisposing factors that would be most difficult a priori for the hypothesis in question to surmount. If the hypothesis is largely supported in a context unfavorable to it, the result is likely to be reliable. On the other hand, if the hypothesis is supported where all predisposing factors are a priori in favor of it, the test has much less significance (see Eckstein, forthcoming).

Research Paradigms

Finally, even if data, contexts, and procedure are the same, investigators will reach different results unless they adopt common research paradigms and hypotheses. Scholars do not always look for the same relationships in the data; they have different preconceived notions of expected results. Some are interested in charting the impact of power, economic, industrial, and modernization variables upon outcomes in the international system. They will look to the *infrastructure* of world politics to explain the variance in behavior. Others, particularly those interested in arms races, will look at the action-reaction phenomenon: the degree to which the *interaction* at time t_1 explains or helps to predict interaction at time t_2. Still others place special emphasis upon the role of national *belief systems,* opinion, and domestic political processes as causative factors. It may be that a nation responds more to its own internal and bureaucratic impulses than it does to the behavior of the opponent. Further, some will see linkages proceeding in directions different from those perceived by others. The proponents of infrastructure will tend to see it not only as determining interactions at different time periods, but also ultimately determining belief systems and processes of response. Those who espouse explanations centered around interaction phenomena will often contend that it determines belief systems and attitude. Students of national belief systems and processes will usually assert that these forces directly influence interaction, and ultimately, by mobilizing governmental resources, affect infrastructure.

In any event, the choice of the paradigm will greatly influence the results derived. Certain possible connections will be overlooked. Certain hypothetical linkages will be tested for at the expense of others. Thus, even if data, context, and procedures are uniform, the results will vary, because analysts are in effect examining differing questions.

CURES?

The very complexity of the difficulties confronting quantitative analysis in international politics suggests that there is no simple solution. There are few standard data bases open to all investigators. Those which do exist have difficulties, and in most instances have not been extended to cover a wide range of geographic and chronological contexts. Events data, proxy data, and data on wars and alliances remain largely in the hands of their compilers. The theoretical interests of investigators are parochial. Far from attempting to consider hypotheses formulated in other studies, many analysts tend to ride their own theoretical hobbyhorses; the development of their thought appears to stem more from the progress and results of their own project than from an attempt to relate their work and findings to those of the discipline as a whole. Specific techniques of investigation have become associated with specific investigators, and there seems little disposition to consider alternative techniques. Tools like factor analysis, causal modeling, and collective goods approaches become preferred modi operandi in individual cases, regardless of the work of others. There is no consensus on the best investigative or manipulative procedures.

Ideally, of course, disagreements among investigators and a narrow and idiosyncratic view of international reality could be reduced or even eliminated if all agreed on paradigms, data, context, and manipulative procedure. But few specialists are willing to tailor their work to the usages proposed by others. And as we have seen, if precisely the same decisions were made on these four categories of research procedure, the results would be mathematically the same. *Isomorphic* replication then is neither necessary, nor desirable. Of great importance, however, would be an agreement

between two investigators to seek to hold three of the four factors constant. Specifically, if different types of data sources are to be used, the context hypotheses and procedures should be the same or as nearly identical as possible. If the paradigms are to be varied, it becomes all the more important to use the same data base context and procedures. In other words, *only one of the four possible sources of divergence should be varied at a time.*

The three-variable conceptual paradigm can also be much more fully developed, helping to reduce divergence at the hypothesis and concept formation level. Logically, of course, the three variables of infrastructure, behavioral interaction, and processes and belief systems can be seen as completely interdependent as shown in Figure 1. But the most sensitive and theoretically profitable linkages are likely to be more restricted and specific, as shown in Figure 2.

The hypotheses involved in this second formulation assume that infrastructure (in the short run at least) is not affected by belief systems; that belief systems and processes both affect and are affected by interaction patterns; and that patterns of interaction at one stage may affect patterns of interaction at another. There may, however, be changes in belief systems and processes which will also influence subsequent patterns of interaction.

One of the problems in current research strategies is that investigators have tended to concentrate on a single type of data, procedure, time period, and theoretical linkage. North and Chouri, Wallace, and Singer and Bremer have worked

Figure 1. Total Interdependence of Three Variables

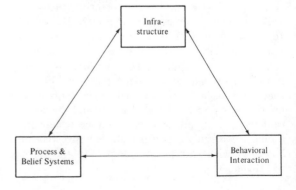

Figure 2. Partial Interdependence of Three Variables

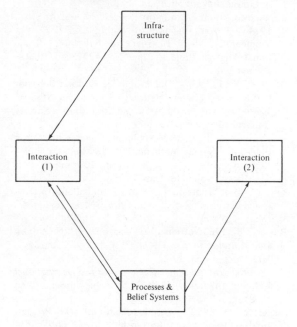

on linkages between infrastructure and interaction. Alker is focusing on arms race and other systemic processes in which INTERACTION (1) together with infrastructure determine INTERACTION (2). George, Allison, and Holsti have pursued the connection between belief systems and processes and inter-action; Azar has concentrated upon the INTER-ACTION (1) ⟶ INTERACTION (2) linkage. A useful recommendation then would be to ask investigators to use their data sets, procedures, and contexts to examine (where possible) an additional linkage. A collaboration between those who have emphasized infrastructure as an explanation and those who use event-interaction as an explanation would be perhaps most fruitful. The events data contributed by the latter could provide a much better test of the ability of infrastructure to ex-plain the variance in outcomes than exists at pres-ent. At the same time, the addition of infrastruc-ture data on power, economic development, modernization, and miliatry factors, would help remedy the often slightly ephemeral quality of events data manipulation, as if those systemic out-comes were self-determining and self-sustaining,

independent of the real national worlds on which they are based. At a later stage the incorporation of studies and data on belief systems and processes could add a further element of reality.

Despite the difficulty of quantitative analysis in international politics, it is apparent to date that there has not been an appropriate test of the validity of quantitative research. Since investiga-tors have chronically disagreed on methods, data, and hypotheses, the divergence in conclusions is entirely to be expected. If, however, the diver-gence in procedures, paradigms, contexts, and data is reduced both through highly necessary collab-oration and the further extension of data sets, conclusions will likely tend to converge. If this happens, the only remaining criticism that antag-onists can present is that the measures used are not valid, that they do not capture international re-ality. That criticism will be much easier to answer than the largely justified critiques of present con-tradictory results.

REFERENCES

Alker, H. R., Jr., and P. G. Bock. 1972. "Propositions about International Relations: Contributions from the *International Encyclopedia of the Social Sciences.*" In *Political Science Annual*, ed. J. A. Robinson, vol. 3, pp. 385-496. New York: Bobbs-Merrill.

Allison, G. T. 1971. *Essence of Decision.* Boston: Little, Brown.

Azar, E. 1970. "Analysis of International Events." *Peace Research Reviews* 4 (Nov).

Bull, H. 1969. "International Theory: The Case for a Classical Approach." In *Contending Approaches to International Politics*, ed. K. Knorr and J. N. Rosenau, pp. 20-38. Princeton: Princeton Univ. Press.

Burns, Arthur. 1974. Book review. *Survival* 16 (Mar-Apr): 104.

Choucri, N., and R. C. North. 1972. "Alternative Dynamics of International Conflict: Population, Re-sources, Technology and Some Implications for Pol-icy." *World Politics* 24 (Spring): 80-122.

Denton, F. H. 1966. "Some Regularities in International Conflict, 1820-1949." *Background* 9 (Feb): 283-96.

Deutsch, K. W., and J. D. Singer. 1964. "Multipolar Power Systems and International Stability." *World Politics* 16 (Apr): 390-406.

———, L. Edinger, R. Macridis, and R. Merritt. 1967. *France, Germany and the Western Alliance: A Study* of Elite Attitudes on European Integration and World Politics. New York: Scribner's.

Doran, C. F. 1971. The Politics of Assimilation: Hegemony and Its Aftermath. Baltimore: Johns Hopkins.

Eckstein, H. Forthcoming. "The Critical Case Study." In Handbook of Political Science, ed. F. Greenstein and N. Polsby. Reading, Mass.: Addison-Wesley.

George, A. L., and R. Smoke. 1974. Deterrence in American Foreign Policy. New York: Columbia Univ. Press.

Haas, E. 1964. "Technocracy, Pluralism and the New Europe." In International Regionalism, ed. J. S. Nye, Jr., pp. 149-76. Boston: Little, Brown.

Haas, M. 1970. "International Subsystems: Stability and Polarity." American Political Science Review 64 (Mar): 98-123.

Hoggard, G. D. 1973. "The Development of the Events Data Movement." Paper presented at the Annual Meeting of the International Studies Association, New York.

Holsti, O. R. 1972. Crisis, Escalation, War. Montreal: McGill-Queen's Univ. Press.

Leng, R. J. 1973. "The Future of Events Data Marriages: A Question of Compatibility." Paper presented at the Annual Meeting of the International Studies Association, New York.

Lipset, S. M. 1960. Political Man: The Social Bases of Politics. Garden City, N.Y.: Doubleday.

McClelland, C. A. 1966. Theory and the International System. New York: Macmillan.

McNamara, R. S. 1968. The Essence of Security: Reflections in Office. New York: Harper & Row.

Mueller, J. E., ed. 1969. Approaches to Measurement in International Relations: A Non-evangelical Survey. New York: Appleton-Century-Crofts.

Peterson, S. 1973. "Research on Research: Events Data Studies." Paper presented at the Annual Meeting of the International Studies Association, New York.

Phillips, W. R. 1973. "Critique of the State of Theory in the Events Data Movement." Paper presented at the Annual Meeting of the International Studies Association, New York.

Ray, J. L. 1974. "Status Inconsistency and War. Involvement among European States, 1816-1970." Ph.D. dissertation, Univ. of Michigan.

Rosecrance, R., A. Alexandroff, B. Healy, and A. Stein. 1974. "Power, Balance of Power, and Status in Nineteenth-Century International Relations." Situational Analysis Project, Paper No. 4. Mimeo. Ithaca: Cornell Univ.

Rummel, R. J. 1963. "Dimensions of Conflict Behavior within and between Nations." In General Systems Yearbook, vol. 8, pp. 1-50. Bedford, Mass.: Society for General Systems Research.

———. 1969a. "Field and Attribute Theories of Nation Behavior: Some Mathematical Interrelationships." Dimensionality of Nations Project, Research Report 31. Mimeo. Honolulu: Univ. of Hawaii.

———. 1969b. "Indicators of Gross National and International Patterns." American Political Science Review 63 (Mar): 127-47.

Russett, B. 1963. Community and Contention: Britain and America in the Twentieth Century. Cambridge: MIT Press.

———. 1967. International Regions and the International System: A Study of Political Ecology. Chicago: Rand McNally.

Singer, J. D. 1972. "The 'Correlates of War' Project: Interim Report and Rationale." World Politics 24 (Jan): 243-70.

——— and M. Small. 1968. "Alliance Aggregation and the Onset of War, 1815-1945." In Quantitative International Politics, ed. J. D. Singer, pp. 247-86. New York: Free Press.

———, S. Bremer, and J. Stuckey. 1972. "Capability, Distribution, Uncertainty, and Major Power War, 1820-1965." In Peace, War, and Numbers, ed. B. Russett, pp. 19-48. Beverly Hills: Sage.

Tanter, R. 1966. "Dimensions of Conflict Behavior within and between Nations, 1958-1960." Journal of Conflict Resolution 10 (Mar): 41-64.

Wallace, M. 1971. "Power, Status, and International War." Journal of Peace Research 8: 22-35.

19. Cumulation, Correlations, and Woozles

Robert Jervis

Before discussing why the quantitative analysis of international relations has not cumulated, two preliminary points should be made. First, cumulation is not identical with increased understanding. Increasing numbers of people can follow the same blind alleys or misleading paths of research, each building on the theories and findings of others. We should not forget about Winnie-the-Pooh's well-known Woozle hunt.[1] Pooh is searching for Woozles and sees what he is sure is a valid track in the snow. He follows it and finds to his delight that his Woozle is joined by another. He calls to his colleagues and two of them join him. Soon they see that the two Woozle tracks are joined by three more and they call in more friends, confident that they are on to something really big that is worthy of concerted effort. The trouble is that they are walking in a big circle and the growing number of tracks is produced by their own efforts. In the same way, we cannot by fiat exclude the possibility that some fields of research may grow, both in terms of the number of people with shared conceptions and in terms of interrelated findings, because scholars are following each other around in circles.

Without reopening the old and generally sterile debate, I would like to note that this is more of a danger with quantitative than with nonquantitative research. First, once some basic ideas have been developed and much data laboriously collected, it seems (at least to an outsider) relatively easy to run replications, variants, and extensions of previous work without asking oneself whether the whole line of inquiry is productive. Second, it seems to me that many new Ph.D.'s working with quantitative techniques are very narrowly trained.

Not only are they unfamiliar with more traditional lines of research, but they often know little about other parts of political science or even about the quantitative approaches that are not represented at the institutions where they are trained. Education by apprenticeship moves students into research quickly, but it has high opportunity costs and may leave the student prematurely committed to one line of work.

It can be argued, of course, that the self-correcting mechanisms of critical science prevent, or at least limit, this wasteful process. If the work is not deepening our understanding of international politics it will not attract new researchers. I find this view a bit overoptimistic. Even when the academic incentive system does not drive the Woozle hunt, the self-correcting mechanisms may operate slowly. Indeed this guards against the danger of lines of work being dropped too quickly, before they have had a chance to show their fruitfulness. But the costs are also significant. The spread of structural-functional analysis in comparative politics is a good object lesson.

It should also be noted that if any approach became dominant, the chances of cumulation would be increased, but a risk would be incurred. Unless we are awfully sure which are the best lines of research, it is vital that the discipline as a whole hedge its bets by pursuing a wide variety of approaches. Even if there is no cross-fertilization, this will both decrease the danger that fruitful inquiries will be overlooked and will maximize the ability of the individual researcher to weigh alternative approaches and choose the one that he thinks appropriate, rather than uncritically adopt a predigested analysis. From this perspective the "closed-mindedness" of various individuals and groups of scholars is a Good Thing since it prevents premature homogenization of the field (not that this seems to be much of a danger today).

[1] See Milne (1957), pp. 36-44. Purists will note that I have slightly altered Milne's account to make my point. For this interpretation of the story I am indebted to Robert Tufts.

A second prefatory comment concerns the fact that there is an assumption behind the question "Why hasn't quantitative international relations research cumulated?" that may be incorrect. The assumption is that cumulation has been slower in quantitative international relations than in other branches of science. Part of the problem may be that the grass always looks more cumulative in other pastures. Most political scientists would be surprised that a psychologist reviewing a biography of one of the greats in that field notes the "notoriously noncumulative nature of psychological research" (Tuddenham, 1974, p. 1072). And I remember reading a psychology review article covering one small sub-area of the impact of affect on perception that cited over 150 experiments and concluded that very little could be concluded. The review was written 15 years ago and it is also instructive to note that the lines of research reviewed were not continued and the debates not resolved. Instead, people's interests shifted to other questions. Furthermore, the situation in international relations as a whole, if not in quantitative international relations, may not be as bad as we sometimes think. A glance at old articles and textbooks is I think sufficient to convince us that we know much more about international politics than we did 20 years ago. If we each made a list of this new knowledge we would probably mention very different things, and many of us would feel that our own lists do not do justice to the developments of the last generation. But I do not think our general feeling that there has been some sort of progress is totally unjustified. In a field I know fairly well—bargaining theory—not only have we seen a series of founding works which illuminated previously little-understood or misunderstood phenomena, but several recent and forthcoming studies definitely build on what was said before, deepening, elaborating, and extending our understanding. The recent formulations are more subtle and contingent than the earlier ones. They point to places where we misunderstood the logic of the models, too quickly jumped to conclusions, concentrated on the wrong variables, and overlooked areas of choice.

But even if outsiders exaggerate the rate of cumulation in fields like psychology, it is still almost certainly true that this rate is higher than that prevailing in quantitative international relations (or than that in the more successful parts of political science). However, this does not call for an explanation, or rather does not call for an explanation couched in terms of the special problems with international relations and quantitative approaches to it, if the difference can be accounted for by the relatively small number of workers in the field. In other words, it is at least possible that the rate of cumulation, expressed in terms of a ratio of progress to number of man-hours of work, could be the same for quantitative international relations as it is for the hard sciences. It should also be acknowledged that (a) the relations might not be linear—e.g., a critical mass might be required before any progress could be made; (b) progress attracts more workers to a field; and (c) one would also have to take account of the range of problems being examined. In calculating the ratio referred to above we should not assume that the size of each field is the same. Not only are there few people doing quantitative international relations work, but perhaps their attention is spread over a range of subjects that is wider than that in other fields.

But if we assume, and I suspect the assumption is valid, that the slow rate of cumulation in the field cannot be completely accounted for by the small number of workers, and if we further assume that the researchers in this field are as smart as those in other areas, there are at least three explanations for the lack of progress. The first deals with the nature of the field and the familiar arguments about the inapplicability of quantitative approaches to the subtle and complex subject of international relations. These cannot be treated in this short chapter. Another explanation holds that quantitative techniques can work, but that temporary obstacles are now preventing progress. These obstacles can be such things as problems with the data and data-collecting methods, limitations of available mathematical and statistical techniques, failures of imagination and conceptualization, and, most importantly, the inadequacy of the theories—largely borrowed from other disciplines and other parts of political science—that we have elaborated and sought to test. That most theories have not fared very well does not automatically mean that future attempts will fare no better. Even if we exclude the possibility that current efforts are learning experiences that will make later cumulation possible, as long as there are few workers in the field, few theories are explored, and most theories are not very good (the latter is a safe assumption in any field), then it is not surprising that cumulation is slight. Thus, a major reason for the lack of cumulation simply may be that the best theories either have not yet been developed or have not been given sufficient attention. One reason is that time and effort are often wasted because data are collected and analyzed before a theory has been carefully examined and elaborated to see whether it is worth testing. Sometime strenuous efforts to produce cumulation are needed before it is clear that the attempt will fail, but many other times giving more thought to the problems of the theory itself would be sufficient to show that it is not likely to be fruitful.

A final explanation lies in the academic incentive system. By and large, someone who tests or builds on someone else's theory receives less credit than someone sho can claim to have developed his own. Of course, if we could easily tell which new approaches were silly and if those who proposed them lost credit, the stress on developing new theories would create fewer problems and could be more easily controlled. Even though this is not the case, it is not possible to say whether the existing incentive system on balance serves us better or worse than alternative ones. But I think it is clear that the system discourages "normal science." And so it is possible that many theories that might have produced cumulation have been abandoned too soon.[2] We can turn to comparative politics, and especially political development, to see the unfortunate effects of the need for academic product differentiation. (Indeed before anyone concludes that international relations is the most confused and depressed part of political science, he should look at comparative politics.)

In closing, some suggestions for improving scientific international relations can be outlined. First, scholars should give at least as much thought to their theories as to their data. Even when scholars have avoided the obvious pitfall of correlating everything with everything else, the theories being tested usually remain underdeveloped. Most quantitative international relations studies spend relatively little time and attention on explaining why their findings should be true—i.e., in linking them to broader theories, elaborating the probable causal linkages, and developing their implications. The problems are of course even greater when the data is bad, the operational definitions questionable, and the percentage of the variance that is explained is low. This means that even when the data yield generalizations, any number of explanations could account for what has been found. By developing richer and more detailed theories, we can increase both the number and variety of propositions produced and the range of data to which they can be applied. The hypothetico-deductive model may have been idealized, but whether we are using quantitative or qualitative evidence, we should not stop when we can say, "My explanation can account for these findings," but should go on to ask ourselves, "If this explanation is true, what else should follow? What are the implications of the explanation? What other events should, and should not, occur? What does the theory say about cases so far unstudied or data not yet analyzed?" Although the role of "critical experiments" seems to have been exaggerated (Lakatos, 1970), we should pay especial attention to cases where our explanation leads us to form expectations that contradict those of other accounts.

"Converging operations" involving both quantitative and traditional studies of individual cases can play a major role in the elaboration and testing of our theories. Detailed investigations into the causes of a particular event that is the dependent variable in an aggregate study can show the plausibility of various explanations, locate important variables that were ignored in the aggregate studies, and lead to new and better interpretations of the original correlations. (This is not to deny that claims about causation, even in a single case,

---

[2]The greater the effort that has gone into a project, the slower people will be to abandon it. Although the costs of throwing good resources after bad are obvious, sometimes obstacles that at first seem insurmountable can in fact be overcome with sufficient effort. For a fascinating discussion of this phenomenon and the workings of the "hiding hand" in the context of economic development, see Hirschman (1967, pp. 9-34). As Hirschman has noted, this argument puts an interesting twist on one aspect of cognitive dissonance theory. For a related discussion, see Jervis (1976, chap. 12).

always involve implicit or explicit comparisons.) Several scholars have argued that high-density theories—those that examine many links in a causal chain—have no privileged status (Hirschi and Selvin, 1967, p. 38; Jervis, 1976, chap. 1; Kaplan, 1965, p. 146). They are not automatically more fruitful than those that leave unexplicated the details of the ways in which one variable affects another, but there are often important practical advantages in such explication. Even in those instances (rare in international relations) in which low-density generalizations (e.g., those linking a state's external environment with its response) are valid with few exceptions, an understanding of detailed linkages is not only intellectually satisfying but can permit us to examine new classes of cases, perhaps in other fields of human interaction, and to subsume behavior that previously seemed unrelated. In the more frequent instances when generalizations are valid for but a few cases, high-density studies can help explain why an independent variable has different effects in different sets of instances. Examining the conditions under which domestic turmoil leads to foreign aggression, to quiescence, or to neither may be more interesting (and valuable) than knowing the exact correlation between turmoil and aggression. Or exploring other variables that influence the effect of alliances on the occurrence of war may be more rewarding in the long run than simply establishing a direct relationship between alliance membership and war.

Unless we have isolated the important confounding and intervening variables, the overall correlations are likely to be highly misleading. To take a non-political example, I have been told that there is a positive correlation between the effectiveness of Allied bombing raids during World War II and the degree of fighter opposition. Testing for the impact of every conceivable variable eventually might have revealed what was wrong, but knowing quite a bit about the question and examining several successful and unsuccessful raids more quickly focuses attention on the weather conditions that affect both the ability of the bombers to hit their targets and the ability of the fighters to attack the bombers. Too little quantitative international relations research has reached this stage of sophisti-

cation. (For a partial exception, see Wilkenfeld, 1968.)

Looking at a few cases carefully and trying to find detailed cause-and-effect relationships may enable us to see why certain correlations appear in aggregate studies and what determines the impact of the independent variable, especially if there are interaction effects among the variables. We could then reexamine our aggregate data with the aid of new distinctions and possibly explain more of the variance. For example, it is possible that domestic unrest increases the chance of foreign aggression if a decision maker believes that a quick victory is likely, but decreases it if he expects defeat or even short-run reverses. Unrest may lead to war when decision makers favor greater internal radicalization but may not lead to war when they want to dampen public excitement.[3] Constructing high-density theories also allows us to see similarities; cases may have similar causal linkages even though they are triggered by different antecedent variables (e.g., we can look at cases where causes other than domestic unrest lead the decision maker to seek relatively safe aggressions). Or we may search for outcomes that differ from those involved in the original study (e.g., we can examine cases where the state engaged in dramatic and diverting, but not hostile, foreign policy actions). Such operations can deepen our understanding of the processes at work and explain a wider range of phenomena than did the original formulation. These usages of the details of individual cases also show that both those who argue that case studies cannot cumulate and those who believe that the distinctiveness of each case defeats understanding by means of comparative analysis are unduly pessimistic.

Intensive examination of several cases will facilitate the scrutiny of our concepts to see whether they are really useful for answering our questions. It is probable that many of the terms we commonly use (e.g., "bipolarity," "war," "alliance," "deterrence") carve out categories that are not homogeneous on crucial dimensions. Both quantitative and qualitative analysts employ coding

---

[3]The fact that the examples of linkages given here involve decision making should not be taken to imply that all such linkages must involve this level of analysis.

rules, and they cannot afford to gloss over the crucial decisions that those rules imply. For example, Waltz (1964) has shown that the question of the stability of bipolar systems cannot be adequately examined unless two kinds of bipolarity are distinguished—one in which each pole is composed of one dominant actor and several minor satellites (e.g., the postwar era) and the other in which each pole is composed of several roughly equal states (e.g., the pre-World War I period). Similarly, Siverson reminds us that alliances that aim at deterrence or some other public good should often be distinguished from those that seek divisable values.[4] Thus, if we simply look for alliances or bipolarity, many investigations will yield meager results because our concepts and the resulting coding rules are ill designed for coming to grips with the phenomena we are trying to explain.

Several of the suggestions I have made can be applied to nonquantitative as well as quantitative research. In many instances traditional scholars have failed to examine their concepts carefully, ignored many of the important links between what are believed to be causes and effects, and neglected to develop and test their explanations by looking at their implications. That some of my comments apply to traditional work as well as to quantitative

[4]See Chapter 22.

work is not surprising; the two bodies of literature have much in common. Despite differences in techniques, most international relations scholars ask similar questions and face similar problems.

REFERENCES

Hirschi, T., and H. Selvin. 1967. *Delinquency Research.* New York: Free Press.

Hirschman, A. 1967. *Development Projects Observed.* Washington: Brookings Institution.

Jervis, R. 1976. *Perception and Misperception in International Politics.* Princeton: Princeton Univ. Press.

Kaplan, A. 1965. "Noncausal Explanation." In *Cause and Effect,* ed. D. Lerner, pp. 145-56. New York: Free Press.

Lakatos, I. 1970. "Falsification and the Methodology of Scientific Research Programmes." In *Criticism and the Growth of Knowledge,* ed. I. Lakatos and A. Musgrave, pp. 91-196. Cambridge: At the Univ. Press.

Milne, A. A. 1957. *The World of Pooh.* New York: Dutton.

Tuddenham, R. D. 1974. Review of *Alfred Binet* by Theta Wolf. *Science* 183 (Mar): 1071-72.

Waltz, K. 1964. "The Stability of a Bipolar World." *Daedalus* 93 (Summer).

Wilkenfeld, J. 1968. "Domestic and Foreign Conflict Behavior of Nations." *Journal of Peace Research* (1): 56-69.

20. Theory for and about Policy
Richard Smoke

Walter Lippmann, followed by many others, has suggested that the totality of thought about international relations can be divided into three broad categories. They overlap somewhat, but are quite distinguishable.[1] There is the approach which, in a

[1]Lippmann's tripartite distinction has been widely repeated approvingly, for instance by Hoffmann (1960), whose terminology I employ here.

scientific spirit, takes international relations as a detached object of study. The result of this approach (which is the dominant orientation of most of the essays in this volume) is called scientific theory, or often, empirical theory. There is the approach which inspires us with a vision of an ideal or a much better world, argues for actions by which we can reach it, or tells us how our values must change and be applied to realize a better world. Immanuel Kant's *Perpetual Peace* (1957) and Clark and Sohn's *World Peace through World Law* (1960) are examples. The result of this approach is called normative theory. Finally, there is the approach which begins from the perspective of today's policy makers looking out from government capitals upon today's world, and tries to help them do a better job of making foreign policy. Emphasizing different aspects of it, this approach has been called "policy theory" (Hoffmann, 1960), the problem of "undertakings" (Rosenau, 1968), "design theory" (Simon, 1969), "engineering analytical frameworks" (Bobrow, 1972) and other things. Let me call it "policy theory" here.

These three categories are far from watertight. Although any particular piece of work almost has to emphasize one of them, most work suggests implications, explicitly or implicitly, for the other two. A very important, and almost entirely neglected, problem in the development and cumulation of research in international relations, is the question of how work emphasizing any one of these three approaches can best serve the needs of one or both of the other two. For instance, what are the greatest needs of normative theorists, for scientific, empirical knowledge about the international system? We do not know. And unquestionably, part of the reason why normative theorists have made little progress and have had little impact in recent times, is that a great deal of scientific, empirical research goes forward with little or no consideration given to what kind of results would be of most value to building normative theory.

Aside from putting a flag on this question of the triangular relationship among empirical, normative, and policy theory, I cannot, for reasons of space, deal with the complicated issues it raises. But there are also intricate and difficult problems inhibiting the development and cumulation of *each one* of the three kinds of theory about international affairs, and this paper focuses upon one of these. Let me try to discuss succinctly some of the most salient aspects of the cumulation problems we are experiencing in the creation of *policy theory*.[2]

In contemplating the past and future development of policy theory, one enjoys an important advantage, over someone contemplating the similar development of empirical theory. For in the context of policy theory, one has a somewhat clearer and more vivid image in mind of what one is seeking—improved policy making. This is not to say that there is universal agreement on exactly what that would be, and still less of course on what, substantively, "better policy" would be. Nevertheless a considerable implicit consensus exists, I think, among those who try to make policy and those who try to study how to make policy, about what improvement might look like.

This stands in distinct contrast to the situation in the domain of empirical theory, where there is hardly any consensus at all about the form the goal might take. On the contrary, enormous disparity reigns, and has long reigned, among empirical theorists regarding what level at which to pitch theory, what units of analysis to employ, what kinds of analytic operators or processes or dynamics to embrace, and indeed, what methodologies and approaches would be most useful, and even what ones should or should not count as scientific. In the empirical domain the problem of cumulation swirls unhappily in the vortex of these disputations, for logically it is completely dependent upon the prior questions of what it is that one is trying to cumulate, and toward what.

In the domain of policy theory, however, we perhaps can be somewhat more sanguine about our ability to cumulate consensually. The Aristotelian maxim is that to build theory one must first decide exactly why one needs theory. The existence, presently, of some consensus on needs for policy theory, gives us some hope for progress in creating it.

I think it is useful to distinguish three main varieties of policy theory, or topic areas within policy theory, because the cumulation problem is somewhat different from one variety to the next. My three are: theory aimed at the improvement of the decision-making process; knowledge and models of other nations' and one's own nation's goals, capabilities, and (overlapping the first) cur-

---

[2]Alexander George's essay in this book (Chapter 11) substantially concerns itself with this theme also. My paper draws heavily upon some of his work (notably George, 1968, and George, Hall, and Simons, 1971) and upon work he and I have done together (Smoke and George, 1973, George and Smoke, 1974).

rent decision-making processes; and theory about inter-nation influence instruments.

THEORY AIMED AT THE IMPROVEMENT OF THE DECISION-MAKING PROCESS

We have witnessed impressive development in one aspect of policy theory, although in other aspects the cumulation of research findings is only now perhaps, approaching what might be called the take-off stage. Cumulation has been impressive in the work done on the objective analytics of quantitative dimensions of policy problems. Particularly in the military context, such techniques as cost-effectiveness analysis, "decision theory" more generally, strategic-exchange and some similar kinds of modeling, and such planning and managerial devices as PERT have enjoyed many important successes. These theories and methods cumulate readily because their highly objective and quantitative nature permits them to interlock with few difficulties.[3]

There has not been nearly so much cumulation to date in investigation of less objective aspects of policy: the dimension of values and goals in policy problems, and the organizational, bureaucratic, and other social and social-psychological dimensions of the policy process. Although there have been many efforts in the past to improve policy making by reorganizing the governmental machinery, only in recent years have theorists begun to adapt the combined results of behavioral organization theory, "political science" insights into bureaucratic bargaining, and conclusions from social, personality, and cognitive psychology to the IR context. (See, for instance, Allison, 1971; Janis, 1972; George, 1972; Halperin, 1974; Steinbruner, 1974.)[4]

[3]For example, modelling techniques for force posture planning that developed in the 1950s and 1960s turned out to be easily married to the Planning-Programming-Budgeting System (PPBS) for decision making.

A civilian example in the IR field where cumulation has occurred in quantitative theory for policy might be the fairly good quantitative analysis that can be done concerning the effects of postulated alternative economic aid options for a particular Less Developed Country (LDC).

[4]As theory is developed suggesting how to improve the IR decision-making process, there still remains the political problem of getting these suggestions accepted. But decision makers have a standing interest in such things. The adoption by McNamara's Defense Department of PPBS is an example, on a smaller scale and in a

This, however, is an area of rapidly growing interest for IR theory, and one has the impression that research of this kind is beginning to cumulate in a fairly satisfactory way—almost certainly cumulating more than is IR theory in general. This may be due in part to the manner in which some of this research adapts conclusions from other disciplines which have already gone through the cumulation process within those disciplines. It also may be somewhat temporary; the progress has been mostly in different "cells" of the overall psycho-social decision process, and we have not yet begun to formulate the general theory that would unite the cells. It would be possible (though not, I think, likely) for us to end up with a warehouse full of well-machined parts which could not be fitted together.

Incidentally, this suggests a useful general distinction between two kinds of cumulation: There is the kind of cumulation which represents the steady "filling out" of explanatory hypotheses, vis-à-vis a particular class of problems, until a reasonably comprehensive theory or model is attained. For example, it is quite straightforward to relate Holsti's work on stress and crisis decision making (1972) to, viz., Janis's work on "groupthink" (1972). The other kind of cumulation represents the integration of several different models of several different problems, into a unified overall theory. It is much less easy, at least at present, to relate the work on stress, crisis decision making and "groupthink" to, for instance, the particular class of political and psychological phenomena known, à la Allison (1971) and Halperin (1974), as "bureaucratic politics."

But IR policy theory must attend not merely to the decision-making process, but to the two kinds of "substances" which that process takes as its subject matter: units or actors—the nations and their operationally significant subdivisions—and the policies, or "instruments", that these actors employ to influence each other.

KNOWLEDGE AND MODELS OF ACTORS

From the policy-theoretic viewpoint the cumulation problem with respect to actors is of a lesser order of magnitude; from that viewpoint not much

somewhat specialized context, of a new administration adopting improved decision-making methods orginally developed by theorists.

abstract theory about nations and subnational actors is either desirable or possible. What good policy making requires here is high-quality concrete information, information which is *au courant* and which is richly detailed in ways relevant to the policy problem at hand. This is partly an intelligence problem, notably so where one is concerned about other national players' current capabilities, military and otherwise. And partly this is a problem for national and area specialists such as Kremlinologists and Sinologists, notably so where one is concerned with other national players' current and long-term intentions, and with decision-making processes and personalities within those governments.[5] Cumulation in this context, then, is more a matter of *accumulating* information than the kind of cumulation represented by new, more powerful or more parsimonious theory.

The most important exception to this generalization may be the need in this area for straightforward and explicit *models* of players' decision-making processes, goals, and assumptions. The national specialist, of course, embraces within his expertise more of all these kinds of information than any simple model can contain. But there is a good case to be made for the need of decision makers themselves to have within their own minds simple but accurate models of the principal international players they are dealing with. Indeed there is a good case to be made that, implicitly, they already have simple models, but that these need to be explicated, tested, and rationalized by policy theorists, and then returned to the decision maker. Only then, perhaps, can the decision maker make the maximum, most efficient, and most sophisticated use of the national specialist at his elbow.

The problem of generating a reasonably simple model of another nation and its important subplayers which will not make operationally significant distortions in its subject, is an example of a particular kind of cumulation problem that might be called "encapsulization". A generally accepted and widely employed technique for generating such encapsulizations has not yet emerged.[6] Traditionally theorists have considered the policy tools available in given situations in such a way that a "rational, unitary, national actor" was implicit. This tradition may have had the effect of diverting theoretical attention from the actually nonunitary nature of other states, whose elements may pursue diverse notions of what "rationality" means.[7] This brings us to our third and final problem area, the one most scholars probably think of first when they hear phrases like policy theory.

THEORY ABOUT INTER-NATION INFLUENCE INSTRUMENTS

The nature of inter-nation influence is, of course, one of the grand traditional problems in empirical IR theory. Indeed, interpreting broadly one could say that resolving this problem is the single basic objective of that theory. Much recent work in empirical IR theory continues this tradition.

But from the viewpoint of policy theory—and from the viewpoint of the policy maker who hopes for assistance from theorists—a very large fraction of this work, traditional and current, is of extremely marginal relevance. This is equally true, on the whole, of more traditional qualitative, and the more recent quantitative, empirical research. In both cases the empirical search for comprehensive generalizations and "laws" about inter-nation in-

[5] For logical completeness one must also note the question of the capabilities, intentions, and processes of the various parts, and the whole, of one's *own* government—which may or may not be adequate for the pursuit of certain otherwise plausible lines of policy. However, high-level policy makers normally feel, not necessarily always rightly, that they already possess sufficient information about these things, through personal experience and through standard reporting routines such as force-status and disposition reports.

[6] Probably the best-known effort along these lines is the "operational code" technique invented by Leites (1951) and refined by George (1969). The operational code method can be applied to either states or groups or individuals—perhaps at the present state of the art most interestingly to individuals.

[7] "Rationality" is not, except in some very abstract sense, a single, unified desideratum. As experienced by policy makers, rationality is more a goal to be sought, under serious procedural and cognitive constraints, than a premise to be assumed. Specialists interested in policy theory supplement abstract ideas of rationality with empirical research into how rationality is approached and operationalized under differing circumstances.

fluence has not revealed much that is policy-relevant about the *instruments* of that influence.[8]

But it is the instruments which the policy maker and policy theorist are interested in. If successful policy is to be made, they must know what tools can, and cannot, be used in a given set of circumstances to influence a given international player, or situation, in desired directions. However, the existing literature on this class of problem is too narrow in scope and yet, paradoxically, too deductive in approach, to have cumulated nearly as well as one could wish. Let me discuss these points separately; and in the available space, only summarily.

For various historical reasons, research since World War II on IR policy instruments has focused heavily on negative sanctions, especially on sanctions involving the use or threat of force. Such policy instruments as deterrence, crisis-management techniques, and coercive strategies have received the lion's share of attention from analysts who were understandably caught up in the dilemmas and challenges of the Cold War. Most of all, attention has been paid to the special case of strategic deterrence—special both in its compelling urgency and in its peculiar intellectual simplicity which has allowed mathematical techniques to be employed with striking usefulness. After strategic deterrence, other policy instruments have received theoretical attention roughly in the order in which they embrace force: general foreign policy deterrence, limited war, crisis management, and coercion in diplomacy, in that order. Extraordinarily little thought has been given to the admittedly more difficult problems represented by what might be called crisis-preventive diplomacy, and the wide range of instruments residing within the realm of positive influence: i.e., influence by positive sanctions—by offers and rewards rather than by threats and punishments. Only very recently, with the end of the acute Cold War, has policy-theoretic attention begun to extend to positive influence instruments.

A degree of cumulation is visible in work on policy instruments, primarily, I suggest, through a series of heuristic arguments by analogy. Theoretical ideas, perhaps first derived and honed in the

strategic deterrence context, were extended by analogy to more general deterrence, and thence to crisis management. The analogies did not always apply rigorously, but they did to a degree which was at least useful; and then more was learned through observation of the ways they did apply, and why they didn't to a greater degree.

This may be a general way that cumulation proceeds in the universe of policy theory, where the somewhat restricted context (from the viewpoint of empirical theory) provides a kind of unified a priori ideational background.[9] It applies even in the extension of theoretical ideas first derived from the nature of powerful negative sanctions, to the realm of positive influence, where one can go a certain distance toward an inducement theory by simply rewriting the propositions of general deterrence theory with the minus signs changed to plus signs, and then a certain distance further by observing why that method only goes a certain distance.

Nevertheless one must conclude that cumulation might have proceeded further and faster had not the scope of the problem areas been defined so narrowly for such a long time. We might have learned more that was better, quicker, about deterrence theory *as well as* inducement theory if we had given much more attention to the nature of inducement 15 or 20 years ago, along with the attention to deterrence. More useful policy theory would have cumulated, I think, by playing positive against negative influence theory interactively and "dialectically," than by creeping slowly forward from the extreme negative pole.[10]

---

[8]For an outline of an argument why, in terms of methodologies, this should be so, see Smoke and George (1973, sections 6 and 7).

[9]One of the more difficult aspects of the cumulation problem in empirical IR theory may be on the substantive a priori's rather than on the formal methodologies, which may actually be a less intractable part of the problem.

[10]For instance, one of the deficiencies of a good deal of deterrence theory has been a tendency to take the deterrent "commitment" implicitly as an either/or phenomenon—either one is committed or one is not—and on this basis to proceed at once to the "technical" problem of how to "signal" the commitment credibly. In the context of inducement, it is somewhat clearer and more obvious that the commitment is usually a matter of degree. If this had received the proper emphasis in the inducement context, it seems likely that the recognition of it would have "reflected back" into the deterrence context, where it would then have also received a more appropriate emphasis.

The study of those policy instruments which are especially adapted to the influence of the international system *over the long term* has cumulated even less, partly for the same reason. I think it is fair to say that policy theory is almost nonexistent regarding efforts to influence the evolution of the international system toward alternative futures more than five years ahead. There are several reasons for this, including the lack of much good empirical theory about change in the international system, and the lack of useful normative theory about long-term goal selection. But another reason, again, has been the way in which policy theory has failed to cumulate in the appropriate direction. Instruments for long-term influence of the system necessarily are almost entirely positive rather than negative in character, and the traditional emphasis in policy theory on negative influence has impeded the cumulation of findings. Ideas and theories on the subject of long-term development have remained scattered.[11]

We should also observe that even *within* the scope defining most *present* policy theory, work on influence instruments has failed to cumulate well for methodological reasons; the relationships between deductive logic and inductive empiricism have been defined unsatisfactorily. The most vigorously attacked case, that of the deterrence of strategic thermonuclear war, may have led us astray, for this case is a special one methodologically. Lacking, mercifully, any historical experience of the subject, scholars were obliged to formulate theories abstractly and deductively. However, the habit carried over into other problem areas. For instance, the literatures on general deterrence and on escalation are quite striking for the absence of empirical studies. There are, in fact, a vanishingly small number of theoretically motivated empirical studies of either, despite the wealth of evidence available.[12]

Rather, theorists have contented themselves largely with the construction of abstract models on both topics, models which can be and have been refined and elaborated, but which have *cumulated* only a quite modest number of policy-relevant, operational conclusions and perhaps an even fewer number of puzzles inviting research. Or, where empiricism does exist, it is not to test hypotheses or solve puzzles; it is very largely configurative. Case studies are designed primarily to illuminate the case, and only secondarily to adduce theoretically interesting conclusions, and they are carried out on sufficiently different terms and from sufficiently different points of view, as to render cumulation very difficult.[13] Cumulation of policy-relevant theory, here as elsewhere, has fallen between the nomothetic and configurative stools.

Let me conclude these remarks by mentioning one possible method for coping with some of these problems in policy theory about influence instruments. A possible methodological advance proposed, and attempted, by a number of authors might be called the method of "focused comparison." It is very similar to what, in the context of comparative government, Eckstein (1975) has called a "disciplined-configurative" study. In essence, with this technique one performs case studies in moderate depth on a manageably small number of instances of a phenomenon, employing either qualitative or quantitative methods. One then compares the cases against each other with reference to explicit hypotheses or questions, which are applied in the same standardized way to each case study. (The hypotheses or questions may be derived from abstract models or from any source.) Some comparisons will suggest similarities among the cases, of course, which provide the basis for generalizations. But other comparisons will point out differences, which can lead to equally valuable generalizations when their context is well-specified and when the reasons for the variation are explicitly identified.

[11]Perhaps the principal exception to this generalization would be the domain of political and economic development. On the whole, however, the linkages between development theory and the much larger problem of the long-term evolution of the system generally, have remained largely rhetorical.

[12]On the whole this is true of the much smaller literatures concerning other negative influence instruments as well, where in addition there is also a general lack of abstract models.

[13]There are a few exceptions to this generalization. Both the general theme of this and the succeeding paragraph, and the exceptions to the generalization, are discussed in George and Smoke (1974, chap 4) and Smoke (1977, pt. 1 and app. 2).

Space does not permit a fuller elaboration, but this approach has been described in detail elsewhere and employed a number of times recently in the IR field, mostly in efforts to create policy theory.[14] The method does not normally reveal the frequency with which any particular combination of variables occurs, and therefore the breadth of generality of the research conclusions remains, from the viewpoint of the empirical theorist, to be shown by other tests. From the viewpoint of empirical theory the method is mainly useful as a generator and refiner of interesting hypotheses.

But policy makers, who make up the policy-theorist's main audience, normally do not much care how often a particular combination of factors arises in history. What they are interested in are any combinations which resemble present situations. The focused comparison method, by allowing the researcher wide latitude in his choice of case material, makes it possible to focus on issues particularly relevant to present circumstances. For this and other reasons described in the literature on this method, focused comparison may be a particularly useful research tool for the creation of theory for and about policy.

REFERENCES

Allison, Graham. 1971. *Essence of Decision*. Boston: Little, Brown.

Bloomfield, Lincoln, and Amelia Leiss. 1969. *Controlling Small Wars*. New York: Knopf.

Bobrow, Davis. 1972. *International Relations: New Approaches*. New York: Free Press.

Clark, Grenville, and Louis Sohn. 1960. *World Peace through World Law*. Cambridge: Harvard Univ. Press.

Ekstein, Harry. 1975. "Case Study and Theory in Political Science." In *Political Science Handbook*, vol. 7, pp. 79-138. Reading, Mass.: Addison-Wesley.

George, Alexander L. 1968. "Bridging the 'Gap' between Scholarly Research and Policy-Makers: The Problem of Theory and Action." Mimeo. Stanford: Stanford Univ.

———. 1969. "The 'Operational Code': A Neglected Approach to the Study of Political Leaders and Decision-Making." *International Studies Quarterly* 13 (Jun): 190-222.

———. 1972. "The Case for Multiple Advocacy in Making Foreign Policy." *American Political Science Review* 66 (Sep): 751-85.

———, David K. Hall, and William E. Simons. 1971. *The Limits of Coercive Diplomacy*. Boston: Little, Brown.

——— and Richard Smoke. 1974. *Deterrence in American Foreign Policy: Theory and Practice*. New York: Columbia Univ. Press.

Halperin, Morton. 1974. *Bureaucratic Politics and Foreign Policy*. Washington: Brookings Institution.

Hoffmann, Stanley, ed. 1960. *Contemporary Theory in International Relations*. Englewood Cliffs, N.J.: Prentice-Hall.

Holsti, Ole. 1972. *Crisis, Escalation, War*. Montreal: McGill-Queen's Univ. Press.

Janis, Irving. 1972. *Victims of Groupthink*. Boston: Houghton Mifflin.

Kant, Immanuel. 1957. *Perpetual Peace*. Trans. Lewis W. Beck. New York: Bobbs-Merrill.

Leites, Nathan. 1951. *The Operational Code of the Politburo*. New York: Greenwood.

Paige, Glenn. 1972. "Comparative Case Analysis of Crisis Decisions: Korea and Cuba." In *International Crises*, ed. Charles F. Hermann, pp. 41-55. New York: Free Press.

Rosenau, James N. 1968. "Moral Fervor, Systematic Analysis, and Scientific Consciousness in Foreign Policy Research." In *Political Science and Public Policy*, ed. Austin Ranney, pp. 197-236. Chicago: Markham.

Russett, Bruce M. 1970. "International Behavior Research: Case Studies and Cumulation." In *Approaches to the Study of Political Science*, ed. Michael Haas and Henry S. Kariel, pp. 425-43. San Francisco: Chandler.

Simon, Herbert. 1969. *The Science of the Artificial*. Cambridge: Harvard Univ. Press.

Smoke, Richard. 1977. *Controlling Escalation*. Cambridge: Harvard Univ. Press.

——— and Alexander L. George. 1973. "Theory for Policy in International Affairs." *Policy Sciences* 4 (Dec): 387-413.

Steinbruner, John. 1974. *The Cybernetic Theory of Decision*. Princeton: Princeton Univ. Press.

Verba, Sidney. 1967. "Some Dilemmas in Comparative Research." *World Politics* 20 (Oct): 111-27.

Young, Oran R. 1968. *The Politics of Force*. Princeton: Princeton Univ. Press.

[14]Discussions advocating an approach of this kind may be found, besides in Eckstein (1975), in Verba (1967) and Russett (1970). George discusses it briefly in Chapter 11 of this volume. It is treated at greater length in George, Hall, and Simons (1971), Smoke and George (1973), George and Smoke (1974), and Smoke (1977). Variations on this approach have been employed by Young (1968), Bloomfield and Leiss (1969), Holsti (1972), and Paige (1972).

21. Identifying, Formulating, and Solving Puzzles in International Relations Research

P. Terrence Hopmann

As international relations has taken on an increasingly scientific approach in the last two decades or so, scholars have become increasingly concerned about the problem of the accumulation of knowledge in this field. Those among us who wish to establish a scientific foundation for international relations place considerable emphasis on a scientific model in which knowledge is seen as accumulating in a somewhat organized fashion. This definition of scientific progress does not necessarily mean, however, that cumulation only occurs when all studies are building directly upon one another to create a single, unified edifice, brick by brick. Such a rationalistic and orderly conception of the way science progresses does not adequately describe the growth of knowledge in any scientific discipline. On the other hand, it is clear that science progresses only when there is some process of orderly accumulation of knowledge.

While Kuhn's conceptions of the progress of science have perhaps often been overemphasized as a model for international relations, he does make at least one fundamental point which seems to have considerable validity in our field. I am referring to his notion that normal sciences accumulate knowledge as a result of the common acceptance of a paradigm which guides research primarily through suggesting puzzles which need to be solved. Thus Kuhn notes that a paradigm "is a criterion for choosing problems that, while the paradigm is taken for granted, can be assumed to have solutions" (1962, p. 38). Thus a science becomes cumulative primarily because researchers in the field recognize a common set of problems or puzzles which need to be solved, and they also recognize a set of rules "that limit both the nature of acceptable solutions and the steps by which

they are to be obtained" (Kuhn, 1962, p. 38). Once one has such a paradigm one may engage in research which will be interrelated and cumulative primarily because its importance and its boundaries are defined by the problem itself. Furthermore, the puzzles themselves become interconnected, so that the solution of one puzzle will suggest to the community of researchers another set of puzzles which must be solved, and so forth. This then is the primary function of a scientific paradigm, namely, to guide the selection of puzzles and to provide clues as to their possible solution. Within such a framework, according to Kuhn, science grows through dealing with three kinds of problems, "determination of significant fact, matching of fact with theory, and articulation of theory" (1962, p. 34).

Therefore, the problem faced by those who seek to enhance cumulation in international relations research is more basic than simply encouraging researchers to engage in a process of replication and brick building, step by step. In other words, the primary obstacle to cumulation in international relations research does not seem to be that we have totally ignored one another's work, although that has at times been the case; rather the major obstacle seems to be that we have lacked any broadly shared conceptualizations of the important puzzles or problems to be solved and any adequate theory to guide us in the solution of those problems.[1] Therefore, our theory testing has often in fact been confined to the

---

[1] By emphasizing this essentially intellectual problem, I do not intend to underestimate the many practical problems limiting cumulation, such as the structure of our discipline, the shortage of research funds, and so forth; my focus in this chapter, however, is solely directed to the intellectual obstacles and requirements for enhancing cumulation in international relations research.

testing of isolated hypotheses and our data gathering has often taken place without any theoretical end in mind, so that the scientific enterprise in general has lacked any conceptual unification and the scientific work of researchers has thus too often remained conceptually unrelated to that of others in the field.

It seems to me that there are several possible explanations for this problem, namely, on the one hand, an excessive preoccupation with constructing "general theories" of international relations and, on the other hand, excessive attention devoted to collecting data to describe phenomena without any explicit concern for explanation or prediction.

The problem of excessive concern with the development of a general theory of international relations characterized much of the work in the field during the 1950s and the early 1960s. Candidates for general or "grand" theories of international relations included, among others, the systems approach, the communications approach, the power orientation, the decision-making approach, and field theory. All of these orientations have had a significant impact on the field of international relations, and all have served to a greater or lesser degree as conceptual frameworks to guide the work of numerous researchers in the field. It would thus be unfair to underestimate their importance in suggesting some interesting avenues of research and in at least providing a common vocabulary for scholars in the field. Nevertheless, none of these approaches has succeeded in fulfilling the functions Kuhn attributes to a scientific paradigm. None has clearly defined a set of puzzles to be solved; none has actually led to the construction of a theory, if by a theory we mean a deductively related set of propositions; and none has provided a satisfactory and widely shared guide for the gathering of data in the field. One of the reasons these approaches have failed to become more than loose conceptual frameworks is probably that they were overly ambitious: they tried to apply a few central concepts to such a wide and variable range of substantive problems that they simply could not suggest a logically related set of propositions which could in fact be tested and confirmed in relation to such disparate phenomena. Furthermore, they failed to define specific aspects of

international relations which were to be explained, so that in most cases it was difficult to identify specific dependent variables other than such broad and open ones as international interactions or foreign policy outputs. Hence the approaches were not readily adaptable for empirical research, and it is interesting to note the dearth of actual empirical research in almost 20 years of utilizing, for example, Kaplan's impressive attempt to develop a general theory in *System and Process in International Politics* (1957). Thus general theory seems to have failed to generate cumulative research largely because of its excessive generality, so that no meaningful sets of theoretical propositions could be derived therefrom. Too often general theory attempted to explain everything and thereby failed to explain the crucial differences in specific international relations phenomena, so that in fact it explained nothing.

A second obstacle to the growth of cumulative scientific research has come from the opposite side, namely, from an excessive preoccupation with data collection and data analysis at the expense of theory development. Indeed, in some instances data collectors have virtually attributed the characteristics of a paradigm to data collection and analysis techniques themselves. For example, claims by some of the most enthusiastic proponents of the events data movement almost seem to be suggesting that one can construct a theory around events data and that events data can somehow become a primary foundation for the field of international relations (see, for example, Azar quoted in Rosenau, 1973, p. 57). Similar claims for data analysis techniques providing the foundation for a theory of international relations are often made, for example, by proponents of factor analysis, and Rummel has argued explicitly that this methodology may provide a paradigm for international relations research (see Rummel quoted in Rosenau, 1973, p. 38). Of course, these and other data collection techniques and data analysis methods have made an important contribution to the growth of the field of international relations. But the assertion that they somehow become substitutes for a theoretical paradigm, or that they take on the attributes of such a paradigm, appears to me to be unfounded. Certainly events data may be collected and used to test many partial theories of international relations, but the patterns of event interactions become meaningful only when examined in the light of a theory. As a collection of events they remain a-theoretical. Similarly, factor analysis may provide a method for analyzing data to test many alternative theories, and while it, like all other methods, carries certain theoretical implications, it does not in and of itself generate theoretical propositions. Therefore, to base the hopes for cumulation of scientific research in international relations upon either a data collection or a data analysis technique seems to me to be unfounded.

An alternative to these approaches seems to me to lie in a concentration upon the development of middle-range theories about specific processes in international relations. Indeed, this approach appears to have characterized a good deal of the most productive research in the field in recent years, although there is still a need for greater systemization and rigor in the theories being developed at this level. Merton (1968, p. 39) has defined middle-range theories as those which "lie between the minor but necessary working hypotheses that evolve in abundance during day-to-day research and the all-inclusive systematic efforts to develop a unified theory that will explain all the observed uniformities." Thus middle-range theories fall between general theories, which are too remote from actual phenomena to explain observed behavior, and specific hypotheses, which tend to remain isolated from one another. In short, they "deal with delimited aspects of social phenomena" (Merton, 1968, pp. 39-40). Examples of such phenomena in international relations which may be dealt with within the framework of middle-range theory are the causes of war, the dynamics of arms races, the processes of crisis decision making, alliance behavior, international integration, bargaining and negotiation among nations, and many other similar phenomena.

It seems to me that the trend toward increased concentration on theory development at this level is likely to lead to increased cumulation in international relations research, providing that such work is in fact guided by systematic theories which lead groups of researchers from puzzle to puzzle in a logically coherent fashion. In the absence of such a theoretical structure, however,

explanation at this level is likely to remain limited and is not likely to attain the characteristics which I have just attributed to middle-range theories. On the other hand, if these conditions are met in our theoretical efforts, then this approach might enable us to avoid some of the problems discussed above which have arisen from the other two dominant orientations in the field to date.

First, the narrowing of the range of phenomena under discussion, in contrast with the approach of those pursuing the development of general theories of international relations, is likely to enhance our ability to identify viable paradigms around which we could construct theory and carry on observations. Of course, this orientation could also lead to a greater fragmentation of the field than would be likely if we pursued the strategy of developing general theory. Thus there might develop a tendency to treat different phenomena, like alliance behavior and the onset of war, with different theories, even though both common sense and some empirical data tend to suggest that they are closely interrelated. Although these phenomena obviously cannot be completely separated and each may play a role in theories seeking to explain only one of these phenomena, the middle-range approach would still assume that an explanation of a phenomenon like the onset of war was sufficiently different from the explanation of alliance cohesion to require an essentially different theoretical orientation. Different theoretical orientations would not necessarily preclude, for example, variables like the degree of alliance cohesion serving as important independent variables in any theory about the causes of war. The middle-range-theory approach, however, would mean that we could begin searching for candidate paradigms without requiring that they be made applicable to all of the disparate phenomena which we consider under the general heading of international relations.

Second, the middle-range-theory approach places the focus primarily on the development of theory rather than on a particular set of data or technique for collecting or analyzing data. Furthermore, it readily defines what it is that we want our theory to explain. In this instance, it is clear that what we want to explain are specific phenomena like the causes of war rather than vague and general phenomena like all of international relations. Given such a theoretical orientation, we may search for alternative kinds of data and data analysis techniques to test our theories, rather than making these the central focus of the research paradigm. For example, research on the causes of war may profitably make use of data collection devices as diverse as events data, content analysis, experimental analysis and simulation, and aggregate data, using data analysis techniques such as factor analysis, multiple regression analysis, or even simple nonparametric tests of significance. The type of data and analytical methods should then be dictated by the particular theory being tested or more generally by the paradigm concerning the causes of war (or any other similar subject) which the researcher adopts and not by any particular commitment to a single source of data or a single research methodology. This is also likely to enhance the development of multimethod approaches to the analysis of single important puzzles, since the research will be driven by the puzzle to be solved rather than by the availability of a particular methodology.

An additional indicator that this approach may contribute to cumulation in international relations research is that it in fact seems to encompass the general orientation taken by those scholars who seem to me to have actually made the greatest gains (modest though they may be) in the area of cumulation, especially over the last decade or so. Although most of the research to which I am referring has occurred in the absence of an adequate theory, there has been a convergence of researchers around sets of propositions in important areas of research, such as the causes of war, alliance behavior, and crisis decision making. For example, Hermann (1972) has identified 311 propositions concerning the conditions under which crises are likely to escalate or de-escalate, and Holsti, Hopmann, and Sullivan (1973) have summarized 417 propositions dealing with the formation, cohesion, disintegration, and effects of international alliances. Of course, these sets of propositions are not sufficient to create a middle-range theory. Many of these propositions are unrelated or contradictory, and others are largely untested. Nevertheless, some efforts have been made to synthesize these kinds of propositions into some kind of logically coherent framework,

and this represents an important step in the right direction. Still further, however, we need to develop more rigorous theories, based upon some fundamental sets of axioms, which may provide tighter conceptual unity to research in these areas. Thus what we still need to do—and this is the most important as well as the most difficult point—is to develop within these substantive areas a set of unifying theoretical assumptions which will provide us with sets of logically interrelated propositions rather than isolated and ad hoc propositions. If we give more attention to the logical structure of our theories in these areas we do, I think, have the basis for some meaningful cumulative development of theory in several of these substantive problem areas, including the causes of war, dynamics of crisis decision making, sources of alliance cohesion and disintegration, preconditions and processes of international integration, and bargaining processes in international negotiations, to name just a few of the most salient examples.

Having just made the general point that cumulative research in international relations can be best fostered by focusing on the development of theories applicable primarily to specific processes within international relations rather than to the field as a whole, let me suggest a general outline of how we might proceed in the development of such middle-range theory and thereby enhance the cumulativeness of international relations research. The following discussion is not meant to imply that there is only one road, or even a limited set of roads, to cumulative international relations research, but only to suggest one possible road which I find congenial.

First, if middle-range-theory development is to be more systematic and cumulative than it has been in the past, then it must be founded upon some shared set of assumptions or axioms which form the core of the theoretical paradigm. These axioms and assumptions may provide the basis from which testable hypotheses may be derived deductively, and they thus provide the foundation for the development of theory in a logically coherent manner. In practice, however, many theories in international relations probably cannot be rigorously deduced in their entirety from such a fundamental set of axioms, and we may often have to borrow propositions which have been developed more inductively either from within international relations or from other related disciplines such as social psychology. Nevertheless, random borrowings of this nature should be prohibited, since the logical consistency with the fundamental axioms on which the theory is based provides a criterion for the admissibility of propositions into the theory. This keeps the development of the theory contained within some bounds and also forces those who accept these axioms to be concerned about logical coherence rather than "doing their own thing" independent of the work of other researchers.

This orientation also implies that the development of cumulative international relations theory is not likely to come through purely inductive data gathering or through beginning with descriptions unencumbered by explanatory or predictive theory. Unless the standard of logical interrelatedness is upheld, the solution of one problem or puzzle will tell one nothing about where to turn next. The testing and subsequent confirmation or disconfirmation of an ad hoc proposition tells us nothing about what should be investigated next and hence provides no basis for cumulative research. On the other hand, the deductive interdependence upon which scientific theories depend should suggest the logical nature of the interrelationships among puzzles. This means that the solution of one puzzle may suggest new puzzles to be solved, particularly as one goes about refining the initial generalization and following the logical consequences of one's discoveries. It is, therefore, through the logical interrelationships of these puzzles provided by a fundamental set of axioms that research is likely to become cumulative, since the answer which one researcher obtains to his or her particular puzzle will have important implications for himself or herself as well as for other researchers in solving other puzzles and in suggesting new puzzles which require solution.

Given these fundamental axioms and logically consistent sets of propositions, we may then engage in empirical research to test the middle range theory which has resulted. The principal objective of this aspect of the research is not only to either accept or reject the theory in total, but rather to refine the theory and to enhance its complexity to make it better correspond with empirical reality.

This process may be facilitated through the search for "scope conditions" which limit the applicability of theoretical generalizations. For example, we may begin with a generalization believed to be applicable to all nations and then find, on the basis of empirical research, that it is applicable only to the set of developed nations with, say, a per capita GNP of $1000 per year; we have thus identified the limiting conditions for the applicability of our theory. Identifying scope conditions, however, is not sufficient. This then leads us to questions about why the original generalization is applicable under one set of conditions and not applicable under another set of conditions. In answering this question, a new and logically consistent hypothesis may be generated to explain this difference, and this hypothesis itself may be subjected to empirical testing. As these new hypotheses are tested and new scope conditions are discovered, the original theory may become less general but it is also likely to become more refined and complex. And, because we started with a logically related set of axioms and followed through with the development of our theory, taking into account the interplay between empirical reality and the deductions from our theory, the theory should grow in a logically coherent and parsimonious fashion rather than in ad hoc directions. Scholars should have significant clues about where to begin explaining the scope conditions identified by previous researchers and in following through the logical consequences of those explanations. This process, of course, may proceed continually over long periods of time until finally some distinction cannot be explained within the logical confines of the operating paradigm. This then may become an anomaly which could give rise to a search for a new organizing paradigm, or in Kuhn's words, to a scientific revolution.

As should be evident, the process of theory construction which I have been describing involves a close interaction between deductive and inductive strategies, with both contributing to cumulation. Deductively, cumulation is driven by the logical interdependence of puzzles, so that the solution of one puzzle leads logically to the investigation of another puzzle. Inductively, the limits on the empirical applicability of one set of deductively derived theoretical generalizations leads to the refinement of the generalizations and to the search for logically consistent explanations for such limitations; these explanations must then be tested empirically, again leading to cumulative research as these further refinements follow logically from the initial empirical findings and introduce complexity into more general theories.

In this context, replication and research building upon previous research can be more dynamic and more theoretically motivated than the kind of mechanical replication procedures which characterize much of experimental social psychology, for example, where seemingly endless numbers of studies are often undertaken with only trivial modifications over previous studies and with no overarching theoretical justification for a particular variant. On the contrary, studies building upon others should seek to improve the match between theory and data while still remaining logically consistent with the initial axioms or assumptions of the theory.

The most important criterion for cumulation to occur in this approach then becomes the widespread acceptance of the fundamental assumptions or axioms and the general paradigm which identifies the puzzles as important ones and provides a guide for formulating and solving puzzles. At present, such consensus is still rare in the field of international relations, so there has been a lack of genuine cumulative research in the field. But, in conclusion, I maintain that the prospects for consensus about paradigms and fundamental assumptions are greater in those cases where scholars have identified limited and concrete research problems rather than when they have tried to solve all of the puzzles of international relations at once. Cumulative gains are thus most likely to be made by groups of scholars focusing on common problems of substantive and theoretical interest on the basis of a common though limited paradigm and sets of fundamental axioms.

REFERENCES

Hermann, Charles F., ed. 1972. *International Crises: Insights from Behavioral Research.* New York: Free Press.

Holsti, Ole R., P. Terrence Hopmann, and John D. Sullivan. 1973. *Unity and Disintegration in International Alliances: Comparative Studies.* New York: Wiley.

Kaplan, Morton. 1957. *System and Process in International Politics.* New York: Wiley.

Kuhn, Thomas S. 1962. *The Structure of Scientific Revolutions.* Chicago: Univ. of Chicago Press.

Merton, Robert K. 1968. *Social Theory and Social Structure.* Enlarged ed. New York: Free Press.

Rosenau, James N. 1973. "Success and Failure in Scientific International Relations Research: A Report on a Workshop." Mimeo. Los Angeles: Univ. of Southern California.

22. Some Suggestions for Improving Cumulation

Randolph M. Siverson

The task of this paper is to set forth views about the obstacles to cumulation in scientific international relations research and to outline the possible means of overcoming these obstacles. Before undertaking this, however, I think it appropriate to offer a short discussion of the notion of cumulation and a few comments on the extent to which international relations is cumulative.

It appears that scientists see cumulation as taking place in essentially two ways. For some, cumulation consists of the collection of increasing numbers of empirical generalizations in which we may have a fairly high degree of confidence.[1] One example of this type of cumulation may be found in Berelson and Steiner's *Human Behavior: An Inventory of Scientific Findings* (1964). Examples more relevant to international relations may be found in Robinson's (1970) inventory of the literature on crisis decision making and McGowan and Shapiro's (1973) survey of findings in the field of foreign policy.

An alternative view of cumulation, and the one to which I generally adhere, suggests that like the first approach cumulation consists of a growing body of statements which have received empirical support; but, unlike the first approach, in this case the statements are all directly related to a single conceptualization of the phenomenon of interest. As the statements receive increasing support, the precision of the conceptualization increases and it becomes more useful for the purposes of science. Rather than being just a collection of statements, the relationship of the statements to each other is accomplished through their joint linkage to the conceptualization.

My reasons for accepting this second type of cumulation as the type toward which we ought to strive are several. First, by linking the statements to a single conceptualization, rather than allowing them to stand alone, the statements gain theoretical coherence. Second, in social relations it is not uncommon for the conditions activating the process described in an empirical generalization to change, thus producing a change in the accuracy of the empirical generalization. By connecting this generalization to abstract concepts in a theoretical structure, change becomes a reflection of the processes in the abstract theory and not a puzzle confounding the empirical generalization.

If international relations research conformed to either of these types of cumulation, the task of this paper would be relatively simple; in fact, it might not be necessary to discuss the problem. The unfortunate fact is that the current state of research in international relations is a mixture of both of these types of cumulation. While a number of investigators are interested in increasing the collection of empirical generalizations (such as, large nations participate in more wars than small nations), it is also evident that numerous others are interested in extending the number of statements relevant to particular theories. But the situation is even more mixed, since those interested in the latter alternative are not themselves agreed upon which theory is preferred as an explanation of some facet of international relations, or even (as discussed below) which level of analysis should be used to the greatest theoretical advantage. These splits among students of international relations,

[1] An empirical generalization may be loosely defined as an assocational or causal abstract statement in which investigators have a degree of confidence less than that accorded a law but more than that given an hypothesis (Reynolds, 1971).

caused largely by an inability to agree upon concepts, are perhaps the primary, but not sole, reason for the lack of greater cumulation in the field. If, to use part of a venerable example, the various observers are not only looking at different parts of the elephant, but most are looking through differing conceptual lenses, then cumulation will take place slowly and in very small segments.

But given the youth of international relations as a science, perhaps this is not particularly unusual. Notwithstanding Rogowski's (1968) argument, it is really only within the last two decades that there has been a sustained, moderately widespread interest in the scientific investigation of international relations. Given this, along with the general rejection of earlier conceptualizations of international relations which emphasized international law and organization, it is perhaps to be expected that the study of international relations would consist of an "unruly flock of activities."[2]

While there are various "schools" of international relations (Russett, 1970b), they are so numerous and offer so little to each other that the present state of international relations research is not very cumulative.[3] However, the condition need not persist. Some modest suggestions may be advanced which, if they have merit, could reduce some of the splits among international relations researchers and consequently increase the amount of cumulation. Generally, the factors which inhibit cumulation in international relations may be classified in two groups: (1) the professional-sociological and (2) the intellectual. However, since the former are also present in other disciplines which somehow manage to remain cumulative (and are also well discussed in other papers in this section), I will address myself only to the intellectual problems of our field which render cumulation difficult. In this regard I offer a discussion of (1) the need to integrate existing theories, (2) the need to develop linkages between the various levels of analysis, (3) the advantages of

testing alternative models, and (4) the necessity of increasing the amount of research in the field of international relations.

[1] *There needs to be increased effort toward integrating various models and theories of international relations.* This, it may be argued, is the single most important step we can take to increase the amount of cumulative research in the field. To the extent possible, existing theories which purport to explain the same or similar phenomena should be carefully examined to determine the extent to which they may be fruitfully integrated.

A reading of the international relations literature may lead one to believe that in many cases various investigators are talking about the same thing, or are overlooking a broader perspective which would serve to unify different theories. For example, in recent years the area of alliance theory has been very active. Not only has there been substantial activity, but the level of rigor in many of the models and theories has been very high relative to other areas of international relations. Notable in this regard are Riker (1962) and Olson (1965). For the readers of this chapter there is no need to recapitulate the basic ideas of their theories. The relevant point is that while both employ rigorous methods, they, like many other theorists, offer different assertions about certain attributes of alliances. Consider their respective predictions about the size of alliances. Riker advances the notion of the minimum winning coalition and argues that alliances will tend toward the minimum size necessary for the achievement of their goal and no larger. Olson, on the other hand, suggests that alliances will tend to be large in order to minimize the burden each member must carry. Thus, we have two very interesting theories which suggest quite different sizes for alliances. What may be overlooked is that these theories may be referring to two *different types* of alliances. Riker's minimum winning coalitions have the purpose of gaining something which may then be divided up among the members. In this sense they may be seen as redistributative alliances. Olson's alliances are apparently interested only in dividing up the burden of the alliance and not in sharing in the fruits of some redistribution. The intervening variable which *may* serve to unify these two theo-

---

[2] A phrase used a number of years ago by McClelland (1963) to characterize the field. While we are now somewhat better off, the condition is basically the same.

[3] Further, many of these "schools" are united by their particular methodology, and common methodology probably should not be seen as cumulation unless the methods derive from or refer to common concepts.

ries is the *purpose* of the alliance. The introduction of this variable may serve to produce coherence in two apparently contradictory theories.[4]

It might also be possible to integrate several of the theories which have status as an important concept. A number of research papers suggest that status is an important variable in determining international behavior (Wallace, 1971, 1973; East, 1972). Moreover, Galtung's (1964) major contribution to international relations theory is centered around the concept of status. Further, it might be suggested that Rummel's (1965) notions of field theory are laden with the implicit conception of status; when Rummel asserts that two of the prime variables influencing a nation's behavior are power and economic development he is certainly using two of the factors which would determine a nation's rank relative to others. If these various efforts can be drawn together, it may be possible to formulate a single theory of status which would be more powerful than the individual efforts.

In addition to the above, the need to reduce our inventory of theories and concepts can be seen unfortunately well in the case studies which pervade our field. Methodologically speaking, the case study is one of the time-honored approaches to empiricism. The observer puts into words a report of what he has observed in a particular situation, event, or pattern of events. The empiricism of the case approach becomes scientific as increasing numbers of observed cases reveal the same characteristic relationships as the other cases. As observations of the phenomena become quantifiable and as hypothesized relationships reveal a high incidence, predictability improves (or error decreases). Any laboratory experiment, after all, is a numerous reproduction of the factors observed in an initial case study. Significantly, these case studies are held together by a set of concepts. Unfortunately, in international relations, where the number of concepts in use is large, it is not usual to find case studies which are cumulative. Consequently, we accumulate more and more case studies which have relatively little to do with each other, even when approaching the same problem.

Despite this, case studies have already contributed to cumulation. Russett (1970a) not only furnishes an extremely useful discussion of the uses of case studies in searching for general patterns, but also offers examples of the use of case studies as cumulative devices in the areas of political integration, deterrence and escalation. Haas (1969) provides another example of the uses of case studies in his coding of the findings of a number of case studies of international crises. Qualitative findings are thus quantified and subjected to statistical analysis. The work of Russett and Haas, however, would have been greatly facilitated if the various case studies used were explicitly related to the same or roughly similar set of concepts.

[2] *Synthesis and integration also need to be improved across levels of analysis.* Researchers in international relations frequently work on different levels of analysis. Singer (1969), McClelland (1961), and others focus their attention upon the interaction of nations within the international system. Others, such as Rosenau (1971), Hermann (1972), Rummel (1965), are inclined to seek their explanations of national foreign policy behavior in the attributes of nations. Finally, still others, such as Holsti (1971) and George (1969), look for explanatory factors in the decision-making systems of nations. None of the above levels of analysis lays claim to being the only approach to the study of international relations, but, despite this, most of the work being done today does not work across levels or attempt to find linkages between them.

Rosenau, for example, in a recent review of two books on decision making (1972), comments that in "the long run, if not the short run as well, the course of international history seems likely to be shaped mainly by the convergence of forces in which the talents, aspirations, and perspectives of particular individuals are of relatively minor importance." From Rosenau's comparative foreign policy perspective or from the view of those interested in the international system, this is probably a correct assertion, for the types of questions in which they are interested will not likely yield very interesting answers if the decision-making approach is used. The partisans of comparative foreign policy are persuaded that national attributes such as development, penetration, and size

---

[4]Incidentally there may be some empirical support for this position. Horvath and Foster (1963) suggest that there is a different size function for various types of groups; aggressive groups tend to be smaller than peaceful groups.

are better predictors of a nation's foreign policy than are the factors associated with the decision-making approach. While it may be granted that the comparative foreign policy approach will explain a certain amount of the variance in foreign policy *between* categories of nations, it *may* not be able to explain the residual variance *within* categories. The amount of this variance may differ between particular issue areas or situations. However, by integrating or linking appropriate decision-making factors into the scheme, it may be possible to improve the explanation. Eventually, linkages should be sought across all three levels. In so doing previous research on one level may become relevant (or cumulative) with previous or ongoing research on other levels.

[3] *Alternative models need to be tested.* In many cases, because of basic incompatabilities it will simply be impossible to synthesize or integrate various models and theories. In these instances one viable alternative is to formulate the research problem in such a manner that the data will enable the investigator to make a judgment as to which theory or model is most consistent with the data. Generally this is the technique Platt (1964) described as strong inference. According to Platt the procedure of testing carefully chosen alternative hypotheses is likely to lead to rapid progress in scientific knowledge since empty theories may be identified and discarded.[5]

Unfortunately it is not yet as easy to design critical experiments in international relations as it is in Platt's field of biophysics. Still, this type of procedure is not absent from our field. Brody and Verba (1973), for example, have tested alternative hypotheses concerning the public's policy preferences toward the Vietnam War. Tanter (1972) has also attempted a test of two alternative theories of foreign policy behavior.

The paper by Brody and Verba, as well as that by Tanter, illustrate not only the potential use of the technique of testing alternative theories, but also indicate some of the difficulties involved. Brody and Verba are able to draw conclusions, but from their closing comments it is evident that they

are not completely satisfied with the results of their research. While Tanter offers an imaginative formulation of two testable alternative hypotheses, the results of his data analysis are, at best, disappointing. Difficulties such as these are caused primarily by our lack of experimental research designs which clean up the data by controlling variance. However, it would be foolish to treat difficulties as insurmountable obstacles. If one is willing to accept Snyder's (1962) notion of probing theories, then the INS type simulation can go far toward offering clearer answers to difficult questions. Moreover, the use of quasi-experimental designs (Campbell and Stanley, 1963) and computer simulation, when used in conjunction with standard research techniques, may yield results which will increase our cumulation by rejecting theories that are either empty or have low explanatory power relative to their alternatives.

[4] *The need for more researchers and better financial support.* A further reason that the science of international relations is not more cumulative is perhaps related to the small number of scientists and the relatively modest financial support available for the field. If we compare international relations to the "mature" sciences, we clearly have far fewer people involved in scientific activity and less in the way of resources for research support. While the actual number of international relations scientists is unknown to me, it was all too easy for Jones and Singer (1972) to provide lengthy abstracts of the literature in a single volume. Similarly, the list of journals which regularly carry scientific international relations research is small.

Certainly there are reasons for these lacks. Scientific international relations is, after all, relatively young and undeveloped and the sources of financial support are often (though not always) in a similar condition.

The avenue we might take to increase our numbers and improve our support is by no means easily found. We have relatively little direct control over the numbers of investigators entering the field; since we cannot shanghai students into the field, there appears to be little we can do save attempt to communicate to them the excitement of research and knowledge in international relations. Similarly, outside of exhorting our case to various funding agencies, there is little that can be

---

[5] Platt also points out that the method has the happy consequence of inhibiting the scientist's attachment to a particular theory or hypothesis.

done to increase our sources and amount of support.

Indirectly, however, there is much that can be done. We can probably increase both our numbers and support level if we are able to achieve measurable scientific success in addressing our problems of interest. One measure of success is the extent to which our findings are cumulative. But if cumulation is to be increased, then the limited number of investigators already working will perhaps need to focus their attention on removing the obstacles to cumulation identified above.

If we are able to reduce the number of competing theories, establish linkages across levels, and test alternative models, then we will in effect have begun to reduce the number of concepts in the field of international relations. By reducing these, we will increase our cumulation. One hopes that this in turn will lead to better theory and the demonstration to funding agencies that research money will not go toward one more effort standing by itself.

Let us suppose that students of international politics are able to reduce the number of concepts used in explaining their subject matter. A consequence of this will be, as already suggested, a concentration on those concepts shown to be more viable than others. Will this development bring any undesirable side effects? Azar (1973), for example, emphasizes the fear that "cumulativeness can lead to or become a criterion for the *rejection* of research activities." In this lamentation Azar is probably correct.

The history of science is filled with example after example of scientists rejecting theories or findings because they did not fit with the then current state of science, that is, with the cumulated knowledge of a field or discipline. The point often made in this regard by Kuhn (1962) and his followers in political science (Wolin, 1968) is that science is not objective in the sense that many think of it. The value of a theory or finding, they assert, is not evaluated by objective standards, but by the extent to which it fits into the state of existing knowledge. Heretics and doubters are likely to be sanctioned in some way by the establishment. The emphasis on cumulation, therefore, might actually retard the actual growth of knowledge in a field by emphasizing the well-worn rut of

normal science as opposed to revolutionary science.

This fear of cumulation as an inhibitor of scientific change could be sufficient reason to abandon cumulation if it were as broad and pervasive as some think. First, while it is true that the structure of a discipline or field may not reward those who question its tenets, revolutions and change do take place in scientific knowledge, although undoubtedly not as rapidly as some would like. Science is *not* stagnant. Moreover, it is no longer so clear, as Kuhn apparently argued, that a scientist's change from one set of ideas to another is akin to a religious conversion the scientists are unable to explain (Landau, 1972). In many cases, but probably not all, scientists do employ standards in accepting or rejecting new research.[6] In short, science is perhaps not so rigid as Azar and others might fear. Moreover, it seems probable that intersubjective standards are most likely to be employed when the concepts and methodologies used are held in fairly widespread agreement, so that scientists are able to communicate with little ambiguity.

Finally, it seems highly unlikely that at any time in the near future will international relations research become so monolithic that new ideas will have difficulty in finding expression. To reduce our "unruly flock of activities" to a more orderly group which will allow research to go forward seems a worthwhile price. Also it is only when we have order in the discipline that the anomalies and puzzles creating "revolutionary science" can come forward. In our present circumstances, it is not possible to distinguish revolutionary research, when virtually all research claims this title.

Another problem is more real. If the number of theories and conceptualizations is reduced and the number of investigators increased or held constant, then there will be more scientists per question. Under these circumstances the focus of activity in the field will narrow and the investigations of various scientists will begin to overlap. Assuming that most or many of the scientists are roughly equal in talents and resources, instances of simultaneous discovery will begin to occur.

[6]However, there are extreme cases of resistance. For a discussion of scientists' resistance to scientific discovery, see Barber (1961).

As these instances take place, students of international relations are likely to become concerned about others in the field anticipating their research. Hagstrom (1974) presents data on a sample of American scientists indicating that more than 60 percent of the sample have been anticipated in their research by another scientist and that about one-third were concerned with being anticipated in their current work. These concerns of anticipation lead to three consequences: (1) a shifting of a scientist's field of specialization, and (2) secretiveness, and (3) increased competition.

While the secretiveness among scientists is unfortunate—if understandable—the increased competition and the shifting of fields of specialization may have beneficial side effects as Hagstrom suggests. The shifting of fields of specialization may bring fresh minds to a field which brings about important advances in knowledge (Reynolds, 1971). Further, the competition which may follow from cumulation tends to be associated with innovation and high productivity.

International relations research is by no means close to the type of cumulation which obtains in many other scientific disciplines. In time, however, it may come to pass and we should not fear it. Quite the contrary, cumulation will mean that common ground is being investigated and that a true science of international relations is finally emerging.

REFERENCES

Azar, Edward E. 1973. "The Issue of Cumulativeness in Events Data Research." Mimeo.

Barber, Bernard. 1961. "The Resistance of Scientists to Scientific Discovery." *Science* 134 (Sep): 596-602.

Berelson, Bernard, and Gary Steiner. 1964. *Human Behavior: An Inventory of Scientific Findings.* New York: Harcourt, Brace & World.

Brody, Richard A., and Sidney Verba. 1972. "Hawk and Dove: The Search for an Explanation of Vietnam Policy." *Acta Politica* 7 (Jul): 285-322.

Campbell, Donald, and Julian Stanley. 1963. *Experimental and Quasi-experimental Designs for Research.* Chicago: Rand McNally.

East, Maurice A. 1972. "Status Discrepancy and Violence in the International System." In *The Analysis of International Politics,* ed. James N. Rosenau, Vincent Davis, and Maurice A. East, pp. 299-319. New York: Free Press.

Galtung, Johan. 1964. "A Structural Theory of Aggression." *Journal of Peace Research* (2): 95-119.

George, Alexander L. 1969. "The 'Operational Code': A Neglected Approach to the Study of Political Leaders and Decision-Making." *International Studies Quarterly* 12 (Jun): 190-222.

Haas, Michael. 1969. "Communication Factors in Decision Making." *Papers, Peace Research Society (International)* 12: 65-86.

Hagstrom, Warren D. 1974. "Competition in Science." *American Sociological Review* 39 (Feb): 1-18.

Hermann, Charles F. 1972. "Policy Classification: A Key to the Comparative Study of Foreign Policy." In *The Analysis of International Politics,* ed. James N. Rosenau, Vincent Davis, and Maurice A. East, pp. 58-79. New York: Free Press.

Holsti, Ole R. 1971. "Crisis Stress and Decision-Making." *International Social Science Journal* 22: 53-67.

Horvath, William, and Caxton Foster. 1963. "Stochastic Models of War Alliances." *Journal of Conflict Resolution* 7 (Jun): 110-16.

Jones, Susan, and J. David Singer. 1972. *Beyond Conjecture in International Politics.* Itasca, Ill.: Peacock.

Kuhn, Thomas. 1962. *The Structure of Scientific Revolutions.* Chicago: Univ. of Chicago Press.

Landau, Martin. 1972. *Political Theory and Political Science.* New York: Free Press.

McClelland, Charles. 1961. "The Acute International Crisis." *World Politics* 14 (Oct): 182-204.

———. 1963. "An Unruly Flock of Activities: Comments on the State of International Studies." *Background* 7 (May): 3-11.

McGowan, Patrick, and Howard Shapiro. 1973. *The Comparative Study of Foreign Policy.* Beverly Hills: Sage.

Olson, Mancur. 1965. *The Logic of Collective Action.* Cambridge: Harvard Univ. Press.

Platt, John R. 1964. "Strong Inference." *Science* 146 (Oct): 347-53.

Reynolds, Paul D. 1971. *A Primer in Theory Construction.* Indianapolis: Bobbs-Merrill.

Riker, William. 1962. *The Theory of Political Coalitions.* New Haven: Yale Univ. Press.

Robinson, James. 1970. "Crisis Decision-Making." In *Political Science Annual,* ed. James Robinson, vol. 2, pp. 111-48. Indianapolis: Bobbs-Merrill.

Rogowski, Ronald. 1968. "International Politics: The Past as Science." *International Studies Quarterly* 12 (Dec): 394-418.

Rosenau, James N. 1971. *The Scientific Study of Foreign Policy.* New York: Free Press.

———. 1972. Review of *Dag Hammarskjöld's United Nations* and *The New Nations in the United Nations. American Historical Review* 77 (Dec): 1415-16.

Rummel, Rudolph J. 1965. "A Social Field Theory of

Foreign Conflict." *Papers, Peace Research Society (International)* 4: 131-50.

Russett, Bruce M. 1970a. "International Behavior Research: Case Studies and Cumulation." In *Approaches to the Study of Political Science,* ed. Michael Haas and Henry Kariel, pp. 425-43. San Francisco: Chandler.

———. 1970b. "Methodological and Theoretical Schools in International Relations." In *A Design for International Relations,* ed. Norman Palmer, pp. 87-105. Philadelphia: American Academy of Political and Social Science.

Singer, J. David. 1969. "The Global System and Its Subsystems: A Developmental View." In *Linkage Politics,* ed. James N. Rosenau, pp. 21-43. New York: Free Press.

Snyder, Richard C. 1962. "Experimental Techniques and Political Analysis." In *The Limits of Behavioralism in Political Science,* ed. James Charlesworth, pp. 94-123. Philadelphia: American Academy of Political and Social Science.

Tanter, Raymond. 1972. "International System and Foreign Policy Approaches: Implications for Conflict Modeling and Management." *World Politics* 14 (suppl.): 7-39.

Wallace, Michael. 1971. "Power, Status and International War." *Journal of Peace Research* (1): 23-36.

———. 1973. *War and Rank among Nations.* Lexington, Mass.: Heath.

Wolin, Sheldon. 1968. "Paradigms and Political Theory." In *The Politics of Experience,* ed. Preston King and B. C. Parekh, pp. 125-52. Cambridge: At the Univ. Press.

23. Obstacles to the Accumulation of Knowledge

Stuart A. Bremer

Few would question the assertion that cumulative knowledge is desirable in a field of study. The principal disagreements seem to concern what cumulative knowledge is, how it is generated, and when is the proper time to seek it. It is with some reluctance that I leave these questions and turn to the somewhat narrower, but nevertheless important, question that I have been asked to consider; that is, why hasn't international relations research been more cumulative in nature? In the following I will advance some tentative hypotheses about why more cumulative knowledge has not been generated within our field. I will avoid the temptation to ascribe all of our difficulties in achieving cumulativeness to our lack of a paradigm and attempt, instead, to discuss more specific and concrete conditions which may, or may not, be manifestations and consequences of this basic problem. Proceeding from the most abstract to the most concrete, I will discuss ten factors which may constitute obstacles to the generation of cumulative knowledge

in international relations research. They are to be considered hypotheses, and although they vary considerably in the degree to which they seem to be supported by evidence, I will try to assert each in the strongest terms and with equal vigor.

ONTOLOGICAL DIFFERENCES

This refers to different conceptions of what "reality" is, and in particular, the degree to which it is knowable in any final sense. While I do not pretend to be a philosopher of science, I will attempt to delineate two different conceptions of the reality of world politics, representing polar positions on an ontological continuum.

One end of this continuum asserts that reality is not directly knowable or observable. There are no such things as hard facts, only imperfect sensor readings. Plato's "cave allegory" contains such a view, but it may manifest itself in other forms.

The assertion that reality is so complex that the human mind cannot possibly comprehend it is compatible with this position, as is the slightly more moderate view that, even granting the existence of reality, it is still unknowable by observation in any final sense.

The other end of this continuum, of course, represents a contradiction of all the statements above. There is a real world, and it is patterned according to relatively simple rules. It can be observed with sufficient precision such that these rules may be discovered. The quality of our observations is a matter to be settled technologically and empirically, not philosophically. The history of science clearly reveals a progressive improvement in our ability to observe things which were previously considered inherently unmeasurable.

I must admit that I am unable to cite an example of this kind of cleavage in our field. I suspect, however, that this stems from our inattention to such fundamental questions as "Does God play dice?" rather than from consensus as to the answers. It is ironic that the field of physics, which enshrined mechanical determinism as *the* model of science for centuries, has more recently given us Bohr's principle of complementarity, which states that a phenomenon can be looked at in each of two mutually exclusive ways, with both outlooks nevertheless remaining valid in their own terms, and Heisenberg's better-known principle of uncertainty, which destroyed the purely deterministic philosophy of the universe.

Perhaps as our science advances, we, too, will be forced to debate openly such fundamental questions. What is certain is that to the degree that such differences in ontological orientations are present in our field, cumulativeness suffers. Communication is difficult, to say the least, between those who cannot agree on the fundamental nature of what they are talking about. There is little they believe they can learn from one another and each is unlikely to find the other's work useful in his individual efforts to accumulate knowledge about world affairs.

EPISTEMOLOGICAL DIFFERENCES

A more obvious obstacle stems from the lack of consensus among researchers and practitioners of international relations about the proper epistemological orientation. This differs from the ontological question since it is possible for two people to have the same fundamental ontological orientation yet to have radically different epistemological orientations. An epistemological orientation specifies one's preferred strategy for generating knowledge, as exemplified in our field by the differences between the traditionalists and behavioralists. These have been frequently discussed before, and I will not dwell on them here.

Perhaps the division within the field of international relations which best reflects different positions on this continuum is the statesman versus the scientist. In their stereotyped forms, the statesman relies principally on intuition and insight, rather than on hard evidence, and he acquires *wisdom* about world affairs only after extensive, highly personal experience. The stereotyped scientist, on the other hand, relies strongly on hard evidence, rejecting all else as speculation. He acquires *knowledge* about world affairs by systematically collecting and analyzing inter-subjectively verifiable facts.

The implications of this split are similar to the ones above. Different epistemological orientations restrict communication and learning, which in turn, inhibit the accumulation of knowledge. I sense that a more balanced epistemological orientation is developing within our field as some traditionalists begin to use quantitative techniques and the behavioralists, having become more accustomed to their mathematical and statistical tools, are better able to see their strengths and weaknesses. The growth of Bayesian inferential methods also encourages the fusion of these two views, since these methods recognize that intuition and casual observation are useful sources of knowledge.

PROFESSIONAL CONSIDERATIONS

Some aspects of the reward structure of our profession clearly discourage cumulative research. Most international relations researchers are paid for teaching, but *rewarded* for research. The part-time aspect of research activity reduces the amount of research produced, but in addition, its episodic nature also impedes cumulativeness. It must yield to the school calendar, and there are times when university obligations absorb all of one's time. At these times, research stops until other obligations are met. This pattern of fits and starts is generally not conducive to coherent, cumulative research, since one is never quite able to return to the point where one left off.

However, the research preferences which seem to be implicit in the reward structure are more important obstacles to cumulativeness. Certain kinds of research activity are viewed more favorably than others; some activities which contribute directly to the accumulation of knowledge, such as data gathering and replication, are not sufficiently rewarded, while others which contribute much less, in a cumulative sense, are favored.

Finally, the emphasis on "visibility" and "scholarly productivity" as criteria for professional advancement are not altogether compatible with careful craftsmanship, which is essential if research is to be truly cumulative. The temptation to assess quality by quantity is difficult to resist. The field of history, I am told, differs considerably from ours in this regard. The emphasis is much more on the long-term significance of the research contribution of a scholar, rather than short-term productivity. As long as the careful craftsman must yield his share of professional rewards to the effusive dilettante, cumulative research in international relations will suffer.

STRUCTURAL FACTORS

Our field is structured in a quasi-feudal nature, centered on a relatively few major scholars located in various parts of the country. At best, this system can be considered a pluralistic, polycentric system, but at worst, it sometimes resembles a group of warring states. It is not unlike the state of affairs which tends to obtain during the disintegration of an empire. The center has lost its power to several major peripheral centers, none of which is strong enough to organize the others.

This kind of structural arrangement both encourages and discourages cumulativeness. Within the "invisible colleges" which constitute the principal nodes in the structure, considerable coherence and cumulativeness can be attained in reasonably efficient ways. There seems, however, to be little interaction between these units themselves and even less between them and the periphery. Harold Guetzkow seems to have been the most successful at attending to, and building upon, the work of other projects, but his case is exceptional.

SOCIOLOGICAL CONSIDERATIONS

The recent emergence of the quantitative sector of our field was accompanied by factional disputes which are not conducive to cumulativeness. The partial split within the field and mutual disallowance of what each side considers knowledge have impeded developments on both sides. Those who use the classical approach, to use Hedley Bull's term, are inclined to consider the work of the nonclassically oriented as trivial, while the latter are inclined to consider the former "mere speculators" and "inside-dopesters." During an upheaval such as this grievances, jealousies, rivalries, and interpersonal differences are bound to develop, and to the degree that these factors impede mutual learning, they inevitably impede cumulativeness.

FINANCIAL CONSTRAINTS

To a certain extent, our failure to produce much cumulative research in international relations is a direct consequence of the extent and nature of its financial base. First, there clearly have not been enough funds available in the past, and it certainly appears there has been a sizable decrease recently. With the exception of a few fortunate senior scholars who occupy institutionalized research positions, most scholars must seek research support from external agencies. This requires the researcher to tailor his proposals so that they conform to the kind of research that the agency is currently interested in fostering. (Population studies, for example, seem to be in vogue now.) This is clearly counter-productive to the creation of cumulative knowledge about international relations.

Another aspect of the financial structure of international relations research which slows down cumulation is the nature of the limitations many of the agencies set. Some simply state that their funds cannot be used to provide released time for the investigator but may be used only for research assistants and supplies. Others do not state this in principle but in practice show an extreme reluctance to provide such support. Some require that the recipient spend his tenure somewhere other than his home base, even if this is the best place to do the research. Others are reluctant to provide computer funds, assuming, erroneously, that computer time is a free good in all universities.

All these factors, the insufficiency of funds, the dependence on inconstant funding agencies, and the implicit and explicit limitations on how funds may be used, operate in such a manner that truly cumulative research is, at best, difficult.

COMMUNICATION PROBLEMS

Our communications network is clearly inadequate for the job that it must perform, if we are to be cumulative. It is inadequate in three ways. First, information is unevenly disseminated throughout the field; those who are distant from one of the structural nodes receive far less information about what others are doing than those who are close. Second, the transmission of information is too dependent on informal channels, such as the "mimeo circuit" and periodic but fleeting face-to-face discussions at conferences. If a person were restricted to only the formal part of our communications network—books and journals—for information about what others in the field are doing, he would be aware of only a fraction of the research which is being carried out, and even this fraction would be less useful, since it would represent research that was carried on one or more years ago, rather than what is current. The third principal problem with our communications network follows directly from the above. The formal channels have insufficient channel capacity for the job that they must perform, if more cumulative research is to be fostered. One of the consequences of this is the large publication lags that we are now witnessing.

INSTITUTIONAL LIMITATIONS

The basic research unit tends to be a "project," as contrasted with more permanent organizations like centers or institutes. This tendency seems es-

pecially pronounced in the quantitative parts of our field. Projects are usually short-lived and center around the activities of one or perhaps, at most, two individuals. If the individual or individuals move, the project moves also. Their financial base is composed of "soft" money and, therefore, especially susceptible to the vagaries of funding agencies. Several centers in the United States are involved in international relations research, but most seem to be oriented toward applied rather than basic research, and employ traditional rather than modern methods of inquiry.

The lack of sufficient institutional bases to support ongoing research activities has resulted in the adoption of the more ad hoc project organizational form. I suggest that such an organizational arrangement is not conducive to cumulative research in international relations. I think it encourages short-term, product-oriented research rather than concerted and sustained exploration of a particular problem area. The need to constantly justify one's work by the citation of results encourages the propagation of "point" knowledge rather than "pattern" knowledge. The latter contributes much more directly to cumulativeness than does the former.

ORGANIZATIONAL PROBLEMS

Although my experience is limited, it seems to me that the way we organize and carry out our research projects is clearly inefficient and suboptimal. Perhaps it is inherent in the knowledge generation process that affairs always seem to be on the edge of, and sometimes beyond, chaos, yet I am not convinced that this is necessarily so. It is easy to overstate the efficiency of business and military organizations, for example, yet it seems clear to me that, by and large, they are better organized and more efficient than we are when it comes to research activities. There are those who argue that research is a creative enterprise which does best in a relatively unfettered state, yet I suspect we pay a tremendous price for this freedom.

There are some powerful factors in operation which make efficient organization very difficult. Part-time employees, consultants, and volunteers make up a significant proportion of the work forces, and these groups tend to have a high turn-over rate. Since many of these individuals are students, a significant proportion of project funds essentially serve an educational function. Since the research work is largely defined in terms of individuals, rather than roles, changes in personnel inevitably introduce discontinuities in research within a particular project. The implications for this are that pressures are generated which work against a concerted, sustained, programmatic research effort, which is conducive to the accumulation of knowledge.

METHODOLOGICAL FACTORS

Methodological factors operate in two different ways to impede the accumulation of knowledge. The less important obstacle stems from the way we use our statistical tools. Too often, we have become fascinated with a particular analysis procedure and have selected problems which could be addressed using this method, rather than vice versa. Some of the most frequently used methods, correlation and contingency coefficients, for example, generate findings which are cumulative only in a propositional sense. In my own work on a computer simulation of international behavior, I found much of this correlational knowledge useless because it specifies only the *degree* of association, rather than the *functional nature* of the association. If one is building a propositional inventory, it is helpful. If, on the other hand, a more complex and integrated structure is desired, then additional information about the mathematical structure of the relationship is essential.

The second methodological impediment to cumulativeness concerns the type of tools that we have available. John Tukey, a prominent statistician, has frequently argued that statisticians have concentrated upon the easy problems which involve simple, linear, additive relationships between variables with random measurement error measured on a sample generated by random selection procedures. Tukey chides his fellow statisticians to direct more of their energies to problems where these conditions do not obtain, and if they do so, the social sciences are likely to be the principal beneficiaries. The implications for cumulativeness are that we often need to redefine problems in order to make them susceptible to analysis and when we put them back together, they do not quite cohere in the way they should. For example, it is awkward and difficult to introduce linear and nonlinear associations in the same model, threshold effects are hard to evaluate, and mixing nominal and interval variables in the same analysis is a very involved process. All these constraints distract us from the development of the theoretical considerations which are essential for cumulativeness.

In spite of what I have said, I do not think that, as a field, we have anything to apologize for with regard to our apparent lack of cumulativeness in international relations research. Given sufficient amounts of time, money, and manpower, virtually all of the problems I discussed above would disappear. After all, if it took billions of dollars, thousands of men, and more than a decade of concerted work to solve the relatively simple problem of getting men to the moon and back, what will be needed to solve the much more complex problem of establishing a reasonably high probability that our spacemen will have an earth to return to?

24. Environmental Fertility and Cumulative Growth

Russell J. Leng

Most of us would agree that the goal of social science is explanation for the purpose of controlling social phenomena, not just for the sake of knowing. The goal places a heavy burden on us because both knowing and controlling are more difficult in social science than in either the physical or biological sciences. The reasons for this are familiar to us all. Nonetheless, I think it is wise to begin a discussion of the problems of achieving scientific cumulation by recognizing the obvious—that we deal with a subject matter that places extraordinary strains on the scientific enterprise.

If we accept Boynton's definition of cumulation as occurring when "a second research effort on a topic can rely on findings of a first research effort in such a way that it does not have to start from scratch,"[1] it appears as an expected phase in the advancement of scientific knowledge from one level of discovery and validation to the next. This is not something that can be legislated or programmed. As Rosenau (1974) has suggested, cumulation is ultimately a matter of confidence, the confidence that one scientist has in another's work. The best that one can do to facilitate this is to provide a more fertile environment for research and discovery. My own opinion is that this would be an intellectually open environment, an environment which would not constrain imagination by doctrinaire methodological requirements.

The question then is "What can be done to increase the fertility of the environment without imposing contraints on the scientific enterprise?" I can think of five prominent requirements for the growth of cumulation which might be stimulated. These are (1) a large body of data accepted as valid and reliably generated, (2) accepted testing pro-

cedures appropriate to the research problem and available data, (3) a good deal of professional intercourse among scholars pursuing similar paths of investigation, (4) adequate support to allow scholars to commit themselves to long-term investigations, and, most important, (5) committed scholars of outstanding imagination, intelligence, and persistence.

I think it is safe to say that a decade ago there were virtually no empirical data on international conflict behavior. During the past ten years we have seen pioneering efforts to generate that data, beginning with the Stanford research on the pre-World War I crisis,[2] and the events data movement begun with McClelland's work on the WEIS project.[3] These efforts could be called breakthroughs, but because this was the first wave, it has been only natural that these data would have a limited life. The next wave of investigators found that the early data collections were not sufficiently discriminating to answer the more pointed questions they wished to ask. A question that has interested me, for example, has been the likelihood of compliance with different types of influence attempts. This was a question that could not be answered with data generated for more general analyses of the conflict process, so I constructed a new coding scheme (Leng and Singer, 1970), but in doing so I started where the previous efforts had left off. By the same token, when Legault, Stein, Sigler, and Steinberg (1974) launched the CADIC project for the comparative analysis of dyadic interstate conflict, with heavy stress on measuring the influence

[1] Quoted in Rosenau (1974, p. 14).

[2] The early work on the Stanford project was undertaken by Robert C. North, Ole Holsti, and Richard Brody. For an example see Holsti et al. (1968).

[3] For an early statement of the research design, see McClelland (1968).

of national objectives on conflict behavior, the earlier efforts served as the basis for new coding rules to meet the new data requirements. My point is that these efforts represent cumulation at the early stages of the scientific enterprise.

The major drawback to this is the enormous investment, both in time and money, that the generation of events data requires. In the first three years of my work on the Behavioral Correlates of War project, I estimate that over 80 percent of my time was devoted to the data generation effort. With this in mind, we attempted to construct a coding scheme to produce data which could be exploited for the testing of a variety of behavioral models of international conflict. We were "hedging our bets" with regard to where we expected our own research to take us and, at the same time, generating data of use to other scholars interested in studying conflict behavior. The data have been generated in a two-stage effort, with the first stage consisting of a verbal chronology of events, backed up by detailed "Conflict Summary Papers," describing the quality and possible biases of the data sources. Similar approaches have been taken by the WEIS, COPDAB,[4] and CADIC projects.

In a paper presented to the International Studies Association (Leng, 1975), I offered the following conclusions regarding the compatibility of extant events data generation efforts. First, that there is sufficient compatibility among major events data generation efforts today, with regard to the identification of international events and their principal components, to make an exchange of verbal chronologies worthwhile. And second, that it would not be difficult for the principal investigators of a number of events data projects to agree upon a standard format for verbal chronologies. If this could be done, a standard format could be published for the transmission of chronologies to a central archive, such as the Interuniversity Consortium for Political Research archive at the University of Michigan. Separate funding should be provided expressly for this purpose. If this could be done, it would result in an enormous reduction in expense without discour-

aging creativity in the construction of new coding schemes.

A second requirement for a cumulative scientific effort is a body of accepted testing procedures appropriate to the data being measured and the questions being asked. Like most of my colleagues, I consider myself a political scientist by choice and a statistician by necessity. Nevertheless, what knowledge of statistics I have has made me cautious about accepting the published results of scientific research on international conflict behavior, or international politics in general. Too often too much has been claimed for what appear to be questionable results, sometimes from dubious data. Fortunately, the changes that have been occurring the the last few years are cause for optimism. Besides some valuable new techniques which have begun to appear with increasingly regularity in the last few years,[5] students of international relations are becoming more and more aware of the possibilities—and problems—associated with statistical techniques from other disciplines, especially economics.

Nonetheless, I share Dina Zinnes's concern with an uninformed dependence on certain statistical techniques,[6] and I am even more concerned with what I see as a rather large gap between the few scholars using highly sophisticated mathematical and statistical techniques and the rest of the members of the field. As statistical advances and innovations increase, this gap will grow. The result may well be an increase in accessibility coupled with a decrease in relative knowledgeability. The answer to this problem seems straightforward enough: periodic, formal "re-tooling" is required by almost all of us. This is an accepted procedure in less intellectually prestigious occupations, for example, the airline industry. (Perhaps that is because the costs of ignorance are more visible.) I see no good reason it should not be expected in our own profession, especially when one considers the good fortune of having three months of every year conveniently set aside to allow for just such opportunities. My own career has benefited greatly from two such summer experiences. I think that it is in

---

[4] A brief description of the COPDA project appears in Azar (1974).

[5] A good example of this would be the nonparametric statistical routines developed recently by the Institute for Social Research at the University of Michigan.

[6] See Chapter 16.

the interest of the health of the profession for us to encourage both universities and outside funding agencies to place greater emphasis on the value of these efforts.

The third requirement for a cumulative science is professional interchange among scholars pursuing similar paths of investigation. History suggests that major discoveries occur most often when several scholars are tackling similar research problems. The traditional means of interchange of ideas is supposed to be the professional journal, but I doubt that anyone in the field needs to be reminded of the extraordinary time lag between the completion of a piece of research and the day when it appears in one of our journals. This is hardly an asset to hastening the process of cumulation. Yet finding some way of facilitating professional interchange may be one of the most practical means of hastening the process of replication and cumulation.

One of the most valuable inputs to my own research in conflict behavior, and I am sure, of many others, came from the 1970 and 1971 conferences on events data research at Michigan State University. The meeting of a relatively small group of researchers employing roughly the same methodology and, as it turned out, working at about the same stages of their respective investigations, produced a quality of interchange that I have not experienced at any other meetings. I think a good deal of the momentum the "events data movement" has achieved can be traced to those meetings. They were a far more effective way of exchanging ideas than our national conventions.

As for the fourth requirement, that of adequate support, I can add little that has not been said by others. "If only we had adequate funding" is the perpetual refrain of every man and woman with a research problem. Nevertheless, I suggest that the process of cumulation might be accelerated if funding priorities were directed more toward two ends. First, to provide adequate funding for those projects promising to produce data useful to a wide range of scholars, and, second, to provide smaller grants to scholars beginning new projects or experimenting with new methodological approaches.

This leads to the last and most important of the requirements for achieving scientific cumulation in international relations research, that is, engaging intelligent and imaginative scholars in the research effort. In addition to younger scholars at major universities, who may have the good fortune to become associated with one of the larger ongoing research efforts, there is an increasingly large number of very able young scholars at small colleges far from a research center who have not had an opportunity to commit their talents to an ongoing research effort. The neglect of their talents in a system Stuart Bremer has characterized as "quasi-feudal"[7] may be our greatest waste of resources. Increasing the number of summer re-tooling programs, as I suggested above, is one step which may be taken to encourage wider participation in the scientific enterprise. Another would be to urge funding agencies to offer and advertise a larger number of small "seed" grants for new research efforts. Few ingredients are more important to the growth of knowledge in any field than the continuing infusion of new perspectives and new ideas.

The foregoing suggestions are, at best, common-sensical ways of accelerating a process that cannot be controlled by benign intervention. The pace of cumulation in international relations research must be judged in light of the difficulties presented by the subject matter and the amount of time and effort that has been devoted to the scientific enterprise. If we take these variables into account, I think the progress that has been achieved to date is cause for excitement rather than despair. How much further we will be able to go in the foreseeable future will depend on the quality and quantity of scholars who commit their talents to the effort. As for recruiting able scholars, I think the challenge presented by the problems of international politics and our present lack of cumulative knowledge may well be the best incentives. All that remains is to provide the conditions to make a long-term commitment to serious research possible.

REFERENCES

Azar, Edward E. 1974. "Quantitative Events Research at the University of North Carolina." *International Studies Notes* 1 (Spring): 28-30.

[7]See Chapter 23.

Holsti, Ole R., Robert C. North, and Richard Brody. 1968. "Perception and Action in the 1914 Crisis." In *Quantitative International Politics,* ed. J. David Singer, pp. 123-58. New York: Free Press.

Legault, Albert, Janice Stein, John Sigler, and Blema Steinberg. 1974. "The Comparative Analysis of Dyadic Interstate Conflict: Project Description." Mimeo. Quebec: Centre Quebecois de Relations Internationales.

Leng, Russell J. 1975. "The Future of Events Data Marriages: A Question of Compatibility." *International Interactions* 2: 1-18.

——— and J. David Singer. 1970. "Toward a Multitheoretical Typology of International Behavior." Paper presented at the International Events Data Conference, Michigan State Univ.

McClelland, Charles A. 1968. "International Interaction Analysis: Basic Research Design and Some Practical Applications." World Event/Interaction Survey Technical Report No. 2. Mimeo. Los Angeles: Univ. of Southern California.

Rosenau, James N. 1974. "Success and Failure in Scientific International Relations Research: A Report on a Workshop." Mimeo. Los Angeles: Univ. of Southern California.

25. Cumulation, Cooperation, and Commitment
Wayne Richard Martin

One of the most important questions raised at the Santa Monica Conference on Cumulation in Scientific International Relations was whether research in international relations can be considered scientific if it does not cumulate substantive knowledge within the framework of a general theory. The concern was that scientific research requires evidence of a linked series of deductive and interdependent propositions to which research adds, and that in the discipline of international relations there is no clear evidence of such an accomplishment. In the words of the NSF director for political research, G. R. Boynton, "I see a significant problem for our discipline."

The concern over the noncumulativeness and the nonscientific features of much international relations research has been expressed previously (Levy, 1969; Rosenau, 1971), and the intent of the Santa Monica conference was to consider if there has been a failure to accumulate rapidly a substantive knowledge of international relations. As one might expect, the factors perceived to inhibit cumulation were not agreed upon completely by the conference attendees, although there was an impressive degree of shared concern.

INTERNATIONAL RELATIONS THEORY

The study of international relations is in a period of transition in which the systematic analysis of particular concepts is replacing attempts, at least temporarily, to integrate the study of international relations into a single theoretical framework (McClelland, 1972a). This problem orientation of current research is data-based, technically oriented, and directed toward the testing of limited ranges of concepts. Examples of the products of such research can be found throughout the current journal literature in the discipline, and a recently published collection of abstracts from a number of data-based studies provides a good review of some of this research (Jones and Singer, 1972). While there is ample evidence of the rigor in many contemporary studies, the question still remains whether these research efforts provide evidence of a cumulation of substantive international relations knowledge. In disagreement with some of the conference members, I believe that significant progress has been made in the development of a scientific approach to the study of international relations, and that this progress can be found in both the attitudes of many of those involved in international relations research and in the products of their labor.

One indication of the scientific direction of current research is the acceptance of the argument that although international relations problems appear complex they are amenable, nevertheless, to description and explanation. Scholars are identifying problem areas (escalation processes, crisis behavior, threat processes, rank disequilibrium, national-international linkages, etc.) in which traditional concerns have been high and statements of explanation frequent, and testing these statements as hypotheses for the expected relationships with historical or simulated data and systematic research procedures. The results of these efforts have included an increased likelihood that unsupported statements can be eliminated from the international relations lore, the production of a growing body of tested hypotheses (a few of which have been supported in replicative studies), an increasing familiarity with the data with which we must work, and a growing understanding of the techniques of analysis most suitable for international relations analysis. There is also increased confidence that a rigorously supported body of descriptive and explanatory statements can be accumulated for a number of interesting and important international relations phenomena, and that these supportable statements can be used to build international relations theory.

The inability of the observer, or the researcher for that matter, to easily link together this work within a general theoretical framework should not be taken as a sign of weakness at this time, but rather as an indication that research is in progress and that the assumed complexity of international politics is under attack. Furthermore, it seems premature to suggest that there has been a failure among international relations scholars to apply the scientific method correctly to their problem solving and thus to conclude that the lack of cumulative knowledge can be laid to such a failure. It is noted in several of the other Santa Monica conference papers that international relations research is poorly funded, lacks fully developed channels of communication, and is undermanned. It can also be pointed out that the scientific study of international relations is nascent, and that all of

these factors tend to inhibit rapid advancement. The apparent complexity of international politics, the lack of accumulated substantive findings, and the absence of a general theory are not due to a failure to apply the scientific method properly during the past ten years; they are instead evidence of the state of the art, which in no way should be taken as a gauge of either the direction or objectives of the individuals involved in international relations research.

This point is especially important for those who deem it necessary to explain "how science is done." There may be more than one approach to improving our substantive knowledge of international relations and members of the discipline must be cautious in their desire to guide and direct the work in the field. The history of international relations research *looks* like a series of Kuhnian "revolutions," and the discipline is not one bit better off for all of this activity. While it is necessary for scholars to provide critical evaluations of theory and research offerings within their discipline, major confrontations among international relations scholars have done more to restrict than to build international relations theory. The unnecessary bitterness of the disputes has split departments and harmed both colleague and faculty-student rapport. Major confrontations have created unnecessary debates among specialists and discouraged the transfer of knowledge.

The vigorous demand by some scholars for perfect, abstract, parsimonious, and general international relations theory is easy to understand, but not very easy to accomplish. There is no need to stress this point unduly, but if international relations theory is to take on the above characteristics a great deal more must be understood about international relations processes, and it is premature at this time to suggest that any one approach is more likely than any other to provide such understanding. The utility of a concept, method, procedure for analysis, or a data set must be proved by repeated tests and against new cases or situations. Argument itself without such tests is simply unproductive as well as unscientific. Contemporary international relations research shows a lack in not integrating other research in a cumulative and developmental manner not only because there is poor communication among international relations scholars, as others have pointed out, but also because there is a general failure to examine concepts and hypotheses cooperatively without demanding the predominance of any one approach before rigorous testing is begun.

CUMULATION WITHOUT A GENERAL THEORY

Without a general theory to guide international relations research, specialists in the field have directed much of their attention toward identifying the area of study which should provide the best explanation of international relations phenomena. There are three main outlooks. First there is the contention that the study of international relations should focus on the international politics of nation-states. Second, there is the approach which says that the concept of international politics is outdated and should be replaced by models and conceptualizations of a world society (Burton, 1972). And finally, there is the widely shared view "that across-systems-level theory has much greater explanatory power than within-systems-level theory" (Rosenau, 1973).

There is good reason to support the notion that of the three perspectives the focus on the nation and its international politics offers the best potential for providing a base from which a cumulative knowledge of international relations can be systematically and rapidly built. Sims (1973) has made a strong argument that a focus on "atomistic" approaches (territorial permeability, informal penetration, and linkage politics), world society perspectives, or "great power" relations, while "useful in themselves, have all complicated the status of the formal diplomatic system by calling into question its composition, autonomy, and supremacy" (p. 285). Sims does not argue that the international system is static nor that scholars should pay no attention to non-state actors. He does stress, however, that interstate relations still dominate the international system, and that these relations "remain the most useful point of departure, and point of reference, for those who seek to understand human behavior that involves the passage of state boundaries" (p. 287.)

I fully agree with Sims that we have failed generally to provide an adequate understanding of international politics as political interactions among states. We do have a number of unlinked quantitative analyses of crises interactions, alliance patterns, arms races, and so forth, but nowhere in our work is to be found a complete body of knowledge which describes or explains systematically and thoroughly how nation-states relate to other nation-states. Where does the student or policy analyst go, for example, when he wants an explanation or even a description of the "typical" activity of a state in the international system over time and during peace, crisis, or war? There is no complete and rigorous typology of international threats or threat relations. There is no data-based model for identifying reliably international commitments. In fact we almost completely lack the ability to answer, with systematic empirical analysis, the important questions which have been asked traditionally about international relations. Simply stated, we have very few adequate findings, models, or data on international politics. It might indeed be very productive cumulatively for the discipline if we worked on finding answers to these questions, and for the present concentrated our research efforts on accumulating information and knowledge about international politics.

We can report that research is in progress which should greatly increase our ability to describe and reliably explain international politics. Among the most important of these efforts is events data analysis. Events data analysts have conceptualized national foreign policy output as the international control or regulatory behavior of national decision-making processes. Preliminary work in this area has shown that the foreign policy outputs of states can be observed and measured, and that national foreign policy behavior can be characterized (McClelland et al., 1967) and even tested against hypotheses about interstate behavior (Rummel, 1968; Tanter, 1966; Wilkenfeld et al., 1972). Research findings from events data analyses and the data sets and category schemes for these data are under intensive examination, and there is evidence that work in progress will contribute cumulatively to our knowledge of international relations.

The success of events data analysis is important for more than just its substantive contribution to international relations knowledge. Events data analysis is also important as an indicator of the amount of investment that must be made in time, money, and effort to accomplish even preliminary research findings. There are at least 11 major events data research projects that have surfaced recently (Burgess and Lawton, 1972), and among these projects only a relatively few substantive findings can be counted at this time. While researchers within each of the projects may see a tremendous potential for events data research, others view the paucity of substantive output more critically. This is an important recognition, but not an indication of failure. The inherent difficulty in producing rigorously substantiated international relations findings suggests that before we are able to collect a storehouse full of interrelated knowledge we will need concentrated research efforts on specific conceptual problems, cooperative sponsorship of large-scale data collection projects, continuous and progressive empirical testing, and a general understanding that the cumulation of substantive international relations findings, even within limited conceptual foci, will come only after arduous and long-term research efforts.

If there is a significant problem of noncumulation in the field of international relations, it is due in part to a general failure among international relations scholars to carry through to completion their research efforts in this period of transition. Too often we find evidence of the collection of incomplete data sets, partially tested propositions, incomplete models, and findings so inadequately tested that other researchers are unwilling or unable to accept the work as a basis for their own. The events data movement is perhaps an exception to this general observation. The events data movement is now ten years old (McClelland, 1972b), and while a great body of substantive findings has not yet come from this research, the directed and focused work of the individuals involved in events data research, the cooperativeness evident in the enterprise, the adherence to long range research objectives, and its direct focus on international politics promises great payoff for the study of international relations.

REFERENCES

Burgess, Philip M., and Raymond W. Lawton. 1972. *Indicators of International Behavior: An Assessment of Events Data Research.* Beverly Hills.: Sage.

Burton, John. 1972. *World Society.* Cambridge: At the Univ. Press.

Jones, Susan D., and J. David Singer. 1972. *Beyond Conjecture in International Politics: Abstracts of Data-based Research.* Itasca, Ill.: Peacock.

Levy, Marion J., Jr. 1969. " 'Does it Matter If He's Naked?' Bawled the Child." In *Contending Approaches to International Politics,* ed. Klaus Knorr and James N. Rosenau, pp. 87-109. Princeton: Princeton Univ. Press.

McClelland, Charles A. 1967. "The Communist Chinese Performance in Crisis and Noncrisis: Quantitative Studies of the Taiwan Straits Confrontation, 1950-1964." China Lake, Calif.: U.S. Naval Ordnance Test Station.

———. 1972a. "On the Fourth Wave: Past and Future in the Study of International Systems." In *The Analysis of International Politics,* ed. James N. Rosenau, Vincent Davis, and Maurice A. East, pp. 15-40. New York: Free Press.

———. 1972b. "Some Effects on Theory from the International Events Analysis Movement." In *International Events Interaction Analysis,* ed. Edward E. Azar, Richard A. Brody, and Charles A. McClelland, pp. 15-41. Beverly Hills: Sage.

Rosenau, James N. 1971. *The Scientific Study of Foreign Policy.* New York: Free Press.

———. 1973. "Theorizing across Systems: Linkage Politics Revisited." In *Conflict Behavior and Linkage Politics,* ed. Jonathan Wilkenfeld, pp. 25-56. New York: McKay.

Rummel, R.J. 1968. "The Relationship between National Attributes and Foreign Conflict Behavior." In *Quantitative International Politics,* ed. J. David Singer, pp. 187-214. New York: Free Press.

Sims, N. A. 1973. "Implications of Commitment: Reflections on the Study of International Relations in Britain." *International Relations* 4 (May): 274-85.

Tanter, Raymond. 1966. "Dimensions of Conflict Behavior within and between Nations, 1958-1960." *Journal of Conflict Resolution* 10 (Mar): 41-64.

Wilkenfeld, Jonathan, Virginia Lee Lussier, and Dale Tahitinen. 1972. "Conflict Interactions in the Middle East, 1949-1967." *Journal of Conflict Resolution* 16 (Jun): 135-54.

Part Three

Comparative Foreign Policy

Substantive Perspectives

26. The Future of Comparative Studies: An Evangelical Plea

Patrick J. McGowan

A discussion of the future of a field of study presupposes that the field already exists. While I have no difficulty with this presupposition, many readers of this chapter may well doubt that a distinct field of comparative foreign policy analysis has an existence, much less a future. On the basis of experience, I believe a strong case can be made that comparative foreign policy studies now comprise a significant field of policy research, linking comparative and international politics.[1] Thus, let us first establish the fact that our field exists and then proceed to describe its salient characteristics before we offer normative proposals about its future.

SPECIAL NOTE: An earlier version of this paper was presented to the Summer Workshop of the Inter-university Comparative Foreign Policy (ICFP) Project, June 1973. Thanks are due the Department of Political Science, Syracuse University, and the School of Politics and International Relations, University of Southern California, for financial support. I wish also to thank Stewart S. Johnson, who helped in the revisions of the present chapter.

[1] These experiences have been (1) my participation in the ICFP group since 1969, (2) my collaboration with James N. Rosenau and John V. Gillespie in editing the recent ICFP volume (Rosenau, 1974), (3) my coauthorship of a volume that surveys the empirical literature, *The Comparative Study of Foreign Policy* (McGowan and Shapiro, 1973), and (4) my editorship since 1972 of the *Sage International Yearbook of Foreign Policy Studies* (McGowan, 1973).

A DEFINITION OF COMPARATIVE FOREIGN POLICY STUDIES

Rosenau (1968) once asked if comparative foreign policy was a fad, field, or fantasy. He concluded that some fantastic claims had been made, that faddish practices were being engaged in, but that in the end a field could and should emerge as long as it was conceived of as "the comparative study of foreign policy" and not "comparative foreign policy." Rosenau argued that our movement was primarily methodological in direction, that we were engaged in applying the comparative method to the study of foreign policy and that no substantive field called comparative foreign policy exists or could exist. Readers familiar with controversies in the allied field of "comparative politics" will find nothing new about all of this. I, for one, agree with Rosenau. Since no intelligible difference can be made between the comparative and scientific study of naturally occurring political phenomena, the scientific study of foreign policy and comparative foreign policy studies are synonymous terms signifying the same set of activities.[2] However, it may be wiser for us to talk about the comparative study of foreign policy, for the use of "comparative" probably does not create expectations in others that the use of "scientific" does. Be this as it may, I shall henceforth assume that as practitioners of the comparative study of foreign policy we have made the *value choice* of accepting the scientific method as the "best" way to study foreign policy.

It should be noted that I have said that we accept *the* scientific method, not *a* scientific method. This, if you will, puts my epistemological cards on the table. I hold what the philosophers of

science call a nonseparatist doctrine, that there is only one scientific methodology, that there is only one way of producing and communicating knowledge in a scientific manner (Rudner, 1966; Graham, 1971; Mayer, 1972). To quote an economic theorist (Mansfield, 1970, p. 15):

> This methodology is much the same ... in any ... type of scientific analysis, the basic procedure being the formulation of models. A model is composed of a number of assumptions from which conclusions—or predictions—are deduced. For example, suppose that we wanted to formulate a model of the solar system. We might represent each of the planets by a point in space, and we might make the assumption that each would change position in accord with certain mathematical equations. Based on this model, we might predict when an eclipse would occur.

Thus, nonseparatists believe that the *intellectual* and *social* activities of stating assumptions, deducing consequences, empirically checking these predictions, and reporting the results are logically similar whether the subject matter be solar eclipses, market demand, or foreign policy interventions. Scientific fields certainly vary in their research technology—compare the cloud chamber to the sample survey—but not in their methodology.

Thus, the field of the comparative study of foreign policy represents the activities of researchers around the world who study what they call foreign policy by using scientific methods of inquiry. *The objective of comparative studies of foreign policy is to state and to check against systematically created data general, explanatory sentences about the causes and consequences of foreign policy behavior.* We do this because of our value commitment to scientific methodology as the preferred way to produce knowledge. Since there is only one scientific methodology, we agree that relevant knowledge represents empirically based findings about the external behavior of states that are hierarchically organized by a theoretical structure of deductively related generalizations.

It goes without saying that many students of foreign policy phenomena do not share this *value commitment* to the scientific method nor do they share the *philosophical doctrine* of the unity of scientific method which is its basis. A comparison of *Foreign Affairs* and *Foreign Policy* to *The Journal of Peace Research* and *The International*

---

[2] As Almond (1970, p. 254) has remarked in this regard with respect to "comparative politics": "Comparison, whether it be in the experiment, in the analysis of the results of quantitative surveys, or in the observation of process and behavior in different contexts in the real world, is the very essence of the scientific method. It makes no sense to speak of a comparative politics in political science, since if it is a science, it goes without saying that it is comparative in its approach."

Or, to quote another authority of even greater prestige: "For anyone with a scientific approach to political phenomena the idea of an independent comparative method seems redundant. Isn't the scientific approach unavoidably to verify generalizations by comparing all relevant data?" (Lasswell, 1968, p. 3).

Studies Quarterly will confirm this. Depending upon one's values, this pluralism is healthy or pathological, but diagnosis of the state of foreign policy studies in general is not my concern in this chapter. I am only concerned with that part of the broader field which goes under the name of the comparative (scientific) study of foreign policy and I hope by now it is clear what I mean by that term.

THE SOCIOLOGY OF THE FIELD

Having defined our subject matter, I shall now try to describe some of its principal characteristics. Howard Shapiro and I recently completed a book in which we attempted to survey the findings of all comparative studies of foreign policy we could identify (McGowan and Shapiro, 1973). Together, I am sure we have read most, but probably not all, publications that met our criteria of being comparative studies of foreign policy.[3] Our effort and the bibliographies in McGowan (1973, 1974a) provide the data base for my subsequent comments.

We surveyed 326 articles, books, and dissertations published between 1940 and late 1973. Two facts are immediately apparent about our list of publications. First, all but three titles were published in English, although this was not a criterion for inclusion. There probably are some studies in the major European and Asiatic languages which we missed in our survey, and several items in our list are translations into English, but our finding replicates that of Jones and Singer (1972) who abstracted data-based articles in the general field of international politics. That the independent efforts of two teams of writers agree almost exactly suggests that very little work on foreign policy or international politics of a scientific sort is being done outside the English-speaking world. As I shall point out shortly, scholars who are engaged in systematic foreign policy research are not all members of the narrow Churchillian "English Speaking Peoples," but if their mother

tongue is Hindi or Swedish, they tend to publish in English anyway. I, for one, am surprised by the relative scarcity of French, and the complete lack of Spanish- and German-language works. This suggests that our field is narrowly parochial, for not only is nearly all the work apparently being done in English, but the vast majority of our authors are North Americans. On the other hand, one might optimistically argue that "social scientific English" has become the worldwide language of scholarly communication in our field, as Latin was at one time in other fields, and that this should ease the burden of scientific communication. In my view there is evidence to support both arguments.

The second fact of some interest is that we were not able to identify a single work published prior to 1940 which met our criteria, nor did we find more than six which were published before 1960. As Table 1 illustrates, our field of inquiry is quite new, with real growth in scholarly output only getting under way in 1963. Another way to view this fact is to note the publication dates of the "readers" and books of essays which were a

Table 1. Frequency of Comparative Publications on Foreign Policy

Pub. Date	Number	Percent
1940	2	0.6
1949	1	0.3
1952	2	0.6
1959	1	0.3
1960	4	1.2
1961	4	1.2
1962	4	1.2
1963	9	2.8
1964	10	3.1
1965	17	5.2
1966	13	4.0
1967	27	8.3
1968	25	7.7
1969	37	11.4
1970	34	10.4
1971	36	11.0
1972	58	17.8
1973 (incomplete)	42	12.9
TOTAL	326	100.0

Source: Reference and bibliography sections of McGowan and Shapiro (1973) and McGowan (1973, 1974a).

[3]These criteria were (1) the works must be published, (2) the works must be data-based, but not necessarily quantitative, (3) the works had to be comparative, examining two or more cases, (4) the works must relate two or more variables, one of which had to be the external behavior of nation-states.

frequent source of surveyed works: (Kelman, 1965; Rosenau, 1967; Singer, 1968; Kriesberg, 1968; Butwell, 1969; Rosenau, 1969a, 1969b; Gillespie and Nesvold, 1971; Hanrieder, 1971; Hermann, 1972; and Wilkenfeld, 1973). The histogram of Figure 1 is another way to present these data. The growth curve of the field of comparative foreign policy studies is clearly similar to the exponential law (or the law of natural growth, $Q = Q_O e^{at}$), found in so many fields (Bertalanffy, 1968, pp. 60-63) and known to be descriptive of growth in human knowledge (Hersh, 1942).

These publishing trends are likely to continue throughout the 1970s. A new journal edited by Edward Azar of the University of North Carolina, *International Interactions,* and the present author's new annual, *The Sage International Yearbook of Foreign Policy Studies,* appeared in 1973;

each features comparative studies of foreign policy. Moreover, many books related to our field are in press or recently published (Rummel, 1972; Russett, 1972; McGowan and Shapiro, 1973; Rosenau, 1974; Kegley et al., 1975). Thus, judged solely by the criterion of quantitative output, a field of comparative foreign policy studies has unquestionably emerged.

We can learn more about the sociology of the field by looking at where these works have been published. All of the books cited in the previous paragraph were published in the United States and 11 out of 16 by three publishing houses (Sage, 5; Free Press, 4; McKay, 2). Thus by this standard not only is our field parochial, it is also an oligopoly. The picture is somewhat brighter, however, when we turn to the journals that published the original articles we surveyed.

Figure 1. Growth of Scientific Publications on Foreign Policy

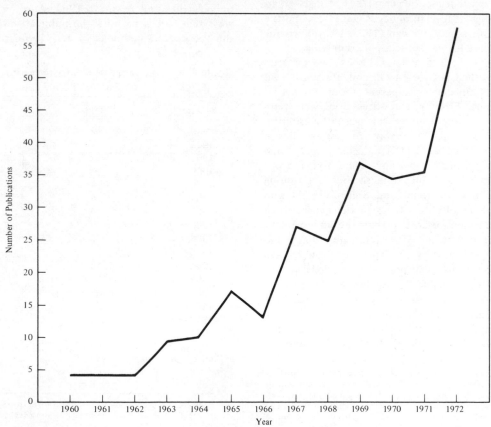

Far more diversity is apparent in Table 2 than in the data we have so far presented. While 16 journals and yearbooks account for 88 percent of our surveyed articles, 22 other journals contributed at least one article. Again, all but one are English-language reviews, but three are edited outside North America, two in Norway: *The Journal of Peace Research* and *Cooperation and Conflict;* one in Great Britain: *Journal of Common Market Studies.* Quite significant, I think, for the sociology of our field is the prominent place of three journals which account for 37 percent of all our articles. Three of the top four journals are explicitly devoted to the normative concerns of peace research and conflict resolution.

In part, their high rank is caused by the willingness of their editors to publish complex quantitative type studies before more traditional journals such as *World Politics,, International Organization,* and *Orbis* were willing to accept this type of work.

On the other hand, their large contribution to the comparative literature on foreign policy represents *prima facie* evidence that our field contains many scholars with strong commitments to normatively oriented research. Moreover, this concern with peace research is not in any way inconsistent with our earlier definition of our field. There is no logical reason why the methodology of science cannot be applied to normative questions like war and peace; indeed the history of science shows that scientific fields and applied problem solving have often developed together. What has been amiss is that the wrong problems are often attacked with the tools of science. But however one feels about that issue, I would argue that our evidence does demonstrate the existence of a field of study we can call the comparative (scientific) study of foreign policy.

Our field now comprises what I estimate as somewhat over 150 active researchers, located

Table 2.   Journals and Yearbooks Publishing Comparative Studies of Foreign Policy, 1940-1973

Rank	Journal/Yearbook	Number of Articles	Percent
1.0	*Journal of Peace Research* (Olso)[a]	27	15
2.0	*Journal of Conflict Resolution* (New Haven)	23	13
3.5	*Peace Science Society Papers* (Philadelphia)	15	9
3.5	*International Studies Quarterly* (Vancouver)	15	9
5.5	*American Political Science Review* (Berkeley)	13	7
5.5	*World Politics* (Princeton)	13	7
7.5	*International Organization* (Boston)	10	6
7.5	*Sage International Yearbook of Foreign Policy Studies* (Syracuse)	10	6
9.5	*Orbis* (Philadelphia)	5	3
9.5	*Western Political Quarterly* (Salt Lake City)	5	3
11.0	*Cooperation and Conflict* (Oslo)	4	2
13.0	*Études Internationales* (Quebec)	3	2
13.0	*General Systems Yearbook* (Ann Arbor)	3	2
13.0	*Journal of Politics* (University, Ala.)	3	2
15.5	*Journal of Common Market Studies* (Oxford)	2	1
15.5	*Social Science Quarterly* (Austin, Tex.)	2	1
	SUBTOTAL	153	88
	Journals with only one article	22	12
	TOTAL	175	100

[a]Cities in parentheses indicate where the publication was edited as of December 1973, not necessarily where it is published.
Source: Reference and bibliography sections of McGowan and Shapiro (1973) and McGowan (1973, 1974a).

primarily in North America and Scandinavia.[4] This is a small but productive group of people, largely male, white, middle-class, and English-speaking. In these respects it is no different from the broader field of political science. However, the smaller number of researchers is distinct, for they are tied together by personal acquaintance, personal communication networks, and face-to-face encounters at such events as the annual meetings of the International Studies Association each spring and the Peace Science Society (International) meetings each fall. Sociologically, we must often appear to be an invisible college, with all the odious implications that this term represents.

The data we have examined indicate that our field is a recent development of the 1960s. A significant turning point in its history was Rosenau's well-known essay "Pre-theories and Theories of Foreign Policy," written and widely circulated in 1964 and published two years later (Rosenau, 1966). The comparative study of foreign policy would seem to be characterized by normative commitments to the application of scientific methods in foreign policy studies (as persuasively argued by Rosenau in 1966) and to peace research (as that is rather idiosyncratically defined by each researcher).

MAIN CHARACTERISTICS OF PREVIOUS COMPARATIVE FOREIGN POLICY RESEARCH

In order to more fully understand the intellectual characteristics of a field of inquiry we must have some sort of a conceptual framework or typology whose categories will provide boxes into which we can sort the variety of studies that comprise our field. Figure 2 presents the framework that Shapiro and I found useful in undertaking our *Survey* (1973). Foreign policy patterns represent measured official outputs of states. These are seen to be "caused" by features of the decision-making system and by nine attribute variables of the society.

Individual attributes, such as biological factors, relate to leadership personality and other features

[4]The geographical distribution of specialists in our field is underscored by the fact that only one paper by a non-U.S. citizen was submitted for consideration in the first edition of my *Yearbook*.

unique to the decision maker (Wiegele, 1973). Elite variables, such as the proportion of military men in the elite, measure the aggregate characteristics of the group of people who make policy. Establishment variables refer to the organizational features of a state's foreign policy departments, their size, level of bureaucratization, or internal competition. Political attributes refer to political processes such as the competitiveness of the party system as measured by changes in party control, whereas governmental variables refer to structural features of the polity such as the form of government—presidential or parliamentary. Economic, societal, and cultural attributes measure concepts often dealt with by economists, sociologists, and anthropologists such as wealth, modernization, and religion. Finally, linkages refer to past foreign policies which determine current behavior.

The national society itself and its foreign policies may be "influenced" by three "external" factors. First are the policies of other societies directed specifically at the actors under investigation. Second are changes in the structure and processes of the international system and subsystems to which the states studied belong, such as the degree of polarity or the density of international organizations in the systems. Finally, the actor may be "affected" by its own policies almost simultaneously (F_1) or indirectly via their impact on its environment (F_2). The framework is elaborated in more detail in our *Survey* (McGowan and Shapiro, 1973, chap. 2), here I want to use it merely to focus on what we have been studying over the past dozen years.

Shapiro and I were able to formulate 118 propositions on the basis of the innumerable findings contained in the 203 comparative studies of foreign policy surveyed. These propositions range from the rather trivial No. 51, "The greater a nation's population size and density, the greater its support of the United Nations," to the very vague No. 78, "Variations in the external environment tend to be related to variations in foreign policy over time." However, interesting and complex propositions were also established such as Nos. 18 and 67, "The less the political unity of a state, the less are its aggressive tendencies" and "The existence of an alliance increases the possibility of a

Figure 2. A Framework for Comparative Foreign Policy Analysis

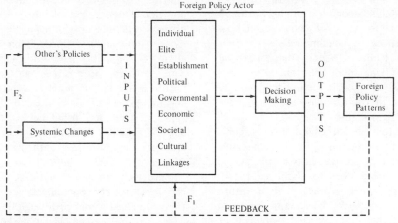

Source: McGowan and Shapiro (1973, p. 41).

nation supporting its ally (and becoming involved in conflict) according to the terms of the pact between them." Whatever the vagaries of our propositions, what is now in question is how they distribute themselves over the categories provided by Figure 2.

Table 3 gives us a frequency distribution of recent research across the 13 variable clusters. Each category represents a chapter in our survey and in every case we framed propositions to cover as many discrete findings as possible without reference to the total number under each variable cluster. It is evident from the table that there is no single type of independent variable that dominates the attention of systematic foreign policy research. To the extent that there is one, it is the combined cluster of political and governmental variables, for our distinction between process (political) and structural (governmental) attributes of political systems is surely artificial. If we combine these two categories, they account together for 23 propositions or 19.5 percent of the total.

On the other hand, several types of independent variables have received scanty attention at best. The elite category has been most neglected, but the variable clusters relative to establishment, individual, and cultural variables have not been well researched either. In part this may be accounted for by the relative difficulty of gathering data on individuals which is necessary for three of

these clusters—individual, elite, and aspects of the cultural. Let us look more closely at the work done in each category.

One caveat must be immediately introduced. Since this is intended as a critical essay, I shall dwell more on the weaknesses of the literature than on its several strengths. Given this proviso, what do we find?

Research on individual characteristics of leaders which relates measured individual traits to foreign

Table 3. Distribution of Comparative Foreign Policy Propositions by Conceptual Categories

Conceptual Category	Number	Percent
Individual variables	5	4.2
Elite variables	2	1.7
Establishment variables	4	3.4
Political variables	13	11.0
Governmental variables	10	8.5
Economic variables	10	8.5
Societal variables	8	6.8
Cultural variables	6	5.1
Linkage variables	10	8.5
Others' policies	9	7.6
Systemic variables	15	12.7
Decision-making variables	13	11.0
The feedback process	13	11.0
TOTAL	118	100.0

Source: McGowan and Shapiro (1973).

policy behavior is technically very sophisticated but limited to the work of the Stanford Group of Robert North and his associates on the outbreak of World War I. Thus, what we know about how idiosyncratic features of leaders relate to their policies is mainly limited to one crisis situation. What about other leaders in different situations, including noncrises? While the methodological and technical expertise of the Stanford team can serve as a model to us all, we must admit that we know very little of a systematic sort about this category.

Shapiro and I found only five comparative studies that related collective elite attributes to their policies. We were able to frame only two propositions for this cluster. Given the attention devoted to elites in sociological and political science literatures, this is shocking. At present we know next to nothing about how this category may affect foreign policy.

Almost as harsh a conclusion can be reached for the establishment cluster where we were able to come up with only four propositions. Studies of "bureaucratic politics and foreign policy" are very much *à la mode* at present, but of course they have so far utterly failed to be comparative between countries and they are rarely comparative over time within a single state (e.g., Halperin and Kanter, 1973). Hence, they are not scientific by our criteria. I believe that this category is potentially very fruitful, but until it becomes comparative its input will be minimal. For example, the following proposition cries out to be tested: "The influence a foreign aid donor gains in determining the domestic and foreign policies of the recipient state is inverse to the bureaucratic capabilities of the recipient." What we do know about the influence of organizations on foreign policy derives largely from comparisons of the U.S. and the U.S.S.R. Nothing of worth seems to have been done on the less modern states. Moreover, the field of public administration has apparently added nothing to our stock of hypotheses or findings.

The conceptual category of political variables is the best researched in our field. Three propositions, because of adequate replication, are fairly well established. First, the works of Rummel (1963, 1967, 1968), Tanter (1966), East and Gregg (1967), Jensen (1969), and Weede (1970) all support the proposition "There is little or no relationship between domestic conflict and foreign conflict at one point in time." Second, the rather diverse research of Collins (1967), Haas (1965), Gregg and Banks (1965), Feierabend and Feierabend (1969), and Wilkenfeld (1969, 1971) gives support to the proposition "For certain classes of nations, there is a positive relationship between certain types of domestic conflict and certain types of foreign conflict behavior at one point in time." Finally, Wilkenfeld's work (1969, 1971) and his collaboration with Zinnes (Zinnes and Wilkenfeld, 1971) demonstrate the proposition "For certain classes of nations, there is a positive relationship between some types of domestic conflict and some types of foreign behavior at a lag of one and/two years." What has happened here is most interesting. A bit of conventional wisdom, that domestic and foreign conflict are related, was put to a series of empirical tests and found wanting. Then, modifications were introduced. Instead of looking at all states for which data were available, types of states and types of domestic and foreign conflict were introduced into the analysis. It was found that the traditional wisdom did hold, but only for certain classes of states. Finally, time lags were used with similar results. This is the one really cumulative research area in our literature and I urge that these studies be reexamined for what they can teach us about how to *do* social science, despite any individual faults they may contain.

However, other than this rather bright spot, the political category shows many gaps. In particular, except for a few over-time case studies of single countries, little has been done to relate such interesting phenomena as interest groups, political parties, and civil wars to foreign policy behavior.

The category of government variables, including such national attributes as size and political accountability, has been extensively researched, but it does not manifest the cumulative results associated with research on domestic and foreign conflict behavior. In addition, little attempt has been made to use the many typologies of political systems as developed by Almond and Powell (1966), Apter (1965), Shils (1962), and others in comparative research on foreign policy.

The cluster of economic variables as they relate to foreign policy behavior is an interesting category. Ten propositions, such as No. 44, "The greater a nation's trade, the more ties of other kinds it will have with other nations," have been researched with some degree of replication. In contrast to the preceding category, the economic variables are often precisely defined, such as Gross National Product and total trade (exports and imports). It would appear that the superior empirical specification of concepts and the degree of replication so far achieved are the consequence of the superiority and relative availability of economic data in comparison to many other categories in our framework.

When we come to societal variables we find that most research has related population measures, such as size and density, to foreign policy outputs. Many central concepts in the sociological literature like social stratification, anomie, ethnic conflict, and modernization have not yet received the attention they deserve. The concentration on demographic aspects of societies would appear to be the consequence of using what data is at hand rather than as the result of theoretical concerns.

Very little work indeed has been accomplished on cultural variables and their relationships to foreign policy behavior. Shapiro and I were able to frame only six propositions for this category, and some of them, such as No. 57, "There is a relationship between a nation's religious composition and its voting in the United Nations," are vague and of little apparent theoretical import. Cross-cultural comparison is a basic aspect of our methodology (see Przeworski and Teune, 1970), yet explicit attention to cultural differences has been lacking. We were surprised to find no use as yet of the concept of political culture as developed by Almond and Verba (1963) in the field of scientific studies of foreign policy. An attempt to examine variables from the culture cluster for black Africa by the present author illustrates the difficulties of valid measurement in this cluster (McGowan and Lewis, 1973).

The cluster of linkage variables—the state's past behavior as it determines present behavior—has been studied to a considerable extent. However, replication has been scanty and studies of the relative potencies of different types of linkages in "causing" foreign policy are regrettably rare. The linkage concept is especially fruitful because it forces the analyst to think in dynamic terms, how behavior now (t) is influenced by past behavior (t-n). But our field remains exceedingly cross-sectional, where all variables are measured at one point in time. Diachronic and truly longitudinal studies are infrequent and much needed if we are to check against data the dynamic theories of foreign policy we seek to construct.

There has been a variety of research on the influence of other's policies on states' foreign policies. However, other's policies can be used in two ways: (1) to predict the foreign policy of the targets and (2) to predict the domestic policies of the targets. In the light of this, not much research has been done. Moreover, concepts that are widely referred to such as spheres of influence, intervention, and penetration, which are all instances of this class of variables, have not been systematically investigated.

The systemic cluster contains a rather rich literature which yielded 15 propositions, the most frequently recorded category. Proposition No. 81 is typical: "The greater the amount of status discrepancy in the international system, the greater the level of foreign policy conflict," which is both specific and theoretically interesting (East, 1972; Wallace, 1971). However, it must be noted that little replication has been achieved so far for this category.

Feedback is an important category because it compels the analyst to ask what difference different policies have for the acting state and its environment. As research on foreign policy has become more systematic, there has been a tendency to adopt the behavioralist research design where a dependent policy variable is accounted for by a set of independent ecological variables. Thus, if one compares the research designs of much voting behavior research (e.g., Campbell et al., 1964) with research on political development (Lipset, 1959; Cutwright, 1963) and foreign policy, one finds they all share the same "conformist" conception of behavior. Hardly anyone has asked what the effect on the actor of a voting decision or a foreign policy pattern may be. The work Shapiro and I surveyed covered three areas illustrating the effects of the actor's policies on (1) its domestic structure, (2) its other foreign policies, and (3) its environment. Little has therefore been accomplished to date in this vital research area.

The three clusters of feedback, other's policies, and systemic variables are, in my view, extremely important areas for further research because they permit one to integrate into one framework the nation-state and international system levels-of-analysis (Singer, 1961). The feedback cluster concerns how actor behavior affects the international system and the actor itself. The systemic cluster examines how changes in the system over time affect state behavior. Examination of the interconnections between other's policies and foreign policy patterns comprises a form of interaction analysis frequently undertaken by specialists in international politics. Given the possibilities of research on these three clusters, the amount accomplished to date is negligible.

The final cluster of our framework is that of decision-making variables. This category was at one time conceived almost synonymously with foreign policy behavior itself (Snyder, Bruck, and Sapin, 1962). However, the strongly phenomenological orientation of early decision-making frameworks, which led to detailed case studies of single decisions, has resulted in little cumulative comparative research on this cluster of variables. A common fault of research on decision-making variables is the failure to explicitly relate the variable attributes of decision-making units and processes to foreign policy outputs. Far more common are findings which relate one decision-making variable to another, such as those which support proposition No. 104, "The longer the time taken in formulating a policy decision, the more alternatives will be considered and the more rational will be the process." Many clearly important decision-making variables, such as the information available to decision makers and the costs of decision making, have not been examined comparatively.

This summary of recent research in our field may appear overly negative. While there is surely much to fault, even in areas of some sustained effort like the domestic-foreign conflict relationship, the total picture is not all that bad. In con-

cluding our *Survey of Findings* (1973) Shapiro and I pointed out that considerable progress has been made. We have, during the past 12 years, learned that concepts comprising both independent and dependent variables can be operationalized and validly measured; that analyses using these scales can yield generalizations applicable across different political systems; in brief, that a complex political phenomenon like foreign policy can be accounted for by a number of types of independent variables. The comparative study of foreign policy is, indeed, an emerging field within the social sciences. I believe that *its faults are common to most social sciences*. Our job is to help in its emergence via a more self-conscious awareness of what we have been doing, are doing, and possibly can do.

GENERAL PROBLEMS OF THE FIELD

Up to this point I have been rather detailed in my criticisms of comparative foreign policy studies. If one stands back a bit and tries to draw up a list of general faults in the field, it seems to me that there are six main problem areas.

[1] First and foremost is the lack of general and middle range theory in our discipline. This absence of deductively organized theory in our field has serious consequences. Without theory we cannot explain the relationships we discover and we can only make predictions of the crudest sort based upon projections from empirical trends, not upon a profound understanding of foreign policy behavior. Without theory to guide our research we must depend on luck and educated guesses to come up with worthwhile research hypotheses. Without theory research becomes ad hoc in the extreme, with no justification provided for the selection of cases, with no system to the definition and measurement of concepts, and with no consistency in the use of research techniques and data processing routines. In brief, a field without theory is hardly an area of disciplined scientific inquiry. Since the comparative study of foreign policy lacks both middle range and general theories of foreign policy behavior, it fails to meet the basic objective of any science—a body of

theoretically organized knowledge that is based on cumulative empirical research.

Rather, what one finds in our literature are extremely narrow, albeit partially validated, propositions which state, for example, that a state's participation in international politics is a consequence of its economic development and national power (Participation = b_1 development + b_2 power). These propositions are not integrated in any sort of deductive hierarchy. When one turns to the so-called theoretical literature one finds that it is not recognizably scientific theory. Either it is a monism, where all behavior is attributed to one concept, such as the desire for power or economic necessity, and hence is either true but meaningless or meaningful but false (Levy, 1969, p. 93); or it is so vaguely sketched as not to be open to measurement and testing (e.g., much of Hoffmann, 1960; Aron, 1966; Hanrieder, 1967, 1965); or finally, it is policy recommendation pretending to be theory.

I have argued elsewhere (McGowan, 1974b) that the one sustained attempt to construct a recognizably scientific (i.e., falsifiable) general theory of foreign policy by Rosenau suffers from such serious logical faults that is merely a weakly related set of typologies. If Rosenau's work is the closest our discipline has so far come in its search for general and middle range theory, we have a long way to go. A theory is a deductively related set of generalizations, some of which are taken for granted and called axioms or assumptions and others which are deduced from these and are called theorems, consequences, propositions, predictions, or hypotheses. Whatever terms one prefers to employ, we have not got such a deductive model in foreign policy studies. And, to repeat myself, without such theories we hardly have a field.

[2] The second general fault, which is also of a theoretical character, but which overlaps with much empirical work, is the great power bias of our literature. Perhaps this is a sin apparent only to someone like myself who was also trained in African studies. Moreover, I would not deny for an instant that the great powers are important, both to theory and to policy; on the other hand, I do assume that we are trying to create general explanatory theory. Economists can theorize about the

behavior of any consumer and they can take into account differences between poor and rich consumers by reference to such concepts as marginal utility. We do not as yet seem able to do this. I have repeatedly read the general theoretical works for ideas that I might incorporate into a model of the foreign policy behavior of small, less modern states and I have not found much of use. When one approaches the literature with such an objective in mind, the theoretical and case selection biases are striking (but see East, 1973).

The simple fact of the matter is that our theorizing is ethnocentric. Most specialists in our field live in and do research on modern societies and their policies. True, some of us work in small, modern societies like the Scandinavians, but most of us are concerned as citizens and scholars with the foreign affairs of super powers or great powers. It should not be surprising that our work is considered irrelevant by most Asians, Africans, and Latin Americans. From their perspective it is!

[3] Further evidence of the weakly developed character of the comparative study of foreign policy is the ideographic nature of much of our literature. All of the comparative case studies Shapiro and I surveyed, and many of the more statistical works as well, employ spatial-temporal terms for their explanations of behavior that drastically limit the scope of any generalizations that can be derived from the research. The goal of comparative research is to substitute variables like level of modernization for spatial-temporal terms like Nigeria and France (Przeworski and Teune, 1970, pp. 5-11, 24-30).

The idiographic character of our field can be accounted for by two reasons. First, qualitatively oriented scholars have continued to do single case studies rather than comparisons of two or more cases. One does not have to use numbers to generate scientifically useful findings, but one has to be comparative to make such findings. Many excellent scholars have failed to appreciate this and they have continued to do single country case studies, although it is easy to demonstrate the scientific uselessness of such research (Zelditch, 1971). The second reason is that quantitatively oriented scholars have tended to collect data prior to theorizing and have then proceeded to analyze these data in a mainly bivariate fashion. In the end we must recognize that a theoretical justification is the only acceptable reason to collect a given set of data or to apply a particular technique to the analysis of the data collected. Much of the most technically sophisticated work in comparative foreign policy studies has been theoretical *ex post facto*. When this happens, place names and time periods are introduced to make sense out of the "significant" but unexpected "findings." This is a salient feature of UN voting behavior studies, for example.

[4] The techniques that we have used so far in our quantitative research have been largely inappropriate for the tasks we have set ourselves. Foreign policy behavior, its causes and consequences, comprises a complex set of interacting variables that are not necessarily related in a linear fashion and whose interrelationships are open to change over time. Yet, our field persists in using cross-sectional, bivariate correlation techniques as the principal mode of quantitative hypothesis testing. The world is not bivariate, it is probably not linear, and it is not static! Our use of static, two-variable correlations may fairly represent the technological sophistication of the majority of researchers in our field, but it does not represent reality in a fair manner.

Only multivariate analysis can examine the relative potencies of competing independent variables. Only nonlinear regression analysis and computer simulation can cope with nonlinear relationships. Only the explicit measurement of variables at different points in time can permit the testing of dynamic hypotheses. Only simultaneous-equation estimation techniques and computer simulations force the researcher to state a series of relations among a set of variables in an *explicit model* of the behavior in question. The proportion of research in our field that has exploited these techniques is very small indeed.

Up to this point I have dwelt on sins of commission: our theories are not genuinely theoretical, they are biased toward explaining great power behavior; our research is idiographic not nomothetic; and our statistical techniques and use of the computer have been largely inappropriate. But, theologians tell us there are also sins of omission, and we have committed these as well.

[5] We have omitted replication as a basic scientific activity. My discussion of the research so far accomplished within each category of independent variables repeatedly pointed to the lack of replicated findings in most categories. Only through this painstaking process can we build a body of cumulative knowledge in foreign policy studies, yet most of our research is original and unreplicated.

Why are there not more replications? One simple reason is that most studies in foreign policy are not replicable. Researchers usually fail to be specific and detailed enough in the writing of their research reports to permit someone else to replicate their work. As Deutsch has commented (1966, p. 42):

> We suffer from the curse of enforced originality which makes it a crime for a graduate student to replicate somebody else's experiment and forces the unhappy man to think up a new wrinkle on every experiment. I wish we could get an inter-university agreement that we expect everybody who earns a degree to do two things: first, to replicate honestly one experiment in social science and then, if he must, invent a new one. If physicists and chemists had not replicated each other's experiments, they would still be in the age of alchemy.

Of course, Deutsch is using the word experiment in the broadest possible sense here, to signify any type of scientific study, and he has hit upon a vital problem that is both sociological and intellectual. Our present disciplinary reward structures rarely reward the *original* replication of someone else's work. Our field needs more Tanters (1966) and Wilkenfelds (1971).

But if we are to replicate each other's work, we must have access to the same data base. While certain research projects such as WEIS, DON, and the Correlates of War (McClelland and Hoggard, 1969; Rummel, 1972; Singer, 1972) and the members of ICFP have generously shared their data, the attitudes described by Deutsch (1966, p. 55) are more typical of the field:

> So long as data are thought of as reposing in archives, and the custodians of these archives think of themselves as librarians—and if possible as librarians of rare medieval books which can only be let out with infinite caution—we will not have much in the way of social science.

Thus, without a mechanism for routine data sharing we shall never achieve the frequency of replicated research that our field so desperately needs.

[6] Finally, there is a series of neglected problems that have not received the attention they deserve by members of our field of study. In my view four stand out:

1. First, certain plausible independent variables have hardly been studied. My earlier summary of recent research highlighted these gaps. Little of worth has been done on the individual, elite, establishment, and cultural variable clusters.

2. Second, our dependent variable of foreign policy is in need of further specification. Yes, we have talked about "What Is a Foreign Policy Event" and "The Unit-of-Analysis Problem in Comparative Foreign Policy," perhaps *ad nauseam*. What I am pointing to here is our need for a widely accepted *empirically grounded* typology of foreign policy output behavior and our need for *cross-culturally valid* quantitative scales of selected dimensions of foreign policy behavior. Important typological work has been undertaken by Kegley (1971) and Salmore (1972), but no one has yet pulled these and related efforts together into a single workable classification scheme (but see Kegley, Salmore, and Rosen, 1974). The early scaling efforts of Moses et al. (1967) and Corson (1969) have not been built upon except perhaps by Azar et al. (1972). I cannot think of a single area of research that should have greater priority at this time. What is needed is hard thinking—creative theorizing—not more data manipulation.

3. We have utterly ignored the levels-of-analysis problem in the comparative study of foreign policy. The best-known published work that specifically addresses itself to this topic is insightful but not systematic (Singer, 1961, but see also Moul, 1973). The problem of fallacious inference across different levels is an aspect of the larger problem of the analysis of parts and wholes (Alker, 1969). If the comparative study of foreign policy is to progress, intensive analyses need to be made of the conditions under which characteristics of a foreign policy elite (a part) may be used to explain the behavior of nation-states (the

whole) or how aspects of the international system (the whole) can be used to predict the behavior of its member-states (the parts) (Hannan, 1970; Ray and Singer, 1973).

4. The normative use of our scholarship remains unexamined, and as often said, the unexamined life is not worth living. Certainly, we have accepted the normative assumption that a scientific approach to our subject is worthwhile. But assuming that we can correct our multitude of errors and create a science of foreign policy studies, what will we do with our creation? Will it be for sale to the highest bidder? (As things stand now, that means the U.S. federal government, if it wants to buy.) Or, should we adopt the position of some peace researchers, that social science is a tool in the struggle for a better world and that we should apply our methods and techniques to creating a world that is less violent, more just, and more abundant in a more equitable fashion?

Let us be frank: most research published in the peace research and conflict resolution journals is very remote from explicit problem solving. It is in these journals because their editors are competent to evaluate these complex research papers and willing to publish them. Moreover, the central premise of peace research, the eventual limitation or elimination of war as a tool of foreign policy, is both so all-encompassing and politically difficult that our meager research efforts are absurd in comparison to the task. If this is the case, then what possibly achievable values ought our research to focus on over the next decade? Can we at least do a better job in making our value premises explicit when we write up our research? We have tended to omit this too.

RECOMMENDATIONS

The simplest recommendation to make is to avoid all the errors I have discussed in the preceding three sections! However, I have mentioned so many that some sort of a ranking of priorities is necessary. In establishing such a ranking we must recognize that the comparative study of foreign policy is an activity carried out by people; therefore, it has sociological and institutional dimensions as well as intellectual strengths and weaknesses. Let us first be normative about the sociology of our field of inquiry.

Too many of us are middle-class, white, male Americans teaching at relatively prestigious universities in North America. I expect that when one becomes a competent social scientist one becomes bourgeois, even in socialist societies, but there is no necessity that these other attributes must hold. Within North America we should seek ways to bring into our field younger scholars *who are not like ourselves.* Outside our continent we need to identify scholars, particularly in the Third World, with whom we share interests and who can join with us in genuinely multinational comparative research projects. We need to share our data with these people, to make available resources for their research·efforts and publication outlets for their research. Most importantly, we need to recruit and train graduate students from abroad, again particularly from the Third World. This does not necessarily have to be a form of cultural imperialism either, for these students should be encouraged to learn from us only what can be of use to them. And we can also learn from them. I can·see no way for us to become less parochial in our interests and less enthnocentric in our theories if we do not truly internationalize our discipline.

In today's world one of the most inequitably distributed values is social scientific knowledge and the wherewithal to produce it. Almost all of this knowledge (whatever its quality) is produced and consumed in North America and Western Europe—even knowledge about the Third World! This is but one manifestation of a larger problem, but it is a part academic specialists in foreign policy studies can and should address themselves to resolving. It is also an instance where good intentions and self-interest coincide, for our field of study can only benefit by the infusion of different, and therefore comparative, perspectives on foreign policy behavior.

The fact that there has been little genuine replication and not enough data sharing is a sociological and institutional problem. Perhaps the M.A. thesis which has now been dropped in many political science departments should be reinstituted and designed to serve as a replication of an already published study. It would be an excellent idea if one of the journals in our field established a Replications Section where graduate students *and faculty* could publish short research notes on their replications. This might affect the reward structure for the better and encourage more replications.

The fact that there are no validated middle-range and general theories of foreign policy is also in part a sociological problem. The fact of the matter is that scholars who are reputed to be theorists rarely undertake empirical comparative studies of foreign policy, the only type of research that can validate their theories. On the other hand, the empirically oriented data gatherers and manipulators seldom sit down and think long enough to write substantial theoretical essays. This is an instance where the division of labor has not been beneficial, but it is characteristic of much of political science and the related disciplines of sociology and anthropology. It may ·not be so typical of psychology and economics, which suggests there is hope.

Since, at the present time, very few people combine the talents of theoretical creativity and technical research expertise, there is a continued need for team research and collaborative efforts of all kinds. Second, our students must be better trained than we were! By better training I mean literacy in the related languages of logic, mathematics, and computer programming combined with substantial experience in ongoing research projects as junior colleagues. The languages we must learn to use are not those like French and Swahili, but mathematics and logic, for only these are general and appropriate to the task of theory construction.

Now, if a community of scholars comes into being such as the one I have just projected that is international, mathematically literate, and dedicated to replication and data sharing, what would we have the community study? The intellectual tasks that confront the comparative study of foreign policy are enormous, but really no different from any other area of political science and international relations that I am familiar with.

Foremost, completely new departures in the area of theory construction must be undertaken. Our past theoretical efforts are at a dead end. Holt and Richardson's (1970) critique of comparative political theory applies equally well to our field.

We have borrowed too much and not wisely from sociology and anthropology in constructing functionalist and conformist approaches to foreign policy behavior. Levy (1969) may be cynical, but he is right, the emperor is indeed naked. Our field does not have a single middle range scientific theory, much less a general theory. At best, as in the work of Rosenau, we have a number of weakly related typologies of types of actors, types of actor attributes, and types of foreign policy behavior. I am not aware of a single deductively implied general proposition that has been operationalized and validated by comparative empirical research with the possible exception of studies of Richardsonian arms race models.[5]

Now, a scientific theory of foreign policy would be a positive theory as that term is used in economic science (Friedman, 1953). It would contain a set of well-defined, but not necessarily measured or measurable, concepts. These would be related in a set of axiomatic statements whose truth is assumed initially. By applying logic or the appropriate branch of mathematics to the axioms, theorems would be deduced, some of which would be expected to be testable. It would then be necessary to state rules of interpretation whereby the theoretical concepts were measured so that the selected theorems could be checked against data. What would be the advantage of such theories?

First, as part of the theoretical structure we would want the theory to contain a set of decision rules specifying the conditions under which foreign policy decision makers would act to generate observed behavior (Simon, 1966). To take a trite example, considerable comparative empirical research has now established the fact that the bigger and more modern the state, the more active it is in foreign affairs. Rosenau (1966) originally suggested that size and wealth were important characteristics of nation-states, but he did not say why. Empirical researchers following Rosenau's lead have now demonstrated that size and wealth or modernization are associated with aspects of foreign policy activity. Like Rosenau, however, they have not said why! But if they had a deductive theory which contained decision rules that re-

sulted in the prediction that the bigger and wealthier the state, the more active it would be, they would have an explanation. They could answer the vital questions "Why?" and "So what?"

The second advantage of such theories would be the possibility of integrating into one structure our diverse and so far unrelated findings. Until some sort of hierarchical structure is created, we really do not know if our findings are contradictory or reinforcing. Finally, if we possessed theories that served us well as explanatory and organizing schemes, they should serve us equally well as tools of normative prescription and empirical prediction. Positive theories in economics are frequently used in both fashions, and if we are self-conscious about what we are doing, as some economists are not, confusion need not arise.

Now, to borrow, a phrase, let me make one thing perfectly clear. I am not recommending that the comparative study of foreign policy ransack the field of economics for concepts the way political science has raped sociology and anthropology for the past 20 years. What I am suggesting is that we learn to apply the economist's methodology of abstract model building with its proven power of deductive rigor and elegant explanation. It may well be that we should start with the economist's premise of rational choice; this is what the few political scientists and political economists that have used the methodology of positive economics have done (e.g., Downs, 1957; Riker, 1962; Olson, 1971; Frohlich, Oppenheimer, and Young, 1971), but at least one prominent economist has persuasively argued for a more complex set of assumptions involving contingent rational choice (Harsanyi, 1969). That this approach has very great potential may be doubted. I would refer the doubters to the now classic essay by Olson and Zeckhauser, "An Economic Theory of Alliances," (1966) and the recent provocative essay by Frohlich and Oppenheimer, "Enterpreneurial Politics and Foreign Policy," (1972).

It further seems to me that genuine theorists of foreign policy can exploit at least three quite rich areas of social science literature in their attempts to develop positive theories of foreign policy. Two go under the head of exchange theory, but each is different. The first is microeconomics (Mansfield, 1970; Ferguson, 1966) as it has developed in the

---

[5]I am aware of the problems of getting from theoretical or postulational concepts contained in theorems to measured variables, but it can be done (Blalock, 1968).

areas of welfare economics and the theory of public finance. The best introduction to this approach, with a good bibliography, is provided by Curry and Wade (1968). Particularly important is the theory of public or collective goods (Olson, 1971; Frohlich et al., 1971). The second is the social-psychological exchange theory based upon the work of Homans (1961), Blau (1964) and Thibaut and Kelley (1959). Simon (1957) showed early on the possibilities of formalizing Homans's work and Waldman (1972) has recently presented an explicitly political theory of exchange based on Homans, with an interesting comparison to the economic exchange theorists.

The third area is a bit of a catchall, but I would call it systems design theory to distinguish it from the systems approach of Parsons, Easton, Almond, and Kaplan. Engineers and many applied social scientists have become concerned with modeling what Simon has called the organized complexity of artificial systems, that is, man-made institutions such as cities and governments. They often resort to the computer and model the processes in question via simulations. The recent work of Brunner and Brewer (1971) in modeling political development is general enough to warrant careful study by foreign policy specialists. Thorson (1974) has written a paper which explicitly relates systems design ideas to foreign policy matters and which can eventually be simulated once specification has proceeded somewhat. Choucri, Laird, and Meadows are applying these simulation approaches to foreign policy at present (1972).

In my view the advantage of positive theories, whatever their origin, is that they require the theorist to state his assumptions explicitly, particularly concerning the motivations of the actor. Even among our most talented theorists of the present these assumptions are half-hidden or entirely implicit. By forcing the theorist to state his assumptions, exchange theories and computer simulations make it necessary that the relations of every variable in the model with every other variable be specified. Getting our cards on the table in this fashion would be a great advance; we might even be dealt a few winning hands if our theories were at least in part supported by data.

To conclude this chapter I must reiterate my belief that new departures in theory construction represent the primary intellectual need of the comparative study of foreign policy at this time. Only if progress is achieved in this area can we come up with better typologies and indexes of foreign policy behavior which are also pressing needs. But the establishment of typologies and scales of foreign policy behavior is basically a measurement exercise, and measurement without theory to guide it is a sterile exercise. Finally, I am convinced that it is only the type of theory that I have recommended we try to construct that will permit us to address responsibly the pressing normative questions that confront our field. I simply do not see how we can suggest policies to achieve a less violent and more just world without theories of the causes of conflict and income distribution among states.[6]

REFERENCES

Alker, H. R., Jr. 1969. "A Typology of Ecological Fallacies." In *Quantitative Ecological Analysis*, ed. M. Dogan and S. Rokkan, pp. 69-86. Cambridge: MIT Press.

Almond, G. A. 1970. *Political Development: Essays in Heuristic Theory*. Boston: Little, Brown.

――― and S. Verba. 1963. *The Civic Culture*. Princeton: Princeton Univ. Press.

――― and G. B. Powell, Jr. 1966. *Comparative Politics: A Developmental Approach*. Boston: Little, Brown.

Apter, D. E. 1965. *The Politics of Modernization*. Chicago: Univ. of Chicago Press.

Aron, R. 1966. *Peace and War: A Theory of International Relations*. Garden City, N.Y.: Doubleday.

[6]Quite clearly, then, I disagree with those who would push comparative studies of foreign policy into the arena of policy recommendation prior to the development of at least partial theories of foreign policy behavior. It has been demonstrated by econometricians that predictive policy recommendation *without* theoretical knowledge of the causal structure involved will work only as long as the structure does not change. Since we have no reason to believe that the causal structures that produce national foreign policies are static, we had best try to gain theoretical understanding of the changing patterns of relationships that form the structure before we recommend action to national decision makers or counter-elites. On the other hand, that comparative studies of foreign policy ought to focus on more specific foreign policy issues rather than on highly aggregated patterns like cooperation-conflict—as argued by Michael K. O'Leary in Chapter 34—in no way contradicts what I have pleaded for in my essay. His argument is sound.

Azar, E. E., S. H. Cohen, T. O. Jukam, and J. McCormick. 1972. "Making and Measuring the International Event as a Unit of Analysis." In *International Events Interaction Analysis,* ed. E. E. Azar, R. Brody, and C. A. McClelland, pp. 59-77. Beverly Hills: Sage.

Bertalanffy, L. von. 1968. *General System Theory: Foundations, Development, Applications.* New York: Braziller.

Blalock, H. M., Jr. 1968. "The Measurement Problem: A Gap between the Languages of Theory and Research." In *Methodology in Social Research,* ed. H. M. Blalock, Jr., and A. Blalock, pp. 5-27. New York: McGraw-Hill.

Blau, P. 1964. *Exchange and Power in Social Life.* New York: Wiley.

Brunner, R. D., and G. D. Brewer. 1971. *Organized Complexity: Theories of Political Development.* New York: Free Press.

Butwell, R., ed. 1969. *Foreign Policy and the Developing Nations.* Lexington: Univ. Press of Kentucky.

Campbell, A., P. E. Converse, W. E. Miller, and D. E. Stokes. 1964. *The American Voter.* New York: Wiley.

Choucri, N., M. Laird, and D. L. Meadows. 1972. *Resource Scarcity and Foreign Policy: A Simulation Model of International Conflict.* Cambridge: MIT Center for International Studies.

Collins, J. N. 1967. "Foreign Conflict Behavior and Domestic Disorder in Africa." Ph.D. dissertation, Northwestern Univ.

Corson, W. H. 1969. "Measuring Conflict and Cooperation Intensity in International Relations." Mimeo. Cambridge: Harvard Univ.

Curry, R. L., Jr., and L. L. Wade. 1968. *A Theory of Political Exchange: Economic Reasoning in Political Analysis.* Englewood Cliffs, N.J.: Prentice-Hall.

Cutwright, P. 1963. "National Political Development: Measurement and Analysis." *American Sociological Review* 28 (Apr): 256-64.

Deutsch, K. W. 1966. "Recent Trends in Research Methods in Political Science." In *A Design for Political Science,* ed. J. S. Charlesworth, pp. 149-78. Philadelphia: American Academy of Political and Social Science.

Downs, A. 1957. *An Economic Theory of Democracy.* New York: Harper & Row.

East, M. A. 1972. "Status Discrepancy and Violence in the International System: An Empirical Analysis." In *The Analysis of International Politics,* ed. J. N. Rosenau, V. Davis, and M. A. East, pp. 299-316. New York: Free Press.

–––. 1973. "Size and Foreign Policy Behavior: A Test of Two Models." *World Politics* 25 (Jul): 556-76.

––– and P. M. Gregg. 1967. "Factors Influencing Cooperation and Conflict in the International System." *International Studies Quarterly* 11 (Sep): 244-69.

Feierabend, I., and R. Feierabend. 1969. "Level of Development and Internation Behavior." In *Foreign Policy and the Developing Nations,* ed. R. Butwell, pp. 135-88. Lexington: Univ. Press of Kentucky.

Ferguson, C. 1966. *Microeconomic Theory.* Homewood, Ill.: Irwin.

Friedman, M. 1953. *Essays in Positive Economics.* Chicago: Univ. of Chicago Press.

Frohlich, N., and J. A. Oppenheimer. 1972. "Entrepreneurial Politics and Foreign Policy." In *Theory and Policy in International Relations,* ed. R. Tanter and R. Ullman, pp. 151-78. Princeton: Princeton Univ. Press.

–––, J. A. Oppenheimer, and O. R. Young. 1971. *Political Leadership and Collective Goods.* Princeton: Princeton Univ. Press.

Gillespie, J. V., and B. V. Nesvold, eds. 1971. *Macroquantitative Analysis.* Beverly Hills: Sage.

Graham, G. J., Jr. 1971. *Methodological Foundations for Political Analysis.* Waltham, Mass.: Xerox College Publishing.

Gregg, P. M., and A. S. Banks. 1965. "Dimensions of Political Systems: Factor Analysis of a Cross-polity Survey." *American Political Science Review* 59 (Sep): 602-14.

Haas, M. 1965. "Societal Approaches to the Study of War." *Journal of Peace Research* 2 (4): 307-24.

Halperin, M. H., and A. Kanter, eds. 1973. *Readings in American Foreign Policy: A Bureaucratic Perspective.* Boston: Little, Brown.

Hannan, M. T. 1970. *Problems of Aggregation and Disaggregation in Sociological Research.* Chapel Hill: Univ. of North Carolina, Institute for Research in Social Science.

Hanrieder, W. F. 1965. "Actor Objectives and International Systems." *Journal of Politics* 27 (Feb): 109-32.

–––. 1967. "Compatability and Consensus: A Proposal for the Conceptual Linkage of External and Internal Dimensions of Foreign Policy." *American Political Science Review* 61 (Dec): 971-82.

–––, ed. 1971. *Comparative Foreign Policy: Theoretical Essays.* New York: McKay.

Harsanyi, J. C. 1969. "Rational-Choice Models of Political Behavior vs. Functionalist and Conformist Theories." *World Politics* 21 (Jul): 513-38.

Hermann, C. F., ed. 1972. *International Crises: Insights from Behavioral Research.* New York: Free Press.

Hersh, A. H. 1942. "Drosophila and the Course of Research." *Ohio Journal of Science* 42: 198-200.

Hoffmann, S., ed. 1960. *Contemporary Theory in International Relations.* Englewood Cliffs, N.J.: Prentice-Hall.

Holt, R. T., and J. M. Richardson, Jr. 1970. "Competing Paradigms in Comparative Politics." In *The Methodology of Comparative Research,* ed. R. T. Holt and J. E. Turner, pp. 21-71. New York: Free Press.

Homans, G. C. 1961. *Social Behavior: Its Elementary Forms.* New York: Harcourt, Brace & World.

Jensen, L. 1969. "Levels of Political Development and Interstate Conflict in South Asia." In *Foreign Policy and the Developing Nations,* ed. R. Butwell, pp. 189-208. Lexington: Univ. Press of Kentucky.

Jones, S. D., and J. D. Singer. 1972. *Beyond Conjecture in International Politics.* Itasca, Ill.: Peacock.

Kegley, C. W., Jr. 1971. "Toward the Construction of an Empirically Grounded Typology of Foreign Policy Output Behavior." Ph.D. dissertation, Syracuse Univ.

———, G. A. Raymond, R. M. Rood, and R. A. Skinner. 1975. *International Events and the Comparative Analysis of Foreign Policy.* Columbia: Univ. of South Carolina Press.

———, S. A. Salmore, and D. Rosen. 1974. "Convergences in the Measurement of Interstate Behavior." In *Sage International Yearbook of Foreign Policy Studies,* ed. P. J. McGowan, vol. 2, pp. 309-39. Beverly Hills: Sage.

Kelman, H. C., ed. 1965. *International Behavior.* New York: Holt, Rinehart & Winston.

Kriesberg, L., ed. 1968. *Social Processes in International Relations.* New York: Wiley.

Lasswell, H. D. 1968. "The Future of the Comparative Method." *Comparative Politics* 1 (Oct): 3-18.

Levy, M. J., Jr. 1969. " 'Does It Matter If He's Naked?' Bawled the Child." In *Contending Approaches to International Politics,* ed. K. Knorr and J. N. Rosenau, pp. 87-109. Princeton: Princeton Univ. Press.

Lipset, S. M. 1959. "Some Social Requisites of Democracy: Economic Development and Political Legitimacy." *American Political Science Review* 53 (Mar): 65-105.

Mansfield, E. 1970. *Microeconomics: Theory and Applications.* New York: Norton.

Mayer, L. C. 1972. *Comparative Political Inquiry: A Methodological Survey.* Homewood, Ill.: Dorsey.

McClelland, C. A., and G. D. Hoggard. 1969. "Conflict Patterns in the Interactions among Nations." In *International Politics and Foreign Policy* (rev. ed.), ed. J. N. Rosenau, pp. 711-24. New York: Free Press.

McGowan, P. J., ed. 1973. *Sage International Yearbook of Foreign Policy Studies.* Vol. 1. Beverly Hills: Sage.

———, ed. 1974a. *Sage International Yearbook of Foreign Policy Studies.* Vol. 2. Beverly Hills: Sage.

———. 1974b. "Problems in the Construction of Positive Theories of Foreign Policy." In *Comparing Foreign Policies,* ed. J. N. Rosenau, pp. 25-44. Bevery Hills: Sage.

——— and R. I. Lewis. 1973. "Culture and Foreign Policy Behavior in Black Africa: An Exploratory, Comparative Study." Africa Project Research Report No. 4. Mimeo. Syracuse: Syracuse Univ., Dept. of Political Science.

——— and H. B. Shapiro. 1973. *The Comparative Study of Foreign Policy: A Survey of Scientific Findings.* Beverly Hills: Sage.

Moses, L., R. Brody, O. Holsti, J. Kadane, and J. Milstein. 1967. "Scaling Data on Inter-Nation Actions." *Science* 156 (May): 1054-59.

Moul, W. B. 1973. "The Level-of-Analysis Problem Revisited." *Canadian Journal of Political Science* 9 (Sep): 494-513.

Olson, M., Jr. 1971. *The Logic of Collective Action.* Rev. ed. New York: Schocken.

——— and R. Zeckhauser. 1966. "An Economic Theory of Alliances." *Review of Economics and Statistics* 48 (Aug): 266-79.

Przeworski, A., and H. Teune. 1970. *The Logic of Comparative Social Inquiry.* New York: Wiley-Interscience.

Ray, J. L., and J. D. Singer. 1973. "Measuring the Concentration of Power in the International System." *Sociological Methods and Research* 1 (May): 403-38.

Riker, W. H. 1962. *The Theory of Political Coalitions.* New Haven: Yale Univ. Press.

Rosenau, J. N. 1966. "Pre-theories and Theories of Foreign Policy." In *Approaches to Comparative and International Politics,* ed. R. B. Farrell, pp. 27-92. Evanston: Northwestern Univ. Press.

———, ed. 1967 *Domestic Sources of Foreign Policy.* New York: Free Press.

———, ed. 1969a. *International Politics and Foreign Policy.* Rev. ed. New York: Free Press.

———, ed. 1969b. *Linkage Politics.* New York: Free Press.

———, ed. 1974. *Comparing Foreign Policies: Theories, Findings and Methods.* Beverly Hills: Sage.

Rudner, R. S. 1966. *Philosophy of Social Science.* Englewood Cliffs, N.J.: Prentice-Hall.

Rummel, R. J. 1963. "Dimensions of Conflict Behavior within and between Nations." In *General Systems Yearbook,* vol. 8, pp. 1-50. Bedford, Mass.: Society for General Systems Research.

———. 1967. "Some Attributes and Behavioral Patterns of Nations." *Journal of Peace Research* 4 (2): 196-206.

———. 1968. "The Relationships between National Attributes and Foreign Conflict Behavior." In *Quantitative International Politics,* ed. J. D. Singer, pp. 187-214. New York: Free Press.

———. 1972. *The Dimensions of Nations.* Beverly Hills: Sage.

Russett, B. M., ed. 1972. *Peace, War, and Numbers.* Beverly Hills: Sage.

Salmore, S. A. 1972. "Foreign Policy and National Attributes: A Multivariate Analysis." Ph.D. dissertation, Princeton Univ.

Shils, E. 1962. *Political Development in the New States.* The Hague: Mouton.

Simon, H. A. 1957. *Models of Man.* New York: Wiley.

———. 1966. "Political Research: The Decision-Making Framework." In *Varieties of Political Theory,* ed. D. Easton, pp. 15-24. Englewood Cliffs, N.J.: Prentice-Hall.

Singer, J. D. 1961. "The Levels-of-Analysis Problem in International Relations." In *The International System,* ed. K. Knorr and S. Verba, pp. 77-92. Princeton: Princeton Univ. Press.

———, ed. 1968. *Quantitative International Politics: Insights and Evidence.* New York: Free Press.

———. 1972. "The 'Correlates of War' Project: Interim Report and Rationale." *World Politics* 24 (Jan): 243-70.

Snyder, R. C., H. W. Bruck, and B. Sapin, eds. 1962. *Foreign Policy Decision-Making.* New York: Free Press.

Tanter, R. 1966. "Dimensions of Conflict Behavior within and between Nations, 1958-60." *Journal of Conflict Resolution* 10 (Mar): 41-64.

Thibaut, J. W., and H. H. Kelley. 1959. *The Social Psychology of Groups.* New York: Wiley.

Thorson, S. 1974. "Adaptation and Foreign Policy Theory." In *Sage International Yearbook of Foreign Policy Studies,* ed. P. J. McGowan, vol. 2, pp. 123-139. Beverly Hills: Sage.

Waldman, S. R. 1972. *Foundations of Political Action:* *An Exchange Theory of Political Life.* Boston: Little, Brown.

Wallace, M. D. 1971. "Power, Status, and International War." *Journal of Peace Research* 8 (1): 23-36.

Weede, E. 1970. "Conflict Behavior of Nation-States." *Journal of Peace Research* 7 (3): 229-35.

Wiegele, T. C. 1973. "Decision-Making in an International Crisis: Some Biological Factors." *International Studies Quarterly* 17 (Sep): 295-335.

Wilkenfeld, J. 1969. "Some Further Findings Regarding the Domestic and Foreign Conflict Behavior of Nations." *Journal of Peace Research* 6 (2): 147-56.

———. 1971. "Domestic and Foreign Conflict Behavior of Nations." In *A Multi-method Introduction to International Politics,* ed. W. D. Coplin and C. W. Kegley, Jr., pp. 189-203. Chicago: Markham.

———, ed. 1973. *Conflict Behavior and Linkage Politics.* New York: McKay.

Zelditch, M., Jr. 1971. "Intelligible Comparisons." In *Comparative Methods in Sociology,* ed. I. Vallier, pp. 267-307. Berkeley and Los Angeles: Univ. of California Press.

Zinnes, D. A., and J. Wilkenfeld. 1971. "An Analysis of Foreign Conflict Behavior of Nations." In *Comparative Foreign Policy,* ed. W. F. Hanrieder, pp. 167-213. New York: McKay.

27. Optimal Control Theory: A Promising Approach for Future Research

John V. Gillespie

The intellectual historian of fifty years from now, looking back and reflecting on the research efforts in comparative foreign policy, may view the past five years or so as a period in which scholars learned to apply statistical routines to large bodies of data for the purposes of confirming (let's hope that in fifty years "confirmation" will be passé and that the term "confidence" will carry its rich and nonscientism meaning) hypotheses generated by other scholars whose task it was to speculate, i.e., piece together in a more coherent way the reasonable ideas relating aspects of the world in which they lived. If such is our epitaph, we may have accomplished something. But in that something we have accomplished, we should and must be distressed that as scholars of foreign policy we

SPECIAL NOTE: This paper has been prepared under Research Grant GS-36806 from the National Science Foundation. I wish to express appreciation to Dina A. Zinnes who read a previous draft and provided numerous helpful suggestions. Jose Cruz, G. S. Tahim, Philip A. Schrodt, and Richard Rubison provided assistance with technical problems.

have not contributed more to an accumulated body of knowledge than larger data archives, more efficient computer programs, and many hypotheses which reflect the way the world "was." To avoid depression, we must think about problems we can solve and answers we can generate; our problems must be substantive in nature and, like an engineer designing a bridge, we must be able to state how much stress can be tolerated and what the equilibrium and stability attributes of the proposed structure are.

My purpose here is not to state that we have erred in our endeavors to understand foreign policy; my purpose is to argue that if we continue to do the same things we have in the past few years, we may never realize that there are many important and significant questions to ask. My claim is that the present trend in comparative foreign policy research is leading to too many variables, too many concepts, too many frameworks, too many hypotheses, too much data in machine-readable form, and not enough knowledge that can be considered well reasoned and logical—not commonsensical as in social science common sense—but logical and conclusive and, most of all, convincing; we need knowledge that goes beyond empirical generalizations yielding convincing arguments about the yet unrealized properties of foreign policy decision-making systems.

One cannot say that the past several years of endeavor to understand foreign policy have been fruitless. As social scientists we have carefully collected data on everything from national defense expenditures to discrete foreign policy events, from international trade to personnel employed in the diplomatic services of nations. We have used the sophistication of contemporary multivariate statistical routines to analyze these large bodies of accumulated data. The goal of these many data-gathering and data-analysis exercises has been to arrive at empirical generalizations guided by insightful categorizations of the interplay of variables and by frameworks attempting to make some sense of those things that seem to have some effect on foreign policies.

Even though we have defined, hypothesized, operationalized, and data-analyzed, there still seems to be a sense of dissatisfaction that our many efforts have not yielded any real new understandings. Our dissatisfactions seem to stem from the fact that the product of our labors does not meet with our desired goal to develop a codified body of knowledge about foreign policy, a body of knowledge which will provide answers to the question "Under a given set of conditions, what consequences will follow?" We have used the empirical world, at least that portion of it that could be coded into data files without too great a cost, as the guide to understanding. It has been an intellectual exercise which, for the most part, has meant sorting out variables to assess the strongest correlates of a given foreign policy activity in order to yield results which, to varying degrees, supported social science hunches about the way the empirical world is.

Confirming our hunches has not been too rewarding. We have not been able to uncover findings that counter our commonsensical understandings in any real way to build greater awareness of the determinants of foreign policy behavior. Perhaps we have gained greater confidence, or at times reduced the degree of faith we have in our common sense, but in general we have not been stunned except, perhaps, by the idiosyncratic behaviors of foreign policy decision makers which, when analyzed, become outliers in our statistical generalizations, and are forgotten as long as the data analysis meets accepted criteria of statistical significance. Although it would be silly, if not sacrilegious, to claim that we do not need more frameworks, more hypotheses and propositions, greater data-collection efforts, more valid statistical and measurement devices, etc., there is a need, if not an imperative, to attempt to find new ways of talking about foreign policy. The data-based analyses we have been performing give us a foundation, a "confidence base," from which we can isolate basic dynamics of foreign policy decision making. Using this information, we need to build models which will allow us to reason beyond our mere observations of the way the system works, to move to statements that assess the equilibrium, stability, and sensitivity properties of the system, which then will allow us to use what we know to be true about the empirical world to arrive at conclusions that go beyond our hunches about what variables relate to other variables.

THE REASONING BEHIND RECENT EFFORTS IN COMPARATIVE FOREIGN POLICY

Our present efforts in comparative foreign policy research have given us series of generalizations about the attributes of the empirical world. These generalizations are confirmed hunches. The logical structure underlying the process through which empirical generalizations are obtained is of the generic family of cause-and-effect reasoning. The classical notion of cause and effect is reflected in the contemporary use of the "if-then" statement and the desire of researchers to establish the empirical truth or acceptability of the conditional sentence. Exercises to establish this acceptability take three basic forms under the generic family of causal reasoning.

First, there is the finding-the-cause-or-causes-of-the-effect form. Exercises of this form are essentially sorting activities in which several "if-then" sentences are hypothesized, the sentences differing only with respect to the antecedent condition, and generally offering but one consequent. A number of independent variables is commonly offered (in more sophisticated analyses researchers are often concerned with the interaction effects between the independent variables and with the resulting multicolinearity) and are postulated to have some effect (linear or nonlinear) on some dependent variable. The effort is an attempt to assess the "significance" or "importance" of the independent variables, either in groups or separately, on the dependent variable. The complete analysis may contain more than one dependent variable, but typically each dependent variable is considered separately in association with the independent variables. These exercises commonly use statistical techniques such as bivariate and multivariate regression and correlation analysis, factor analysis, discriminate function, and similar forms of data reduction. Many quasi-experimental designs fit into this form of cause-and-effect reasoning. Researchers using it are able to reduce the set of variables explaining some effect (consequent), by sorting out those independent variables which do not relate to the effect. In this way, the analysis essentially reduces the number of hunches the researcher has about "cause-and-effect relations" into a smaller, and perhaps more refined, set of confirmed (or accepted) hunches.

A second kind of cause-and-effect analysis can be called "maximizing the amount of variance explained." In such exercises the researcher attempts to include many relevant independent variables, to increase the variance explained in some dependent variable. In the sorting exercises referred to above, the goal is to eliminate potential independent variables so as to isolate the set of independent variables that best explain the dependent variable; in the maximization of variance exercises, the goal is to include many independent variables, using some criterion of "significance," so as to increase the completeness of the accounting for the dependent variable. In maximization-of-variance designs, one "if-then" sentence is the result of the analysis. The antecedent part of the conditional sentence is the conjunction of a number of independent variables, i.e., if X_1 and X_2, and . . . , and X_n, then Y. In such analyses control variables may be used to isolate contaminous conditions, and a variety of additional elaborations on the same basic theme can be found in the comparative foreign policy literature. The researcher attempts to give the most complete list of causes of some effect so that the analysis will essentially yield a single statement combining the various hunches the researcher has about cause-and-effect relations. The single statement gives the most complete accounting of causes for the effect.

A third kind of cause-and-effect analysis is that typified by the techniques popularized by Blalock and others in "causal modeling." These exercises attempt to solve more complex systems of variables and they differ from the two types outlined above in that there are no real independent and dependent variables; the variables must be characterized as exogenous and endogenous variable sets. In causal modeling there is an interlocking system of "if-then" sentences in which the variables in one sentence reappear in another sentence, i.e., the dependent variable in one sentence may be an independent variable in another. Most causal modeling exercises are performed for the purposes of tracing the flow of variance (or some similar measure of dependency) along a variety of possible paths in order to assess which path provides the greatest explanatory power.

It should be noted that many corollary formats of the three kinds of cause-and-effect reasoning appear in the comparative foreign policy literature. For example, many computer simulations, other than those that attempt to describe the empirical world in a language the computer understands, use all forms of cause-and-effect reasoning, especially that of simultaneous linear equations commonly associated with causal modeling. On occasion in computer simulations, once parameter estimates have been computed, the researcher uses these estimated values in a further cause-and-effect-reasoning design.

Our search for causes of those effects we desire to explain has not led us to any really stunning findings. However, rather than reviewing the findings for further investigation, the more common discussion among scholars of comparative foreign policy is about methodological issues, reformulating hunches (hypotheses), and repeating the search for causes of the things we want to explain. We have been satisfied with the empirical generalizations as end products.

I do not want to suggest that we abandon the search for causes and correlates. I do, however, want to argue that there are other productive forms of reasoning which have not been explored in the comparative foreign policy literature and which are beyond the mere enumeration of empirical generalizations. To abandon the search for causes and determinants is to abandon the desire to explain the empirical world. It would neglect the desire of many of us to piece together a more coherent, simplified, and parsimonious representation of the empirical world than that provided by historical accounts and intensive verbal descriptions based upon evidence quite often assessed through more interpretive and intuitive methods. However, an area of study such as comparative foreign policy can become stagnant if it becomes so singular in its basic form of reasoning that it fails to ask what can be done with the product rendered from its intellectual efforts.

One form of analysis developed primarily by electrical engineers does seem to have numerous applications to those problems which concern many scholars in comparative foreign policy. This form of analysis generally goes under the rubric of "Optimal Systems," "Optimization with Controls," or "Optimization in Feedback Systems," or some such similar title. Optimal control methods are now occasionally being applied in economic and in business research. My purpose here is to provide a layman's description of optimal control thinking and to discuss its potential for the analysis of foreign policy questions.

THE REASONING BEHIND OPTIMAL CONTROL SYSTEMS

Engineers have a vast number of physical problems to solve. For example, an engineer in metals and materials may be assigned to produce a concrete that can withstand a certain weight and can also serve as the foundation for flooring material in a building of a certain number of stories. Such a task is typical of an optimal control problem. The object is to optimize a certain system part (the concrete) to a variety of constraints and, often, provide it with properties whereby the system (in the above example the building design, the needed capacity for holding weight, etc.) can be controlled so that it is stable and performs optimally. In a sense the plumber who repairs piping is using optimal control methods, although he may not be too successful in his endeavors. He is often assigned the task of locating a leak in a set of pipes and patching the leak in such a way that it will not fault again. The consumer of the plumber's services obviously also desires to minimize the cost of the repair. In this example, there is an objective, namely to minimize the cost of the repair, but there are also constraints, namely to maximize the probability that the leak will not develop again and that the appropriate water pressure will be maintained. Given his assignment, the plumber attempts to meet the goal, subject to the constraint and further subject to the control that he introduces into the system of pipes, namely the patch on the leak.

The basic reasoning underlying optimal control thinking is that the cause-and-effect relations are known, that the question of what causes what (not the degree of causal linkage, however measured) is known. This is to say that optimal control reasoning *begins* with a set of confirmed empirical generalizations. In the example of the plumber patching a leak, we know, or a competent plumber knows, the cause-and-effect relations between patching the leak and water pressure and circulation. Optimal control theory assumes we know the relevant basic cause-and-effect relations in the empirical world. These empirical generalizations are called the "plant" or the "system."

Not only do we have a plant but we must also have an objective. An objective is a goal or a performance criterion, or in optimal control terminology an "objective function" or a "performance index." The performance index states what we desire to get out of the system at some future time. In the example of the plumber, his objective function, depending on business, may be to stop the leak only long enough to secure payment for his services, hoping then to secure another contract to stop the leak again.

The process of utilizing optimal control thinking begins with a statement, however vague, of an objective to be satisfied either by an existing social or political process or by one that is to be constructed. For example, one may want to improve the efficiency of a given organizational structure by altering certain patterns of communication and demand or one may want to design a system to provide equitable distribution of goods and services to participating nations in some international organization. What is necessary is that a set of goals or objectives which broadly describes the desired performance of the social or political process be defined. Second, a set of constraints (the plant) which represents the limitations that are either inherent in the political reality of the process or artificially imposed must be defined. For example, in most political problems there are always requirements relating to cost, reliability, size, etc., as well as the idiosyncratic tastes of decision makers.

The goal of optimal control thinking is the answer to the question "Given the plant, how can the goal or objective be satisfied?" With appropriate mathematical representations, this question can be answered; it will yield the best strategy or action for a decision maker to follow in order to arrive at his objective. However, the question of what the best strategy or action is is not the sole interest; also of interest are the analytical properties of the plant and the objectives. For example, does the system have an equilibrium, i.e., a point at which the rate of production of output of the plant (the dependent variable) ceases to change $(dx/dt = 0)$ or obtains a steady state of change $(dx/dt = c;$ where c is a constant)? The system may not have an equilibrium; it may blow up $(dx/dt \rightarrow \infty)$, or it may decay into nothing $(x(t)=0)$. Another interesting analytical problem concerns the stability of the equilibrium: given slight fluctuations in the equilibrium parameters, will the system return to equilibrium or will it seek a new equilibrium, blow up, or decay? Analytical questions can be raised concerning the sensitive properties of the objective function. The objective function is defined by a set of parameters and variables. Sensitivity analysis assesses the consequences of slight perturbations in each parameter in the objective function on the best strategy or action, that is, given slight changes in the objective, it assesses the consequences for the preferred action or behavior.

One might ask why go to all the bother of optimal control analysis when, for many problems, common sense tells us what course of action should be followed to gain a desired result? Why cannot foreign policy decision-making problems be addressed directly? Is there not an "art of political reasoning" which instructs decision makers to follow certain courses of action in solving their problems? In the art of political reasoning, the decision maker, or his consultant acting as a "political scientist," combines his experience, know-how, ingenuity, and the results of empirical research and experimentation to suggest a set of actions which will yield the desired result. He does not develop mathematical or rigorous representations for the component parts of the plant or system, nor does he rigorously define his goals and objectives, but instead he relies upon his knowledge and understanding of the political process to arrive at a solution to his problem. Such an approach often works and solves the problem at hand. For many social and political problems the art of political reasoning is satisfactory.

However, for complicated systems and stringent performance requirements (objectives), the art of political reasoning is frequently inadequate. Moreover, the risks and costs involved in extensive experimentation and empirical research may be so great as to render the art of political reasoning useless. It may be based on uninformed hunches. For example, one would not attempt, or should not attempt, to control inflation in an economy by experimenting with interest rates. The art of political reasoning, although it may sharpen the political scientist's intuition, rarely yields broad and general decision criteria which can be applied to a variety of problems.

SOME LIMITATIONS ON THE APPLICABILITY OF OPTIMAL CONTROL SYSTEMS

Control theory does have its limitations. First, as observed above, the control systems approach to problem solving begins with the representation of the real-world problem involving mathematical relationships. In other words, the first step consists in formulating a suitable mathematical model of the social process, the objectives for that social process, and the imposed constraints. The adequate mathematical description and formulation of a decision-making problem is an extremely challenging and difficult, if not a creative, task. Features of the objectives and of the system or plant may be so vague that they are almost impossible to translate into a mathematical language. Moreover, mathematical models, which are idealizations and approximations of the real world, are not unique and are not intensive descriptions of the real world. In this sense, the mathematical model may be a broader generalization that is useful for a specific foreign public policy problem.

Second, not all decision problems are control problems. The essential elements of a control problem are (1) a mathematical model (system) to be controlled, (2) a desired output of the system, (3) a set of admissible inputs or controls, and (4) a

performance or cost (objective) function which measures the effectiveness of a given control action. The mathematical model consists of a set of relations which represents the response or output of the political system being modeled for various inputs. Constraints based upon the social situation are incorporated into this set of relations. In translating the decision-making problem into a control problem, the scientist is faced with the task of describing desirable political behavior of the system in mathematical terms. The objective or performance index is often translated into a requirement on the policy output. Not all problems can be forced into this neat format; it may be that for many decision-making problems the four essential elements cannot be isolated.

Third, control theory does not assure an answer. Sometimes the desired objective can be attained by many admissible inputs, or, on the other hand, it may be the case that the desired objective cannot be attained by the use of any admissible input. If several controls produce the desired objective, it is necessary to construct more refined objectives or to add criteria, such as cost effectiveness, for the purpose of selecting which signal or control input is to be used to bring the system to its desired state. Even with such additional criteria, definitive conclusions may not be reached; expert judgment and similar intuitive skills may be the only solution to the problem. However, it should be noted that the solution set has been narrowed to a smaller set of signals and intelligent decisions can be made by those responsible for a given foreign policy action.

If there are no solutions in the solution set, i.e., if no signal will bring the system to the desired state of equilibrium, there are several courses of action the researcher can take. First, the objective or performance index can be altered to that of a lower preference or a less satisfying state of affairs. This reduction of preference does not necessarily produce a solution set or a unique solution. A satisfactory state of affairs cannot always be obtained. However, such a result is an important and significant piece of information and does represent, at least for the researcher, the impossibility of the achievement of the stated goal or the reduced preference outcome.

A second procedure to be followed if the desired goal cannot be attained is to ask the question "What systems can be created to attain the objective?" Certainly it is important for the researcher to know that there is a set of systems under which the goal may be attained. This procedure is arduous, but very important for the purposes of expanding theoretical understanding.

A third procedure to be followed if the desired objective cannot be attained is to relax the social and political constraints on the problem in order to assess whether, given the alterations in the constraints, a solution set can be obtained. Perhaps in the original modeling of the constraints the mathematical representations were expressed too rigidly and a less restrictive solution is necessary. A fourth procedure would be to combine the three noted above.

There is never an assured solution to an optimal control problem. Control systems theorists have solved many mathematical systems for us; however, they are generally the kind in which the objective function is in quadratic form and the system or plant is a set of linear differential equations. In addition, there are many control systems problems for which the solutions can only be estimated by numerical methods; hence, understanding the properties of the solution set can only be obtained by examination of the numerical results. This is especially true of highly complex systems of mathematical representations.

Optimal control theory is still a growing enterprise, and applied mathematicians are hard at work on systems for which numerical estimation is still the best means of solution. Other frailties of optimal control applications need to be noted. First, solutions do require considerable mathematical knowledge, a scarce resource among political scientists. Second, and most important, the underlying notion that we know the objectives of foreign policies and that we can assert cause-and-effect relations runs counter to the guiding spirit under which many political analysts pursue their research. I present no solution to these more disciplinary problems, but I do want to argue that in optimal control we have the elements for a new kind of research in comparative foreign policy and the promise of greater policy relevance for our research.

REVIEW OF THE BASIC THEOREM OF OPTIMAL CONTROL THEORY: FINITE TIME HORIZON

Let us review. First, we have an identified system, i.e., a set of elements and relations between the elements. These elements, however vaguely defined, comprise a complete system. It may be a system such as the defense relations between two nations, or a system describing the civil-military decision structure of some nation. The system as identified is the object of study. We are interested in the system as it evolves through time. At any moment in time the system is in some *state*, i.e., a particular configuration of the relationships between the elements of the system which can be described by a finite-dimensional vector, $x(t)$. In an optimization problem there may be a possibility of controlling this system as it moves through time. Controlling the system means that there is a selection of some objective or performance index for the system that is deemed desirable. For any time, t, there is a vector, $u(t)$, which can be chosen by a decision maker from a set of vectors which may, in general, vary with both t and the state, $x(t)$. The vector $u(t)$ will be called the *control variable(s)*.

It is assumed that the state and control variables at any point in time completely determine the rate of change of the state of the system. This is to say that the system is closed and complete and all relevant variables and conditions have been contained within it. The evolution, or change in the system, is governed by three elements: $x(t)$, the state variables; $u(t)$, the control variables, and t, time. In general, using the standard notation of optimal control as applied in many areas of scientific research, the change in the state of the system is governed by a set of differential equations[1] of the form

$$\dot{x} = \int_{o}^{T} [x(t), u(t), t] \, dt. \qquad (1)$$

[1] The notation $\dot{x}$ should be read as dx/dt.

Given the state of the system at some time, t_o, and the choice of control variables as a function of time, $u(t)$, the whole course of the system is determined for the finite time horizon, T.

By selecting various values for the control variables over time, a set of future "histories" can be built for the system. However, the objective of the analysis is not to select any single history by less than rigorous methods. What is needed is the addition of some objective or performance index to judge which of the histories is desired. By selecting an objective function the researcher is stating what he or some decision maker, wants the system to exhibit during the time horizon. This represents the yield from the system that the decision maker desires at each moment in time. It is expressed as a differential equation. Let

$$J(x,u,t), \qquad (2)$$

be the objective function at time t for the state x and the control vector u.

With the finite time horizon, the general statement of the optimization problem is

$$\int_{o}^{T} J[x(t),u(t),t]\,dt \qquad (3)$$

with respect to the choice of control variables over time subject to (1), and possibly some constraints on the choice of controls depending on the values of the state variables, and the initial conditions, $x(t_o) = x$.

Pontryagin and his associates, as well as many others, have shown that for some choice of control variables, $u^*(t)$, there exist auxiliary variables, functions of time, $p(t)$, with the same dimensionality as the state x, such that, for each t,

$u^*(t)$ maximizes $H[x(t),u(t),p(t),t]$, where $\qquad$ (3a)
$H(x,u,p,t) = J(x,u,t) + p'\,F(x,u,t)$;

and the function $p(t)$ satisfies the differential equations

$$\dot{p}_i = -\partial H/\partial x_i,\text{ evaluated at} \qquad (3b)$$
$$x=x(t),\ u=u^*(t),\ p=p(t).$$

$$\partial H/\partial u = O \qquad (3c)$$

$$\dot{x} = F[x(t),\ u(t),\ t] \qquad (3d)$$

The function H is known as the Hamiltonian. The auxiliary variables, p, contain the constraints. Various constraints, equality or inequality constraints, can be placed on the system. Solving the Hamiltonian, H, we can achieve the maximization of our objective function, J, subject to the nature of the system and the constraints on the control variables, by regulating the values of the control variables, or signals.

The above is only the most general and primitive representation of a control systems approach. Indeed, for a more complete treatment we need to consider infinite time horizons and a variety of constraint conditions. We have outlined here only the basics of the maximum principle subject to constraints. However, it is the core of reasoning behind optimal control theory.

A SIMPLIFIED EXAMPLE USING RICHARDSON'S ARMS RACE MODEL

A simple example of optimal control systems can be constructed using Richardson's (1960) arms race model.

Let

x: the armaments of nation X
u: the armaments of nation U
ℓu: the threat which nation U's arms pose for nation X
βx: the fatigue and expense which nation X's arms pose for itself
h: grievance of nation X toward nation U (h is a constant)

the Richardson model is

$$\dot{x}=\ell u(t)-\beta x(t)+h. \qquad (4)$$

The Richardson model will serve as the linear plant. We now need to construct an objective function for nation U. Let us agree that nation U desires to maintain some arms advantage over nation X and also wants to minimize the total amount of arms between itself and nation X. However, nation U is more concerned about its arms advantage over nation X than with the total amount of arms.

Figure 1. Block Diagram of System

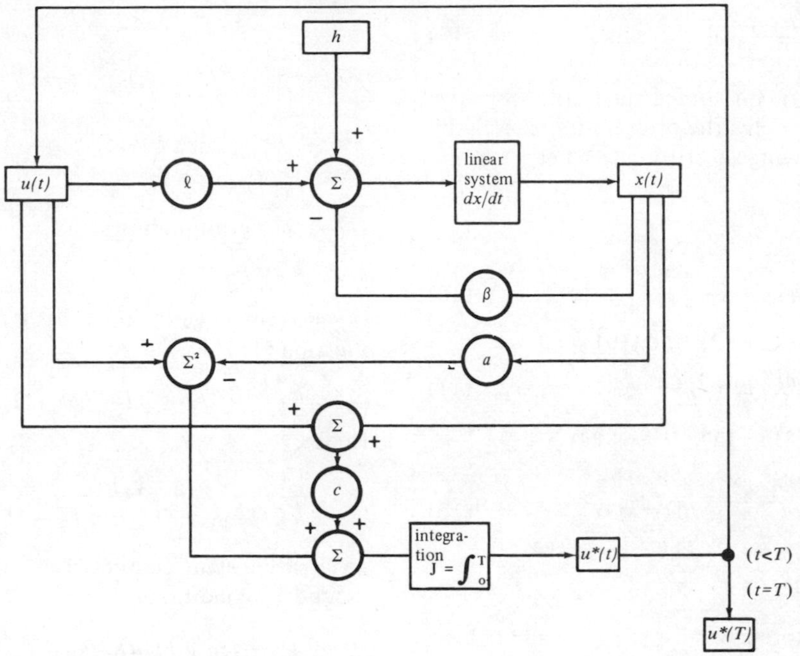

Nation U's objective function can be written as

$$J = \int_O^T \left[\left\{ u(t) - ax(t) \right\}^2 + c \left\{ u(t)+x(t) \right\} \right] dt \quad (5)$$

where

$(u-ax)^2$:   nation U's arms advantage over nation X and its importance relative to the overall objective, J

$c(u+x)$:   total arms held by nations U and X.

Since we are concerned with the objective of nation U, the variable u is the control variable and the variable x is the state variable. The problem is to find u^* to minimize[2] the objective function (5) subject to the plant (4). (It should be noted that this problem has been simplified for the purposes of demonstration.) One way of visualizing the system with which we are operating, is to recast it as a block diagram as shown in Figure 1.

[2] The maximum principle can be simply be adapted to problems of minimization. It is generally mathematically more convenient to state problems in terms of minimization.

Examination of the block diagram shows that the system is a closed loop with feedback. Given that the initial conditions of $x(t_o)$ and $u(t_o)$ are known, the system can be solved for any t.

The first step of the solution is to form the Hamiltonian (3a).

$$H(x,u,p) = \left[(u-ax)^2 + c(u+x) \right] + p \left(\ell u - \beta x + h \right)$$

where

p: auxiliary variables

For simplicity the time notation of variables will be eliminated but it should be understood that x, u, and p are all time-variant.

From the Hamiltonian:

$$\frac{\partial H}{\partial u} = 2(u - ax)+c+p\ell=0 \quad (6)$$

$$\dot{p} = - (\partial H / \partial x) \quad (7)$$

$$= 2a(u-ax)+p\beta-c$$

$$\dot{x} = \ell u - \beta x + h \quad (8)$$

Using (6) to solve for u

$$u = \frac{2ax - p\ell - c}{2} \qquad (9)$$

For a linear plant and a quadratic objective function, we can solve the problem more easily by making the following substitutions.[3] Let

$$p = k_1 x + k_2$$

Then:

$$\dot{p} = k_1 \dot{x} + \dot{k_1} x + \dot{k_2}. \qquad (10)$$

Using expressions (7), (9), and (10) we have:

$$\dot{p} = (\beta k_1 - a\ell k_1)x + (\beta k_2 - a\ell k_2 - ac - c). \qquad (11)$$

Using expressions (4) and (10) we have

$$\dot{p} = (k_1 \ell a - \frac{k_1^2 \ell^2}{2} - \beta k_1 + \dot{k_1})x \qquad (12)$$

$$+ (\dot{k_2} k_1 h - \frac{k_1 \ell c}{2} - \frac{k_1 k_2 \ell^2}{2})$$

Using the two expressions for $\dot{p}$ in (11) and (12) we have

$$0 = \dot{p} - \dot{p}$$

$$0 = (2k_1 \ell a - 2k_1 \beta - \frac{k_1^2 \ell^2}{2} + \dot{k_1})x + \qquad (13)$$
$$(k_2 \ell a - \beta k_2 + ac + k_1 h$$
$$- \frac{k_1 \ell c}{2} - \frac{k_1 k_2 \ell^2}{2} + c + \dot{k_2})$$

Solving for $\dot{k_1}$ and $\dot{k_2}$ in (13), we have

$$\dot{k_1} = 2(\beta - \ell a)k_1 + \frac{\ell^2}{2} k_1^2 \qquad (14)$$

[3]The method of proof here is known as the Ricatti method and expression (10) is the Ricatti equation. This is a very handy device in solving many optimal control problems because Ricatti equations have very desirable properties. The reasoning is to pose an equation for the auxiliary variables, p, which is compatible with the Hamiltonian and gives a structure which poses no additional assumptions. Much of the craftsmanship of quadratic-linear differential equations problems surrounds the productive use of such techniques. The difficulty is that there are few hard and fast mathematical principles to follow. In the final solution (17) note that none of the elements of the Ricatti equations appears and that the auxiliary variables used in constructing the Hamiltonian have also disappeared.

$$\dot{k_2} = (\beta - \ell a)k_2 + \frac{\ell^2}{2} k_1 k_2 \qquad (15)$$
$$+ (\frac{\ell c}{2} - h)k_1 - (a+1)c$$

The boundary solution is

$$k_1(T) \equiv 0$$

(k_1 is the zero function), and

$$k_2(T) = 0$$

(k_2 evaluated at $t=T$ equals 0). Therefore from expression (15)

$$\dot{k_2} = (\beta - \ell a)k_2 - (a+1)c.$$

Hence,

$$k_2(t) = Ke^{(\beta - \ell a)t} + (a+1)c/(\beta - \ell a)$$

(K is a constant composed of several terms). The boundary conditions require $k_2(T) = 0$,

$$K = -[(a+1)c/(\beta - \ell a)]e^{(\beta - \ell a)(-T)}$$

and we can write:

$$k_2(t) = [(a+1)c/(\beta - \ell a)] \qquad (16)$$
$$[1 - e^{(\beta - \ell a)(t-T)}].$$

From expression (9) and (16), we can now write the solution $u^*(t)$:

$$u^*(t) = ax(t) - \frac{1}{2}[\ell c(a+1)/(\beta - \ell a)] \qquad (17)$$
$$[1 - e^{(\beta - \ell a)(t-T)}] - \frac{1}{2}.$$

To write (17) in more parsimonious terms define

$$g(t) \overset{\Delta}{=} -\frac{1}{2} - \frac{1}{2}[\ell c(a+1)/(\beta - \ell a)]$$
$$[1 - e^{(\beta - \ell a)(t-T)}].$$

Then,

$$u^*(t) = ax(t) + g(t) \qquad (18)$$

Expressions (17) and (18) provide the optimal value of the control variable u for each moment in time for the purpose of satisfying the objective function (5) and constrained by the plant (4). What is substantively interesting about (17) is that as t approaches the terminal time T, the value $g(t)$ becomes very small and hence, the nation U begins only to respond, if it chooses to follow its optimal or best value, to maintaining an advantage over nation X. When t is small, the response of nation U to nation X is muted, at least to some degree by its concern for the total amount of arms between X and U. Examining expression (17) one can see, however, that the term "a" (the advantage in arms of U over X) is far more a determinant of u^* than is the term "c" (the term referring to the importance of the total armaments in the system). As the terminal time T approaches, the decision maker will increase the investment in arms. It is also interesting to note that the term "$\beta - \ell a$" appears in several places in expression (17). β is the fatigue and expense of nation X, ℓ is the threat nation U poses for nation X, and a is nation U's desired advantage over X. Its significance is that the comparison is between fatigue and expense (how much economic hardship for nation X's population) and a combination of threat and advantage terms.

The analysis presented here could be expanded to an analysis of the equilibrium, stability, and sensitivity properties of the model. Using the fiction of an infinite time horizon, one could assess the analytical attributes of the modeled system. However, this is beyond the purpose of this chapter; the example presented should provide evidence of the kinds of problems which can be examined by an optimal control approach.

OPTIMAL CONTROL THEORY AND COMPARATIVE FOREIGN POLICY

Although the above example is a simple one, optimal control methods can be used for the analysis of large-scale systems, hierarchical systems with one- and two-way communications, game models (matrix and differential games, two-person and n-person games), and a variety of other systems with regulators, moderators, etc. The mathematics is powerful enough to be cast into several settings compatible with the ways in which we conceptualize the world of foreign policy.

Optimal control thinking is, without question, different from the kind of thinking we have conventionally employed in comparative foreign policy. It is a problem-oriented approach that moves beyond standard analyses for the purposes of testing hypotheses; with it potentially we can begin to evaluate policy decisions, assess the attributes of systems underway and how they might be altered to provide greater likelihood of achieving desired results, and also we can construct, design, and assess the attributes and behaviors of alternative systems not known to the empirical world. The thinking always pertains to dynamic processes and it always attempts to assess the attributes of the process and where it is leading.

Too often in any kind of public policy research our effort is "to explain," and once we have achieved our explanation we abandon further research. Using our commonsensical notions and "confirmed" hypotheses as to what causes what, we can begin to model systems and assess their attributes. Such assessments are convincing because they translate our problems from the world of the manipulation of words into a new language, the grammar for which is well defined. Proofs can be challenged on grounds of the assumptions (the statements of the model) employed, but if correctly stated, they cannot be disclaimed. Such analyses or proofs, I contend, lead to lasting pieces of knowledge, that when accumulated are likely to comprise a coherent whole.

REFERENCES

Athans, M., and P. L. Falb. 1966. *Optimal Control: An Introduction to the Theory and Its Applications.* New York: McGraw-Hill.

Bellman, R. 1965. *Dynamic Programming and Modern Control Theory.* New York: Academic Press.

Bryson, A. E., and Y. C. Ho. 1969. *Applied Control Theory.* Waltham, Mass.: Ginn.

Dyer, P., and S. R. McReynolds. 1970. *Computation and Theory of Optimal Control.* New York: Academic Press.

Hsu, J. C., and A. U. Meyer, 1968. *Modern Control Principles and Applications.* New York: McGraw-Hill.

Isaacs, R. 1965. *Differential Games.* New York: Wiley.

Koppel, L. B. 1968. *Introduction to Control Theory.* Englewood Cliffs, N.J.: Prentice-Hall.

Lasdon, L. S. 1970. *Optimization Theory for Large Systems.* New York: Macmillan.

Lee, E. B., and L. Marcus. 1967. *Foundations of Optimal Control Theory.* New York: Wiley.

Mesarovic, M. D., D. Macko, and Y. Takahara. 1970. *Theory of Hierarchical, Multi-level Systems.* New York: Academic Press.

Ogata, M. 1970. *Modern Control Engineering.* Englewood Cliffs, N.J.: Prentice-Hall.

Richardson, L. F. 1960. *Arms and Insecurity.* Pittsburgh: Boxwood.

Sage, A. P. 1968. *Optimal Systems Control.* Englewood Cliffs, N.J.: Prentice-Hall.

Varaiya, P. P. 1962. *Notes on Optimization.* New York: Van Nostrand Reinhold.

28. Some Conceptual Problems in Constructing Theories of Foreign Policy Behavior

Stuart J. Thorson

Theories of foreign policy behavior—like theories of most anything else—are developed with a variety of purposes. In this chapter I will discuss three such purposes: (1) description, (2) policy, and (3) design. It will be argued that the three are interrelated in various ways and that it will be helpful in constructing theories to be aware of some of these interrelations. To make this argument, I must first clarify what I mean by a theory. Within political science (at least) the concept of a theory is one which takes on many meanings. To argue that one concept is more correct than others would be arrogant (and probably pointless). However, to assume that "everyone knows what a theory is" and thus not to define it is dangerous.

SPECIAL NOTE: An earlier version of this paper was presented to the Inter-university Comparative Foreign Policy Project Conference on the Future of Comparative Foreign Policy Analysis, Ojai, California, June 1973. Support for this paper was provided in part by the Advanced Research Projects Agency (DAHC15 73 C 0197). The helpful comments of the ICFP conference attendees, Warren Phillips, Philip Miller, and Steven Yarnell are gratefully acknowledged.

Therefore, at the risk of appearing arrogant, let me make as precise as I can the way I will be using the term "theory." Further, since this is a paper on the study of foreign policy and not on the definition of theory, I want to accomplish this task as briefly as possible. One way to achieve this is to identify some attributes of "theories" and then to specify the exact set of attributes possessed by what I will be calling theories.

To begin, most of uses of theory entail that theories are linguistic. That is, they are sets of sentences. Thus one attribute of a theory is the kind of language (e.g., semantically closed or open, natural or artificial, etc.) in which it is expressed. Without pursuing the point here, it should be noted that the kind of language chosen to express the theory has consequences for what can be asserted in the theory (i.e., it is generally not simply a matter of translating a theory from one language to another).

This leads to a second characteristic of theories. Theories are composed of assertions that some thing(s) is true. The sentences in a theory are assertions that some state of affairs obtains. For example, "Force is equal to mass times acceleration," or "Variations in the structure of a nation are related to changes in the nation's external environment." When sentences such as the above two appear in a theory (e.g., the second is in Rosenau's, 1970, adaptation theory), I want to be able to say that they are being asserted to be true. That the sentences which comprise a theory are asserted to be true would seem to be fairly unobjectionable (for an opposing position see Friedman, 1953, or perhaps, by implication, McGowan, 1974). Note that to assert a sentence to be true is not to make it true. Whether a particular sentence is accepted as true will depend in large part upon ones epistemological and methodological positions. These questions will not be considered here.

Having defined the term "theory" as a set of sentences (in some language) each of which is asserted to be true, there remains one additional distinction to be made. In this paper, I will be considering two senses of the term—a technical one and a nontechnical one. A technical theory is a set of sentences asserted to be true where the set is closed under deduction. That is, the set contains any sentence that is logically implied by any other sentence in the set. This concept requires some preassigned logical framework or "calculus axioms" (e.g., first-order predicate calculus). Any time we deal with an axiomatic theory, this technical sense is being employed.

On the other hand, there is an important non-technical use of "theory." A nontechnical theory is simply a set of sentences asserted to be true. In this usage, no position is taken on the truth of any sentences "implied" by the theory sentences (indeed, "implied" may be undefined since no calculus axioms need be assigned to the theory). Thus the entire body of knowledge about some subject may be referred to as the theory of that subject, as in "foreign policy theory." However, in this paper, unless otherwise specified, I will be using "theory" in its technical sense.

Having defined "theory," it is important to provide a definition of a related and commonly encountered term—"model." In very rough terms, a model is that "thing" which makes the sentences in a theory true. In scientific theorizing we generally want to order or account for some aspects of a perceived reality. Thus we must first represent reality in terms of some posited objects and relations. Whether these posited objects and relations

indeed represent reality is, of course, in many senses moot and is certainly contingent upon both our perceptual system and our ability to make and hold to distinctions.

However, a well-specified collection of objects and relations is not linguistic in this sense. Indeed, it is a set-theoretic structure and not a theory. In a theory, object *symbols* and relation *symbols* are used to make assertions about the objects and relations in the "perceived reality." This well-specified collection of objects and relations (or, loosely, the "reality") is termed a *model* for the theory. A model is a set-theoretic structure which makes the sentences in the theory true.

More precisely, a set-theoretic structure M is a set of elements (objects), $A = (a_1, a_2, \ldots)$ together with a set of relations of order i, $P_1{}^i1, P_2{}^i2, \ldots,$ and may be expressed

$$M = \langle A; P_1{}^i1, P_2{}^i2, \ldots, P_n{}^in, \ldots \rangle.$$

A formal language **L** in which properties of M can be expressed will consist of formulas generated by a specific set of rules, say the predicate calculus, from an alphabet consisting of relations symbols $(R_1, R_2, \ldots)$, variable symbols $(x_1, x_2, \ldots)$, connectives $(\neg, \vee, \wedge, \ldots)$, and quantifiers $(\forall, \exists)$. Since functions and constants are special kinds of relations, function symbols $(f_1, f_2, \ldots)$ and constant symbols $(c_1, c_2, \ldots)$ will also be used in **L**. The language **L** will be assumed to be first order, that is, its variables range over the elements of A (as opposed to ranging over the subsets of A, or sets of subsets, etc.). Sentences in **L** are formulas containing no free variables.

Let T be a set of axioms in a language **L**. If ϕ is a mapping of constant symbols occurring in T into the set of objects A, and also a mapping of relation symbols occurring in T into the set of relations in M, then M provides an interpretation of T under ϕ. If this interpretation results in the sentences in T being true, then M is said to satisfy T and M is a model of the axiom set T. A model for a set of axioms then, is a set-theoretical mathematical structure which interprets the axioms in such a way that the axioms are true.

The above definition of "model" leaves us with an obvious problem: what is meant by a sentence being "true." Rather than provide an extended discussion of truth, the reader is referred to Tarski (1944). The important question here is not how do we know whether a particular sentence is in fact true, but rather what is meant by asserting a sentence to be true. This latter semantic question is treated in considerable detail by Tarski for important classes of formal languages.[1]

This definition of "model" is completely general. Its utility lies both in its enabling us to distinguish very precisely between a theory and that which is being theorized about and in its "fit" with certain of the systems notions currently being employed in the theoretical study of foreign policy behavior. In this chapter we will be making direct use of this second property of the model definition, while we will be exploiting the first only indirectly. Ashby (1952), for example, has defined a (abstract) system as a collection of objects together with the relations defined upon them.[2] Thus a system is a mathematical (i.e., set-theoretic) structure. A task for systems theorists of foreign policy then becomes the identification of systems which can serve as models for theories of foreign policy behavior. Further, to adopt a systems vocabulary for the ensuing discussion will not limit the range of theories which might be developed (or more precisely will not limit the range of structures we may theorize about).

In order to get on with the discussion, we can consider a government from an artificial systems perspective (Simon, 1969; Thorson, 1974). Under this view, a government (including the foreign-policy-making mechanism) is assumed to be an inner environment attempting to achieve various (perhaps poorly articulated and inconsistent) goals. At least a part of these goals will have to be achieved in some outer environment. The outer environment may include domestic aspects of the "government's" nation as well as the rest of the "international system." The governmental players, together with the (not always well-coordinated) relations between them may be thought of as being "located" in the inner environment.[3] In

other words, the artificial systems framework argues that a government can be viewed as an adaptive control mechanism and the rest of the "world" as the process the government is attempting to control.

From this perspective, there are several sorts of questions the theorist might choose to address. First, for particular nations, what do the goals, inner and outer environments, look like? Second, given an inner and outer environment (that is holding the structure of the inner environment fixed), how can certain goals be "best" achieved? And third, given some set of objectives, what sorts of inner and/or outer environments can "best" achieve them. These can be termed questions of description, policy, and design, respectively. In the next sections I will argue that these questions can be ordered in the sense that answering policy questions will generally require having fairly good answers to descriptive questions and that solutions to problems of political design will usually require prior work in the policy and descriptive areas. I will examine each of these separately, moving from description to policy to design.

DESCRIPTION

"Description" is being used here in a very general fashion to refer to a standard concern in constructing scientific theory—accounting for observations, identifying interrelations among them, and predicting new observations. I do *not* mean to embrace any particular metaphysical position on the possibility of knowing an external world (i.e., have the "correct" description of it). Rather, my use of "description" is Wittgenstein's (1922, para. 6.342 ff.):

> That Newtonian mechanics *can* be used to describe the world tells us nothing about the world. But this *does* tell us something—that it can be used to describe the world in the way in which we do in fact use it.

Thus the task of developing a descriptive theory of foreign policy behavior involves constructing a set of sentences which orders (makes sense of) some set of observations of foreign policy behaviors and which can be used to predict future foreign policy behaviors.

---

[1] This discussion is taken from S. Thorson and J. Stever (1974).

[2] This definition is similar to the more current definition proposed by Mesarovic et al. (1970).

[3] This discussion may suggest more reification of the objects comprising the system than I would like. This is done for the sake of brevity and illustration.

To achieve this goal, the theorist will have to work on the basis of some finite number of observations. With these observations, he will be attempting to identify an underlying structure which might be generating them. And yet, as is well known, there is an infinite number of structures which could have generated the observed strings of behavior. More specifically, to describe a system is to write sentences which relate values of some variables to values of others. These sentences (i.e., the theory) can be used to predict future states of the world. As an example, consider the abstract system of Figure 1. The state of the system at any point in time is given by the vector x.

Figure 1.

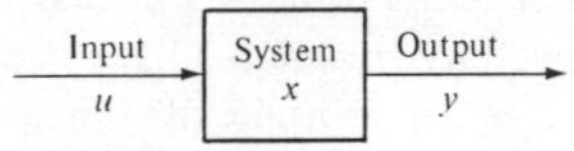

A description of this system might consist of the following equations:

(i) $\dot{x} = f(x,u)$

(ii) $y = h(x,u)$

These equations assert that changes in the internal state $(\dot{x})$ are a function $(f(\cdot))$ of the state of the system (x) and the input (u), and that the output of the system (y) is a second function $(h(\cdot))$ of the internal state and the input. This is important, for in looking at the overtime behavior of a system (in terms of its outputs) it is crucial to take into account internal state changes as well as input-output changes. In other words, output behavior need not be a function (in the mathematical sense) of inputs. The same input can lead to different outputs if the internal state[4] of the system is different.

As a highly stylized example, consider the behavior of a "bully" nation. Suppose it is capable of being in only two internal states—it either is stable (S) or unstable $(\sim S)$. Further, it is capable of emitting and sensing only two sorts of behaviors—

[4]State here is being used in the sense of Ashby (1952) and not of Mesarovic et al. (1970).

aggressive (A) and nonaggressive $(\sim A)$. Thus we have:

u: $\{ A, \sim A \}$

y: $\{ A, \sim A \}$

x: $\{ S, \sim S \}$

Since the nation is a bully, it will behave aggressively whenever it can. And yet, as everyone knows, the only time a bully does not aggress is when it is aggressed upon and in a weak (in our terms, unstable) state. Thus we can write $y = h(x,u)$ as in Table 1.

Table 1.

Input (u)	State (x)	Output (y)
A	S	A
$\sim A$	S	A
A	$\sim S$	$\sim A$
$\sim A$	$\sim S$	A

As can be seen, the output of the bully nation is entirely deterministic. Further, since even a bully gets nervous (and, therefore, unstable) when he is aggressed upon, $x = f(x,u)$ can be written as in Table 2.

Table 2.

Input (u)	State (x)	New State (x)
A	S	$\sim S$
$\sim A$	S	$\sim S$
A	$\sim S$	S
$\sim A$	$\sim S$	$\sim S$

All this most likely seems both absurd and simple. However, further suppose a political scientist is watching the bully nation and trying to relate its behavior (outputs) to the behavior it receives (its input). What might be the result?

First of all, he will generally ignore the internal structure of the system and simply relate inputs and outputs. Thus, he might watch the bully over a long period of time and note that nonaggressive inputs *always* are followed by aggressive outputs on the part of the bully. However, he would note, aggressive outputs are preceded by aggressive inputs only about one-half of the time. Therefore, he writes an article in which he proclaims two general laws.

Law (1) $P(y = A/u = \sim A) = 1$
Law (2) $P(y = A/u = A) = 1/2$

Of course, by this time the world is getting rather sick of the bully's behavior and commissions our political scientist to recommend a policy toward the bully (this policy would consist of generating values of u). Given the two laws above, the optimal policy would, of course, be to always behave in an aggressive way toward the bully nation which would, according to law (2), guarantee that one-half of the bully's responses would be nonaggressive.

Note that our mythical political scientist, like so many of us, ignored the internal state of the bully nation. As a result, he was forced to state his laws in probabilistic terms and to conclude that the "best" that could be done was to reduce $p(y = A)$ to about one-half.

However, by referring back to the transition tables, it can be seen that the bully can be made to act in a completely nonaggressive way. Suppose, first, he is initially in state $\sim S$. Then by always behaving in an aggressive way toward the bully, the bully will never respond in an aggressive way. If, on the other hand, he is initially in state S, then he will respond in an aggressive manner no matter what is done. However, by threatening him, he will be forced into an unstable state and, therefore, continuing aggressive acts will result in no more threats from the bully.[5] Thus, by paying attention to internal states, it becomes possible to eliminate references to probabilities and to suggest a policy which will result in at most one aggressive behavior by the bully. While in this example ignoring internal structure did not result in "wrong" policy advice, it is possible to construct a slightly more complex example for which it would.[6]

The important point here is that developing descriptive theories of foreign policy behavior requires paying close attention to the internal structure of the foreign policy generating mechanism as well as to that of the environment (domestic, as well as international) in which the mechanism is imbedded. We need to know how inputs affect internal states and how inputs together with internal states determine outputs. As Halperin and Kanter (1973, p. 3) suggest, "the scholar requires an understanding of a nation's domestic political structure and of its national security bureaucracy in order to explain or predict the foreign policy actions it will take." Examples of work in this area include Niskanen (1971), Allison (1971), Ellsberg (1972), and Halperin and Kanter (1973).

POLICY

The previous section alluded to the importance of descriptive theory in the making of policy recommendations (as well as in evaluating the impact of a policy). To provide a clarification of what is meant by a "policy", it will be helpful to return to the artificial systems framework mentioned earlier. Here the inner environment (I.E.) seeks to behave in such a way as to maintain the states of the outer and inner environments within specified limits. These desired states can be termed goals of the inner environment. In order to achieve its goals, the inner environment sends outputs to the outer environment. These streams of outputs can be termed the (revealed) policy of the outer environment (O.E.).

If political scientists are going to be able to assist in consistently making "better" policy decisions, we must approach being able to do the following:

1. Identify a set of feasible policies,
2. identify the rules for linking policies to consequences,
3. identify a preference ordering or a utility function over the various dimensions of the consequences,
4. identify a rule for selecting a policy from 1. on the bases of 2. and 3.

A general purpose of policies is to move the state of the entire system to some desired value (or set of values), and it is important to recognize that goals are defined in terms of both the state of the inner environment and that of the outer environment. This allows for domestic and internal bureaucratic goals as well as external "foreign policy" objectives.

[5] Though such a policy might result in your becoming a bully.

[6] For example, see Kanter and Thorson (1972).

In order to identify the impact of a policy upon a system, it is necessary first to have a description of that system of the sort identified in the previous section. Such a theory will describe what happens when something is done to the system. But what can be done to the system? A U.S. president, for example, has many foreign policy options which are, in principle, open to him. In any particular instance these may range from doing nothing to launching nuclear weapons. However, the options a president in principle has and those he considers are not generally the same. Constraints—be they political, economic, etc.—rule out certain policies. Those policies which meet the constraints are called feasible policies.

If we are to make policy recommendations to a unit of government—be it a president or a desk officer—we must first be able to identify a set of feasible policy options. These constraints are often contingent upon the policy maker. It is feasible for the president to take actions not open to a desk officer (and conversely). Additionally, even the relatively simple task of identifying the constraints depends upon a descriptive theory of the system. Policies which might be infeasible under one description may become feasible under a second. For example, it is doubtful that either Nixon or his critics in the early 1970s wanted to greatly increase the risk of nuclear war. His mining of Haiphong Harbor was criticized for greatly increasing that risk. Whether it did or did not greatly increase the risk is, of course, dependent upon the particular descriptive theory being employed. The difference between Nixon and his critics may be viewed less as a disagreement about policy objectives and more as one over the consequences of a particular policy. The predicted consequences depend upon the descriptive theory used to make the predictions. Moreover, the identification of feasible policies is not completely independent of the rules (i.e., the description) for linking policies to consequences. To do even the most simple part of policy analysis, adequate descriptive theory is required.

Associating consequences (or perhaps probability distributions over consequences) with policies is not enough. We must also be able to (in some sense) order the consequences with respect to their "desirability." Generally the approach taken is to represent the ordering with a utility function.[7] Here if $t(\cdot)$ is a utility function and s_1 and s_2 are two consequences (i.e., states of the system) then we want $t(s_1)$ to be greater than $t(s_2)$ if and only if s_1 is more desirable than (i.e., is preferred to) s_2.

In decision theory these utility functions are typically scalar valued. For example, states of the world might be ordered with respect to their value in U.S. dollars. However, in many policy applications it is not possible to identify such a single common "metric" as money. In a foreign policy application, for example, a decision maker might be concerned with such attributes of various states of the system as dollar costs, strategic impact, domestic political impact, and level of benefits to various sectors of the inner environment. These attributes may be seen as being incommensurable and, indeed, may even be themselves composed of incommensurable attributes. Incommensurability might arise, for example, if it is impossible to specify trade-offs (i.e., rates of substitution) among the attributes. Such instances require the use of multiple-valued utility functions. There are few general rules for identifying and manipulating such functions (for an introduction to the problems posed by such situations see Raiffa, 1969). Which is bigger—the vector $<9, 7>$ or the vector $<6, 10>$? Thus, a second problem we may face in assisting in the making of foreign policy is dealing with multiple-valued utility functions.

Even given a set of feasible policies and well-behaved utility functions over their possible consequences, the task of policy selection is not completed. Indeed the most important task remains. This is to define some sort of rule for selecting a policy given the utility function. Approaches to this question are reviewed in great detail by Chernoff (1954). Even if we know a particular actor's set of feasible alternatives and his utility function over their possible consequences, we still cannot advise him how he should act (i.e., what policy he should select). This can be seen more clearly by

---

[7] The conditions under which a (real) single-valued utility function exists are identified in Debreu (1954). It is a simple matter to show reasonable situations (e.g., lexicographic orderings) which violate these conditions.

examining a particular (though not unrealistic) sort of decision problem (one in which the descriptive theory is probabilistic). First define a set U^f of feasible policy alternatives $u_1, u_2, \ldots, u_n$. Second define a set of S of possible systems states $s_1, s_2, \ldots, s_m$ for the O.E. and the I.E. of the artificial system. Clearly the goal state s_i^* belongs to S. Further, to simplify the example, assume the utility associated with any $u_i \in U^f$ to in part depend upon which $s_i \in S$ actually obtains. We will not consider how particular time-ordered sequences of s_i might result from time-ordered sequences of u_i. Thus the utility function t is defined over elements of S and U^f yielding $t(u_j, s_i)$. This formulation can be transferred into a traditional decision problem if risk is viewed as negative utility thus yielding a risk function $r(u_j, s_i) = -t(u_j, s_i)$.

The task now becomes to identify an appropriate decision rule for selecting a best $u_i \in U^f$. The decision rule most often encountered in political science is that of maximizing expected utility. This criterion is a useful one if it is possible to "accurately" assign probabilities to states of the system. Here we need simply to multiply $t(u_j, s_i)$ by the probability (p_i) of s_i for all u_j, s_i and then select that u_j for which

$$\sum_{i=1}^{m} p_i u_j$$

is at a maximum.

As an example consider a situation where the descriptive theory yields three possible states of the system, each of which is equally likely $(p_1 = p_2 = p_3 = 1/3)$. Further, there are two feasible policies u_1 and u_2. $t(u_j, s_i)$ are given as cell entries in the following matrix:

	u_1	u_2
s_1	−30	30
s_2	3000	60
s_3	300	90

The expected utility of u_1 is

$$1/3(-30) + 1/3(3000) + 1/3(300) = 1090$$

In like manner, the expected utility of u_2 is equal to 60. Under the maximize expected utility rule,

policy u_1 ought to be enacted since 1090 is greater than 60.

However this is not the only "reasonable" criterion which might be used. Another plausible one is to minimize your maximum risk. Remembering that risk is equal to negative utility, it can be seen that the maximum risk is obtained under u_1 (and is equal to 30). Thus the policy maker desiring to minimize maximum risk ought to enact u_2.[8]

There are many other equally plausible decision criteria which might be used. That there are such different rules is important since in risky or uncertain worlds, an actors' decisions cannot be predicted simply by knowing his feasible policies and the utility he attaches to their possible consequences. It might even be useful to develop a classification of actors based in part upon the decision rule(s) used in selecting foreign policy strategies. Perhaps, for example, leaders of nations with nuclear weapons would be more inclined to use a minimize maximum risk strategy than would leaders of other nations in certain decision environments.

The importance of specifying the decision rule being used cannot be overstressed. Even descriptive theories of foreign policy decision making often seem to depend upon the particular rule being employed. Thus, for example, a major source of disagreement between "quagmire" theories of U.S. involvement in Vietnam (e.g., Schlesinger, 1966) and the stalemate theory of Ellsberg (1972) may result from different perceptions of the decision rule being employed.

To summarize, in this section I have attempted to sketch some minimal theoretical problems which must be addressed before we can be of much use in giving policy advice. Further, I have argued that the manner in which these problems are resolved is dependent upon a descriptive theory.

DESIGN

Whereas a policy problem (or, alternatively, a policy theory) is concerned with identifying and

---

[8]Ferejohn and Fiorina (1974) provide a very nice discussion of these two decision rules and their impact on people's probability of voting.

implementing feasible strategies to meet some goal(s) in accord with a particular decision rule(s), design problems deal with identifying and describing various mechanisms (e.g., inner environments, outer environments, and interfaces) for the achievement of goals. The distinction I am making here between policy and design is analogous to the distinction between the values of variables (including parameters) and their structure. Policy changes are changes in the level of variables, and design changes are changes in the structure relating the variables. Thus, increasing the rate of an existing tax would be a policy change, while introducing a new tax would be a design change.

The design problem is often viewed in engineering terms (Simon, 1969), where the problem is to design an inner environment (or control mechanism) which can achieve goals (or control) in a particular outer or task environment (process). It is important to note a distinction between the typical engineering approach to design and that being taken here. In engineering the process (or outer environment) is taken to be given. For example in designing an airplane, the "laws" of gravity are fixed. The airframe designer is not free to design new graviational laws which will make it easier for his plane to fly. This is not always true in designing social systems. Oftentimes the structure of the outer environment itself can be changed. Indeed it may sometimes be "easier" to change the O.E. structure than it is to change the levels of various variables.

More generally, a task of design theories might be seen as one of identifying various governmental systems (including, of course, foreign policy mechanisms) which are effective in achieving specified goals in various classes of outer environments. It has been shown, for example, that for a fairly general class of outer environment there can exist no universal inner environment (Thorson, 1974). In other words, given an inner environment (governmental mechanism) there will always exist outer environments to which the inner environment cannot adapt. Thus we are led to consider what classes of inner environments have the capacity to adapt to what classes of outer environments. If viewed this way, important tasks to be

accomplished include developing taxonomies of inner and outer environments and types of goals.

In designing these inner environments, one area which requires additional research are the interfaces between a governmental system and its outer environment. The governmental system can be viewed as a hierarchical information processor. That is, information is gathered about the outer environment and, partially on the basis of this information, policy outputs are generated. Moreover, this information will be processed hierarchically by the inner environment. This hierarchical arrangement of the inner environment is in part related to multigoal "nature" of governments. As Mesarovic et al. (1970, p. 22) note, "the overall goal of the organization as a whole is broken into a sequence of subgoals, so that the solution of the overall goal is replaced by the solution of the family of subgoals." This information is used to select appropriate outputs (policies). Implicit here is the idea that responses are functions of previous information and the present system state.

This hierarchical arrangement and its attendant goal specialization brings with it the problem of coordination. Lower level units process much information but, presumably, consider fewer goals. As one moves up in the hierarchy the detail of the information is reduced and the number of goals considered can thereby be increased. The problem, of course, is to determine what information should be sent up the hierarchy and what coordination inputs should be sent down the hierarchy in order to achieve goals as efficiently[9] as possible. The problem of coordination is discussed at length in Mesarovic et al. (1970).

In order to receive this information the government (inner environment) must have some sort of observation interface. This serves as a perceptual system and determines what aspects of the outer environment the government will have information about. The observation interface may be thought of as sort of screen which may modify and eliminate information in the outer environment. Theoretical work in this area may be found in such works as Julez (1971), Gregory (1969), Fu (1968),

---

[9] "Efficiency" is being used here in the very general sense of getting the most (desired) output for least input.

Minsky and Papert (1969), and Chase and Simon (1973).

The importance of the kind of perceptual screen used by the government is illustrated by the work in designing algorithms by which computers can play chess. Interest in machine chess has been high partly because it has been felt that the principles necessary to playing a good game of chess are similar to the principles necessary for dealing with real world problems such as management and planning. In addition, it has been argued (de Groot, 1965; Chase and Simon, 1973) that what distinguishes chess masters from beginners is more perceptual differences than cognitive processing (i.e., logical skills) differences. Therefore, work in analyzing chess becomes relevant to the foreign policy theorists' interest in identifying how a government's observation interface (its "perceptual system") structures the information on which it operates.

Shannon (1950) first identified the two approaches that algorithms for chess playing might take:

1. Scan all possible moves and construct a decision tree of equal length for each move (length here refers to the number of moves into the future the programs scans). Then, using some weighting function the possible moves can be evaluated and the best one chosen.
2. Scan only certain moves. Eliminate others through the use of some special rule.

The first approach requires the computer to view the chess board in all its complexity. Very valuable information is treated the same as more unimportant information. The price of this synoptic approach is that, for a given memory size, the number of moves into the future that are looked at is severely limited. Much memory is wasted looking at trivial information. The second approach tries to avoid this problem. By precluding weak moves, a longer future can be considered. Unfortunately, the rule for eliminating bad moves is most difficult to discover.

The problem facing designers of chess machines was an interesting one. They had two approaches— one is relatively easily implemented but rather wasteful and the other is very efficient but ex-

tremely difficult to implement. A Russian grandmaster and electrical engineer Mihail Botvinnik, has spent considerable effort to develop an algorithm for chess which is based upon the second principle. Central to Botvinnik's algorithm is the concept of "horizon." At each half-move point the computer generates a mathematical "map" of the chess board. The horizon limits the area of the map scanned by the computer much as natural boundaries limit our horizon. He defines it:

> The horizon is the boundary of the region containing those pieces, and only those pieces, that can take an active role within the given limits of time for movement. . . . An attack falling within the horizon is included in the mathematical calculations–otherwise, it is not.

Rather than having the machine calculate all positions and eliminate some very early, Botvinnik (1970) has developed a means by which the machine's perceptual system is designed to immediately eliminate (by not perceiving it) trivial[10] information. This, of course, should greatly increase the depth to which moves within the horizon may be considered. Some sort of perceptual screen is important even in dealing with problems in which all information is, at least to some degree, relevant.

A less rigorous example of the importance of the observation interface is provided by the U.S. experience in Vietnam. Ellsberg (1972, p. 120) describes the usual Viet Minh and Viet Cong response to increased U.S. military intervention:

> After suffering initial setbacks they would lie low for an extended period, gather data, analyze experience, develop, test, and adapt new strategies, then plan and prepare carefully before launching them.

However, the U.S., according to Ellsberg, monitored enemy strength through its field commanders who in turn equated frequency of enemy contact with enemy strength. If the enemy is strong, the reasoning went, then it will fight. If it is quiet, then it must be weak. Based on these reports, the natural tendency was for the president to view policy changes as successes. However de-

---

[10]Note here what is trivial will depend upon the descriptive theory being employed.

creased contact did not mean a weakened enemy and, indeed, the periods of greatest crisis came at the times of highest U.S. optimism. The observation interface was inappropriate.

Selection of an observation interface is only one-half of the interface design problem. In addition, the theorist must identify an appropriate access interface. Included in the access interface are structures involved with policy implementation. How do actors in the government get their policies into the outer environment? Oftentimes otherwise desirable policies become infeasible because there is no way to get them into the outer environment. The problem of access interface selection is discussed in some detail in Bailey and Holt (1971) and Thorson (1974).

Finally, the design theorist must develop means of distinguishing various mechanisms (inner environments) and relating these distinctions to effectiveness in classes of outer environments. As Hurwicz (1960, p. 28) noted of economic allocation mechanisms, the problem is to treat the mechanism as "the unknown of the problem, rather than a datum." One possible approach might be to identify the dimensions of a "mechanism space." Indeed, one reasonable task in comparative foreign policy analysis might be to specify what dimensions must be used to identify "properly" a foreign policy mechanism. Certain possibilities such as centralized-decentralized, big-small, decision rules employed, and so on come immediately to mind. Again, however, these dimensions cannot be identified (postulated) independently of the underlying descriptive and policy theories. From this perspective, a foreign policy mechanism would be identified as a point in this mechanism space.

If the same sort of spatial analysis could be applied to outer environments, the design theorist might then address questions concerning relations between points in the mechanism space and points in the outer environment space. One thing of concern would almost certainly be effectiveness. Here we would be interested in the competence of a particular mechanism to achieve certain goals in a particular class of outer environments. Competence is not something that can be directly observed (though, of course, performance can). Indeed, if the class of outer environments is restricted, it is often possible to increase performance at the cost of decreased competence. Thus an important task for the theorist is to develop a way of characterizing the competence of a particular mechanism. My guess is that any definition of competence will be contingent upon the outer environment. A particular mechanism may be very competent over one range of environments and much less so over others. Therefore, in designing mechanisms, we must either have good estimates of future outer environments or else build in an effective self-reorganizing capacity (e.g., see Formby, 1965).

Questions of political design are as old as the study of politics. Consider, as an example, this translation of a passage from Plato's *Republic:*

> I understand, said Glaucon: You mean this commonwealth we have been founding in the realism of discourse; for I think it nowhere exists on earth.
>
> No, I replied; but perhaps there is a pattern set up in the heavens for one who desires to see it and, seeing it, to found one in himself. But whether it exists anywhere or will ever exist is no matter. . . .

To me, at least, the development of design theories is one of the most exciting and important areas open to the theorist. Moreover, I have attempted to show in this chapter that to the extent our concern is with *feasible* design, we require prior work in the areas of policy and descriptive theories.

REFERENCES

Allison, G. 1971. *Essence of Decision.* Boston: Little, Brown.

Ashby, W. R. 1952. *Design for a Brain.* London: Butler & Tanner.

Bailey, F., and R. Holt. 1971. "Toward a Science of Complex Systems." Mimeo. Minneapolis: Univ. of Minnesota.

Botvinnik, M. 1970. *Computers, Chess and Long-Range Planning.* New York: Springer-Verlag.

Chase, W., and H. Simon. 1973. "The Mind's Eye in Chess." In *Visual Information Processing,* ed. W. Chase, pp. 215-82. New York: Academic Press.

Chernoff, H. 1954. "Rational Selection of Decision Functions." *Econometrica* 22 (4): 422-43.

Debreu, G. 1954. "Representation of a Preference Ordering by a Numerical Function." In *Decision Processes,* ed. R. M. Thrall, C. H. Coombs, and R. L. David, pp. 159-66. New York: Wiley.

de Groot, A. 1965. *Thought and Choice in Chess.* The Hague: Mouton.

Ellsberg, D. 1972. *Papers on the War.* New York: Simon & Schuster.

Ferejohn, J., and M. Fiorina. 1974. "The Paradox of Not Voting: A Decision-Theoretic Analysis." *American Political Science Review* 68 (Jun): 525-36.

Formby, J. 1965. *An Introduction to the Mathematical Formulation of Self-organizing Systems.* London: E. & F. N. Spon.

Friedman, M. 1953. *Essays in Positive Economics.* Chicago: Univ. of Chicago Press.

Fu. K. S. 1968. *Sequential Methods in Pattern Recognition and Machine Learning.* New York: Academic Press.

Gregory, R. 1969. "On How So Little Information Controls So Much Behavior." In *Toward a Theoretical Biology,* vol. 2, pp. 236-46. Edinburgh: Edinburgh Univ. Press.

Halperin, M., and A. Kanter. 1973. *Readings in American Foreign Policy.* Boston: Little, Brown.

Hurwicz, L. 1960. "Optimality and Informational Efficiency in Resource Allocation Processes." In *Mathematical Methods in the Social Sciences, 1959,* ed. K. Arrow, S. Karlin, and P. Suppes. Stanford: Stanford Univ. Press.

Julez, B. 1971. *Foundations of Cyclopean Perception.* Chicago: Univ. of Chicago Press.

Kanter, A., and S. Thorson. 1972. "The Logic of U.S. Weapons Procurement." *Public Policy* 20 (4, Autumn): 479-524.

McGowan, P. 1974. "Problems in the Construction of Positive Theories of Foreign Policy." In *Comparing Foreign Policies,* ed. J. N. Rosenau, pp. 25-44. Beverly Hills: Sage.

Mesarovic, M., D. Macko, and Y. Takahara. 1970. *Theory of Hierarchical, Multi-level Systems.* New York: Academic Press.

Minsky, M. L., and S. Papert. 1969. *Perceptions and Introduction to Computational Geometry.* Cambridge: MIT Press.

Niskanen, W. 1971. *Bureaucracy and Representative Government.* Chicago: Aldine.

Raiffa, H. 1969. "Preference for Multi-attributed Alternatives." Rand Corp., Memorandum RM-5868-DOT/RC, April.

Rosenau, J. N. 1970. *The Adaptation of National Societies: A Theory of Political System Behavior and Transformation.* New York: McCaleb-Seiler.

Schlesinger, A. 1966. *The Bitter Heritage: Vietnam and American Democracy, 1941-1966.* Boston: Houghton Mifflin.

Shannon, C. 1950. "Programming a Computer for Playing Chess." *Philosophical Magazine* 41 (Mar).

Simon, H. 1969. *The Science of the Artificial.* Cambridge: MIT Press.

Tarski, A. 1944. "The Semantic Conception of Truth." *Philosophy and Phenomenlogical Research* 4: 341-75.

Thorson, S. 1974. "National Political Adaptation." In *Comparing Foreign Policies,* ed. J. N. Rosenau, pp. 71-116. Beverly Hills: Sage.

––– and J. Stever. 1974. "Classes of Models for Selected Axiomatic Theories of Choice." *Journal of Mathematical Psychology* 11 (Feb): 15-32.

Wittgenstein, L. 1922. *Tractatus logico-philosophicus.* London: Kegan Paul.

29. Comparative Foreign Policy: Fads, Fantasies, Orthodoxies, Perversities

Don Munton

The comparative study of foreign policy has proven considerably more than a mere fad or fantasy.[1] The field, if it can be assumed to have reached that ill-defined status, has developed a definite direction and a certain degree of momentum. As with most new fields, it has acquired, as well as a few fashionable practices, a certain amount of ornamental folderol and, above all, a number of well-defined orthodoxies.[2] Reflected in the assumptions of empirical studies and the arguments of leading proponents, these orthodoxies are neither inconsiderable nor ephemeral. They touch on every aspect of the research process: the variables; hypotheses; units of analysis; data-collection, -measurement, and -analysis procedures; and epistemological goals. They have,

SPECIAL NOTE: This chapter is a much revised version of an earlier paper prepared for the Inter-university Comparative Foreign Policy Project (ICFP) Conference on the Future of Comparative Foreign Policy Analysis, Ojai, California, June 1973. I would like to thank the members of the ICFP group for ideas and discussions. Various people provided helpful comments on the contents of the earlier draft, including Linda Brady, Charles Hermann, Charles Kegley, William McGrath, Thomas Milburn, Warren Phillips, James N. Rosenau, and Denis Stairs. I would also like to extend thanks to my colleagues in the Centre for Foreign Policy Studies at Dalhousie University for their continuing support and for collectively creating a challenging and stimulating environment. Ann Jacobs helped more than a great deal to shepherd this all through a difficult process of rethinking and revision.

[1] The phrase is from Rosenau (1968b). The "field" referred to throughout this paper is roughly that fairly recent tradition identified by Rosenau in his article. For an alternative non-American view of a "comparative foreign policy" with its origins in the work of Aristotle and Grotius, see Boardman (1973).

[2] A refreshingly nonorthodox look at the "fads, fashions, and folderol" in psychological research is found in Dunnette (1965).

moreover, in varying degrees achieved an aura of permanence if not sanctity.

The orthodoxies are at least eight in number. Stated simply they include the following: that analysis should focus upon the factors influencing foreign policies; that there is a need for more "if-then" hypotheses which link a particular factor with a particular aspect of policy; that the case-study approach ought to be avoided and these linkages between factors and policies should be compared across a number of states; that there is a paucity of empirical data and thus significant effort should be expended to collect more; that these data should be used in the testing of the "if-then" hypotheses; that there is a "level-of-analysis" problem which must be avoided; that the goal of hypothesis testing should be to determine the relative potencies of individual factors or independent variables; and finally, that the study of comparative foreign policy is now in a take-off stage and should be further developed as an autonomous field. Each of these orthodoxies has traceable roots in the seminal thinking of a decade ago that redirected much analysis of foreign policy. Each of these, when originally stated as a critique of the then existing literature, had a fundamental and beneficial effect. Each of these is still very much evident in current practice and thinking. However, each of them, I will argue, ought now to be abandoned as a guideline for foreign policy research.

What could justify such a perverse line of argument? And furthermore, what could justify inflicting them upon others whose time might be more profitably spent than in reading yet another polemic about the state of the field? To confront the latter question first, the justification for making these arguments here is they may serve to spark debate about undeniably important issues, however misguided the arguments themselves may appear. To some readers, they undoubtedly will seem wrong-headed. To other readers, a smaller group perhaps, they will in contrast seem rather passé. Such are the inevitable consequences of disciplinary eclecticism. Perhaps those who fall in either category will greet all this with forebearance. It is possible, though, that those who fall in neither category will be so few in number as to render this a somewhat bootless exercise.

One person's orthodoxies are often another's radicalism. It is the same with perversities. Moreover, the term itself (**pervers′ity**, n.) has two distinguishable definitions. One is "a persistence in error"; the other is "a difference from what is reasonable or required." Needless to say, the intention here is to pursue a course along the lines of the latter, rather than the former, meaning. The intention is to show that the arguments suggested above are not in fact "in error," that there are good reasons for comparative foreign policy analysis to be different from what has come to be regarded as "reasonable," "required"—and orthodox. The arguments stem in essence from a personal feeling that comparative foreign policy has begun to outgrow its established orthodoxies. Increasingly these appear, to borrow a phrase, more as epitaphs to a successful protest,[3] than as valid signposts for a maturing field.

While the arguments about current orthodoxies may seem perverse and contrary, the suggestions or counter-orthodoxies that emerge here are intended to be constructive. They do, however, fall short of being "evangelical" pleas, or even being genuinely innovative ideas.[4] Virtually none can claim much originality; most have appeared elsewhere in one form or another. Nevertheless, such thoughts are still not fashionable among students of comparative foreign policy. Let me turn now to considering those that are.

[3]The phrase is from Dahl's (1961) evaluation of the behavioral revolution in political science.

[4]See, for example, Chapters 26, 27, and 28 by McGowan, Gillespie, and Thorson, respectively.

Orthodoxy 1: The major intellectual task in the field is conceptualizing the factors which influence foreign policy.

The desire to explain and predict provides the basic intellectual motivation for studying foreign policy. To explain adequately or predict dependably one must of course examine the role of the various factors that exert an influence on policy. Virtually all analyses, whether traditional or scientific, whether qualitative or quantitative, hold this much in common. As a result, virtually all devote most of their attention to identifying, discussing, sometimes defining, and occasionally measuring these "factors," "sources," or "determinants." Black and Thompson (1963), for example, elaborate upon but a few of "the multiplicity of factors which might be classed as determinants"— history, geography, natural resources, industrial development, military capacity, population, government, leadership, and diplomacy. Corresponding if slightly differing attempts at identifying the relevant factors are to be found in a host of other books and articles.[5] Some of the attempts have been more successful than others. The "pre-theory" framework of Rosenau (1966) was one that proved particularly stimulating to large numbers of students, in part because it went further and suggested a systematic way in which possible factors could be grouped into five reasonably distinct categories or clusters. On the whole, however, the field has perhaps "been exhausted as far as inventorying the determinants of external behavior is concerned" (Rosenau, 1966, p. 32).

The problem with this first, and likely the field's longest-standing, orthodoxy is really not what it prescribes, but what it does not prescribe. Because it emphasizes analysis of the factors which influence policy, it ignores, and thus deflects attention from, the nature or content of policy. The disturbing but nonetheless accurate conclusion to be drawn from the contemporary literature is that students of foreign policy do not have even a reasonably clear or generally agreed-upon notion of the very concept "foreign policy." Few have bothered to define the concept at all, and those

[5]The emphasis can be found in works as varied as Morgenthau (1948), Snyder, Bruck, and Sapin (1962), and Brecher, Steinberg, and Stein (1969).

who have done so often leave as much or more confusion in their wake as existed before. When the term appears, it is seldom clear whether it refers to actions, goals, decisions, objectives, strategies, interests, orientations, initiatives, attitudes, plans, undertakings, or whatever. But the confusion extends beyond the fact that the actual meaning remains obscure. The term tends also to mean many things to most users and quite different things at different times. Thus, "policy" will at one point, for example, apparently be used in the sense of long-term strategies, and at another, in the sense of day-to-day actions. Students of foreign policy have presumably been slow to recognize this confusion only because they feel that they know implicitly what the term means.

To conclude from this assessment that a significant effort ought to be made at conceptualizing "foreign policy" would undoubtedly be valid—but not in itself particularly perverse. The reason is that there has been a growing awareness of the term's ambiguity, of the "dependent variable" problem, as it has come to be called.[6] In fact, there is now a small but growing literature on the conceptual question, much of it from persons engaged in event data-based research. The attempt by Meehan (1971) to deal with foreign policy at the philosophical level is one example; the discussion by Hermann (1972) on types of policy classification is another. The increasingly numerous empirical studies using event data, of course, each deal with the behavior measurement problem in some fashion. A variety of techniques have been employed, including factor analysis, Q-sort, judgmental scaling, and circumplex models.[7] Empirical work of this sort has proven sufficiently important and substantial to merit at least one thorough appraisal (Kegley et al., 1974).

And yet, one is left with the perverse feeling that many of the key conceptual questions still have not been asked, much less answered. The sophisticated analytical techniques brought to bear

on event data, while exposing important patterns and interrelationships, cannot escape the limitations of those data to which they are applied. A set of events is merely a record of overt actions taken presumably as a result of conscious decisions to act, and a partial, publicly derived record at that. Event data researchers have not come to grips with the crucial conceptual implications of such questions as: how limited or general a segment of action must be to qualify as an event, what one does about "non-decisions," and so on. No event data collector seems to have advanced the concept "state action" much beyond the pioneering but oft-forgotten work of Richard Snyder and his colleagues (1962). And these matters are of course only part of the overall problem. Overt behaviors do not at all fully encompass what many analysts understand by the term foreign policy. Although there have been some useful attempts to examine "national interests" (Robinson, 1967) and "national roles" (K. J. Holsti, 1970) as aspects of policy, the broader conceptual questions about the term remain largely unexplored.

Thus, despite recognition of the "dependent variable problem" by many scholars, little in the way of a solution appears imminent. Qualitative analysts still seem to assume either that there is no problem or that it can be solved with a few simple, and usually appropriately vague, definitions. Quantitative analysts often seem to assume that the problem has been solved with event data. Both unfortunately are wrong. But both, assuming what they do, usually revert to the orthodox pattern of devoting most of their analytical energies to the independent variables, the sources of policy. Like the remaining orthodoxies discussed below, it is one which should be changed.

Orthodoxy 2: The need in foreign policy analysis is for "if-then" hypotheses which link some factor (the independent variable) with some aspect of a state's external policies (the dependent variable).

There is little argument over the theoretical deficiencies of much of the foreign policy literature both past and present. Moreover, there is little doubt that the most glaring of these deficiencies is the lack of clearly stated, explanatory propositions. The tendency was to identify and sometimes

---

[6]This awareness is reflected in an increasing number of writings; see for example, Rosenau (1968c) and Rosenau, Burgess, and Hermann (1973).

[7]On these methods, respectively, see McClelland and Hoggard (1969), O.R. Holsti (1972), Azar et al. (1972), and Kegley (1973).

to classify factors, but then merely to assert they had an influence on policy rather than to propose the nature of that linkage. In a now classic critique, Rosenau (1966, p. 31) noted that "to identify factors is not to trace their influence. To uncover processes that affect external behavior is not to explain how and why they are operative under certain circumstances and not under others." Foreign policy analysts were simply not pursuing their theoretical task to its necessary completion. The result was apparent:

> Rare is the article or book which goes beyond description of an internal factor and locates it in the ever changing interplay of variables—both external and internal—which combine to produce foreign policies. Even rarer is the work that contains explicit "if-then" hypotheses in which the "if" is a particular form of the internal factor and the "then" is a particular type of foreign policy.

This charge by Rosenau has become perhaps the most oft-quoted evaluation of the literature, and has been registered by many others. Hermann (1968, p. 521), for example, has argued that "instead of offering theories about the conduct of foreign policy, we frequently enumerate categories. . . . Instead of hypotheses . . . we produce detailed studies describing the making of a particular policy."

As stated, this criticism-become-orthodoxy is unassailable. Hypotheses are the backbone of any theoretical enterprise, to be sure. But the endless pursuit of more and more hypotheses, it can be argued, may well serve to misdirect scientific energies and retard the development of sound theory. Whether or not there ever was an actual paucity of hypotheses, the supply now looks abundant indeed. This change is partly due to the fact that more scholars began to formulate and apply such propositions. In addition though, scholars have become more sensitive to the often vague, frequently implicit, but nevertheless identifiable, propositions that lurk in some profusion in what was often dismissed as the "traditional" literature. One of the best examples of abstracting such propositions is a review by Hermann (1968) of Waltz's *Foreign Policy and Democratic Politics* and Brzezinski and Huntington's *Political Power: USA-USSR*. Compiling extensive propositional inven-

tories has more recently become a fairly common procedure. The number of such inventories that has been done, let alone the number of inventoried propositions, is substantial.[8] Moreover, there are now comprehensive surveys of hypotheses and findings in both the quantitative international relations (Jones and Singer, 1972) and comparative foreign policy literatures (McGowan and Shapiro, 1973).

Abundance has nevertheless not been accompanied by convergence. Many of the extant propositions appear directly or indirectly contradictory to one another. Findings from empirical tests often seem inconclusive, if not conflicting. The result is, as Patrick McGowan notes in Chapter 26, a profusion of "extremely narrow, albeit partially validated propositions." The problem for scholars has thus become as much making sense out of a bountiful confusion as searching out new hypotheses.

While this is not a totally disagreeable situation, it does call for something of a reorientation in approach. Rather than thinking of theory building as the chore of accumulating possible relationships, students of foreign policy should begin thinking of it more as the task of discarding empirically weak ones. "It might well be said," notes Kaplan (1964, p. 304), "that the predicament of behavioral science is not the absence of theory but its proliferation. The history of science is undeniably a history of the successive replacement of poor theories by better ones. . . ." Caporaso (1973, p. 2) makes the same point: "Science," he says, "is both a positive process of pointing to confirmations and a backhanded, winnowing process of eliminating rival hypotheses." Whether perverse or not, the argument here is that the comparative study of foreign policy has developed to the point at which its students should seriously embark on a systematic process of discarding hypotheses. The process may not lead us unto Truth, but it ought to deliver us from a few evils.

[8]As a small sample of these efforts, we might note the propositional inventories on alliances (Holsti, Hopmann, and Sullivan, 1973), on crisis behavior (Hermann and Brady, 1972) and from studies in *The International Encyclopedia of the Social Sciences* (Alker and Bock, 1972).

Orthodoxy 3: The single-country case-study approach is inherently deficient and unproductive; foreign policy analyses should focus on comparisons across countries.

A prime target for those who led the revolution in the study of comparative politics was a tradition of manifestly noncomparative single-country studies. Similarly, when the uprising came against the *ancien régime* in the foreign policy field, purveyors of case studies became *discipuli non grata*. Leaders in the movement argued with much justification that "case studies, which should become the basis for generalization, have somehow supported the notion that about any policy or event there is *too much* known, much of it unknowable" (Snyder, Bruck, and Sapin, 1962, p. 44). But the problem involved more than just the amount of detailed knowledge apparently necessary. It also seemed to involve weaknesses inherent in the case-study approach. Rosenau (1966, p. 36) notes:

> Single country analyses are themselves theoretically deficient. By placing a society's foreign policies in a historical and problem-solving context, analysts tend to treat each international situation in which the society participates as unique and consequently, to view its external behavior with respect to each situation as stemming from immediate and particular antecedents. This approach ... does inhibit the construction of if-then models which link the behavior patterns to a systematic set of stimuli.

The solution proposed of course was to systematically compare these linkages across a number of cases. Perhaps not surprisingly, comparative analysis came largely to mean one specific type of comparison; it came "to indicate the scope of inquiry is cross-national" (Hermann, 1972, p. 59). Evidence of this emphasis is not hard to uncover. Most current quantitative studies employ a cross-national, or more precisely, a cross-actor, design.[9] Correspondingly, the substantial majority of propositions[10] which McGowan and Shapiro

(1973) identified in comparative foreign policy studies were strictly cross-national in nature.

Despite this prevailing emphasis on cross-national comparison, it is neither particularly original nor perverse to argue there are severe limitations to such studies. One of the most obvious is an inability to incorporate many types of explanatory variables. Factors which vary across time, such as the changing level of interbureaucratic conflict within a government, cannot be adequately studied cross-sectionally. Nor can many systemic factors, such as the level of interbloc hostility or the extent of bipolarity or multipolarity. While there are some excellent studies of such factors, they are few.[11] The narrow interpretation of comparison has had the unfortunate overall effect of providing students with a set of theoretical blinders.

Moreover, questions of explanation aside, the cross-national focus also renders it difficult to address, let alone answer, some of the most interesting questions of policy evaluation and prescription. Policy makers are presumably and understandably much less interested in static cross-national generalizations, in which their country might well be a deviant case, than in generalizations concerning, for example, changes in that country's performance over a period of time.

Few would likely quarrel with the suggestion of looking at temporal variations, even for a single country. Why then the criticism of case studies? The reason, I would submit, is an obvious though little recognized confusion regarding the term "case study"—at least in the comparative foreign policy literature.[12] The term is applied at various times to a rather wide array of research designs, including those focusing upon a specific event or

---

[9] The dominance of the cross-national perspective is abundantly clear from examining the studies noted in the surveys, cited above, of the quantitative international relations (Jones and Singer, 1972) and the comparative foreign policy literatures (McGowan and Shapiro, 1973).

[10] These calculations are mine. Of the total of 118 propositions, 15 were judged to be ambiguous as to the

type of comparison involved. Of the remaining 103, no less than 55 are clearly cross-national in nature. The next most common varieties are cross-time (18) and cross-dyadic (13) comparisons.

[11] Again, this generalization is supported by referring to McGowan and Shapiro's work. See also the summary tables and discussion in Chapter 26. Representative of the best current studies of systemic factors are those by Choucri and North (1969, 1972).

[12] The discussions by Rosenau (1968b) and Russett (1970) while useful, fail to clarify the meaning of the term.

situation, a particular policy issue, a single bilateral relationship, or an individual country. The term has even been applied to quantitative research such as the Stanford studies on the 1914 situation (e.g., Holsti, North, and Brody, 1968) and Rummel's (1972) analysis of U.S. foreign behavior. The root of the confusion is a nonappreciation of the simple fact that there are three possible analytical dimensions (i.e., entities, characteristics, and time),[13] and that virtually all systematic research has been restricted to analyzing two of the three at any one point. Cross-national studies, for example, usually analyze variations in behavior (one dimension) across actors (another dimension). From that pattern seems to have emerged the feeling that any study which does not similarly compare across a large number of actors is somehow not really comparative, and much worse, is actually a case study.

Now a proper, if strict, definition of the term would be a research design in which there is no variation in the independent variable.[14] If there is none, no antecedent conditions have changed, and there cannot logically be any effect on some dependent variable. If there is variation in the independent variable, then, whatever the design might be, it is not a case study. Thus, neither the Stanford studies, which largely compare behavior across time periods, nor Rummel's work on the U.S., which compares behavior across a large number of targets, nor many similar examples, can be correctly classed as case studies. This point should underscore one fact: the theoretical limitations ascribed to the beleaguered case-study approach simply do not apply to many types of research heretofore characterized by that label.[15]

In sum, it is likely that the emphasis on cross-national (i.e., cross-actor) comparison and the confusion as to what constitutes a case study have

combined to discourage alternative types of comparison. I would argue that much more emphasis should be given to cross-dyad, cross-behavior, and especially cross-time designs.[16]

The present juncture is probably as good a place as any to voice a general lamentation, one somewhat broader than, but related to, the case-study issue. It is as follows. All of the techniques and paraphernalia of social science—the independent variables, "if-then" hypotheses, cross-dyadic comparisons, multivariate models, and others mentioned above or below—are tools, presumably employed for a purpose. And presumably that purpose has something to do with extending our understanding of certain real-world phenomena. Much of the time these tools are indeed useful, and serve the purpose well. At other times, though, as some critics have charged, they do not seem to serve much at all, let alone extend our understanding. Perhaps the key factor differentiating the productive times from the others is simply the substantive knowledge and intuitive "feel" for the particular phenomena which the analyst brings to his task. If these are considerable—whatever that means—the tools can be used to best advantage. If they are less than adequate, the tools are unlikely to compensate for the lack.

There is nothing at all original in this lamentation—although I must confess that my personal sympathies with it are now greater than in the past. The point of voicing it here is simply to introduce an additional perversity. Most foreign policy analysts obviously do not have what could be regarded as a considerable knowledge of the foreign policies and processes of a large number of countries. Thus, studies based on large cross-national samples are more likely than other varieties to suffer what might be termed substantive malnutrition. The current literature offers abundant evidence of this malady. As Verba (1967, pp. 112-113) said in a superb review of similar work in comparative politics: "the general theoretical works float well above reality, and they often are so abstract as to suggest no clear problem focus. . . . [They provide] us with many general-

[13]On this point see the discussion in Rummel (1970, chap. 8).

[14]Caporaso (1974) discusses this point with regard to "good" and "poor" research designs in international relations.

[15]There are many examples of qualitative foreign policy studies which, while not formally testing hypotheses, do develop and examine some general propositions, and thus take on theoretical significance. See, for example, Boardman and Sharma (1974) and Barry (1975). For an insightful analysis of one "case" of great-power-small-power relations, see Stairs (1974).

[16]On the advantages and limitations of comparisons across directed dyads, see the discussion by Kegley and Skinner in Chapter 33.

izations that do not seem to fit many or any of the relevant cases."

All this is not to argue that cross-national studies ought to be discontinued, for they have obvious and unique analytical advantages. Nor is it to argue that all students of foreign policy ought to be area or country specialists, for that is an unreasonable and potentially harmful expectation. It is rather to argue that because substantive knowledge is important, more students ought to be doing country- and perhaps regional-based comparative studies.[17] Verba (1967, p. 117) nicely identified the horns of the dilemma: "Reality seems to demand a configurative approach; generalizability seems to demand a more analytical approach." The comparative study of foreign policy has clearly been more responsive to the demands of generalizability. Reality should now be given more of a chance.

Orthodoxy 4: There is a lack of empirical data available for comparative foreign policy analysis; a significant and continuing effort should be made to collect more.

If the theme of the challenge mounted against traditional foreign policy analysis concerned the importance of developing rigorous theory, then the subtheme was the importance of systematically collected data. Students came to recognize that frameworks should be held up to reality and hypotheses should be submitted to empirical test, even if that recognition did not lead in all cases to practice. There was, at any rate, considerable agreement "on the need for more empirical and data-gathering research as a prerequisite to theory-building" (Singer, 1961, p. 91). The need was not an illusion, nor was it soon diminished. Recent years have witnessed a continuing call for more, and more varied types of data, especially quantitative data.

The calls have not been in vain. Vast amounts of time and effort—and money—have been invested in data-collection activities. Once students of foreign policy realized that data are not heaven-sent, that their field was not dealt some trick of congenital data impoverishment at birth, and instead that data have to be "made" from facts, then the gap began to be filled. And filled it was; by any standard the field has gone from being data-poor to being data-rich. One measure of the change is that the mid-1960s blush of excitement over the first generation of quantitative data handbooks (e.g., *World Handbook of Political and Social Indicators, Cross-Polity Survey*) gave way in the early 1970s to matter-of-fact acceptance of enlarged and improved second-generation versions. Collections of international event data have been surfacing so quickly that a recent review of this "new" frontier (Lawton and Burgess, 1972) was somewhat outdated only months after it was published. The major institutional computer data banks have not only greatly expanded but actually have experienced such a run on deposits that at least one seriously began to consider criteria for screening would-be depositors. The push for data collection, in short, became a stampede.

Indeed, so drastically has the situation changed that the need for more data has become a decidedly second-order one. There is, I would argue, much less need for a continued effort at data collection than for a self-conscious effort at data measurement. The emphasis should be shifted from concerns about acquiring data properly to concerns about using it thoroughly. Exhaustive utilization demands in part the increasingly familiar techniques of sophisticated data analysis—regression, analysis of variance, nonlinear modeling and the like. But it also demands the less familiar, yet no less crucial, techniques of data measurement—multiple indicators, validity testing, index construction, and the like.[18] Some work has been done along these lines, for example on the source validity of international event data.[19] Some innovative but preliminary work has also been carried out on the complementarity of different event

---

[17]The richness which results from a strong substantive knowledge of the situations being analyzed is evident in such studies as Rosenau (1968a), Holsti (1972) and Choucri and North (1969, 1972).

[18]Some of the best discussions of data-measurement problems in international relations are found in the work of Caporaso (1971, 1974). See also Blalock (1968) for a useful general perspective on measurement.

[19]A reasonably up-to-date review of this work was contained in Munton (1976).

data collections.[20] Much more work needs to be done. However, this will require some redirecting and even retraining. As Firestone (1971, p. 579) points out:

> We have all absorbed in the early days of our education the necessity of confronting our constructs with reality. What was not emphasized to us is that it is not just observational specifications, but the form of the relations implied in our particular observational specifications which count in constructing other than trivial tests of our theoretical networks. From the point of view of such networks, measurement relations are as important as theoretical and empirical relations.

In the orthodox perspective, they are not perceived as such. The argument here is that they should be.

Orthodoxy 5: The comparative study of foreign policy will advance through the empirical testing of "if-then" hypotheses.

Hypothesis testing is the *sine qua non* of empirical social science. Graduate students, and even undergraduates, learn that something called the scientific method prescribes how one goes about doing empirical research: first state a hypothesis, then choose a sample of cases, then go out and collect the relevant data, test the hypothesis with these data, and finally, draw the appropriate inferences as to whether the hypothesis has been supported or disconfirmed. The findings from this and similar research then serve as a foundation or stimulus for further research.

In only somewhat less idealized fashion, such is the underlying methodological orthodoxy among students of comparative foreign policy. The hypothesis-testing approach is a basic premise emerging explicitly from many, if not all, state-of-the-field discussions. It is the assumption implicitly underlying much, if not most, quantitative foreign policy research. It is also clearly reflected in the very organization of the recent survey of scientific findings in the field (McGowan and Shapiro, 1973) which groups these findings under 118 distinct propositions, virtually all of which are bivariate. Hypothesis testing is, however, despite

its pervasiveness, an increasingly dubious formula for theoretical advancement.

The problem rests not with hypotheses per se, but with the bivariate structure they seem most often to assume. Students of foreign policy often gain the impression that political reality is really nothing more than a vast multitude of bivariate relationships. They also tend to assume that bivariate hypothesis testing is somehow the natural, if not the only, appropriate manner in which to go about empirical research. Neither, of course, is the truth. The common everyday bivariate hypothesis is the crudest of all theories. Bivariate hypothesis testing is correspondingly the weakest of investigatory procedures.

Without getting too involved for present purposes in what is a most complex subject, I would argue that more foreign policy analysts should now be thinking in terms of interrelated sets of hypotheses, and in terms of formulating and testing multivariate models.[21] More should be, in Caporaso's (1974, p. 16) words, "moving from a tradition where hypotheses are tested for significance in a bivariate way to one in which many variables are treated simultaneously as both dependent and independent variables and in which the estimation of the parameters (coefficients) of previously specified models may be substituted for tests of significance." Most foreign-policy-related phenomena are too remote from the analyst, and most are too patently unamenable to laboratory manipulation for the extensive use of classical experimental research procedures. The methods which have proved so successful in the physical sciences—which emphasize a very few select variables and rigorous controls—therefore seem largely inappropriate. "Multivariate analysis is essentially a process of controlled comparison of cases," Firestone (1971, p. 598) has observed. "It is the functional equivalent for the social scientist of laboratory experimentation for the physical

---

[20]Two studies which have both confronted the complementarity question, albeit in different ways, are Phillips (1972) and Leng (1973).

[21]Excellent examples of the use of econometric modeling and computer simulation are those of Choucri and North (1969) and Milstein and Mitchell (1969), respectively. Evidence that interval-level measurement is not essential for testing multivariate models is provided by studies such as Brady (1974), which employ multivariate analysis of variance procedures. General discussions of multivariate models in international relations are Alker (1968) and Firestone (1971).

scientist." Since the student of foreign policy cannot validly break reality down into its simplest, most basic relationships, he should instead work with more complex and thus, hopefully, less unrealistic analytical models. Comparative foreign policy should, in short, move from hypothesis testing to model testing.[22]

A short footnote might be added here. The idealized version of the scientific method is not only overly pure, it is also overly strict. It presents a thoroughly routinized and joyless picture of the research process. Unfortunately, students of foreign policy often seem to mistake this picture for reality. They ought not to. Raser (1969, p. 156), in referring to James Watson's narrative on the discovery of DNA, paints a different scene, one which highlights

> the role of "play," and of "messing around," or, as Watson calls it, "fiddling" .... Such are the activities of Nobel prize winners in chemistry—men who have come closer than anyone else to unlocking the ancient riddle of life. Social scientists might do well to take a lesson from them and to refuse to be apologetic about their own fiddling, tentative modeling, gaming and hunch playing.

More than hypothesis testing, perhaps, model testing permits and encourages such an attitude.

Orthodoxy 6: There is a "level-of-analysis" problem which students of foreign policy must recognize and avoid.

The basic formulation of the "level-of-analysis" problem is found in an oft-cited article by Singer

(1961). The premise is that one must distinguish between two widely employed levels of analysis— the international system on the one hand, and the national state on the other. After setting out certain advantages and limitations to both, Singer presents the crux of his argument: "We may utilize one level here and another there, but we cannot afford to shift our orientation in the midst of a study" (p. 90). This "problem," or at least, the usual interpretation thereof, has attained a position of some prominence and has likely had an important and undesirable effect on the basic way students of foreign policy have thought about their research.[23]

The problem with the "problem" is that it does not really refer to levels of analysis at all. It refers instead to what are commonly termed "units" of analysis, that is the units or cases across which one compares. What Singer is saying therefore, and quite correctly, is that one cannot analyze across both nations and systems as though they were comparable units. What he is not saying, but what many interpretations seem to imply, is that one necessarily encounters an analytical problem when dealing simultaneously with variables at different levels of aggregation. Singer does not deny the possibility of cross-level relationships—for example, relating a state's foreign policy to both national characteristics and aspects of the international system. To be sure, the level of these two variables is different; but there is certainly no logical fallacy, and presumably some theoretical merit, in positing such relationships.

Whether or not due to errant interpretations of Singer's "level-of-analysis problem," the fact is that there are very few attempts indeed to analyze cross-level relationships quantitatively. Analysts trying to explain aggregated measures of national behavior tend to do so in terms of aggregate national attributes. Analysts trying to explain temporal variations in national behavior tend to do so in terms of responses to other nations' behavior. And analysts focusing upon variations in systemic-level characteristics tend to relate these to other

---

[22]Since the focus here is on largely methodological orthodoxies, no attempt will be made to elaborate the content these models might have. One possible form is that of "design" or "optimal control" theory, discussed in Chapters 27 and 28 by Gillespie and Thorson, respectively. A number of suggestions about types of "positive theory" that might be applied are made by McGowan in Chapter 26. While one could raise questions about whether nations can in any sense "control" or "design" their environments, and thus about the ultimate utility of these notions, there is the more practical problem of short-term feasibility. In brief, many of these "theories" assume that we now have much more and much better knowledge about foreign policy than is the case. An alternative, and more likely successful, approach to modeling is to integrate and build upon existing propositions and findings. Examples of this approach include Hermann and Brady (1972) and Choucri and North (1969, 1972).

[23]Critical but somewhat different interpretations of the "level-of-analysis" problem than that provided here are to be found in Moul (1973), Rosenau (1973) and McGowan (Chapter 26 of this volume).

systemic-level characteristics.[24] There are, however, very few quantitative studies in which variations in national behavior are related both to
domestic factors and to factors arising in the international system.[25] Logically, there is no necessity
for this; there is, to repeat, no level-of-analysis
problem involved. But the tendencies persist
regardless.

As long as they do, the models that are developed and the explanations they provide are almost
certain to be incomplete. Foreign policy is seldom,
if ever, the result of national or international factors acting alone. To the extent that both exert an
influence in reality, both should be included in the
models which are constructed to explain that
reality. Two researchers who have developed and
tested such multilevel models, Choucri and North,
have argued this point (1969; 1972, pp. 117,
105):

> A model focusing either on national or on interna-
> tional effects is likely to be vulnerable on theoretical
> terms (by reducing everything to internal factors or to
> considerations external to the system) and incomplete
> in operational terms. . . . What we are suggesting,
> therefore, is that optimum specifications would, by
> necessity, include both internal and external variables.
> A "mixed" model of this sort is likely to yield greater
> payoffs in the long run. . . .

Combining both types of factors will not, of
course, insure a more theoretically valid model; a
trivial model will yield trivial results no matter
what type of factors comprise the model. But the
interesting and encouraging results with multilevel
models recently obtained by some analysts,[26] only
a few of whom would profess to be doing comparative foreign policy, are sufficient grounds on
which to recommend such strategies to those who
would so profess.

[24]Again, this pattern emerges in the survey by
McGowan and Shapiro (1973). It is also evident in a
review of "systemic model" explanations of foreign
policy (Munton, 1975).

[25]Exceptions include Choucri and North (1969) and
Wilkenfeld, Lussier, and Tahtinen (1972). The simulation-
based study by Crow and Noel (1965) is perhaps unique
in its multiple focus on personality, organizational, and
situational factors.

[26]In addition to those cited earlier, see some of the
recent studies in the *Sage International Yearbook of
Foreign Policy Studies* and in Russett (1972).

*Orthodoxy 7: The goal of hypothesis testing is to
determine the relative potencies of individual factors or independent variables.*

The quest for the most potent variable is not a
recent crusade. Among contemporary students of
foreign policy it can be traced back through Morgenthau (1948, p. 105)—"Of all the factors which
make for the power of a nation, the most important . . . is the quality of diplomacy"—and beyond
him to most of his intellectual predecessors. The
quest is common to both the cross-nationally
oriented student and his country-oriented breth-
ren. As two reviewers of the (Western) literature
on Soviet foreign policy note: "Most of these
theories contend that one or more factors are
especially important determinants of Soviet behavior . . . that certain factors consistently influence Russian actions more than others" (Hoffman
and Fleron, 1971, p. 6). Quantitative analysts have
been no less concerned with determining the relative importance of individual variables; moreover,
they have the perhaps dubious advantage over
their nonquantitative colleagues of being able con-
cretely to operationalize "importance," a trick
usually performed using the magnitude of correlation or beta coefficients.

Perhaps the most forceful argument for asking
the relative potency question is made by Rosenau
(1966, p. 43): after the initial task of identifying
clusters of independent variables, "one has to
assess their *relative potencies.* That is, one has to
decide which set of variables contributes most to
external behavior, which ranks next in influence,
and so on through all the sets." This task is seen as
not merely useful, but essential. Rosenau (1968a,
p. 17) argues and others (e.g., McGowan and Shapiro, 1973, p. 223) agree that "only after the
relevant variables have been identified and their
relative potency assessed through quantitative
analysis is it possible to fashion a coherent body of
empirical theory."

To this argument in particular there is an increasingly strong alternative view. Stated simply, it
is that the quest should be less for assessing relative potencies and more for determining the degree
of overall empirical "fit" of theoretical models.[27]

[27]The attempt to assess relative potency may not only
be somewhat unproductive, but also be a very question-

The primary emphasis should thus be on the extent to which the model accounts for variance in the phenomena being analyzed.[28] This focus flows quite naturally from the strategy of testing multivariate models rather than bivariate hypotheses. While not implying that the relative strength of particular relationships (i.e., the relative potency of particular variables) is in any way irrelevant, the focus does imply that the overall adequacy of the model is a prior and more fundamental question. In addition, it implies that the strength of empirical relationships can only be assessed subsequent, rather than prior, to the fashioning and testing of the models. Only within a theoretically coherent set of factors—however that might be determined—does the question about the relative strength of any one factor become meaningful.

The quest for relative potency has also had the unfortunate effect of accentuating the fruitless debate as to whether factors external or internal to the nation-state are more important for its external behavior. This debate is very much analogous to the nature-versus-nurture, heredity-versus-environment, and personality-versus-situation debates in psychology and social psychology. The consensus is apparently that these debates are "dead" (Anastasi, 1958), that the question as to which factor is more influential is "a meaningless one" (Raush et al., 1959). Acceptance of this verdict has freed researchers to address the centrally important question—that of the extent and nature of the interactions between different factors. Students of foreign policy would be well advised to follow suit.[29] The study of interaction terms holds the promise of improving our knowledge by emphasizing not only that policy must be per-

ceived as necessarily the result of a variety of factors, but also that it is important to understand how these factors themselves combine and interact. As Kaplan (1964, p. 326) has said:

> In the present state of our knowledge, human behavior is often seen as the outcome of the joint working of a number of distinct and often unrelated factors, as in the choice of a mate, or in the outbreak of war between nations. . . . In a sense, we know too much to be able to unify it in a single theory, and we do not know any of it with sufficient sureness. . . . We need to know, not only the separate factors that are determinative of behavior, but also how they interact with one another.

In sum, newer methodological perspectives again throw doubt on present orthodoxies. The argument—perverse or not—I am making here is that assessing the relative potency of specific variables is no more important than assessing the interactions between variables, and certainly less important than determining the overall empirical adequacy of specific theoretical models.

CONCLUSION

Throughout this brief polemic I have attempted to identify what appear to be the prominent, underlying, orthodox assumptions among students of comparative foreign policy. Generally, the orthodoxies appear to reflect the historical legacy and initial intellectual stirrings of the field better than some of its nascent trends and emerging needs. This disjunction between past, present, and future prompted a series of seemingly perverse counter-orthodoxies. These perhaps merit restatement, not so they might gain pride of place, but merely so they might attain a semblance of clarity:

1. There is a continuing overemphasis on the sources of, or factors which influence, foreign policy. A major effort should be made to formulate and explore alternative conceptualizations for various aspects of "policy," including actions, objectives, and roles.

2. There is no shortage of propositions about foreign policy. More attention should be given to systematic elimination of those propositions which appear empirically weak.

---

able epistemological venture. Stairs (1975) argues convincingly that while it is possible to identify necessary or unnecessary and sufficient or insufficient conditions for some phenomena, there is no logical basis for putting any number of similarly necessary—but—insufficient conditions into some rank order of potency.

[28]The analysis by Tanter (1974) of Corson's data on the Berlin Crises is one example which begins by formulating models, but ends with conclusions pertaining only to the relative potency of variables. One possible reason that studies take such a route is that the amount of variance being explained sometimes turns out disturbingly low.

[29]See the discussion of personality-situation interactions by Margaret Hermann in Chapter 35.

3. There is an overemphasis on rather abstract cross-national comparison. More analyses should be undertaken that are cross-time, cross-dyad, and cross-behavioral in design, and more should be undertaken that have a firmer basis of substantive knowledge into the phenomena being analyzed.

4. There is no shortage of data for foreign policy analysis. More extensive and more careful use should be made of existing data through more self-conscious data-measurement procedures.

5. Bivariate hypothesis testing is not the best route toward building theory. More attempts should be initiated to construct and test multivariate models.

6. There is no level-of-analysis problem. More theorizing should be attempted which links national and systemic level variables.

7. There is an overemphasis on assessing the relative potency of particular predictor variables. More attention should be given to assessing both the interactions among variables and the overall empirical "fit" provided by well-specified models.

Stated outright, few of these seem to comprise the stuff of which controversy, let alone perversity, is made. Some may, actually, appear even acceptable. Nevertheless, the fact remains that individually each differs from its parallel orthodoxy, and, taken collectively, they propose a rather different future direction for students of comparative foreign policy.

Although eight orthodoxies were claimed at the outset of this paper, only seven have so far been subjected to scrutiny. The eighth and final one has been left for the simple reason that it is the most general of all. It concerns not methods and procedures, but the viability of the field.

Orthodoxy 8: The comparative study of foreign policy is now in a take-off stage and should be further developed as an autonomous field.

The distinction between foreign policy, or the external behavior of a state, and international politics, or the interaction behavior of two or more states, has long been a widely accepted one. Recognition of a more or less separate comparative study of foreign policy is presumably based in part

on this distinction. It is worth noting that this recognition has been beneficial in many respects—in stimulating thinking about foreign policy theory, in fostering communication among students, and in encouraging the beginnings of a cumulative research tradition. The comparative foreign policy community has been a lively and self-conscious one. In quasi-organizational terms, the morale has been very high and the goal orientation very strong. As a result, many within the community would agree that "the comparative study of foreign policy is an emerging field in the social sciences. . . . It is the present task . . . to build upon that foundation" (McGowan and Shapiro, 1973, p. 224). And yet, one can question the utility of the field's continued distinctness.

To argue against sovereignty for comparative foreign policy so soon after its liberation would seem the ultimate of perversities. Nonetheless, that is precisely what I would argue. The benefits of intellectual separatism have been reaped; it is the costs which now appear most evident. Among these is the maintenance of artificial boundaries between foreign policy analysis and international systems analysis. To be sure, a conceptual distinction, useful for some purposes, can be made between them, but it ought not to be an inviolable boundary.

The division discourages cross-level theorizing and the development of models linking national and systemic level variables.[30] To a lesser extent it discourages the diffusion of methodological innovation. More importantly, it also tends to reduce the amount of useful communication between students of both schools.[31]

The eighth and final perversity, then, is that a distinct comparative study of foreign policy ought to disappear, not by withering away, but by merging with a scientific study of international politics. The combined field—whether called interpoli-

[30]On this point, see the perceptive discussions by Rosenau (1968c, 1973). Brody (1971) argues persuasively for the complementarity and convergence of foreign policy and systems models.

[31]While surveys such as that of McGowan and Shapiro (1973) provide an excellent means of communication between students of international politics and foreign policy, my hunch is that the authors of a few of those studies surveyed would be surprised by their apparent inclusion in the "comparative foreign policy" school.

metrics, as some have suggested, or any other name—would hopefully prove a productive union. It would broaden the perspectives of comparative foreign policy analysis, and might well even encourage reexamination of its present orthodoxies. To be specific, integration may even encourage students of foreign policy to conceptualize systematically the policies or interactions of states as well as their sources; to discover and better utilize existing stocks of propositions and data; to explore relatively little used methods of comparative inquiry; to consider and experiment with multivariate, multilevel model building; and to emphasize the overall empirical adequacy of these models.

I frankly do not know whether these changes in approach and method will in fact happen, let alone whether they will succeed in substantially improving our knowledge if they did. Predicting trends through social science is still a problematic exercise. Predicting trends *in* social science is no less problematic. The likelihood of such changes coming about, however, does seem fairly high. The arguments for them are gaining currency among students of international politics and other fields, and the trends themselves are to some extent discernible in various empirical studies being done on foreign policy questions. Where they are not yet as readily discernible is in our orthodox rhetoric about the field. That may not matter a great deal. However, if students of foreign policy do become convinced that the changes mean improvement, then revising the old orthodoxies will be necessary to sustain development.

REFERENCES

Alker, Hayward R., Jr. 1968. "The Long Road to International Relations Theory: Problems of Statistical Nonadditivity." In *New Approaches to International Relations,* ed. M. Kaplan, pp. 137-69. New York: St. Martin's.

——— and P. G. Bock. 1972. "Propositions about International Relations: Contributions from the *International Encyclopedia of the Social Sciences.*" In *Political Science Annual,* ed. J. A. Robinson, vol. 3. Indianapolis: Bobbs-Merrill.

Anastasi, Anne. 1958. "Heredity, Environment, and the Question 'How?'" *Psychological Review* 65: 197-209.

Azar, Edward, et al. 1972. "Making and Measuring the International Event as a Unit of Analysis." In *Sage Professional Papers in International Studies,* vol. 1, pp. 59-77. Beverly Hills: Sage.

Barry, Donald. 1975. "Interest Groups and the Foreign Policy Process: The Case of Biafra." In *Pressure Groups in Canadian Politics,* ed. P. Pross. Toronto: Copp Clark.

Black, Joseph E., and Kenneth W. Thompson, eds. 1963. *Foreign Policies in a World of Change.* New York: Harper & Row.

Blalock, Hubert M. 1968. "The Measurement Problem: A Gap between the Languages of Theory and Research." In *Methodology in Social Research,* ed. H. Blalock and A. Blalock, pp. 5-27. New York: McGraw-Hill.

Boardman, Robert. 1973. "Comparative Method and Foreign Policy." In *Yearbook of World Affairs,* pp. 372-82. London: Stevens.

——— and Kunjar Sharma. 1974. "Patterns of Actor Involvement in Foreign Policy Issues: A Comparative Study of Britain and Nepal." Occasional Paper. Halifax: Dalhousie Univ., Centre for Foreign Policy Studies.

Brady, Linda P. 1974. "Threat, Decision Time, and Awareness: The Impact of Situational Variables on Foreign Policy Behavior." Ph.D. dissertation, Ohio State Univ.

Brecher, Michael, Blema Steinberg, and Janice Stein. 1969. "A Framework for Research on Foreign Policy Behavior." *Journal of Conflict Resolution* 13: 75-101.

Brody, Richard A. 1971. "Convergences and Challenges in International Relations." In *International Studies,* Monograph 12, ed. F. W. Riggs. Philadelphia: American Academy of Political and Social Science.

———. 1972. "International Events: Problems of Measurement and Analysis." In *Sage Professional Papers in International Studies,* vol. 1, pp. 45-48. Beverly Hills: Sage.

Caporaso, James A. 1971. "Theory and Method in the Study of International Integration." *International Organization* 25: 228-53.

———. 1974. "A Philosophy of Science Assessment of the Stanford Studies in Conflict and Integration." Paper prepared for a meeting of the International Studies Association, St. Louis.

Choucri, Nazli, and Robert C. North. 1969. "The Determinants of International Violence." *Papers, Peace Research Society (International)* 12: 33-63.

——— and Robert C. North. 1972. "Dynamics of International Conflict: Some Policy Implications of Population, Resources, and Technology." *World Politics* 24 (suppl.): 80-122.

Crow, Wayman J., and Robert C. Noel. 1965. "The Valid

Use of Simulation Results." Mimeo. Western Behavioral Sciences Institute.

Dahl, Robert. 1961. "The Behavioral Approach in Political Science: Epitaph for a Monument to a Successful Protest." *American Political Science Review* 55: 763-72.

Dunnette, Marvin D. 1965. "Fads, Fashions, and Folderol in Psychology." *American Psychologist* 21: 343-52.

Firestone, Joseph M. 1971. "Remarks on Concept Formation: Theory Building and Theory Testing." *Philosophy of Science* 38: 570-604.

Hermann, Charles F. 1968. "The Comparative Study of Foreign Policy." *World Politics* 20: 521-34.

———. 1971. "What Is a Foreign Policy Event?" In *Comparative Foreign Policy*, ed. W. F. Hanrieder, pp. 295-321. New York: McKay.

———. 1972. "Policy Classification: A Key to the Comparative Study of Foreign Policy." In *The Analysis of International Politics*, ed. J. N. Rosenau, V. Davis, and M. A. East, pp. 58-79. New York: Free Press.

——— and Linda P. Brady. 1972. "Alternative Models of International Crises Behavior." In *International Crises*, ed. C. F. Hermann, pp. 281-320. New York: Free Press.

Hoffmann, Erik P., and Frederic J. Fleron, Jr., eds. 1971. *The Conduct of Soviet Foreign Policy.* Chicago: Aldine-Atherton.

Holsti, K. J. 1970. "National Role Conceptions in the Study of Foreign Policy." *International Studies Quarterly* 14: 233-309.

Holsti, Ole R. 1972. *Crisis, Escalation, War.* Montreal: McGill-Queen's Univ. Press.

———, Robert C. North, and Richard A. Brody. 1968. "Perception and Action in the 1914 Crisis." In *Quantitative International Politics*, ed. J. D. Singer, pp. 123-58. New York: Free Press.

———, P. Terrence Hopmann, and John D. Sullivan. 1973. *Unity and Disintegration in International Alliances.* New York: Wiley.

Jones, Susan D., and J. David Singer. 1972. *Beyond Conjecture in International Politics.* Itasca, Ill.: Peacock.

Kaplan, Abraham. 1964. *The Conduct of Inquiry.* San Francisco: Chandler.

Kegley, Charles W. 1973. "A General Empirical Typology of Foreign Policy Behavior." In *Sage Professional Papers in International Studies*, vol. 2. Beverly Hills: Sage.

———, Stephen A. Salmore, and David J. Rosen. 1974. "Convergences in the Measurement of Interstate Behavior." In *Sage International Yearbook of Foreign Policy Studies*, ed. P. J. McGowan, vol. 2, pp. 309-39. Beverly Hills: Sage.

Lawton, Raymond W., and Philip M. Burgess. 1972. "Indicators of International Behavior: An Assessment of Events Data Research." In *Sage Professional Papers in International Studies*, vol. 1, pp. 5-96. Beverly Hills: Sage.

Leng, Russell. 1973. "The Future of Events Data Marriages: A Question of Compatibility." Paper presented at a meeting of the International Studies Association, New York.

McClelland, Charles A., and Gary D. Hoggard. 1969. "Conflict Patterns in the Interactions among Nations." In *International Politics and Foreign Policy*, ed. J. N. Rosenau, pp. 711-24. New York: Free Press.

McGowan, Patrick J., and H. B. Shapiro. 1973. *The Comparative Study of Foreign Policy: A Survey of Scientific Findings.* Beverly Hills: Sage.

Meehan, Eugene J. 1971. "The Concept 'Foreign Policy.'" In *Comparative Foreign Policy*, ed. W. F. Hanrieder, pp. 265-94. New York: McKay.

Milstein, Jeffrey S., and William Charles Mitchell. 1969. "Computer Simulation of International Processes: The Vietnam War and the Pre-World War I Naval Race." *Papers, Peace Research Society (International)* 12: 117-36.

Morgenthau, Hans J. 1948. *Politics among Nations.* New York: Knopf.

Moul, William B. 1973. "The Level-of-Analysis Problem Revisited." *Canadian Journal of Political Science* 6: 494-513.

Munton, Don. 1975. "External Sources of Foreign Policy: A Review and Critique." Mimeo. Halifax: Dalhousie Univ., Centre for Foreign Policy Studies.

———, ed. 1976. "Measuring International Behavior: Validity Problems in Event Data." Occasional Paper. Halifax: Dalhousie Univ., Centre for Foreign Policy Studies.

Phillips, Warren R. 1972. "Two Views of Foreign Policy Interaction: Substantially the Same or Different?" Paper presented at a meeting of the International Studies Association (Midwest) and the Peace Research Society, Toronto.

Popper, Karl R. 1959. *The Logic of Scientific Discovery.* London: Hutchinson.

Raser, John. 1969. *Simulation and Society.* Boston: Allyn & Bacon.

Rausch, H. L., A. T. Dittmann, and T. J. Taylor. 1959. "Person, Setting, and Change in Social Interaction." *Human Relations* 12: 361-77.

Robinson, Thomas W. 1967. "A National Interest Analysis of Sino-Soviet Relations." *International Studies Quarterly* 2: 135-75.

Rosenau, James N. 1966. "Pre-theories and Theories of Foreign Policy." In *Approaches to Comparative and*

International Politics, ed. B. Farrell, pp. 27-93. Evanston: Northwestern Univ. Press.

———. 1968a. "Private Preferences and Political Responsibilities: The Relative Potency of Individual and Role Variables in the Behavior of U.S. Senators." In *Quantitative International Politics,* ed. J. D. Singer, pp. 17-50. New York: Free Press.

———. 1968b. "Comparative Foreign Policy: Fad, Fantasy, or Field?" *International Studies Quarterly* 12: 296-329.

———. 1968c. "Moral Fervor, Systematic Analyses, and Scientific Consciousness in Foreign Policy Research." In *Political Science and Public Policy,* ed. A. Ranney, pp. 197-236. Chicago: Markham.

———. 1973. "Theorizing across Systems: Linkage Politics Revisited." In *Conflict Behavior and Linkage Politics,* ed. J. Wilkenfeld, pp. 25-26. New York: McKay.

———, Philip M. Burgess, and Charles F. Hermann. 1973. "The Adaptation of Foreign Policy Research: A Case Study of an Anti-Case Study Project." *International Studies Quarterly* 17: 119-44.

Rummel, R. J. 1970. *Applied Factor Analysis.* Evanston: Northwestern Univ. Press.

———. 1972. "U.S. Foreign Relations: Conflict, Cooperation, and Attribute Distances." In *Peace, War, and Numbers,* ed. B. Russett, pp. 71-114. Beverly Hills: Sage.

Russett, Bruce M. 1970. "International Behavior Research: Case Studies and Cumulation." In *Approaches to the Study of Political Science,* ed. M. Haas and H. S. Kariel, pp. 425-43. San Francisco: Chandler.

———, ed. 1972. *Peace, War, and Numbers.* Beverly Hills: Sage.

Singer, J. David. 1961. "The Level-of-Analysis Problem in International Relations." In *The International System,* ed. K. Knorr and S. Verba, pp. 77-92. Princeton: Princeton Univ. Press.

Snyder, Richard C., H. W. Bruck, and Burton Sapin. 1962. *Foreign Policy Decision Making.* New York: Free Press.

Stairs, Denis. 1974. *The Diplomacy of Constraint: Canada, the Korean War, and the United States.* Toronto: Univ. of Toronto Press.

———. 1975. "Analytical Relativism and the Single Case." Paper presented at the Inter-university Seminar on International Relations, McGill Univ., Montreal.

Tanter, Raymond. 1974. *Modelling and Managing International Crises.* Beverly Hills: Sage.

Verba, Sidney. 1967. "Some Dilemmas in Comparative Research." *World Politics* 20: 111-27.

Wilkenfeld, Jonathan., V. Lussier, and D. Tahtinen. 1972. "Conflict Interactions in the Middle East, 1949-1967." *Journal of Conflict Resolution* 16: 135-54.

30. Laws, Explanation, and the X→Y Syndrome

James E. Harf ▪ Bruce E. Moon ▪ John E. Thompson

The principal purpose of this article is to demonstrate how the comparative study of foreign policy, now devoid of any viable theories or theorizing to guide its enterprise, might develop an agenda for coping with this omission. The thrust of our arguments focuses primarily upon the role of the external environment.

Specifically, we argue that the lack of viable theories in all aspects of international politics is primarily a function of both the discipline's approach to the role of laws in explanation and, paradoxically, the rapid development of data banks and techniques for ordering such information.

We suggest a need for greater attention to a framework of analysis which allows us to *begin* the process of explaining how, why, and through what mechanisms foreign policy decisions are made (e.g., outputs) and their consequences (outcomes) generated for both participating actors and for larger aspects of the international system.

We hope eventually to show the imperative of deductive reasoning, particularly with reference to external influences on foreign policy making. The inadequacy of prior system-level research and theorizing suggests the strongest rationale for such a deductive strategy, and we hope that our survey of the extant literature will document such inadequacy. Unfortunately, this stage cannot be implemented until a framework in which such a deductive theory might be imbedded is developed.

THE STATE OF THE ART

Critical Overview

In a recent study of over 200 research efforts in the comparative study of foreign policy, McGowan and Shapiro (1973) conclude that we have no theories of foreign policy, and wonder why. More specifically, they ask why there are no middle-range or general theories of foreign policy based on deductive reasoning. Such theories, defined as bodies of theoretically organized knowledge based on cumulative empirical research, represent the essential goal of any science. The discipline's lack of any such accumulation suggests a much lower stage of growth than had been predicted a few years ago.

Other authors make similar observations. In their survey of propositions from *The International Encyclopedia of the Social Sciences* (1972), Alker and Bock assert that the most outstanding lack of empirical research in international politics has been the researchers' failure to explicate the context in which a relationship is assumed to be operative. They argue that students of international relations quickly adopted the *"X → Y"* syndrome without specifying when and under what conditions such a relationship may exist; consequently, critical tests of a relationship are rarely found.

Young (1972) alludes to the same omissions. He suggests that there is no viable theory in international politics, and that even the few existing logical models fare badly in their capacity to explain behavior. Young also argues that current research enterprises are not only failing to develop viable theory, but may be obstructing the entire approach to such development by inappropriate responses to dilemmas confronting the scholar of international politics.

And, finally, another author observes that expanded data banks and more sophisticated computer programs are the only recent contributions to the study of foreign policy. John Gillespie, in Chapter 27 of this volume, concludes that our intellectual activity has been limited to "sorting out variables in order to assess which are the strongest correlates of a given foreign policy activity."

The essence of these authors' indictments might be captured by posing the analogy of foreign policy theory as a game of chance. Data banks are represented by the roulette wheel or the blackjack table; the variety of canned computer programs may be likened to the procedures and permutations of the gaming table and the resident programmer to the house dealer. The researcher is of course the gambler. If the gambler is lucky, and if his luck is augmented with intuition or a little knowledge about probable outcomes, he may hit the right permutation. If the researcher is lucky, he may ask for the correct number of rotated factors, he may control for the right mediating factors, or he may cover every contingency by programming the computer to examine *every alternative* so that the one meaningful relationship can emerge. Jackpot! Instant theory has been created. Variance has been explained, or the statistical significance of a correlation coefficient has been established.

The past twenty years have not been without progress, however; we have seen the development of comprehensive data banks, imaginative measurement techniques, and a rather impressive level of sophistication in statistical procedure, particularly with respect to regression analysis and analysis of variance. But the entire enterprise is now only as intellectually strong as is the most primitive stage in the path from theory building through verification to the question of *quo vadimus*. And, unfortunately, this foundation may be so rickety that all the skills of the computer programmer and the statistican cannot salvage the enterprise. Therefore, to make these advances useful they must be combined with the researcher's decision to eliminate excessive preoccupation with nonproductive emphases in the initial stages of research design.

But why have these authors indicted the state of the art? What has happened to the promises of the early practitioners of foreign-policy-as-a-science? Why do we find many of these scholars presently engaged in intellectual soul searching? And most important, how might we now develop an agenda to allow the construction of viable theories—in our particular case, middle-range theories linking the external environment and foreign policy making? This article attempts to find answers to these questions.

Environmental Concerns and Foreign Policy

Although the above indictments are applicable to all aspects of foreign policy analysis, the situation is even more depressing when one examines those factors affecting foreign policy decision making which emanate from beyond a nation's borders. The scholar who wishes to focus upon factors physically close to the decision maker—be they idiosyncratic, role or elite variables—can draw upon a large body of social science literature pertaining to such factors. Armed with widely held beliefs and reasonably well tested notions about the behavior of individuals and small groups, the scholar finds it a manageable task to model these theories to foreign policy behavior. The causal links between antecedent factors and the decision-making process become less obvious as research moves further and further away from this core. Consequently, we have the obligation to explicate these links much more fully, and in so doing to reveal the rationale for such relationships as we may find.

Two distinct types of approaches to defining the foreign policy role of extranational factors are found in the literature. *The first approach suggests that the foreign policy behavior of nation A is essentially triggered by a perceived need to respond to an immediate stimulus in the external environment.* This stimulus is assumed to impact either directly or indirectly upon nation A within a relatively short period of time. This familiar stimulus-response (S-R) model was initially popularized in international relations by two research enterprises, the Stanford 1914 studies and the interaction analysis of Charles McClelland's WEIS project at the University of Southern California. Although numerous scholars have tried to build upon these first efforts in various ways, only

minimal attempts have been made to seek out the rationale underlying this S-R mechanism. In contrast, every other aspect of these research endeavors—from data collection to analysis—shows remarkable progress over earlier work.[1]

The second approach to the role of extranational influences focuses upon some set of structural and/or behavioral attributes. These sets have been viewed in one of the following ways:

1. The *aggregation* of a structural or behavioral attribute for the entire *global system* at a given moment in time (e.g., the number of alliances or the amount of war),
2. The *distribution* of an attribute in the global *system* (e.g., the distribution of power or trade),
3. An aspect of a *specific* nation's structural or behavioral pattern viewed, in turn, in one of three ways:
   (a) a nation's prior foreign policy *behavior pattern expressed in absolute* terms,
   (b) a nation's prior foreign policy *behavior pattern* expressed in *relational* terms (i.e., in comparison to the behavior of other actors in the system),
   (c) a nation's *structural* attribute (such as its level of development) vis-à-vis other actors in the system.[2]

Research using either the S-R or the extranational attribute approach has followed a predominantly inductive strategy, wherein all permutations are examined until findings that are judged significant—usually in a statistical sense—are uncovered. Consequently, when all the methodological trappings are removed, about all we know is that behavior begets behavior (and particularly, hostility begets hostility), and that certain systemic conditions (operationalized and measured in particular ways) are sometimes, but not always, associated with other systemic conditions.

Thus our basic position now is that even with all the advances in data generation and manipula-

---

[1] See, for example, the works of Dehio (1963), Feierabend and Feierabend (1969), and Phillips (1971).

[2] In this case, and the previous one, the structural or behavioral attribute of a nation might be compared to one of three groups: all contiguous nations (or those constituting its immediate environment), those actors involved with the nation in the decision sequence, or all other actors in the system.

tion, we have not produced a middle-range or general theory which explicates the causal links between extranational phenomena and the foreign policy process.

DIAGNOSIS OF THE PROBLEM

The X → Y Syndrome

Throughout the first part of this article we have emphasized three major shortcomings now prevalent in international politics research:

1. The absence of general or middle-range theories,
2. A lack of sufficient knowledge concerning the conditions under which relationships we postulate are true,
3. An inability to trace the linkages (usually causal) between the independent and dependent variables of our propositions even when we assume their existence.

It is our contention that these shortcomings are all produced in large part by the $X \to Y$ syndrome—an excessive preoccupation with the discovery of statistical associations among variables without a companion thrust to determine the *reason* for such associations. Our objection is not so much to the use of statistical methods to further understanding of political phenomena; rather, we do not subscribe to the goal which implicitly guides much contemporary research namely, the discovery of and statistical accounting for patterns in the data. Again, the argument is not that such goal is never appropriate, but that it is almost never appropriate as the *sole* goal of research. It is at best a necessary step in the process of progressing from hunch to theory, but not the end product in itself. If the discovery of patterns in data is to serve a valuable function, it must be through the utilization of these findings to further understanding of the processes manifested in the data.

More important, perhaps, than the way research is presently being conducted, are the criteria invoked in evaluating the final product of research. Here too the $X \to Y$ syndrome has become the dominant paradigm: we begin (and usually end) evaluation with questions of the form "How much

variance is explained?" or "Is the correlation coefficient statistically significant at .05?" Our preoccupation with these issues is demonstrated by the frequency of debates such as the appropriateness of significance tests when the universe of nations is being examined. Another manifestation of this syndrome can be found in the increasingly longer sections of research papers being devoted to the rationale for the choice of e.g., one-tailed rather than two-tailed tests, or the use of the maximum distance hierarchical clustering technique rather than an obliquely rotated factor analysis solution, as opposed to the increasingly shorter summaries which merely sketch the theoretical implications of the research.

At first glance this phenomenon may be seen as a simple, but relatively harmless, overzealousness in reporting research methodology; however, the problem of the $X \to Y$ syndrome is both more dangerous and more complex than the above explanation reflects. The syndrome is a consequence of three conditions:

1. The acceptance of one particular view of the role of laws in explanation of empirical phenomena,
2. The lack of a research mission built upon a framework of analysis which posits the linkages among the vast number of potentially relevant variables,
3. The disappearance of traditional concepts which have guided the study of political phenomena for years, and their subsequent replacement, not with concepts based on theory, but with quasi-concepts which are fundamentally "data-based."

The Role of Laws in Explanation

The acceptance of the covering law interpretation of explanation has enabled researchers to engage in a subtle kind of self-delusion with enormous consequences for the study of international politics. They have uncritically accepted a view of the explanation of empirical phenomena which places heavy emphasis upon the discovery of quasi-laws linking two or more variables. This covering law view of explanation, as represented by Carl

Hempel's deductive-nomological model,[3] may be summarized as follows.

The explanation of the occurrence of any empirical event takes the form of a logical argument (in the simplest case, one of the *modus ponens* form) in which the event to be explained is shown as a logical consequence of (1) the existence of a law which links one or more initial conditions with the occurrence of an event of the particular type to be explained, and (2) the presence of the stipulated initial conditions. Thus the explanation of event *y* consists of the following argument.

1. Whenever an event of type X occurs, an event of type Y will also occur.
2. An event *x* (of type X) occurred. Therefore,
3. An event *y* (of type Y) occurred.

Hempel further argues that only four conditions must be met in order to justify the assertion that event y has been explained: (1) the *explanadum* (statement 3) must be a logical consequence of the *explanans*[4] (statements 1 and 2), (2) the *explanans* must contain a nontrivial law, (3) the *explanans* must be empirical, and (4) all statements in the *explanans* must be true. These criteria emphasize the degree to which Hempel's concern is with the logical form of the explanation, rather than its substantive content.

Given the acceptance of this approach to explanation and Hempel's four criteria, it is not surprising that the task of research has been taken to be the discovery of empirical generalities which link two or more variables. And it is no wonder that, with the help of statisticians and computer programmers, we have developed hundreds of imaginative ways—Pearson's *r*, tau *b*, betas, etc.—of asking the same fundamental question, "What empirical generalization can we derive from the

data?" However, even though we can derive generalizations we are unable, on the basis of form alone, to determine their status as causal laws.

It seems to us that, after twenty years of research based on this approach, we now need to reexamine the estate (in terms of knowledge and understanding of political events) left to our progeny, and to question the adequacy of this predominant philosophy of inquiry. Our position is that this view of explanation is detrimental to the development of general theory; when we create or evaluate an explanation it encourages us to focus only upon the *logical form* of the explanation and not upon its *content*. In so doing, we are sacrificing our expertise in dealing with political phenomena because we do not bring it to bear upon the evaluation of research; in its place we have utilized the skills of logic, mathematics, and statistics, skills which are not highly developed in the typical political researcher.

A competing view of explanation, one which we think discourages a reliance upon the $X \rightarrow Y$ syndrome, is that ascribed to Michael Scriven by Hempel (1965). In this account Hempel has confused two concepts which ought to remain distinct, namely, the explanation of an event and the justification for that explanation. Scriven claims that an explanation is not an argument at all (and it is particularly not a *modus ponens* argument), but that an explanation is an assertion. For Scriven, the explanation of the occurrence of event *y* in the above example would take the form of the assertion "*y* because *x*." The role of the law "Whenever an event of type X occurs, an event of type Y also occurs" is not to serve in the explanation of the occurrence of *y*, but rather to serve as a justification for asserting the explanation "*y* because *x*." Thus laws belong in the province of justification, not in the province of explanation. The above law is not the only evidence which could be cited in support of the explanation (although it is extraordinarily good evidence), and further, some explanations may not admit of any supporting laws. In sum, to explain an event is to assert those conditions or events which produced it, while to discover constant conjunction between these antecedents and the type of event to be

---

[3]Hempel (1965) is by no means the only advocate of the "covering law" interpretation. See also Cohen and Nagel (1934) and Popper (1959, 1962) for samples of the large number of philosophers of science who accept this view.

[4]Simply stated the *explanadum* is the sentence(s) that expresses the occurrence of the phenomenon to be explained, while the *explanans* consists of those sentences invoked to explain it. In the simplest *modus ponens* explanation, the *explanans* consists of the sentence expressing a law and the sentence asserting the existence of the necessary initial conditions.

explained is to marshal support in justification for the assertion that the causal links are as posited.

According to this interpretation research which seeks to uncover constant conjunctions (or covariation) is attempting to justify the claim that the asserted causal connection between the independent and dependent variables exists. But if there has been no assertion of a particular causal link—and therefore no explanation—what has been justified by the law which the researcher has worked so hard to establish? The crux of our argument is simply that researchers, by failing to distinguish between an explanation and the justification for that explanation, have allowed themselves to engage in a kind of empiricism which *describes* a particular pattern of covariation but in no way seeks to *explain* it. And, more importantly, this subtle philosophical difference has enabled researchers to accept as valid and valuable research findings which, when viewed from any perspective other than that of logical form, are inadequate to the task of theory building.

An example will illustrate the shortcomings inherent in this approach. A recent research effort investigated the empirical link between a nation's physical size and its amount of foreign conflict behavior (Feierabend and Feierabend, 1969).[5] Its principal finding, stated in Hempelian form, is that "large nations engage in more foreign conflict than do small nations." If one ignores the fact that this generalization does not constitute a deterministic law (since the correlation is not 1.0), the research in question has provided an explanation for the foreign conflict behavior of any pair of nations. One needs only to establish their relative sizes in order to predict logically their relative foreign conflict levels.

Stated in its covering law form, the research appears to be a valuable contribution to our knowledge of the foreign policy behavior of nations. Viewed from the Scriven perspective, however, the evaluation looks considerably less

impressive. In this latter form (*y because x*) the explanation would be presented as follows: "The United States engages in more foreign conflict than Venezuela because it is larger." The justification for the explanation—the assertion of this causal link—is that a constant conjunction has been observed between size and conflict.

Viewing the explanation in this latter form has many implications. Consider, for example, this final examination question for an undergraduate course in comparative foreign policy: "Why does the United States engage in more conflict than Venezuela?" The answer provided by this explanation, "Because it is larger," would be universally unacceptable. Yet, by expressing the explanation in Hempelian form—"Large nations engage in more foreign conflict than do small nations"—we can have this research evaluated positively by a journal's jurying procedures. This is but one instance in which an author has slipped into the $X \rightarrow Y$ syndrome by mistaking a statistical correlation between patterns in data with an explanation of political phenomena; others have followed him into the trap by observing only the strength of the coefficient. The example illustrates the three inadequacies resulting from the prevalence of the $X \rightarrow Y$ syndrome.

First, it is difficult to foresee, particularly given the record of the past twenty years, how such research could contribute to the building of general or middle-range theory of nation behavior. Second, with no explication of the ways in which largeness is related to conflict, we have no systematic way of even guessing under what conditions such a relationship will hold. No doubt there will be deviant cases, presumably because of intervening factors; however, without some knowledge of these factors we are unable to determine what variables may intervene, and we certainly have no way of knowing what values of these variables are critical in determining whether a nation will be an *instance* of the law or an *exception* to it. Third and most important, although we have gained some knowledge about a behavioral pattern, we have been unable to acquire even a minimal *understanding* of the processes which generated it. Consequently, we can neither transmit to students a greater understanding of the foreign policy decision-making process, nor can we provide

[5]The cited work is but one example of the research strategy which seeks to discover statistical relationships between nation attribute variables and foreign policy behavior variables. Others are Rummel (1969), Moore (1970) Salmore and Hermann (1969), Choucri and North (1969), Singer (1972), Wright (1964), Alker and Russett (1965), Vincent (1968), McGowan (1968), Deutsch (1960), and Alger (1968).

recommendations to policy makers. We have only deluded ourselves that we are making progress toward the day when the discipline will reach the level of a logically elegant science.

This is not to say that our work has been wasted entirely. In discovering such general laws, we have identified that *some* process occurs which translates largeness to conflict. We have thus marked out an area of research which is potentially profitable in explaining the behavior of nations. Our urgent need is to search beyond the mapped surface, probe the process at work, and investigate the causal link (if any) in order to acquire a better understanding of these political phenomena and how they come about. In this fashion we can stipulate the conditions under which such a relationship exists, identify manipulatable variables for policy makers, and subsequently build more general theories of nation behavior based upon the process that we have uncovered.

The Role of Meta-Theory

It should be evident from the above discussion that a framework (meta-theory) for analysis is the necessary initial step toward the creation of valid theory. Such a framework provides the premises upon which our research is based. Without it we have no choice but to engage in highly inductive empiricism, to wander through our data banks searching for relationships among variables. Without it we are unable to establish any criteria for distinguishing between merely accidental empirical generalizations and statements of causal laws which are genuine contributions to our understanding. Stated another way, we must create an abstract model of the foreign policy decision-making process which will suggest the general character of the causal links which produce the eventual foreign policy decision. Once this has been accomplished we can begin to speculate about the effect of specific variables upon the foreign policy behavior of nations.

Thus we have a critical criterion by which to judge research: "To what extent does this particular piece of research link two stages of the decision making process, or some stage of the process, with an exogenous variable?" Using this criterion we can minimize the relevance of research which only links national attributes (size) to particular behaviors (conflict) by noting that both independent and dependent variables fall outside the process, demanding instead that at least some of these causal links be explicated. In particular, we must ask what distinguishes the decision-making processes of large and small nations which warrants the conclusion that they will behave differently? Until we can begin to stipulate the character of those processes, at least in very general form, we shall be unable to answer that question. In so stating, we reject the view that the comparative study of foreign policy is an infant science that will continue to develop, however slowly, if only we are diligent in our efforts to carry on with our present research paradigm. We strongly argue that our current strategy is not moving us nearer to the kind of theory for which an empirical science strives, but in fact it is carrying us slowly in quite the opposite direction.

The Role of Concepts

A third reason for the discouraging state of foreign policy theory (and the chief reason why the development of frameworks has been slow) is the dearth of theoretically meaningful concepts. With the advent of the behavioral revolution, those committed to the use of quantitative techniques were anxious to divorce themselves from what they regarded as the bankruptcy of the traditional approach. In the midst of this turmoil one important ingredient of theory building—namely, fundamental political concepts such as goals, strategies, objectives, interests, alternatives, and the like—was swept aside. Most concepts were thought to be inappropriate to the study of politics as envisioned by this new breed; some seemed unresearchable, others were based upon fundamental assumptions which they were no longer willing to grant, and still others were rejected or simply ignored solely because of guilt by association. Why, for example, were we unwilling to employ the notion of a goal to explain foreign policy behavior? Goals are *difficult* to research; we do not deny that, but their high degree of face validity and obvious utility in explaining behavior would seem to justify their inclusion in a framework which models foreign policy decision making. The contemporary approach has, however, almost completely abandoned this concept, insisting upon searching for explanations elsewhere precisely for the same reasons as the man who searched for his lost keys under the streetlight, not because he dropped them there but because the light was better.

The loss of these concepts, which might be fundamental in our intuitive meta-theory of the behavior of the decision-making unit, is not as distressing as is their replacement by concepts not rooted in theory but rather in data banks. These data bank concepts are useful either because they are observable and easily operationalized, or because they are typological entities. The variable clusters of Rosenau, for example, are fundamentally atheoretical and typological; they are based upon the notion that behavior influences can be distinguished by observing their distance from the decision maker. No claim is made or implied that variables far from the decision making core act upon the process differently, under different conditions, at different times, through different mechanisms, with different impacts. Rather, these concepts serve as data typologies, with emphasis on levels of analysis, such that idiosyncratic variables are acquired through biographical sketches or content analyses of speeches and the like; governmental and societal variables are available through aggregate data banks; and systemic variables are generated by introspection or by impressionistic readings of history. Given that such concepts were meant to be independent of theory, how can we expect them to form the foundation for theory building in comparative foreign policy?

REQUIREMENTS OF A FRAMEWORK

Let us now summarize the requirements of a viable framework or meta-theory for modeling the process of foreign policy decision making. This framework, by serving as an abstract sketch of the causal chain which produces foreign policy behavior, constitutes a structure and language within which our theory may be imbedded.

First, the framework must allow us (indeed, force us) to utilize such fundamental concepts as goals, perceptions, capabilities, and strategies. These concepts hold strong face validity at other levels of analysis (the individual, for example) and, consequently, offer great promise in helping to understand the behavior of nations.

Second, the framework, *at a minimum,* must allow us to distinguish among (1) the policy-making process, (2) the policy itself, and (3) the consequences of the policy. Moreover, we must be able to identify distinct stages of the process wherein each stage is open to the impact of a number of variables. These stages may be delineated temporally (occurring at different times and probably arranged sequentially), spatially (occurring in different places and probably involving different personnel), or analytically (serving different functions). Furthermore, the stages must operate in a dynamic manner which will allow feedback and learning. Whatever distinctions are made, they must serve as plausible (however gross) links in a causal chain leading to the implementation of a policy.

Third, the framework must be capable of sustaining and accommodating a large number of premises that reflects hunches about behavior and its antecedents. It must also be capable of generating or suggesting additional premises; in short, it must serve as a "pre-theory."

Our own suggestion for a framework models the foreign policy decision-making process as a goal-seeking system. As such, this strategy draws upon systems theory, particularly upon recent literature which treats decision making as adaptive behavior.[6]

A SUGGESTED FRAMEWORK

The prime focus of our framework is upon the activities of one decision making unit within the decision-making structure—a unit, termed D, which is distinguished from others within the bureaucratic structure on the basis of (1) its level within this hierarchy, (2) its jurisdiction over specific problems or issue areas, and (3) the particular segment of the external environment which it monitors. The decision-making unit is linked to the external environment through a monitor func-

[6]Most prominent among these are Rosenau's adaptation theory (1970) and Mesarovic's theory of hierarchical systems (1970).

tion as well as through a series of interactions with the environment. These interactions consist of *inputs (X)* to *D* and *D*'s outputs *(M)*. An input *X* is a policy action undertaken by some segment of the environment (usually a decision-making unit of another state), which is perceived by *D* to involve, either directly or indirectly, *D*'s goals. An output *M* is a policy action or decision made by *D in response to* input *X*. *M*, in turn, may have consequences for other nations' goals and will thus produce a response from some segment of the environment.

Interaction theorists would suggest that the framework is essentially complete, claiming that behavior begets behavior and, therefore, that foreign policy may be adequately conceptualized as a system of billiard balls i.e., each nation's behavior being purely a response to its collision or interaction with another. We contend, however, that it is also essential to focus upon the process by which the decision maker produces an output in response to an input. Without referencing this intervening process, we are unable to account for the seemingly acausal multiplicity of outputs produced at various times in response to the same input, a fact which has been apparently overlooked in the work of the interaction theorists. Moreover, until we can at least begin to sketch the causal links of the process whereby inputs are mapped to outputs, we are not entitled to claim that an explanation has been given, nor have we necessarily increased our understanding of the phenomena. Further, we affirm that even when they react to inputs, nations do so in pursuit of goals; thus nations or national decision-making units intend that certain outputs produce consequences for the achievement of goals. Specifically, there exist particular variables—goal variables—whose values are ordered by some preference relation; that is, each value corresponds to a particular state of affairs, each of which is desired differentially by the nation or unit in question. Changes in the value of these goal variables are part of the consequences of choosing outputs; these consequences of policy are termed *outcomes* and are referenced by the symbol *Y*.

The specific outcome *(Y)* of the interaction, which is produced by the environment (termed *E*) in conjunction with the output, bears upon the immediate goals of the decision-making unit. The environmental process can be represented as a function in set-theoretic notation: $E: M \otimes Z \to Y$, where *Z* is the representation of the state of the environment.

Only two objects are responsible for the outcome—the decision *(M)* or output of *D*, and the state representation of the environment *(Z)*. If the state of the environment is known, the relation between output and outcome is purely functional. Obviously, if the goal is precise and the function *E* is known, the choice of the "best" *M* is routine; *D* simply chooses that *M* which produces the most valued *Y*. The decision is rarely that easy, of course, since seldom will either premise be met fully; ordinarily a decision will require both a *theory* of the environment and a *precise statement of the goals* (objective function).

While *E* may never be known exactly, some approximation of *E*, theory of *E*, or hunch about *E* must be present if *D* is to choose intelligently among the plausible alternatives. In particular, every decision-making unit has some theory, E_D, which has the same form as *E*, namely, $E_D: M \otimes \widehat{Z} \to \widehat{Y}$ where $\widehat{Z}$ is the estimated state representation of the environment, *M* is the contemplated decision of *D*, and $\widehat{Y}$ is the predicted outcome. The decision by *D* can now be viewed as the simple process whereby *D* places every plausible *M* into the equation and derives the expected outcome of each in turn. The selection of the output *M* is then accomplished via the use of an objective function, that is, a function which assigns to each output-outcome pair the utility value associated by *D* with that state of affairs represented by the output-outcome pair. Formally, the objective function *(G)* may be represented as follows: $G: M \otimes Y \to V$ where *M* is the set of contemplated outputs, *Y* is the set of resultant outcomes, and *V* is the value set whose elements are ordered by some preference relation. Thus the process of selecting an outcome from the set of plausible alternatives consists of utilizing first the theory of the environment *(E_D)* to determine the likely outcome of each alternative output, and then the objective function *(G)* to assign a value to each of the outcomes. *D* simply chooses that *M* which is believed to produce the most valued *Y*. With the selection and implementation of a specific *M* the decision situation ends.

The next step in this sequence is the production of an outcome by the environment through the function E. Upon the appearance of the actual or observed Y, the decision-making unit compares the observed outcome with the expected outcome $(\widehat{Y})$. On the basis of the discrepancy between Y and $\widehat{Y}$, the decision-making unit maintains or alters certain of its processes—for example, the theory of the environment or the objective function.

The above discussion of the framework is rudimentary. The constraints of space dictate no further elaboration; however, in brief, the temporal process of this framework may be sketched from the following outline.

1. Receipt of input X
   (a) X interpreted as relevant to nation's goals
   (b) jurisdiction within bureaucracy determined
2. Definition of the situation
   (a) relevant goals to be considered in deciding upon response selected
   (b) plausible alternative list selected
   (c) theory of the environment (E_D) selected
   (d) objective function (G) defined
3. Forecasting of output-outcome pair
   (a) refinement of E_D for specific situation
   (b) estimation of the state of the environment $\widehat{Z}$
   (c) derivation of the expected outcome of each plausible alternative output
4. Predecision evaluation of alternatives (use of the objective function to determine most preferred outcome and, therefore, most preferred output)
5. Implementation (choice of M)
6. Postdecision evaluation (juxtaposition of Y and $\widehat{Y}$)
   (a) errors in E_D determined and corrected
   (b) errors in plausible alternative list for this type situation suggested (omission or commission)
   (c) errors in objective function determined and corrected
   (d) errors in $\widehat{Z}$ determined and corrected
   (e) errors in definition of the situation suggested in terms of goals which ought to be considered in this type of situation.

The process may also be shown in set theoretic notation.

x is an element of X, the set of all possible inputs from the environment to D

m is an element of M, the set of all possible outputs from D to the environment

y is an element of Y, the set of all possible outcomes

z is an element of Z, the set of all possible state representations of the environment

$D: X \otimes \widehat{Z} \otimes \widehat{Y} \to M$
$E: M \otimes Z \to Y$
$E_D: M \otimes \widehat{Z} \to \widehat{Y}$
$G: M \otimes Y \to V$

And finally, the process may also be illustrated by the classic input-output model as shown in Figure 1.

Figure 1. Input-Output Model

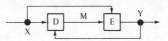

CONCLUSION

This article has attempted to pinpoint the reasons for the dearth of viable theories in the comparative study of foreign policy, and to suggest one framework which might allow researchers to rechannel their intellectual resources in an effort to remedy these conditions. This reordering of research priorities is essential if we are ever to achieve the level of explanation which characterizes a mature science.

REFERENCES

Alger, C. F. 1968. "Interaction in a Committee of the United Nations General Assembly." In *Quantitative International Politics,* ed. J. D. Singer, pp. 51-84. New York: Free Press.

Alker, H. R., Jr., and P. G. Bock. 1972. "Propositions about International Relations." In *Political Science Annual,* ed. J. A. Robinson, vol. 3, pp. 385-495. Indianapolis: Bobbs-Merrill.

――― and B. R. Russett. 1965. *World Politics in the General Assembly.* New Haven: Yale Univ. Press.

Choucri, N., and R. C. North. 1969. "The Determinants of International Violence." *Papers, Peace Research Society (International)* 12: 33-63.

Cohen, M. R., and E. Nagel. 1934. *An Introduction to Logic and Scientific Method.* New York: Harcourt, Brace & World.

Dehio, L. 1963. *The Precarious Balance: The Politics of Power in Europe, 1944-1945.* London: Chatto & Windus.

Deutsch, K. W. 1960. "The Propensity to International Transactions." *Political Studies* 8: 147-55.

Feierabend, I., and R. Feierabend. 1969. "Level of Development and Internation Behavior." In *Foreign Policy and the Developing Nation,* ed. R. Butwell, pp. 135-88. Lexington: Univ. Press of Kentucky.

Hempel, C. G. 1965. *Aspects of Scientific Explanation: And Other Essays in the Philosophy of Science.* New York: Free Press.

McGowan, P. J. 1968. "Africa and Non-alignment: A Comparative Study of Foreign Policy." *International Studies Quarterly* 12: 262-95.

――― and H. B. Shapiro. 1973. *The Comparative Study of Foreign Policy: A Survey of Scientific Findings.* Beverly Hills: Sage.

Mesarovic, M. D., D. Macko, and Y. Takahara. 1970. *Theory of Hierarchical, Multi-level Systems.* New York: Academic Press.

Moore, D. W. 1970. "Governmental and Societal Influences on Foreign Policy: A Partial Examination of Rosenau's Adaptation Model." Ph.D. dissertation, Ohio State Univ.

Phillips, W. R. 1971. "The Dynamics of Behavioral Action and Reaction in International Conflict." *Papers, Peace Research Society (International)* 17: 31-46.

Popper, K. R. 1959. *the Logic of Scientific Discovery.* London: Hutchinson.

―――. 1962. *Conjectures and Refutations.* New York: Basic Books.

Rosenau, J. N. 1970. *The Adaptation of National Societies: A Theory of Political System Behavior and Transformation.* New York: McCaleb-Seiler.

Rummel, R. J. 1969. "Some Empirical Findings on Nations and Their Behavior." *World Politics* 21: 226-41.

Salmore, S. A., and C. F. Hermann. 1969. "The Effect of Size, Development, and Accountability on Foreign Policy." *Papers, Peace Research Society (International)* 14: 15-30.

Singer, J. D. 1972. "The 'Correlates of War' Project: Interim Report and Rationale." *World Politics* 24: 243-70.

Vincent, J. E. 1968. "National Attributes as Predictors of Delegate Attitudes at the United Nations." *American Political Science Review* 62: 916-31.

Wright, Q. 1964. *A Study of War.* Chicago: Univ. of Chicago Press.

Young, O. R. 1972. "The Perils of Odysseus: On Constructing Theories of International Relations." In *Theory and Policy in International Relations,* ed. R. Tanter and R. H. Ullman, pp. 179-203. Princeton: Princeton Univ. Press.

31. Reconceptualizing the Sources of Foreign Policy Behavior

William O. Chittick ▪ Jerry B. Jenkins

The comparative (scientific) study of foreign policy has emerged in the last decade as a distinct field of analysis. A recent survey of the published findings of some 200 such studies reveals 118 vague and loosely related propositions based on scattered and sometimes contradictory evidence (McGowan and Shapiro, 1973). Although the number of such studies itself is quite impressive, given their paucity prior to 1965, the survey demonstrates that we have made relatively little progress toward building a theory of foreign policy.

What is most alarming about the present state of the field is not that we lack an accepted theory of foreign policy but rather that there seems to be a sizable gap between our theorizing about foreign policy and our empirical analyses of foreign policy (McGowan and Shapiro, 1973, pp. 214-15). If science involves a confrontation between theory and data, it may well be that we are not yet practicing science! In this essay, we shall argue that one reason why contemporary studies of foreign policy are not sufficiently scientific (comparative) is because they do not adequately incorporate the international environment into their analyses.[1]

This essay is divided into three sections. In the first section we examine the status of contemporary efforts to explain foreign policy behavior scientifically. We argue that although most of those who theorize about foreign policy behavior take the international environment into account, most of those who conduct empirical studies of foreign policy fail to do so. In the second section we explain why the data used in these empirical studies must be reanalyzed in order to test the hypotheses offered and, generally, how that can be done. In the third section we indicate how we can avoid the need for reanalysis of data by reconceptualizing our independent variables initially.

STATUS

The desire for a science of politics has fostered a large number of comparative studies. Comparative analysis is an essential part of the scientific method because we must be able to compare two or more cases in order to offer any generalizations about them. Unfortunately, the requirement for at least two, preferably more, cases is regarded by some as the only objective criteria for a compara-

tive study. Moreover, there is a tendency to identify the requirement for two or more cases exclusively with cross-sectional designs, whereas it would be equally valid to develop cases with longitudinal research designs. In short, many researchers confuse a general method of analysis with a particular subject matter and type of research design; they associate the comparative method with the field of comparative national politics.[2]

This association is particularly dangerous for those interested in the comparative study of foreign policy behavior because it leads them to explain the external behavior of nation-states solely in terms of the internal characteristics of those states. This approach fails to recognize that the comparative method (and for that matter the field of comparative politics) requires that cases for analysis be compared inclusively with respect to all of the factors that may account for the phenomena to be explained. If our comparisons are not inclusive in this sense, we can no longer have confidence that the differences we are trying to explain (the *explanandum*) can be accounted for by the differences in those conditions (*explanans*) we have included in our comparison.

What conditions must be taken into account in order to explain foreign policy? The answer to that question depends on our definition of foreign policy. In our view, foreign policy is a combination of both *intra*national and *inter*national politics. Intranational (or what is more commonly referred to as domestic, national, or comparative—in the subject-matter sense) politics is concerned with the relations between people and their government, that is, it concerns interdependencies within the boundaries of the state. International politics is concerned with the interactions and relationships among states as well as other extranational entities, that is, with interdependencies among states and other aspects of the international system. Foreign policy is best understood in terms of the exchanges between intra- and international politics or between states and their international environments (Chittick, 1975).

---

[1] By international environment we refer to the collectivity of countries' orientations toward their external environments. The referent for "countries' orientations toward their external environments" is quite inclusive. For any given country, the phrase refers to the orientations of individuals of that country who *can* affect the continuation, modification, or discontinuation of actions taken by persons outside the country. Further, "Orientations" refers to perceptions and evaluations of such external stimuli, to the intentions of those perceiving and evaluating, and to the responses to the external environment.

[2] Rosenau anticipated this problem in part in his discussion of the difference between the comparative study of foreign policy and comparative foreign policy (Rosenau, 1971, pp. 76-78).

We believe that the international environment is an essential component of any explanation of foreign policy behavior because the international environment of every state is somewhat different. This follows from the fact that each state is part of every other state's international environment but cannot be part of its own. Thus, nations neither constitute nor are contained in identical test tubes. When we fail to take nation A's and nation B's intra- or international aspects into account, we are actually comparing A and B in an effort to explain differences in their behavior which reflect A plus or times... with B plus or times.... Assuming that both intra- and international factors are important in the explanation of foreign policy phenomena, such comparisons are simply not valid.

Most theorists of international politics and foreign policy recognize the close relationship between intra- and international politics even if they measure the two sets of variables separately. For example, Rosenau has written at length about the linkages between intra- and international politics (1969). In his original pre-theory he emphasized the extent to which members of some societies participate directly and authoritatively in the decisions of other societies—the penetrated states (1966). Further, Rosenau's theory of adaptation explicitly focused upon the relations between the state and its international environment (1970). And, in one of his more recent articles, Rosenau devotes his attention exclusively to the importance of environmental variables in foreign policy studies (1972).

It is true that some approaches to the study of foreign policy seem to ignore the international environment. To the extent that they do so, however, we believe that the propositions tendered by these approaches are only valid when there is a close correspondence between the empirical assumptions underlying each of these approaches and the respective situations in the real world to which they are applied. Indeed, one reason they are "approaches" and not "theories" is that they are so data-bound that they are useful only if we are willing to make some rather strong empirical assumptions.

For example, the decision-making approach introduced by Snyder, Bruck, and Sapin focused its attention primarily upon processes at work within the decision-making unit of the state (1962). These authors acknowledged that the international setting might determine foreign policy actions "irrespective of whether or how the decision-makers perceive them" (1962, p. 67). If the international setting did determine the actions of a state, there were no apparent reasons why we would want to use the decision-making approach to study that phenomenon.

Similarly, Allison has illuminated three different models for explaining foreign policy behavior—the rational model, the organizational process model, and the bureaucratic politics model (1971). Although Allison's rational model necessarily implies a consideration of the international environment (Sigal, 1970), he discusses each model in terms of a single actor. To the extent that the international environment is important in the explanation of foreign policy behavior, we would not want to use any of Allison's models as he presents them.

Since various approaches make different empirical assumptions about what data are more relevant for understanding foreign policy, it follows that we must make a determination as to which of these assumptions seems to be appropriate in a particular case or set of cases. This requirement has been recognized by a number of authors. For example, Allison suggests that some of his models will be more appropriate than others under some, but not all, circumstances (1971, pp. 275-77). Similarly, Pruitt indicates that our interpretation of an interaction system will depend largely upon knowing in which of several general situations we find ourselves (1969, pp. 405-6). It is also commonplace for game theorists to acknowledge that the best course of action depends on the proper identification of the game we are playing (Snyder, 1971, pp. 91-102). Thus, to the extent that various approaches treat the international environment as a given, rather than as a variable, theorists of international politics and foreign policy usually recognize this as a limitation on the applicability of those approaches.

In view of the fact that most theorists recognize the importance of the international environment in the explanation of foreign policy behavior, we find it puzzling that the international environment of states is either not considered at all or not considered very adequately in comparative studies of foreign policy. We base this rather sweeping indictment on two recent surveys of these studies. One source, as indicated, describes some 200 empirical studies published between 1955 and mid-1972 that involved at least two countries and that sought to explain either the causes or consequences of foreign policy behavior (McGowan and Shapiro, 1973, pp. 35-36). Another source provides a list of all papers written through 1971 under the auspices of the Inter-university Comparative Foreign Policy (ICFP) project (Rosenau et al., 1973).[3] Between them, these two sources probably cover a large portion of the relevant studies.

If there is a dominant approach to the explanation of foreign policy behavior in these studies it is the attempt to explain the behavior of states in terms of state attributes, i.e., "attribute theory," "field theory," and "status field theory." Of the twelve categories of independent variables used to explain state behavior in McGowan and Shapiro, for example, at least five represent attribute data at the level of the state, i.e., political, governmental, economic, societal, and cultural (1973, p. 41). Thus, the most common research design relates the attributes of a state with its behavior.

The emphasis on national attributes as *explanans* of foreign policy behavior is equally apparent if we examine the ICFP papers. Most of these studies build upon Rosenau's original pretheory identification of three national attributes of the state—size, economic development, and political accountability—as genotypic variables which would enable us to order the potencies of all other sources of foreign policy behavior (1966). Therefore, many ICFP papers relate one or more of these state attributes with state behavior.

We would argue that none of the studies based exclusively on attribute data are truly comparative because they do not consider the international environment. First, attributes cannot adequately measure the interactions and relationships between specific states (at best, attributes can reflect only the total interactions and relationships of states with others), and consequently they cannot specify

the situational factors that are generally believed to affect foreign policy.[4] Second, although attribute data can be aggregated to reflect characteristics of the international system as a whole, this is probably the least effective way of describing that system for the purpose of measuring its politics.

Of the seven remaining categories of independent variables used in the explanation of foreign policy behavior, four deal with intranational units below the state level, i.e., individual, elite, establishment, and decision-making (McGowan and Shapiro, 1973, p. 41). Only two of these categories of variables can reflect aspects of the international environment; they are individual and decision-making variables. To the extent that variables in either of these categories reflect aspects of the international environment, we believe that these aspects of the environment should also be represented by variables based on the interactions and relationships among states.

This leaves only three categories of independent variables, out of a total of twelve, which attempt to measure aspects of a state's international environment directly; they are linkage variables, systemic variables, and other nations' policies (McGowan and Shapiro, 1973, p. 41). Of the 60 ICFP papers, two deal explicitly, but not exclusively, with variables that depict aspects of the international environment (East, 1970; Harf, Hoovler, and James, 1974). Although many of these variables describe some aspect of the international environment, they either employ variables at the level of the state which do not allow them to measure important aspects of the international environment or they employ variables at the level of the system as a whole which do not allow them to distinguish among the international environments of different states.

Moreover, since most analysts try to distinguish between variables at the level of the state and variables at the level of the international system, they would have to employ multiple levels of analysis in order for their studies to be truly comparative (Przeworski and Teune, 1970, p. 48). This

---

[3]At the time this essay was written most of these papers were unpublished but familiar to one or both of the authors.

[4]There is some evidence that attribute distances are associated with state interactions (McGowan and Shapiro, 1973, pp. 170-74). For a more complete discussion of the distinction between attribute data and relationship data, see the section on reconceptualization.

requirement is gradually being recognized, and a few of the studies surveyed attempt to test the relative potency of intranational and international variables on foreign policy (e.g., East and Gregg, 1967; Choucri and North, 1969; Rosenau and Hoggard, 1974; Rosenau and Ramsey, 1973; Tanter 1972).

Although these studies represent a step in the right direction, most of them also fail to be truly comparative because they do not adequately take the international environment of the state into account. Once again, it may be instructive to employ Rosenau's attempts to test his extended pre-theory as our illustration of this type of study (Rosenau and Hoggard, 1974; Rosenau and Ramsey, 1973). In the extended pre-theory Rosenau introduces three "relational" variables—geographic distance, sociocultural homogeneity, and military balance—as the international counterparts of his three national genotypic variables—size, economic development, and political accountability.

There are several reasons why we do not believe that these more comparative studies are truly comparative. First, we note that these studies seldom measure the interactions and relationships between states. The difficulty stems from the type of variable employed to depict the international environment. In all too many cases the variables selected are attribute variables. For example, two of the three variables employed by Rosenau to depict international factors—sociocultural homogeneity and military balance—are state attribute variables. Even if the distance between states on these two attributes were correlated with the foreign policy behavior of states, we would argue that they could not help us to explain this behavior at the international level because these measures do not transcend the nation-state.[5] The reason for this is that these variables show differences among states; they cannot show whether there are linkages, or *lack* of linkages, between these same states.

Second, we note that none of these studies comes close to taking the total international envi-

ronment of a state into account. This difficulty arises from the rather restricted conception of the environment employed by most of us. For example, the emergence of event data sets has led us to look at the interactions between two states (dyads). However, we seldom consider the general context within which these interactions take place. Although the use of dyadic data is a step forward, it is not very satisfactory from the standpoint of introducing the international environment into studies of foreign policy both because it frequently looks only at bilateral behavior and because it does not fully tap relationships between these states. It is like explaining United States policy toward China by studying the interactions between the United States and China apart from the interactions and relationships of both these countries with the Soviet Union and other aspects of the international environment.

Third, few of these studies simultaneously examine the effect of intra- and international factors on foreign policy behavior. This problem emerges in part because of the extent to which many researchers are now wary of the levels of analysis problem (Singer, 1961; Ray and Singer, 1973). Many of the studies which employ both intranational and international *explanans* of foreign policy behavior analyze the effect of each *explanan* on the *explanandum* separately. This type of design actually precludes one from making useful inferences about the relative strengths of variables at multiple levels to say nothing of possible interaction effects among these variables.

Since we believe that most contemporary studies of foreign policy are not truly comparative because they do not adequately take the international environment into account, it is incumbent upon us to explain more systematically how we feel the international environment can be more effectively introduced into foreign policy analyses. This is the subject of the next two sections of this paper. The following section visits familiar terrain in the form of two well-known studies.[6] The visit is made in order to show how existing data (1) *can* be reanalyzed in such a way that the international environments of states are included to a greater

[5]McGowan and Shapiro state that "correlating distance on different variables to interactions is a vacuous exercise without a theory that explains why a relationship is expected" (1973, p. 173).

[6]This section is based upon two forthcoming studies for which data analysis is currently underway (Jenkins, forthcoming a, b).

extent than was the case in the original studies, and (2) *must* be reanalyzed in order to attain more valid tests of the hypotheses examined in those studies.

REANALYSIS

The first study that we visit is "National Alliance Commitments and War Involvement, 1815-1945," one of the initial products of the Correlates of War project that has so greatly stimulated the thought and work of the present authors and many others (Singer and Small, 1966). In this study, Singer and Small reported their findings on the extent to which the alliance relationships that states enter into predict their proneness to war. For each country, they summed their measures of state alliance and war participation over time (1815-1945), and correlated the pairs of summed figures (or their ranks).

Now clearly, the authors are cognizant of the need to take into account alliance participation in the international environment, generally, in order to more fully explicate the relationship between states' alliance and war participation. That is, they suggest, among other things, using aggregated, system level alliance participation to predict to state war participation (Ray and Singer, 1973). But the hypothesis at the state level could have been more thoroughly examined than it was by state level data, alone. Search as one might, there is no reference to the alliance relationships of a state's war opponent(s). Suppose that a state, allied with no other, is consistently involved in wars with countries that are allied. Why should this be considered a deviation from an expected positive relationship between alliance and war at the state level? True, that state's *own* alliance participation (or lack thereof) deviates from the expected relationship, but if the Singer-Small hypothesis has any merit, the alliance relations of its opponents may have been critical to its having any opponents at all.

Lest the reader think the preceding is too remote a possibility to be given serious consideration, let us introduce the case of Turkey for the years 1815-1939. Turkey was allied with at least one other country during 30 of those years, none

of which was followed within three years by war. It was also a deviant (relative to expectations) case in that, like our hypothetical country, almost one-third of its years not in alliance were followed within three years by interstate war participation. Turkey shared further characteristics of our hypothetical country. Of the eleven interstate wars in which it was engaged, nine were fought against countries that *were* in alliances (in five of these instances, the opponent country[ies] were in defensive alliances with others or one another). In addition, Turkey is adjudged as having initiated only one of the interstate wars in which it was involved (Singer and Small, 1972, pp. 368-369).

The net impact of these considerations can be expressed in the form of an axiom for the conduct of state level research: Where the dependent variable (*explanandum*) of a hypothesis involves the interaction of states, a valid examination of that hypothesis with state level variables cannot be conducted by relating only each state's values on the independent variable(s) with its own values on the dependent variable. In all such cases, the values of each state on the independent variables must be related to the values on the dependent variable(s) of each other state with which it engages in the interactive behavior of the *explanandum*. In short, where one's research involves state-level data and an interactive dependent variable, more of each state's international environment must be incorporated into the design of the research (except for those states having zero values on the dependent variable).

Whatever confusion exists on the preceding points will be clarified, hopefully, after visiting a second study, Rummel's "Dimensions of Conflict Behavior within and between Nations" (1963). Rummel's finding that "foreign conflict behavior is generally completely unrelated to domestic conflict behavior" (1963, p. 24) is based upon data that are analyzed in such a way that the slight relationships discerned between the two domains of conflict behavior can be expected regardless of their strength of relationship in the "real world."

The major problem with the existing results,[7] and the data analyses from which they come, is

[7]The extant analysis that comes closest to being an exception to this perspective on the domestic-external conflict studies is that of Phillips (1973, pp. 124-47).

that the latter fail to take into account the time-honored "aggression problem." That is, the existing analyses of the relationship between foreign and domestic conflict do not distinguish between countries initiating hostilities and those that are attacked. Clearly, to the extent that countries initiating hostilities have high domestic conflict, and those being attacked have low domestic conflict, then we have (1) real-world confirmation of the "push" proposition (i.e., that countries experiencing domestic strife are more likely than others to engage in foreign conflict, establishing an external enemy for increasing internal cohesion) that is not reflected in (2) statistical analyses that fail to distinguish aggressors from among those countries engaging in interstate conflict.

The simplest response to the analysis problem regarding the internal-external conflict relationship, one that avoids the operational problem of defining, and adjudging, "aggressors," is to relate the amount of conflict between each country-dyad with the domestic conflict of whichever dyad member is experiencing the greater amount. This is a more valid measure of the relationship between domestic and foreign conflict than those conducted to date. Recognize that, once again, we were faced with state level data and a dependent variable that involved interaction between states, and, once again, we improve our analysis by acknowledging that the domestic conflict extant in a given state's international environment may better account for that state's external conflict (by another being "pushed" toward it) than will its own domestic conflict.

RECONCEPTUALIZATION

Among other things, the preceding section has revealed the less than total independence of states. To acknowledge that the characteristics of *other* states must be taken into account in order to improve our explanations and predictions of any given state's behavior is to acknowledge that a state's environment provides the parameters for whatever degree of fate control it possesses. We believe, however, that this recognition comes more easily because of the nature of the interactive dependent variables that were considered (interstate war and conflict). They were forceful inter-

actions where the will of one state could readily be viewed as being imposed on another. But the force involved should be viewed as incidental; the interaction involved in the *explanandum* is what compels us to include the international environment of a state in accounting for its behavior. Substitute "international integration" for conflict, and we are no less compelled. It is this perspective that leads—indeed, pushes—us in the direction of using relationship data,[8] in preference to variables at the two traditional levels of analysis (state and systemic). Relationship variables manifest in the independent variable the interactive process among states that can only be grossly inferred from systemic data, and that can only be found in the dependent variables of state level analyses. In turn, we are encouraged to try to reconceptualize states in terms of their situation in the international environment by the employment of relationship variables. Our perspective on such reconceptualization will be elaborated upon subsequently in this section. First, we engage in a bit of stocktaking. This involves stating, with greater specificity, the requirements of comparative foreign policy that we ultimately wish to fulfill.

In order to study foreign policy comparatively, we contend that our *explanans* must reflect both the intra- and international sources of foreign policy behavior. We believe that existing studies fail to be comparative both because the *explanans* represent only one aspect of the state, that is, they are either intranational variables or international variables, and, that being the case, because they do not explain behavior in terms of multiple levels of analysis. In order for us to identify the kinds of variables and levels of analysis that we think are required for comparative analyses of foreign policy, it may be useful to first describe four distinct aspects of foreign policy data: (1) units of analysis, (2) cases for analysis,[9] (3) types of variables, and (4) levels of analysis.

[8] Relationship variables describe the more established patterns of relations among states, such as military alliance, diplomatic exchanges, and shared memberships in international organizations (Bernstein and Weldon, 1968).

[9] This particular aspect of foreign policy data has received extensive consideration by Kegley and Skinner as the "case-for-analysis problem." See their study in this volume, Chapter 33.

Units of analysis are the objects whose attributes or behaviors are observed and analyzed. In most foreign policy studies we are interested primarily in explaining the behavior of the governments of nation-states. Thus, the nation-state or more accurately the government of the state becomes the unit whose behavior we study. As the salience of other actors (units) becomes recognized, we will become more interested in analyzing their behavior. For example, we may become even more interested in the behavior of groups of multinational corporations or blocs of states in the future.

In order to explain these behaviors, we may refer to attributes and behaviors of the same or additional units of analysis, such as individuals and groups. Moreover, we may observe the attributes and behaviors of one set of units and then aggregate them so as to represent another unit of analysis. For example, we may observe the opinions of individuals and then aggregate these opinions to reflect public opinion within a nation. The foreign policy behavior of a state may be explained in terms of the attributes and behaviors of one or more of the following: individuals, groups, states, international nongovernmental organizations, international intergovernmental organizations, and the international system as a whole.

Once we have selected the unit or units of analysis in terms of which we shall attempt to explain foreign policy behavior, we must decide how these units will be treated to form the *cases* for analysis. If each unit is treated as a separate case, then the number of such units and the number of cases are the same. However, if we are interested in the relations between pairs of states, then the case for analysis is the dyad, and we may have many more cases for analysis than we have numbers of such units. For example, if we are studying four states (state is the unit of analysis) and our case for analysis is the monad, then there is a total of only four cases, whether we study them individually or comparatively. If we are studying four states and our case for analysis is the dyad, however, there is a total of six dyads, or cases, for our study. The situation is compounded, further, if our case for analysis is the directed dyad where we are only interested in the behavior which a given state is directing toward a particular target

state.[10] In that event there would be a total of twelve directed dyads among only four states.

It is important to distinguish between these various cases for analysis because they determine in part the *types* of variables we can employ in our study. If our case for analysis is the monad, then we are concerned with two general types of variables, attributes and behaviors (Singer, 1971). Attributes are the static characteristics of entities, such as their size, state of development, and stability; behaviors are the dynamic characteristics of these same units. For example, the size of a state is one of its attributes, but if the state uses its size to bully another state by various means, those actions are behaviors. We may compare the attributes and behaviors of two or more states when states are treated as monads as in "field theory" and "status field theory," but we cannot properly infer from this information alone that there is any connection between these combinations of states because of their similarities or differences. The reason for this becomes clear when we identify the types of variables which are involved when the case for analysis is the dyad, triad, or polyad.

When our case for analysis is at least the dyad, we may consider two additional types of variables, interactions and relationships (Singer, 1971). Interactions refer to the sequence of actions and reactions among two or more units. Interactions are different from behaviors in that the latter are part of an interaction sequence only if the target entity or entities are affected by this behavior and subsequently respond to it. Relationships refer to the connections between two or more entities (not just to the similarities and differences between them, which is the situation when the case for analysis is the monad). Since two entities or units may share a bond without any clear sequence of actions and reactions between them, a relationship may exist without any apparent interactions. In addition, we would expect identical interactions between each of several pairs of states to have the same consequences for the interacting states only if their relationships with one another were identical. Moreover, the existence of a relationship between two or more entities allows us to infer the presence of some interactions. Thus, an alliance

10See Chapter 33.

demonstrates a political relationship between two states, and we can infer that some form of diplomatic interaction occurs between alliance partners.

It is important to realize, then, that these four types of variables have been introduced in order of greater inclusiveness. As we move from attributes to behaviors, to interactions, to relationships, we take into account more and more about the context in which foreign policy occurs. For instance, if we compare the attributes of two states, we are only able to identify similarities and differences which may *potentially* have some effect on the behavior of one or more of these states. Even if we can show correlations between the attributes and behaviors of these states, either individually or collectively, we still do not know if the behavior of one or more states is in any way responsive to the behavior of other states. Only if we can determine that there is an interaction between two or more states are we justified in claiming, on the basis of state level data, that we are taking both intra- and international factors into account. And only if we employ a valid measure of relationship can we claim to represent both intra- and international factors that go beyond explicit interactions.

Thus, it is important to recognize that as we move from the more observable, concrete attributes of individual states to the more abstract relationships among all states, we are likely to maximize our explanation of foreign policy behavior because we are taking into account more of what we believe can account for that behavior. Since the relationships among states or groups of states are not so concrete as attributes of states, it is reasonable to infer that we shall have to build some assumptions into our models for explaining foreign policy behavior in terms of these variables (but no more assumptions than we now make by employing attribute data). Moreover, the more of these kinds of assumptions we are willing to make, the more, not less, theoretically interesting these models are likely to become.

The variables which are incorporated into our explanatory models may also be arrayed according to various *levels* of analysis. Such levels are usually associated with levels of aggregation so that units at a lower level of analysis, such as the state or nation, can be combined to form a higher level of analysis, such as the interstate or international system.[11] As long as our data are lodged at two distinct levels of analysis, we must incorporate *explanans* that are appropriate to the respective levels (state and system) in order to provide general-law-type explanations of foreign policy behavior.

The problem with using attributes and behaviors to measure state and systemic conditions is that they cannot tap the dynamics of the more inclusive types of variables—interactions and relationships among states. This difficulty is particularly serious in the case of variables at the state level because these data usually fail to represent the international environment at all. Attribute data cannot be used to measure the relations among states except in those cases where we can clearly make inferences about relationships from attribute data, such as the number of foreign embassies in a country. Moreover, the use of attribute data to measure changes in the international system is disturbing because attributes are by definition the more static characteristics of states. No wonder foreign policy analysts believe that they can safely treat the international system as a constant; they measure state and systemic variables in ways that are likely to obscure whatever changes in the international environment actually occur!

If we are going to conduct comparative studies of foreign policy, we should either employ traditional variables at both the state and systemic levels of analysis or make use of relationship data to depict the total situation of each state in the system. The latter course of action should allow us to avoid using variables at two levels of analysis since these new situational variables would be directly affected by traditional measures at both state and systemic levels.

One inference that can be drawn from this conclusion is that concepts, such as sovereignty, independence, and commitment which are frequently defined as attributes of states, need to be reconceptualized in terms of the relationships among states. For example, the state itself is tradi-

[11]Although the state and international system levels of analyses are most common in foreign policy analyses, it may also be useful to consider intermediate levels of analysis, such as international regions.

tionally defined in terms of its attributes, that is its population, territory, and government. The sovereignty or independence of a state is based on the recognition by others of these intranational attributes. Thus, independence is treated as a nominal variable. As suggested in beginning this section, we propose that "independence" connote a relationship between two or more states in which the actions of each state are truly independent of the actions of other states. This will allow us to treat the independence of states as a variable which reflects the full range of possibilities, including complete independence of, complete dependence upon, and complete interdependence with, other actors.

Our view is that to the extent a state is in an interdependent and/or dependent relationship with any other state(s), its parameters of choice vis-à-vis the other state(s) is restricted, and it is less independent of the other state(s). This perspective is employed in our ongoing research wherein a conception of positive political interdependence is imposed on two types of relationships among states—shared membership in intergovernmental organization and diplomatic exchange (Jenkins and Chittick, 1975, p. 87). Our expectation is that by employing this conceptualization of relationship data, we are taking into account the interactive dynamics among states in our *independent variable*. If this is the case, we are not faced with the necessity of data reanalysis that was considered in the preceding section. Rather, our *explanans* are expected to manifest, in common with the *explanandum* (where the dependent variable involves interaction among states), the effects of the state's international environment.

We believe that such a movement toward measurement of states in situations will enhance our predictive capability, but, perhaps more importantly, we should be in a better position to markedly close the sizable gap between extant theorizing about foreign policy and its empirical analysis.

REFERENCES

Allison, Graham T. 1971. *Essence of Decision: Explaining the Cuban Missile Crisis.* Boston: Little, Brown.

Bernstein, A. Robert, and Peter D. Weldon. 1968. "Structural Approach to the Analysis of International Rela-

tions." *Journal of Conflict Resolution* 12: 159-81.

Chittick, William O. 1975. *The Analysis of Foreign Policy Outputs.* Columbus, Ohio: Merrill.

Choucri, Nazli, and Robert C. North. 1969. "The Determinants of International Violence," *Papers, Peace Society Research (International),* 12: 33-63.

East, Maurice A. 1970. "The Influence of Size and System Polarity on Foreign Policy Acts, 1946-1967." Paper presented at the Annual Meeting of the International Studies Association, Pittsburgh.

——— and Phillip M. Gregg. 1967. "Factors Influencing Cooperation and Conflict in the International System." *International Studies Quarterly* (Sep): 244-68.

Harf, James E., David G. Hoovler, and Thomas E. James. 1974. "Systemic and External Attributes in Foreign Policy Analysis." In *Comparing Foreign Policies,* ed. James N. Rosenau, pp. 235-49. Beverly Hills: Sage.

Jenkins, Jerry B. Forthcoming a. "The Independence of Conflict Behavior within and between Countries as Methodological Artifact."

———. Forthcoming b. "State Alliance and Violence: Testing a Hypothesis."

——— and William O. Chittick. 1975. "Reconceptualizing Foreign Policy Behavior: The Problem of Discrete Events in a Continuous World." In *Foreign Policy Analysis,* ed. Richard L. Merritt, pp. 79-92. Lexington, Mass.: Heath.

McGowan, Patrick J., and Howard B. Shapiro. 1973. *The Comparative Study of Foreign Policy: A Survey of Scientific Findings.* Beverly Hills: Sage.

Phillips, Warren R. 1973. "The Conflict Environment of Nations: A Study of Conflict Inputs to Nations in 1963." In *Conflict Behavior and Linkage Politics,* ed. Jonathan Wilkenfeld, pp. 124-47. New York: McKay.

Pruitt, Dean G. 1969. "Stability and Sudden Change in Interpersonal and International Affairs." In *International Politics and Foreign Policy,* ed. James N. Rosenau, pp. 392-408. New York: Free Press.

Przeworski, Adam, and Henry Teune. 1970. *The Logic of Comparative Social Inquiry.* New York: Wiley.

Ray, James L., and David Singer. 1973. "Aggregation and Inference: The Levels Problem Revisited." Paper prepared for the Annual Meeting of the International Studies Association, New York.

Rosenau, James N. 1966. "Pre-theories and Theories of Foreign Policy." In *Approaches to Comparative and International Politics,* ed. R. Barry Farrell, pp. 27-92. Evanston: Northwestern Univ. Press.

———. 1969. *Linkage Politics: Essays on the Convergence of National and International Systems.* New York: Free Press.

———. 1970. *The Adaptation of National Societies: A Theory of Political System Behavior and Transforma-*

tion, pp. 1-28. New York: McCaleb-Seiler.

———. 1971. *The Scientific Study of Foreign Policy*. New York: Free Press.

———. 1972. "The External Environment as a Variable in Foreign Policy Analysis." In *The Analysis of International Politics,* ed. James N. Rosenau, Vincent Davis, and Maurice A. East, pp. 145-63. New York: Free Press.

———, Philip M. Burgess, and Charles F. Hermann. 1973. "The Adaptation of Foreign Policy Research: A Case Study of an Anti-Case Study Project." *International Studies Quarterly* 17 (Mar): 119-44.

——— and George R. Ramsey, Jr. 1973. "External vs. Internal Sources of Foreign Policy Behavior: Testing the Stability of an Intriguing Set of Findings." Paper prepared for the Ninth World Congress of the International Political Science Association, Montreal.

——— and Gary Hoggard. 1974. "Foreign Policy Behavior in Dyadic Relationships: Testing a Pre-theoretical Extension." In *Comparing Foreign Policies,* ed. James N. Rosenau, pp. 117-49. Beverly Hills: Sage.

Rummel, Rudolph J. 1963. "Dimensions of Conlict Behavior within and between Nations." In *General System Yearbook,* vol. 8, pp. 1-50. Bedford, Mass.: Society for General Systems Research.

Sigal, Leon V. 1970. "The 'Rational Policy' Model and the Formosan Strait Crisis." *International Studies Quarterly* 14 (Jun): 121-56.

Singer, J. David. 1961. "The Level-of-Analysis Problem in International Relations." In *The International System,* ed. Klaus Knorr and Sidney Verba, pp. 77-92. Princeton: Princeton Univ. Press.

———. 1971. *General System Taxonomy for Political Science*. Morristown, N.J.: General Learning Press.

——— and Melvin Small. 1966. "National Alliance Commitments and War Involvement, 1815-1945." *Papers, Peace Research Society (International)* 5: 109-40.

——— and Melvin Small. 1972. *The Wages of War, 1816-1965: A Statistical Handbook,* pp. 71-75. New York: Wiley.

Snyder, Glenn H. 1971. " 'Prisoner's Dilemma' and 'Chicken' Models in International Politics." *International Studies Quarterly* 15 (Mar): 91-102.

Snyder, Richard C., H. W. Bruck, and Burton Sapin. 1962. *Foreign Policy Decision-Making*. New York: Free Press.

Tanter, Raymond. 1972. "International System and Foreign Policy Approaches: Implications for Conflict Modeling and Management." *World Politics* 24 (suppl.): 7-39.

32. Epistemology, Theory, Data, and the Future

Charles A. Powell · David Andrus
Helen Purkitt · Kathleen Knight

EPISTEMOLOGY

Although there is a considerable risk of getting lost in airy verbosity, the questions of why and how (we think) we know what we know are always implicitly present; attempting to find answers has a certain utility in moving forward at the edges of our ignorance. Philosophic excursions can be abstruse and irrelevant, and none of us considers himself or herself a philosopher of science. But, as

Lazarsfeld has observed: "Philosophers of science are not interested in, and do not know what the work-a-day empirical research man does. This has two consequences: we have to become our own methodologists, or we have to muddle along without benefit of the explicating clergy" (1962, p. 470).

Our focus here will be comparative foreign policy (CFP), and we will first examine the philosophic or meta-theoretical aspects of this "movement" so as to establish some helpful points of reference in thinking about CFP and its future. Looking for the origins of this movement, we can refer to the short history provided by Rosenau, Burgess, and Hermann (1973). They point out that CFP explicitly intended to produce a convergence between certain empirical approaches on one hand and, on the other, contemporary theoretical developments in the study of foreign policy and the international system. These latter developments themselves represent a convergence of many notions and ideas which have surfaced in the theoretical ferment of the last 20 years. The particular synthesis which has had the role of translating these developments into a coherent framework or point of departure was one proposed by Rosenau (1971b), in the well-known "Pre-theories and Theories of Foreign Policy" originally published five years earlier. This should not be regarded as *the* theory, or even *a* theory, but rather as an instance of synthetic consolidation. As McClelland (1972, p. 29) notes:

> When we look in the cupboard for explicit, well-developed international system theory to *use* in research and in the pursuit of new theory, we find it almost bare. What is to be found is a rich supply of inchoate theory that was accumulated for a purpose different from that of orienting specific empirical research. If international system theory currently has little to offer in the way of specific hypotheses for testing by research, it has much to offer by way of directing choices of areas of research and of limiting objectives in research undertakings.

Much has been made of the transition from the state of synthetic consolidation (the "third wave") to the state in which theory building is accomplished by data confrontation (the "fourth wave")–these terms were applied by McClelland (1972). The CFP convergence can be seen as an example of the fourth wave in terms of the general convergence between the methodological and technological developments which have spilled over into the social sciences generally and the (rather inchoate) wisdom and thought which has been generated within the substantive area of foreign policy analysis and international relations. From an epistemological point of view, there are two aspects of particular importance in this kind of convergence. First, there is the possibility of basic incompatabilities between the approaches adopted by empirical researchers and the "theoretical" synthesis, such as that proposed by Rosenau. Second, there is the question of whether the "theoretical" synthesis does indeed provide a coherent organizing framework.

In the study of CFP, a convincing case can be made that a philosophical incompatability exists, and, further, that it has relevance for the day-to-day operation of CFP research. First, let us look at the basic "systems theoretical" view of reality which pervades, consciously and unconsciously, aggregate macro-analytic research. There are two quantitative approaches which have dominated empirical research of the "generalist" (as opposed to area studies or case study) variety. Both are somewhat diffuse, at least to the degree that one must be careful in lumping researchers into categories which might overstate the actual degree of coordination or similarity in research approach. This is particularly true when we are trying to link such categories with basic views of reality. With that qualification in mind, we will take a brief look at the meta-theory which pervades the two main quantitative approaches: aggregate indicators and events data.

While attempts to describe international behavior using aggregate indicators preceded a formal statement of "systems theory" in international relations, a common conceptualization is apparent. Thus, in 1955 Quincy Wright, spoke of the need to determine "*factors* significant in international relations, *indices* disclosing the changes of these variables . . . and *regulators* [institutions, ideas, procedures, and relations susceptible of human manipulation], continuous survey of which would yield both understanding of, and the power to control international affairs" (1961, p. 401). The most ambitious attempt to develop data compatible with this "field theory" was undertaken by R. J. Rummel who, unfortunately, found it necessary to sacrifice much of Wright's intuitive clarity in favor of the methodological rigors of factor analysis (Thurston, 1947). Some notions of Rosenau's extended pre-theory (Rosenau and Hoggard, 1974) can be found in Rummel's suggestion, first published in 1965, that "foreign conflict behavior, is not internally derived. . . . It is a relational phenomenon depending on the degree of economic, social and political similarity between nations, the geographic distance between them, and their power parity" (1969, p. 612).[1]

The second quantitative approach which has been tapped by CFP is events data research. As in the case of Rummel and "field theory," events data research has an identifiable meta-theoretical context within which the original stimulus sparked its macroanalytical empiricism. The context for events data research was the attempt to introduce and adapt "general systems theory" (GST). Charles McClelland, who began the movement to collect and analyze large sets of events data, was among a small group of influential scholars who in the mid-1950s were much impressed with GST. As Rapoport has noted: "General systems theory is best described not as a theory in the sense that this word is used in science but, rather, as a program or a direction in the contemporary philosophy of science" (1968, p. 452; see also McClelland, 1972, p. 35).

GST thus was at the core of the "behavioral revolution" at the international level of analysis, which, as in every area of social science, stimulated a countervailing wave of vehement criticism and opposition. Much of this was directed at Kaplan, probably because of his vigorous advocacy of the approach. This has tended to give the mistaken impression of a monolithic consensus on what the "scientific approach" dictated in terms of research techniques and the empirical questions to which these techniques can be applied, as well as a failure to understand and explore the epistemological foundations of the "movement." Expressed most simply, the opposition to "science" has been rationalized primarily in terms of the feeling that a scientific empiricism was necessarily reductionist, ignoring the nuance and substantive texture of the mass of information available in the historical and documentary record. Ironically, if the systems approach has had any common thrust at all in international relations, it has been to redirect attention back to the minutiae and painstaking cognitive

procedures of historical research. McClelland et al. (1971), Sherwin (1973), and Rosecrance (1963) are salient and contrasting examples.

Even a cursory review of the literature shows great differences, as for example, between Kaplan and McClelland. Kaplan was concerned with closed systems as definable states of the international system and the transformations from one state to another. McClelland, while also concerned with stable patterns of international action and transformation processes, was more oriented toward dynamic and open-ended systems evolution—i.e., process. There is, unfortunately, no published account of the time which Charles McClelland, Morton Kaplan, and Harold Guetzkow spent with Ross Ashby at the Center for Advanced Studies in the Behavioral Sciences in Palo Alto during the mid-1950s. That GST and Ashby's influence could have initiated the distinctly different research traditions associated with each of these three scholars (as well as others, albeit less directly) is remarkable. We have not dealt with Guetzkow and the simulation approach in this discussion, particularly since the Ashby influence is not so overtly obvious. Also the relation with CFP is more tenuous, although it might be noted, if only to complete the circle, that Rummel acknowledged his debt to Guetzkow for his aid in selecting the variables employed in his 1964 study published as "Some Dimensions of International Relations" (1969, p. 600). (For a similar epistemological analysis of the Guetzkow-stimulated simulation approach, see Powell, 1969, 1971, 1973, 1976, forthcoming.) At a deeper philosophical level, the central notion of reality which has pervaded empirical research (especially events data research) has been carried over from the Ashbyian GST. In Ashby's words (1970, pp. 94-95):

> I would like then to start from the basic fact that every model of a real system is in one sense second-rate. Nothing can exceed, or even equal, the truth and accuracy of the real system itself. Every model is inferior, a distortion, a lie. . . . Here I want to adhere to the . . . point of view that the truth is the *whole* system, not any extract from it. I would point out here that however vigorously Newton's equations of motion are defended as the extreme in truth, the astronomer must always reintroduce the discrepancies, such as (until Einstein's work) the rotation of the

---

[1] There are many criticisms of Rummel's work, but we will not get into that controversy here. An interesting technical criticism which relates directly to our comment above can be found in Vincent (1974). We are also aware of the fact that a passing reference to Rummel does not constitute an adequate review of the rather varied field of aggregate indicators research, which began with Wright (1942) and Richardson (1960a, 1960b).

perihelion of Mercury, when he would make *real* predictions. Ultimately, the raw facts are final.

Ashby and all of the international relations researchers who have been influenced by him take what has been called by C. West Churchman the "non-systematic" position that "reality," as they perceive it "has a truth and accuracy that no model can attain." They believe that there is a "real world," very complicated and largely unknown, from which they want to abstract (because it is convenient to do so), or which they want to map, or model, realistically (Churchman, 1970, pp. 134-35). The contrasting, "systematic" position would see "reality" as a mental construct, in which theory and relevant data together constitute a complete formal system. Churchman has noted that "philosophers, of course, have discussed this matter endlessly. Being prone to paradox, they have pointed out that reality must be and must not be a mental construct. It must be a mental construct, because otherwise reality is all mental, which is silly" (1970, p. 134).

Churchman's (1963, 1970) distinction between "systematic" (not to be confused with the "*systems* approach" or GST) and "non-systematic" view allows for a division of scientific labor in which theory building can proceed without theory testing (i.e., without an intimate connection with empirical problems), but where, ultimately, reality is the final judge of the value of any assertion. This allows free-form theorizing along with a feeling of a concrete reality which would be the final authority. It defers actual theorizing, because it permits "theory" to be a set of non-systematic assertions and avoids stating explicitly what the shape of the ultimate reality would have to be. Most succinctly, this position asserts that "*x* models *y*" when *x* is a system, and by means of *x* one can predict realistic assertions about *y*. The assertions in *x* must match the ultimate facts which constitute *y*, or *x* must be rejected. In contrast, the "systematic" position requires that *y*, the "reality construct," also be an explicit formal system, just as *x* is a formal system. In addition, to be complete systems, both *x* and *y* include not only empirical components (data), but also the logic of induction (empirical validity criteria). If *x* contradicts *y*, there is no automatic assumption that *y* involves the "ultimate facts," and *x* is

therefore invalid. The process of scientific analysis is one of making competing theoretical/empirical systems converge, following the twists and turns which contradiction and uncertainty set out in the researcher's path. In this view of the research process, the roles of theorist and researcher are inextricably woven together, and both tasks have to be performed simultaneously.

The "systematic" position requires that the reality construct be stated as a formal system, which, however, cannot be considered to be logically superior to the model. In contrast, the "non-systematic" position assumes that the observing mind validates the model by checking its assertions against the "known facts," and if the assertions are thereby shown to be deficient, they are altered. Model building, in this view, consists of writing down, or otherwise agreeing upon, a set of realistic assertions (Churchman, 1963, pp. 8-10). The realism of these assertions is established externally (validated). A formal system is then constructed and manipulated to see if it can predict the realistic assertions within the required degree of accuracy. It is this "non-systematic" view which has been so precisely stated by Ashby and which has carried over into the events data approach from GST. The "non-systematic" position leaves the scholar open to control by an external clientele whose view of "reality" constitutes the "ultimate facts." Churchman (1970, pp. 135-36) has given a delightful illustration of this particular consequence:

Suppose someone comes into your well-stocked shop and says, "I want an oregue to spanilize the franfran." You understand the beginning of the sentence, but the rest is mystifying. However, you don't want to lose a well-heeled client. You ask him to explain, but he keeps talking in a frustrating manner: "An oregue is not a franfran, but it can be made to spanilize a franfran; answer me, do you have one that does this?" Now if you're wise you'll begin to try some things, and at first he'll say, "Not that, for heaven's sake: that doesn't spanilize *anything*!" But after a bit, you'll develop a model for this customer. The model will suggest some items to try, and he'll admit you're getting closer. Finally, he may say, "That's it! There's an oregue that really does spanilize the franfran." At that point you might have some idea of what your client really did want.

Of course this example must seem unfair. Everybody understands so well what reality is, because the feeling of reality is a deep-seated psychological force. Hence the idea of "representing reality" by a model is also well understood. But it's this very fact of common understanding which makes the client's wishes so hard to satisfy in this case. Since everyone knows so well what it means to represent reality, no one is willing or able to articulate his demand. It is as though we had traveled the circle of meaning: the empty "an oregue to spanilize the franfran" and "a model to represent reality" turn out to be very close in terms of their meaningful content.

If the "non-systematic" position is adopted, then the only thing that would endow "a model to represent reality" with meaning is the metaphysical feeling that reality is a fixed entity, "out there," which a formal theory would seek to predict—always imperfectly, of course. Reality is a set of fixed observational facts, which the formal theory attempts to reproduce as accurately as possible. Even if a formal theory is developed which produces assertions which have no "real-world referent" yet, it is assumed, or hoped, that they will turn out to be "realistic" when an opportunity for empirical validation occurs. But what are facts (data)? Observations or perceptions have to be interpreted in order to become facts (data). And what is the basis upon which this interpretation rests? The logic of induction is a central problem of the "non-systematic" approach, and its difficulties result from an essential vagueness as to how assertions about reality which validate formal theories are themselves authenticated.

Unless the theoretical component of the data generation process is recognized and explicitly related to the overall theoretical context, and unless it is recognized that perception is distorted by both internal constraints and external position, then the research learning process (the struggle for convergence) will not cycle. Or, at least, this is the conclusion dictated by the "systematic" position. Whether its criticisms are useful depends upon how compelling you find its view of reality. On the other hand, while the criticisms offered by the "systematic" position may be valid, it can be argued that the "systematic" criteria for proper research are so stringent as to be unrealistic. (Either that, or knowledge in this area is at the

"first ripple" stage where it cannot stand up to scientific scrutiny at all.) It might be felt that "bad" theory is better than no theory, or that "bad" research is better than no research. In the great burst of social science theorizing and empirical research of the last two decades, this last assertion would have been accepted as a matter of course. Such automatic acceptance is no longer so easily assumed. A period of scientific soul searching is upon us, and it is frequently suggested that perhaps research ought to stop while considerable thought is given to intellectual and social premises, as well as to the use to which allegedly scientific knowledge may be put.

We feel that such soul searching can only be done usefully in the context of ongoing research, so that the termination of research per se is hardly the answer. Similarly, bad theory is difficult to diagnose and repair (or reject) without seeing if it "works" in an empirical context which the theory itself, along with explicit scientific beliefs about formal and empirical validity, can be made to generate. Comparison of the resultant complete formal/empirical system with competing reality constructs then leads to the struggle for convergence—the "ninth wave" to which all science aspires. Bad *research*, on the other hand, is an unsatisfying delusion in which data crunching goes on mindlessly and endlessly (at least until the client's money and/or patience is at an end.) We feel that the "non-systematic" view of reality and the attitudes associated with it which we have identified above have and will continue to encourage the sort of research which has impelled many scholars to call for a halt to large-scale aggregate empiricism. Unless some approximation of the "systematic" position is adopted, specifically its emphasis upon explicit theory and the role of such theory in empirical research, the argument for the End of Empiricism is, regrettably, compelling.

It should be noted that the barrenness of the theoretical cupboard—empty even of bad theory—will not lead either to despair or to an urge to theorize on the part of those who follow the path of the purely inductive historian. If we reject the extreme purism of those who declare the impossibility, and therefore, the irrelevance of theory in the analysis of the flow of events, there remains the view that theory can arise from pure induction. In this view, no theory is distinctly better than bad theory. The Ashby conception of "reality" found in GST approaches fits this view extremely well. If there is such a "reality" which serves as the ultimate arbiter—the "naked facts"— then assertions about "reality," its structure and patterns, can surely emerge without the benefit of theoretical midwifery. Indeed, theory, in this view, serves only to distort and obstruct the scientific process of knowing "reality." However, it is not denying the value of collections of historical data to point out that no empirical exploration has ever been conducted which did not require a theoretical component through which material and perceptions were screened, sorted, and translated into factual assertions. Both the observer and the observed have a theoretical context without which there is no meaning. Calhoun (1974, p. 85) has put this well with regard to events data:

> The common view of international events is that they are objective pieces of empirical reality—perhaps distorted a bit by various national biases—which they are not. They are first and most importantly communicative acts about a social reality in which they are embedded. It is this social reality that determines what an event is, how it is defined, what meaning is attached to it and how important it is, and not whether *it is*, or *is not*, an empirically objective fact. The source of confusion in depicting events as wholly empirical arises mainly because only man has the creative capacity to live simultaneously in two realms of experience, the physical and the symbolic.

THEORY

The original Rosenau position and the derivative CFP approach contained a commitment to theoretical explicitness and coherence. None of those involved would claim that either has hewn very close to such theoretically stringent crtieria. On the other hand, it is reasonable to say that there is a clear gap between the sort of explicit theoretical commitment made by the CFP researchers and the atheoretical (or omnitheoretical) stance taken by most aggregate indicator and events data researchers.

It would be possible to dismiss the point that we have been laboring to make by asserting that the theoretical base of CFP is either wrong and misleading or simply irrelevant and as amorphous

as the "non-systematic" view of reality. This can be put squarely, it would seem, in terms of whether Rosenau's pre-theoretical formulation is formally valid and useful as an orienting and directing framework for research. It can be extremely tedious to try to synthesize working conceptual definitions for such vague and general terms, of course. The question can be raised as to whether an attempt at such a definition is worth the effort. The answer is yes for two reasons. First, conceptual problems always turn up in the long run in spite of efforts to ignore or suppress them. Second, it can be argued that definitions are not purely arbitrary, but can be true or false; conceptual definitions are useful devices for crystallizing and refining goal-oriented research activities. A purpose-related "teleologically real" definition will assist a subarea of research to become "self-supporting" by translating working procedures into explicit and coherent norms (Churchman, 1963, p. 1).

In CFP, the question is whether the emphasis on explicit theory or "pre-theory" has accomplished its purpose in leading research away from the trap of mindless data crunching. This is a major question, and one over which substantial doubt and difference of opinion has been expressed; but one which must be given a positive answer (however diluted) in order for there to be a future for CFP, or indeed, for there to have been a useful *past* for CFP.

Rosenau's original article (1971b) attempted to make explicit and coherent the implicit, and possibly inconsistent, conventional wisdom about foreign policy and the international system. It also reflected a concern previously expressed by Rosenau about the dysfunctional separation of the study of the international system from the study of comparative politics (1971a). This separation is often reflected at a bureaucratic and academic politics level in the struggle of international relations to remain independent from the suffocating (presumably) embrace of the unidisciplinary orthodoxy and national/subnational emphasis of political science.

It is possible to assert the irrelevance of the internal environment by emphasizing those states of the international system which can be called system-dominant. In these situations, readily generalizable to other levels of societal aggregation, the logic of the situation takes over and the actors are drawn into irretrievable interaction processes, as illustrated by the well-known case of the Richardson process of hostile escalation. The demonstrable existence of such system-dominant states of the international system should not, however, be generalized into an a priori assumption that all interaction patterns at the international level have a similar property. This error has led to an exclusive concern for *intergovernmental* "events" taken out of context and considered in analytical isolation. Research into events forecasting tends to be practically identical to the sort of atheoretical mysticism one finds in the stock market forecasts of the Wall Street "chartmen." The "market" is imputed with motives, reactivity, and in general a life of its own in explaining and extrapolating the ups and downs of indicator or events fluctuations (trends).

Atheoretical projections, coupled with the implicit feeling about a concrete reality which is anthropomorphically organic in nature, can result in the worst sort of pseudoscientific crystal balling. The lack of process models, other than the formal model of arms races suggested and empirically explored by Richardson (1960a, 1960b) and a few others following his lead, and particularly the lack of bargaining (cooperative) process models, makes the system dominance argument

not only hypothetical, but vague and conjectural. The a priori objection to foreign policy process models is unconvincing. This does not mean, of course, that a contrary emphasis upon internal national or societal factors in foreign policy and international processes is necessarily valid.

In Rosenau's original articles (1971a, 1971b) there was an interest in the comparative approach itself which had done so much to rehabilitate cross-national research from the drear of "modern foreign governments," as well as an interest in utilizing the substance of cross-national research in modeling and specifying the linkages between internal politics, foreign policy behavior, and international interaction. The ordering of these last three elements, although it could be regarded as semantically nominal, suggests a directional flow. This flow from within-group to between-group behaviors is usually illustrated by frieze-like representations which purport to show the paradigm of foreign policy adaptation. Although not inconsistent with the postulation of between-group processes which dominate within-group behavior, (system dominance) such processes are noticeably de-emphasized by this sort of paradigmatic display.

Rosenau originally got beyond this error in a rather explicit fashion, suggesting a paradigm (see Figure 1), in which foreign policy output was

Figure 1. The Full Pre-theory

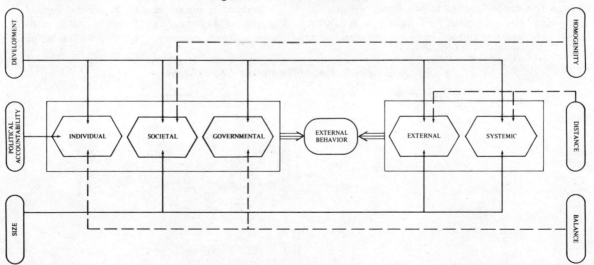

determined by a set of five sources (perhaps "sectors" would be a better term) whose "relative potency" was modulated at first by a cluster of three national attributes, later extended to include the cluster of three relational variables suggested by Rummel (1969, p. 612) which described the nature of the dyadic relationships between any country and all other countries. This part of the "pre-theory" not only had the appropriate scope for a CFP model, but also included an intriguing set of factors, sectors, and/or variables, arranged in a nonsimplistic fashion. The first problem encountered in evaluating the pre-theory (as extended to include "relational" variables) is whether it was ever fully carried over into operational use. In an earlier paper (Powell et al., 1974a) it was suggested that the original structure of the pre-theory was substantially simplified. Here there is sure to be an argument, as in both of the specific papers (Rosenau and Hoggard, 1974; Rosenau and Ramsey, 1975) in which the extended pre-theory is explored empirically, there are indications that the authors assume that the original form has been preserved. Nonetheless, we feel that the actual data analysis does not reflect the full paradigm because variables within the sources/sectors were never operationalized nor extensively discussed in subsequent empirical extensions. The model implied by the data analysis (see Figure 1) contained in both papers (see Figure 2) includes the modulating conditions or variables as the independent variables—the determinants of foreign policy. Nor is this model limited to just these two specific instances. The empirical CFP literature in general uses these same variables in much the same way,

while the link with the original paradigm is (usually implicitly) presumed to be still existent.

Accepting our point, for the sake of argument if nothing else, we can then ask whether the simplification is good or bad, and why it happened. Perhaps it is our ignorance, but we have never found the original paradigm particularly persuasive, despite its conceded utility as a point of departure, and thus we do not feel particularly inclined to try to maintain the original link. Moreover, it may be overlooking an empirical accomplishment to keep up the appearance that the original formulation has survived intact. And finally, it may be possible to pick up some of the original elements later in an altered form. Thus, it is by no means necessarily bad that the original paradigm never made it out into the field, even though it is unfortunate and misleading that this has not been recognized.

Why the pre-theory was simplified has at least two answers. First, it was much easier to handle in a simplified form; it conformed with available measures and analytical procedures, particularly the latter. It may indeed be the case that the original paradigm could never be transformed into a model and operationalized, especially in a nonexperimental context. Second, the simpler formulation was more consistent with the felt need to plug into the events data approach. Given the arguments presented in the first section of this paper, the question immediately occurs as to whether this second reason implies a sell-out to the "nonsystematic" philosophical position implied in aggregate indicator and events data research, which, from our point of view, would be unfor-

Figure 2. The Extended Pre-theory, Causal Model

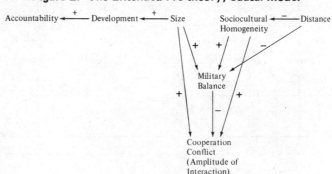

tunate. It would tend to lead CFP into the atheoretical bog in which such research has floundered.

In the aggregate indicators and the events data approaches, descriptive rather than inferential statistical analysis has been the dominant mode of data analysis (not meaning to imply that one mode of data analysis is inherently superior—they are just different). This means that one is proceeding inductively, throwing as wide a net as possible to capture indicators or events, put them into a common correlational pot, and then try to tease out a more parsimonious set of descriptions. Anything that cannot be easily committed to the common pot tends to fall by the wayside. In the "pretheory," the original modulating, and now independent, variables were the same variables as those found in aggregate analysis, while the original foreign policy determinants (internal and external sectoral sources) were not. Whether they could or should be made compatible is a question that has been passed over rather than faced.

If an unkind critic would then assert that CFP has foundered in the mindless data-crunching bog, would he be making a valid judgment? Our feeling is that this would have to be conceded in part, but that probation rather than condemnation would be a more just sentence. The justification for this is that there are important philosophical and theoretical distinctions between CFP and events data and other aggregate macroanalytical research.

DATA[2]

Criticism has been expressed concerning much of the contemporary events data "revisionism" (multiple source comparisons and the like). Calhoun (1974, p. 86) has said:

> The question of source bias becomes a nontrivial one, whereas the question of multiple sources becomes a

[2]Our comments in this section may be limited because of our concentration on an extension of only one data analysis (however general and central) in the CFP literature. However, Rosenau and Ramsey (1975) suggest that the WEIS-derived events data base in the initial analysis is essentially equivalent to other events data collections, although some of these data sets have attempted to get away from the original WEIS schema. (For a more thorough discussion of possible structural differences between WEIS and subsequent data sets, see Kegley et al., 1974).

somewhat trivial one. That is to say, source bias is then more than just a question of inaccurate reporting; it becomes a question of structuring a particular kind of reality, the reality of the socio-political culture in which it is embedded. In the same way, the term "multiple sources" seems to lose its meaning. The concept of uncovering a common reality among different ways of structuring such a reality begins to lose its force.

Some of the original events data researchers have also felt that the CFP attempt to link aggregate indicators and foreign policy output was unlikely to come up with much. McClelland (1971, pp. 379-80), for example, has written:

> From the standpoint of prudence and common sense, the advocacy of linkage is to be advised. One gains approval or respect from colleagues by observing that domestic processes and national-unit characteristics sometimes account best for what occurs in international relations and that sometimes international situations and events dominate, even to the extent of actually changing, domestic processes and nation traits. The thing to acknowledge is national-international linkage, and the action to take is to trace through the whole intra-inter unit circuitry. This may be good social commentary but it is not good international relations theorizing until the linkage begins to describe and predict that which will be found empirically about the specific balances of the two influences and when specified balances may be expected to exist. One might argue that the drive to find the linkages is premature and that the linkage conception will emerge without exhortation as the field and system approaches eventually converge after a generation or so of basic research and theory elaboration.

On the other hand, Skrein, also on the basis of the WEIS data, concluded that "despite the lack of success encountered in previous years ... it appears that we can indeed detect relationships between national attributes and foreign policy output" (1970, p. 68).

A simple model using countries as the units of analysis misses the relational and interactive aspects of the international system. The use of the directed dyad (Skinner and Kegley, 1973) makes for a less dubious data base with which CFP theory, such as it is, can be conjoined. It is this which excepts CFP, and other events data research that utilizes the directed dyad, from the criticisms.

THE FUTURE OF COMPARATIVE FOREIGN POLICY

Two key points occur to us at the conclusion of the above review of CFP. One refers to the data structure based on the directed dyad as an analytical unit, and the other refers to the theoretical direction in which our own work in CFP (Powell et al., 1974a, 1974b) seems to be impelling us. Since we have already devoted a section to data, the first point can be dealt with briefly. We find the sort of data sets generated by the use of the directed dyad extremely promising. They escape the criticism posed by the events data researchers concerning the inefficacy and theoretical intractability of national characteristics as determinants of foreign policy behavior, even if we have not (and may never) succeeded in incorporating the fuller version of Rosenau's pre-theory. This sort of data structure, despite theoretical problems which we will discuss next, allows the analysis of indicator, relational, and behavioral variables in the same domain, which no previous data structure permitted. We have not fully explored this kind of data structure, but while it is always possible to hit a deadend, at least considerable forward momentum in data analysis has been created. (See Powell et al., 1974b, for further progress along these lines.)

The second point derives from a data problem, but ultimately becomes a major theoretical question. In the discussion of the extended Rosenau "pre-theory" and the related data analysis, there was an a priori distinction between the national characteristics or attributes cluster and the relational cluster. This distinction is, in an important regard, clearly artificial and arbitrary. For example, take the two variables of size and military balance, the former an attribute, the latter a relational variable. One could, however, transform size into a relational variable of relative size between the two countries in the dyad, and transform military balance back into an attribute by using the original trichotomous ranking of military capability (for operationalizations of all of these variables, see Rosenau and Hoggard, 1974). Indeed, one could say that the use of the dyad constrains the researcher into transforming all attributes into relational variables.

On the other hand, important information is lost when this is done. Not only is the relative position of the two nations important, but also the absolute position of each nation, and perhaps even the degree or amount of relative disparity.[3] While the relational variable carries some of this over, particularly in cases of larger disparities and where ordinal (dichotomous or trichotomous) rankings are used, considerable information is still lost. The size and military balance example shows this in that size and *absolute* military capability are correlated, explaining why size and relative military balance are linked empirically (see Figure 2), but, on the other hand, controlling for size does not result in the disappearance of the impact of military balance. Both the absolute and relational information is important to understanding the structure of the data and explaining the variation in the foreign policy output variable. As in the case of the amplitude/differentiation (proportion) problem in the dependent (output) variable, this will persist as a difficulty, particularly where technical or data analytical remedies to handle the problem are so clumsy.

The larger theoretical implications of the attribute/relational variable problem can be seen in the question of how to improve the causal model suggested in Figure 2 by indicating more clearly how size and the antecedent (to military balance) relational variables of sociocultural homogeneity and distance are to be ordered. In our earlier paper (1974a), we suggested a way of handling the overall model by extending it into a dynamic model (see Figure 3). Upon reflection, it is clear that this does not handle the problem in question. It presumes that the attributes will have an impact on output, both in terms of the originator and the target of foreign policy action. We pencilled in the relational variables as crossing the lines leading from the two actors to each other's output (the impact of the target nation's attributes), but this was sort of an easy evasion of the problem. Figure 4 represents an attempt to confront the problem, which is, however, still far from satisfactory.

Both of these paradigms show what would be the results of carrying out our suggestion about completing the partial equilibrium model and then

---

[3]While handling the latter might seem difficult in the case of ordinal variables, Coombs (1964) has suggested a technique ("unfolding") for obtaining the relative ranking of such distances even where they cannot be given absolute values via internal measures.

Figure 3. A Paradigm for Dyadic Interaction in in the International System

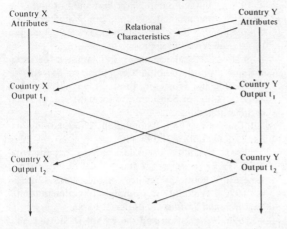

Figure 4. A Revised Paradigm for Dyadic Inter-action in the International System

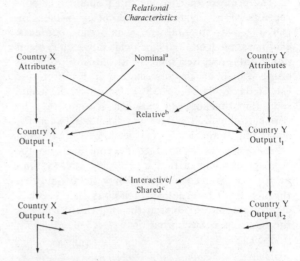

[a] Nominal refers to those relational characteristics which are not derived from (determined by) the comparison of two countries' attributes (i.e., distance).

[b] Relative refers to those characteristics of a dyad which are dependent/determined by the relative position of the actor and target (expressed as either ordinal or interval values) on a given dimension (i.e., military balance).

[c] Interactive/shared refers to those characteristics which are determined by the direct effect of the interaction of the countries' outputs and/or certain shared characteristics. These may be relatively fixed and not perceived by the dyad such as the "unobserved (non varying) controls" suggested by Thorson in Chapter 28 of this volume.

expanding this into a dynamic model. (Such paradigms are by definition vaguer than models, and represent attempts to sketch out what some of the characteristics of a model might be, without spelling out all elements). These paradigms tie together the complete equilibrium model with the type of dynamic process model exemplified by Richardson's processes and negotiated solutions. As we noted in our description of the original paradigm, the open end suggests the possibility of systems dominance in which interaction processes effectively escape the original exogenous determinants. These may, of course, eventually feed back and influence the original exogenous factors in a way familiar to historians of the international system, even though these feedback linkages are not noted in Figures 3 and 4. While the development of such processes may take some time in a single dyad and even at times in larger dyadic webs, such development, even allowing for low interaction in a majority of dyads, can be relatively quick, explosively so. This can also be seen as an extension of the theorem that in complex systems original direct effects are dominated and overcome by interaction (both static and dynamic) effects. Such a paradigm suggests the possibility of high volatility, even though the exogenous variables vary much more slowly, if at all.

The paradigm is not only a preliminary theoretical map, but indicates some elements of an even more extended data set. This reflects the

initial philosophical point that we are concerned with the logic of induction, so that theoretical and data analytical considerations are linked *intimately*. It, in effect, suggests a path for convergence based on the work done so far, and the desire to extend the scope of the model to provide a framework for interaction processes, and, by implication, policy analysis. The model or models envisioned by the paradigm are international systems models in which processes can be imbedded within a known or knowable environmental content. This suggests that there is no necessary dissonance between the end product of CFP and the theoretical vision of the systems (GST) theorists, but rather a difference of approach and philosophy which have important effects on the *process of research.*

The promise of CFP lies in an operational conception of a "systematic theoretical attack on (the) environmental problem"—the contexts, ecologies, environments, or fields in which systems dominant processes such as Richardson processes erupt—which has been so lacking in the literature (McClelland, 1971, p. 381). Moreover, it would seem that this sort of a paradigm accomplishes the connection which Wright envisioned between the geographical and analytical fields, i.e., "that international processes need to be considered in the context of their particular ecologies, that systems need to be located in their proper fields, and that the theory of international relations must be sufficiently complex to match the empirical variety in the relations between nations" (McClelland, 1971, p. 385).

REFERENCES

Ashby, W. Ross. 1970. "Analysis of the System to the Modeled." In *The Process of Model-Building in the Behavioral Sciences,* ed. Ralph Stogdill, pp. 94-114. Columbus: Ohio State Univ. Press.

Calhoun, H. L. 1974. "Events: Reality, Context, Importance." *World Studies* 1: 84-99.

Churchman, C. West. 1963. "An Analysis of the Concept of Simulation." In *Symposium on Simulation Models,* ed. Austin Hoggatt and Frederick Balkerston, pp. 1-13. Cincinnati: South-Western.

———. 1970. "When Does a Model Represent Reality?" In *The Process of Model-Building in the Behavioral Sciences,* ed. Ralph Stogdill, pp. 133-38. Columbus: Ohio State Univ. Press.

Coombs, Clyde. 1964. *A Theory of Data.* New York: Wiley.

Kegley, Charles W., Jr., Stephen Salmore, and David Rosen. 1974. "Convergences in the Measurement of Interstate Behavior." In *Sage International Yearbook of Foreign Policy Studies,* ed. Patrick J. McGowan, vol. 2, pp. 309-39. Beverly Hills: Sage.

Lazarsfeld, Paul F. 1962. "Philosophy of Science and Empirical Social Research." In *Logic, Methodology, and Philosophy of Science,* ed. E. Nagel et al., pp. 463-73. Stanford: Stanford Univ. Press.

McClelland, Charles A. 1971. "Field Theory and System Theory in International Realtions." In *The Search for World Order,* ed. Albert Lepawsky et al. New York: Appleton-Century-Crofts.

———. 1972. "On the Fourth Wave: Past and Future in the Study of International Systems." In *The Analysis of International Politics,* ed. James N. Rosenau et al., pp. 15-40. New York: Free Press.

——— et al. 1971. "Management and Analysis of International Events Data: A Computerized System for Monitoring and Projecting Event Flows." Mimeo. Los Angeles: Univ. of Southern California, Dept. of International Relations.

Powell, Charles A. 1969. "Simulation: The Anatomy of a Fad." *Acta Politica* 3: 299-330.

———. 1971. "Validity Issues in Complex Experimentation." Paper presented at the Annual Meeting of the American Political Science Association, Chicago.

———. 1973. "Validity in Complex Experimentation." *Experimental Studies in Politics* 2: 61-95.

———. 1976. "Simulation and the Events Data Approach: Some Comments." In *Emerging Data Sources of Comparative and International Studies,* ed. Neal Cutler and Charles Powell. Pittsburgh and Los Angeles: International Studies Association and *World Studies.*

———. Forthcoming. *Simulation in International Relations: A Critique and a Reconstruction.*

———, David Andrus, Kathleen Knight, and William Fowler. 1974a. "Determinants of Foreign Policy Behavior: A Causal Modeling Approach." In *Comparing Foreign Policies,* ed. James N. Rosenau, pp. 151-70. Beverly Hills: Sage.

———, C. Benjamin, K. Knight, H. Purkitt. 1974b. "Further Exhaustion of an 'Intriguing Set of Findings': Models and Data Analysis of the Determinants of Foreign Policy Behavior." Paper prepared for the Annual Meeting of the Southern Political Science Association, New Orleans.

Rapoport, Anatol. 1968. "Systems Analysis: General Systems Theory." In *International Encyclopedia of the Social Sciences,* ed. David L. Sills, vol. 15, pp. 452-58. New York: Macmillan and Free Press.

Richardson, Lewis F. 1960a. *Arms and Insecurity.* Chicago: Quadrangle.

———. 1960b. *Statistics of Deadly Quarrels.* Chicago: Quadrangle.

Rosecrance, Richard N. 1963. *Action and Reaction in World Politics: International Systems in Perspective.* Boston: Little, Brown.

Rosenau, James N. 1971a. "Comparative Foreign Policy: Fad, Fantasy, or Field?" In *The Scientific Study of Foreign Policy,* by James N. Rosenau. New York: Free Press.

———. 1971b. "Pre-Theories and Theories of Foreign Policy." In *The Scientific Study of Foreign Policy,* by James N. Rosenau. New York: Free Press.

———, Philip M. Burgess, and Charles F. Hermann. 1973.

"The Adaptation of Foreign Policy Research: A Case Study of an Anti-Case Study Project." *International Studies Quarterly* 17: 119-44.

––– and Gary Hoggard. 1974. "Foreign Policy Behavior in Dyadic Relationships: Testing a Pre-theoretical Extension." In *Comparing Foreign Policies,* ed. James N. Rosenau, pp. 117-49. Beverly Hills: Sage.

––– and George R. Ramsey. 1975. "External vs. Internal Sources of Foreign Policy Behavior: Testing the Stability of an Intriguing Set of Findings." In *Sage International Yearbook of Foreign Policy Studies,* ed. Patrick J. McGowan, vol. 3. Beverly Hills: Sage.

Rummel, Rudolph J. 1969. "Some Dimensions in the Foreign Behavior of Nations." In *International Politics and Foreign Policies,* ed. James N. Rosenau, pp. 600-621. New York: Free Press.

Sherwin, Ronald G. 1973. "WEIS Project Final Report." Mimeo. Los Angeles: Univ. of Southern California, School of International Relations.

Skinner, Richard A., and Charles W. Kegley, Jr. 1973.

"The Use of the Directed Dyad in the Comparative Study of Foreign Policy." Mimeo. Ojai, California: Inter-university Comparative Foreign Policy Project.

Skrein, Michael. 1970. "National Attributes and Foreign Policy Output: Tests for a Relationship." World Event/Interaction Survey, Support Study No. 4. Mimeo. Los Angeles: Univ. of Southern California, School of International Relations.

Thurston, L. L. 1947. *Multi-factor Analysis.* Chicago: Univ. of Chicago Press.

Vincent, Jack E. 1974. "Some Problem Areas in Dyadic Research as Developed in Social Field Theory." Paper prepared for the Annual Meeting of the Southern California Political Science Association, New Orleans.

Wright, Quincy. 1942. *A Study of War.* Chicago: Univ. of Chicago Press.

–––. 1961. "The Form of a Discipline of International Relations." In *International Politics and Foreign Policies,* ed. James N. Rosenau, pp. 399-411. New York: Free Press.

33. The Case-for-Analysis Problem

Charles W. Kegley, Jr. · Richard A. Skinner

The advent of truly scientific studies of interstate relations less than two decades ago was regarded by proponents of that path to knowledge to constitute a fruitful endeavor promising high payoffs. Although some of the claims were indeed "fantastic," it is nevertheless clear that a field of scientific (comparative) foreign policy analysis has not only emerged but is also proceeding in the

SPECIAL NOTE: Earlier versions of this chapter were presented at the Peace Science Society (International) Southern Section Meeting, Lake Cumberland, Kentucky, April 1973, and at the Inter-university Comparative Foreign Policy (ICFP) Project Meeting on the Future of Comparative Foreign Policy Analysis, Ojai, California, June 1973. The authors are appreciative of comments on an earlier draft of this paper provided by J. David Singer, William O. Chittick, and Patrick J. McGowan; none of them, of course, should be burdened with responsibility for any deficiencies of the present text.

"mopping-up" activities of a "normal science" (Rosenau, 1975; McGowan, Chapter 26, this volume). And yet, despite its remarkable achievements in so brief a time span, one of the most conspicuous characteristics of the behavioral research community has been the prevalence and persistence of in-house criticism and debate. Adherents to the scientific approach have consistently been their own worst critics, thereby perpetuating the self-consciousness and stock-taking mood that has typified the movement since its inception. However, the enduring nature of such internecine dissension might be due to more than the academic's predilection for self-scrutiny. It seems reasonable to suggest that the criticism is symptomatic of dissatisfaction with the amount of progress which the scientific endeavor has managed to achieve thus far, as well as indicative of lingering doubts from ardent supporters about the ability of the method to fulfill its promise (Rummel, Chapter 2, this volume).

Many sources of dissatisfaction are readily identifiable, including the paucity of available data, the persistence of methodological eclecticism, the lack of consensus regarding definitions of basic concepts and frameworks for utilizing them, the questionable utility of the prevailing paradigm (Handelman et al., 1973), and the unwillingness to undertake policy-relevant research (Bobrow, 1972). Perhaps most disturbing has been the general inability of comparative research thus far to uncover strong empirical relationships among variables, to develop models possessing high predictive capacities, or to build positivistic theories at the general or middle-range levels.

While it would be premature to conclude that the construction of "empirically grounded theory" will never get off the ground, it is obvious that there are no panaceas, notwithstanding the appearance of a Kepler in the near future (Munton, 1974), and that the acquisition of verifiable knowledge in our field will require the sort of patience demonstrated by physics in its 300-year struggle to obtain knowledge that is at once elegant and relevant, persuasive and predictive. We should not expect ultimate success to be quick or easily attained.

Thus, the identification of problem areas in the scientific study of interstate phenomena, and prescriptions for the solution to those problems, should begin with the recognition that such problems and debate over their resolution are to be expected in any field in its incipient stage of scientific development (Kuhn, 1970). Rather than being frustrated by the persistence of a plethora of problems and distressed by the extent to which debate over their resolution dominates the literature, it might be more appropriate to interpret such quarrels over how best to study our subject matter as healthy and necessary. While "theorizing about theory" and building a case for one framework over another can become tedious, time and attention to pretheorizing, the examination of contending approaches, and the esoterics of methodology and measurement problems can contribute greatly to the formation of a shared perspective on the nature of the phenomena under

analysis and to the probability of an eventual innovative breakthrough occurring. Scientific knowledge is built, history suggests, through a lengthy incremental process in which cumulation is achieved at the cost of painstaking effort. Progress is rarely rapid and sure.

One salient problem area retarding progress in the acquisition of empirical knowledge about the behavior of nations pertains to the confusion surrounding the vocabulary employed by researchers to describe the form in which behavioral data is organized analytically and conceptually. While other issues are certainly equally important, it would seem that common agreement is crucial on the terminology with which researchers describe and discuss alternate conceptions of cases-for-analysis. The current language used to describe these conceptions fails to convey intersubjectively transmissible meaning, and encourages researchers to continue talking at cross purposes and past each other. Consequently, just as clarification of such terms as the "universe of discourse" (Kerlinger, 1973), the "level-of-analysis" (Singer, 1969; Singer and Ray, 1973), and the "unit-of-analysis" and "unit-of-observation" (McGowan, 1971) served to enhance scientific communication, so the establishment of a common vocabulary for describing this feature of the research enterprise should contribute to the advancement of comparative studies of external behavior beyond its present stage of development. It is the purpose of this chapter to seek clarification of this problem so that we may get on with the task of building better theories about the behavior of nations.

In pursuing this objective, a cluster of issues concerning how to organize our perceptions about "cases-for-analysis" must be addressed. In the first instance we face the choice of definition: what is meant by the term, "case-for-analysis" and, more importantly, what are the most prominent categories for the classification of alternate conceptions of cases-for-analysis? In addition, the theoretical assumptions of each of these delineated analytic categories need to be identified, and their implications and consequences assessed. And finally, we need to evaluate the relative utility of each of these alternatives for various research questions. In this way the potentials of these various conceptions of cases for positive theory construction need to be highlighted, and empirically informed suggestions about the relative advantages and costs of choosing one or another case should be provided.

THE CASE-FOR-ANALYSIS CONCEPT

Generally, when social scientists speak of cases, they refer to the object or analytic entity they are studying. For instance, by tradition the most conventional case for study in the field of comparative politics has been the nation-state; an in-depth analysis of a particular nation constitutes a case study, whereas a cross-national study of two or more states entails a comparative analysis for the purpose of deriving generalizations that are not specific to a particular nation for their validity.

However, this convention is by no means a necessary one. The political investigator is free in principle to choose any arrangement of phenomena to focus upon for analysis; the definition of case is limited only by the investigator's imagination. (For instance, the case-for-analysis may range from particular individuals, through aggregates of individuals comprising nations, to larger collectivities such as regional groupings or international organizations in the global system.) The case to be subjected to inquiry may be defined in any manner regarded by the investigator as a meaningful description of his phenomena; that is, the case is defined in terms of the observer's mental model of the most relevant distinguishing features of the phenomena.

Because cases are necessarily products of the manner in which the observer organizes his perceptions about his subject, three characteristics of case definition necessarily obtain. First, since case definition is dependent upon observations, no definition of the case-for-analysis will be without some distortion. It is impossible[1] to define a case-

for-analysis which will encompass, with full representational accuracy, the complete objective picture of the phenomena to be studied. As a consequence, it may be noted secondly that when the phenomena under examination is as complex as is interstate behavior, we may expect to find many competing definitions of the most meaningful cases with which to study that behavior.[2] Analysts of international behavior have indeed found a variety of useful ways for slicing up and differentiating that behavior for study (Singer, 1969). And finally, it is only proper to evaluate the appropriateness of a particular definition in terms of the research problem under consideration. How satisfactory a particular definition of case is will depend on the extent to which that definition minimizes the amount of distortion, and the relative distortion may be expected to vary with the dimension of international relations being researched.

With these prefatory observations in mind, we submit that in the comparative study of foreign policy field an intersubjective consensus prevails regarding the most meaningful way to conceptualize cases-for-analysis. However implicit, this consensus reflects the predilection of behavioral scientists to define *interaction* between nations as the principal focus and distinguishing characteristic of international relations research. That is, analysis has come to concentrate on observed *behavior*—whether it entails interactions or transactions (McClelland, 1968)—that spans national boundaries.[3] We are primarily interested in exploring the behavior of various types of actors which crosses national boundaries in the international system, rather than with an examination of the characteristics of those actors themselves. Thus, unlike the field of comparative politics, the unit-of-analysis is not the actor, but the actor's behavior.

As McGowan (1971) stated it: "Actors are individuals, aggregates, and collectivities whose attri-

[1]Rosenau (1971, pp. 11, 12) has lucidly couched this feature of the observation process thus: "Unable to perceive and depict the universe of international phenomena in its entirety, the observer is forced to select some of its dimensions as important and in need of close examination, while dismissing others as trivial and unworthy of further analysis ... Though there may be an objective truth about world politics, the observer can never know it. He must select in order to know reality, and in so doing he must distort it."

[2]This expectation is based on the psychological finding that individuals manifest different cognitive styles in observing and classifying objects (Gardner, 1953, pp. 214-33; Mischel, 1968, pp. 16-20).

[3]This follows Sears (1951, p. 469) contention that "the basic events to which behavior theory must have reference are *actions* ... actions are the events of most importance, and actions are most available to observation and measurement."

butes we measure and which we relate to the actor's behavior. It is this behavior which is our unit-of-analysis—the phenomenon we are primarily concerned with describing and explaining." Consequently, what we study are *acts*, or behavioral activities, and in foreign policy research this means our focus is on the things states say and do abroad. Adoption of foreign policy acts as units-of-analysis places the study of comparative foreign policy within the philosophical and theoretical tradition of those scholars such as Mead (1938), Parsons and Shils (1962), and Riker (1957) who emphasize the act in the scientific analysis of social behavior.[4]

If the primary actor in foreign policy research is the nation-state (Singer, 1969; Sondermann, 1961; Rosenau, 1971) and the fundamental unit-of-analysis is the behavior emanating from those polities and directed to their external environment, then the problem confronting the empirical investigator is that of selecting some basis for analytically organizing, observing, and classifying that behavior. The boundaries surrounding the behavioral activity must be delineated. How the investigator performs this conceptual task determines and defines his case-for-analysis, for cases-for-analysis refer primarily to the manner in which indicators of interstate relations are put into a format for data analysis. The choice of alternate formats for treating the external behavior of nations depends on the location of the parameters of that behavior; and the investigator's selection of parameters determines what his analytic case unit will be.

Three Conceptions of Cases-for-Analysis

This conceptual problem is best clarified with illustrations of contending definitions of cases for the

comparative study of foreign policy. A nonexhaustive listing of the major definitions of cases currently employed in empirical foreign policy studies includes three conceptual modes as cases-for-analysis: the monad, the directed dyad, and the summed dyad.[5] As will be seen, the distinction between them rests with the analyst's choice of format for the "does what" segment of Harold Lasswell's classic definition of political behavior—"who does what to whom." The decision the investigator makes about what to include and exclude in his definition of behavior ("what is done") structures his definition of the analytic case unit and thereby determines which of these three formats his analysis will be based on.

Perhaps the most traditional conception of the case-for-analysis in foreign policy research has been the "actor-action" paradigm which characterizes the aggregate behavioral output of a nation with no reference to *whom* those behaviors are directed. Termed the *monad*, this format for the organization of observations treats external behavior without identifying the recipients of those actions. The case, therefore, becomes the total identifiable action emanating from a particular national actor and directed outside its borders, but aggregated in such a way so as not to specify the external targets of the actions.

The monad is conventionally employed to profile the behavior of a particular nation and longitudinally describe fluctuations in that performance over time (e.g., Brown, 1968). However, when the comparativist employs this case, his purpose is to classify each nation's foreign policy behavior along some explicit dimensions. In such classification, each nation is categorized by the type of behavior it manifests toward all other actors in the international system. The taxonomic

---

[4] This focus conforms to the conceptual pretheorizing of many social scientists, such as Coser and Rosenberg (1959, pp. 65), who point out that "It is one of the tenets of sociology that the behavior of human beings can never be fully understood if one does not realize that the social actions of individuals are always oriented toward other human beings. . . . Thus, the simplest unit of sociological . . . analysis consists not of solitary individuals but of at least a pair of individuals mutually influencing each other's behavior." Such a conception is central to social psychology, where it is taken as axiomatic "that any item of social behavior is understood only as it is seen as a functional part of a situation composed of interacting selves" (Cottrell, 1942, p. 370), or in international rela-

tions itself where Galtung's (1968, p. 270) reasoning prevails that we "can never deal with the single unit; history may perhaps deal with one personality, but international relations will have to interpret one nation in the context of the nations with which it interacts."

[5] The reader will note that this classification of types of cases is a common one. The literature is replete with quantitative studies listing monads (Rummel, 1963; Tanter, 1966), directed dyads (Rummel, 1972), or alternately, summed dyads (Cobb and Elder, 1970) as the cases on which the analysis is based. Any cross-national, comparative design requires the designation of some such case.

works of Young (1975) and McClelland and Hoggard (1969) are exemplary. Again, what renders this case different from alternate conceptions is that in monadic studies all observed behavior is aggregated and measured without differentiating the target of the behavior. As Rummel (1972, p. 78) described studies employing monadic cases-for-analysis, the emphasis

> is on the characteristics and behavior of the nation itself and not on the nation in relation to some particular other one. The concern is with the policy of the nation, the development of the nation, the conflict behavior of the nation, the relationship between the nation's trade and development, or internal unrest and foreign conflict, or power capability and foreign policy.

An alternate way of treating behavior for data analysis is through employment of a dyad as a case-for-analysis. With the dyad, behavior is ordered in terms of the target toward which that behavior is directed. Dyadic organizations of behavioral data assume that behavior flows are affected by, and at least partially specific to, the type of actor with whom the initiator is interacting.[6] The data are collected not in terms of gross output, but rather are recorded according to "who is doing what with whom." The underlying inference of this dyadic perspective is that "a nation's behavior is dependent on whom one is interacting with" (East, 1972, p. 3).

By differentiating the targets of a nation's acts, the dyadic conception acknowledges the interaction dimension of most behavior and therefore enables investigation of the *relations* between interacting pairs of nations. Moreover, conceptu-

alizing the lines of a dyadic relationship (what country A does to country B: A→B) as the case-for-analysis disaggregates the coding of internation behavior data into the smallest unit of social action. Thus, by treating behavior in terms of the target to which that behavior is directed, the data analyst adheres to a conception formulated by Simmel (1950, p. 122):

> The simplest sociological formation, methodologically speaking, remains that which operates between two elements. It contains the scheme, germ, and material of innumerable more complex forms. Its sociological significance, however, by no means rests on its extensions and multiplications only. It itself is a sociation. Not only are many general forms of sociation realized in it in a very pure and characteristic fashion; what is more, the limitation to two members is a condition under which alone several forms of relationship exist.

Implicit in such a conception as well is Skinner's (1953, p. 297) contention that "social behavior may be defined as the behavior of two or more people with respect to one another in concert."

Two variations of dyadic cases prevail[7] in current foreign policy research: the *directed dyad* and the *summed dyad*. The former, labeled either a directed dyad (Goodman et al., 1972) or a directional dyad (Cobb and Elder, 1970), is the one utilized in most event data projects (Burgess and Lawton, 1972). It specifies that the external behavior of a national actor have an identifiable foreign target, and records that behavior exclusively in terms of its direction from initiator to recipient. Thus, the data are in the format of the who-did-what-to-whom structure because the subject of that declarative sentence refers to the initiator of the act (who), the verb refers to the type of foreign policy action engaged in (did what), and the object refers to the recipient (whom) of the behavior. The latter conception (i.e., summed dyad), on the other hand, treats behavior flowing between the actor pair (the partners to the dyad) without indicating the direction of the behavioral transaction. The ordering arrangement of actor-

---

[6] This assumption underlies much of the work of social psychologists, who contend that an understanding of the individual personality can be measured meaningfully "by reference to dyadic situations or symbolic representations of them" (Sears, 1951, p. 469). The inference is that people act differently with different types of individuals, and that their characteristic response set (e.g., personality) is molded in part by the attributes of the object of their intention. Timothy Leary's classic *Interpersonal Diagnosis of Personality* (1957) provides an excellent discussion of the empirical and theoretical basis for such an assumption. Needless to say, it is reasonable to inquire if the behavior of nations might not be affected as well by the type of foreign actor with which it interacts, and moreover, to ask if the behavioral profile of nations varies with the nature of the target. Unfortunately, not much work on this subject has been undertaken as yet.

[7] Theoretical studies in the comparative foreign policy field which employ dyadic measures are relatively rare. Those breaking from the traditional monadic focus include Rummel (1972), Kegley (1973), Rosenau and Hoggard (1974), Rosenau and Ramsey (1973), and Munton (1974).

target is not identified. As the term implies, the actions or transactions of the two actors are aggregated without differentiating between the level of activity sent by one unit to the other. Instead, a single value is given which provides a measure of the total interactions or transactions between the two parties to the dyad within some time frame. Consequently, when a summed dyad is employed as the case-for-analysis, the direction of foreign policy behavior is not specified, so that behavior treated in this way serves primarily as an indicator of the overall relationship pertaining to the two parties of the dyad.

In order to visualize the differences among these three conceptions of cases-for-analysis more readily, Figure 1 is provided. As the diagram clearly suggests, what distinguishes these three definitions of analytic case units is the manner in which foreign policy *behavior* is organized for analysis. While both the definition of primary actor (i.e., nation-state) and the definition of what constitutes external behavior, (i.e., the acts initiated by government officials on behalf of their societies and targeted to actors in their external environment) remain consistent across the case types, the delineation of the conceptual boundaries of the behavior varies. These boundaries specify how the behavior data are to be collected

and organized. The cases delineate alternate ways of treating the unit-of-analysis, behavior, rather than the actors emitting behavior. Hence it would be mistaken to call conceptions such as these "actors." The dyad, for instance, manifests no behavior; the actors within the dyad remain the *sources* of behavior. The dyad does not act, but is an analytical arrangement for the recording of foreign policy behavior. Consequently, when we speak of the case-for-analysis in foreign policy research, we refer to the manner in which the behavior of nations is defined for analytical purposes.

Assumptions of Alternate Cases-for-Analysis

The choice of one or another of these analytic case units carries with it a set of assumptions which serves to influence and restrict their utility. In deciding which type of case to employ, the researcher should take cognizance of the assumptions and theoretical implications associated with each, for these have a direct bearing on the type of case which would be of most use in addressing particular research questions in foreign policy studies. These assumptions will be briefly outlined here so that the relative potential of each conception of cases can be assessed for specific research goals.

In choosing the *monad* as his case, the researcher employs a conception which implies that an actor's foreign policy is, to a very large degree, undifferentiated in the type of behavior it directs to its external environment. It is assumed that a nation's foreign policy may be characterized on some dimension, such as *affect*, by the aggregate number of conflictual and cooperative acts involved in that behavior, regardless of target. The nation is assumed to be predisposed to act in some characteristic way, and that behavior pattern is regarded as invariant with respect to any foreign actor. According to such conceptions, it is assumed that it is meaningful to classify the policies of states according to generic labels (e.g., country X is expansionist, country Y is a status quo power). Implicit in the assumption is the notion that an expansionist state will seek to expand its domain of influence over most other states in the system, and that likewise, a status quo

Figure 1. Three Possible Cases-for-Analysis in Foreign Policy Research

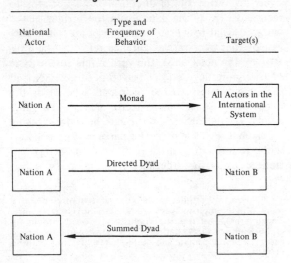

National Actor	Type and Frequency of Behavior	Target(s)
Nation A	Monad →	All Actors in the International System
Nation A	Directed Dyad →	Nation B
Nation A	← Summed Dyad →	Nation B

nation will seek to perpetuate its present relationships with most other countries. Hence a nation's foreign policy orientation is presumed to be descriptive of its typical behavior disposition with respect to all external actors.

Such a conception tends to "black box" or to discount differences among national actors, since it assumes that they are sufficiently similar to minimize the effect which any differences might exert on a particular nation's foreign conduct. If pressed to its logical conclusion, such a view results in the absurdity of suggesting that how the United States acts with the Soviet Union resembles how it behaves toward Great Britain or Iceland. While it may be meaningful to talk about the policies of certain states as being revisionist (just as we describe the personalities of some individuals as paranoid or authoritarian), it would be dangerous to allow those dispositional typifications to suffice as descriptions of the relations that a country maintains with specific foreign targets. Obviously, revisionist states are not revisionist with respect to all actors (or issues), any more than paranoid individuals are fearful of all other people or problems. And yet, monadic conceptions, by homogenizing the characteristics of other actors, tend to encourage this image. The literature is replete with monadic studies classifying the foreign behavior of nations according to the measured aggregate level of its conflict. What must be recognized is that such a conception assumes that actors fail to discriminate in directing their cooperation or conflict toward other states (Goodman et al., 1972, p. 31). Such an assumption is an empirical question, and those employing the monad should recognize that they are taking the assumption as a given fact.

A final assumption inherent in monadic conceptions of foreign policy is that a nation is capable of exerting a significant influence over its external environment, over other members of the system and the system as a whole. By denying that a state's policy is relatively affected by the behavior of other states toward it, the theorist who adheres to a monadic conception is prone to exaggerate the impact of the actor on the system. This view underestimates not only differences among nations, but the interdependence and interconnectedness of members of the global system as well. Such a way of looking at foreign policy may

not be cogent, but it is common. Why scholars and practitioners alike should cling to such a dubious image is unclear, but Rummel (1972, p. 79) cites one plausible explanation.

> Students of international relations share with their fellow social scientists this monadic lock-in—this overemphasis on the individual, group, or nation. Kaplan (1964: 323) has commented on this bias. "I believe that one of the sources of this tendency is the image of the self as monadic. The principle of local determination may appear to us to be naturally and necessarily true of our own behavior, as a reflection of our sense of individuality and freedom. It is easier for us to accept a theory of behavior with complex predicates than one which introduces complex subjects for its propositions. The subject of a theory of behavior may be complicated, but not complex—it is just 'me,' a unitary self."

When the theorist replaces the monad as his case-for-analysis with a dyadic conception he jettisons the previous set of assumptions about foreign policy behavior and perforce takes on another set. With a dyadic case-for-analysis, the researcher employs a conception of behavior which accentuates the relational characteristics of interstate behavior. Studying interaction relationships requires a case-for-analysis which incorporates, at a minimum, two international actors. Since it describes the behavior of one actor as it is directed toward another, the dyad facilitates interaction, as opposed to action analysis.[8] Moreover, it encourages differentiation among the actors (or dyadic partners) in the international system, rather than assuming their similarity and commonality. Whom an actor interacts with is presumed to make a difference. The assumptions implicit in this focus are that (1) behavior tends to be target-specific rather than generalized; (2) the international system conforms to a "billiard ball" model to the extent that the behavior of particular members of the system is influenced by the pattern of the

[8]It was noted above that adoption of the dyad does not involve a change in the unit-of-analysis: whether molar or molecular units, behavior remains the unit-of-analysis (Sears, 1951, Kerlinger, 1973; McGowan, 1971). Likewise, the use of the directed dyad does not necessarily involve a shift in the level-of-analysis. Because the directed dyad specifies only the target of an actor's external behavior and not the target's response (as in the case of the summed dyad), we remain at the action analysis level (Burgess et al., 1972).

behavior of others and by the configuration of interaction operative in the system as a whole,[9] and (3) inasmuch as a dyad specifies a target of the actor's behavior, that behavior may be interpreted as goal-directed and a manifestation of influence or calculated control-type activities (Rosenau, 1971; Kegley et al., 1975).

When the dyad is broken down into its *directed* and *summed* variants, several additional assumptions become noteworthy. While the directed dyad is relatively flexible and free of assumptions which restrict its use (for reasons which will be discussed below), the summed dyad is built on an assumption of reciprocal and symmetrical interaction in behavior exchange. The summed dyad fails to specify the direction of behavior transpiring between dyadic partners, and consequently carries with it the assumptions (1) that behavior initiated to a foreign target will be reciprocated (behavior sent will be responded to), and (2) that such behavior will be returned in kind (i.e., symmetrical). As Goodman et al. (1972, p. 30) have pointed out; "the use of the (summed) dyad presumes a high degree of dyadic symmetry. It is assumed that if nation A is cooperating with nation B, then nation B is cooperating with nation A. There, therefore, can be no asymmetrical relationships." Obviously, this gross assumption about the nature of interstate behavior exchange is a dangerous one; whether reciprocity and symmetry do indeed tend to obtain between states in interaction is an empirical question. Given the lack of convincing evidence supporting this assumption, the researcher must be cautious about the employment of the summed dyad as a case-for-analysis for some research questions.

RESEARCH UTILITIES OF ALTERNATE CASES-FOR-ANALYSIS

Since the discovery of an all-purpose way of investigating interstate phenomena is improbable, we fortunately are not faced with a final choice

[9]This assumption is a traditional one in the literature. Indeed, emphasis on the relational quality of international politics is explicit even in normative approaches. Morgenthau (1960, p. 29) for example, defines political power in relational terms, whereby "political power is a psychological *relation* between those who exercise it and those over whom it is exercised" (emphasis added).

between these alternate types of analytic case units. Similarly, we are not burdened with the necessity of selecting one of these conceptions for the analysis of all types of theoretical questions. However, it should be evident from the preceding discussion of the assumptions of these cases that such assumptions serve to restrict the uses to which the cases can profitably be put. What follows is an inventory of the relative advantages and costs associated with the application of one or another case-for-analysis; the assessment of research utilities is made with respect to two broad research activities in the comparative study of foreign policy: (1) the conceptualization and measurement of foreign policy behavior and (2) the formulation of research designs for various types of analysis.

The Conceptualization and Measurement of Foreign Policy Behavior

Under this general class of research activities, three issues seem particularly sensitive to the selection of alternate cases-for-analysis. The first concerns the *conceptualization* of foreign policy behavior. A necessary task for scientific studies of foreign policy is the formation of an intersubjective consensus regarding definitions of what constitutes foreign policy phenomena. Unfortunately, there is no current agreement on the meaning of foreign policy (Hermann, 1971, p. 70) and there exist nearly as many definitions as there are foreign policy researchers. While any of the case-for-analysis options delineated here are amenable to, and felicitous of, a scientifically useful concept of foreign policy, the directed dyad appears particularly attractive for definitions emphasizing the behavioral component of policy output. Because it organizes behavior in a who-does-what-to-whom format, it is possible to employ the directed dyad as a unit in a meaningful manner to conceptualize foreign policy activity. Thus events data researchers, in adopting this format, have devised an explicit concept of foreign policy (Hermann, 1971; Kegley et al., 1975; Phillips, 1973). Such a definition is useful because unless the researcher can observe that the target of an actor's behavior is indeed a separate, distinct, and recognizable international actor, he cannot know whether he is actually observing behavior that spans national boundaries. Of course, if the researcher is primarily interested in studying how foreign policy is formulated (i.e., foreign policy decision making à la Allison, 1971), then a monadic concept may serve equally well.

A second major concern to the comparativist is the *dimensionality* of interstate behavior. The comparativist does not study the behavior of nations, but attributes of that behavior. A traditional and important characteristic of external behavior is the dimensionality of its *affect,* i.e., the distinct types and degree of hostility obtaining in behavior. Studies concerned with the measurement of interstate behavior have converged on several empirical findings. Repeatedly it has been found that (1) foreign policy behavior is multidimensional (e.g., conflict, cooperation, and participation form statistically independent types of external behavior) and that (2) the dimensions of foreign policy behavior are conditioned by the target of that behavior (Kegley, Salmore, and Rosen, 1974; McClelland and Hoggard, 1969; Rummel, 1969). This second point says that how a nation acts is a function of, and varies with, who the recipient of the act is. These empirical findings have important implications for the study of foreign policy. They suggest that the choice one makes of his case-for-analysis will significantly affect his research results, because the kind of behavior initiated is different in the monadic case than in the dyadic case. That is, the dimensionality of behavior sent is target-specific. More specifically, this finding suggests that it makes sense to study foreign conflict behavior only with directed dyadic measures, since it is meaningless to speak of the hostility of an actor without specifying the object of hostility. Brody (1975) has commented on the implications of this.

> In order to test these two constructions of the relationship between conflict and cooperation, behavior directed in a *specific dyad must be the unit of analysis*—the unidimensional hypothesis does not argue that nations specialize in behavior at one end of the scale or the other; rather, it argues that in its relations with another nation one mode of action or the other will be characteristic [emphasis added].

The conclusion we derive is that the student of foreign policy behavior would do well to consider

shifting investigation of the sources of conflict behavior from monadic to directed dyadic measures of that behavior. Rather than discarding the traditional focus on the study of conflict (Handelman, et al., 1973), the reasoning reported here indicates that our capacity to arrive at strong empirical relationships might be enhanced if behavior were treated in an explicitly dyadic fashion. The success of some initial efforts in this direction (Rosenau and Hoggard, 1974; Rosenau and Ramsey, 1973) supports this conclusion.

The third fundamental problem confronting the data analyst is the number of cases upon which he bases his study, i.e., the *size of the population* subjected to analysis. The nomothetically inclined investigator is naturally interested in maximizing the number of cases for statistical tests in order that empirical descriptions may be derived, hypotheses tested, and generalizations developed. One inhibiting factor has been the small number of cases researchers of interstate behavior have had to analyze statistically. Etzioni has argued that "There probably will never be a science of international relations as there is one of physics or chemistry, if for no other reason that . . . the number of cases is too small for a rigorous statistical analysis" (1965, pp. 88-89). As McClelland (1970, p. 5) has commented:

> The point the critics of statistical analysis of international relations have in mind is that numbers between 100 and 200 which represent the upper limit of the numbers of actors in the international system are too small. A *sample* size of 30 or so might be satisfactory but it is a whole *population* of 100 or 200 that is being approached. It is this low numerosity of the population that is said to invalidate statistical analysis.

If research retains its emphasis on nations as its units-of-analysis, the population size resulting does indeed cast some doubts on the capacity of statistical analysis to uncover meaningful contingency statements. This would also be the case where the monad is employed in research on foreign policy behavior.

One way of redressing this problem is to shift from monadic to dyadic conceptions of foreign policy as cases-for-analysis. For instance, the number of cases for the monad is limited to the number of national actors in the system (about

140); if the summed dyad is employed, the following data base would result:

$$\frac{n(n-1)}{2} \quad \text{or} \quad \frac{140(140-1)}{2} = 9,730 \text{ cases}$$

The directed dyad, though, would result in:

$$n(n-1) \quad \text{or} \quad 140(140-1) = 19,460 \text{ cases}$$

McClelland (1970, p. 6), noting this increase in the size of the population, has observed that

> it is sufficiently large to require the assistance of descriptive statistics in any actual, empirical investigations of the 'configurations of relations.' Further, the number is large enough to make random sampling a sensible approach in the study of 'dyads.' Studies that produce estimates about the population of all dyads from analysis of random samples are statistical in the exact sence.

This relationship between the case-for-analysis and the number of cases available for statistical treatment certainly recommends selection of the directed dyad as the most useful analytic case. However, such a prescription must be qualified by cognizance of the inverse relationship obtaining between population size and quantity of behavioral data; that is, while the directed dyad maximizes the number of cases available, it diminishes the quantity of behavior which will be observed flowing between partners to a dyad. Hence, adoption of a directed dyad as a case-for-analysis, because it restricts attention to the number of acts initiated by states to specific foreign targets, risks the possibility of leaving the researcher with insufficient data for a meaningful analysis. A "missing data" problem may result, wherein the quantity of observed behavior recorded is too small. This is not a necessary consequence,[10] however, but the possibility should be acknowledged. Certainly in

choosing one case-for-analysis over another, the researcher should consider the potential trade-offs in terms of data availability.

A corollary problem to that of population size as it relates to the management of data is that concerning the best strategy (and case-for-analysis) to maximize the amount of data retained. One critical need within our discipline is the availability of data. Although the number of data collection projects for interstate relations has increased tenfold, the continued scarcity of data makes it imperative that behavior is treated in a format wherein the amount of information is maximized to as great an extent as possible. International relations scholars are not so data-rich that they can afford to employ cases which, by the nature of their format, lose potentially useful information. Here, the directed dyad seems most advantageous because it offers the possibility of richer data collections. By collecting and organizing behavioral data in terms of the lines of a directed dyad (A→B), flexibility for research is enhanced because "the directed dyad can be aggregated while it is not possible to disaggregate the [summed] dyad or the monad" (Goodman et al., 1972, p. 31).

---

[10]Previous research (Kegley, 1973) indicates that data may not be "lost" by adoption of the directed dyad case-for-analysis; evidence was found confirming the conclusion of McClelland and Hoggard (1969) and Young (1975) that a relatively small set of national actors, defined monadically, account for most of the behavior flowing in the international system. By eliminating from consideration those actors included in the World Event Interaction Survey data set which were neither sovereign foreign policy actors nor interacted with at least one other actor a minimum of five times, the study derived a population of only 91 "active" states (pp. 17-20, Table 2). From this population of actors, a population of 452

directed *dyads* was identified, which accounted for 81 percent of the national foreign policy events of the WEIS data. This suggested that a relatively few number of dyads account for a large proportion of the total international activity in the system. This finding should encourage us to employ the dyad in our studies of the international system, because the data problem is not so severe with that unit of investigation, and the dyad tells us most about the pattern of relationships among national units in the system.

These findings will undoubtedly dismay some researchers encouraged by the nearly 20-fold increase in the number of cases potentially derived by the adoption of the directed dyad as a research case, since it diminishes the ability to sample randomly from the universe of all dyads. But we would be misdirected in our efforts if our decision to adopt a particular type of case were predicated only on the basis of whether or not adoption entailed an increase in the size of our population. Our interest lies not with the analysis of actors as much as it aims at the explanation and prediction of interstate behavior, and in such a vein it becomes clear that we should employ that case which allows us to say something about that behavior. It is possible that by relaxing the criterion of five events per dyad, we might increase our population significantly, but only at the cost of reducing our capacity to say *anything* about interstate behavior. Moreover, the fact that the 452 dyads account for such a large proportion of the total international activity offers us the possibility for investigating many hypotheses central to the interest of comparative foreign policy studies.

Designs and Objectives of Inquiry

In addition to problems regarding the conceptualization and the measurement of foreign policy behavior, the uses to which alternate case units can be put depend upon the analytic objectives and research designs of the investigator. The alternate cases-for-analysis are not equally applicable to descriptive, explanatory, or predictive inquiries, nor are all amenable to use in *micro* and *macro* designs.

When the student of foreign policy is primarily interested in *describing* rather than explaining external behavior, the validity of his analysis is contingent to a large degree on the extent to which representational accuracy and comprehensiveness is achieved. He needs to provide as complete a picture of foreign policy behavior, in all its manifest complexity, as possible, while concurrently minimizing distortion and the obscuration of important aspects of the phenomena. When the descriptive task is pursued in either studies of a particular nation's foreign policy or in intersocietal surveys, a monadic conception is superior to either variant of dyadic cases-for-analysis. Descriptive studies of foreign policy aim at coverage of the totality of a nation's external interactions between initiator and target. Many of the behavioral externalities of a national actor include things other than relations with another target, e.g., the signing of multilateral treaties, voting on UN resolutions, and a promise of aid to another nation in order that the recipient might combat the infiltration of still another actor's forces. Thus by selecting a dyadic conception which specifies that the action of an international actor have a distinct target, the researcher fails to capture those external actions which have no direct target[11] and therefore loses much of the "stuff" of foreign conduct. While aggregating behavior across directed dyads may

recover some of this information,[12] only a monadic case unit is capable of approximating a representationally accurate portrayal of the actors' repertoire of foreign behavior.

When the researcher turns to the more theoretically interesting and difficult goal of constructing explanations of foreign policy behavior, the nature of the task shifts as well. By *explanation,* social scientists generally mean some variant of the nomological model of explanation (Isaak, 1969, pp. 101-8) which necessitates inclusion of causal nomothetic statements (McGowan, 1975; Raymond, 1975). Generally, explanatory theory tends to necessitate sacrificing representational accuracy and exhaustiveness for parsimony, generalizability, and validity (Coplin and Kegley, 1975, p. 366). Moreover, explanatory theories of foreign conduct necessarily require the inclusion of independent variables at all levels-of-analysis (Singer, 1969; Rosenau, 1971) if they are to be valid and cogent, for it is intuitively obvious that both subsystemic (i.e., national attributes) and systemic (i.e., characteristics of the actor's global environment) factors serve to condition the kind of behavior emanating from the national actor.

These qualities of the explicative task suggest the inherent inadequacy of monadic conceptions of foreign policy behavior in constructing theories which account for that behavior. Monadic case units "black box" much of the external environment of the actor by failing to take into account differences in the foreign actors comprising that environment. The predominant paradigm of comparative studies of foreign policy (Rosenau, 1971, pp. 95-149) contends that there is explanatory capacity associated with knowledge concerning who an actor interacts with and what the attributes of that target are. The monad fails to tap any of this information, which greatly diminishes its utility in the construction of explanatory theory. While the monad enables us to test hypotheses focused exclusively in national attribute theory, such as the connection between internal turmoil and external conflict (e.g., Wilkenfeld, 1969) or the association accruing between size and

---

[11]Some forms of external behavior have no readily identifiable target. An example might be a statement by the prime minister of nation X that "our nuclear forces are at top efficiency." In this instance, the researcher is forced either to make inferences about the "real" target of the verbal action or ignore it. Another example is one where the president of nation Y promises support for all peace-loving people in the world. Again, the researcher is faced with a dilemma.

[12]That is, nothing prohibits the researcher from aggregating the behavior collected along the lines of a directed dyadic relationship into larger units reflecting multiple objects of the actor's behavior.

external performance (e.g., East, 1975), it is devoid of explanatory power for theories incorporating interactions between units as explanatory variables.

Four central aspects of interstate relations which the monad is incapable of explaining are noteworthy.

1. Interstate *relations:* explanations accentuating the relational character of international phenomena, incorporating at a minimum two international actors, can only be provided by dyadic cases describing the behavior of one actor as it is directed toward another. Simply stated, the relations of nations cannot be investigated unless the behavior flowing *between* actors can be monitored. Monadic studies are incapable of tapping this behavior. If we agree with Rosenau (1968, p. 311) that "at the heart of foreign policy analysis is a concern with *sequences of interaction,* perceptual or behavioral, which span national boundaries," then it is clear that such analysis is contingent upon adoption of a dyadic case unit. The directed dyad captures this component most satisfactorily.

2. The *consequences* of foreign policy output: in order to study the effects of policy outputs, both foreign and domestic, dyadic cases are superior because they identify the targets to those outputs and thereby enable the investigator to probe the consequences of those actions on the intended recipient. Hence the dyad in general, and the directed dyad in particular, allow one to devise explanations of what Rosenau (1968, p. 320) has termed the "responsive" stage. If we are to study this stage, we must acknowledge that "a concern for foreign policy cannot be sustained without the question of its effectiveness and consequences arising. . . . Foreign policy analysts cannot avoid assessing the likelihood of one or another type of undertaking bringing about the desired modifications." Such a concern with behavior modification can only be addressed by observing foreign policy behavior as it is directed to specific targets (i.e., with a directed dyad case unit).

3. *Reciprocity* in interstate behavior: explanations of interstate *interaction* must include some attention to the extent to which behavior sent is returned (i.e., reciprocated)

by the recipient of the behavior. As Singer has said, "Whenever a nation behaves vis-a-vis another nation (or any other entity) and the second nation responds to that behavior, we may speak of an interaction." The identification of both action and reaction is thus necessary for interaction analysis. Only analysis which treats behavior in terms of the directed dyad case permits investigation of such interaction. A monadic case unit is hopeless because no target is specified, and a summed dyad fails to capture such interaction exchanges because it loses information regarding the direction which behavior flows between the actors. The summed dyad forecloses research because it denies the possibility of testing for reciprocity. For instance, in terms of foreign aid between two nations, the summed dyad would provide the following (hypothetical) information about the transactions between Taiwan and South Vietnam:

Taiwan—South Vietnam (1975)—$500 million

The obvious disadvantage to this type of information is that an observer would be unable to tell exactly what the relationship was: donor/recipient, recipient/donor, roughly equal, etc. This example illustrates that information about the direction of behavior is extremely important in telling the student something about the nature of the interactions obtaining between two polities.

4. *Symmetry* in interstate interaction: as with reciprocity, only the directed dyadic case permits the analyst to study the relationship between the *kind* of behavior sent and the kind received. Symmetry is conventionally defined as a response to a previous action in which the affective component or intensity of the previous action is duplicated by the respondent. Like reciprocity, symmetry is an empirical feature of interaction. When actions are organized in a directed dyad format, symmetry can be tested empirically: "The use of the directed dyad—which express cooperation or conflict going in one direction—allows one to test for more detailed and sensitive relationships—for symmetry for example" (Goodman et al., 1972, p. 31). Or, as East notes: "The directed dyadic perspective allows the researcher to determine whether the behavior directed from Nation A to Nation B is differ-

ent from the behavior directed from B to A. This conceptualization allows one to move from consideration of factors such as participation or activity (non-directed or symmetric variables) to factors such as dominance and reciprocity" (1972, pp. 9-10).

Hence, the directed dyadic case has a decided advantage over monadic and summed dyadic cases in the analysis of this important feature of interstate relations.

Prediction and forecasting of foreign policy behavior do not require the sophistication of explanatory analyses (Singer, 1969, p. 22), and consequently it is rather difficult to come to any conclusions about the relative utilities of alternate case units to lead to reliable predictions about foreign policy behavior. We may predict the performance of a nation in its external environment equally well from its internal characteristics (for which a monadic conception may be employed), from its level of integration with another national society (a summed dyadic measure would be useful for this purpose), or from the type of acts received from a particular foreign target (directed dyad). How a nation will act may be predicted from any of these sources without having an explanatory model specifying why these factors reliably predict that behavior. Given the absence of knowledge regarding if, and why, external behavior is most conditional on (a) its own prior behavior, (b) the previous behavior received from others, or (c) its own internal structure, all three cases-for-analysis are of use in making predictive statements.

We suggest that it would be best to reserve judgment expressed on behalf of one or another case until future research can demonstrate that greater predictive capability results from utilization of a particular case unit. In the last analysis, the fecundity of any research case must be evaluated in terms of its ability to facilitate the construction of powerful explanatory models. However, for some preliminary evidence that predictive power is indeed enhanced through utilization of directed dyadic measures, see Moore and Young (1969).

A final, but by no means exhaustive, research issue concerns the kind of *research design* most appropriate for alternate cases-for-analysis. Here it is clear that the utility of both monadic and summed dyadic cases is restricted; adoption of the monad necessitates a *micro* design whereas adoption of the summed dyad as the case-of-analysis necessarily involves a shift in the level-of-analysis to the *macro* level,[13] since in this latter case the researcher has chosen to investigate the exchange of behavior between two international actors. In other words, the adoption of the summed dyad as the case-of-analysis necessitates the simultaneous adoption of an interaction perspective (one which the researcher may neither be aware of nor desire) and shifts the level-of-analysis to the *macro* level. Because the directed dyad remains, by nature of its specification of a target of one actor's behavior and not the target's response, at the *micro* level, the researcher is able to avoid the necessary adoption of an interaction perspective and a shift in the level-of-analysis, although as a research alternative the directed dyad may be employed in an interaction framework if aggregated—i.e., if A → B is studied in terms of B → A. It is this independence of research objectives and methodological flexibility which recommends the directed dyad as a case on this research design issue.

CONCLUSION

While the choice of alternate cases-for-analysis and approaches is an enjoyable freedom for analysts of interstate behavior, it is eclipsed by a recognition

[13] Because the directed dyad specifies only the target of an actor's external behavior and not the target's response (as is the case with the summed dyad) we remain at the *micro* level (Singer, 1969); or as Burgess et al. (1972) term this research mode, *action analysis*.

It may be helpful in clarifying the problem of the level-of-analysis as related to cases-for-analysis by noting that the *macro* level-of-analysis is described or determined not by the number of actors included in a research design, but by the relationship produced by the exchange of behavior *between actors*. What distinguishes macroanalysis from microanalysis is that the former involves interaction between parties while the latter does not. The analysis of interaction (inasmuch as reciprocity is deemed an essential characteristic), whether in the name of international systems research or foreign policy research, constitutes a shift in the level-of-analysis from the micro to the macro level. Hence, the monad is at the micro level (no interaction is entailed) and the summed dyad is at the macro level of analysis. The directed dyad—despite its binary composition—remains at the micro level since there is no exchange of behavior, but rather, the identification of a target of one actor's behavior. Only when the directed dyad is summed (A → B + B → A = A ↔ B) does analysis shift to the macro level.

that in adopting one or the other case the researcher must be mindful of the assumptions he makes and the analytical burdens he takes on. In this discussion, we hope to have made some of these issues clearer.

Moreover, in providing a review of the relative advantages and costs associated with the case-for-analysis options delineated here, we would be remiss if we failed to emphasize that this review indicates that the directed dyad has much to recommend it as a case-for-analysis in foreign policy research. The methodological flexibility associated with its use renders it attractive for the investigation of many aspects of foreign policy research, and in particular for the construction of relational models of interstate behavior. While the utility of any one case-for-analysis is relative to the problem being investigated, it should be clear from the foregoing that greater attention to dyadic measures of foreign policy behavior is worth considering. The concentrated focus on monadic concepts of external behavior has yet to produce the hoped-for-payoff, as we noted in our opening remarks, and we thus suggest that a profitable avenue for future studies might reside with dyadic concepts. As Hermann has noted: "We have various alternative units and measures to shed a little light in the murky darkness of foreign affairs, but we cannot be sure that the keys to unlock explanations of foreign policy behavior will be found under any of the existing methodological lampposts" (1971, p. 296).

In the absence of any compelling methodological lampposts it appears to us worth discovering if adoption of a directed dyadic case unit might provide us with a possible key. Regardless of whether the reader is persuaded by this prescription and the reasoning behind it, this article will nevertheless have accomplished its purpose if it has sensitized the researcher to the conceptual implications of the research case he selects for analysis. As a final note to this analytic problem, it is helpful to gain perspective by recalling North's (1968, p. 304) remarks on the objectives of theories of international politics and foreign policy:

> Given a particular environmental event, we want to know in the short run what types of behavioral outputs we can expect from various nation-states, and we want to try to account for such outputs when they

occur. For the longer run, we want to know which of the more stable elements—relatively constant in the short run—are likely to change and how and why.

In the brief interlude since North's statement, research in these two directions has already begun.[14] These efforts have been made possible in no small measure by the increasing availability of empirical data about interstate behavior. Given the retarded state of our would-be science and more importantly, the urgency of the issue of conflict and cooperation which confronts our daily lives, it may seem obstinate and ill timed for questions of research cases to be presented and debated. But the very urgency of these two issues indicate that it is of extreme importance that our means of obtaining necessary knowledge not be impediments. The "handles" we seek for the organization and analysis of data may ultimately be the ways that allow us to learn of, and control for, the profusion of conflict. A common understanding of the meaning of these analytic case units should, at the very least, enhance the prospects for better communication and more cumulativeness in the comparative study of foreign policy.

REFERENCES

Allison, G. T. 1971. *Essence of Decision.* Boston: Little, Brown.

Bobrow, D. B. 1972. "The Relevance Potential of Different Products." *World Politics* 24 (suppl.): 204-23.

Brody, R. A. 1975. "Problems in the Measurement and Analysis of International Events." In *International Events and the Comparative Analysis of Foreign Policy,* ed. C. W. Kegley, Jr., et al., pp. 120-31. Columbia: Univ. of South Carolina Press.

Brown, S. 1968. *The Faces of Power: Constancy and Change in United States Foreign Policy from Truman to Johnson.* New York: Columbia Univ. Press.

Burgess, P. M., R. W. Lawton, and T. P. Kridler. 1972. "Indicators of International Behavior: An Overview and Re-examination of Micro-Macro Designs." Paper

[14]An example of the former research suggested by North is Moore and Young (1969), while the latter is exemplified by the work of Choucri and North (1972).

presented at the Annual Meeting of the International Studies Association, Dallas.

––– and R. W. Lawton. 1972. *Indicators of International Behavior: An Assessment of Events Data Research.* Beverly Hills: Sage.

Choucri, N., and R. C. North. 1972. "Dynamics of International Conflict: Some Policy Implications of Population, Resources and Technology." *World Politics* 25 (Spring): 80-122.

Cobb, R. W., and C. Elder. 1970. *International Community: A Regional and Global Study.* New York: Holt, Rinehart & Winston.

Coplin, W. D., and C. W. Kegley, Jr., eds. 1975. *The Analysis of International Relations.* New York: Praeger.

Coser, L. A., and B. Rosenberg, eds. 1959. *Sociological Theory: A Book of Readings.* New York: Macmillan.

Cottrell, L. S., Jr. 1942. "The Analysis of Situational Fields in Social Psychology." *American Sociological Review* 7: 370-82.

East, M. A. 1972. "Stratification of World Society and the International System." Paper presented at the Annual Meeting of the International Studies Association (South), Atlanta.

–––. 1975. "Size and Foreign Policy: A Test of Two Models." In *International Events and the Comparative Analysis of Foreign Policy*, ed. C. W. Kegley, Jr., et al., pp. 159-78.

Etzioni, A. 1965. *Political Unification: A Comparative Study of Leaders and Forces.* New York: Holt, Rinehart & Winston.

Galtung, J. 1968. "Small Group Theory and the Theory of International Relations: A Study in Isomorphism." In *New Approaches to International Relations*, ed. M. A. Kaplan, pp. 270-302. New York: St. Martin's.

Gardner, R. W. 1953. "Cognitive Styles in Categorizing Behavior." *Journal of Personality* 22: 214-33.

Goodman, R., J. Hart, and R. Rosecrance. 1972. "Testing International Theory: Methods and Data in a Situational Analysis of International Politics." Situational Analysis Project, Paper No. 2. Mimeo. Ithaca: Cornell Univ.

Handelman, J., J. Vasquez, M. K. O'Leary, and W. D. Coplin. 1973. "Color It Morgenthau: A Data-based Examination of Quantitative International Relations Research." Paper presented at the Annual Meeting of the International Studies Association, New York.

Hermann, C. F. 1971. "What Is a Foreign Policy Event?" In *Comparative Foreign Policy,* ed. W. F. Hanrieder, pp. 295-321. New York: McKay.

Isaak, A. C. 1969. *Scope and Methods of Political Science.* Homewood, Ill.: Dorsey.

Kaplan, A. 1964. *The Conduct of Inquiry.* San Francisco: Chandler.

Kegley, C. W., Jr. 1973. *A General Empirical Typology of*

Foreign Policy Behavior. Beverly Hills: Sage.

–––, S. A. Salmore, and D. Rosen. 1974. "Convergences in the Measurement of Interstate Behavior." In *Sage International Yearbook of Foreign Policy Studies,* ed. P. J. McGowan, vol. 2, pp. 309-39. Beverly Hills: Sage.

–––, G. A. Raymond, R. M. Rood, and R. A. Skinner, eds. 1975. *International Events and the Comparative Analysis of Foreign Policy.* Columbia: Univ. of South Carolina Press.

Kerlinger, F. N. 1973. *Foundations of Behavioral Research.* 2d ed. New York: Holt, Rinehart & Winston.

Kuhn, T. S. 1970. *The Structure of Scientific Revolutions.* 2d ed. Chicago: Univ. of Chicago Press.

Leary, T. M. 1957. *Interpersonal Diagnosis of Personality.* New York: Ronald.

McClelland, C. A. 1968. "Access to Berlin: The Quantity and Variety of Events, 1948-1963." In *Quantitative International Politics,* ed. J. D. Singer, pp. 159-86. New York: Free Press.

––– and G. D. Hoggard. 1969. "Conflict Patterns in the Interactions among Nations." In *International Politics and Foreign Policy,* ed. J. N. Rosenau, pp. 711-24. New York: Free Press.

–––. 1970. "Two Conceptual Issues in the Quantitative Analysis of International Events Data." Mimeo. Los Angeles: Univ. of Southern California.

McGowan, P. J. 1971. "The Unit-of-Analysis Problem in the Comparative Analysis of Foreign Policy." Mimeo. East Lansing: Michigan State Univ.

–––. 1975. "Meaningful Comparisons in the Study of Foreign Policy." In *International Events and the Comparative Analysis of Foreign Policy,* ed. C. W. Kegley, Jr., et al., pp. 52-87. Columbia: Univ. of South Carolina Press.

Mead, G. H. 1938. *The Philosophy of the Act.* Chicago: Univ. of Chicago Press.

Mischel, W. 1968. *Personality and Assessment.* New York: Wiley.

Moore, J. A., and R. A. Young. 1969. "Some Preliminary Short-Term Predictions of International Interaction." World Event/Interaction Survey, Working Paper No. 1. Mimeo. Los Angeles: Univ. of Southern California.

Morgenthau, Hans J. 1960. *Politics among Nations: The Struggle for Power and Peace.* 3d ed. New York: Knopf.

Munton, D. 1974. "Waiting for Kepler: Event Data and Relational Model Explanations of Canadian Foreign Policy Behavior." In *Sage International Yearbook of Foreign Policy Studies,* ed. P. J. McGowan, vol. 3. Beverly Hills: Sage.

North, R. C. 1968. "The Behavior of Nation-States: Problems of Conflict and Integration." In *New Approaches to International Relations,* ed. M. A. Kaplan, pp. 303-56. New York: St. Martin's.

Parsons, T., and E. A. Shils, eds. 1962. *Toward a General*

Theory of Action. New York: Harper & Row.

Phillips, W. R. 1973. "Theoretical Underpinnings of the Events Data Movement." Paper presented at the Annual Meeting of the International Studies Association, New York.

Raymond, G. A. 1975. "Comparative Analysis and Nomological Explanation." In *International Events and the Comparative Analysis of Foreign Policy,* ed. C. W. Kegley, Jr., et al., pp. 41-51. Columbia: Univ. of South Carolina Press.

Riker, W. H. 1957. "Events and Situations." *Journal of Philosophy* 54 (Jan): 57-70.

Rosenau, J. N. 1971. *The Scientific Study of Foreign Policy.* New York: Free Press.

———. 1975. "Comparative Foreign Policy: One-Time Fad, Realized Fantasy, and Normal Field." In *International Events and the Comparative Analysis of Foreign Policy,* ed. C. W. Kegley, Jr., et al., pp. 3-38. Columbia: Univ. of South Carolina Press.

—— and G. R. Ramsey, Jr. 1973. "External vs. Internal Sources of Foreign Policy Behavior: Testing the Stability of an Intriguing Set of Findings." Paper presented at the Ninth World Congress of the International Political Science Association, Montreal.

—— and G. D. Hoggard. 1974. "Foreign Policy Behavior in Dyadic Relationships: Testing a Pre-Theoretical Extension." In *Comparing Foreign Policies,* ed. J. N. Rosenau, pp. 117-49. Beverly Hills: Sage.

Rummel, R. J. 1963. "Some Dimensions of Conflict Behavior within and between nations." In *General Systems Yearbook,* vol. 8, pp. 1-50. Bedford Mass.: Society for General Systems Research.

———. 1969. "Some Empirical Findings on Nations and Their Behavior." *World Politics* 21 (Jan): 226-41.

———. 1972. "U.S. Foreign Relations: Conflict, Cooperation, and Attribute Distances." In *Peace, War, and Numbers,* ed. B. M. Russett, pp. 71-113. Beverly Hills: Sage.

Sears, R. F. 1951. "Social Behavior and Personality Development." In *Toward a General Theory of Action,* ed. T. Parsons and E. A. Shils, pp. 465-78. Cambridge: Harvard Univ. Press.

Simmel, G. 1950. *The Sociology of George Simmel.* Trans. and ed. K. H. Wolff. New York: Free Press.

Singer, J. D. 1969. "The Level-of-Analysis Problem in International Relations." In *International Politics and Foreign Policy* (rev. ed.), ed. J. N. Rosenau, pp. 20-29. New York: Free Press.

—— and J. L. Ray. 1973. "Aggregation and Inference: The Level-of-Analysis Problem Revisited." Paper presented at the Annual Meeting of the International Studies Association, New York.

Skinner, B. F. 1953. *Science and Human Behavior.* New York: Free Press.

Sondermann, F. A. 1961. "The Linkage between Foreign Policy and International Politics." In *International Politics and Foreign Policy,* ed. J. N. Rosenau, pp. 8-17. New York: Free Press.

Tanter, R. 1966. "Dimensions of Conflict Behavior within and between Nations, 1958-1960." *Journal of Conflict Resolution* 10 (Mar): 41-64.

Wilkenfeld, J. 1969. "Some Further Findings Regarding the Domestic and Foreign Conflict Behavior of Nations." *Journal of Peace Research* 6: 147-56.

Young, R. A. 1975. "A Classification of Nations According to Foreign Policy Output." In *Theory and Practice of Events Research,* ed. E. E. Azar and J. Ben-Dak, pp. 175-96. New York: Gordon & Breach.

34. The Role of Issues

Michael K. O'Leary

In a paper presented at the 1973 convention of the International Studies Association I argued, along with my coauthors, that, in effect, the overwhelming empirical work in the field of international relations constituted a kind of "new conservatism." We argued that empirical work tended to accept as its dominant conceptual paradigm a notion of the international system as described by Hans J. Morgenthau and other spokesmen of the power-politics view of international affairs. We also argued that this viewpoint, while possibly appropriate in some contexts, has helped explain the general lack of progress of quantitative studies of international relations (Handelman et al., 1973). This chapter is an attempt to focus our argument specifically on the comparative study of foreign policy, and to add some observations about the future of that subject.

In the earlier paper my colleagues and I argued that quantitative scholars shared, along with the adherents of power politics, a threefold view of the world which was so persuasive as to warrant its being called a paradigm. The three components of this paradigm jointly shared by quantifiers and traditionalists were:

1. The most important subject of study was the behavior of people acting in the name of various nation-states.
2. Social behavior within the boundaries of a nation-state was conceptually separable from social behavior which crossed nation-state boundaries. In other words there was a fundamental distinction between domestic and foreign policy.
3. Interactions between governments were concerned with a unidimensional relationship variously called "the struggle for power and peace" or generalized conflict and cooperation.

In the earlier paper we presented an analysis based on coding a sample of published articles to support our contention that quantitative international relations scholars did in fact overwhelmingly conform to the three-part paradigm. As we have all been told in our basic statistics training, we must be careful to avoid the ecological fallacy of concluding that a relationship which holds for an entire system also holds for subsets of that system. However, in the present situation I do not think that the ecological fallacy offers an escape hatch. If anything, the field of comparative foreign policy is probably more heavily dominated by the power-politics paradigm than the rest of international relations studies. Indeed, the very name and definition of the field associates it with assumption No. 2 of the paradigm, the foreign-policy-domestic-policy distinction.

In general, it hardly seems questionable that the overwhelming proportion of systematic work in the field has conformed to the international politics paradigm. Governments are the chief unit

of analysis studied. The official behavior of governments is either the independent variable, the dependent variable, or both. The foreign-domestic distinction pervades all analysis. And the behavior studied is dimensionalized along conflict and cooperative scales without regard for the topics giving occasion to the cooperation or conflict.

Some possible exceptions to these generalizations merely help prove the point. One of the most innovative steps concerning the domestic-foreign policy distinction has been made by James Rosenau. He, however, does not question the foreign-domestic distinction but merely says that domestic variables should be looked at as dependent variables rather than solely as independent variables as has previously been the case (Rosenau, 1970, 1972).[1]

The events data branch of comparative foreign policy has marched in step with other methods in the study of comparative foreign policy. It has been written "by their coding rules, yea, we shall know them." And so it is, in the World Event Interaction Survey (WEIS) coding scheme for example, that subnational groups are not coded as actors, although in early discussions of the subject, McClelland (1970) acknowledged that national actors were usually merely collectives or many separate actors. The same nation-state bias has pervaded other events data coding schemes.

The point of this, of course, is not what the factual situation concerning the thrust of comparative foreign policy studies is; the important question is "What difference does all this make?" The exceedingly low percentage of variance explained in the work done is one general consequence of the paradigm employed by quantitative international scholars. Once again, it may be that those studies which could be classified as foreign policy analysis might fare better with respect to variance explained, but that is highly doubtful.

Of course, attacking a particular study, or a general field, solely on the basis of variance explained is neither fair nor particularly enlightening. A work may contribute little in the explanation of

[1] In the more recent article, Rosenau refers to the blurring of the domestic-foreign distinction but nevertheless argues that "increasingly . . . 'internal' events and trends are sustained by 'external' events and trends" (1972, p. 156).

variance but may still be admirable for other purposes—the elegance of its deductive reasoning, its
relevance to policy makers because of the variable
it deals with, because it suggests to other researchers new directions they might take, or for
many other reasons. But if the present study of
comparative foreign policy is a worthwhile field,
despite its low statistical results, such redeeming
social qualities are not immediately obvious.
Indeed, when one looks at those instances of findings based on high correlations, the vitality of
comparative foreign policy becomes even more
suspect (Rosenau and Hoggard, 1974). This is
because the dependent variable, which from time
to time has been found to be systematically associated with various independent variables, is so
highly aggregated as to render it without theoretical content. And, from a policy-making point of
view, it holds little interest.

A survey, admittedly unsystematic, of some
available studies of comparative foreign policy
leads to the observation that such things as
"participation," "total conflict," and "total
cooperation" are all proudly displayed as being
systematically associated with different attributes
of governments, societies, and decision-making
systems (Munton, 1973; Peterson, 1973). Interestingly enough, the dependent variable in these
studies is scarcely even defined in conceptual
terms. Such attention as it does receive is devoted
to methodological and operational concerns—the
scale on which it was measured, its distributional
properties, the sources and cavalier theoretical
treatment of the variable to be explained. One is
left with one of two conclusions. Either there is no
theoretical interest in the variable being studied,
other than that persuasive theoretical attractiveness of availability, or—especially in the case of
conflict and cooperation—it is not necessary to
provide a careful conceptual discussion of the variable since, having read Morgenthau's *Politics
among Nations,* we are fully aware of what it
means.

The critic is constantly told that he must do
more than simply criticize. No matter how often
he observes others egregiously, enthusiastically,
and persistently beating their heads against deadend signs, it is not sufficient simply to point out
this fact. It is necessary, so the argument goes, to

demonstrate the proper road to be traveled. The
critic might reply that if people would stop beating their heads in the same spot they could find
their way themselves. But the charge is well taken,
nonetheless. If for no other reason than to finish
on the upbeat, it is worthwhile to direct some
attention to where we might go from here.

Each of the basic assumptions listed above as
characterizing the international politics paradigm,
if examined carefully, ought to provide guidelines
for directions in which systematic social science
investigations could profitably proceed. Assumption No. 1 would lead us to consider actors other
than governments as being important in the allocation of values on a worldwide scale. Assumption
No. 2 would lead us to reject the notion of an a
priori distinction between domestic and foreign
policies. Each of these two points could, by itself,
provide the basis for extended discussion. But I
would rather postpone such discussion for another
time and concentrate instead on some guidelines
suggested by the third assumption. It could lead us
to reject the notion that it is useful to study
relations between states in terms of unidimensional measures of cooperation and conflict, or of
other grossly aggregated measures.

In order to begin breaking away from the con-
strictive power-politics paradigm, it appears to me
that we need a new basic assumption in order to
begin a fruitful alternative course of action. This
new assumption is "Foreign policy is that set of
actions by governments (and other actors) directed
toward affecting the allocation of values in two or
more nation-states." On the surface this definition
may appear quite similar to traditional definition
of foreign policy as behavior by some intended to
influence the behavior of others. But the definition offered here will at least point researchers to
the problem of identifying the sorts of values
whose allocation is the occasion for foreign policy
behavior.

This definition also leads us naturally to consider the allocations of values which are in dispute
among various actors. Let us define such disputed
value allocations (actual or potential) as issues.
Issues thus become the unit of analysis of foreign
policy studies. To make the point as clearly as
possible, an issue is a proposed—and disputed—
specific allocation of values. It is assumed that

resolving the issue—allocating the values—is what motivates state behavior. It may be possible to speak usefully of an issue area, for example, "disarmament," as long as all of the issue outcomes that comprise that issue area are specified, e.g., a nonproliferation treaty, a Russian-American ceiling on missile production, a nuclear-free zone in Latin America, etc. But to speak of an "issue area" as, for example, a "military issue area" without specifying what value outcomes are in dispute is merely to label a category whose content is vague.[2]

There are several ways in which actors can be related to issues. An actor's power or capabilities on each issue and the importance of each issue to an actor, are relationships worthy of important measures. However, a measure we have found to be one of the most useful is the relative position taken by each actor on each of a series of issues. Recall that we define an issue as an actual or proposed allocation of values which is in dispute. Actors can thus be recorded as taking a position in favor of, or opposed to, the proposed outcome. These issue positions may be correlated as dependent variables with nation types, with other actors' issue positions, or with other variables.

We do not want to present a complete outline for the study of issue-based foreign policy or the theoretical underpinnings of such a study;[3] we merely want to emphasize that issues are important and should be made a part of the systematic study of foreign policy.

The foregoing statement is interesting, not because it is radical or insightful, but because it is so obvious. After all, "everybody knows" that issues are important, that at a given point in time, for example, the United States and the Soviet Union may be bargaining over implementing European political agreements, achieving economic agree-

ments, mutually reducing arms spending, and resolving conflict in the Middle East—to take just four of the more visible categories of values whose distribution is at issue between the two countries. But what is equally obvious is that this "obvious" fact has made little, if any, impact upon systematic research in the field.

Two difficulties must be faced when moving out of the simplistic power-politics-dominated mode of research on foreign policy. The first is the difficulty of obtaining issue-related systematic data.

There are several ways of obtaining issue-related data. Two promising ones are surveying experts on the nature of relations between states with respect to a specified set of issues, and using trade journals and related sources to abstract and code issue-related events. Preliminary work has been undertaken on both of these activities. Surveys of experts have been conducted to assess the relative issue positions of the actors in bargaining between North and South Korea (O'Leary and Coplin, 1975). And a modest events data collection has been assembled to study the politics of the international oil system by using, among other things, petroleum trade journals (O'Leary and Coplin, 1975).

Still a third method is to code for issues in the generally available events data sources. A limited effort has been undertaken in this direction using the most accessible events data set, WEIS of the University of Southern California. This coding, based on the raw sentences of the WEIS data, classified each event as to the value allocation in dispute for each particular interaction. The issue classification was twofold, identifying (1) the value or values whose allocation was in question and (2) the physical location of the value-allocation struggle. Thus, the most specific coding of an issue identifies the value at stake—for example, the value of arms reduction also involves the location of the struggle to achieve that value i.e., Latin America, Western Europe, throughout the world, or, indeed, in outer space (O'Leary and Shapiro, 1972).

Of course, the empty cell problem so bedeviling to events data research is compounded by coding for specific categories from such a general data source. Consequently, the following discussion will

---

[2]In his definition of "issue areas" Rosenau says they consist of in part of "a cluster of values, the allocation or potential allocation of which motivates behavior" (1966, p. 81). In our view, Rosenau and others have been overly relaxed in allowing the specific values to be allocated to remain unspecified within general issue-area categories. The issue-area concept was, we feel, a major contribution to the field. But its contribution has remained limited until greater specific substance can be attached to it.

[3]For further elaboration of some of these ideas see Coplin et al. (1974).

deal with a subset of the data we have made, using only the functional coding for issues, and dealing with only the richest dyads in the WEIS data set.

The first inquiry made of the data was whether or not our initial hunch made sense concerning the existential narrowness of the international politics paradigm. To test this, we performed two simple analyses of the data. We first examined the width of the issue spectrum in the interactions of 115 actor countries that sent events targeted to the United States. This distribution, as shown in Figure 1, indicates that there is a large number of countries in the WEIS data which, as initiators of action, deal with several identifiable issues in their relations with the United States. There is also a substantial number, the single largest category in fact, recorded as interacting over only a single issue. (These single-issue countries were also the ones with the least number of total interactions reported.)

Suppose it is accepted (on the basis of the limited argument presented so far) that there are

systematically identifiable issues in foreign policy behavior, and that the nature of these issues far exceeds the outlines of the field suggested by the power-politics paradigm.

It must still be asked whether "issues make a difference," that is, whether notions can be identified as exhibiting different patterns of behavior across a range of issues. As a simple test of variation in dyad behavior across issues, we have performed the following analysis. Each interaction which was issue-coded was also coded on a +10/-10 scale, as to the level of friendship or hostility exhibited by the actor toward the target in that particular act. For each directional dyad we then computed the mean and standard deviations across the range of issues comprising that actor's interactive agenda toward that target. The higher the standard deviation for an actor in a dyad, the more that its friendship-hostility pattern varied across issues.

Using these two measures, mean and standard deviation, we have begun to develop an issue-based

Figure 1. The Number of Separate Issues Sent by 115 Countries Sending Interactions in the WEIS Data Set

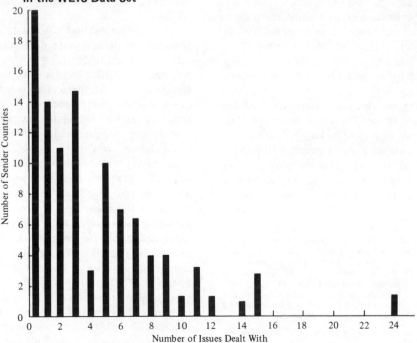

typology of transnational relations. Category I is the relationship conforming to the traditional competitive interaction pattern, with unfriendly (negative) hostility-friendship scores, and little variation across issues—low standard deviation.

Category II is an early transitional stage from category I. It is a relationship marked, as in category I, by hostility (although at somewhat diminished levels), by greater variation of friendship-hostility across issue categories. Nations characterized by this stage of relationships are in the process of establishing the procedures, understandings, and institutions for nonpower politics relationships between them. States in category II still find much to be hostile about, but they also find areas in which they perceive mutual interests, or issues on which they have the same, or similar, issue positions. Consequently, their relationships are marked by moderately hostile interactions and relatively high standard deviation across issues.

Category III is the second transitional stage. In this case, dyads are still in the process of establishing patterns of contracts by which they can work to resolve issues. Greater areas of cooperation lead to more friendly interactions, but areas of unresolved issues lead to some disagreements and thus a high standard of deviation.

Category IV is the stage where, at the level of highly visible government interaction, the general relationships is friendly, and there is little difference in this friendly pattern from one issue to another; standard deviation is accordingly low.

Figure 2 summarizes this fourfold typology. The cells of the table also contain examples of countries which exhibit the characteristics of each of the categories in their relationship to the United States, according to our coding of the WEIS data.

The WEIS data, and similar events data sets which rely upon general news sources for reports of government behavior, can be used to identify the classification of each national dyad. However, these sources become less relevant for anything more than placing a dyad in one of the four categories as one proceeds from category I through category IV. The reason is that only in category I are the issues reported in the press likely to be the major component of relations between a given dyad. In the other categories, especially category IV, the major transnational interactions for a given

Figure 2. An Issued-based Typology of Inter-actions between States, Based on Friendship-Hostility across All Issues

Mean	Standard Deviation (S.D.)	
	High	Low
Positive	Category III Japan Mean = 2.4 S.D. = 4.4	Category IV United Kingdom Mean = 1.4 S.D. = 2.9
Negative	Category II U.S.S.R. Mean = -0.03 S.D. = 4.8	Category I China Mean = -4.4 S.D. = 2.7

Note: The country named in each cell is representative of the particular type of interaction with the United States, according to issue coding of the WEIS data.

dyad take place through the activities of foreign policy ministries at low levels, non-foreign-policy bureaucracies at all levels, and through nongovernmental groups or other agencies not likely to be covered by the general news media.

Therefore, when the WEIS data indicate that a dyad such as the U.S. and the U.K. are engaging in relatively friendly interactions with little variation across issues, they are correct with respect to high-level public diplomatic interaction. But they say nothing about transnational bureaucratic interaction, competitive or otherwise, between the two countries. Assuming a minimal level, or general contact, between two societies, it is only for dyads in category I (hostility, low standard deviation) that the patterns of normal events data can be given substantive meaning. Events data can be used to classify dyads in the other three categories, but in these cases the scholar must look to other sources to estimate the richness of dyad interactions.

There are at least three dimensions along which the relationships posited above may vary. In the first dimension, the number of any given nation's dyadic relationships may vary within each of the categories. Israel, for example, is in a competitive, single-issue category I relationship with its neighbors and with many other nations. Contrast Israel with Denmark, which interacts with its neighbors and other countries in terms of a multiple-issue agenda characterized by category IV. Many such relationships involve conflict, but only at levels of bureaucratic competition involving the allocation of wealth and social values, rather than the so-called high politics of strategic intergovernmental conflict in the line of international politics. Figure 3 shows the relationship of the United States to the countries with which it interacts, according to one or more issues in the WEIS data. As this figure indicates, the great bulk of interacting partners is found outside category I, which is the only category in which standard events data can be used for substantive or theoretical purposes.

A second dimension is that a given dyad may vary over time. Perhaps the most dramatic example of the evolution of a dyad from category I to category IV is that of France and Germany. At the beginning of the twentieth century they were highly competitive antagonists in international politics; today they are involved in a wide range of multiple-issue relationships. It may be presumed, in looking at a single dyad over time, that there is a natural evolution of the relationship

starting in category I and terminating in category IV. It is natural only in the sense that, other things being equal, a dyad is *likely* to move from category I through category IV. In actual situations of course, many factors may intervene to fix relations at a particular stage or to move relationships "backward" away from category IV and toward category I. When considering issue-based relations according to the dimension of time, the task becomes one of considering the variables associated with a dyad's being in one category or another.

A third dimension along which the categories may vary is in the resource or value, whose allocation constitutes the issue area. In the first of two extreme examples, we would expect to find that disposition of territory would take place according to category IV interaction. The second, and more complex, example, is that it is probably true that the disposition of worldwide petroleum resources prompted patterns of behavior consistent with category I power-politics behavior, at least until recently. Access to, and denial of, petroleum resources was dealt with as part of the overall struggle for power among states. More recently, however, action in the realm of oil policy has involved the resolution of specific issues concerning the actual and future allocation of oil and related energy values. This has not made a decline in the conflict surrounding distribution of oil, but it has created different patterns of cooperation and conflict at the governmental level. It also has introduced new actors, in addition to the traditional diplomatic representatives who previously dominated the decision-making process.

These arguments are, of course, largely speculative and do not advance the development of social science theory any more than the research which has been criticized for ignoring issues does. However, the purpose of this chapter is merely to point out the possibility of adopting an issue-orientation method for doing systematic research in place of elaborating on the theoretical implications of such research. Other work is being done on the subject. It has been shown, for example, that states' issue positions on nuclear proliferation is sytematically related to their national attributes (Kegley and Andrews, 1973). Other findings indicate that the genotypical variables of high national wealth help significantly to explain the extent to which states

Figure 3. Distribution of Dyads Involving the United States and Other Nations According to the Issue-based Typology from WEIS Data

Mean	Standard Deviation (S.D.)	
	High	Low
The United States as Sender to Other Countries		
Positive or Neutral	Category IV Mean = 21 S.D. < 3.5	Category III Mean = 9 S.D. > 3.5
Negative	Category I Mean = -10 S.D. < 3.5	Category II Mean = -15 S.D. > 3.5
The United States as Receiver from Other Countries		
Positive or Neutral	Category IV Mean = 17 S.D. < 4.0	Category III Mean = 18 S.D. > 4.0
Negative	Category I Mean = -29 S.D. < 4.0	Category II Mean = -16 S.D. > 4.0

are active with respect to economic issues more than to other types of issues (Downing and Green, 1973). Canadian-U.S. relations have shown significant differences in military, as opposed to economic, issue areas (Munton, 1973). These findings offer more theoretical and explanatory payoff than the atheoretical findings concerning such generalized concepts as nonsubstantive "participation," conflict and cooperation. Likewise, both theoretical and empirical work is also underway to develop and test propositions about issue position over time among nations and other actors concerning transnational issues.

This short statement, of course, is far from confirming any answer to the question of where the study of comparative foreign policy should be moving. But it at least fails to falsify the hypothesis of this chapter, that there is a range of quantitative and qualitative richness to foreign policy behavior which has not yet been measured systematically, much less analyzed. To move systematically and rigorously into the complex field of issue analysis is not easy. But in the long run the costs may not be as great as continuing in the present path of statistical impotence and theoretical vacuity.

REFERENCES

Coplin, W. D., S. L. Mills, and M. K. O'Leary. 1974. "The PRINCE Concepts and the Study of Foreign Policy." In *Sage International Yearbook of Foreign Policy Studies*, ed. P. J. McGowan, vol. 1, pp. 73-103. Beverly Hills: Sage.

Downing, B., and J. E. Green. 1973. "National Attributes and Foreign Policy: An Issue-based Study." Mimeo. Syracuse: Syracuse Univ.

Handelman, J. R., J. A. Vasquez, M. K. O'Leary, and W. D. Coplin. 1973. "Color It Morgenthau: A Data-based Assessment of Quantitative International Relations Research." Paper prepared for the National Convention of the International Studies Association.

Kegley, C. W., Jr., and C. N. Andrews. 1973. "National and Systemic Determinants of Proliferation." Paper prepared for the National Convention of the International Studies Association.

McClelland, C. 1970. "Two Conceptual Issues in the Quantitative Analysis of International Events Data." Mimeo. Los Angeles: Univ. of Southern California, Dept. of International Relations.

Morgenthau, H. J. 1973. *Politics among Nations.* New York: Knopf.

Munton, D. 1973. "Issue-Areas in Canadian-American Relations: An Extension of the Situational Model." Paper prepared for the Annual Meeting of the Peace Science Society (Northeast).

O'Leary, M. K., and H. B. Shapiro. 1972. "Instructions for Coding Foreign Policy Acts." Mimeo. Syracuse: Syracuse Univ., International Relations Program.

――― and W. D. Coplin. 1975. *Quantitative Techniques in Foreign Policy Analysis and Forecasting.* New York: Praeger.

Peterson, S. 1973. "Research on Research: Events Data Studies, 1961-1972." Paper prepared for the National Convention of the International Studies Association.

Rosenau, J. N. 1966. "Pre-theories and Theories of Foreign Policy." In *Approaches to Comparative and International Politics*, ed. B. Farrell, pp. 27-92. Evanston: Northwestern Univ. Press.

―――. 1970. *The Adaptation of National Societies: A Theory of Political System Behavior and Transformation.* New York: McCaleb-Seiler.

―――. 1972. "Adaptive Politics in an Interdependent World." *Orbis* 16 (Spring): 153-73.

――― and G. D. Hoggard. 1974. "Foreign Policy Behavior in Dyadic Relationships: Testing a Pre-theoretical Extension." In *Comparing Foreign Policies*, ed. J. N. Rosenau, pp. 117-49. Beverly Hills: Sage.

35. When Leader Personality Will Affect Foreign Policy: Some Propositions

Margaret G. Hermann

Fortune varying and men remaining fixed in their ways, they are successful so long as these ways conform to circumstances, but when they are opposed then they are unsuccessful.

—Machiavelli, *The Prince*

As a relative newcomer to the comparative study of foreign policy—an interloper from another discipline (psychology)—let me register my surprise at the lack of interest in exploring the interrelationships among the independent or so-called determinants of foreign policy. There are studies of how attributes of nations affect foreign policy, of how bureaucracies affect foreign policy, of how changes in regimes affect foreign policy, of how leader personality affects foreign policy, but little attempt has been made to indicate how these variables might interrelate in their effects on foreign policy. In fact, the few studies (e.g., Rosenau, 1968; Stassen, 1972) which examine two or more of these determiners of foreign policy focus on the relative potency of various clusters of variables rather than their interaction. Surely, this state of affairs is like the blind men and the elephant. Examination of the relationships between only one type of independent variable and foreign policy may represent a distortion of the reality present with a mix of independent variables. Exploration of the interrelationships among various types of independent variables in the ex-

planation of foreign policy seems a valuable next step in the comparative study of foreign policy.

Along this line, this chapter sets forth some propositions indicating under what circumstances leader personality will have an effect on foreign policy. The conditions include variables from other groups of independent variables. The propositions are intended to suggest some possible linkages between leader personality and other types of independent variables.

Leader personality is probably a good independent variable to begin with, since its influence on policy has generated much controversy (see, e.g., Bronfenbrenner, 1960; Greenstein, 1969; Hook, 1943; Leontief, 1963; Verba, 1969). The critics argue that leader personality has little effect on political behavior because individual actors "are severely limited in the impact they can have on events" and "because individuals with varying individual characteristics will behave similarly when placed in common situations" (Greenstein, 1969, p. 34).

The first argument concerns the centuries-old debate of "great man" versus *Zeitgeist*. In other words, must the times be right for the man or will the man be great regardless of the times? For example, would Lincoln have had as much impact on domestic policy had he been president in the 1920s instead of the 1860s? This debate has also raged among psychologists and sociologists interested in the study of leadership. Research on leadership indicates that neither position is tenable by itself (see Gibb, 1969; Stogdill, 1974). While most leaders do seem to be self-confident, extroverted, and to exhibit interpersonal sensitivity (or empathy), a leader in one situation is not necessarily a leader in a different situation. Moreover,

SPECIAL NOTE: This chapter represents a revised version of a discussion paper prepared for the Inter-university Comparative Foreign Policy Project Conference, Ojai, California, June 18-22, 1973. The writing of this chapter was supported by National Science Foundation Grant GS-40356 and the Mershon Center at Ohio State University. Comments on an earlier draft of this material by Maurice East, Charles Hermann, Barbara Salmore, and Stephen Salmore are gratefully acknowledged.

leadership is often bestowed on the basis of the values and needs of a constituency, both of which can change. Students of leadership propose that it is the interaction between the characteristics of the individual and the characteristics of the situation which determines who will become a leader and the kind of behavior the leader will exhibit (see Fiedler, 1967; Hollander and Julian, 1970). In this tradition Paige (1972, p. 69) defines political leadership as "the interaction of personality, role, organization, task, values, and setting as expressed in the behavior of salient individuals" who can have an effect on policy.

The second criticism that "individuals with varying individual characteristics will behave similarly when placed in common situations" is at the heart of this chapter. As proponents of this position Kolko and Kolko (1972) argue that political leaders merely reflect the views, beliefs, and ideologies of the constituencies they lead and, as a result, react to common situations in a similar manner. Interestingly, however, even advocates of this position (e.g., Shils, 1954; Verba, 1969) grant that in certain situations the effects of personality on political behavior are probably enhanced rather than reduced. Moreover, they have suggested some conditions which enhance the impact of personality on political behavior. Greenstein (1969, p. 47) has rephrased this objection in a manner appropriate to the discussion to follow: "Under what circumstances do different actors (placed in common situations) vary in their behavior and under what circumstances is their behavior uniform?" It is toward the task of proposing the conditions under which leader personality will have an effect on foreign policy that the rest of this chapter is addressed.

Building on Paige's definition of political leadership, a first decision to be made concerns who are the salient individuals who can have an effect on foreign policy. Specifically, for which policy makers do we think personality characteristics could have an impact on national foreign policy. Let me propose that the personality characteristics of a policy maker have a greater potential for influencing national foreign policy the higher in the foreign policy organization his role is. Snyder and Robinson (1961, p. 158) have

observed from research on organizations "that when asked if personality plays as great (or greater) a part in behavior as organizational factors such as communication, officials who are at lower echelons tend to say no, while those at high echelons tend to say yes." Roles are less likely to be well defined the higher in an organization one climbs; the role occupant has more responsibility for delimiting and/or expanding his functions. Furthermore, there are fewer, if any, people above one to change or modify the decision. Recall the famous sign on Truman's desk: "The buck stops here." As Stassen (1972, p. 118) notes in discussing foreign policy: "Top-level executives are not under tight hierarchical constraint. . . . They must be persuaded and bargained with rather than simply commanded. . . . Therefore, preferences and belief-sets are likely to be important for top-level executive decision makers." In sum, (1) the more authority the policy maker has over a nation's foreign policy machinery, the fewer the people there are above him in the foreign policy bureaucracy to change his decision; and (2) the less well defined the policy maker's role, the more likely his personality characteristics are to influence foreign policy. Based on this rationale, the personalities of heads of state and foreign ministers will probably have more impact on the foreign policy behavior of their governments than the personalities of the occupants of most other governmental positions.

To date my research (M. Hermann, 1974) has focused only on heads of state and not on the comparison between heads of state and policy makers lower down in the foreign policy bureaucracy. It is noteworthy, however, that 50 percent (7 out of 14) of the predicted relationships between leader personality and foreign policy were significant or approached significance ($p < .10$; rank order correlations of .44 or greater) using heads of state. The percentage of such bivariate relationships for policy makers lower in the foreign policy organization is expected to be much less than 50 percent.

Given a sample of policy makers who personally have the ability to influence foreign policy—that is, heads of state—under what conditions will they try to influence national foreign policy? Another way of asking this question is under what conditions do heads of state participate in making foreign policy. And, more specifically, under which of these conditions would we expect their personality characteristics (their views of the world, their motivations, their ways of dealing with other people) to influence the decisions which are made? The following eight propositions are advanced in an attempt to answer this last question. These eight propositions concern the past experience of the head of state, his present relationship with his constituency, the governmental setting in which he finds himself, and the situation he faces.

[1] The more general interest the head of state has in foreign policy, the more likely his personality characteristics are to affect foreign policy behavior (cf. Greenstein, 1969, p. 54; Verba, 1969, p. 221).

General interest in foreign policy appears to vary among heads of state. In wanting to be his own secretary of state, Kennedy exhibited a great interest in and paid a great deal of attention to foreign affairs (see Schlesinger, 1965; Sorensen, 1965). He hoped to set the tone and direction of U.S. foreign policy. Bourguiba (see Merlin, 1968), in his 1965 initiatives to bring peace to the Middle East, focused all his attention on foreign affairs and, in effect, made Tunisian foreign policy as he traveled from one Middle Eastern capital to the next. At the other extreme is a head of state like Eisenhower, who preferred to let Dulles handle most foreign policy issues.

The Kennedy and Bourguiba examples suggest that one consequence of interest in foreign policy will be increased participation in the making of foreign policy. (In fact, one operationalization of interest might be the percentage of events in which the head of state participates relative to the bureaucracy.) The head of state will want to be consulted on decisions and will want to be kept informed about what is happening in foreign affairs. If nothing else, his beliefs about the world and his preferred ways of dealing with other people will influence the areas of the world and the issues which are addressed. Moreover, the reasons behind the head of state's interest in foreign policy—he places value on good external relations,

he fears an enemy takeover, he sees it as a way of gaining reelection—may predetermine the course of action he will seek to implement.

Interest is probably a more general variable than those involved in the seven propositions to follow. A certain level of interest may be necessary before any of these proposed intervening variables will enhance the leader personality-foreign policy relationship. Interest acts as a motivating force. Moreover, interest may take the form of increased attention to a specific foreign policy issue (for example, Eisenhower's "Atoms for Peace" proposal) rather than to foreign policy in general. The head of state who has little interest in foreign affairs is likely to delegate authority to other people, negating any effect of his personality on the resultant policy except as his spokesman's personality is similar to his own.

[2] The more dramatic are the means of assuming power, the more likely the personality characteristics of the head of state are to affect foreign policy behavior.

Revolutions, assassinations, and elections by an overwhelming plurality of the people or parliament (landslide elections) are considered dramatic means of assuming power. Following revolutions, assassinations, and landslide elections there seems to be, at least for a time, a honeymoon period in which the new head of state can implement his policy—both domestic and foreign—with ease. Constituency criticism is held in abeyance during this period of time. In such a setting the head of state is relatively free to chart the direction foreign policy will take. And the new head of state will probably have some beliefs and feelings about foreign policy which he will want to institute. Unless one of the other seven intervening variables is present, however, the influence of the head of state's personality will diminish as the honeymoon period ends. This proposition is expected to hold for only six to twelve months following the dramatic accession to power.

One might argue that there is some brief honeymoon period following any regime change to let the new head of state get adjusted to his role and to see what his policies will be. As a consequence, personality factors may have an effect on foreign policy for a short period of time. Along this line,

Hollander and Julian (1970) have found, in their research on small groups, that immediately following their election, leaders are more confident and willing to deviate from the group.

[3] *The more charismatic is the head of state, the more likely his personality characteristics are to affect foreign policy behavior.*

Willner and Willner (1965, p. 79) define "charisma" (following Max Weber) as the "leader's capacity to elicit from a following deference, devotion and awe toward himself as the source of authority." The leader is master, the followers are disciples. Tucker (1968) suggests that charisma develops because people are experiencing some distress for which the leader indicates he has a solution; the leader believes he was chosen to solve the problem and radiates confidence; only through him will the masses attain salvation from the dire predicament in which they find themselves. Both Nkrumah and De Gaulle are examples of charismatic heads of state (see Apter, 1968; Hoffmann and Hoffmann, 1968). Charismatic leadership flourishes in times of disturbance and distress. It is not clear that the charismatic leader can survive as the initial problems are alleviated and the nation moves into a more routine and less crisis-prone condition. Hoffmann and Hoffmann (1968) propose that only through routinizing charisma by constantly provoking stressful situations can the charismatic leader retain his power as the nation moves out of the revolutionary state.

Given the deference and devotion of the charismatic leader's constituents, such a leader can exercise much influence over the nation's domestic and foreign policy (if not generally, certainly in the problem areas for which he achieved his charisma). The charismatic leader is expected to be able to solve any problems. His beliefs, attitudes, values, and desires become the beliefs, attitudes, values, and desires of his followers.

Charisma is a hard variable to operationalize since, as the definitions presented earlier imply, it is as much in the "eye of the beholder" as a characteristic of the leader. Byars (1973) has recently suggested that like the "great man" in small group research (see Borgatta, Couch, and Bales, 1962), the charismatic leader performs both the task-oriented and interpersonal or affect-oriented functions required by the nation so well that he is rewarded by the people of the nation (in a similar fashion to their small group counterparts) with the leadership role. In other words, the charismatic leader is able to appear to conduct the business of the nation effectively as well as to provide enough personal satisfactions to his constituents that they keep clamoring for him to remain in power. Going further, Byars (1972) has designed a measure of the orientations of political leaders called the Task/Affect Quotient. Combining this Task/Affect Quotient with some measure of follower adulation—for example, number of people who come out to see the head of state when he appears in public or some rating of the enthusiasm of such crowds—might provide a way of assessing both components of charisma.

[4] *The more authority a head of state has over foreign policy, the more likely his personality characteristics are to affect foreign policy behavior.*

Some heads of state appear to have more authority and power over policy than others—for example, heads of state in nations with closed, as opposed to open, political systems. In closed political systems such as China and East Germany, there are fewer elite groups to satisfy or to attempt to influence any decision than in open systems such as the United States and Canada. The leaders in closed political systems are less politically accountable to their constituents. As a result, what these leaders believe, desire, and feel is likely to give direction to the foreign policy decision-making process. Tucker (1965, p. 583) has argued that in totalitarian states the political machinery becomes "a conduit of the dictatorial psychology"—that there is a relatively unimpeded conversion of the whims of the dictator into governmental actions as a result of his authoritarian control of the bureaucracy.

A distinction needs to be made here between authority as used in this proposition and authority as discussed in deciding which group of policy makers to select. In choosing heads of state as the group of policy makers to focus on we were interested in the relative authority of the head of state vis-à-vis other foreign policy officials in his government. In the present proposition we are interested in the relative position power of one head of state vis-à-vis other heads of state.

This proposition has received some support in my own research (M. Hermann, 1974). For a sample of heads of state the open or closed nature of their nation's political system was distinguished by use of an index of political accountability developed by Cutright (1963) and Olsen (1968). Whereas 43 percent (6 out of 14) of the correlations for heads of state in closed nations were .50 or higher, only 14 percent (2 out of 14) of the correlations for heads of state in open nations were .50 or higher. Moreover, one of the correlations for heads of state in open nations was in the opposite direction from that predicted.

[5] The less developed and differentiated is the foreign policy organization of the nation, the more likely the personality characteristics of the head of state are to affect foreign policy behavior.

A less developed foreign policy organization is probably characteristic of new nations and under-developed nations. Such nations are unlikely to have the resources to expend on establishing an organization or to have had time to establish one. As a result, foreign policy decisions probably include the head of state. Furthermore, it is easier to consult with the head of state and for the head of state to initiate foreign policy activity. What the head of state thinks and feels can affect policy. In the new nation, particularly, there are few plans or previous actions—no organizational memory—to predetermine responses to actions initiated by other nations. Thus, the head of state has more latitude to put his personal mark on the foreign policy behavior of his nation. As Dettman (1974, p. 245) argues in his discussion of Third World political leaders (Nehru, Nyerere, Kenyatta, Nkrumah, U Nu, and Sukarno), the student of Third World politics "must give due consideration to the impact of the leadership variable." One way to assess the development of a nation's foreign policy organization is by the number of persons employed in governmental positions dealing with foreign policy.

[6] The more crisislike is the national situation, the more likely the personality characteristics of the head of state are to affect foreign policy behavior.

"Crisis" is used here as defined by C. Hermann (1969). A crisis involves the perception by the decision makers of a high threat to national goals, of short time in which to respond, and of surprise (or lack of anticipation of the event). Literature on crisis (see Cleveland, 1963; C. Hermann, 1969, 1972; Hilsman, 1959; Pruitt, 1964-1965) suggests that there is a contraction of authority during such situations, decisions being made by fewer individuals than normally. The contraction of authority is generally to higher levels in an organization. "As a period of tension grows towards its crisis point, the handling of decisions becomes more centralized and elevated within national governments" (Buchan, 1966, pp. 40-41). Thus, the head of state is likely to be actively involved in the decision-making process during a crisis. Furthermore, the rules of the game are less well defined for such decisions—there is little time to search for information about the situation within the organizational memory or to follow usual bureaucratic procedures; the decision makers must rely on their own abilities and experiences. As Charles Hermann (1969, p. 144) states: "Those individuals who do exercise authority in crisis situations tend to be at the highest levels of government; therefore, they are able to commit agencies without seeking the approval of others." The ways in which the head of state deals with stress, the kinds of coping mechanisms he uses—for example, overreaction or underreaction, attempts to flee or withdraw from the scene, projection—can set the tone for the decision-making process.

The next two hypotheses differ from the previous six in that they are *not* concerned with when the head of state will participate in foreign policy making. Instead they focus on variables which lead to some interpretation of the foreign policy arena on the part of the policy maker. These variables enhance the effect which the head of state's methods of processing information have on foreign policy. The specific methods of processing information of interest here are the policy maker's cognitive styles (his general ways of interpreting incoming stimuli) and his beliefs about the world.

[7a] The less training in foreign affairs the head of state has had, the more likely his cognitive

styles are to affect foreign policy behavior. [7b] The more training in foreign affairs the head of states has had, the more likely his beliefs about the world are to affect foreign policy behavior.

By training in foreign affairs is meant that before becoming head of state, the policy maker had been a foreign minister, a diplomat, in the foreign ministry, or in the general community dealing with the foreign policy of the nation. The head of state with little or no training in foreign affairs may show little or no interest in the foreign policy of his nation. If, however, he does show interest or is forced by circumstances to attend to foreign policy, he has no expertise to call on. He has no previous experience to suggest possible alternatives or plans of action. His natural problem-solving predispositions come into play. For example, does he usually view objects and persons along many dimensions or along a few dimensions, how flexible is he, does he generally search for information or use what is at hand, what kind of level of risk does he prefer, does he rely on experts or loyal supporters for information?

The head of state with training, on the other hand, probably has some interest in foreign policy and has some knowledge about what will succeed and fail in the international arena. As a result of his experience he has very likely developed strong beliefs about the effects of certain strategies in foreign affairs and about his nation's ability to be successful in its foreign policy.

My exploratory research (M. Hermann, 1974) has some results that bear on these two propositions. Of the head of state personality-foreign policy correlations over .50 for heads of state without training, 67 percent (6 out of 9) involved cognitive style variables (cognitive complexity, dogmatism) while 75 percent (6 out of 8) of the correlations over .50 for heads of state with training involved beliefs about the world (nationalism, belief in ability to control events).

[8] *The more ambiguous the external national situation is perceived to be, the more likely the information-processing systems of the head of state are to affect foreign policy behavior.*

This hypothesis has been proposed by a number of writers on personality and politics (e.g., Goldhamer, 1950; Greenstein, 1969; Jervis, 1969; Levinson, 1958; Verba, 1969). Budner (1962) suggests that there are at least three types of ambiguity: the situation which is completely new and never experienced before, the situation which is highly complex with a great number of cues to consider, and the situation with contradictory cues. A fourth type of ambiguous situation is that with relatively few cues to define it.

In a completely new event, Goldhamer (1950) argues that the individual's initial reaction reflects his own cognitive styles and cognitive mapping of the situation; there is no previous experience to rely on. The head of state meeting the completely new event is much like the head of state without training. In the complex event, Levinson (1958, p. 9) states "the person can choose on the basis of personal congeniality." In order to make the complex situation easier to handle, the attitudes and beliefs of the leader may selectively influence what he perceives as important. Similarly, the situations which provide contradictory cues or few cues also invite interpretation in terms of the leader's attitudes and beliefs about the nature of the world. As Holsti (1962, p. 244) indicates, "a decision maker acts upon his 'image' of the situation rather than upon 'objective' reality." The leader's interpretation of "objective reality" is probably particularly pronounced in ambiguous situations where there are relatively few cues and some definition of the situation is demanded.

The following example shows the effect of information processing systems on political behavior in ambiguous situations. In September 1963 Kennedy sent Marine General Victor H. Krulak of the counter-insurgency task force and Joseph A. Mendenhall of the Far Eastern Bureau in the State Department to Vietnam on a fact-finding mission. In reporting to the National Security Council on their trip, Krulak indicated that antiwar demonstrations had little effect on the success of the war effort, while Mendenhall argued that political dissent threatened to unravel the war. "Were you two gentlemen in the same country?" was Kennedy's reply (see Schlesinger, 1965, p. 993).

One caution with regard to this hypothesis is that the situation *must* be perceived as ambiguous by the head of state. Probably situations perceived as ambiguous at the lower levels of the foreign policy bureaucracy are already interpreted and defined by the time they reach the foreign minister or head of state. Ambiguous situations which are considered to involve some threat to high-priority goals may be the only such situations reaching higher-level decision makers before being interpreted and defined.

The eight propositions just discussed represent a first cut at stating under what conditions leader personality will affect foreign policy. They suggest, in effect, that if one focuses on a highly select group of policy makers who are in a position to influence foreign policy—heads of state—and looks at those times when these policy makers will almost certainly be participants in foreign policy making or at the conditions which lead to some interpretation of the foreign policy arena by these policy makers, leader personality will have an effect on foreign policy. These propositions suggest the dependence of leader personality on characteristics of the political regime as well as bureaucratic and situational variables for its effect on foreign policy. These propositions are illustrative of the kinds of interrelationships among the independent variables or "determinants" of foreign policy which it seems important for students of comparative foreign policy to be exploring if we are to achieve a well-balanced and integrated theory of foreign policy.

REFERENCES

Apter, David E. 1968. "Nkrumah, Charisma, and the Coup." *Daedalus* 97: 757-92.

Borgatta, Edgar F., Arthur S. Couch, and Robert F. Bales. 1962. "Some Findings Relevant to the Great Man Theory of Leadership." In *Small Groups,* ed. A. Paul Hare, Edgar F. Borgatta, and Robert F. Bales, pp. 568-74. New York: Knopf.

Bronfenbrenner, Urie. 1960. "Personality and Participation: The Case of the Vanishing Variables." *Journal of Social Issues* 16: 54-63.

Buchan, Alastair. 1966. *Crisis Management.* Boulogne-sur-Seine, France: Atlantic Institute.

Budner, Stanley. 1962. "Intolerance of Ambiguity as a Personality Variable." *Journal of Personality* 30: 29-50.

Byars, Robert S. 1972. "The Task/Affect Quotient: A Technique for Measuring Orientations of Political Leaders." *Comparative Political Studies* 5: 109-20.

———. 1973. "Small-Group Theory and Shifting Styles of Political Leadership." *Comparative Political Studies* 5: 443-69.

Cleveland, Harlan. 1963. "Crisis Diplomacy." *Foreign Affairs* 41: 638.

Cutright, P. 1963. "National Political Development: Measurement and Analysis." *American Sociological Review* 28: 253-64.

Dettman, Paul R. 1974. "Leaders and Structures in 'Third World' Politics." *Comparative Politics* 6: 245-69.

Fiedler, Fred E. 1967. *A Theory of Leadership Effectiveness.* New York: McGraw-Hill.

Gibb, Cecil A. 1969. "Leadership." In *The Handbook of Social Psychology* (2d ed.), ed. Gardner Lindzey and Elliot Aronson, vol. 4, pp. 205-82. Reading, Mass.: Addison-Wesley.

Goldhamer, Herbert. 1950. "Public Opinion and Personality." *American Journal of Sociology* 55: 346-54.

Greenstein, Fred I. 1969. *Personality and Politics.* Chicago: Markham.

Hermann, Charles F. 1969. *Crises in Foreign Policy: A Simulation Analysis.* Indianapolis: Bobbs-Merrill.

———, ed. 1972. *International Crises: Insights from Behavioral Research.* New York: Free Press.

Hermann, Margaret G. 1974. "Leader Personality and Foreign Policy Behavior." In *Comparing Foreign Policies,* ed. James N. Rosenau, pp. 201-34. Beverly Hills: Sage.

Hilsman, Roger. 1959. "The Foreign Policy Consensus: An Interim Research Report." *Journal of Conflict Resolution* 3: 361-82.

Hoffmann, Stanley, and Inge Hoffmann. 1968. "The Will to Grandeur: De Gaulle as Political Artist." *Daedalus* 97: 829-87.

Hollander, E. P., and J. W. Julian. 1970. "Studies in Leader Legitimacy, Influence, and Innovation." *Advances in Experimental Social Psychology* 5: 33-69.

Holsti, Ole R. 1962. "The Belief System and National Images: A Case Study." *Journal of Conflict Resolution* 6: 244-52.

Hook, Sidney. 1943. *The Hero in History.* New York: John Day.

Jervis, Robert. 1969. "Hypotheses on Misperception." In *International Politics and Foreign Policy* (rev. ed.), ed. James N. Rosenau, pp. 239-54. New York: Free Press.

Kolko, Joyce, and Gabriel Kolko. 1972. *The Limits of Power: The World and United States Foreign Policy, 1945-1954.* New York: Harper & Row.

Leontief, Wassily. 1963. "When Should History Be Written Backwards?" *Economic History Review* 16: 1-8.

Levinson, Daniel J. 1958. "The Relevance of Personality for Political Participation." *Public Opinion Quarterly* 22: 3-10.

Merlin, Samuel. 1968. *The Search for Peace in the Middle East.* New York: Yoseloff.

Olsen, M. E. 1968. "Multivariate Analysis of National Political Development." *American Sociological Review* 33: 699-712.

Paige, Glenn D., ed. 1972. *Political Leadership.* New York: Free Press.

Pruitt, Dean G. 1964-1965. *Problem Solving in the Department of State.* Monograph Series in World Affairs, No. 2. Denver: Univ. of Denver, Social Science Foundation and Dept. of International Relations.

Rosenau, James N. 1968. "Private Preferences and Political Responsibilities: The Relative Potency of Individual and Role Variables in the Behavior of U.S. Senators." In *Quantitative International Politics,* ed. J. David Singer, pp. 17-50. New York: Free Press.

Schlesinger, Arthur M., Jr. 1965. *A Thousand Days.* Boston: Houghton Mifflin.

Shils, Edward A. 1954. "Authoritarianism: 'Right' and 'Left.'" In *Studies in the Scope and Method of "The Authoritarian Personality,"* ed. Richard Christie and Marie Jahoda. Glencoe, Ill.: Free Press.

Snyder, Richard C., and James A. Robinson. 1961. *National and International Decision-Making.* New York: Institute for International Order.

Sorensen, Theodore C. *Kennedy.* New York: Harper & Row.

Stassen, Glen H. 1972. "Individual Preference versus Role-Constraint in Policy-Making: Senatorial Response to Secretaries Acheson and Dulles." *World Politics* 25: 96-119.

Stogdill, Ralph M. 1974. *Handbook of Leadership Research.* New York: Free Press.

Tucker, Robert C. 1965. "The Dictator and Totalitarianism." *World Politics* 17: 55-83.

———. 1968. "The Theory of Charismatic Leadership." *Daedalus* 97: 731-56.

Verba, Sidney. 1969. "Assumptions of Rationality and Non-rationality in Models of the International System." In *International Politics and Foreign Policy* (rev. ed.), ed. James N. Rosenau, pp. 217-31. New York: Free Press.

Willner, Ann R., and Dorothy Willner. 1965. "The Rise and Role of Charismatic Leaders." *Annals of the American Academy of Political and Social Science* 358: 77-88.

36. Resources in Comparative Analysis

John D. Sullivan

The late 1960s saw the development within the United States of an ecological or environmental movement concerned with the degradation of the nation's physical environment as a result of population growth and economic development. Near the end of the decade and in the first two years of the 1970s, this concern moved beyond the borders of this country and became an international issue. The reasons were quite simple. It became obvious to many observers that we were living on a "spaceship earth" with limited room and limited physical resources. In addition, it also became obvious that pollution ignored political boundaries and that it could be the case that existing political institutions would be incapable of resolving environmental and resource conflicts and that new institutions would have to be created. This chapter addresses itself to this topic and makes a strong plea that students of comparative foreign policy will increasingly have to incorporate resource and environmental variables in their analyses and proposes a framework for such analyses.

One dominant mode of thought in international relations theorizing views the international political system as one in which actors compete for scarce resources. The resources over which the actors compete include such things as territory, allies, material resources, political stability—intra-state, regional, and global—military security, etc. In the past, the structure of that competition has been almost anarchic in that neither the international system nor any regional system had anything approaching a parallel to a government or organized political system which played a role in conflict reduction and conflict management. Rather, nations engaged in what might be called a process of "strategic interaction" in efforts to resolve or manage conflicts which arose between them. While this mode of interaction often had catastrophic results—such as World War I and II—it did produce global and regional stability much of the time.

Many observers point to recent trends in international politics which they deem such as to insure the collapse of the international system as we know it if steps to develop transnational organizations are not taken. Phenomena such as arms races between superpowers and between lesser powers (Falk, 1971), the burgeoning problem of rapid population growth, particularly in underdeveloped countries (Erlich and Erlich, 1970), and the increasingly large problem of resource depletion, maldistribution of global resources, and environmental degradation, have been viewed as problems almost beyond human control at this point in time.[1] Thus, many have called for a drastic rethinking of man's current mode of social, economic, and political organizations and point to a pressing need for action to forestall disaster.

While the picture in many respects does look extremely bleak—witness the recent "cod war" between Great Britain and Iceland—there are signs which suggest that the so-called environmental crisis may provide a basis for international and regional cooperation in decision making about resource and environmental matters. Here one can point to the United Nations Stockholm conference as well as indications of regional cooperation in such areas as the Mediterranean and the Baltic Sea.

Whatever the prospects of conflict and cooperation and whatever one's view of the proximity or distance of "global system collapse," it seems quite clear to many observers that the nations which comprise the international system can no longer pursue goals and resolve conflicts in unilateral, bilateral, or limited multilateral fashion. It seems increasingly clear that regional and global cooperative schemes will have to be worked out and that nations will have to forego the mode of "strategic interaction" in conflict reduction. While the prospects for increased regional and global cooperation seem rather dim at present, it is likely that the force of events will impel nations in this direction and that efforts to reinforce current cooperative efforts will be made and new approaches initiated.

In part, this may involve the search for and the implementation of strategies to develop positive "collective goods" at the regional and international level (Russett and Sullivan, 1971). In any event, the "ecology of micromotives" which Schelling discussed (1971) applies equally to nations as to individuals; that is, individual actors in pursuit of private goals (micromotives) will often produce social effects, effects which are often negative in character and which, in the long run, work against the attainment of private goals. One clear way to avoid such negative social consequences—negative externalities, to employ a more technical term—is to construct some sort of a social decision system which includes provisions for the identification of possible negative social effects of nation-state action and the development of strategies to avoid such consequences.

Given the judgement that issues of resource allocation and environmental quality are—among many other factors—likely to play an increasingly important role in the foreign policies of nations—both developed and underdeveloped—it is appropriate to inquire into ways in which analytical tools can be developed to permit the analyses of such factors. One purpose of this paper is to propose a conceptual framework which permits the identification of certain types of linkages between societal variables in a nation and resource factors both in foreign policy target nations and in "shared environments."

Let us turn now to an examination of the proposed framework, which is presented in Figure 1, and its implications for the comparative study of foreign policy. Only a very small number of the total possible linkages between the actors in the framework have been identified in this paper. It is

[1] For two statements of this view see Forrester (1971) and Meadows et al. (1972). Sullivan et al. (1973) attempt a less pessimistic analysis.

Figure 1. A Resource-oriented Foreign Policy Framework

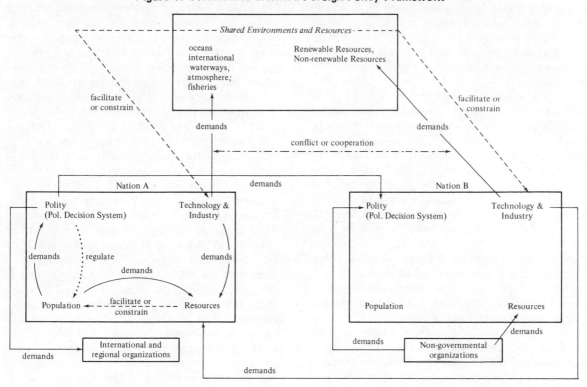

clear that one could complicate this framework enormously by identifying additional linkages and linkages which connected rather a large number of factors both within and between nations and between nations and "non-national" elements of the framework. For the purposes of this brief note, the linkages identified in Figure 1 will suffice.

Consider, in addition, the level of abstraction contained in Figure 1. In some respects it is rather more concrete than some existing frameworks, such as McGowan and Shapiro (1973) in that it identifies concrete linkages within and between actors in terms of demands, constraints, or facilitating linkages. On the other hand, it is rather more abstract than a Forrester-type model (1971) in that it has fewer elements and feedback loops and it does not have the dynamic character that the Forrester model has. It is clear that this is one direction in which future development of this framework will have to move.

Let us examine now the various aspects of this framework. First, this scheme assumes that there are three general types of linkages between the various elements: behaviors or linkages which *demand* a certain class of responses; behaviors or linkages which *facilitate* or *constrain* a certain class of responses; and behaviors or linkages which *regulate* a certain class of responses. Thus, it is postulated that there are three general classes of linkages between elements in the system, but at this stage of development no claim is made that only certain linkages can be associated with certain elements in the framework.

Consider now some specific linkages as presented in Figure 1. First, looking at Nation A, we note that population makes demands on the polity, which in turn makes an effort to regulate the population (or some subset of the total population). If the demand directed at the polity involved some aspect of the population's lifestyle, this might result in a foreign policy output from Nation A to another nation or to a nonnational element such as an ocean resource. Thus, population demands regarding food products might result in outputs to a nonnational element such as an international fishery in the form of a demand or exploitation of that fishery for food products. Alternatively, it might result in a demand to another polity for food products such as wheat, meat, oil, etc. In either case, the response will be a linkage which either facilitates or constrains the behavior of the nation making the demand. In the case of an international fishery, for instance, the fish stock may be sufficiently depleted so as to make it impossible for the nation to have its demands met; thus, its behavior will be constrained. The polity, in turn, may be forced to regulate the behavior of the segment of the population making the demand and attempt to channel its behavior in a different direction, perhaps to consider the consumption of an alternative, previously unpalatable, food product.

It is obvious that one could explore a wide range of additional linkages involving a variety of substantive problem areas in addition to demands by a population for a certain type of food product. Thus, the framework is amenable to the examination of linkages in many of the areas of interest to one concerned with resource management between nations; it can easily be extended to include issues such as military security and political stability. It is obvious that one important area of future development of this framework will be the further specification of the three types of linkages and the identification of testable hypotheses. Let us now turn to some aspects of this framework which provide some interesting points of departure for analysis.

The framework explicitly identifies classes of *targets* of foreign policy outputs in addition to other nation-states. Three types of targets other than nation-states are identified: shared environments and resources, international and regional organizations, and nongovernmental organizations. A word is in order about these four targets. It is obvious that students of comparative foreign policy will continue to devote much of their attention to the nation-state as a target of the foreign policies of members of the international system. This focus makes considerable sense in that an

important concern of nations is, and will continue to be, the actions and goals of other nations. Increasingly, however, it is becoming apparent that other actors and arenas are emerging as important for the foreign policies of nation-states and these actors and arenas should be incorporated into frameworks for competitive foreign policy analyses.

Looking at the linkages between the different types of actors and targets, we observe that this framework suggests the following things. First the linkages between nations as actors are similar to those found in other frameworks in that it is assumed that nations emit certain kinds of actions to other nations, in this case demands, and that the response may take the form of a subsequent demand or an activity designed to facilitate or constrain the behavior of the original actor. Thus, this framework represents no major departure from previous efforts in this respect. Turning to the other targets and arenas, however, it seems that this framework does suggest focusing on aspects of foreign policy not heretofore made as explicit in comparative foreign policy schemes.

It is increasingly obvious that the general arena of shared or common resources will continue to be one in which nations will find the opportunity, and in many cases the necessity, of either cooperative or conflictual interactions and arrangements. As noted above, there is currently a conflict between the United Kingdom and Iceland over fisheries off the coast of Iceland. This particular conflict is a clear example of an international conflict with linkages to domestic factors in that both countries depend rather heavily on that particular fishery. Fishery disputes are not limited to these two countries, however, and the expectation is that the demand upon international fisheries will increase and that more conflicts such as those between Iceland and the United Kingdom and between the United States and Peru over tuna fishing in the Pacific will emerge.[2] Conflicts over ocean food resources are not the only areas of existing and future differences between nations. There is currently an ongoing debate about the presumed sea-bed mineral resources and how they should be exploited and for whose benefit. In turn, this has led to considerable conflict over the

2See Christy and Scott (1972) for a complete discussion of this problem.

whole issue of the length and nature of ocean territorial boundaries of the nations of the globe. In short, the oceans as a shared or common arena are currently an important source of international conflict and cooperation, and the expectation is that they will continue to grow in importance to nations with growing resource and food needs.

Other shared arenas will continue to grow in importance in the foreign relations of nations in the international system. Regional and international waters, for instance, are of growing importance to nations and in Europe, in particular, some efforts have been made to establish cooperative arrangements for the management and distribution of water derived from certain international waterways.[3] Again, the potential exists for both cooperation and conflict and it is increasingly clear that efforts will have to be made to both analyze the potential for cooperation and to begin to foster such cooperative efforts.

Another resource area which has been the source of conflict between nations recently is the oil resources of the Arab countries. In the fall of 1973, the Arab oil-producing countries imposed an embargo on the sale of crude oil to the West which resulted in an energy "crisis." Aside from its domestic repercussions in the United States, the crisis caused Japan radically to change its policy toward the Middle East conflict to support of the Arab countries and it caused many European nations to adopt a stance independent of the United States. Thus, the fact that the Arab nations controlled a resource necessary to the economic well-being of Japan and Europe *constrained* the foreign policy positions of these countries and affected the relationships between the United States and these countries. The repercussions of this issue continue to affect both United States domestic and foreign policy.

Thus, it is suggested that this proposed framework points to one important national-international linkage that has been somewhat ignored in the recent past but that will, in the contemporary environment of international politics, become increasingly important to nations and hence an important concern for the foreign policy analyst. In particular, it will become important for the

analyst to begin to devise ways in which he can begin to incorporate such factors into his schema and to derive testable hypotheses about the impact of these factors on the foreign policies of national actors. This framework only suggests the necessity of doing so at the present, but this will be discussed below.

The remaining two nonnational actors are rather obvious and need only be noted in passing. International organizations are obvious targets of national foreign policies as well as factors which may facilitate or constrain national action. Similarly, such nongovernmental organizations as multinational corporations, ecology organizations, peace research groups, etc. are coming to play an increasingly important role in international politics. Accordingly, this framework suggests the necessity of identifying them as separate factors in comparative foreign policy analyses. This will become increasingly important if as, this writer estimates, questions of resource exploitation and distribution become paramount and international and regional organizations come to play larger roles in the resolution of conflict over such issues. Again, it seems necessary for a foreign policy analyst to begin to deal explicitly with such linkages.

From a broader perspective, it is increasingly clear that traditional "cold war" coalitions are breaking up partly as a result of conflict over resources. The maneuvering among nations before and during the recent Law of the Sea Conference at Caracas provides one important example (Brown and Fabian, 1974). That conference found the United States and the Soviet Union aligned on some issues and China siding very forcefully with the Third World on other issues, while the Soviet Union and Japan coalesced on yet other issues. Given the expectation that this trend will continue, it becomes imperative that comparative foreign policy analysts attend more completely to the growing role of resources and the environment in international conflict *and* cooperation. The framework discussed above provides one starting point for such analyses.

REFERENCES

[3]See Kneese and Bower (1968) for a discussion of management of European waterways.

Brown, Seyom, and Larry L. Fabian. 1974. "Diplomats at Sea." *Foreign Affairs* 50 (Jan): 301-21.

Christy, Francis T., and Anthony Scott. 1972. *The Common Wealth in Ocean Fisheries*. Baltimore: Johns Hopkins.

Erlich, Paul R., and Anne H. Erlich. 1970. *Population, Resources, Environment*. San Francisco: Freeman.

Falk, Richard. 1971. *This Endangered Planet*. New York: Random House.

Forrester, J. W. 1971. *World Dynamics*. Cambridge, Mass.: Wright-Allen.

Kneese, A., and B. Bower. 1968. *Managing Water Quality: Economics, Technology, Institutions*. Baltimore: Johns Hopkins.

McGowan, P. J., and H. B. Shapiro. 1973. *The Comparative Study of Foreign Policy: A Survey of Scientific*

Findings. Beverly Hills: Sage.

Meadows, Donella, et al. 1972. *The Limits to Growth*. New York: Universe Books.

Russett, B., and J. D. Sullivan. 1971. "Collective Goods and International Organization." *International Organization* 25 (Autumn): 845-65.

Schelling, T. 1971. "On the Ecology of Micro-motives." *Public Interest* (Fall).

Sullivan, J. D., et al. 1973. "Identifying Alternative International Systems: Modifications of Forrester's World Dynamics Model." Paper presented at the Annual Meeting of the International Studies Association of the West, San Francisco.

37. Politics and Ecology, Easton and Rosenau: An Alternative Research Priority

Eugene R. Wittkopf

The comparative study of foreign policy is a relatively young field of inquiry born of the perceived need to bridge the gap between specialists in comparative politics and specialists in international

SPECIAL NOTE: Numerous individuals and institutions have contributed to the research presented in the paper. All share in my gratitude, but none is responsible for the analyses or interpretations presented here. The UN roll-call data were made available by the Inter-university Consortium for Political Research. The data were originally collected by Charles Wrigley. The UN budget, delegation, permanent mission, and sponsorship data were made available by Kurt Jacobsen of the International Peace Research Institute, Oslo. Acquisition of the federal budget data was made possible by a grant from the Division of Sponsored Research of the University of Florida. The Department of Political Science of the University of Florida also lent support to the research, including the funds necessary for acquisition of the PRIO data. Alfred B. Clubok and Eric M. Uslaner provided many helpful suggestions; Arthur G. Haller, D. W. Jolley, and Dwight Lambert all provided valuable assistance during various phases of the research.

relations (Rosenau, 1966, 1971a). The seminal work in the field is probably Rosenau's "Pretheories and Theories of Foreign Policy" (1966), for it was with the appearance of this article that a body of theoretical propositions and related empirical research began to focus on the question of how foreign policy outputs of nation-states are determined by the combined impact of internal and external considerations. What Rosenau did was to generate a typology of states based on their physical resources and geography, the state of their economy, and the state of their polity based on the assumption that the combined impact of these variables would affect the "relative potency" of five "source variables"—individual, role, governmental, societal, and systemic—which in turn were assumed to be the primary determinants of foreign policy outputs.

For all its innovation and insight, quite apart from the research it has spurred (Rosenau, Hermann, and Burgess, 1973), the Rosenau pre-theory looks strikingly similar to the framework for political analysis developed by David Easton. What Easton argues, of course, is that the political system is that part of the social system that converts demands stemming from the intra- and extra-societal environment into policy outputs. Although Rosenau takes Easton to task for arguing that the "authoritative allocation of values" necessarily occurs in a "society" (Rosenau, 1966, p. 61), he leaves largely unscathed the notion that the critical role of the political system is the conversion process whereby inputs are translated into outputs. Instead, Rosenau's primary contribution in the "pre-theories" article appears to lie in the argument that type of nation may explain foreign policy behavior. Conversion, then, remains the important function of politics. Unfortunately, however, much of the empirical work in comparative foreign policy has ignored this essential function of politics, focusing instead on patterned variations in environmental inputs, particularly as they are reflected in Rosenau's genotypic categories, as they relate to variations in foreign policy outputs.[1]

Clearly, any adequate understanding of phenomena as complex as foreign policy requires multidisciplinary expertise; the economist, the geographer, and the psychologist may well have contributions to make to our understanding that are equally or more important than the contributions made by political scientists. Clearly also, disciplinary boundaries may obscure rather than illuminate those behavioral phenomena we are seeking to understand. It is unfortunate, however, that political scientists have rather willingly abandoned their own area of expertise, concentrating on "ecological" rather than political explanations of foreign policy outcomes. At the same time, it must be recognized that political scientists have been in the forefront of efforts aimed at the development of measureable empirical referents of

foreign policy. Indeed, the "events data movement" represents a substantial contribution toward the delineation and description of foreign policy outputs. As our ability to describe foreign policy outcomes increases, it seems necessary to turn—or return—to the task of relating policy outcomes to the critical role that political factors play in the conversion of inputs into outputs.[2]

What follow are two examples of research design that attempts to relate foreign policy outcomes to reasonably explicit measures of political phenomena. Both are addressed to what is believed to be one of the causes for the dominant emphasis on ecology, rather than politics, in comparative studies of foreign policy. Before proceeding with these examples, however, it would perhaps be useful to provide at least some evidence for the rather bold assertion that ecology rather than politics has indeed been the dominant focus.

In part, this assertion is based on an intuitive feeling about the work being done by the Interuniversity Comparative Foreign Policy Project (ICFP), a group of scholars whose work over the course of several years has in some respects tended to "define" the comparative study of foreign policy. Thus a perusal of the titles included in the Rosenau, Hermann, and Burgess (1973) account of the intellectual history of ICFP suggests a persistent, if not dominant, concern with foreign policy explanations linked to Rosenau's genotypic variables. (A growing concern for events analysis appears to be another dominant concern.) This is all the more interesting since the Rosenau et al. history of ICFP suggests that the initial research strategy agreed upon was to test the foreign policy behavior of states falling *within* each of the eight genotypic categories, which presumably means that the focus was on the relative potency of the source variables rather than on the genotypic categories themselves (Rosenau, Hermann, and Burgess, 1973, pp. 123-24).

[1] Interestingly, specialists in comparative politics appear to be moving in the direction of focusing attention on variations in policy outcomes exhibited by various political systems rather than on political systems per se, with the explanatory emphasis placed on variations in the type of policy. Groth (1971) is illustrative of this trend. Nothing comparable exists in the comparative foreign policy field.

[2] The experience of analysts working in comparative state politics should be instructive. After an initial burst of enthusiasm for environmental explanations, which has been supported by an impressive array of empirical research documenting the importance of socioeconomic explanations, many political science analysts have turned their attention to a delineation of those policy areas in which political factors either are dominant or add important explanatory power. Fry and Winters (1970) provide a brief review of these trends.

Somewhat less impressionistic evidence about the relative emphasis in comparative foreign policy can be gleaned from the propositional inventory recently published by McGowan and Shapiro (1973). As a device for organizing their summary of the current state of the comparative foreign policy field, McGowan and Shapiro provide a framework which suggests that foreign policy outputs can be "accounted for by a set of independent variables, of which nine categories are attributes of the actor and two are attributes of the external environment." Also, they add a category called "decision-making," and a second called "feedback." The former is conceptualized as an intervening variable through which the eleven categories of independent variables must operate in order to affect foreign policy; and the latter is conceptualized as the process whereby national actors' foreign policy behavior affects the environment as well as the way in which foreign policy affects the initiating actor itself.

Rosenau (1966, p. 42) argues that "all foreign policy analysts either explain the external behavior of societies in terms of five sets of variables, or they proceed in such a way that their explanations can be recast in terms of the five sets." These five sets are, of course, the source variables cited earlier. Following Rosenau's argument, we should be able to collapse the eleven categories of independent variables used by McGowan and Shapiro to determine the relative research emphasis in comparative foreign policy analyses to determine whether greater emphasis has been placed on ecological than on political explanations.

Table 1 shows the relative proportion of attention in McGowan and Shapiro devoted to their eleven explanatory variables, rearranged according to Rosenau's five source variables. Rosenau's three genotypic variables have also been merged with what seems the most appropriate source variable. If we regard the first three Rosenau categories as those most closely akin to "political" variables and the last two as reflecting essentially an "ecological" perspective, the evidence, while hardly overwhelming, does rather clearly point to the underrepresentation of political explanations of foreign policy phenomena.

McGowan and Shapiro's "decision-making" and "feedback" variables have been excluded from Table 1, largely because neither seems to fit very

Table 1.   Proportion of the McGowan-Shapiro Propositional Inventory Devoted to Rosenau's Analytical Categories

Source Variable, Rosenau Category	Explanatory Variable, McGowan-Shapiro Category	Proportion of Pages		Proportion of Propositions	
		No.	%	No.	%
Individual	Individual	10	8.9	5	5.4
Role	Elite	4	3.6	2	2.2
Governmental	Establishment	5	4.5	4	4.3
(State of the	Political	15	13.4	13	14.1
polity)	Governmental	12	10.7	10	10.9
SUBTOTAL		46	41.1	34	37.0
Societal	Economic	10	8.9	10	10.9
(State of the	Societal	7	6.3	8	8.7
economy)	Cultural	7	6.3	6	6.5
Systemic	Linkage (history)	12	10.7	10	10.9
(Geography)	Others' policies	12	10.7	9	9.8
	Systemic	18	16.1	15	16.3
SUBTOTAL		66	58.9	58	63.0
TOTAL		112	100.0	92	100.0

well with Rosenau's assertion that "all foreign policy analysts either explain the external behavior of societies in terms of five sets of variables, or they proceed in such a way that their explanations can be recast in terms of the five sets." But if we follow Rosenau's assertion, it seems most appropriate to place decision-making with the political variables and feedback with the ecological. Following this procedure, the proportion of political to ecological explanations changes only slightly, and does not remove the relatively greater emphasis given to nonpolitical explanations. What is especially interesting, however, is that both of these variables themselves represent very small proportions of the overall attention in the propositional inventory. Since the decision-making variable is the only explanatory category that clearly and unambiguously taps the conversion process that Easton calls the critical role of the political system, this very small emphasis only serves to underscore the point of this brief perspective on the state of comparative foreign policy—ecology has received more emphasis than politics.

The relative underemphasis on feedback mechanisms suggests another feature about comparative foreign policy analyses, namely, that they have ignored the impact of foreign policy outputs on the initiating actors (McGowan and Shapiro, 1973, p. 211). The reason appears to lie in the overwhelming emphasis given to cross-sectional research designs (McGowan and Shapiro, 1973, p. 14) in studying foreign policy comparatively. This emphasis, in turn, appears to lie at the heart of any explanation of the causes of the ecological emphasis in the field. Indeed, in some respects it would appear that cross-sectional, or *cross-national*, was initially conceived as the distinguishing feature of comparative foreign policy. Thus Rosenau et al. (1973, pp. 123, 127, 128) at several points use terms like "genuinely comparative" to describe the commitment of ICFP members, and they explicitly define "genuinely comparative" as "cross-national" (p. 122; see also Hermann, 1972, p. 59). Moreover, they illustrate the meaning of the terms by describing the initial work of the ICFP as being directed toward analysis of the foreign policy behavior of two or more national societies.

A movement away from the excessively restrictive definition of comparative foreign policy

analysis as cross-national inquiry can be discerned in many quarters. Certainly the definition used by McGowan and Shapiro (1973, p. 36) to guide their propositional inventory is not restricted to cross-national analyses. Instead, they define foreign policy analyses as being comparative if they "examine either two or more actors, i.e., states or subunits of states, or two or more comparable instances of behavior of one or more actors." This is a much more open-ended conceptualization of the comparative study of foreign policy, one that we hope will enable us to move rapidly away from the dominant cross-national emphasis which has in turn limited the attention that comparative foreign policy studies have given to explicitly political phenomena.

The research examples that follow measure foreign policy outputs as (1) roll-call votes in the UN General Assembly; and (2) budgetary expenditures of the federal government for foreign policy activities as they are distributed domestically. The roll-call example will utilize longitudinal analysis to examine the foreign policy behavior of a single actor (the United States);[3] the budgetary example conceptualizes foreign policy as one form of public policy and is based on the assumption that foreign policy has a measureable impact on the acting society itself. In both examples an effort is made to relate the outputs analyzed to reasonably explicit measures of political phenomena. It should be noted at the outset, however, that the results of the analyses are generally unexciting and disappointing. This is less important, however—as, indeed, are the examples themselves—than is the argument that greater priority in terms of our research should be given to political phenomena, and that moving away from research designs that conceptualize comparative analysis as cross-national analysis may provide a vehicle for shifting research priorities from ecology to politics.

POLITICAL SUCCESS IN THE UN GENERAL ASSEMBLY

Fifteen years ago roll-call votes in the UN were a widely used source of quantifiable information

---

[3]Wittkopf (1975) uses longitudinal analysis comparable to that reported here to compare Soviet and American political success in the UN General Assembly.

on the foreign policy behavior of nations. Since that time, however, roll calls have been replaced by other measureable referents of foreign policy.

A number of good reasons can be adduced for the movement away from roll-call studies. Principal among these is the relative lack of richness of the data, which in turn limits the number of research questions that can be asked of the data. Roll-call votes do not provide information on the nuance of behavior presumed to be so much a part of foreign policy. They do not provide information on why states vote in the way they do or on the intensity of their convictions on different issues. They do not provide information that would enable researchers to link the choices made by states to the various proponents or opponents of policy alternatives within a national society. They in no way exhaust all, and perhaps not even the most relevant, issues on the "international agenda" at any particular point in time. And even those issues that are on the intra-organizational agenda will not necessarily be decided by a roll call.

These are all compelling arguments for searching out new sources of information on foreign policy. At the same time, however, the advantages that were first seen in looking at voting behavior still seem appropriate. UN roll calls provide an easily accessible source of information about the positions that nearly all extant states take on a wide range of international issues within known institutional procedures and constraints. Also, we now have such information going back for more than a quarter of a century, which means we have a clear opportunity to analyze at least one aspect of states' foreign policy behavior longitudinally. By the end of 1970 over 3,550 roll-call votes, by between 55 and 127 states, had been taken in the plenary meetings of the General Assembly and its seven main committees. This is an impressive array of information that, at least in my judgment, deserves some additional attention.

For purposes of illustrating how UN roll calls might be analyzed longitudinally, I have chosen as the dependent variable the "support level" (SL) index developed by Brams and O'Leary (1970). The index measures the proportion of times that an individual Assembly member votes with the majority across a set of roll calls above or below an expected value, where the expected value is calcu-

lated on the basis of the proportion of all Assembly members that support the majority across a set of roll calls. SL is a probabilistic measure calculated according to two criteria: the more frequently a member votes in support of the majority, the higher will be its support level score; *and* the fewer the number of members voting with the majority, the higher will be the score of those that did vote for the majority position. In other words, the support level index is a weighted measure that accounts for the size of the winning coalition on each roll call. If we make a rational actor assumption about states' voting behavior— that all states will attempt to maximize the number of times that they can vote with the majority coalition, for whatever reason, and that all states will attempt to minimize the number of times they vote with the minority—then we can interpret the SL index as a measure of states' *political success* in the General Assembly.

I have calculated SL scores—political success scores—for all UN members in 24 of the first 25 sessions of the General Assembly (1946-1970). (The one-vote nineteenth session has been excluded.) The resulting calculations for the United States are shown in Figure 1. Zero indicates the point at which the United States would have agreed as often with the majority as expected on the basis of the behavior of all Assembly members in each session. Points lying above zero represent sessions in which the U.S. agreed more often than expected (i.e., enjoyed a greater degree of political success), and points below zero represent agreement less often than expected (i.e., a lesser degree of political success).

Two features about the political success of the U.S. in General Assembly over the last 25 years are apparent from Figure 1. First, although there is considerable variation in the SL scores from one session to the next, more often than not (in 18 of the 24 sessions) the U.S. has agreed with the majority *less* often than one would expect on the basis of the behavior of the entire body. Although this result might be expected for the sessions occurring in the 1960s (sessions 17 to 25), the low points for 1951-1956 (sessions 6 to 10) certainly do not conform to conventional wisdom about UN politics during these early years. Presumably the U.S. at this time was the dominant power in the organization, and Soviet references to the Ameri-

Figure 1. U.S. Support Level Scores, 1946-1970

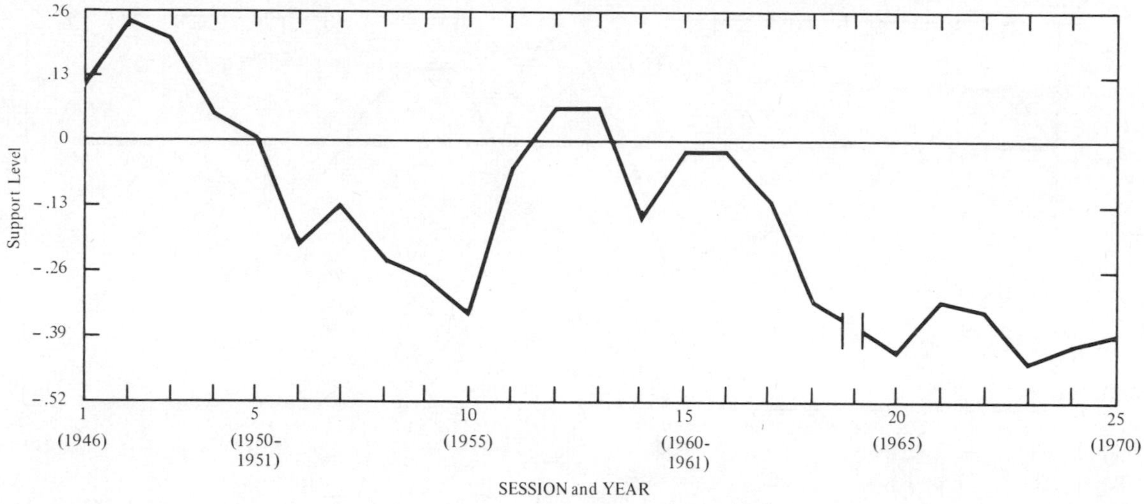

can "mechanical majority" abound in various UN documents. The *SL* scores raise some question about the nature of this dominant "majority." In fact, one questions whether such a majority ever existed. Indeed, the point for session 10, indicating U.S. agreement with the majority 33 percent less often than expected, is not "surpassed" until the *SL* of -0.37 in the twentieth session. Moreover, if Soviet *SL* scores are plotted against those of the U.S. (Wittkopf, 1975), one finds that in 5 of the 14 sessions prior to 1960 (session 15), the Soviet Union actually enjoyed a *greater* degree of political success than did the U.S. In 3 of these 5 sessions the Soviet *SL* scores in fact moved slightly above zero.

The second fact readily apparent from Figure 1 is that over time the United States has enjoyed progressively less political success in the General Assembly, something that does conform to conventional wisdom. A regression line fitted to the *SL* scores shows a statistically significant association between *SL* and time (defined as the number of the Assembly session), with an average decline of 1.98 percent per session. This suggests that the United States has found it more difficult to agree with majority positions over time as the Assembly has grown in size and changed in composition. To account for these factors, the *SL* scores can be "detrended" by using the deviations from the regression line as a new dependent variable. The resulting scores are plotted in Figure 2.

Having defined the dependent variable as detrended *SL* scores, how might we account for fluctuations over time in this measure of U.S. political success? An ecological analysis might search for similarly patterned variations in the size, level of development, and degree of political accountability represented by the U.S. But since these factors are unlikely to vary much given the absence of a cross-national design, they are not very useful explanatory variables. Similarly, the relative impact of role, governmental, societal, or idiosyncratic source variables is unlikely to vary considerably. Instead, then, we might turn to variables relating to the U.S. position within the United Nations in an effort to explain longitudinal variations in its political success.

Kay (1970, pp. 11-42; also Keohane, 1967) has argued that states' missions and delegations to the United Nations, the formal caucusing groups in the Assembly, the limited membership organs of the organization, the negotiations among member states, and the process of presenting and finally voting on resolutions before the world body all represent instruments of influence in the sense that they are used to shape policy outcomes in the United Nations. The empirical utility of some of these variables has been demonstrated by Weigert and Riggs (1969), who use a series of "UN participation indicators" to explain the distribution of Assembly offices among African states. Interestingly, their analysis shows (Weigert and Riggs,

Figure 2. U.S. Support Level Scores with Trend Removed, 1946-1970

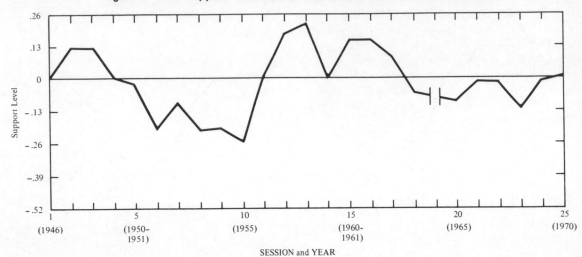

SESSION and YEAR

1969, p. 12) that the UN participation variables account for, on the average, more variation in officeholding than either capability or development indicators. Hence, we might develop specific empirical measures of states' activities in and toward the United Nations and correlate them with their *SL* scores to ascertain whether political success covaries with measures of states' influence or participation in the UN. Some suggestions along these lines as they relate to fluctuations in U.S. political success follow; the results of the correlation analyses are summarized in Table 2.

Table 2.   Correlations between U.S. Political Success in the UN General Assembly, 1946-1970, and Measures of U.S. Influence and Participation in the General Assembly

Independent Variable	r[a]	N[a]
Deviation of U.S. budget assessments from average	.031	24
Deviation of U.S. permanent mission size from average	−.062	24
Deviation of U.S. delegation size from average	.030	24
U.S. sponsorships as a proportion of total sponsorships	−.296	20
Deviation of average U.S. cosponsors from Assembly average	−.017	20
Arab political backing	−.266	20
Benelux political backing	−.125	20
Commonwealth political backing	−.291	20
Latin America political backing	−.082	20
Scandinavia political backing	.122	20
Soviet political backing	−.009	20
Afro-Asia political backing	.362	16
Western Europe political backing	.238	10
Africa political backing	−.729	8

[a]Correlations are Pearson Product-Moment coefficients. *N* refers to the number of Assembly sessions included in the calculations.

The financial and human resources that states devote to the UN are clearly related to the concepts of influence and participation (Clark, O'Leary, and Wittkopf, 1971). These resources can easily be measured by the proportion of the total (regular) UN budget paid by each state, by the number of permanent mission personnel assigned to UN activities, and by the size of the delegation each state sends to the annual Assembly meetings. Assuming that money and personnel represent instruments of influence, we can also assume that the more of such resources that a state devotes to the UN, the more it is likely to be able to influence the content of voting issues in such a way that it can vote in accordance with the majority position across a set of roll calls. In propositional form, then, we would expect a positive association between a state's *SL* scores and the proportion of the UN's regular budget that it supports, the size of its permanent mission, and the size of its Assembly delegation. Because the *SL* scores measure deviations from expected behavior determined by the Assembly as a whole, it seems most appropriate to measure each explanatory variable as the deviation for each state from the average for the Assembly as a whole. Correlations between these measures and the detrended *SL* scores for the U.S. are displayed in Table 2.

My expectations were not well founded. One possible reason, in the case of the assessments, is the absence of substantial fluctuations in the data values. In contrast to the *SL* scores, budget figures change relatively little over short periods of time due to the method employed by the UN Contributions Committee, which sets assessment levels for three-year periods. Little additional variation is introduced even if U.S. assessments are measured as deviations from the average for the body as a whole. In the case of the mission and delegation size variables, however, the absence of variation does not seem to account for the negligible correlations. It is an empirical question whether the absence of meaningful results for the United States would be replicated if the analyses were extended to other members of the U.N.[4] But, insofar as

these results can be generalized, there appears to be little relation between financial and human resources as instruments of political influence and political success in the General Assembly.

States also seek to influence political outcomes in the General Assembly by offering formal proposals for consideration by the body. Presumably, the more proposals it sponsors, the more it is seeking to influence the outcome of Assembly deliberations in such a way that it can vote in accordance with the majority position on issues that come up for roll-call votes. To examine this proposition, the number of U.S. sponsorships in each Assembly session as a proportion of the total number of sponsorships in each session was correlated with the detrended U.S. *SL* scores.[5] The result, as shown in Table 2, is $r = -0.296$.

Again my expectations have clearly not been supported. In part, the magnitude of the negative correlation is due to the outlier effect of the tenth session, in which the U.S. accounts for 19.2 percent of all sponsorships and its detrended *SL* score is -0.258. This sponsorship level compares with an average of 11.7 percent for the U.S. across the 20 sessions for which data are available. Even if the tenth session is excluded from the correlation, however, the relationship remains an inverse one ($r = -0.082$, $N = 19$). It appears, then, that sponsorship activity is also unrelated to political success in the General Assembly.

Perhaps the important relationship is not so much sponsorship activity as *cosponsorship*. States actively seek to build support for their policy proposals by asking other states to back their positions. To the extent that states are successful in their efforts to build such support, we would expect them to vote in accordance with the majority position on issues that come up for roll-call votes. That is, we can hypothesize a positive association between the number of cosponsors of a state's proposals and its level of political success in the General Assembly.

---

[4] The analyses have been extended to India with little difference in the results. The correlations between India's detrended *SL* scores and the assessments, mission, and delegations variables are -0.15, -0.09, and -0.17, respectively.

[5] Sponsorship data are available only for sessions 1 to 21. Sponsorships are defined (Jacobsen, 1969, p. 237) as "any written communication from a UN member presented in any of the organs of the General Assembly, which has received a code number so that it is listed in the 'Check List of Documents' of the *Official Records of the General Assembly,* and which contains a specific proposal, suggestion, etc."

This proposition has been examined for the United States in two different ways. First, the average number of cosponsors of U.S.-supported proposals in each Assembly session have been measured as deviations from the average for the body as a whole. Second, the number of U.S. sponsorships shared with members of the nine formal caucusing groups in the General Assembly has been measured. The groups examined are the Soviet bloc plus the Scandinavian, Benelux, Arab, Latin American, Commonwealth, Afro-Asian, Western European, and African caucusing groups. The first six of these groups have been operative since the first Assembly session, the Afro-Asian caucus became a formal group in the fifth session, the Western European caucus in the eleventh session, and the African caucus in the thirteenth session (Hovet, 1960). The precise membership was determined from Hovet's (1960) description as supplemented by Plano and Riggs (1967, p. 149). States joining the UN since the Plano and Riggs analysis were assigned to what seems the most appropriate political grouping, meaning African, Afro-Asian, or both.

To measure the *political backing* accorded U.S.-sponsored proposals by these nine groups, the *actual* number of cosponsored proposals were measured as a proportion of the total *possible* number of cosponsorships. The results were then weighted by the proportion of the entire membership of the Assembly represented by the caucusing group in question. For example, in the seventeenth General Assembly the United States sponsored 56 measures. In the same session the Latin American caucus comprised 20 Assembly members. Therefore, the total possible number of sponsorships the U.S. could have shared with the Latin American caucus was 1,120 (56 times 20). In fact, however, the Latin American group shared only 90 sponsorships with the U.S., or 8 percent of the number possible. When weighted by the proportion of the entire Assembly represented by the Latin American caucus (20 of 110 or 18.2 percent), the resulting *political backing* score is 1.46. By way of contrast, the corresponding score for the Afro-Asian caucus, with 6.8 percent of the possible number of U.S. sponsorships actually shared with the U.S., and with 50 percent of the Assembly membership, is 3.40.

The results of the correlations between the detrended U.S. *SL* scores and the 10 cosponsorship measures discussed in the preceding paragraphs are shown in Table 2. Once again, the results are not consistent with expectations. Not only are the magnitudes of the correlations generally small, but most of the associations suggest that the U.S. will enjoy *less* political success the *more* it secures the backing of states comprising the formal caucusing groups in the Assembly. This simply does not make much sense given the presumed importance that coalitions play in legislative bodies. But while it makes little sense, I have no ready explanation for the results. Perhaps the problem is that the measure of political backing used in no way distinguishes among the members in the caucusing group that actually share sponsorships with the U.S. If different members vary in terms of their importance within a group, then using a measure that treats all coalition members as equal, as was done here, is inappropriate.

Perhaps also it would be meaningful to distinguish between those proposals sponsored by a state and those that it actually initiates. It is unlikely, for example, that the United States initiated all 56 proposals it sponsored in the seventeenth session; it was probably a "joiner" on several of these. Unfortunately, however, the available data do not lend themselves to making such distinctions. Finally, it could be that the groups that matter in Assembly politics are not the formal caucusing groups but are much more amorphous groups that shift from one issue to the next. Identifying these groups is not, however, an easy task, nor is the procedure by which it might be done an obvious one.

Might the results be improved if multivariate analysis is used? The answer is "not much." One of the problems is the relatively small number of cases; this is particularly true when, for example, the African political backing scores are included with only eight data points. I have done a series of stepwise multiple regressions, one including all 14 of the variables that have been discussed, a second including all except the African political backing scores, a third including all except the African and Western European political backing scores, and a fourth including all except the African, Western

European, and Afro-Asian political backing scores. The stepwise procedure was used to limit the number of independent variables entering the explanatory equation before all of the degrees of freedom were used. As might be expected, this technique tended to yield rather different results depending on the subset of explanatory variables and points in time that were included in the analysis. About the only reasonably consistent result that emerged is that the variable measuring U.S. cosponsorships as deviations from the Assembly average became positive after controlling for the effects of other variables. In three of the four runs the variable would have been deemed statistically significant if the assumptions underlying such tests had been met.

In sum, then, it appears that none of the variables analyzed here can account for variations in U.S. political success in the General Assembly. Before completely rejecting them, however, it bears repeating that expanding the analysis to other states is in order. Analysis of Indian political success comparable to that done here for the United States, for example, yields many of the same kinds of conclusions regarding the assessments, mission size, delegation size, and sponsorship variables, but the correlations based on the cosponsorship measures were generally found to be in the hypothesized direction. In the case of the Arab, Latin American, and Western European political backing scores, the correlations would be deemed significant according to standard statistical tests.[6]

The results for India notwithstanding, both the reworking of the variables examined here and ex-

ploring alternative lines of inquiry are in order if explaining political success on the basis of political phenomena is to be fruitfully pursued. One of the next tasks that might be undertaken is an analysis of the various issue areas covered in each assembly session to determine whether states' political success varies from one type of issue to the next. It seems likely, for example, that one of the reasons the U.S. *SL* scores have declined over time is that the U.S. has found it increasingly difficult to control the content of agenda items. As the United Nations has become largely an organization of have-not states, the have-nots have been able to influence substantially what items will be discussed in the world body. And their choices may be significantly weighted in favor of those issues that are antagonistic to U.S. policy positions. This seems to be a particularly realistic hunch about why the U.S. *SL* scores declined in the 1960s, during which time the African and Asian nations made decolonialization and economic development issues dominant themes in the General Assembly. It may also help explain the surprising lack of success enjoyed by the U.S. in the early and middle 1950s. Presumably, during this time Latin American nations began supporting issues that were very much like those that dominated UN politics during the 1960s.[7]

To examine these notions, one might calculate *SL* scores for each state based only on those votes comprising each issue area. Alternatively, one might simply use as an independent variable the proportion of all votes taken in each Assembly that comprise different issue areas. Some preliminary work in this latter direction has been done, but the results are as yet too inconclusive to make any generalizations.

It should also be recognized that intra-organizational political variables may ultimately have to be supplemented by environmental variables. Role, governmental, societal, or idiosyncratic variables may vary little over time for a particular state. But systemic or external variables

---

[6]Correlations between India's detrended *SL* scores and the sponsorship and cosponsorship measures are given below. See note 4 for the remaining correlations.

India's sponsorships as a proportion of total sponsorships	−.07	20
Deviation of average Indian cosponsors from Assembly average	.24	20
Arab political backing	.41*	20
Benelux political backing	.18	20
Commonwealth political backing	.13	20
Latin America political backing	.44*	20
Scandinavia political backing	.20	20
Soviet political backing	.04	20
Afro-Asia political backing	−.02	16
Western Europe political backing	.55*	10
Africa political backing	.38	8

*Statistically significant at the .05 level.

[7]Limited evidence in support of this notion is provided in Alker and Russett (1965, pp. 63-64). See also Cornelius (1961) for a qualitative assessment of the divergence between U.S. and Latin American voting behavior on such questions as trade, aid, and colonialism during the first 10 years of the UN.

may fluctuate in such a way as to have an impact on the content of UN issues and on the approach that states take to them. Some of these variables may be operationalized in such a way as to account for political factors external to the United Nations. But it may also prove necessary to account for nonpolitical, or ecological, factors as well, such as the changing distribution of capabilities among national actors. It may prove necessary, in other words, to put Rosenau back into Easton—to complement the political explanations with the nonpolitical.

THE DOMESTIC DISTRIBUTION OF U.S. FOREIGN POLICY EXPENDITURES

The foregoing example of foreign policy analysis conceptualized foreign policy behavior as the recurrent output of a single actor and sought (not very successfully) to account for variations in that behavior manifested over several different points in time. What follows is an example that takes as given the output of a single actor and asks what accounts for variations among internal domestic units which experience the consequences of behavior directed toward actors external to the initiating society.

Specifically, the example is concerned with explaining variations in the amount of money received from the federal government by states and congressional districts in the U.S. as a consequence of the pursuit of ongoing foreign policy activities. The explanatory variables are measures of the relative influence of senators and congressmen, which are hypothesized to be determinants of the level of federal expenditures in senators' and congressmen's constituencies. The example is based on the assumption that external events—perceptions of threat, for example—may determine the level of foreign policy expenditures by the United States as a whole. But these external factors will not explain how the consequences (in this case money, which is assumed to confer benefits on the recipients) flowing from such events will be distributed within society. Hence, it is necessary to look at other factors in order to explain these variations, particularly the way in which the domestic political system structures the allocation of benefits derived from the pursuit of

foreign policy activities. Factors other than congressional influence might appropriately be examined in addressing this question; given the role that Congress plays in the budgetary process, however, Congress seems an appropriate place to begin an inquiry into the domestic determinants of the domestic consequences of foreign policy.

The data analyzed are "federal outlays" gathered by the Office of Economic Opportunity as part of a program begun in 1968 at the behest of the president's executive office. Data were abstracted from two county-level files, each containing approximately 350,000 records. The data were aggregated by agency from the county level to the state level and the district level. Federal outlays reported for multidistrict counties were divided equally among all districts in the county, whether the entire district fell within the county or only part of the county. Consequently, the district data are only estimates of the actual monies received by congressional districts.

The agency expenditures can be thought of as falling into categories of defense, quasi-defense, and nondefense foreign policy expenditures. The first category comprises all monies obligated by the Department of Defense (DOD) in states or congressional districts (thus excluding Washington, D.C., as well as monies obligated abroad); the second category comprises all obligations of the Atomic Energy Commission (AEC) and the National Aeronautics and Space Administration (NASA); and the third comprises all obligations of nondefense foreign policy agencies such as the State Department, the Agency for International Development (AID), and the U.S. Information Agency (USIA). Also included in the nondefense category are obligations of other federal agencies that could reasonably be identified as relating to foreign policy activities other than national defense.[8]

In fiscal year (FY) 1972 a total of $69.6 billion was spent domestically outside of Washington, D.C., for foreign policy activities—$59 billion in the defense category, $5.6 billion in the quasi-defense category, and $5 billion in the nondefense category. The distribution of these expenditures

[8]The rules used to define foreign policy expenditures are described in Wittkopf (1973). This paper and Wittkopf (forthcoming) provide a variety of descriptive information about the expenditure data.

Table 3. Federal Agency Expenditures for Foreign Policy Activities in FY 1972 (in thousands of dollars)

Federal Agency	Total Obligations	Number of States Receiving Money	Number of Districts Receiving Money
Defense Department	$58,969,772	50	435
Civilian pay	10,904,457	50	435
Military active duty pay	11,229,234	50	427
Military Reserve and National Guard pay	985,409	50	434
Military prime supply contracts	19,204,387	50	435
Military prime RDTE contracts	5,727,199	50	378
Military prime service contracts	5,768,527	50	421
Military prime construction contracts	1,183,480	50	344
Civilian functions prime contracts	1,003,780	50	417
Prime contracts less than $10,000	2,963,066	50	308
AEC	2,620,874	49	281
NASA	2,991,935	48	350
Agriculture Department	1,936,586	35	169
Commerce Department	534,754	40	302
Health, Education & Welfare	690,953	50	432
Interior Department	39	1	2
Justice Department	109,412	44	217
State Department	255,255	47	357
Treasury Department	178,317	45	249
Peace Corps	18,344	50	368
AID	1,246,000	48	424
Panama Canal	3,074	1	2
USIA	31,390	41	327
All nondefense agency obligations combined	$ 5,004,126	50	435

among the 14 federal agencies that have been chosen for analysis[9] is shown in Table 3. The data for the Defense Department have been broken into

[9] The Departments of Labor and Transportation, the Federal Maritime Commission, the General Services Administration, and the National Aeronautics and Space Council also incurred obligations as a consequence of foreign policy, but they have been excluded from the agency-level analyses since none of these obligations was incurred outside Washington, D.C., in FY 1972. However, the nondefense total for FY 1971 used later in the analysis does include $2,755 obligated by the General Services Administration in Virginia; and $4,642, $3,248, and $24,683 obligated by the Department of Transportation in Michigan, New York, and Ohio, respectively. The Selective Service System has also been excluded from the analysis since its expenditures tend to correlate almost perfectly with population.

the major DOD subcategories, while the monies for the nondefense agencies (i.e., excluding DOD, AEC, and NASA) have been aggregated into a nondefense category. The number of states and congressional districts receiving federal money in FY 1972 from the corresponding agency or in the corresponding category has also been listed.

One way to analyze the influence of senators and congressmen on the distribution of federal foreign policy expenditures is to use as a dependent variable the amount of money received by states and congressional districts in each of the categories shown in Table 3. Intuitively, however, it seems reasonable that congressional influence will be related more to *changes* in the amounts of money received than to levels; levels are likely to have been determined by historical factors relating to the distribution of industrial, agricultural, and educational capabilities in addition to historical variations in congressional influence. To analyze the effects of congressional influence at any particular point in time, therefore, it seems reasonable to use proportionate changes in the amounts of money received by states and districts as a dependent variable. Hence, the percentage increase or decrease in federal spending between FY 1971 and FY 1972, as well as the level measures, has been used as a dependent variable in the analyses summarized below. For comparative purposes, per capita measures have also been included for the state-level analysis.

Seven indicators of congressional influence based on the 92nd Congress have been used as the independent variables in a regression model(s) designed to explain variations in the distribution of federal money. Although others might have been chosen, these seven are at least reasonable measures that can be linked to much of the literature on legislative behavior.

In the case of the state-level analyses, data for each influence measure were collected for both senators representing the state. In this case, then, the seven influence measures were expanded such that 14 explanatory variables were included as independent variables in the regression model(s). Only seven independent variables were used in the district-level analyses, since each district is represented by only one congressman. A description of the seven measures of congressional influence follows; the prose is cast in terms of representatives rather than senators.

1. The representative's political party (Democrat or Republican);
2. The representative's seniority, defined as the number of years he had been in Congress at the beginning of the 92nd Congress (1970);
3. The rank of the most prestigious standing committee of the house of which the representative is a member, weighted by his seniority on the committee;[10]

4. The number of subcommittees (of standing committees) relevant to foreign policy of which the representative is a member;[11]
5. The number of subcommittees (of standing committees) relevant to foreign policy of which the representative is chairman;
6. A dichotomous variable measuring whether or not the representative is a member of the Joint Committee on Atomic Energy; and
7. The representative's independence from the president, defined as the difference between the representative's proportion of the popular vote cast for him in his last election (1970) and the proportion of the popular vote cast in his district for President Nixon in 1968.[12]

The squared multiple correlation coefficients derived from the regression analyses are reported

---

and the House's Science and Astronautics Committee based on transfers to and from the respective committees between the 86th and 92nd (1st session) Congress. All other committees in both houses were updated to include transfers in the 91st and 92nd (1st session) Congresses. Committee seniority was defined as the representative's or the senator's seniority position on each committee within his party divided by the number of party members on the committee. This figure was then used to weight the committee prestige ranking. In the case of the Senate, the weighting factor was defined as the sum of the senator's seniority on the two most prestigious committees to which he was assigned, where the prestige rankings were also defined as the sum of the ranks of the senator's two most prestigious committees. In the case of the House, where a larger number of members are assigned to exclusive committees, only one committee was used as the index, where the choice was made so as to assign the representative the most prestige possible in the case of those representatives assigned to more than one committee. The Minority Leader in the House (Gerald R. Ford) was assigned a weighted committee prestige score equal to that of the most influential Republican (John W. Byrnes) as defined by this index; the Majority Leader (Hale Boggs) and the Speaker of the House (Carl Albert) were both assigned a score equal to that of the most influential Democrat (Wilbur D. Mills).

[11]All permanent subcommittees of the Senate Armed Services Committee, the Senate Foreign Relations Committee, the House Armed Services Committee, the House Foreign Affairs Committee, and the House Science and Astronautics Committee were defined as relevant subcommittees. In addition, 14 Senate subcommittees and 14 House subcommittees were defined as relevant to foreign policy.

[12]In the case of senators, the last election could be 1966, 1968, or 1970. For both houses of Congress, candidates who were unopposed in their last election were assigned 99.9 percent of the vote in their constituency. The idea for this variable comes from Uslaner (1973), who calls the measure a "lead-lag" variable.

---

[10]The rank order of committee prestige builds on the data and technique reported by Goodwin (1970, pp. 114-115). Goodwin's analysis was updated to include the Senate's Aeronautical and Space Sciences Committee

Table 4. Variations in the Distribution of Foreign Policy Expenditures Explained (r^2) by Variations in Congressional Influence

	States			Districts	
Federal Agency	Total $	Per Capita $	Percent Change	Total $	Percent Change
Defense Department	.362	.217	.484	.026	.014
Civilian pay	.457	.347	.305	.004	.028
Military active duty pay	.361	.193	.447	.011	.007
Military Reserve and National Guard Pay	.341	.212	.215	.016	.019
Military prime supply contracts	.299	.195	.381	.028	.009
Military prime RDTE contracts	.303	.279	.420	.018	.007
Military prime service contracts	.307	.315	.265	.053	.010
Military prime construction contracts	.342	.272	.353	.006	.016
Civilian functions prime contracts	.342	.253	.397	.008	.027
Prime contracts less than $10,000	.417	.137	.354	.012	.009
AEC	.417	.405	.242	.008	.014
NASA	.344	.467	.365	.024	.011
Agriculture Department	.197	.278	.294	.060	.036
Commerce Department	.225	.194	.054	.056	.009
Health, Education & Welfare	.381	.231	.162	.021	.006
Justice Department	.196	.296	.242	.013	.053
State Department	.192	.156	.267	.067	.006
Treasury Department	.196	.236	.190	.079	.005
Peace Corps	.229	.556	.211	.013	.011
AID	.256	.276	.369	.050	.010
USIA	.189	.212	.261	.059	.011
All nondefense agency obligations combined	.203	.318	.362	.070	.011

in Table 4.[13] Additional regression results have not been reported because of (1) the considerable multicollinearity associated with the use of 14 independent variables in the case of the state-level

[13]Zero is considered a meaningful data point throughout the analysis with the exception of those states or districts where the expenditures are zero in FY 1971 and greater than zero in FY 1972. These cases have been eliminated from the analyses using the percentage change as the dependent variable, since any dollar received in FY 1972 is a 100 percent increase over FY 1971. Hence, *N* differs slightly from 50 for the state-level analyses and from 435 for the district-level analyses when the percentage change measure is the dependent variable. The state-level regression results for the nondefense expenditures were reported previously in Wittkopf (1973).

analyses and (2) the generally poor explanatory power of the seven independent variables in the case of the district-level analyses. It should be pointed out, however, that the relationship between each independent variable and the dependent variables was frequently not in the direction expected.

Aside from the question of expected direction, the nearly nonexistent amounts of variance explained in the district-level analyses is a perplexing matter. These results clearly and unambiguously challenge some notions firmly rooted in political science about the factors that contribute to variations in the monies distributed by the federal government among various geographical units. Principal among these is the view that the seniority system in Congress tends to reward those congressmen coming from single-party districts, notably in the South, who in turn are able to win substantial benefits for their districts in terms of federal expenditures as a consequence of their position in Congress. Certainly this proposition has face-validity when one examines the geographic concentration of defense installations in the South (and thus the old saw that if one more military base is placed in South Carolina the state will sink). But the results summarized in Table 4 clearly challenge the proposition that seniority, even after controlling for the effects of other variables, is a generalized explanation of the distribution of federal perquisites.

The results of the state-level analyses appear to be much more encouraging. However, the fact that the variance explained is so much greater than for the district-level analyses leads one to suspect that the results are a consequence of the use of so many explanatory variables as much as they are the consequence of having unearthed the "real" relationship between congressional influence and federal spending.

Finally, it should be noted that in both the state- and district-level analyses the variable measuring the percentage change in governmental expenditures generally does little better than the level variables; indeed, in many cases the reverse is true. Perhaps this is due to the sensitivity of the percentage measure to the base level against which it is computed, thus suggesting the need for an alternative way of controlling for the effects of history. Assuming, however, that congressional influence is more closely tied to incremental changes than to determining the size of the whole pie, the results of the analyses using change as the dependent variable are also far from encouraging.

Similar to the UN roll-call example, then, some additional work is in order if political factors are to be used to explain the domestic consequences of foreign policy. Examining alternative variables, both dependent and independent, may be one way to proceed. Examining alternative explanatory models also seems in order. There is no theoretical reason for assuming that the seven independent variables examined here are related to the distribution of foreign policy expenditures in a linear, additive fashion. On the contrary, some reasons might be advanced in support of a multiplicative model. A congressman's influence may, for example, increase at an exponential rate; after spending several years in a relatively obscure and uninfluential position, a congressman's influence may begin to grow at an exponential rate as he increasingly assumes the trappings of an experienced lawmaker.

Ecology may also have to be explicitly added to the equation. Variations in the capabilities of states and congressional districts may to some extent be held constant by examining changes in the amount of foreign policy resources received by different geographical units for the simple reason that industrial, agricultural, and educational capabilities do not shift appreciably from one year to the next. Despite this, it may still be necessary to explicitly control for ecological factors since all states or districts may not be equally logical candidates for an increase (or decrease) in certain types of resources. Take, for example, a decision by the Defense Department to build a new submarine base. Since not all states and congressional districts possess the requisite capabilities to support the new base (i.e., access to the sea), not all can be considered logical candidates for receiving the increase in DOD spending that is likely to result from the decision. Care must be exercised, of course, lest the desire to control for possible environmental constraints reduces the analysis to case specific explanations. Yet some effort to control for ecological factors would seem to be in order, even if we are concerned only with explaining incremental changes in the distribution of the pie from one year to the next.

CONCLUDING REMARKS

Research priorities are unlikely to shift as a consequence of one isolated plea—particularly if that plea is not supported by demonstrable evidence of the utility of the argument advanced. To return to the point made in the opening paragraphs of this chapter, however, the examples of how reasonably explicit measures of political phenomena might be related to foreign policy variables is less important than the argument that the need exists. The events data movement, which has now been sustained for a number of years in several different research centers, represents a clear challenge to the notion that our prior data on foreign policy behavior were capable of yielding answers to the multifaceted questions being raised about state behavior. So, too, it appears necessary to give a corresponding degree of attention to our explanatory variables. The ready accessibility of socioeconomic data, made possible by the existence of a number of quality publications of the United Nations, should cease to be our primary guide to research into the causes of foreign policy behavior.

As we search out new explanatory variables, my plea is that we give explicit attention to political factors. Having done so, we may well conclude, as have some of our American politics colleagues who are working in the field of comparative state politics, that political variables account for only small amounts of the variation in policy outputs, and that ecological factors tend to be far more potent explanations.[14] Yet we can hardly come to this conclusion without giving explicit attention to political phenomena. Put differently, we can hardly determine the relative potency of Rosenau's five source variables without giving explicit attention to them.

Finally, my plea also carries the suggestion that the process of moving away from genotypic analyses and of giving equal time to all five source variables is likely to be enhanced by moving away from the dominant emphasis on cross-sectional research designs. Conceptualizing our research task in longitudinal or multisocietal-level terms may well facilitate the process of reorienting our research priorities in the direction of giving more attention to the critical role that politics are presumed to play in social systems.[15]

REFERENCES

Alker, H. R., and B. M. Russett. 1965. *World Politics in the General Assembly.* New Haven: Yale Univ. Press.

Brams, S. J., and M. K. O'Leary. 1970. "An Axiomatic Model of Voting Bodies." *American Political Science Review* 64 (Jun): 449-70.

Clark, J. F., M. K. O'Leary, and E. R. Wittkopf. 1971. "National Attributes Associated with Dimensions of Support for the United Nations." *International Organization* 25 (Winter): 1-25.

Cornelius, W. G. 1961. "The 'Latin American Bloc' in the United Nations." *Journal of Inter-American Studies* 3 (Jul): 419-35.

Fry, B. R., and R. F. Winters. 1970. "The Politics of Redistribution." *American Political Science Review* 64 (Jun): 508-22.

Goodwin, G., Jr. 1970. *The Little Legislatures.* Amherst: Univ. of Massachusetts Press.

Groth, A. S. 1971. *Comparative Politics: A Distributive Approach.* New York: Collier-Macmillan.

Hermann, C. F. 1972. "Policy Classification: A Key to the Comparative Study of Foreign Policy." In *The Analysis of International Politics,* ed. J. N. Rosenau, V. Davis, and M. A. East, pp. 58-79. New York: Free Press.

Hovet, T. 1960. *Bloc Politics in the United Nations.* Cambridge: Harvard Univ. Press.

Jacobsen, K. 1969. "Sponsorships in the United Nations: A System Analysis." *Journal of Peace Research* (3): 235-56.

Kay, D. A. 1970. "Instruments of Influence in the United Nations Political Process." In *The United Nations Political System,* ed. D. A. Kay, pp. 92-107. New York: Wiley.

Keohane, R. O. 1967. "The Study of Political Influence in the General Assembly." *International Organization* 21 (Spring): 221- 37.

McGowan, P. J., and H. B. Shapiro. 1973. *The Compara-*

---

[14]It is interesting to note that after reviewing the literature in comparative state politics (see note 2) that points to the importance of socioeconomic variables ir explaining policy outcomes, Fry and Winters (1970, pp. 521, 522) conclude that by "shifting the focus [from taxation and expenditure levels] to an examination of allocations of burdens and benefits in state systems of revenues and expenditures" political variables turn out to be "considerably more powerful than . . . socioeconomic variables in explaining interstate variations in redistributive patterns."

[15]Rosenau's (1971b) own research designed to assess the relative potency of the source variables was set in the American context using two different time periods. Since that time, however, Rosenau (Rosenau and Ramsey, 1973; Rosenau and Hoggard, 1974), too, seems to have abandoned the source variables in favor of a cross-national elaboration of the environmental conditions and constraints within which states operate.

tive Study of Foreign Policy. Beverly Hills: Sage.

Plano, J. C., and R. E. Riggs. 1967. *Forging World Order.* London: Macmillan.

Rosenau, J. N. 1966. "Pre-theories and Theories of Foreign Policy." In *Approaches to Comparative and International Politics,* ed. R. B. Farrell, pp. 27-92. Evanston: Northwestern Univ. Press.

———. 1971a. "Comparative Foreign Policy: Fad, Fantasy, or Field?" In *The Scientific Study of Foreign Policy,* by J. N. Rosenau, pp. 67-94. New York: Free Press.

———. 1971b. "Private Preferences and Political Responsibilities: The Relative Potency of Individual and Role Variables in the Behavior of U.S. Senators." *The Scientific Study of Foreign Policy,* by J. N. Rosenau, pp. 151-93. New York: Free Press.

———, C. F. Hermann, and P. M. Burgess. 1973. "The Adaptation of Foreign Policy Research: A Case Study of an Anti-Case Study Project." *International Studies Quarterly* 17 (Mar): 119-44.

——— and G. R. Ramsey, Jr. 1973. "External vs. Internal Sources of Foreign Policy Behavior: Testing the Stability of an Intriguing Set of Findings." Paper presented at the Ninth World Congress of the International Political Science Association, Montreal.

——— and G. D. Hoggard. 1974. "Foreign Policy Behavior in Dyadic Relationships: Testing a Pre-theoretical Extension." In *Comparing Foreign Policies,* ed. J. N. Rosenau, pp. 117-49. Beverly Hills: Sage.

Uslaner, E. M. 1973. "Congressional Attitudes and Congressional Behavior: The House Decision on the ABM." Paper presented at the Annual Meeting of the Midwest Political Science Association, Chicago.

Weigert, K. M., and R. E. Riggs. 1969. "Africa and United Nations Elections: An Aggregate Data Analysis." *International Organization* 23 (Winter): 1-19.

Wittkopf, E. R. 1973. "Who Gets What? The Domestic Distribution of U.S. Non-defense Foreign Policy Expenditures." Paper presented at the Eleventh North American Conference of the Peace Science Society (International), Cambridge, Mass.

———. 1975. "Soviet and American Political Success in the UN General Assembly, 1946-1970." In *International Events and the Comparative Analysis of Foreign Policy,* ed. C. W. Kegley, Jr., et al., pp. 179-204. Columbia: Univ. of South Carolina Press.

———. Forthcoming. "Incrementalism and Change in the Domestic Distribution of U.S. Foreign Policy Expenditures." *International Interactions.*

38. Conceptualizing Foreign Policy Behavior Using Events Data

Charles F. Hermann

EMERGENCE OF SUBSTANTIVE CONCERNS IN EVENTS DATA

Quantitatively oriented students of foreign policy have displayed considerable interest in the use of events data for the study of their subject. Chief

SPECIAL NOTE: An earlier version of this chapter was presented at the Inter-university Comparative Foreign Policy Conference at Ojai, California, June 18-22, 1973. The events data research described here, as part of the Comparative Research on the Events of Nations (CREON) project, is supported by grants from the Mershon Center at Ohio State University and NSF (#GS40356).

among the attractions of these data are (1) the accessibility of the material, (2) the ability to construct reliable categories and scales using variations on the established techniques of content analysis, (3) the range of behavior that can be included, and (4) the applicability to all nation-states and virtually any other actors for which records of activity are readily produced. Among the liabilities of these data, none has been more thoroughly discussed than validity—particularly as it is affected by the nature of the data source. It is undoubtedly a credit to the early collectors of events data that rather than cover up or ignore this problem, they devoted a substantial proportion of their writing to comparisons of source bias and related topics (Azar et al., 1972; Burrowes, 1974; Doran et al., 1973; Harle, 1972; Hoggard, 1967; Sigler, 1972).

Yet observers of this band of events data advocates may be able to detect a trend away from what some might characterize as methodological navel gazing. Such an unkind characterization of a prominent activity in events data analysis certainly is unfair in the sense that it fails to give credit to data users for quickly recognizing an important shortcoming in their material. It is a problem that must ultimately be adequately handled. Critics may reasonably wonder, however, whether the concern for comparing source bias and studying validity stems from a failure to think of anything else to do with the data that have been so laboriously assembled. It is in response to such expressions—or anticipated expressions—by other foreign policy colleagues and by funding agencies that events data users have begun to shift their topics of research. At the appropriate panel during the International Studies Association meetings in Dallas, Texas, in March 1972, one speaker after another arose to suggest that we should turn more attention to the substantive policy problems that events data can address.[1] The scholars advocating this approach are more likely to have the motivation and the support for improving the quality and validity of their events data, if they can make the case that it provides a means of studying problems of widespread interest and a means for providing new insights to older substantive questions.

The call for setting a substantive research agenda using events data has given new impetus to concerns that various scholars have recognized for some time. In particular, we see attention to the problem of *international conflict processes* and the expression and receipt of hostility (e.g., Harle, 1974). We also find interest in comparing the foreign *behavior of nations that have been typed or grouped* in some way (e.g., East and Hermann,

1974). (Is the within-group variance in foreign behavior less than between-group variance?) Furthermore, renewed concern with using events data to *forecast future occurrences* has emerged to pick up the older idea of using events to construct an international tension or "fever" chart (e.g., Wynn, Rubin, and Franco, 1973). Another concern now receiving considerable attention is the effort *to cluster or group behavior by means of some statistical techniques* (e.g., Kegley, 1973). In addition, we can expect more consideration of a greater *variety of external event behaviors* in which international actors engage (e.g., Kegley, Salmore, and Rosen, 1973).[2]

The latter activity represents a thrust of considerable importance for the comparative study of foreign policy among those of us who have declared that a fundamental weakness of foreign policy research has been the absence of any entirely adequate conceptualization of foreign policy behavior (e.g., Froman, 1968; Hermann, 1972). More specifically, the critical need is for conceptual schemes of behaviors that include a broad range of activities pursued by international actors and which lend themselves to empirical hypothesis testing. Despite the well-established history of scholarship in the foreign policy field, it remains in its infancy with respect to scientific methods of inquiry. This is partly because little attention has been paid to the development of behavioral measures that have both empirical and theoretical import.

At such an early stage, the inductive-statistical approach to identifying patterns or dimensions of foreign policy has much merit. But there are scholars who will look at these initial substantive efforts in the use of events data—particularly, those attempting to map the pattern of foreign policy—and declare, "We need a theory." Few would quarrel over this declaration, especially so

---

[1] The workshop, organized by Robert Beattie and chaired by Edward Azar, was entitled "Problems in Events Data Sources—Event Data Users Meet Events Data Makers." It occurred at the Thirteenth Annual Convention of the International Studies Association, Hotel Adolphus, Dallas, Texas, March 15, 1972.

[2] Kegley, Salmore, and Rosen (1974) found that most event sets tended to use categories that produced conflict and cooperation dimensions when subjected to some type of statistical reduction technique such as factor analysis. However, some of their evidence suggests that when events are initially classified into more diverse types of behavior, then reduction techniques produce dimensions other than conflict and cooperation. The implication may be that collectors of events data in the past have constructed rather restrictive typologies of behavior.

long as "theory" remains an undefined term.[3] Arguments may be expected, however, as to what preliminary steps or procedures should be followed to promote the discovery of a theory that produces empirically verifiable statements. Without squarely addressing these issues, this chapter asserts (1) that no such theory exists now and (2) that it seems reasonable to consider some ways beyond the inductive-statistical pattern approach in order to move the characterization of foreign behavior ahead.

In brief, I contend that the field of comparative foreign policy needs a conceptualization of foreign policy behavior that will stimulate as much research on behaviors as Rosenau's (1966) genotypes stimulated on national attributes and the clustering of nations. I am not in a position to offer such a pioneering scheme as Rosenau's. In the remainder of this essay, however, I shall sketch some conceptualizations of foreign policy behavior that have been operationalized in the Comparative Research on the Events of Nations (CREON) data. The CREON project is a cross-national study of the foreign policy behavior of 36 nations in which scholars in different fields of inquiry and located at several universities are participating. The project has two immediate objectives: (1) to map and compare the range of foreign policy activities initiated between 1959-1968 by the nations under study and (2) to seek explanations of foreign policy behaviors in terms of six alternative theoretical perspectives. The basic CREON data set consists of approximately 11,600 foreign policy events. Over 100 different variables have been coded for each event. The variables concern the decision process and the characteristics of the external behavior. Each event results from a decision by political authorities of the national government.[4]

The ways of conceptualizing foreign policy behavior that will be discussed in the remainder of this chapter are issue areas, event properties, nation-defined properties, and inductive categories of action. The participants in the CREON project are not the only events data collectors who have been experimenting with alternative means of conceptualizing behavior,[5] and I hope that still others will be encouraged to undertake their own efforts. Beyond the relevance of such behavioral measures for users of events data, they should have utility for all scholars interested in the comparative study of foreign policy.

ISSUE AREAS

Defining foreign policy in terms of issue areas has received considerable attention among those interested in classifying foreign policy. In some recent writing, issue areas have denoted any substantive domain of interest to the author—for example, foreign aid, arms control, or alliance policies. However, those who have followed Dahl's (1963) initial work (e.g., Huntington, 1961; Lowi, 1967; Rosenau, 1967) and have applied the concept to foreign policy in a similar manner have not used the term in such a comprehensive way. As did Dahl, they propose that issues can be differentiated by the participants and the decision process. Different types of foreign policy issues are handled by different groups using different skills. Although the substantive topic approach to issue areas also must be explored, it is the participant-process means of classification that will be discussed here. To date scholars have not moved very far in identifying

---

[3]Perhaps this sentence should have been written as "Few of the people who read this paper would quarrel over this declaration." Since most readers are assumed to be interested in the *comparative* study of foreign policy, it is likely that they will subscribe to the value of a general theory of foreign policy. It might be useful to review the question "Why and for what do we want such a theory?" In turn, answers to that question may invite another: "Is the comparative, cross-national approach really the way to proceed, and why?"

[4]A comprehensive overview of the CREON project can be obtained from two monographs: a description of the data appears in Hermann et al. (1973) and the theo-

retical perspectives are advanced in East and Salmore (1976). The six theoretical perspectives are (1) personal characteristics of political leaders, (2) aspects of governmental structure and process, (3) political features of regimes, (4) national attributes of societies, (5) transitory qualities of situations, and (6) properties of the international system. Besides the editors, contributors are Linda Brady, Margaret Hermann, Charles Hermann, Warren Phillips, and Barbara Salmore.

[5]Two illustrations of other attempts to use events data in various conceptualizations of behavior include the work of O'Leary and Shapiro (1972) and Leng (1972). O'Leary and Shapiro are developing a substantive set of issue areas for events data and Leng is continuing his earlier work with Singer to develop a hierarchical classification of events based on properties that can be reliably identified by observers.

foreign policy decisions in this way, but the field may be on the verge of some important developments in this conceptual approach.

Although some of the contributors to these recent advances have not been concerned with establishing issue areas, and although most of the explorations have been case studies in American foreign policy, distinctive issue-area categories are emerging. For example, I might tentatively suggest that each of the following has substantial differences in both actors and/or decision processes:

1. *Crises.* Actors are the highest level of government; actors are few (small group); the process is hierarchical in that decisions are taken by a chief executive.
2. *Internal Resource Allocation.* Actors tend to be drawn from various levels of government and include both executive and legislative personnel; actors are numerous; the process is characterized by log rolling and bargaining.
3. *Protracted International Negotiations.* Actors tend to be middle-level; actors are relatively few; actors tend to be backstopped by a task force composed largely of specialists; the internal process tends to be hierarchically structured.
4. *Policy or Program Design.* Actors tend to be at diverse levels in the executive branch; actors are numerous; the process tends to be a mix of the advocacy process marked by extensive bargaining, but with final decisions involving an executive style.

As stated, these examples of issue areas are not totally satisfactory because the categories are neither mutually exclusive nor exhaustive, but they do denote the kinds of differences that the concept of issue area may originally introduce.

In the CREON data, we have tried to capture the issue-area concept and subject it to empirical investigation. For example, we have classified all events by the skills and type of resources involved. We have also constructed a series of ad hoc categories designed to identify such process distinctions as those involved in negotiation/bargaining behavior, treaty behavior, regional organization behavior, military behavior, propaganda and cultural behavior, and foreign assistance. We have attempted to distinguish crises (defined in terms of threat,

time, and surprise) from other types of situations. Of even greater novelty is the attempt to capture aspects of the internal decision process, such as the size of the decision unit, the nature of the participating decision units, and the level of the participants.[6] Thus, it should be possible to determine whether behaviors differ with respect to these various indicators of the participants and the decision processes.

It is important to recognize that we may wish to move either from decision processes and participants to behavior, or conversely, from behavior to inferences about who might have participated and how. Because behaviors are more readily available from public sources than are aspects of decision processes, it would be of considerable value to reconstruct the process from knowledge of the outputs if some high degree of association can be established.

EVENT PROPERTIES

Issue areas, as they have been conceptualized here, involve the classification of foreign policy behavior according to the participants and decision processes. Alternatively, we can construct foreign behavior measures in terms of attributes of the action component in discrete events. In other words, every event can be classified according to properties determined from the action. Such a procedure for classifying foreign policy is hardly new, yet we want to focus this procedure in a specific way by using it to help answer the question "What is the nature of the minimum information we need to establish the probable intention of the present actor's behavior?" If we assume that foreign policy behavior is purposeful, then we can envision any given behavior as representing a point in space which can be related to some goal(s) or objective(s). We want to determine as best we can the character of this vector. Assume that the behavior is considered analogous to an object moving in space (say, a projectile). We would want to know the direction, accuracy, speed, and force of the projectile. With respect to foreign policy

---

[6]These and all other CREON variables are described in the appendix to Hermann et al. (1973).

behavior the analogous properties are those that provide answers to the following questions.

1. *Direction*. What or who is the actor attempting to influence by his behavior? (What is he aiming at?)

2. *Specificity*. How much information does the actor provide, that is, is his behavior vague and uncertain or clear and specific? (How focused is the action?)

3. *Commitment*. To what extent does the actor display a strong commitment in his behavior? (Is the action relatively weak or strong?)

4. *Affect*. As manifested by his behavior, is the actor positively oriented toward the object of influence (helpful intention) or negatively oriented (harmful intention)? (Is the action designed to obstruct or assist the object?)

These qualities are universal (i.e., present in all actions), determinable solely from knowledge of the events, and can be hypothesized as subject to considerable variation in the theoretical perspectives alluded to earlier (East and Salmore, 1976). As with issue areas, certain problems must still be addressed. For example, specificity may be influenced by the context. The action may seem vague, but the intended receiver knows rather well what is meant. Consider as an illustration Dulles's declaration that the United States might have to undertake "an agonizing reappraisal" of its relations with Europe. Jervis (1970) has alerted us to the deliberate use of vagueness as a tactic in international diplomacy. Despite these cautions, one can argue that something substantial is varied depending on whether actors dispel public uncertainty concerning details of who, what, when, where, and how in their behaviors.

It should be noted that two of the four properties are attributes that can be defined exclusively with reference to the action, whereas two others (direction and affect) require knowledge of both the action and the object of influence and, thus, are relational qualities. Relational properties require either a dyadic mode of analysis (one actor and one target) or some means of aggregation across actors and targets.

With the possible exception of direction—which may be a nominal category—the event properties lend themselves to an ordinal or interval scale. In

the CREON data several items have been designed to abstract aspects of each property in the expectation that scales can be constructed. For example, the data records information on the specificity of (a) the addressee, (b) the problem, (c) the resources, and (d) the timing. Items relevant to intensity of commitment include whether resources are symbolic or significant, the use of words versus deeds, the level of decision makers (e.g., whether head of state is involved), the duration of action, the location of the announcer of the action, the channel by which the action is announced, and so on. In several different ways, we attempted to tap whether the affect was positive, negative, or neutral with respect both to the immediate addressee of the action (target) and the entity whom the actor is trying to influence (object). In addition, some of the ad hoc categories characterize behaviors which, in the vast majority of cases, can be regarded as either positive or negative.

NATION-DEFINED PROPERTIES

Brief reference will be made to two other conceptualizations of foreign policy which are potentially understood through the CREON alternative theoretical perspectives. The first of these—nation-defined properties—are properties for which a value cannot be assigned on the basis of a single event. Instead, it is necessary to aggregate events for a nation across time according to some domain of activity. Such nation-defined properties may be relational qualities or attributes. Examples of relational properties of this kind are the history of the actor's affect toward a given object (or target), another is the consistency with which an actor treats certain entities in its environment.

One property that has an attribute character is the duration, or time, across which similar behaviors are pursued (regardless of target). Another attribute of considerable importance is the goal or objective which the actor pursues through various behaviors. In the CREON data set we have recorded the stated purpose (e.g., "expressed goal") the actor advances for a particular event. Although this is a promising dimension, it must be recognized that the ends which actions are intended to serve cannot be established fully from any one event. The purpose is not stated every time an action is undertaken in pursuit of some goal. Moreover, the actual purposes may deviate from those which are publicly announced. Some other implications of goals will be commented upon in the closing remarks.

INDUCTIVE CATEGORIES OF ACTIONS

A fourth approach to the conceptualization of behavior is that of Charles McClelland and his associates, who made an inductive approach to conceptualizing foreign policy behaviors in their World Event Interaction Survey (WEIS). Over an extended period of time they categorized items in the *New York Times* dealing with international affairs. They continued to revise and expand their classification scheme until they could group approximately 99 percent of all items that appeared in their source into one of their categories. Several attempts to identify underlying themes or differentiating principles have been inspired by the WEIS scheme.

Corson (1970) regrouped all WEIS categories into one of eight clusters. First, he distinguished between conflictful and cooperative events; then he subdivided each of these into four categories of increasing commitment—starting with evaluative comment, desire for action by others, expression of intent to act oneself, and finally, physical deeds. Looking at the same WEIS categories, Stephen Salmore (Hermann et al., 1974) created a Sequential Action Scheme in which he sought to identify the basic action qualities entailed in various WEIS coding rules (e.g., whether the action was verbal or a physical deed, whether action was elicited or unelicited, and whether action involved one actor or collaboration). These distinctions and subdistinctions were then arrayed in a logical sequence so that the coder could move through a decision tree in classifying the event. A variation of the WEIS classification, and the Corson and the Salmore schemes, are included in the CREON data set. They have an undeniable appeal and relevance because they are grounded in observed types of actual foreign policy behavior rather than in a conceptualization of how nations may behave.

EVENTS AND FOREIGN POLICY

This chapter has advanced several schemes for conceptualizing foreign policy behavior using events data. The question remains as to the connection between events and what commonly is understood as foreign policy. I shall conclude with a brief discussion of the problem. There are almost as many definitions of foreign policy as there are scholarly books on the subject. In distilling the common elements in many of these definitions, I have concluded that many commentators view policy as involving actions taken as part of some plan or program in pursuit of certain ends (objectives, goals, or interests). I contend that in developing an operational formulation of policy the critical element is the clustering of all behaviors initiated in response to the same desired end. If events represent discrete actions, then the goals or ends they are intended to serve are missing.

Here one runs into the twofold problem that has long plagued students of formal organizations and other collectivities: What is a goal for a human collectivity and who specifies the goals for a given entity?

It seems to me that there are several possible choices in response to the inquiry as to who determines goals. We can assume that policy makers define goals. Actually, this breaks down into what the policy makers publicly declare as goals and what they may privately select as goals. Alternatively, we can join Morton Kaplan, Hans Morgenthau, and many others who stipulate as observers what the goals of the nations must be if certain things are to happen (e.g., a given system maintained, national power not to be overextended, etc.). Events data can be assembled according to any of these ways of determining goals. When events have been so arrayed, I contend that one can appropriately speak of having operationalized policy. As noted earlier, the CREON data include records of those instances when an actor declares what purpose a given action is intended to serve. If, alternatively, one wishes to establish the policy makers' unannounced goals, then he must resort to content analysis or some similar technique. Should he prefer to stipulate the goals from whatever orientation he desires as an observer, that too can be done. These are tasks that he would confront regardless of whether he employed events data. Once having derived his classification scheme of goals, however, events data can be aggregated accordingly. If the scheme subsequently turns out to be disappointing, a new scheme of goals can be advanced and the events redistributed with a resulting new definition of policy.

REFERENCES

Azar, E. E., et al. 1972. *International Events Interaction Analysis: Some Research Considerations.* Beverly Hills: Sage.

Burrowes, R. 1974. "Mirror, Mirror, on the Wall: A Comparison of Sources of External Events Data." In *Comparing Foreign Policies,* ed. J. N. Rosenau, pp. 383-406. Beverly Hills: Sage

Cohen, S., T. Jukam, and J. McCormick. 1972. "The Problem of Source Coverage in the Use of International Events Data." *International Studies Quarterly* 16 (Sep): 373-88.

Corson, W. 1970. "Conflict and Cooperation in East-West Crises: Measurement and Explanation." Paper presented at the Annual Meeting of the American Political Science Association, Los Angeles.

Dahl, R. A. 1963. *Who Governs?* New Haven: Yale Univ. Press.

Doran, C. F., R. E. Pendley, and G. Autunes. 1973. "A Test of Cross-national Event Reliability." *International Studies Quarterly* 17 (Sep): 175-204.

East, M. A., and S. A. Salmore. 1976. *Theoretical Bases for Comparative Foreign Policy Studies.* Beverly Hills: Sage.

––– and C. F. Hermann. 1974. "Do Nation-Types Account for Foreign Policy Behavior?" In *Comparing Foreign Policies,* ed. J. N. Rosenau, pp. 269-304. Beverly Hills: Sage.

Froman, L. A., Jr. 1968. "The Categorization of Policy Contents." In *Political Science and Public Policy,* ed. A. Ranney, pp. 41-52. Chicago: Markham.

Harle, V. 1972. "Reliability of International Events Data Sources." Mimeo. Tampere, Finland: Univ. of Tampere, Research Institute.

–––. 1974. "Inter-system and Intra-system Tension in the East-West Threat System." Ph.D. dissertation, Univ. of Tampere.

Hermann, C. F. 1972. "Policy Classification: A Key to the Comparative Study of Foreign Policy." In *The Analysis of International Politics,* ed. J. N. Rosenau, V. Davis, and M. A. East, pp. 58-79. New York: Free Press.

––– et al. 1973. *CREON: Foreign Events Data Set.* Beverly Hills: Sage.

Hoggard, G. D. 1967. "Comparison of Reporting for *New York Times Index, Asian Recorder,* and *Deadline Data:* Chinese Interactions January through October, 1962." Mimeo. Los Angeles: Univ. of Southern California.

Huntington, S. P. 1961. *The Common Defense.* New York: Columbia Univ. Press.

Jervis, R. 1970. *The Logic of Image in International Relations.* Princeton: Princeton Univ. Press.

Kegley, C. W., Jr. 1973. *A General Empirical Typology of Foreign Policy Behavior.* Beverly Hills: Sage.

–––, S. A. Salmore, and D. Rosen. 1974. "Convergence in the Measurement of Interstate Behavior." In *Sage Yearbook of Foreign Policy Studies,* ed. P. J. McGowan, vol. 2, pp. 309-42. Beverly Hills: Sage.

Leng, R. J. 1972. "Coder's Manual for Identifying and Describing International Actions." Mimeo. Middlebury: Middlebury College.

Lowi, T. J. 1967. "Making Democracy Safe for the World." In *Domestic Sources of Foreign Policy,* ed. J. N. Rosenau, pp. 295-332. New York: Free Press.

O'Leary, M. K., and H. B. Shapiro. 1972. "A Codebook of International Transactions, Issue-Specific Interactions and Power." PRINCE Research Studies, No. 10. Mimeo. Syracuse: Syracuse Univ.

Rosenau, J. N. 1966. "Pre-theories and Theories of Foreign Policy." In *Approaches to Comparative and International Politics,* ed. R. B. Farrell, pp. 27-92. Evanston: Northwestern Univ. Press.

–––. 1967. "Foreign Policy as an Issue Area." In *Domestic Sources of Foreign Policy,* ed. J. N. Rosenau, pp. 11-50. New York: Free Press.

Sigler, J. H. 1972. "Reliability Problems in the Measurement of International Events in the Elite Press." In *Applications of Events Data Analysis,* ed. J. H. Sigler, J. O. Field, and M. L. Adelman, pp. 9-30. Beverly Hills: Sage.

Wynn, M., T. Rubin, and G. R. Franco. 1973. "New Ways to Measure and Forecast International Affairs." *Futurist* 7 (Dec): 244-49.

39. Targeting Behavior: A New Direction

Maurice A. East · Barbara Kay Winters

The primary purpose of this chapter is to outline and discuss an area of research in the comparative study of foreign policy that seems to have considerable promise but has generally been neglected thus far in the literature. This general research area can perhaps best be characterized as the answer to the following question: "Where do states direct their foreign policy behavior and why?" For convenience, we shall refer to this as targeting behavior. How can we describe the targeting of foreign policy behavior of states? What are the factors that explain variations in the targeting behavior of states? Although we are currently engaged in several empirical studies of targeting behavior, this chapter will not present any findings but rather will attempt to justify and establish the importance of further research in this area.

If one assumes that the foreign policy behavior of states is not random, then it is quite reasonable to assume that there will be discernible differences in the targeting patterns of various states. These differences can be described and analyzed by examining where nations direct their externally oriented influence attempts (i.e., foreign policy behavior). In our attempts to conceptualize this problem in a broader policy context, we asked what seemed like important prior questions: "What are the possible focal points of the attention of foreign policy decision makers? What sort of entities might serve as the objects of attention and/or activity?" Leaving aside for the moment that literature which assumes a primary importance for internal organizational and bureaucratic entities, we posit two general foci for the attention of decision makers: (1) substantive issue areas or (2) other actors in the international system.

It does seem to make some difference whether one assumes issues or other actors as the primary focus for attention. For example, Deutsch and Singer (1964), in a widely quoted article on international system stability, assume that the attention of states is focused primarily on other states in the system. They assert that there is a certain minimal level of attention which one state must focus on another state before war can break out between the two. Thus, according to their argument, the larger the number of actors in the system, the less likely that any nation will receive the "critical amount" of attention, and therefore, there is less likelihood of international warfare. Several criticisms can be made of this line of reasoning,[1] but most important for our purposes is an examination of the assumption that attention is focused on states. If one were to assume that issues rather than actors were the focal point, then of course the Deutsch-Singer argument would no longer hold. In fact, a quite plausible argument can be made that *issues* are the central focus of the deliberations of decision makers, in spite of the fact that the monitoring capabilities of many, if not most, foreign offices are organized in such a manner as to focus on states and geographical regions.

However, when we shift our emphasis from the question of where a nation's *attention* is directed to where *activity* is directed, then the primacy of the role of other actors as targets becomes clearer. Even if one assumes that a nation's foreign policy decision making is in fact structured around issues rather than actors, the importance of other actors as the targets of foreign policy behavior cannot be denied. Coping with issues calls for behavior designed to influence other actors. For example, one

[1] Perhaps one of the most questionable assumptions underlying this model is that every state in the system requires or demands even a miniscule degree of attention from all other states in the system. Yet this assumption is critical to the theory and argument of Deutsch and Singer (1964).

might well assume that a large part of current United States foreign policy deliberations are focused on, and structured by, the energy crisis; but when the United States moves to implement its policy, the subsequent behavior will be directed toward identifiable actors in the international system.

RELATIONSHIP TO OTHER LITERATURE

We have stated above that we feel the study of the targeting of foreign policy behavior has generally been neglected. However, there is one major body of literature and a few other articles which are at least indirectly concerned with similar questions. These studies have the common feature of recognizing that states behave differently toward different targets. However, these studies do not focus their primary attention on the targets per se or on the choice of targets.

The largest body of literature of interest is that referred to as field theory. Social field theory, particularly as developed in international relations by Rummel, conceptualizes units as being embedded in a "force field" with the directed behavior of the acting units being affected by the *distances*—social, psychological, attribute, etc.— between units in the field. In simpler terms, Rummel's analysis assumes that the behavior of an actor is explained in terms of the total social context of the situation (Rummel, 1965, p. 183). Social field theory is of interest to us because Rummel was one of the early international studies scholars to demonstrate the importance of analyzing international behavior, not just in the aggregate, *but in relation to the particular target of behavior* (Rummel, 1967).

However, the models and theories developed by Rummel and others are of limited utility for those interested in targeting behavior. First, field theory is not concerned with *who* the target is. The overarching concern of field theorists is with the concept of distances per se. They attempt to predict foreign policy behavior and international activity based on the measured distances between the actor and the target nation in a total field defined by various dimensions. This emphasis often causes field theorists to overlook differences between

types of targets and actors and leads to losses of information in the process. For example, if two actor states are both equidistant on some dimension from their respective targets, then field theory assumes that the behavior of both actors will be similar. However, a greater emphasis on who the targets and actors are might reveal that one case is that of a Great Power interacting with a Middle Power, while the other case is a Middle Power interacting with a Small Power. Although the power distances may be equal, one can think of numerous reasons why the behaviors may not be similar in the two cases. The study of targeting behaviors attempts to examine these types of questions.

The notion of distance inherent in field theory also makes it difficult to study several other important aspects of targets. First, the logic of distance requires that the dimensions be measured on at least an ordinal scale. Yet some of the more promising dimensions for classifying targets often employ nominal categories, e.g., regional groupings, alignment groups, groups reflecting similar historical experiences, etc. In these cases, the distance measure is often reduced to a simple dichotomy—similar/dissimilar—thus precluding the possibility of working with a nominal scale having multiple categories. Second, the distance requirement of field theory also rules out consideration of nonrelational dimensions, i.e., those attributes of targets defined without reference to the relationship between target and actor. An example of the sort of dimension which would be of interest in understanding targeting, but which is not amenable to distance measures, is the character of the export sector of the target state's economy, e.g., agricultural, nonagricultural raw materials, semifinished goods, etc. This categorization can clearly be considered as an attribute of target states, one which exists and has meaning without positing any relationship between a particular actor and the target state. Finally, attribute distance can be measured only for those dimensions applicable to both the actor and the target. This being so, if the focus of our study is on the behavior of nation-states as actors, then the targets will necessarily be limited to nation-states also. Social field theory cannot easily incorporate intergovernmental organizations (IGOs) within its framework because they do not have national attributes (Vincent, 1972). However, IGOs are the target of a significant proportion of behavior for many states (East, 1973).

Thus, although field theory is clearly a related body of literature, it is not capable of handling many of the questions regarding how and why nations select some entities in the international system to the neglect of others—nor was it intended to examine this question.

Recently, several articles have been written which are relevant to our interests because of their attempts to analyze targets in various ways. These include articles by Rosenau and Hoggard (1974), Hermann and Salmore (1971), Harf (1974), and Wittkopf (1972). These studies all attempt to analyze targets as a means of explaining aspects of foreign policy. Their basic premise is that aspects of the target are related to characteristics and goals of the actor in such a way as to produce certain types of behavior.

However, these studies comprise only the modest beginnings of what is needed. Although each study has value in and of itself, none has systematically addressed the general problem of targeting behavior—and indeed, none of the authors attempted to do so! As in Rummel's work, the emphasis in these articles has been on explaining specific *types* of foreign policy behavior, and the concern with targeting has been indirect at best. For instance, Harf focuses on conflict resolution, and he argues that successful resolution of conflict is more likely if the two parties involved have certain similar characteristics. Wittkopf examines only foreign aid behavior and is not interested in the targeting of any other types of foreign policy behavior. Rosenau and Hoggard examine data on a wider range of behaviors—measures of conflict and cooperation—but again their central concern is with the relative salience of external versus internal variables in explaining foreign policy. Hermann and Salmore do examine the total range of behavior in part of their analysis, but they do so for only those events where the actor and target are different on some attribute dimension.

The very fact that these studies are limited to only certain types of behavior or certain types of events and do not look at the total range of

foreign policy activity means that they are not really useful in analyzing targeting as a general phenomenon. Looking only at certain types of behavior is of little use in either describing or explaining the *total* distribution of behavior across all possible targets.

Two other articles do examine targeting more directly. Kegley (1974) has looked at the raw number of targets addressed in the WEIS data and concludes that states are very selective in their targeting. Winters (1975) has examined the status and regional distribution of foreign policy recipients on a systemic level and has found high-status states and the American-Western European region to be the most popular recipients of behavior.

Finally, in order to answer many of the interesting questions about where a state addresses its behavior, it will be necessary to examine both actual *and* potential targets in the international system. This is necessary because it is impossible to draw valid conclusions about recipient relationships unless all possible types of cases have been included in the analysis. For example, a recent study of African states by Winters (1974) hypothesized a positive relationship between cooperation toward the United States and the amount of aid given by the United States the following year. It is possible to test this hypothesis in one of two ways. If we analyze only those states which already receive U.S. aid, we are actually testing the relationship between amount of cooperation and amount of aid among those states already selected as aid recipients. On the other hand, if we analyze the relationships among *all* states, i.e., both the actual and potential recipients of U.S. aid, we are looking at an aspect of targeting behavior. In fact, when the first analysis was carried out, the original hypothesis was not verified. But in the second analysis using all states, there was a positive relationship of moderate magnitude. Thus, it appears that the previously established level of cooperation toward the U.S. is a factor that influences the selection of an aid recipient and the amount of aid received. This relationship is not, and could not be, revealed except by a study including both potential and actual recipients.[2]

[2]Van Ness (1970), in his study of Chinese endorsements of National Liberation Movements, is inconsistent on this matter. In looking at friendship/hostility toward

In this brief review of work indirectly related to targeting behavior, we can see that researchers are examining foreign policy dyadically, i.e., in terms of actor-target relationships. However, their concerns thus far have directed attention primarily toward explanations of various types of behavior, and they have avoided questions about to whom that behavior is directed and why. At this point, one might well ask, "Why is it important to look at targeting behavior in foreign policy?" It is to this question that we now turn.

WHY STUDY TARGETING BEHAVIOR?

As we mentioned above, it can be assumed that all foreign policy behavior is directed toward some entity or set of entities. These targets can be other states, international organizations, multinational corporations, individuals and organizations within states, or even the entire international system. The primary purpose of studying targeting behavior is to find out where things happen in the international system. Which entities and what kinds of entities are the targets of foreign policy behavior? Do different types of actor-states target their foreign policy behavior differently? Are there differences in the targeting patterns across substantive problem areas? Does targeting behavior change over time?

All these fundamental descriptive questions need to be answered before we can fully understand foreign policy behavior. The answers to such questions are basic descriptive elements upon which can be built more elaborate models and systems for analyzing the relationships between foreign policy behavior and the large variety of causal factors which have been suggested (Rosenau, 1966).

The study of targeting behavior has developed in a manner similar in many ways to the development of social interaction and social exchange theory in sociology. For example, Blau (1968, p. 452) outlines the basic assumptions of social

exchange theory in terms relevant to the study of targeting in foreign policy behavior:

> The basic assumptions of the theory of social exchange are that men enter into new social associations because they expect doing so to be rewarding and that they continue relations with old associates and expand their interaction with them because they actually find doing so to be rewarding.

Blau goes on to indicate how social exchange theory is an important means for describing and studying the structure of a social system.

In a similar manner, one can assume that states interact with other entities because there is some expectation of benefits or rewards. Such benefits can range from simple economic gain to increased power, strategic or tactical advantage, greater prestige, or the attainment of specific foreign policy objectives. The expected rewards may also be conceived of in a negative manner, i.e., the reduction of threat. Thus, the selection of targets for foreign policy behavior can be tied very closely to the widely recognized model in which a nation-state's actions are related to a set of foreign policy goals and objectives.

Interest in the study of targeting behavior can generally be classified in two broad areas: systemic perspective and nation-state-level perspective. From the systemic perspective, the interest in targeting behavior leads one to ask questions about the total distribution of targets of foreign policy behavior throughout the system. The emphasis is upon the structure of the system and the identification of possible subgroups within the system. The types of questions which would be of interest might include "What is the rank ordering of actors according to their frequency of being targets? How does this rank order compare with or relate to rank orderings on other dimensions, e.g., military capabilities or power, economic development level, prestige, etc? Is the rank ordering of targets stable over time? Are there clusters of actors exhibiting similar targeting behavior?"

Perhaps one of the most interesting studies that could be carried out using the systemic approach to targeting behavior would be an analysis of changes in the distribution of power and influence in the international system over time. By assuming that the choice of a unit as a target is in some

China and its relationship to endorsement, he uses only those states receiving endorsements. However, when he examines the feudal nature of the target, he attempts to analyze all possible targets. Wittkopf (1972), in his study of foreign aid distribution by Western countries, has run the analysis for all potential aid recipients but chooses to present these findings only in a footnote.

sense equivalent to ascribing importance to the unit, then it may be possible to recognize shifts in the distribution of ascribed power and influence in the system over time.[3] To refer briefly to a more contemporary example, it would seem likely that the examination of foreign policy targeting over the period 1965-1974 would reveal quite clearly the rising power and influence of the Arab oil states in world politics.

Since we are interested in the relevance of targeting behavior for the comparative study of foreign policy, the nation-state-level perspective on targeting behavior is central to the concerns of this article. From this perspective, targeting-behavior studies focus attention on the differences in targeting found between various national actors or between various *types* of national actors. What kinds of differences, if any, are there in the targeting behavior of the United States and the Soviet Union? How does the targeting behavior of these two superpowers compare over time? Does it reflect the shifting arena of the Cold War, for example?[4]

The central thrust of the comparative study of foreign policy focuses on the relationship of certain characteristics of the national actor to its foreign policy output. Similarly, we expect to find interesting relationships between the characteristics of actors and targeting behavior, which is after all only another aspect of foreign policy behavior. More specifically, we are interested in the variation in targeting behavior across different types of actors classified along various dimensions. Do large and small states, i.e., those with high and low capacities to act, manifest different patterns of targeting behavior? Are there important differences in targeting behavior between developed and developing states? What about between African and Latin American states? Theoretically, we are interested in studying the relationships between targeting behavior and virtually all of the many factors which have been posited as influencing other types of foreign policy behavior.

[3] For a more detailed development of this argument, see East (1972, p. 305) where a similar operationalization is used to generate a measure of ascribed power or prestige.

[4] See Falk (1972) for an interesting discussion of the relationship between geopolitical zones—defined in relation to U.S.-Soviet affairs—and world order.

At this point, we want to comment on the essentially descriptive emphasis in our discussion of targeting up to this point. It is precisely the descriptive aspects of targeting which have been neglected. Furthermore, the call for more descriptive studies parallels the development of sociometry, where the development of the sociogram in the early stages was hailed as a major step forward in the descriptive analysis of social relations (Borgatta, 1968). However, we also contend that the study of targeting behavior is not without analytic or theoretical justification. It is possible to go beyond description, and we hope to demonstrate this below. Before turning to the theoretical aspects, we shall examine briefly some of the ways in which targeting behavior can be measured.

MEASURING TARGETING BEHAVIOR

There are two distinct, but not necessarily independent, strategies for operationalizing targeting behavior. One, the more narrow strategy, looks only at nation-states as targets and generates measures of the frequency and dispersion of foreign policy behavior across the universe of nation-states. The second calls for the generation of a set of typologies for targets and then utilizes measures of frequency and dispersion across the categories of these typologies. Both strategies have problems associated with them. For example, if the first strategy is used, you are limited to measuring targeting behavior directed at nation-states. Furthermore, when looking at the distribution of behavior across nation-states as targets, you are unable to make use of the theory underlying a typology of targets. On the other hand, if the second strategy is used, you are faced with the realization that the number of dimensions or factors for typologizing targets is virtually limitless. There does not yet seem to be any well-developed theory for deciding which factors are most useful for typologizing targets.

At least two different summary measures can be used in the study of targeting. First, there are the simple frequency counts. This often amounts to generating a frequency score for each actor to which behavior was targeted. A variant of this measure is one which counts every target to which an actor directs some minimal number of acts, e.g., five or more acts (Kegley, 1974, p. 2).

A second type of measure of targeting focuses on dispersion—how equally dispersed or concentrated is a nation's foreign policy behavior across targets? This type of measure would allow one to distinguish between a case where an actor generates very many acts distributed rather evenly across n targets and another case where the actor generates few acts directed at n targets but with the majority of acts clustered around one or two targets. Even though both cases have identical numbers of targets, the latter case would have a much more highly concentrated targeting pattern.

Finally, we can mention briefly the matter of typologizing targets. As noted above, it is possible to generate a typology of targets based on any dimension which can be used to classify actors—the choice is virtually limitless. However, we suggest that the following be considered as dimensions for typologizing targets in the early analyses: (1) geography, (2) size, i.e., capacity to act, (3) type of export economy, (4) foreign policy orientation to change, i.e., revisionist or status-quo.

These four dimensions are not the result of an exhaustive theoretical analysis but rather are our best "guesstimates" as to which dimensions for typologizing targets might prove fruitful during the first set of analyses. Geography seems important because of the effects of proximity on the opportunities and costs of interaction (Hare, 1962). The size of the target, or its capacity to act, seems directly related to its ability to provide benefits and rewards to the actor. Typologizing according to the principal nature of exports also seems to tap the target's economic salience and attractiveness to the actor. Finally, the target's foreign policy orientation to change is likely to be the basis upon which allies and adversaries are determined. It also seems to be a salient dimension for tapping the foreign policy equivalent of interpersonal attraction based on sociocultural similarities.

THEORETICAL ASPECTS OF TARGETING BEHAVIOR

In this final section, we want to discuss briefly and illustratively the general relationship between tar-

geting and several clusters of causal factors used in the analysis of foreign policy behavior. Our purpose is to point out some, but by no means all, of the theoretical relationships that could be investigated using targeting as the dependent variable cluster. We shall concentrate on three independent variable clusters, each of which is being utilized in the CREON project[5] and has been discussed with regard to foreign policy behavior elsewhere (East and Salmore, 1976). These three clusters are (1) individual factors, (2) national attributes, and (3) characteristics of regimes.

Individual Factors

The general theoretical thrust of this variable cluster is that individual characteristics and personality traits of the highest level leaders of nation-states will affect the foreign policy behavior generated by those nation-states.[6] In terms of targeting behavior, it is assumed that high-level foreign policy makers will direct more attention toward a wider variety of targets and will also be more selective in their targeting insofar as they have previous experience in international affairs, higher levels of education, more complex cognitive structures, etc. In one sense, there is a clear underlying assumption here—a belief that the world is in fact a complex system and is not a single-issue-single-actor arena. Thus, it is assumed that to be effective, foreign policy leaders will have to deal with numerous issues involving larger numbers of different targets.

Based on the above, it is possible to generate illustrative hypotheses relating individual factors to targeting behavior:

1. The less training or experience a leader has had in international affairs, the smaller the total number of targets to which behavior will be directed.

[5]The CREON project (Comparative Research on the Events of Nations) is a major multiuniversity foreign-events-data project. East and Salmore (1976) contains the theoretical statements upon which the project is based. For a description of the project and the data set, see Hermann et al. (1973).

[6]This section draws heavily on the ideas of Margaret G. Hermann, a member of the CREON project; see especially M. Hermann (1976).

2. Those geographic regions or individual countries with which a leader has had previous experience or training will receive a higher proportion of activity.

3. Leaders with more complex cognitive structures will exhibit a targeting behavior that includes a larger number of targets; at the same time, foreign policy behavior will tend to be more concentrated in areas of high salience.

National Attributes

This variable cluster includes many of those factors most widely assumed to be affecting foreign policy behavior.[7] Characteristics or attributes of the actor state itself are assumed to have a most important effect on that state's foreign policy. For our purposes, we are positing that the effects of various national attributes can be assumed to be operating through the fluctuation of a single conceptual variable—capacity to act. This can be defined as the combined effect of the resources available to the state for allocation in foreign affairs and its ability to utilize them. National attributes such as land area, population, level of economic productivity, degree of social organization, etc. can all be conceptualized as affecting a state's capacity to act in foreign affairs.

How does a state's capacity to act affect its targeting behavior? One assumption is that states which have a greater capacity to act will also have a wider range of interests in international affairs. To put it another way, they will have more to protect and look after. Another assumption is that states with a lower capacity to act will have to husband their resources and utilize them in a more concentrated means to get maximum impact from their efforts. Also, it is generally assumed that states with lower levels of capacity to act will interact more with states having higher levels of capacity; the have-nots will interact with the haves in trying to acquire valued goods and services.

From this perspective, the following illustrative hypotheses can be offered:

1. States with greater capacity to act will direct activity toward a larger total number of targets as well as toward a larger number of different *types* of targets classified geographically, ideologically, and economically.

2. States with less capacity to act will be more likely to direct high amounts of behavior to targets similar in terms of foreign policy orientation, type of economy, and capacity to act. This attraction of similars will be less pronounced in high-capacity states.

3. States with less capacity to act will tend to concentrate their behavior on several types of targets: (a) states having the highest levels of capacity to act, (b) states of a similar capacity level in their own geographical region, and (c) IGOs.

Regime Characteristics

The focus of this theoretical perspective is upon the structures and processes within the governments of the actor states.[8] There is particular concern with the relationships between the various political groups comprising the regime as well as the relationships between the regime and its constituency. Some political features of regimes that are frequently considered include the type and strength of constraints operating on the regime, its internal cohesiveness, and whether the regime came into office by legal or illegal means.

The general relationship between regime characteristics and targeting behavior is based on the assumption that highly constrained regimes are less likely to pursue an activist or expanding role in international affairs. Because of constraints, the primary emphasis of the government's leaders will be on domestic affairs. Even when such regimes do act in the international arena, one could expect to find a very intense, highly concentrated burst of activity designed to solve the immediate problem and then a turning back to domestic concerns. Similarly with regard to the degree of cohesiveness or stability of a regime: An unstable regime has little incentive to expand its role in foreign affairs. On the other hand, traditional wisdom would pre-

---

[7] For a more complete statement of the national attribute perspective, see the chapter written by East entitled "The National Attributes Perspective on Foreign Policy Behavior" in East and Salmore (1976).

[8] The discussion of the regime perspective is based on the work of Barbara G. Salmore and Stephen A. Salmore, two other members of the CREON project. See their more complete statement in Salmore and Salmore (1976).

dict that there would be a tendency for such regimes to use foreign affairs as a means of creating greater cohesion—by creating an "external enemy." In either case, there are clear implications for targeting behavior. With this sort of perspective, we can offer the following hypotheses to illustrate the relationship:

1. The more constrained a regime, the fewer targets it will direct attention toward, and the more concentrated will be the activity it does direct to the international arena.
2. Regimes that have a low degree of cohesiveness will also direct attention toward fewer targets; behavior that is generated is likely to be concentrated in the immediate geographic region, particularly if it is conflictful or hostile behavior.
3. Regimes that come into office illegally are more likely to interact with a large number of targets and also with targets from a wider variety of different regions and ideological orientations in an attempt to gain legitimacy.

Again, it must be noted at this point that these represent only a few theoretically based hypotheses relating targeting behavior to factors affecting foreign policy. Undoubtedly, further consideration could generate many additional hypotheses.

SUMMARY

In this chapter we have made the case for directing more of our energies and efforts toward the examination of the targeting of foreign policy behavior. An increasing amount of evidence, along with an intuitively satisfying intellectual posture, supports the call for studying foreign policy behavior in terms of the targets to which it is directed. However, merely studying actor-target dyads does not mean that targeting will be the focus of research. Field theory and other "dyadic" studies can, and most often do, have a different research goal in mind. What is needed is a significant and concerted effort to begin to map targeting behavior and then to generate and test theoretical explanations for the ways in which various nations target their foreign policy behavior. This research task cannot be successfully completed by looking at only selected types of

foreign policy behavior; it calls for an examination of the total scope of foreign policy activity. Fortunately, the growth and development of the events data movement (Burgess and Lawton, 1972) have provided us with data appropriate for our immediate tasks. Also, we have pointed out by way of illustration several theoretical directions which this research can follow. In our minds, targeting is just another dimension of foreign policy outputs, albeit one that has been sorely neglected. It is in this sense that we see the study of targeting behavior as a major new area to be explored in the continued development of the comparative study of foreign policy.

REFERENCES

Blau, Peter M. 1968. "Interaction: Social Exchange." In *International Encyclopedia of the Social Sciences,* ed. David L. Sills, vol. 7, pp. 452-57. New York: Macmillan and Free Press.

Borgatta, Edgar F. 1968. "Sociometry." In *International Encyclopedia of the Social Sciences,* ed. David L. Sills, vol. 15, pp. 53-56. New York: Macmillan and Free Press.

Burgess, Philip M., and Raymond W. Lawton. 1972. *Indicators of International Behavior: An Assessment of Events Data Research.* Beverly Hills: Sage.

Deutsch, Karl W., and J. David Singer. 1964. "Multipolar Power Systems and International Stability." *World Politics* 16 (Apr): 390-406.

East, Maurice A. 1972. "Status Discrepancy and Violence in the International System: An Empirical Analysis." In *The Analysis of International Politics,* ed. James N. Rosenau, Vincent Davis, and Maurice A. East, pp. 299-319.

———. 1973. "Size and Foreign Policy Behavior: A Test of Two Models." *World Politics* 25 (Jul): 556-76.

——— and Stephen A. Salmore, eds. 1976. *Theoretical Perspectives for Comparative Foreign Policy Studies.* Beverly Hills: Sage.

Falk, Richard A. 1972. "Zone II as a World Order Construct." In *The Analysis of International Politics,* ed. James N. Rosenau, Vincent Davis, and Maurice A. East, pp. 187-206. New York: Free Press.

Hare, A. Paul. 1962. *Handbook of Small Group Research.* New York: Free Press.

Harf, James E. 1974. "Inter-Nation Conflict Resolution and National Attributes." In *Comparing Foreign Policies,* ed. James N. Rosenau, pp. 305-25. Beverly Hills: Sage.

Hermann, Charles F., and Stephen A. Salmore. 1971. "The Recipients of Foreign Policy Events." Paper presented at a meeting of the Peace Research Society, Ann Arbor.

——— et al. 1973. *CREON: A Foreign Events Data Set.* Beverly Hills: Sage.

Hermann, Margaret G. 1976. "Effects of Personal Characteristics of Leaders on Foreign Policy." In *Theoretical Perspectives for Comparative Foreign Policy Studies,* eds. Maurice A. East and Stephen A. Salmore. Beverly Hills: Sage.

Kegley, Charles W., Jr. 1974. "Selective Attention: A General Characteristic of the Interactive Behavior of Nations." Paper presented at a meeting of the Southern Political Science Association, New Orleans.

Rosenau, James N. 1966. "Pre-theories and Theories of Foreign Policy." In *Approaches to Comparative and International Politics,* ed. R. Barry Farrell, pp. 27-92. Evanston: Northwestern Univ. Press.

——— and Gary D. Hoggard. 1974. "Foreign Policy Behavior in Dyadic Relationships: Testing a Pretheoretical Extension." In *Comparing Foreign Policies,* ed. James N. Rosenau, pp. 117-50. Beverly Hills: Sage.

Rummel, R. J. 1965. "A Field Theory of Social Action with Application to Conflict within Nations." In *General Systems Yearbook,* vol. 10, pp. 183-211. Bedford, Mass.: Society for General Systems Research.

———. 1967. "The Relationship between National Attributes and Foreign Conflict Behavior." In *Quantitative International Politics,* ed. J. David Singer, pp. 187-214. New York: Free Press.

Salmore, Stephen A., and Barbara G. Salmore. 1976. "Regime Structure and Foreign Policy." In *Theoretical Perspectives for Comparative Foreign Policy Studies,* eds. Maurice A. East and Stephen A. Salmore. Beverly Hills: Sage.

Van Ness, Peter. 1970. *Revolution and Chinese Foreign Policy.* Berkeley and Los Angeles: Univ. of California Press.

Vincent, Jack E. 1972. "Comments on Social Field Theory." DON Research Report 58. Mimeo. Honolulu: Univ. of Hawaii.

Winters, Barbara K. 1974. "United States Foreign Aid and African Foreign Policy Behavior." Mimeo. Lexington: Univ. of Kentucky.

———. 1975. "Monitoring Activity in the International System." Paper presented at the Southern Section Meeting of the Peace Science Society, Raleigh.

Wittkopf, Eugene R. 1972. *Western Bilateral Aid Allocations: A Comparative Study of Recipient State Attributes and Aid Received.* Beverly Hills: Sage.

40. Restlessness, Change, and Foreign Policy Analysis

James N. Rosenau

All the evidence points to the conclusion that the comparative study of foreign policy has emerged as a *normal* science. For nearly a decade many investigators have been busily building and improving data banks, testing and revising propositions, using and departing from each other's work. It has been an astonishingly rapid evolution, not only because of the steady and growing flow of research products, but also because of the large degree to which there has been convergence around particular variables and methodologies. Our differences now are about small points—the adequacy of an events data scheme or the scope of a governmental variable—and the great "debates" over the role of case studies and the appropriateness of scientific methods have faded into an obscure past. Now we can work at peace, without diverting energy to justifying our existence and beating back challenges from unsympathetic colleagues.

A conspicuous indication that a normal science—consisting of, as Kuhn puts it, "mopping-up operations" (1970, p. 24)—has emerged is the speed with which we have adopted the parenthetic citation rather than the extended footnote as the standard format for documenting evidence in our papers. Some trained in an earlier era may long for the old style that relegates bibliographic detail to the bottoms of pages and allows one's best prose to unfold in an unfettered way, but it seems clear to me that the parenthetic form is a mark of science. The greater the amount of reliable knowledge that a discipline has cumulated, the more is an abbreviated citational form required to accommodate the myriad references necessary to depict the cumulation. At least this would seem to be why variants of the parenthetic form are so prevalent in the hard sciences. In the humanities, in history, and in traditional political science, in contrast, knowledge grows in a number of disparate directions, thus encouraging discursive discussions of tangentially related studies apart from the text. Thus even the format of our writings reflects our development as a normal science and, more important, the pervasiveness of parenthetic intrusions in papers and journal articles indicates that cumulation has proceeded apace, that our mop has been wielded with broad strokes.

Normal science, however, has its drawbacks. It is by definition an enterprise which stresses careful empirical analysis more than innovative theorizing. As Kuhn (1970, p. 24) notes, those who practice a normal science

> attempt to force nature into the preformed and relatively inflexible box that the paradigm supplies. No part of the aim of normal science is to call forth new sorts of phenomena; indeed, those that will not fit the box are often not seen at all. Nor do scientists normally aim to invent new theories, and they often are intolerant of those invented by others. Instead, normal scientific research is directed to the articulation of those phenomena and theories that the paradigm already supplies.

While it is not my impression that those who study foreign policy comparatively are intolerant, neither do they seem generally inclined to invent new theories. We are not lacking in inventiveness, and our responsiveness to new schemes for the creation and analysis of data is extensive, but these predispositions are narrowly confined to those variables and formulations where cumulation has already begun to occur. Except for occasional arguments rejecting the notion that the nation-state is an essential actor in world affairs and that studying foreign policy is thus a worthwhile endeavor (Handelman et al., 1973), our burgeoning literature is devoid of theoretical challenges that attempt to explain foreign policy phenomena in entirely new ways. In effect, we fit Kuhn's description of normal science rather well, and are thus far removed from what he considers a revolutionary science (1970, pp. 92-135).

This is not necessarily an undesirable state of affairs. My own tendencies are toward theory building and I sometimes get anxious about the extent and intensity with which many colleagues are committed to closely reasoned and narrowly structured empirical inquiries. Yet it seems clear, given the complexity of foreign policy phenomena, that our normal science has a long way to go before we tie down all the loose ends and mop up all the stray details. Furthermore, I doubt that it will be undermined by those who challenge the utility of treating nation-states as central international actors. Both subnational and supranational actors are gaining in importance as technology shrinks the world and heightens interdependence, but my own view—admittedly shaped by the prevailing paradigm—is that while the capabilities and influence of nation-states will diminish with mounting interdependence, the future will be an asymmetrical one in which nations are supreme in some areas and other international actors are predominant in other areas (Rosenau, 1972). If so, foreign policy phenomena will be with us for a long time to come and the task of clarifying their operation should thus continue to be satisfying and important.

So the present state of affairs need not be regretted and the ensuing observations thus should not be interpreted as a call to revolutionary science. On the contrary, the suggestions that follow fall within the prevailing paradigm and I for one continue to enjoy the opportunity of working under circumstances where there are a sufficient number of like-minded others as to constitute an informal community of scholars. Widespread consensus on the rules and goals of the game is a rarity in the subfields of political science and we ought to relish every moment of it.

A RESTLESS SCIENCE

Yet, even as we derive satisfaction from participating in the processes of convergence and cumulation, so should we aspire to quickening its pace and expanding its scope. We have developed concepts, data, and methodologies with which to conduct our inquiries, but full comprehension of the dynamics of foreign policy continues to elude us. Nation-states still do the unexpected, officials still engage in unanticipated behavior, and publics still undergo surprising transformations. Thus we are in urgent need of variables with greater explanatory power. I see attempts to fulfill this need as compatible with both acceptance of the prevailing paradigm and rejection of the sufficiency of the variables that presently articulate it. The identification of new variables in the context of the dominant paradigm is neither normal nor revolutionary science but falls between the two. For want of a better term, I suggest we call it a *restless science.*

The inclination of many in the field to turn to the issue-area concept in their search for more penetrating understanding is illustrative of a restless science,[1] but I fear that the results of these efforts may not quell our restlessness. In the first place, there is the danger that, in searching for deeper understanding through greater precision, we may come to define issue areas so narrowly as to, in effect, think in terms of issues, a development that would lead us away from cumulation and parsimony. Second, the quest for an issue-area typology that has the potential for powerful explanation may prove futile. On the one hand, conventional typologies that distinguish among, say, economic, political, cultural, military, and diplomatic issues, or unconventional ones that differentiate among, say, status, territorial, human resource, and nonhuman resource issues, require the specification of essentially artificial issue-area boundaries, since issues rarely fall clearly and exclusively in one area. On the other hand, typologies cast at lower levels of abstraction to achieve mutu-

[1] For a recent published expression of this inclination, see Brewer (1973).

ally exclusively categories tend to equate issues with issue areas, a consequence which, to repeat, is unlikely to resolve our restlessness. Third, if the concept is to have any theoretical utility, issue areas must be treated as independent variables. This requires the specification of those values embraced by an area that evoke attitudes and behaviors different from those related to any other area, a staggering task which may necessitate a revolutionary paradigm to execute. Fourth, if adequate empirical data are ever gathered linking attitudinal and behavioral differences to the values bounded by different issue areas, the issue-area concept may prove not to account for great amounts of variance. I was recently given pause in this respect by the results of a just completed study in which it was found that a clear-cut foreign policy issue (the testing of nuclear weapons) and an equally salient domestic issue (civil rights) did not evoke differences on the part of active citizens across 150 of 152 attitudinal and behavioral dependent variables (Rosenau, 1974, pp. 451-56).

My own restlessness over the possibility that issue-area analysis will lead us away from parsimony (or even back to noncomparable case studies) has led me to search for basic attitudinal and behavioral orientations that are operative in any and all issue areas. My effort to delineate four types of adaptive orientations is a product of this search (1970). Much of the criticism of the adaptation framework, of course, is that it is too general, that officials and nations adapt differently in different issue areas. Empirical investigation of such a hypothesis would help to clarify both the adaptive and issue-area perspectives and would constitute another illustration of a restless science.

THE CONCEPT OF CHANGE

Let me suggest another route that may be fruitful to pursue. I believe a rich payoff might ensue if the concept of change were fashioned into an operational dependent variable. In our search for recurring patterns—for constancies in the external behavior of nations—we tend to treat breaks in patterns as exceptions, as nuisances which complicate our tasks. Yet it is precisely the point at which a trend veers off sharply in a new direction that the interaction of key variables is most fully exposed. Patterns do not change except when the value of one or more variable is altered or when situations arise in which processes that are normally independent of each other become intertwined and must undergo modification. The alterations in the social, economic, political, and diplomatic processes that culminate in changed external behavior may unfold slowly or occur suddenly, but in either event the changed behavior provides an especially useful occasion for observing the interplay of the factors that shape foreign policy and assessing their relative potencies.

Attention to the points at which patterns of behavior change may not only serve to reveal the clash of normally balanced processes, but—and perhaps more importantly—it may also generate puzzles (to use Kuhn's useful term for the foci of theory). Fruitful puzzle-solving (i.e., mopping-up) activities cannot proceed apace unless we have fruitful puzzles to solve and I fear that one of our difficulties is a scarcity of theoretical problems that are so puzzling as to challenge our ingenuities and galvanize our energies. All too often our inquiries are addressed to what or whether questions rather than to why questions. We ask, say, "What is the impact of a x variable on nation-type y's behavior" or "Whether societal variables are more potent than systemic factors"—questions which do not provoke restlessness and sustain curiosity because the only obstacles to their solution pertain to the availability of adequate data and appropriate methodologies. By focusing on those points where old patterns break and new ones develop, however, our attention is drawn to genuine puzzles. For immediately the question of *why* arises—why the change occurs when, how, and where it does. Such questions are especially challenging because the obstacles to their solution lie in our own creativity. Data and methodology are necessary to test the validity of the solutions, but the solutions themselves must come out of our understanding, our grasp of how the factors that culminate in the external behavior of nation-states interact and when they are subject to alteration. Furthermore, the dynamics of change are pervaded with uncertainty—over duration, direction, and outcome—and nothing lends itself to restlessness and curiosity better than uncertainty. If we focus on the change point of patterned behavior, our values, egos, and imaginations will be engaged,

encouraging us to mop up puzzles of our own choosing.

Still another advantage of the change concept is that, virtually by definition, it will compel us to build longitudinal variables into our models. Change cannot be discerned or assessed unless it is analyzed in the context of previously constant—or continuous—behavior. There are no discontinuities without continuities to highlight them, so that of necessity we will have to trace the operation of the variables that interest us across time. We often pay lip service to this necessity but rarely act on it, succumbing instead to the easier procedures of cross-sectional inquiry. But longitudinal analysis cannot be avoided if the problems that puzzle us are rooted in patterned behavior marked by discontinuities.

This is not to imply, in any way, that a concern with the break points in foreign policy patterns requires or confines us to the case history approach. To be sure, a large population of such cases, organized and described in terms of common variables and detailed sequences of interaction, would of course be an invaluable contribution to the pool of available data. One's mind boggles at the thought of what might be done—the hypotheses that might be tested and the understanding that might be developed—if elaborate analyses of, say, 50 major alterations in the external behavior of an equal number of nation-states could be compiled, with 10 in each case drawn from each of the last five decades and with the same operational formulations of the key idiosyncratic, governmental, societal, external, and systemic variables employed in all the cases. Such analyses, however, would be far from the conventional case histories. In addition to chronological sequences that described the perceptions, actions, and interactions of the relevant decision makers and thus facilitate the assessment of the impact of idiosyncratic and governmental variables, they would also include materials that allowed for the comparison of the decision makers and their actions with those of their predecessors who engaged in the prior continuous behavior from which the case being investigated deviates. Presumably such analyses would also include systematic data on any changes in societal and external conditions that may have preceded the altered foreign policy and thus facilitate the delineation of the relative impact of macrovariables.

Of course, the probability of such a data base, or of even one half the size, being created in the foreseeable future is virtually nil. Even if a number of investigators could be prevailed upon to contribute to it, the time and coordination required to compile case analyses of this kind are too great to make the desired results likely. Yet this does not mean that a focus on change would require us to fall back on conventional case histories. Break points can be readily probed through a variety of quantitative techniques that, in effect, bypass the reconstruction of perceptual worlds and detailed interaction sequences. The potency of idiosyncratic variables, for example, can be creatively investigated through cross-national comparisons of the flow of new personnel through the key decision-making roles before, during, and after the period in which the prevailing pattern of behavior underwent alteration. Blake's (1968) analysis of the extent to which prior changes in top decision makers and/or regimes preceded altered votes in the United Nations on the question of seating the delegation from mainland China, an analysis which traced the repeated behavior of many nations over some 15 years, illustrates the way in which breaks in prevailing patterns can be incisively pressed to yield insight into the operation of idiosyncratic variables, not to mention certain important governmental variables. Similarly, content analyses of the announcements and/or accompanying speeches through which break points are made public, defended, and justified could serve as a means of at least assessing how officials perceive the potency of the factors that led them to depart from prevailing policies. Still another approach, elaborated at greater length below, involves the use of events data to trace the role played by governmental, societal, external, and systemic variables as sources of change behavior.

Whatever method is used to quantify the break points, of course, it will be necessary to develop a typology of forms of change which, in turn, can be used as the basis for framing hypotheses about how various types of alterations in foreign policy behavior may be linked to various idiosyncratic, governmental, societal, external, and systemic sources. Distinctions might be drawn, for example,

between tactical and strategic changes, between minor revisions and wholesale reversals. It might then be hypothesized that the former are linked to idiosyncratic and/or external variables and the latter to societal and systemic variables. Other dimensions of the typology might distinguish between changes in which a pattern of behavior is abandoned or a new form of behavior is undertaken, between a change in a nation's view of what others should do or in its view of what it will do, between changes that enlarge commitments or reduce them, between changes that are cautiously negotiated or abruptly announced, and so on. My guess is that an elaborate typology could readily be constructed that allowed for the pursuit of a wide range of theoretical interests.

EVENTS DATA AND THE STUDY OF CHANGE

An insight into the opportunities—and difficulties—provided by the change concept can be gained from a consideration of how events data might be used in this context. Such an approach would require that every event be coded in terms of whether or not it constituted change on the part of the actor and, if so, the kind of change that it represented. The difficulties inherent in such coding judgments would be enormous, but it ought to be possible to develop a lexicon of change that enables coders to judge whether an action is or is not consistent with the prior pattern of behavior. Even if the problem of operationalizing the concept precludes high intercoder reliability, one can always resort to a scheme which relies, not on the coder's interpretation, but on explicit statements by the actors involved in the event or the source describing it that change has occurred. Such a method might not result in the compilation of a large sample of change events (as both actors and sources may tend to avoid using the lexicon of change in reporting events), but it should yield a sufficient number to facilitate assessing the relative potencies of key variables.

The CREON data set suggests both the potentials and the problems of pursuing this research strategy. The coding scheme included a "change position" variable and, with respect to every event, the coder was instructed to answer the question "Does the action represent a major change or reversal of the position taken by the actor's government on the same issue in the past?" If the answer was affirmative, the coder was instructed to "briefly describe the change in the position." The full entry in the CREON codebook (Hermann et al., 1971) for this variable lists six alternative codes and a brief comment on how to identify a "major" change:

> *Actor Changes Previous Position on Issue (CHANG-POS)?* Does the action represent a major change or reversal of the position taken by the actor's government on the same issue in the past? A "major" or "significant" change in policy need not be a reversal, but if it is in the same direction as previous positions, it should involve a shift in means (e.g., from non-military support to military support) or an abrupt change in level of governmental effort.
>
> 1 = decision maker indicates action represents major change
>
> 2 = decision maker indicates action represents no major change
>
> 3 = data source indicates action represents major change–do not use if category 1 is applicable
>
> 4 = data source indicates action represents no major change–do not use if category 2 is applicable
>
> 5 = coder infers that action represents major change–do not use if either category 1 or 3 is applicable
>
> 6 = coder infers that action represents no major change–do not use if either category 2 or 4 is applicable

The problems with such coding are obvious. Will different coders, especially those without training in the foreign policy field, operate with the same or similar conceptions of what constitutes a major or significant change so that the use of code 5 will be reliable? Will they rely on the same lexicon of change to determine whether either the actor or the data source indicates that the action represents major change, making codes 1 through 4 reliable? Do either actors or data sources explicitly characterize action as either altered or constant frequently enough that the resulting sample of data will not be primarily a function of the coders' own substantive judgments of the events rather than of their interpretation of language?

Even a cursory examination of the 10,999 events that comprised the CREON data set at the time of this analysis suggests answers to these questions.[2] The initial results indicate either that major change is a rare foreign policy event or that coders, perhaps aware of the limits of their training, avoid the use of code 5. Only 322 of the 10,999 events, or less than 3 percent, were coded as constituting a major change, and probably no more than 26 of these 322 were judged so by the coder (using code 5). My guess is that this finding reflects the reluctance of coders to conclude that an event represents change more than it does the actual extent of change, but a closer analysis of the data is necessary before a more confident assertion can be made in this regard.[3] Even if the data underestimate the extent of change, however, it is clearly not a typical event. The fact that probably only 296 events in the sample were so characterized by either the actor or the data source suggests the large degree to which patterned behavior and continuity mark the external behavior of nations.

As for the question of whether there is a common lexicon of change that serves as the basis for the coding of events data, an examination of the brief description of the 322 events reveals a number of recurring words or phrases that must have served as guides for the coders. The words "previously" and "formerly" seem to occur with the greatest frequency, but the list also includes "first time that," "originally," "withdraws," "earlier," "revises," "before," "breaking of," "new," "agrees," "now wants," "stopping," "until now," "no longer," "abandons," "renews," "resume," "sever," and so on. Whether or not the coders used such indicators consistently is of course difficult to say (I do not know what the

---

[2] I am indebted to Patrick Callahan for programing the CREON data so that the change variable could be singled out for a separate analysis.

[3] The initial printout collapsed the change data into simple yes (codes 1, 3, and 5) and no (codes, 2, 4, and 6) categories and thus I had to infer that only 26 of the 322 were classified by the coders from the fact that this was the number of classified as "not applicable" when the change variable was cross-tabulated with one in which events were classified by who announced the action that was viewed as a changed position. Besides the 17 percent coded as "not applicable," 63 percent of the 322 were announced by the chief political executive, 13 percent by career bureaucrats, and the remainder by various other types of officials, spokesmen, or journalists.

measure of intercoder reliability was for this variable), but it seems clear that a vocabulary for describing change exists and could be defined further.

While the degree to which change marks foreign policy behavior may not be very great, some crude breakdowns of the 322 change events in terms of other CREON variables hint at the potential that the compilation and analysis of a small sample of such phenomena might hold for enlarging our substantive comprehension. Consider, for example, these findings:

(a) 70 percent of the change actions were classified as based on diplomatic resources, 15 percent on military resources, and 15 percent on "economic-scientific-technological" resources.

(b) 41 percent of the change actions were classified as occurring in meetings between officials of the nation initiating the action and of the nation toward whom it was directed; 59 percent did not occur in such a setting and presumably were unilateral in their origins.

(c) 20 percent of the change actions were classified as occurring through a speech, 12 percent through a press conference, 24 percent through a diplomatic document, and 27 percent through other written or verbal channels; 17 percent were classified as not being applicable to channels of this kind.

(d) 17 percent of the change actions were estimated to be "physical deeds" that required "minutes/hours" to execute, 18 percent were judged to require "days," 3 percent "weeks," 3 percent "months," 4 percent "years," and 8 percent an "indefinite" period; 47 percent were classified as "verbal statements unaccompanied by physical deeds."

(e) 22 percent of the change actions were classified as involving verbal statements in which the actor indicated the possibility of further action in the future and 13 percent involved statements in which the actor indicated "what it would like an external entity to do in the future"; 22 percent were classified as physical deeds involving "symbolic acts," 8 percent as deeds involving "significant" nonmilitary resource commitments, 13 percent as deeds involving either the transfer or use of military resources, and 22 percent were coded as neutral verbal statements.

(f) 53 percent of the change actions were classified as having been unilateral and "unelicited" by another actor, 6 percent as unilateral and elicited, 38 percent as bilateral or multilateral and unelicited, and the remainder as bilateral or multilateral and elicited.

(g) 30 percent of the change actions were classified as involving an increase in relationships and 19 percent a decrease.

(h) 19 percent of the change actions were classified as involving "border behavior," whereas the comparable figure for all 10,999 events was 8 percent; the equivalent percentages for "penetrative behavior" were 15 and 2, for "military behavior" 11 and 18, and for "bargaining behavior" 39 and 61.

(i) 9 percent of the change actions were classified as occurring in the context of a "world organization" (the equivalent figure for all events was 39 percent).

(j) 18 percent of the change actions were classified as involving the "foreign affairs bureaucracy and/or its officials" (the equivalent figure for all events was 31 percent).

(k) 69 percent of the change actions were judged to be part of a sequence in which the actor had been previously involved, whereas only 43 percent of all the events were so coded.

In sum, not only does change in the behavior of foreign policy actors offer an opportunity for probing the interactions of key variables, but there are also good reasons to believe that such interactions are manifest in events data sets. Indeed, change is perhaps the most constant feature of our times and its pervasiveness is probably such as to be traceable in many types of diverse data.

THEORIZING ABOUT CHANGE

The development of techniques to investigate the breaks in foreign policy behavior patterns as dependent variables will not, however, facilitate theory. Extensive data on pattern shifts will not in themselves make clear why nations alter their courses. Nor will the provision of data depicting the circumstances that preceded the alterations lead automatically to explanatory formulations. Rather it bears repeating that, in addition to the empirical focus on change, we shall have to reorient ourselves to be as theoretical about the discontinuities of foreign policy as we presently are about the continuities. Instead of treating the break points as parameters within which patterns unfold, for example, we need to approach them as potentially explanatory of why patterns manage to persist, as the points at which the processes of mutual reinforcement among variables that had previously prevailed are no longer operative.

One concrete area where theorizing about change may prove to be especially useful revolves around the question, noted earlier, of whether or not the influence of the nation-state is declining and that of other actors growing. If the changing status of actors is considered as a process whereby compliance with requests and/or dictates is either given or withheld by those toward whom actors direct their policies, it ought not be difficult to identify conditions when patterns of compliance will tend to emerge or decline and then to derive theoretical and testable propositions which specify how the compliance-evoking capacity (i.e., authority) of different actors is likely to vary across issue areas. At least such an approach would provide a more meaningful point of departure than either insistence that the influence of the nation-state has diminished or simple assertion that issue-centered analysis is preferable to its state-centered counterpart.

Whether it emerges slowly and almost imperceptibly or suddenly and startlingly, in other words, changed behavior arrests attention. It tells us that the parts of the pattern are no longer holding together and that it is undergoing reorganization. Surely these are circumstances that will arouse our curiosities and stimulate the restless quest for new theory.

REFERENCES

Blake, D. H. 1968. "Leadership Succession and Foreign Policy." Ph.D. dissertation, Rutgers Univ.

Brewer, T. L. 1973. "Issue and Context Variations in Foreign Policy: Effects on American Elite Behavior." *Journal of Conflict Resolution* 17 (Mar): 89-114.

Handelman, J. R., J. A. Vasquez, M. K. O'Leary, and W. D. Coplin. 1973. "Color It Morgenthau: A Data-based Assessment of Quantitative International Relations Research." Paper presented at the Annual Meeting of the International Studies Association, New York.

Hermann, C. F., S. A. Salmore, and M. A. East. 1971. "Code Manual for Analytic Deck of Comparative Foreign Policy Events." Mimeo. Columbus: Ohio State Univ.

Kuhn, T. S. 1970. *The Structure of Scientific Revolutions.* 2d ed. Chicago: Univ. of Chicago Press.

Rosenau, J. N. 1970. *The Adaptation of National Societies: A Theory of Political System Behavior and Transformation.* New York: McCaleb-Seiler.

———. 1972. "Adaptive Polities in an Interdependent World." *Orbis* 16 (Spring): 153-73.

———. 1974. *Citizenship between Elections: An Inquiry into the Mobilizable American.* New York: Free Press.

Notes on Contributors

CHADWICK F. ALGER is Mershon Professor of Political Science and Public Policy and director of the program in transnational cooperation in the policy sciences at the Mershon Center, Ohio State University. He has published widely on political processes, communication, and socialization in the United Nations system. He is presently conducting research and public education on the international relations of cities, using Columbus, Ohio, as a laboratory.

HAYWARD R. ALKER, JR., is a professor of political science at MIT, having formerly taught at Yale, Michigan, Columbia, and FLACSO (Santiago). His books include *Mathematics and Politics, World Politics in the General Assembly* (with Bruce M. Russett), *Analyzing Global Interdependence* (with Lincoln P. Bloomfield and Nazli Choucri), and *Mathematical Approaches to Politics* (edited with Karl W. Deutsch and Antoine Stoetzel).

DAVID ANDRUS is director of the special services section in Security Pacific National Bank's Data Processing Division and a Ph.D. candidate in the School of International Relations at the University of Southern California.

RICHARD K. ASHLEY is an assistant professor of international relations at the University of Southern California. A contributor to numerous books and journals in the field, he recently completed his Ph.D. dissertation at MIT, "Growth, Rivalry, and Balance: The Sino-Soviet-American Triangle of Conflict."

RICHARD SMITH BEAL is an assistant professor of political science and coordinator of the international relations program at Brigham Young University. His writings include "The Coalition Strategy of the Powerful" (1973), "Some Personality Correlates in Game Theory Strategy" (with Stan Taylor, 1974) "Crises in a Transforming International System" (1975), and "WEIS's Untold Story" (1976).

G. R. BOYNTON is a professor of political science at the University of Iowa. He is a coauthor of *Representatives and Represented* (1975) and a coeditor of *Political Behavior and Public Opinion* (1974) and *Legislative Systems in Developing Countries* (1975). He has published many articles on public opinion in professional journals.

STUART A. BREMER is an assistant professor of political science at the University of Michigan.

WILLIAM O. CHITTICK is an associate professor of political science at the University of Georgia. He is the author of *State Department, Press, and Pressure Groups: A Role Analysis* (1970) and the editor of *The Analysis of Foreign Policy Outputs* (1975).

NAZLI CHOUCRI is an associate professor of political science at MIT. Her writings include *Population Dynamics and International Violence: Propositions, Insights and Evidence* (1974), *Nations in Conflict: National Growth and International Violence* (with Robert C. North, 1975), and *International Politics of Energy Interdependence: The Case of Petroleum* (1976).

MAURICE A. EAST is an associate professor of political science and the associate director of the Patterson School of Diplomacy and International Commerce at the University of Kentucky. He is a principal investigator on the Comparative Research on the Events of Nations (CREON) project. He is a coauthor of *CREON: A Foreign Events Data Set* (1973), a coeditor of *The Analysis of International Politics* (1972), and the author of numerous articles for such journals as *World Politics, International Studies Quarterly,* and *Policy Sciences.*

ALEXANDER L. GEORGE is a professor of political science at Stanford University. He served as president of the International Studies Association in 1973-1974. His writings include *Woodrow Wilson and Colonel House* (with Juliette L. George, 1956), *Propaganda Analysis* (1959), *The Chinese Communist Army in Action* (1967), *The Limits of Coercive Diplomacy* (with D. K. Hall and W. R. Simons, 1971), *Deterrence in American Foreign Policy: Theory and Practice* (with Richard Smoke, 1974); and *Toward a More Soundly Based Foreign Policy: Making Better Use of Information* (with collaborators, 1976).

JOHN V. GILLESPIE is an associate professor of political science at Indiana University. He is a coauthor of *Comparative Politics Laboratory* (1972) and a coeditor of *Cross-National Research: Macro-Quantitative Analysis* (1971), *Mathematical Models in International Relations* (1976), and *Mathematical Systems in International Relations Research* (1976). Recent articles based on his research have appeared in *Peace Science Papers, Synthese,* and *Modeling and Simulation* and are forthcoming in the *American Political Science Review* and the *Jerusalem Journal of International Relations.*

HAROLD GUETZKOW is a professor of political science and holds the Gordon Scott Fulcher Chair of Decision-Making in International Relations at Northwestern University. He is author, coauthor, and/or editor of such monographs and books as *Multiple Loyalties* (1955), *Simulation in International Relations* (1963), *A Social Psychology of Group Processes for Decision-Making* (1964), and *Simulation in Social and Administrative Science* (1972) as well as the essays "Long-Range Research in International Relations" (1950) and "Simulations in the Consolidation and Utilization of Knowledge about International Relations" (1969). He is consultant in such organizations as the United Nations Secretariat and the U.S. Departments of State and Defense.

JAMES E. HARF is an associate professor of political science at Ohio State University and chairman of the Consortium for International Studies Education. Author of *Instructor's Guide for Introduction to International Politics* and coauthor of *Theory, Data, and Analysis: A Laboratory Introduction to Comparative and International Politics,* he has contributed to numerous books and journals, including *International Association, Quest, International Journal of Group Tensions, Universities and Transnational Approaches to the Solution of World Problems, International Studies Notes, Comparing Foreign Policies, Methods for the Social Studies Teacher,* and *Computers in the Undergraduate Curricula.*

CHARLES F. HERMANN is Mershon Professor of Political Science and Public Policy at Ohio State University and associate director of the Mershon Center. He is the author of *Crises in Foreign Policy,* the editor of and a contributor to *International Crises,* and a coauthor of *CREON: A Foreign Events Data Set.* In addition to research on foreign policy decision making, he continues the research with the other investigators in the Comparative Research on the Events of Nations (CREON) project.

MARGARET G. HERMANN is a psychologist and research associate at the Mershon Center, Ohio State University. She is an editor of and a contributor to *A Psychological Examination of Political Leaders* and a coauthor of *CREON: A Foreign Events Data Set.* Her research focuses on how the personal characteristics of political leaders affect their political behavior.

OLE R. HOLSTI is the George V. Allen Professor of Political Science at Duke University. His writings include *Unity and Disintegration in International Alliances* (1973), *Crisis, Escalation, War* (1972), and *Content Analysis for the Social Sciences and Humanities* (1969).

P. TERRENCE HOPMANN is an associate professor of political science and director of the Quigley Center of International Studies at the University of Minnesota. He received his B.A. from Princeton University in 1964 and his Ph.D. from Stanford University in 1969. He is a coauthor of *Unity and Disintegration in International Alliances: Comparative Studies* and the author of articles on alliance cohesion and on bargaining in international arms control negotiations. In 1975-1976 he was a Fulbright-Hayes research fellow in Belgium.

JERRY B. JENKINS is an assistant professor of political science at the University of Georgia. His major writing deals with the role of uncertainty and uncertainty reduction in global politics.

ROBERT JERVIS is a professor of political science at the University of California, Los Angeles. He is the author of *The Logic of Images in International Relations* (1970) and *Perception and Misperception in International Politics* (1976).

CHARLES W. KEGLEY, JR., is an associate professor of international relations at the University of South Carolina, where he is chairperson of the International Relations Program. He has written "A General Empirical Typology of Foreign Policy Behavior" (1973), "The Dimensionality of Regional Integration" (1975), "Measuring Transformations in the Global Legal System" (1975), and "The Transformation of Inter-bloc Relations" (1974). Among the books he has edited are *International Events and the Comparative Analysis of Foreign Policy* (1975), *Analyzing International Relations* (1975), *After Vietnam: The Future of American Foreign Policy* (1971), and *A Multi-method Introduction to International Politics.*

KATHLEEN KNIGHT is a Ph.D. candidate in political science at the University of California, Los Angeles, where she holds a regent's teaching internship. Her research has been directed toward combining formal modeling and social psychological concepts in a substantive approach to the study of international relations.

RUSSELL J. LENG is an associate professor of political science at Middlebury College. He has written several articles on inter-nation conflict behavior and events data research, including "Behavioral Indicators of War Proneness in Bilateral Conflicts," in *International Yearbook of Foreign Policy Studies* (1974), and "The Future of Events Data Marriages: A Question of Compatibility" in *International Interactions* (1975). His research on the behavioral correlates of war has been closely associated with J. David Singer's Correlates of War project.

WAYNE RICHARD MARTIN is an associate professor of political science at California State College, Dominguez

Hills, and research associate with the Threat Recognition and Analysis project at the University of Southern California.

CHARLES A. McCLELLAND is a professor of international relations at the University of Southern California. His special interests are theory of the international system and computer-environmental research.

PATRICK J. McGOWAN is an associate professor of international relations at the University of Southern California. He edits the *Sage International Yearbook of Foreign Policy Studies* (1973-) and is a coauthor of *American Foreign Policy: An Introduction to Analysis and Evaluation* (1974) and *The Comparative Study of Foreign Policy: A Survey of Scientific Findings* (1973). His writings on international politics, foreign policy analysis, and African affairs have appeared in *African Studies Review, Journal of Asian and African Studies, International Studies Quarterly,* and *American Political Science Review.*

BRUCE E. MOON received his Ph.D. in political science from Ohio State University and is now a lecturer in the International Relations Program at San Francisco State University. Presently engaged in research in the international system area, he is also interested in formal systems theory, modeling of decision-making processes, and international political economy.

JOHN E. MUELLER is a professor of political science at the University of Rochester. He is the author of *War, Presidents, and Public Opinion* (1973) and the editor of *Approaches to Measurement in International Relations: A Non-evangelical Survey* (1969).

DON MUNTON is an assistant professor of political science and a member of the Centre for Foreign Policy Studies at Dalhousie University. He has written articles on Canadian foreign policy, measuring and analyzing external nation-state behavior, the policy relevance of inter-polimetric studies, and forecasting in international politics. He is currently preparing a book, dealing with the external influences on Canadian foreign policy, which attempts to integrate traditional historical analysis and quantitative methods.

ROBERT C. NORTH is a professor of political science at Stanford University. His writings include *Nations in Conflict: National Growth and International Violence* (with Nazli Choucri, 1975) and various other books and articles in the fields of international relations and foreign policy.

MICHAEL K. O'LEARY is the director of the International Relations Program and a professor of political

science at the Maxwell School, Syracuse University. He is the author of *The Politics of American Foreign Aid* (1967) and a coauthor of *Everyman's Prince* (1972), *American Foreign Policy* (1970), and *Quantitative Techniques in Foreign Policy Analysis and Forecasting* (1975). He has also contributed articles to several books of essays and professional journals, including *American Political Science Review, International Organization, Teaching Political Science, Policy Studies Journal,* and *International Studies Quarterly.*

CHARLES A. POWELL is an associate professor of international relations at the University of Southern California. His research has been in the development of theory and methodology for foreign policy analysis, specializing in the areas of simulation, dynamic modeling, and formal conflict theory. Currently, he is working on a systematic critique of the use of simulation in the study of international relations, using data-based complex experimentation.

HELEN PURKITT is a Ph.D. candidate in international relations at the University of Southern California. She is currently conducting research with complex experimental designs for the analysis of foreign policy.

RICHARD ROSECRANCE is Walter S. Carpenter, Jr., Professor of International and Comparative Politics at Cornell University. A former president of the International Studies Association, he is the author of *Action and Reaction in World Politics* (1963) and *International Relations: Peace or War?* (1973).

JAMES N. ROSENAU is the director of the School of International Relations as well as a professor of political science and international relations at the University of Southern California. His writings include *The Scientific Study of Foreign Policy* (1971), *The Dramas of Politics: An Introduction to the Joys of Inquiry* (1973), and *Citizenship between Elections: An Inquiry into the Mobilizable American* (1974). Among the books he has edited are *International Politics and Foreign Policy* (1969) and *Comparing Foreign Policies: Theories, Findings, and Methods* (1974).

R. J. RUMMEL is the director of the PATH Institute of Research on International Problems, vice-president of Political-Economic Risk Consultants, Ltd., and a professor of political science at the University of Hawaii. His works include *Applied Factor Analysis* (1970), *Dimensions of Nations* (1972), *The Dynamic Psychological Field* (1975), *Field Theory Evolving* (1976), *The Conflict Helix* (1976), *Peace Endangered: The Reality of Détente* (1976), and *National Attributes and Behavior* (1977).

BRUCE M. RUSSETT is a professor of political science at Yale University and the editor of the *Journal of Conflict Resolution*. He is author, coauthor, or editor of a dozen books on international relations, among them *Power and Community in World Politics* (1974) and *Interest and Ideology: The Foreign Policy Beliefs of American Businessmen* (with Elizabeth Hanson, 1975).

J. DAVID SINGER is a professor of political science at the University of Michigan, a member of its Mental Health Research Institute, past president of the Peace Research Society, and director of the Correlates of War project at Michigan. He has published many articles on quantitative history, world politics, and disarmament; among his books are *Deterrence, Arms Control, and Disarmament* (1962), *Quantitative International Politics* (1968), and *The Wages of War, 1816-1965* (with Melvin Small, 1972).

RANDOLPH M. SIVERSON is an associate professor of political science at the University of California, Davis. During 1974-1975 he was a Fulbright-Hayes lecturer and visiting professor at the Center for International Studies, El Colegio de Mexico. His articles have appeared in *International Studies Quarterly, Journal of Conflict Resolution, Youth and Society, International Organization, Western Political Quarterly,* and *Mathematical Models of International Relations.*

RICHARD A. SKINNER is an assistant professor of political science at Old Dominion University. He is author of "Research in the Predictive Mode" and coeditor of *International Events and the Comparative Analysis of Foreign Policy* (1975).

RICHARD SMOKE is author of the forthcoming *Controlling Escalation* and of the chapter "National Security Affairs" in the *Political Science Handbook*. He is coauthor with Alexander L. George of *Deterrence in American Foreign Policy: Theory and Practice*. During 1974-1975 he was a fellow at the Center for Advanced Study in the Behavioral Sciences.

JOHN D. SULLIVAN is an associate professor of political studies at Pitzer College and Claremont Graduate School and is director of the Program in Public Policy Studies of the Claremont Colleges. He is a coauthor of *Unity and Disintegration in International Alliances* (1973). He has written articles on international alliances and alignments and on the "limits to growth" controversy and is currently working on the problem of resource management on the regional and international levels.

JOHN E. THOMPSON is a Ph.D. candidate in political science at Ohio State University majoring in international politics with interests in the merger of general systems theory and phenomenology to political inquiry and the design of alternative societies.

STUART J. THORSON is an associate professor of political science and director of the Polimetrics Laboratory at Ohio State University. He has contributed to a variety of journals and books in the areas of comparative foreign policy and formal theory.

BARBARA KAY WINTERS received her B.S. from Illinois State University in 1970. She is currently a graduate student in the Department of Political Science at the University of Kentucky and is completing work on a dissertation entitled "Actor/Target Attribute Relationships and the Selection of Foreign Policy Behavior Recipients."

EUGENE R. WITTKOPF is an associate professor of political science at the University of Florida. Author of a monograph entitled *Western Bilateral Aid Allocations* (1972), he has published articles in the *American Political Science Review, International Interactions, International Organization,* and *International Studies Quarterly* and has contributed chapters to several books dealing with foreign policy and international politics.

DINA A. ZINNES is a professor of political science at Indiana University. She has recently completed a book surveying the literature in quantitative international relations, entitled *Contemporary Research in International Politics,* a condensed version of which will appear in the *Handbook of Political Science*. She is editing with Frank Hoole and John Gillespie a series of three volumes which present (1) a series of papers evaluating major projects in quantitative international relations, (2) a series of new mathematical models of international politics, and (3) a series of papers exploring applications of control theory and differential games to the study of international politics.

Name Index

Subject Index

386